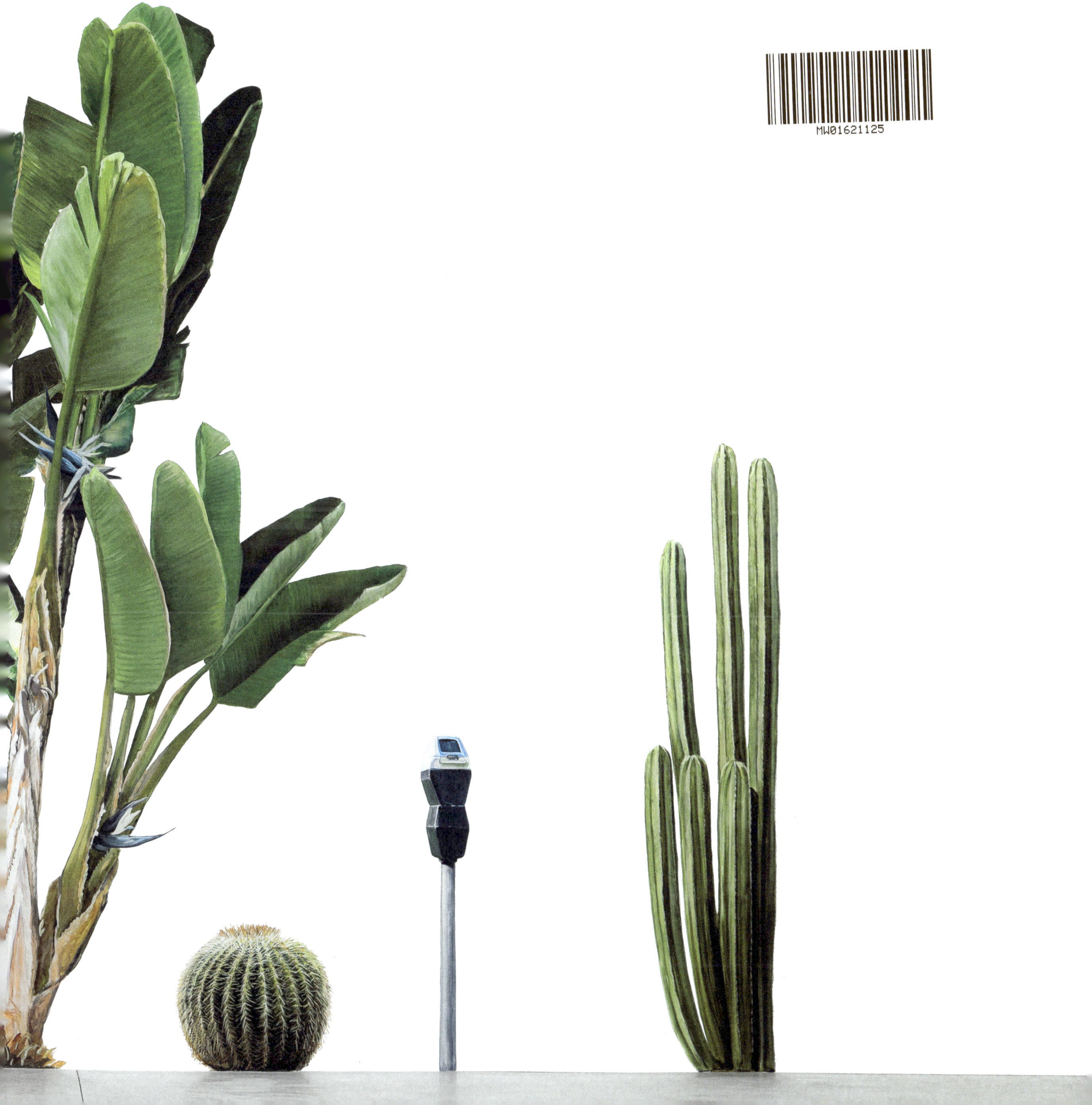

MW01621125

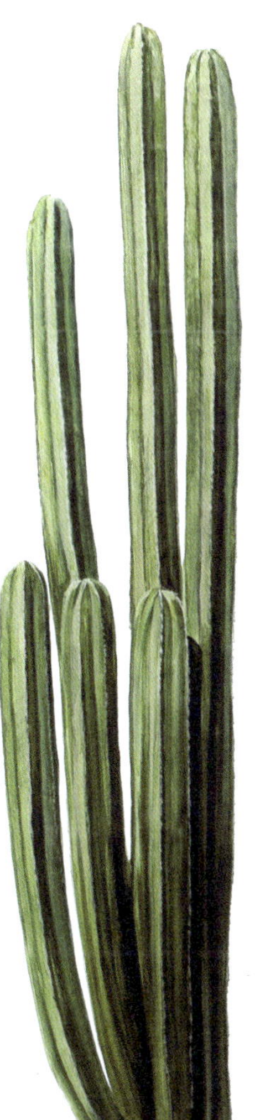

UNPACKING

THE MARCIANO COLLECTION

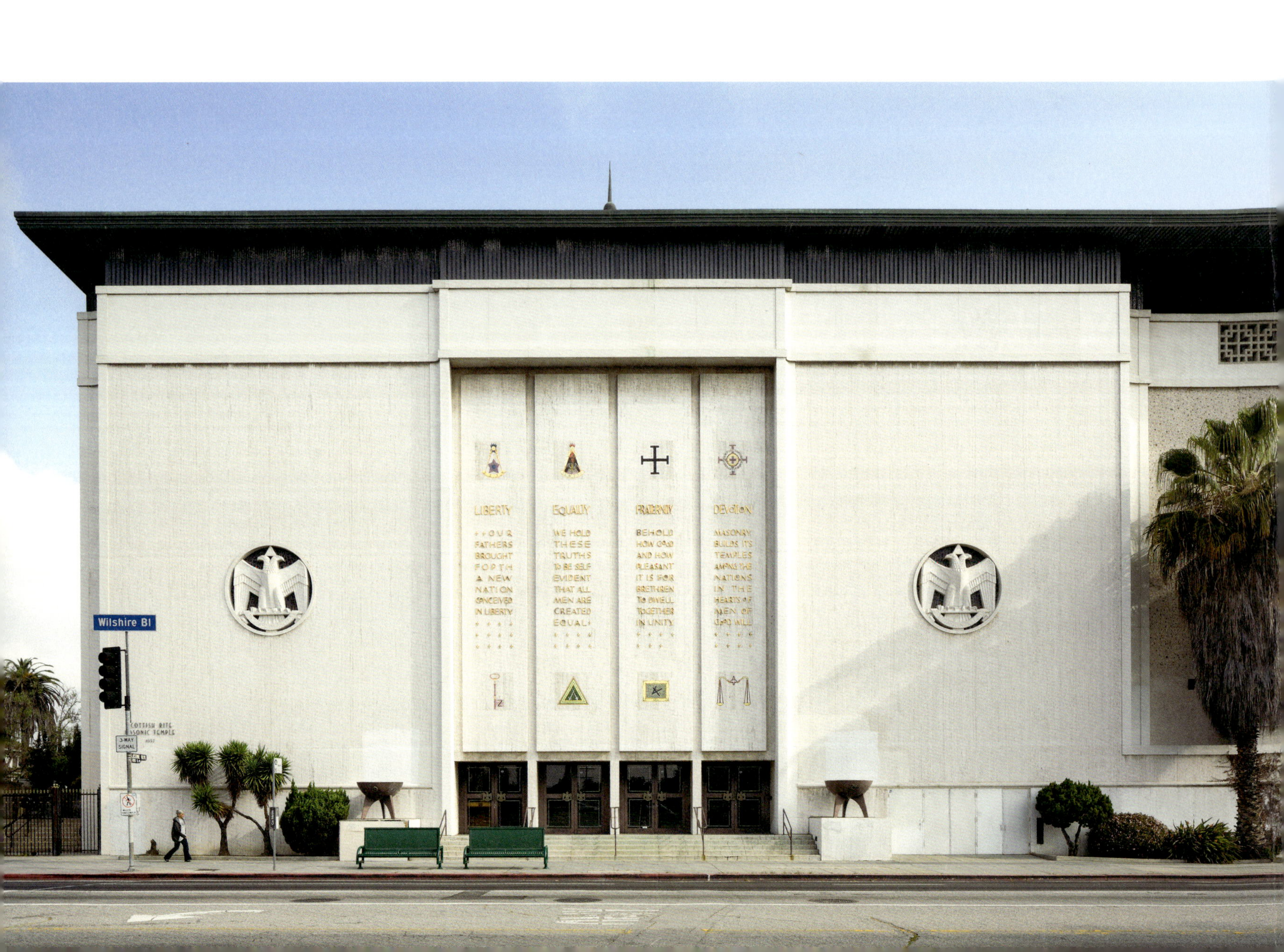
Wilshire Bl
LIBERTY
OUR FATHERS BROUGHT FORTH A NEW NATION CONCEIVED IN LIBERTY
EQUALITY
WE HOLD THESE TRUTHS TO BE SELF EVIDENT THAT ALL MEN ARE CREATED EQUAL
FRATERNITY
BEHOLD HOW GOOD AND HOW PLEASANT IT IS FOR BRETHREN TO DWELL TOGETHER IN UNITY
DEVOTION
MASONRY BUILDS ITS TEMPLES AMONG THE NATIONS IN THE HEARTS OF MEN OF GOOD WILL

UNPACKING THE MARCIANO COLLECTION

EDITED BY
JAMIE G. MANNÉ

WITH CONTRIBUTIONS BY
SUSAN L. ABERTH, PHILIPP KAISER, JIM SHAW, TONY SHEETS, AND KULAPAT YANTRASAST

THE MAURICE AND PAUL MARCIANO ART FOUNDATION, LOS ANGELES

DELMONICO BOOKS • PRESTEL, MUNICH, LONDON, NEW YORK

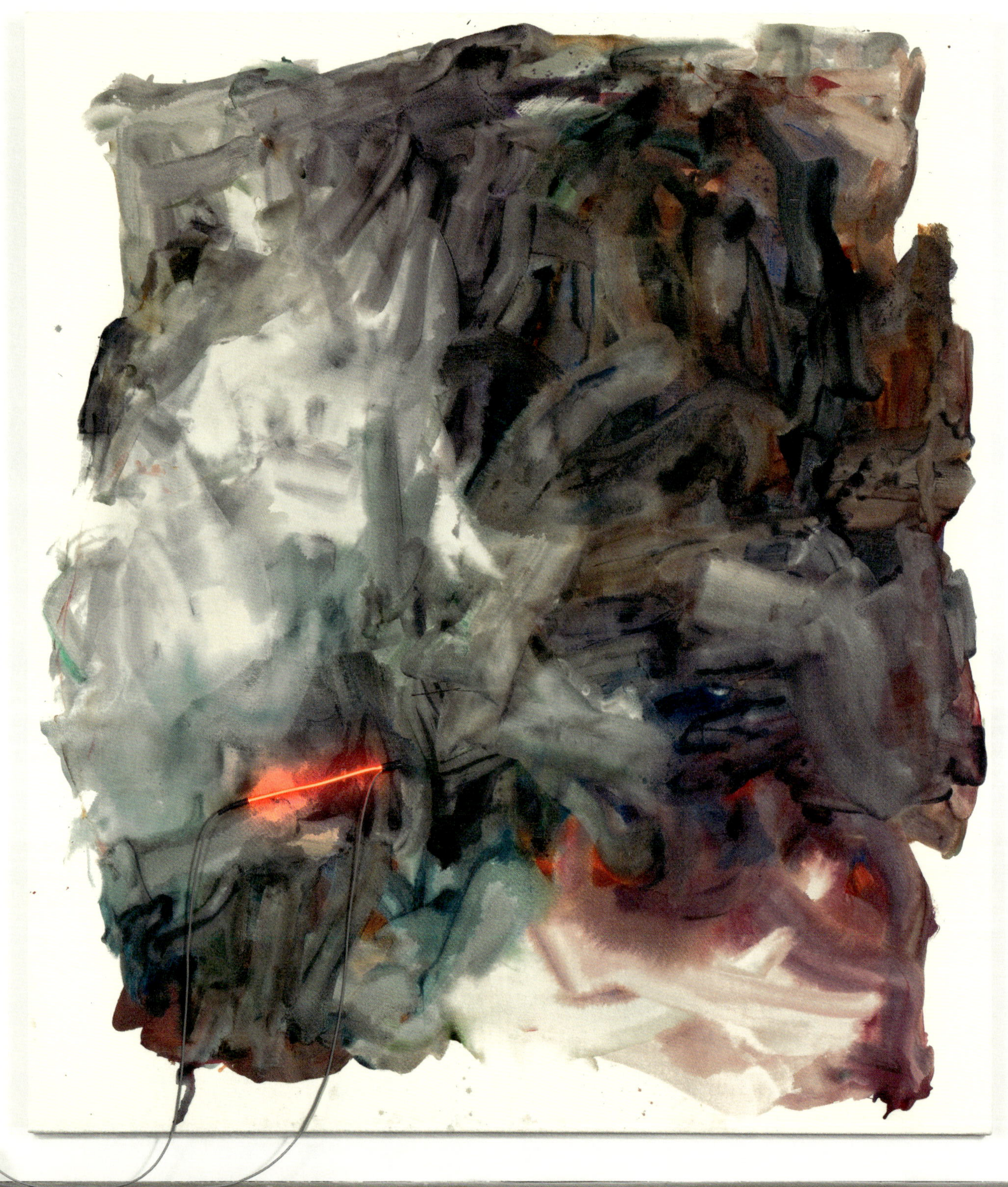

FOREWORD

MAURICE MARCIANO

When Paul and I first began collecting years ago, we could never have imagined that we would one day be opening a foundation where we might share our passion for contemporary art and artists with the public, nor that it would be housed in a monumental former Masonic temple with its own fascinating story and connection to Los Angeles—our home for over thirty-five years. We are thrilled to welcome visitors to this new exhibition space at an exciting moment in Los Angeles's art and civic history.

Our engagement with contemporary art began in the 1980s and developed through visits to galleries and auctions in Paris, New York, and Los Angeles. Early on we were drawn to the work of painters such as Roy Lichtenstein, Gerhard Richter, and Sam Francis. We soon began to spend time with artists in their studio, including Ed Ruscha, and to experience the joys of learning about art directly from the artists creating it.

In 2006, after a nearly fifteen-year hiatus, Paul and I began to think about collecting again. Visiting galleries and exhibitions, including the striking Takashi Murakami retrospective in 2007 at Los Angeles's Museum of Contemporary Art (MOCA), we realized quickly how much the art world had changed and how many compelling artistic developments we had missed—particularly in Los Angeles, which had become an international art capital in its own right. It was like discovering a totally new world, right in our backyard. We began to meet artists and collect in earnest once again, and we've never looked back.

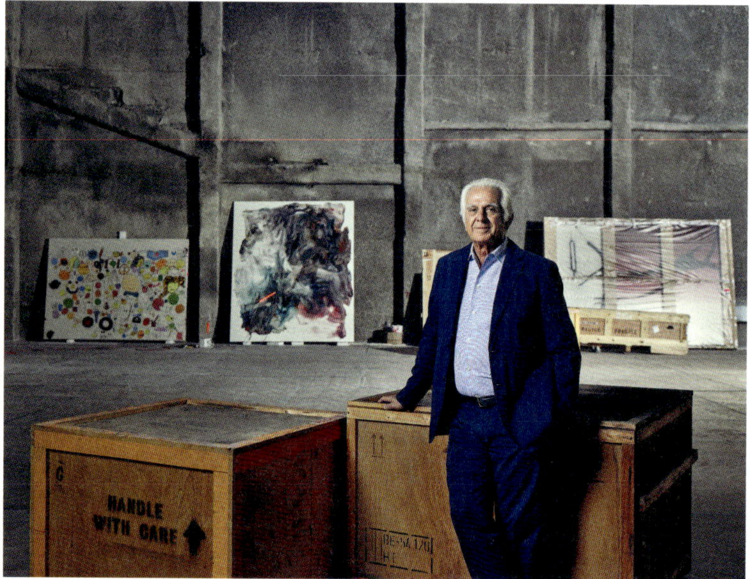

Maurice Marciano, 2016

Since then, what has propelled our collection even further is the incredible vibrancy of artistic activity in Los Angeles over the past decade. Not only is this community thriving, it is continually growing, shifting, and surprising us. We are truly inspired by the artists we collect—both in Los Angeles and around the world—to learn about their process, what drives them, and the ideas they want to share. Their insights are what motivate us, and the personal relationships that we have developed with artists are just as important to us as the works we have collected, which now encompass a range of mediums including painting, sculpture, photography, collage, film and video, installation, and performance.

Collecting for us is not just about buying a work of art but rather about the full experience of watching an artist's practice develop over time. We have been privileged to be able to collect the work of numerous artists in depth, and thus to represent the diverse paths each has followed. Oftentimes we witness artists undertaking a major shift in their work, which is a bold step to take, especially if they have previously found success working in a particular style or medium. Through our sustained support, we hope to encourage artists in making these risky moves, knowing that we are behind them in whatever direction they may go. Following these developments has been one of the most satisfying aspects of building our collection.

This spirit of experimentation, stemming directly from our interactions with artists, is what convinced us to launch the Marciano Art Foundation. Not only will the Foundation provide a venue to display our collection publicly, it will also serve as an experimental forum for artists to develop new concepts, installations, and exhibitions. Embracing the nimble approach of a Kunsthalle, the Foundation will be a place where artists can have visibility within the Los Angeles art community without the pressures and constraints that sometimes come with gallery and museum exhibitions. Young artists can get exposure; more established artists can exhibit a new body of work; or artists might curate an exhibition of work by others who haven't yet had the opportunity to exhibit widely.

It is fitting that we first considered the Scottish Rites Masonic Temple as the site for this new endeavor thanks to an artist. Like so many Angelenos, including Paul and me, Alex Israel had noticed this intriguing building for years while driving along Wilshire Boulevard, and he suggested it to us when we were first exploring the idea of a foundation. Though its size and condition were daunting, we sought artists' feedback and were soon confident in selecting the building when we saw how stimulating they found the temple's interiors and idiosyncrasies. It has been a true pleasure to envision a new space for artists in Los Angeles, while also preserving an example of historic architecture in a city that has so often torn down its links to the past.

What we love about the building in particular is the contrast between its exterior—the historic façade designed by Millard Sheets and the bustle of Wilshire Boulevard—with what is inside. Our galleries will present art at the forefront of contemporary production through displays from the permanent collection, special exhibitions, and site-specific installations. On the first floor, we have transformed a former theater with forty-five-foot ceilings into a massive, raw exhibition space unlike any other in Los Angeles where artists can conceptualize new large-scale installations. On the top floor, we have turned a former ballroom into a series of airy, versatile galleries where we will show the permanent collection in a variety of thematic groupings and monographic presentations, with input from a range of interdisciplinary artists, creators, and curators. Together, these distinctive spaces will offer visitors different types of experiences.

This is an unbelievable moment for art in Los Angeles, and we are honored to contribute to the growing number of institutions that stretch along the Wilshire corridor to downtown, from the Hammer Museum and the Los Angeles County Museum of Art to MOCA and The Broad. We hope to complement them in ways that will illuminate contemporary artistic activity for both new and seasoned art viewers. Yet despite these plans, we have no set course that we want the Foundation to follow; that would be entirely counterintuitive to the experimental approach we are taking. Instead, we will push the Foundation to re-imagine itself continuously, changing shape in response to new developments in the world of contemporary art and functioning as a space where artists can feel free to take risks, push the limits of their practice, and add important new dimensions to their work. It is with them in mind that we open our doors.

SELECTIONS FROM THE COLLECTION

AUTHOR KEY:

J. A. = JAMIN AN
L. C. = LILLY CASILLAS
J. H. = JOSEPH HENRY
J. G. M. = JAMIE G. MANNÉ
C. R. = CHRISTINE ROBINSON
J. T. = JAMES TARMY

DOUG AITKEN

b. 1968, Redondo Beach, CA

Born in 1968 in Redondo Beach, California, Aitken earned a BFA from the Art Center College of Design in Pasadena, California, before gaining critical attention in the mid-nineties in the downtown New York video scene. Aitken now works primarily as a multimedia artist with a focus on photography, film, and sculpture.

Through his upbringing in Southern California, he developed the dual sensibility for the desolate and the sublime. Over the past twenty years, both dynamics have continued to play out in his Happenings, projections, and outdoor works. Exploring contemporary tropes of the picturesque, Aitken works at the intersection of natural and urban landscapes and cinematic, musical, and architectural experience.

He has collaborated numerous times with popular musicians and Hollywood actors, indicating a practice both within and beyond the art world.

Exhibitions at the Vienna Secession, Serpentine Gallery, the Centre Georges Pompidou, The Museum of Modern Art in New York, and The Museum of Contemporary Art in Los Angeles have cemented his position as a major artist. Aitken has also screened his films widely in international festivals, including the New York Film Festival, BFI London, Locarno, and Sundance. His poetic and immersive multi-room video installation, *Electric Earth*, received the 1999 Venice Biennale International Prize. Aitken has also been featured in the 1997 and 2000 editions of the Whitney Biennial, and received numerous prestigious awards, including the 2012 Nam June Paik Center Prize. Aitken lives and works in Los Angeles.

Aitken's series of wall-hanging text sculptures draw on a large bank of images and materials that occupy the inner space of the letters' thick typeface. Unpacking the friction between word and image, Aitken splits signification at its seams. In *Sunset (black and white)* (2011) hand-carved foam, epoxy, and silk-screened acrylic is back-lit by LED lights, with the letters resting on top of each other. The texture of the letters elicits lava rock or cosmic debris—not the idyllic, colorful sunset one might imagine. Aitken questions the actual meaning of the word "sunset" and how its connotations are completely removed from the physical process by which a sunset is formed through the continuous rotation of celestial bodies. The foam letters serve as a sort of post-Pop portrayal for the massive amounts of energy, movement, and velocity intrinsic in the literal meaning of a sunset. In Aitken's world, a "sunset" is simply an idea through which the artist can communicate his interest in the relationship between physical space and meaning.

J. H.

Sunset (black and white), 2011
Hand-carved foam, epoxy with LED lights
and hand silkscreened acrylic
63½ × 78¼ × 8 inches
(161.3 × 198.8 × 20.3 cm)
Edition of 4, AP 1/2

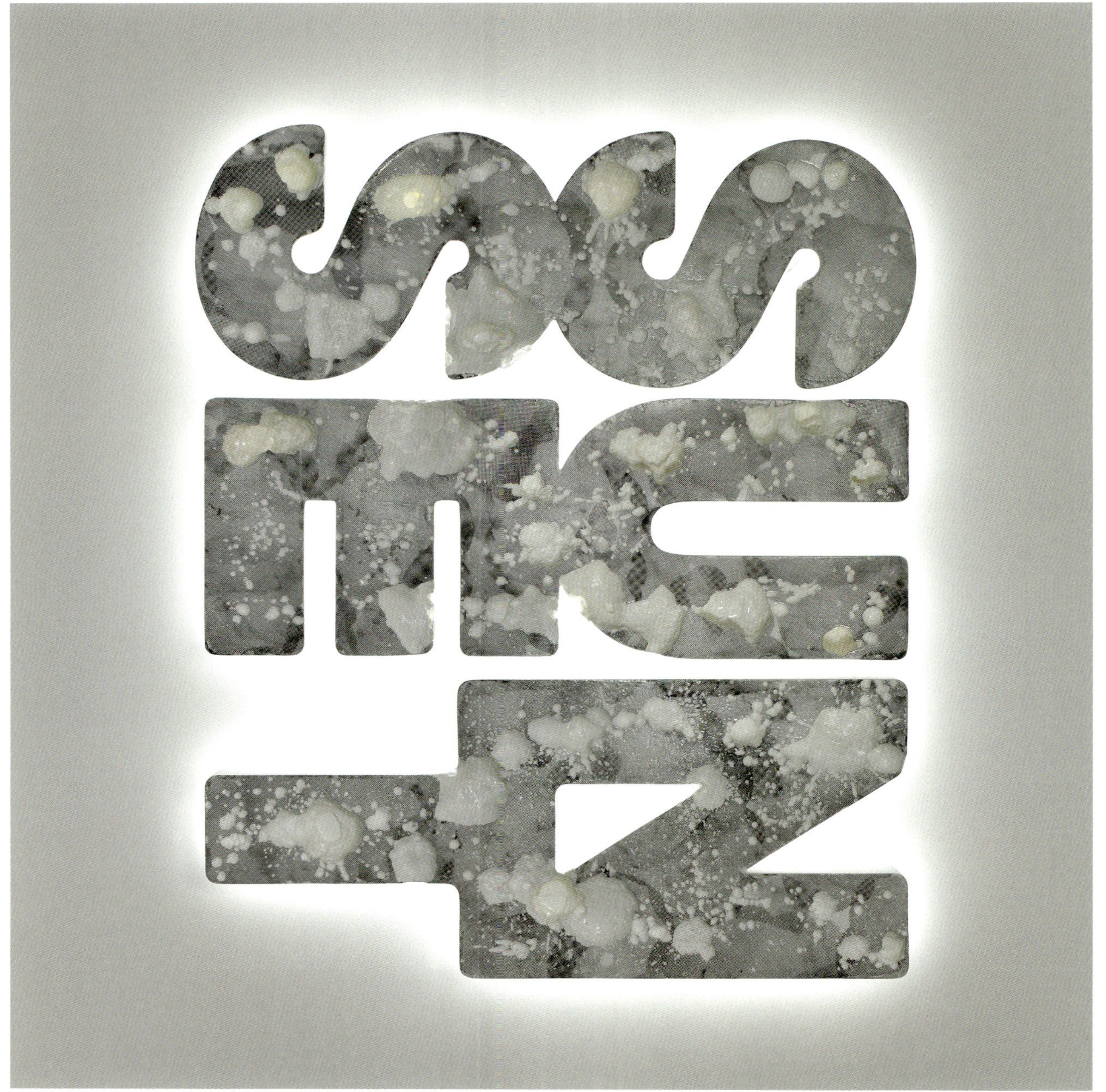

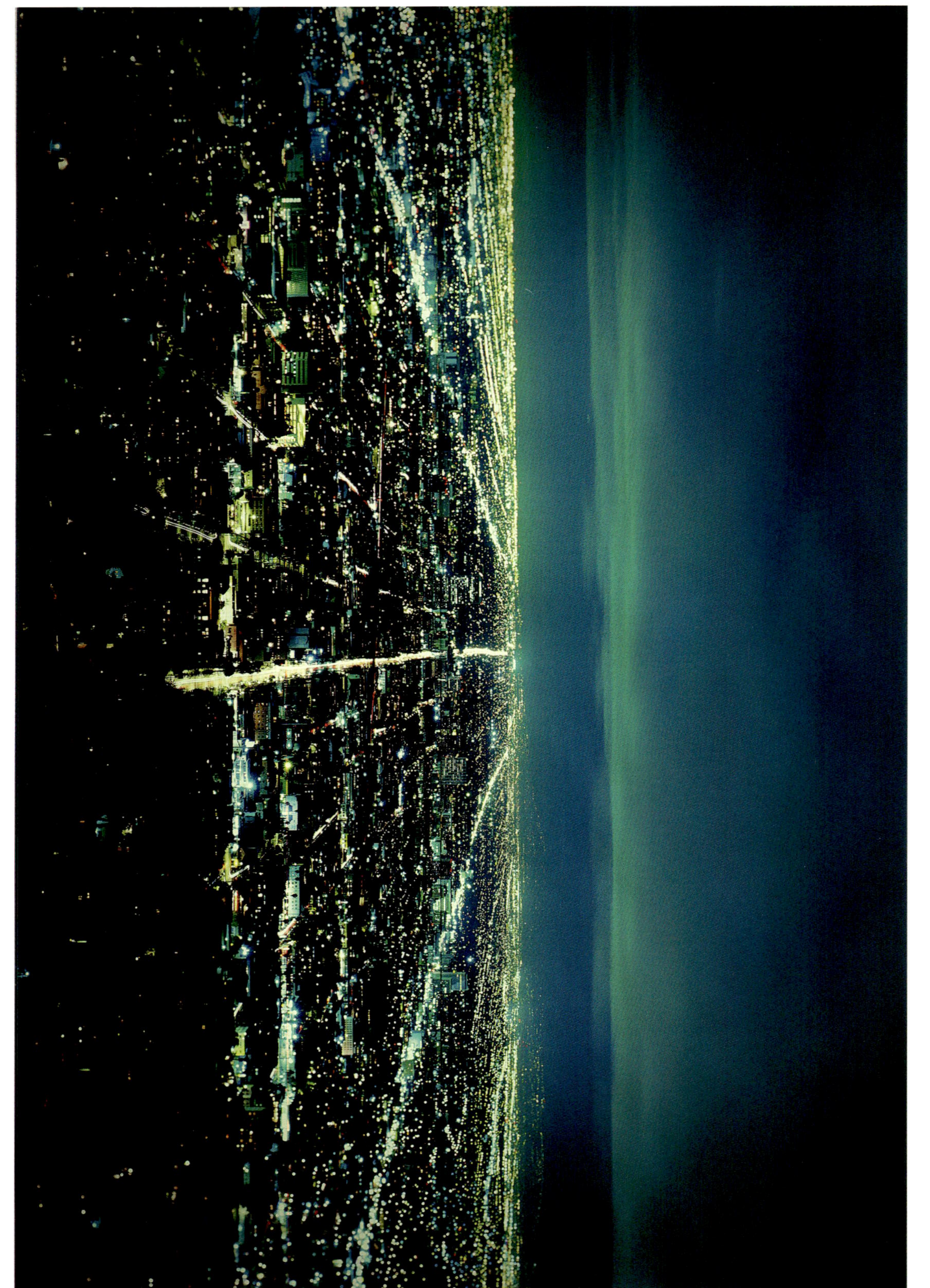

rise, 1998–2001
Chromogenic transparency on acrylic in aluminum light box with fluorescent lights
90 × 132 × 18 inches (228.6 × 335.3 × 45.7 cm)

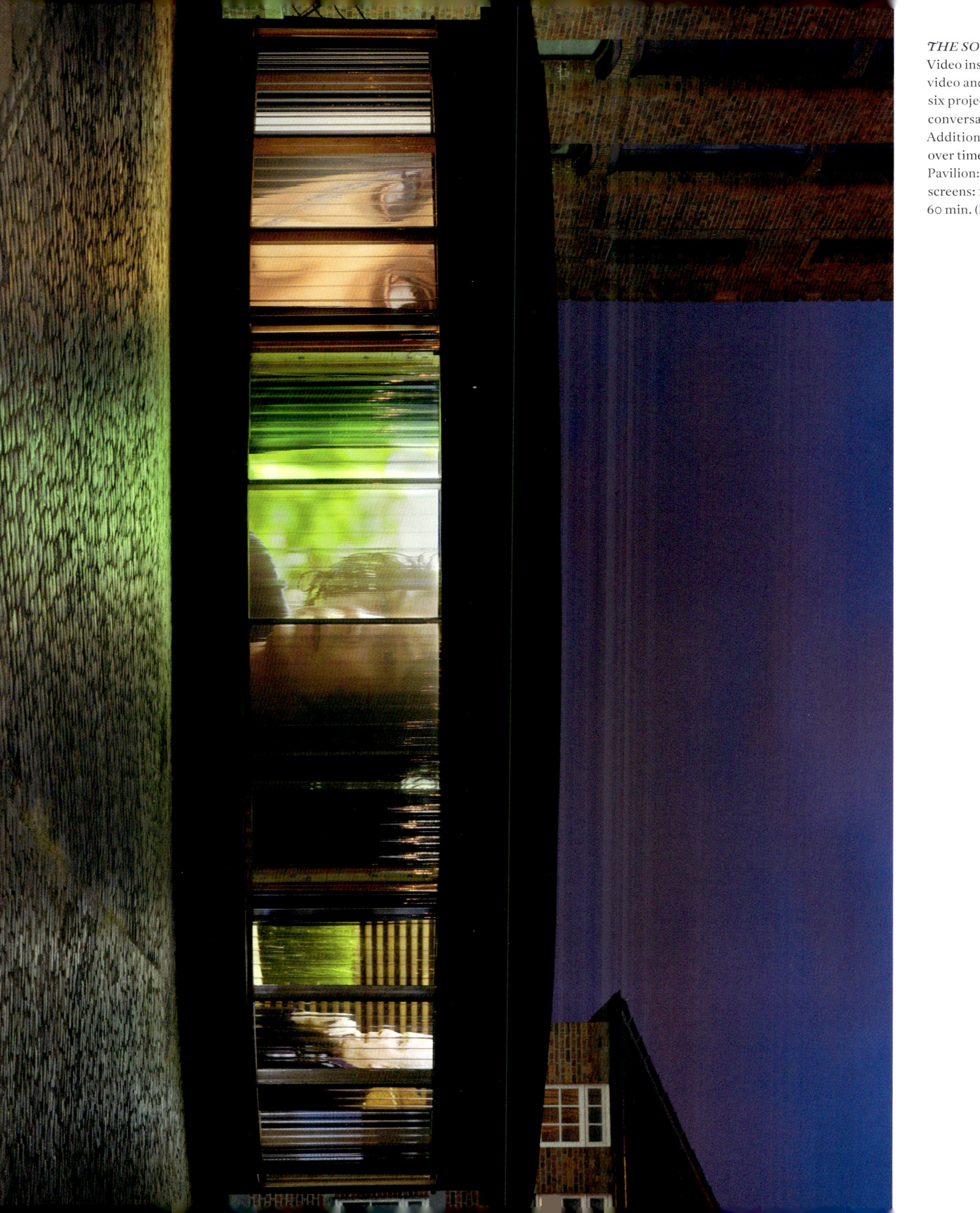

THE SOURCE (evolving), 2012–ongoing
Video installation with six channels of color video and six channels of stereo sound, six projections, featuring twenty-three conversations in an architectural pavilion. Additional conversations may be added over time.
Pavilion: 230 × 686 inches (580 × 1740 cm); screens: 1044½ × 14 inches (220 × 390 cm)
60 min. (loop)

JENNIFER ALLORA b. 1974, Philadelphia, PA
& GUILLERMO CALZADILLA b. 1971, Havana, Cuba

Petrified Petrol Pump No. 2, 2010
Limestone
Dimensions variable; approx.
99½ × 54 × 26 inches (252.7 × 137.2 × 66 cm)

Collaborators since 1995, the San Juan, Puerto Rico–based artists Jennifer Allora and Guillermo Calzadilla address social, political, and cultural issues such as nationhood, environmentalism, authorship, and states of war and resistance through a myriad of media. With the aim of activating social change and bringing greater awareness to the "monstrous dimension of art—the potential in an artwork to exceed the plans and purposes of its creators," the duo relies heavily on metaphor, material, and narrative, while inserting references to pop culture.

This combination of conceptual elements allows the artists to expand the viewer's understanding of the subject at hand by exploiting the ability of the metaphor to transform and the capacity of material to symbolize abstract concepts.

Born in Philadelphia, Pennsylvania, in 1974, Jennifer Allora received a BA from the University of Richmond in Virginia and an MS from the Massachusetts Institute of Technology. Guillermo Calzadilla was born in 1971 in Havana, Cuba, and received a BFA from Escuela de Artes Plásticas, San Juan, Puerto Rico, and an MFA from Bard College. The pair has had several solo exhibitions including the Stedelijk Museum and the Walker Art Center, as well as participating in Documenta 13, the 29th São Paulo Biennial, and Performance 9 at The Museum of Modern Art, New York. Allora & Calzadilla also represented the United States in the 54th Venice Biennale.

In their 2010 limestone sculpture *Petrified Petrol Pump No. 2*, Allora & Calzadilla warn of an apocalyptic future by depicting a common gas pump as a fossilized relic of contemporary culture's dependence on, and exploitation of, natural resources. The work succeeds by commenting on the precarious and often toxic relationship between man and nature, a cynical theme that forms a common thread throughout the breadth of the duo's oeuvre.

In addition to environmental issues, their work deals with the relationship between artistic expression, particularly music, and politics. The biting, blurred, mostly black-and-white images of their *Intermission* series, all made from woodblock prints, depict American soldiers celebrating Halloween at marine camps in Afghanistan and Iraq. Presented in festive costume or playing music, the subjects convey a more relatable side of those serving in the military. The American soldiers in *Intermission (Halloween Afghanistan I)* (2011) run through the camp dressed in comic book superhero costumes, an image that forces the viewer to grapple with America's long history of war and the overall human experience of both compassionate criticality and contemporary culture. L. C.

Intermission (Halloween Afghanistan I), 2011
Woodcut print on linen
120 × 168 inches (304.8 × 426.72 cm)
Edition 1 of 3, 1 AP

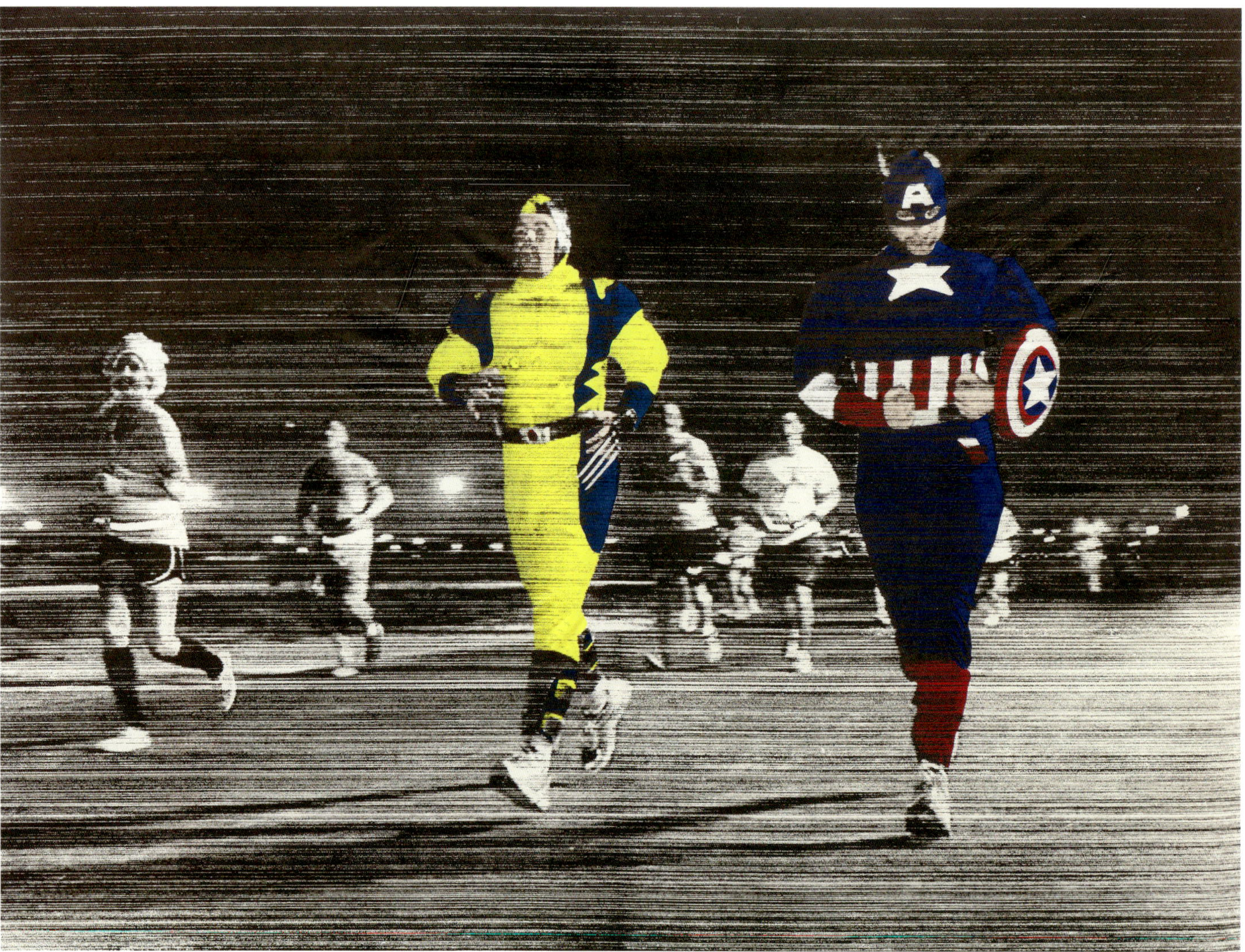

Shape Shifter, 2013
Sandpaper sheets glued on canvas
100 × 73¾ inches (254 × 187.3 cm)

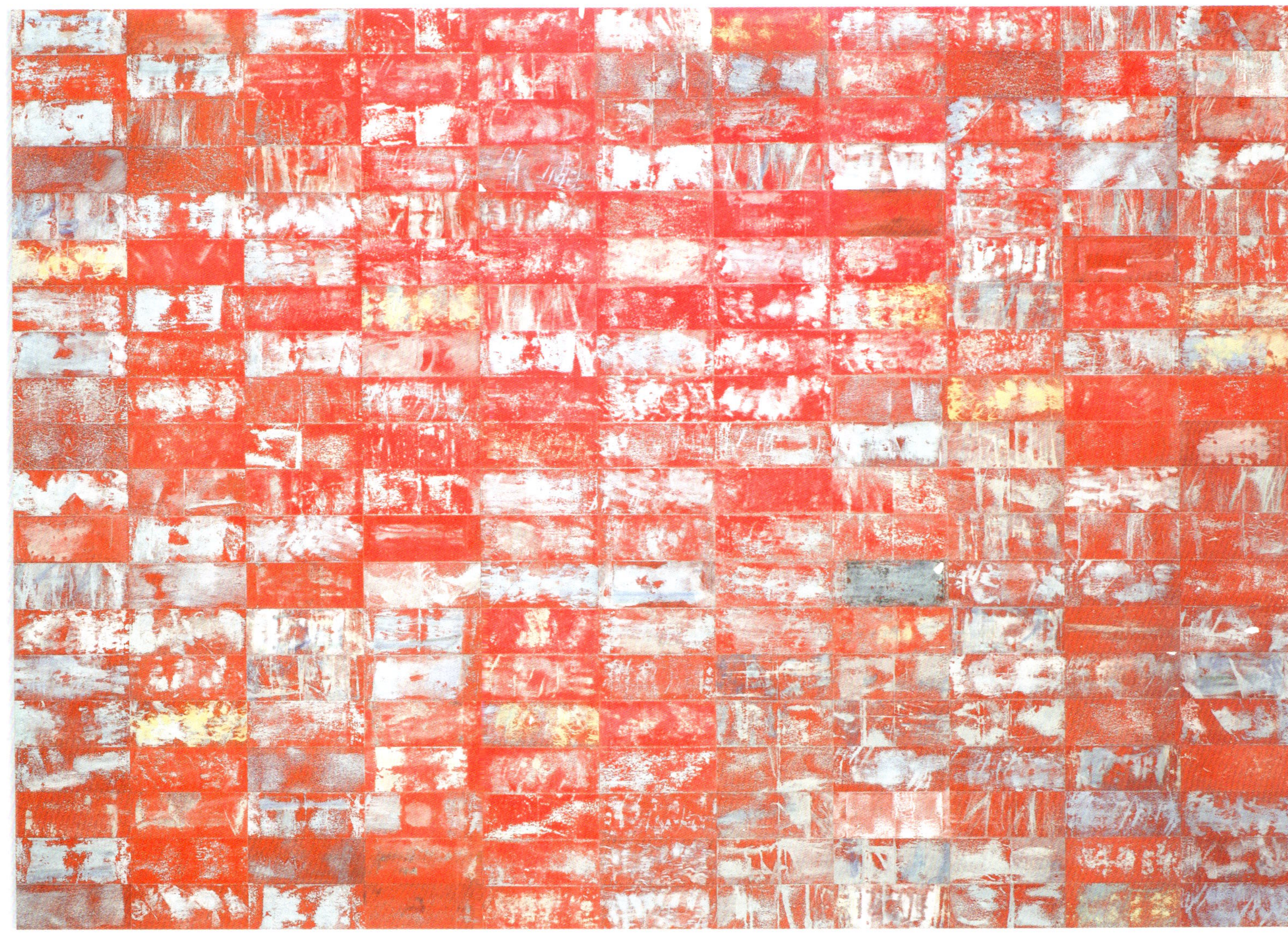

EL ANATSUI

b. 1944, Anyako, Ghana

El Anatsui's career has long straddled Euro-American and African forms of practice. He was born in 1944 in Anyako, Ghana, the youngest of thirty-two siblings. Anatsui received his bachelor's degree from the College of Art at the University of Science and Technology in Kusami, focusing on Western art techniques. He was eventually appointed professor of sculpture at the University of Nigeria in Nsukka in 1975, a position he still holds today. Following earlier decolonization movements, in the 1970s Nsukka became the center of an indigenous African culture revival. Anatsui avidly participated in this renaissance, but as his career saw him travel to the West, his practice accommodated new technological processes as well. His oeuvre achieved renown in the global contemporary art circuit largely due to the success of his bottle-cap sculptures from the late 1990s onward.

Since his early days in Nsukka, Anatsui has sought to critically locate indigenous African practices, like those of the Asante and Ewe peoples, within broader networks of colonialism and globalization.

In his earliest works, Anatsui made ceramic sculptures from the fragments of traditional pots; he would later commission local carvers to fabricate wooden trays typically used for market display and then adorn them with abstract ornamentation. In 1998, he began his most celebrated work: Anatsui collected the disposed tops founded on liquor battles, pounded and punched them, and then stitched the pieces together to create large-scale sculpture—equal parts metal and textile. The reflective sheen of the works belied their humble provenance in an alchemic transposition. Anatsui furthermore granted exhibitors the right to display the works as they pleased, allowing for the contingencies of weight and gravity.

They Finally Broke the Pot of Wisdom from 2011 is one such work. The folds and creases in the work liquidate the found aluminum into an undulating mass. Yet the recycling of cheap commodity also speaks to the broader politics: the kind of liquor from which Anatsui gleans his material historically required slave labor for their manufacturing; these goods would then be used as currency for further human material in the African continent. In the play between sensuous beauty and tragic social meaning, Anatsui opens questions of desire, consumption, and power. J. H.

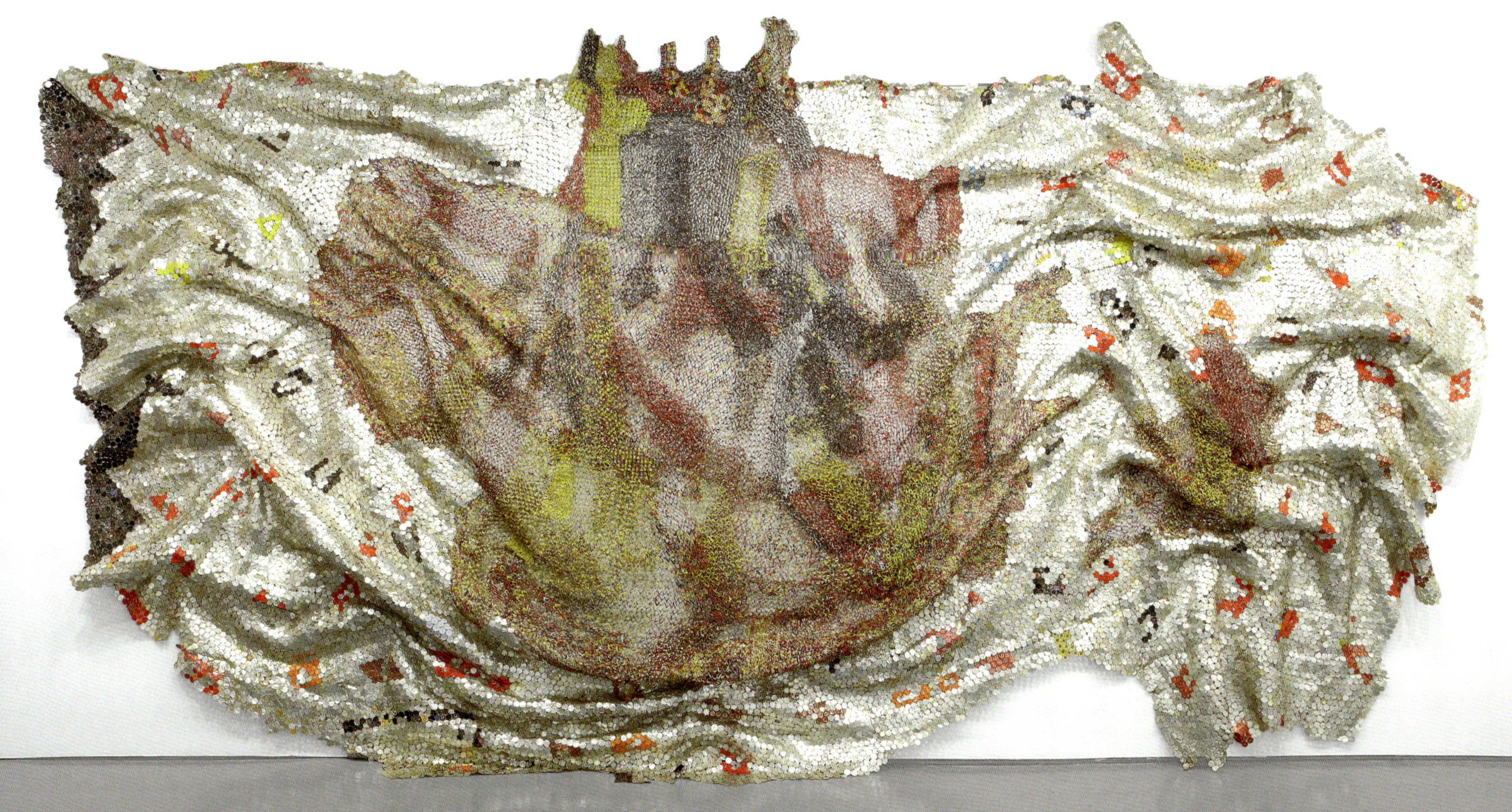

They Finally Broke the Pot of Wisdom, 2011
Found aluminum and copper wire
186 × 276 inches (472.4 × 701 cm) flat
Approx. 136 × 270 inches (345.4 × 685.8 cm)
installed

TAUBA **AUERBACH** b. 1981, San Francisco, CA

New York–based artist Tauba Auerbach dynamically blends media, showcasing interactions between painting, sculpture, photography, weavings, and printed matter. Her work offers new ways of understanding two- and three-dimensional space, order and disorder, representation and abstraction—collapsing these opposing concepts onto a unified surface. She is methodical in her practice, using digital and craft-based techniques to deconstruct conventional ways in which visual and spatial information is conveyed.

Born in San Francisco in 1981, Auerbach received a BA in visual art from Stanford University in 2003. She was included in the 2010 Whitney Biennial, and her work has been exhibited at The Museum of Modern Art, Tate St. Ives, the ICA London, and The New Museum, among many other venues.

Her earliest works of prominence were a series of Fold paintings that garnered attention after her 2011 solo exhibition, *Tetrachromat*, at Bergen Kunstall in Norway. For *Untitled (Fold)* (2012) from this series, Auerbach twisted and folded the canvas before stretching it flat and painting the surface using an industrial spray. The result renders a sort of palimpsest, preserving traces of the now-collapsed third dimension. Subsequently, Auerbach pursued a series of Weave paintings, which employed the medium of weaving to transform the flat picture plane. In *Rupture II* (2011), Auerbach wove strips of white canvas across a wooden frame to create divergent patterns of crosses and squares, disrupting the canvas-as-surface by using it as a craft element to form a new object.

In recent years, Auerbach has worked on a series of large-scale acrylic paintings, each marked by dragging a custom-made instrument across the surface, inscribing patterns derived from chainmail, and a reconceptualization of space she classifies as "four-dimensional" geometry. In *Grain: Wave/Slant Wave* (2015), Auerbach pulls the eye to the upper-left corner of the canvas by contrasting negative space with a rippled pattern, which ironically appears degaussed or even unfocused once the viewer settles on it. L. C.

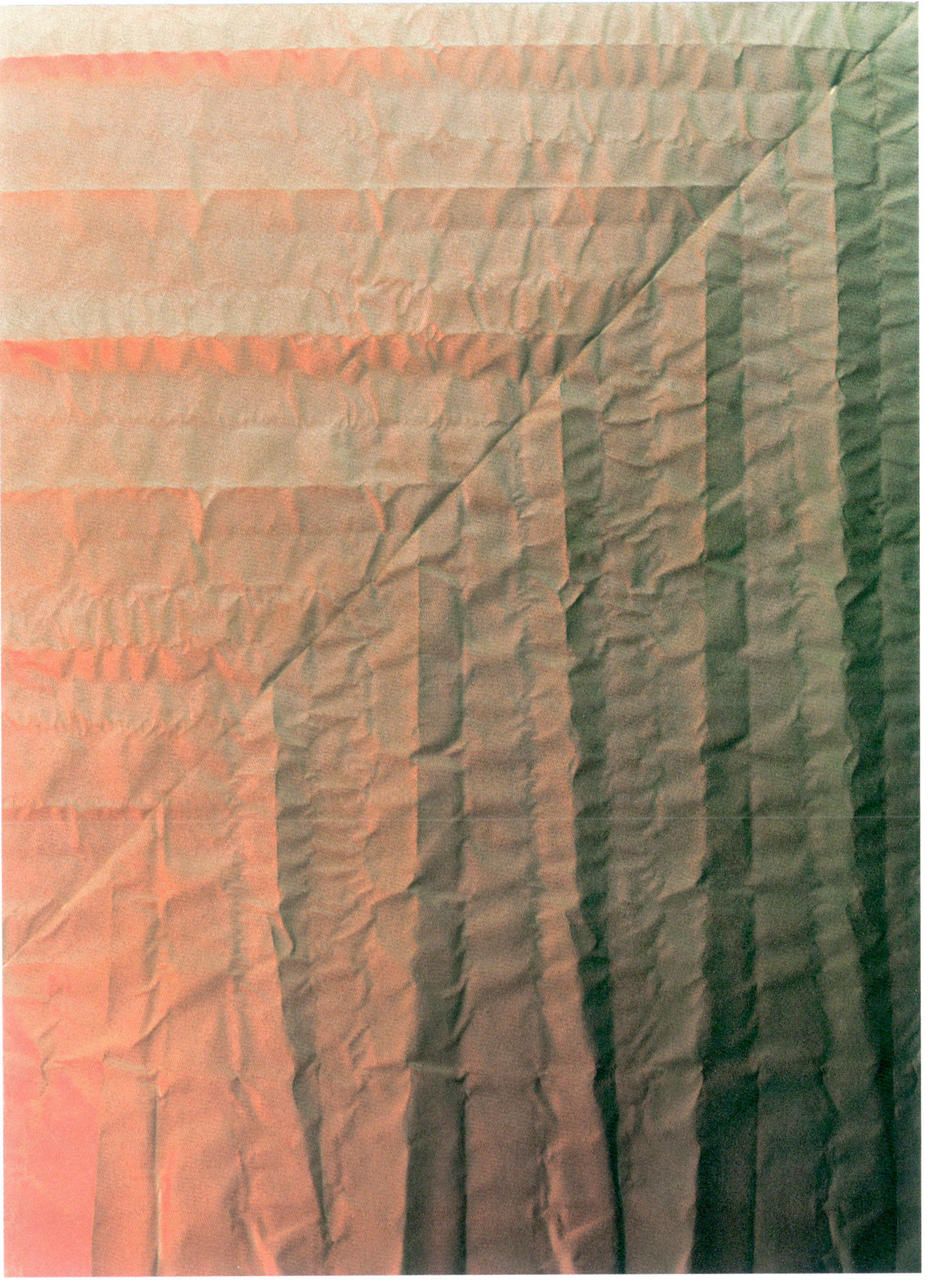

Untitled (Fold), 2012
Acrylic paint on canvas on wooden stretcher
72 × 54 inches (182.9 × 137.2 cm)

Rupture II, 2011
Woven canvas on stretcher
60 × 45 inches (152.4 × 114.3 cm)

Grain: Wave/Slant Wave, 2015
Acrylic on Masonite with Baltic birch cradle
90 × 48 × 2 inches (228.6 × 121.9 × 5.1 cm)

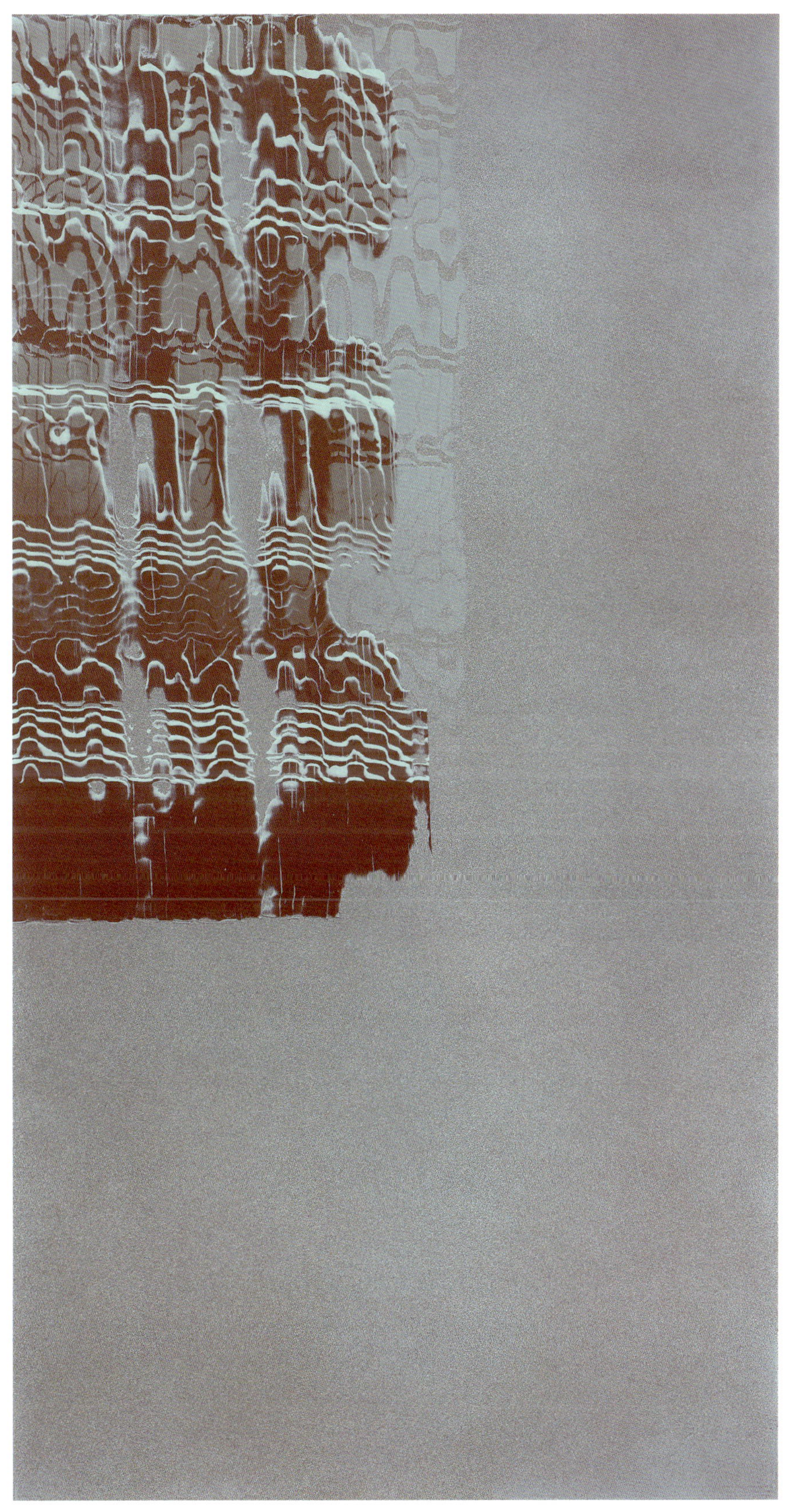

WALEAD **BESHTY** b. 1976, London, England

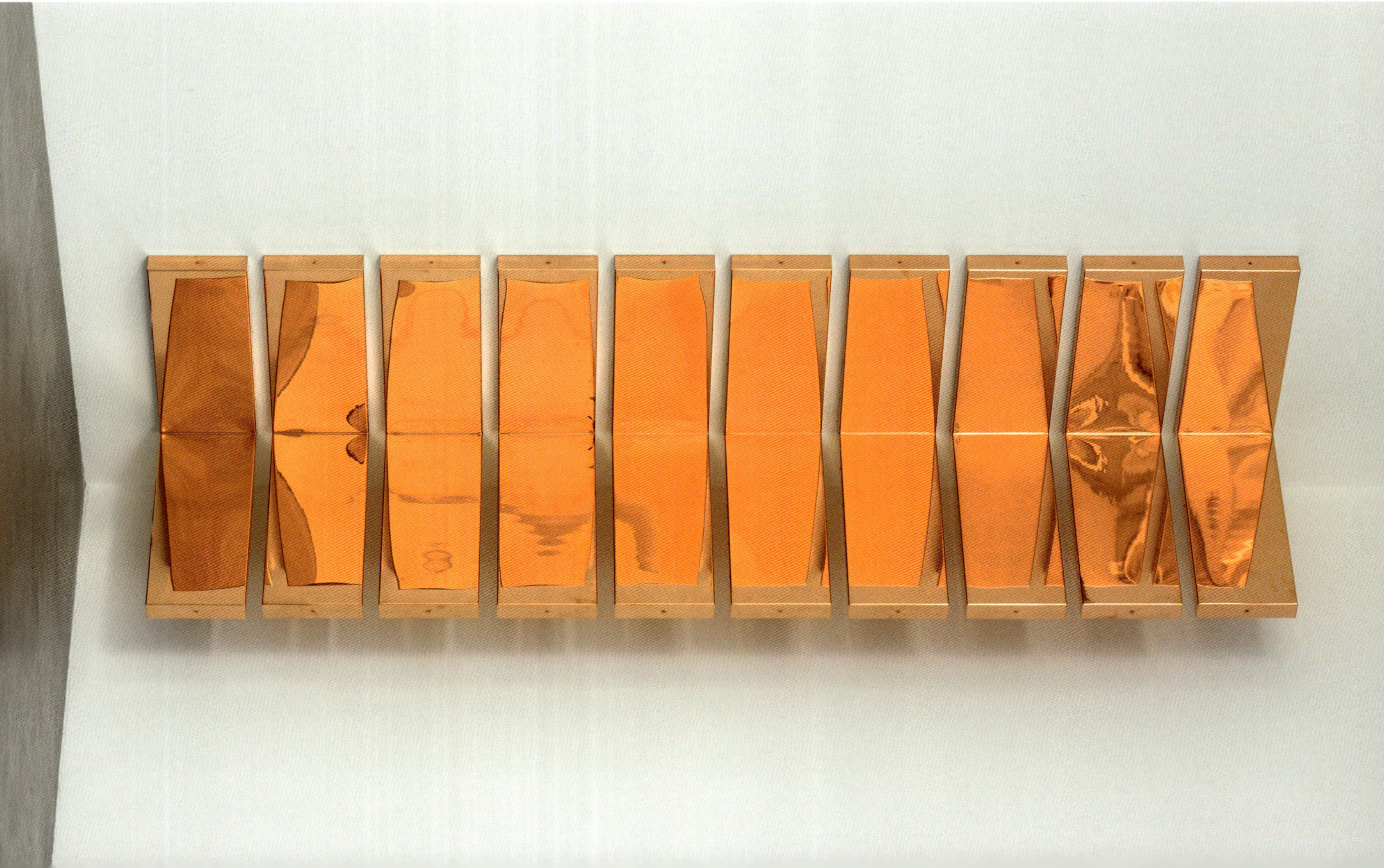

Copper Surrogate (90° Bend, 0°/180° Bisection, 10 sections: July 8, 2016, Beverly Hills, California), 2014
Polished copper
10 parts: 11½ × 30 × 30 inches
(29.2 × 76.2 × 76.2 cm) each

Born in London in 1976, Walead Beshty's practice centers around issues of materiality, technological processes, and the circumstances associated with the production, distribution, and exhibition of art works. In making his work, Beshty often establishes process-based parameters and limitations that determine an unforeseen outcome. He earned a BA from Bard College in 1999 and an MFA from the Yale University School of Art in 2002. Currently a professor at Art Center College of Design, Pasadena, Beshty works with various forms of media but is best known for his sculpture and photography. He lives and works in Los Angeles.

His 2006 series of Travel Pictures offer an entry point to Beshty's later projects. In this series, Beshty documented the abandoned Iraqi Embassy in the former East Berlin with damaged film—undeveloped negatives exposed (unexpectedly, at first) to high-powered airport security X-ray machines during his travel between Los Angeles and Berlin.

In *RA4 Contact Print [Black Curl (YMC/Six Magnet: Los Angeles, California, December 18, 2013, Fuji Color Crystal Archive Super Type C, Em. No. 101-007, 43513), Kreonite KM IV 5225 RA4 Color Processor, Ser. No. 00092174]* (2014), Beshty utilizes the standard RA-4 processing machine used for printing Type C color prints. Bypassing the use of camera and film, he created the photogram in the darkroom using variations of light exposure, the RA-4 machine's chemical development process, and light-sensitive paper. However, Beshty's use of the machine draws attention to the finite lifespan of modes of photographic technology. In the photograph, notched imprints of the machine's parts appear in horizontal strips of color, providing an index of paper jams, misaligned parts, and chance. C. R.

The resulting photographs register not only a complex site of foreign politics but also physical traces of the artist's own international transit. Beshty's subsequent projects include series of photograms and FedEx sculptures that follow predetermined rule-based forms of production—the specific details of which are offered through lengthy technical titles.

BESHTY

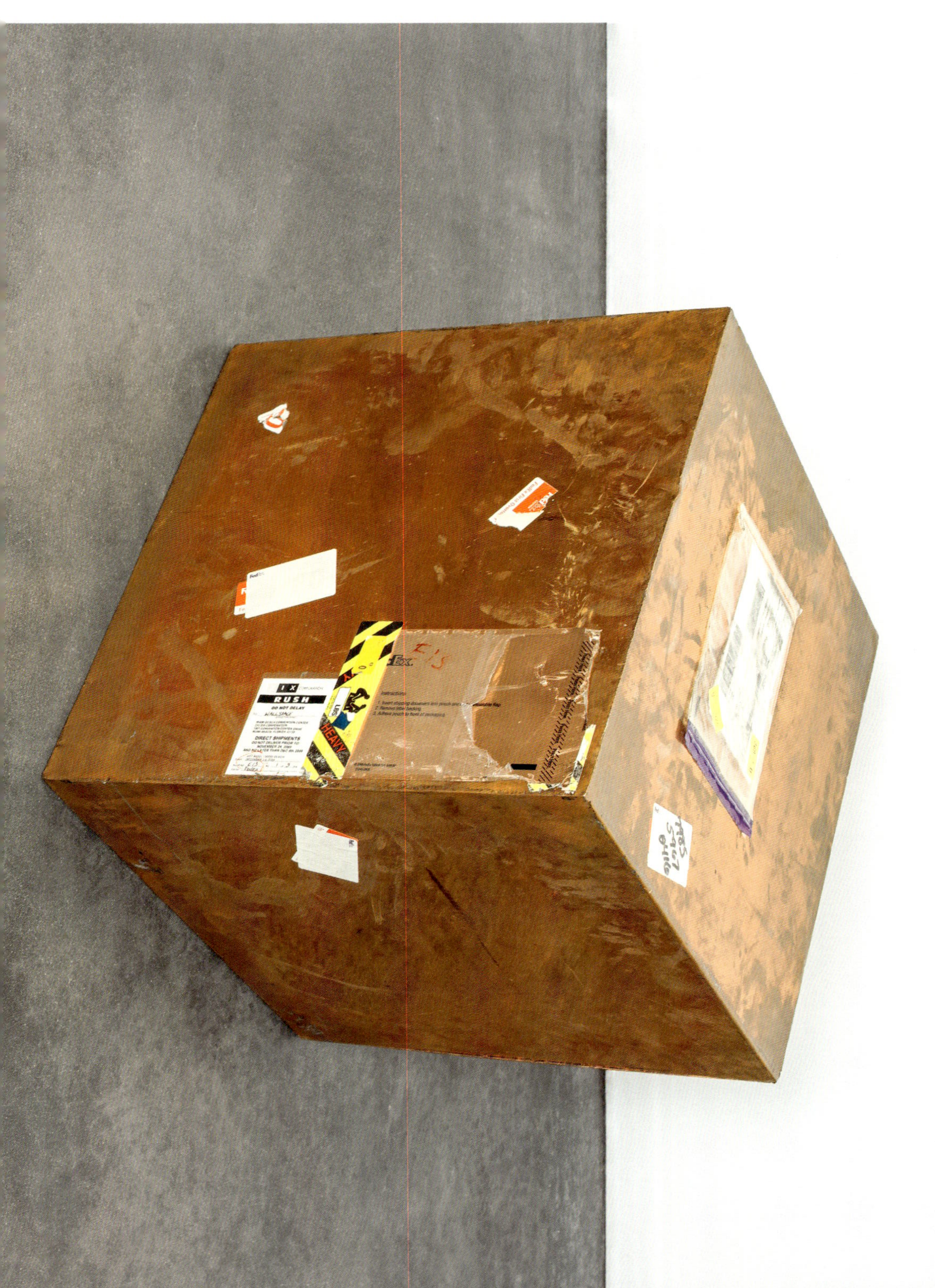

24-inch Copper (FedEx® Large Kraft Box ©2005 FEDEX 330510) First Overnight, Los Angeles–Miami trk#798173003782, November 27–28, 2009, Standard Overnight, Miami–New York trk#798196377030, December 7–8, 2009, Standard Overnight, New York–Beverly Hills trk#793169811939, January 11–12, 2010, Standard Overnight, Beverly Hills–St. Helena trk#793430416294, April 9–10, 2010, Priority Overnight, St. Helena–Beverly Hills trk#798559570416, April 14–15, 2010
2009–, 2014
Polished copper, accrued FedEx shipping and tracking labels
24 × 24 × 24 inches (61 × 61 × 61 cm)

Selected Works (2009–2011/November 15th 2010–March 16th 2011), 2011
Black-and-white fiber-based photographic paper, color photographic paper, and archival inkjet papers
90 × 50 inches (228.6 × 127 cm)

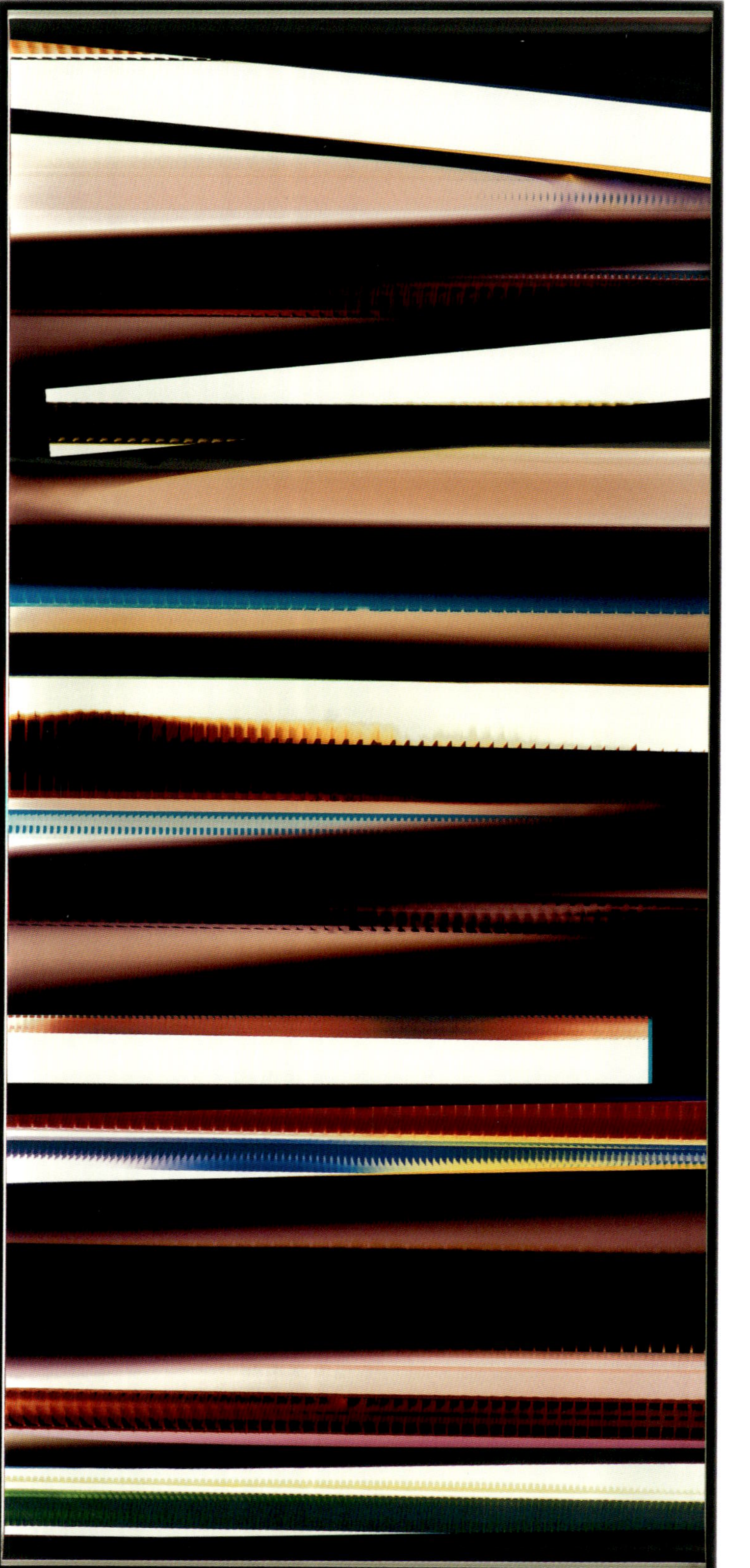

RA4 Contact Print [Black Curl (YMC/Six Magnet: Los Angeles, California, December 18, 2013, Fuji Color Crystal Archive Super Type C, Em. No. 101-007, 43513), Kreonite KM IV 5225 RA4 Color Processor, Ser. No. 00092174], 2014
Color photographic paper
52 × 115½ × 2½ inches (132.1 × 293.4 × 6.4 cm)

Picture Made by My Hand with the Assistance of Light, 2010
Black-and-white fiber-based photographic paper
97 1/2 × 55 1/2 inches (247.7 × 141 cm)

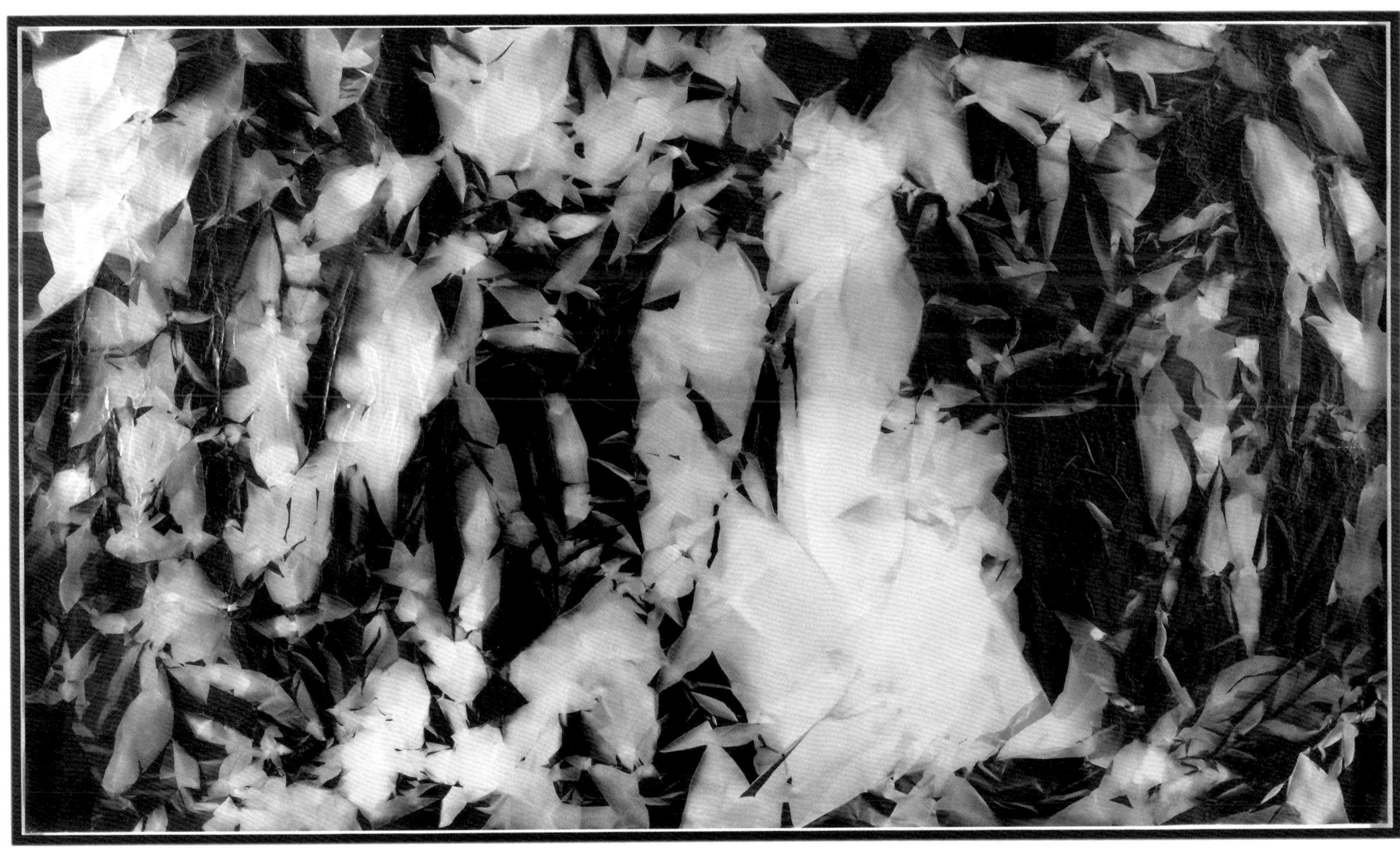

Carol Bove's earliest prominent works, garnering attention shortly after the artist graduated from New York University in 2000, reveal important aspects of her widely celebrated practice. These pieces comprise simple wooden shelves on which she places evocative arrangements of secondhand books—such as Betty Friedan's *The Feminine Mystique*, Kenneth Anger's *Hollywood Babylon*, and *The Writings of Robert Smithson*—alongside found objects. The books' faded covers and dog-eared pages attest to the passage of time since the 1960s, when they first enjoyed public acclaim.

Bove's curious selection of objects—from photographs, metronomes, and seashells to driftwood, crystals, and peacock feathers—also conjures a nostalgic memory of the era's heady mix of sex, politics, and aesthetics. "I have a sense of history being contained by objects," Bove has said, and her practice at the intersection of sculpture, assemblage, and design urges one to encounter worldly things anew.

Raised in Berkeley, California, Bove's upbringing during the waning of the "sixties," in one of the period's hotbed sites, is a key origin point for the artist's sense of objects, their materiality, and the signature way she composes and arranges them to conjure multilayered registers of meaning. Red Hook, Brooklyn, where Bove currently lives and works, has been a more recent source of material and inspiration. While she has departed from her early work and its explicit imprint of the sixties, her recent sculptures and installations continue to engage place, time, and process, in ways that echo artists active in the preceding era. Whether harvesting rusted metal from her postindustrial neighborhood for a sculpture like *Untitled* (2009) or collaborating with nearby jewelers and fabricators to create *Peel's foe, not a set animal, laminates a tone of sleep* (2013), Bove reconceives artistic problems of the 1960s by exposing them to enduring questions of poetics and aesthetics such as sensing and knowing, order and chaos, sight and touch.

Bove has had solo exhibitions at The Museum of Modern Art, New York, the High Line, New York; the Palais de Tokyo, Paris; the Blanton Art Museum, Austin; Kunsthalle Zurich; and the Institute of Contemporary Art, Boston. She has also participated in Documenta 13, the 54th Venice Biennale, and the Whitney Biennial, among many other noteworthy group exhibitions. J. A.

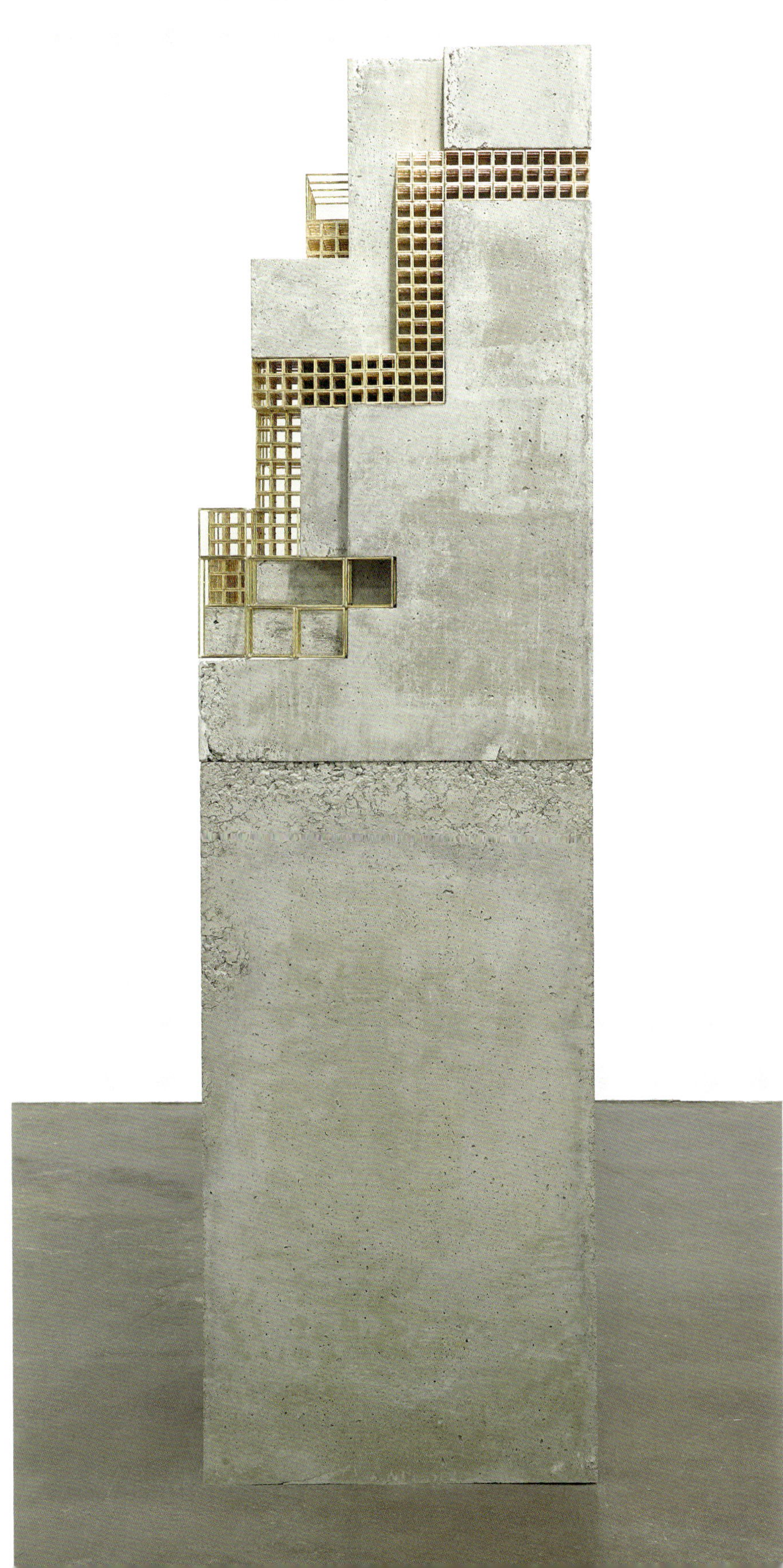

Peel's foe, not a set animal, laminates a tone of sleep, 2013
Brass and concrete
84 × 24 × 24 inches (213.4 × 61 × 61 cm)

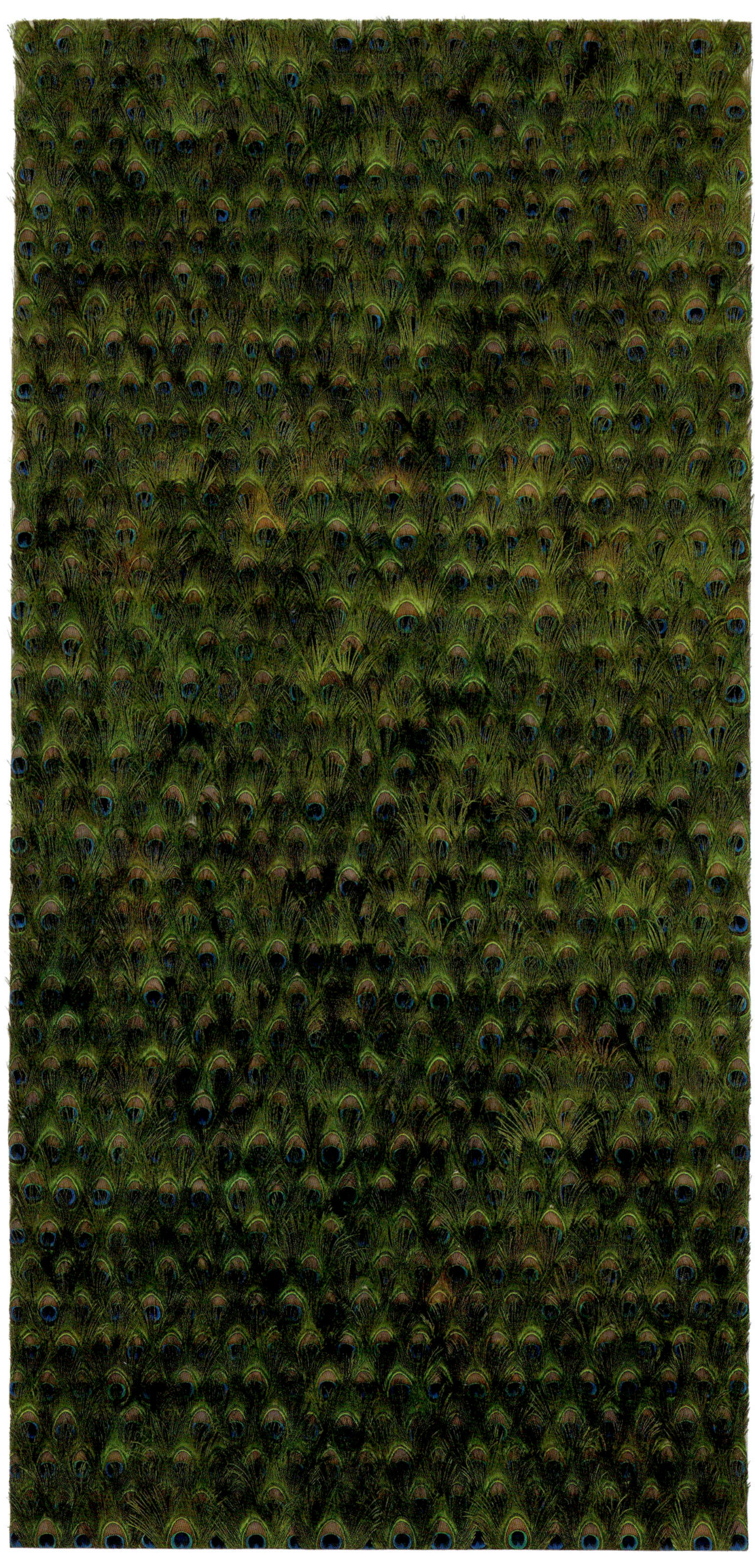

Untitled, 2012
Peacock feathers on linen, Plexiglas vitrine
96 × 48 × 5 inches (243.8 × 121.9 × 12.7 cm)

Eighth Red Sweater Painting, 2015
Acrylic on canvas
48 × 60 × 1¾ inches (121.9 × 152.4 × 4.4 cm)

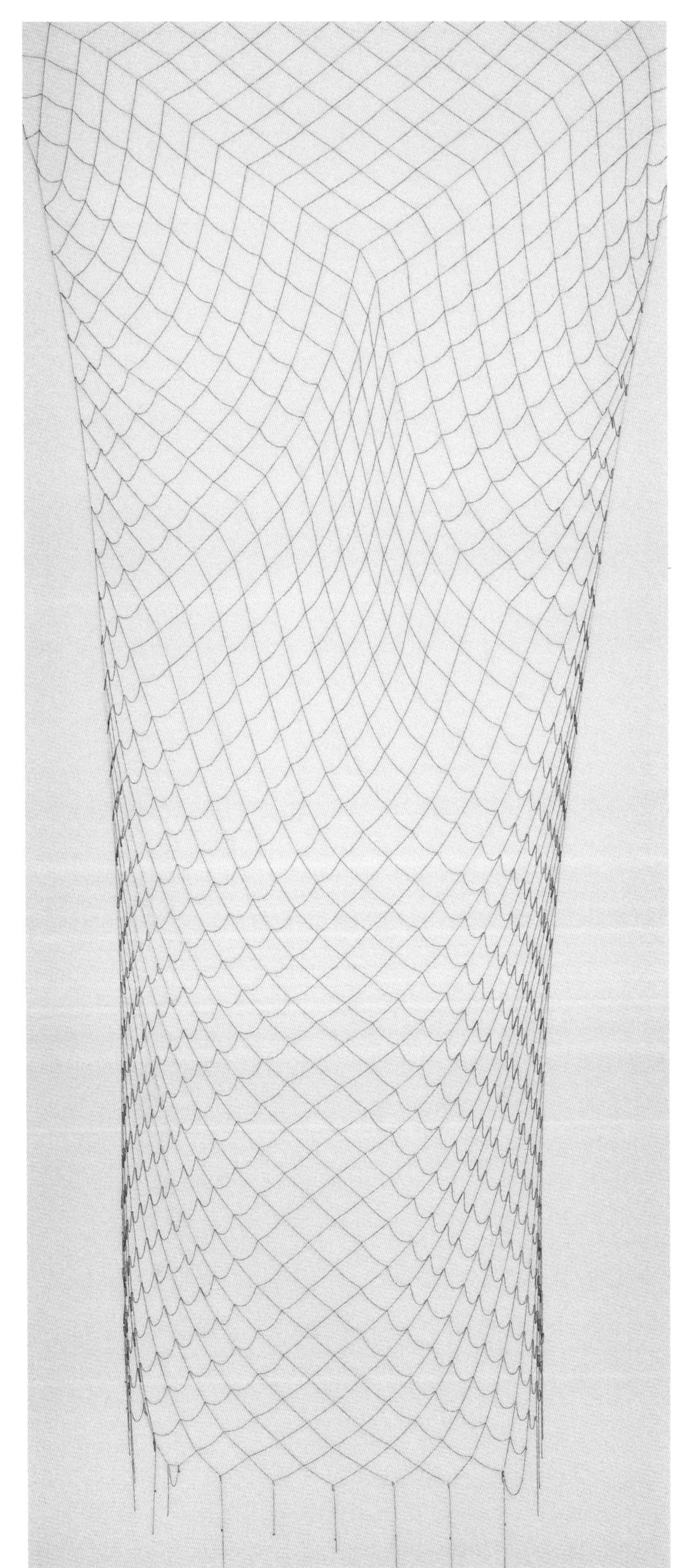

Harlequin, 2011
Acrylic paint on linen
84 × 36 inches (213.4 × 91.4 cm)

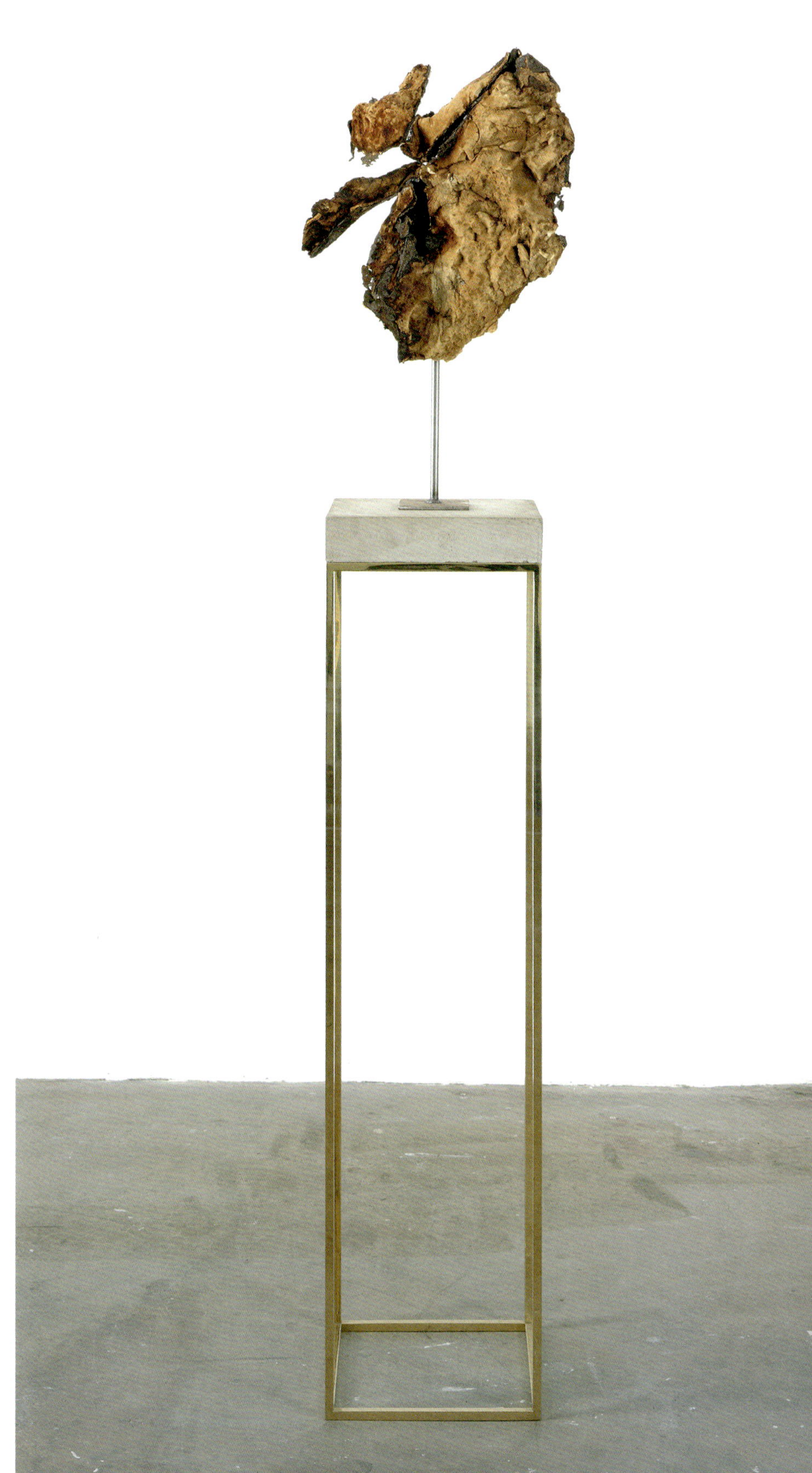

Untitled, 2009
Found metal with insulating foam, steel,
concrete, and bronze
66 × 12 × 12 inches (167.6 × 30.5 × 30.5 cm)

MARK BRADFORD

b. 1961, Los Angeles, CA

Untitled Pink (SFMOMA Benefit), 2016
Mixed media on canvas
60 × 48 inches (152.4 × 121.9 cm)

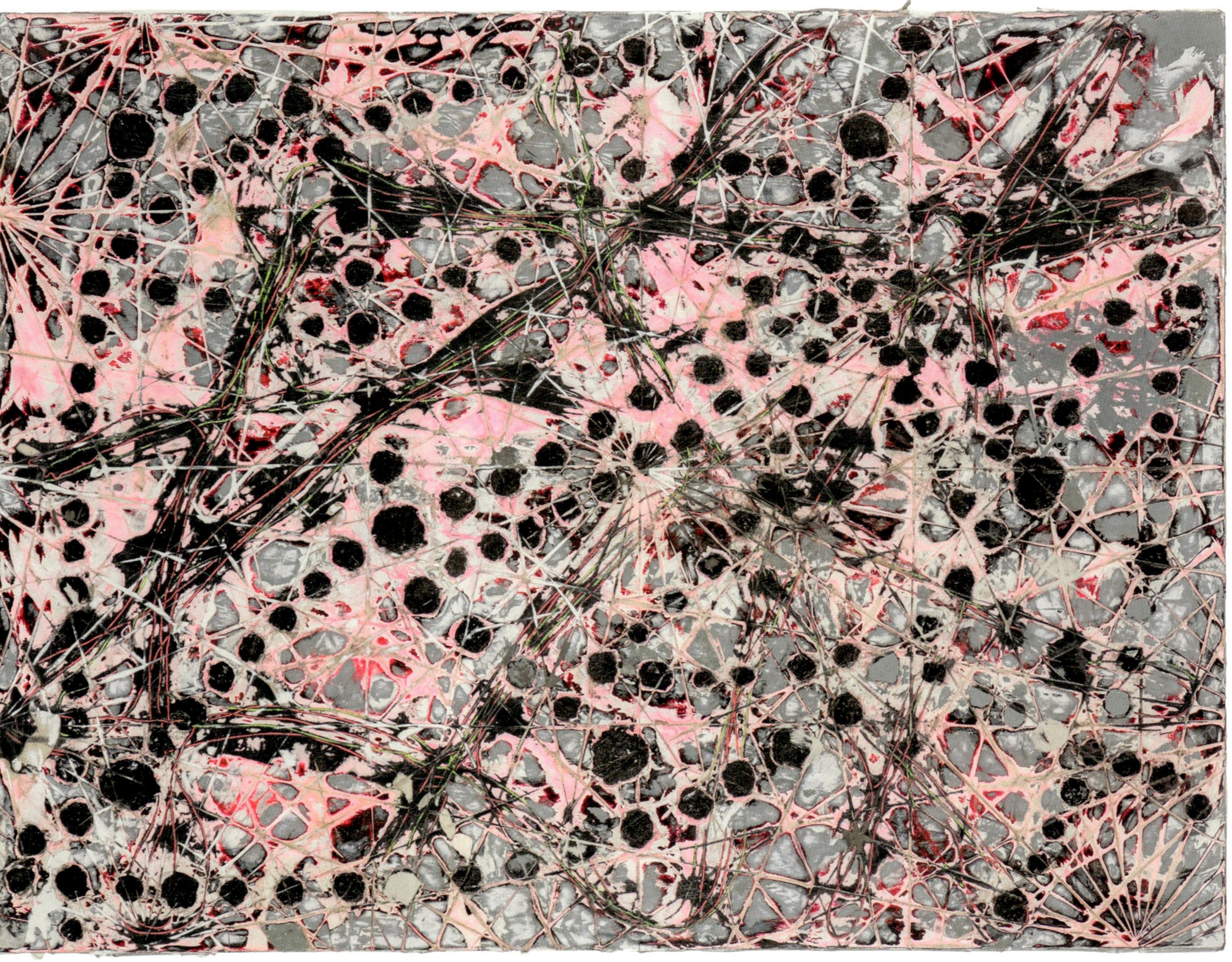

On the face of it, Mark Bradford's large-scale, ebullient paintings are meant to dazzle, and on a purely formal level they do: so layered with paper and paint that they're three dimensional, Bradford's art immerses the viewer in dynamic swirls of color. And yet his practice is at heart an excavation, peeling back layers to reveal maps, grids, even the language of urban and social contexts.

Bradford, who was born in Los Angeles in 1961, spent most of his life in Southern California. He grew up on L.A.'s south side, worked in his family's hair salon to put himself through art school (he graduated with a BFA and MFA from California Institute of the Arts (CalArts) in 1995 and 1997, respectively), and today, his studio is just blocks from that same salon. Bradford was included in the 2001 *Freestyle* exhibition at The Studio Museum in Harlem, and a dizzying number of exhibitions and accolades followed soon after. (That same year Bradford sold his first painting.) Today, he's been the subject a solo show at the Whitney Museum of American Art in New York, received the MacArthur "Genius" grant, created site-specific work for a solo show at the Hammer Museum in Los Angeles, and will represent the U.S. in the 2017 Venice Biennale.

The key to Bradford's rapid, almost unimaginably swift success can be found in his paintings. To make these works, Bradford layers dozens of pieces of paper and ephemera on canvas, occasionally adding layers of paint or other media between each layer. Once these have set, he digs into them with a power sander, attacking the canvas to reveal nuance, depth, and meaning.

Bradford has used this technique to powerful effect, creating works that evoke maps—an evocation of an urban fabric—and paintings with language lifted from fliers, graffiti, and billboards from his neighborhood. This latter technique is in evidence in *Untitled* from 2007, for which Bradford collected posters, paper, and materials from the street, collaged them together, and then used the sander to carve in the language from an advertisement for Promise Land, a group home for low-income L.A. residents struggling with substance abuse. The end effect is trademark Bradford—striking at the outset, and after close inspection, seething with undercurrents of social unrest. J. T.

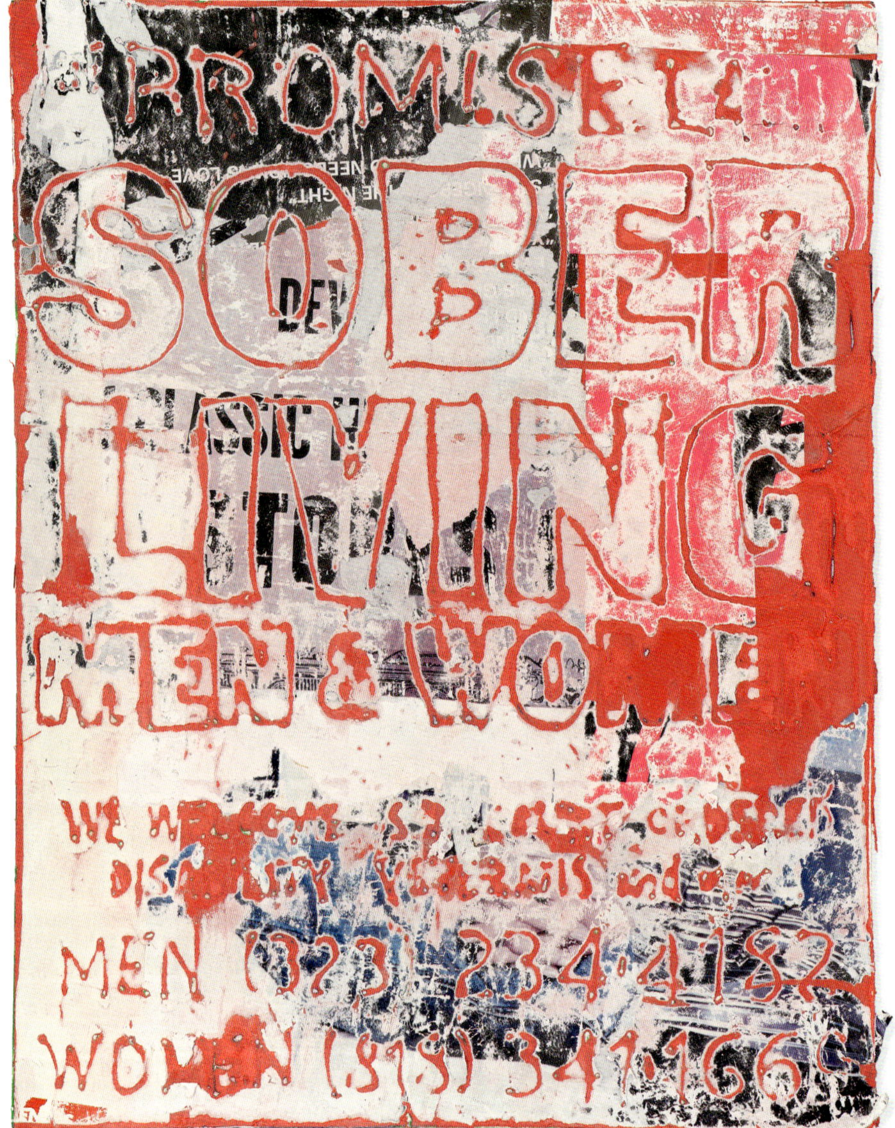

Untitled, 2007
Mixed media on paper
28 ½ × 22 inches (72.4 × 55.9 cm)

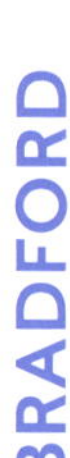

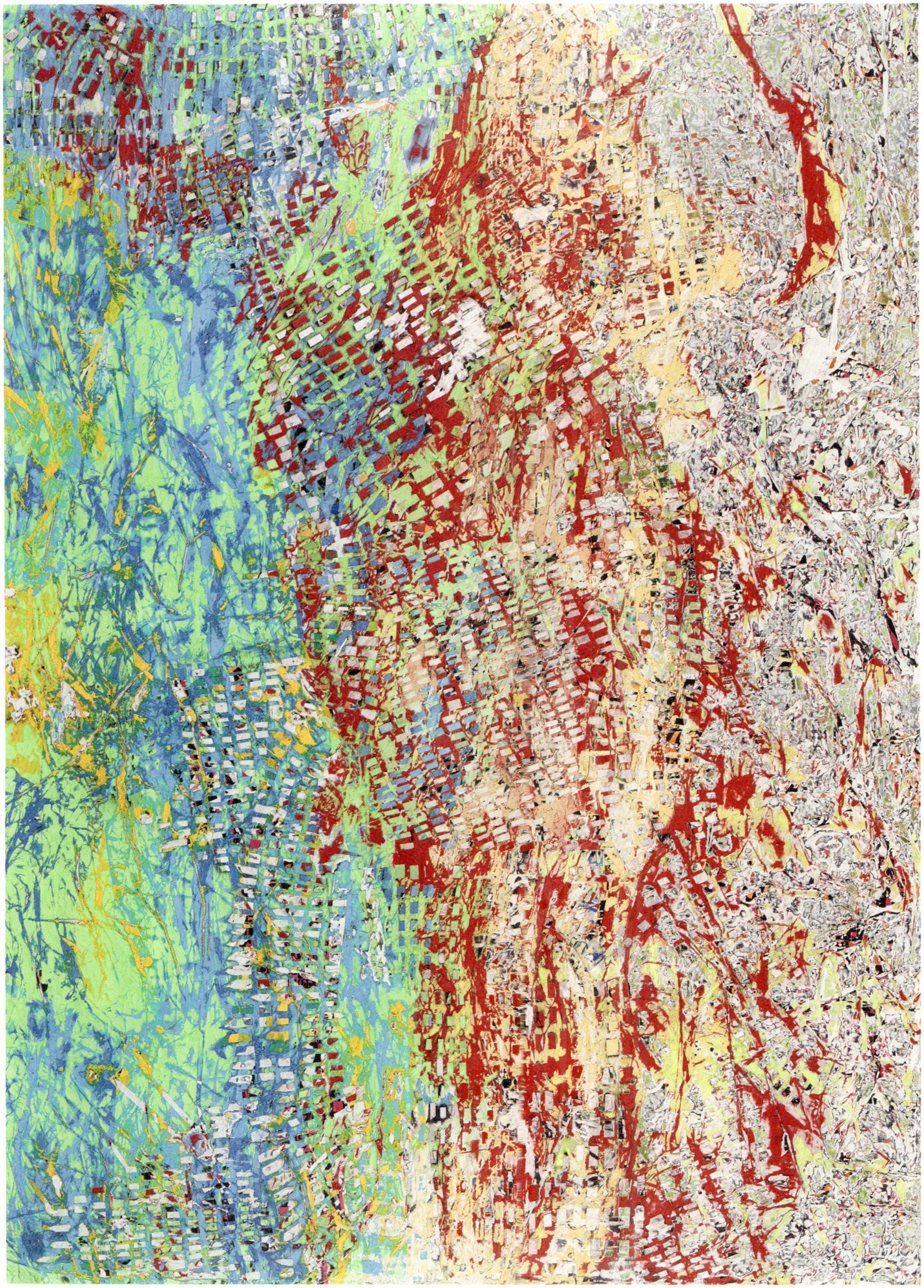

Dragon, 2012
Mixed media on canvas
102 × 144 inches (259.1 × 365.8 cm)

DAN COLEN b. 1979, Leonia, NJ

Dan Colen's art is inextricable from his biography. Born in Leonia, New Jersey, in 1979, he graduated with a BFA from the Rhode Island School of Design in 2001 and moved to New York at a time when the city's art world had been on an unbroken, decade-long growth spurt. Along with Dash Snow, Nate Lowman, and Ryan McGinley, Colen spearheaded the Lower East Side arts scene with unparalleled demonstrations of anti-establishment hedonism—drugs, sex, parties, and more drugs. At the time, Colen's art consisted mainly of hyper-detailed oil paintings of room interiors, though he also collaborated with his friends, most famously working with Snow to shred 2,000 telephone books in the Deitch Projects gallery space in 2007, mimicking a hamster's cage.

In 2008, the art market crashed (briefly, as it turned out), and in 2009 Snow died of an overdose, at which point Colen started to clean up his life and his art. Choosing mediums other than paint—gum, glitter, bird droppings—he began to scale-up his work, creating large sculptures and installations. Today, Colen, who has a studio in Red Hook, Brooklyn, and splits his time between New York City and a farm upstate, has had dozens of solo exhibitions including shows at the Astrup Fearnley Museum of Modern Art in Oslo, Norway, Inverleith House at the Royal Botanic Garden in Edinburgh, Scotland, and the Brant Foundation Art Study Center in Greenwich, Connecticut.

Colen's "bubblegum paintings"—made from store bought and manipulated chewing gum applied to canvas—comprise one of his longest ongoing series. Originally Colen and his assistants chewed each piece of gum themselves, but the process proved far too time-intensive to be scalable as a series. Colen discovered that by heating up the gum, he could achieve the same consistency as if he'd chewed it.

TBT from 2014 is an example of the result: from afar the gum could be heavy oil paint, in the same aesthetic as the Gutai artist Kazuo Shiraga; on closer inspection though, the gum lends a certain webbed texture that would be impossible with paint—layered, fine, and oddly delicate, the work is an example of Colen trying, then succeeding, to create something truly new. J. T.

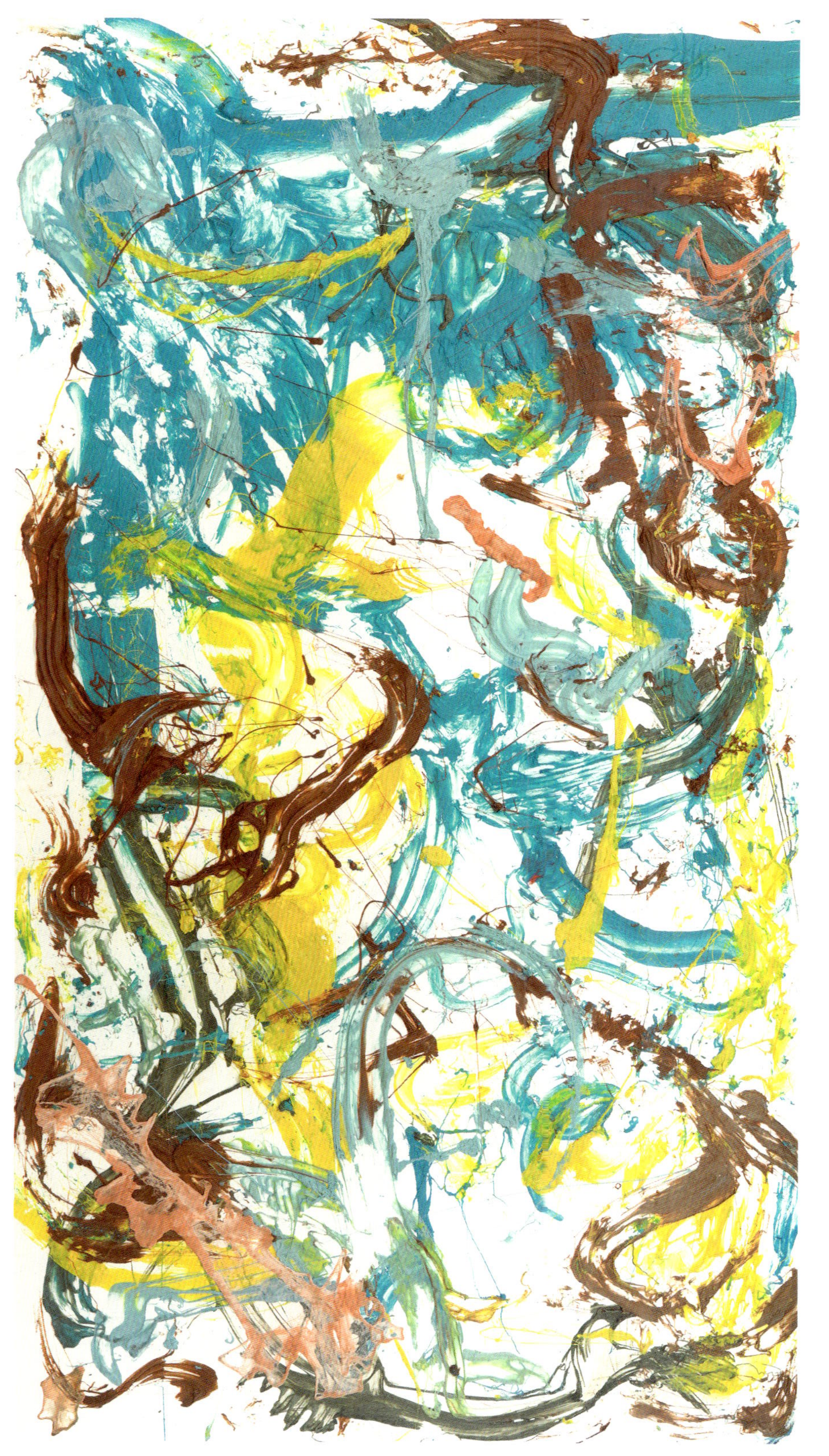

TBT, 2014
Chewing gum on canvas
110 × 207 inches (279.4 × 525.8 cm)

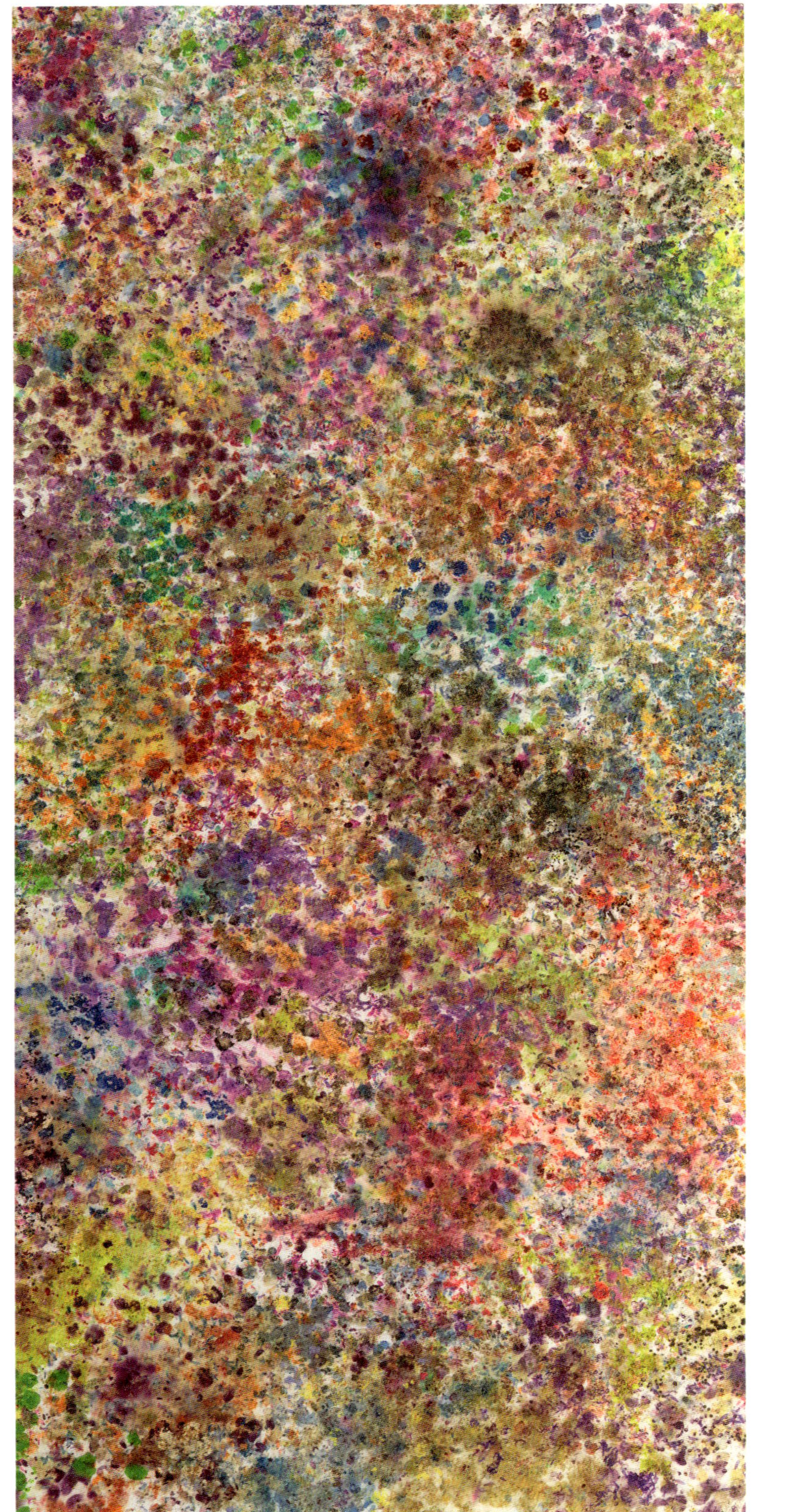

Killed by Death, 2014
Flowers on bleached Belgian linen
96 × 206 inches (243.8 × 523.2 cm)

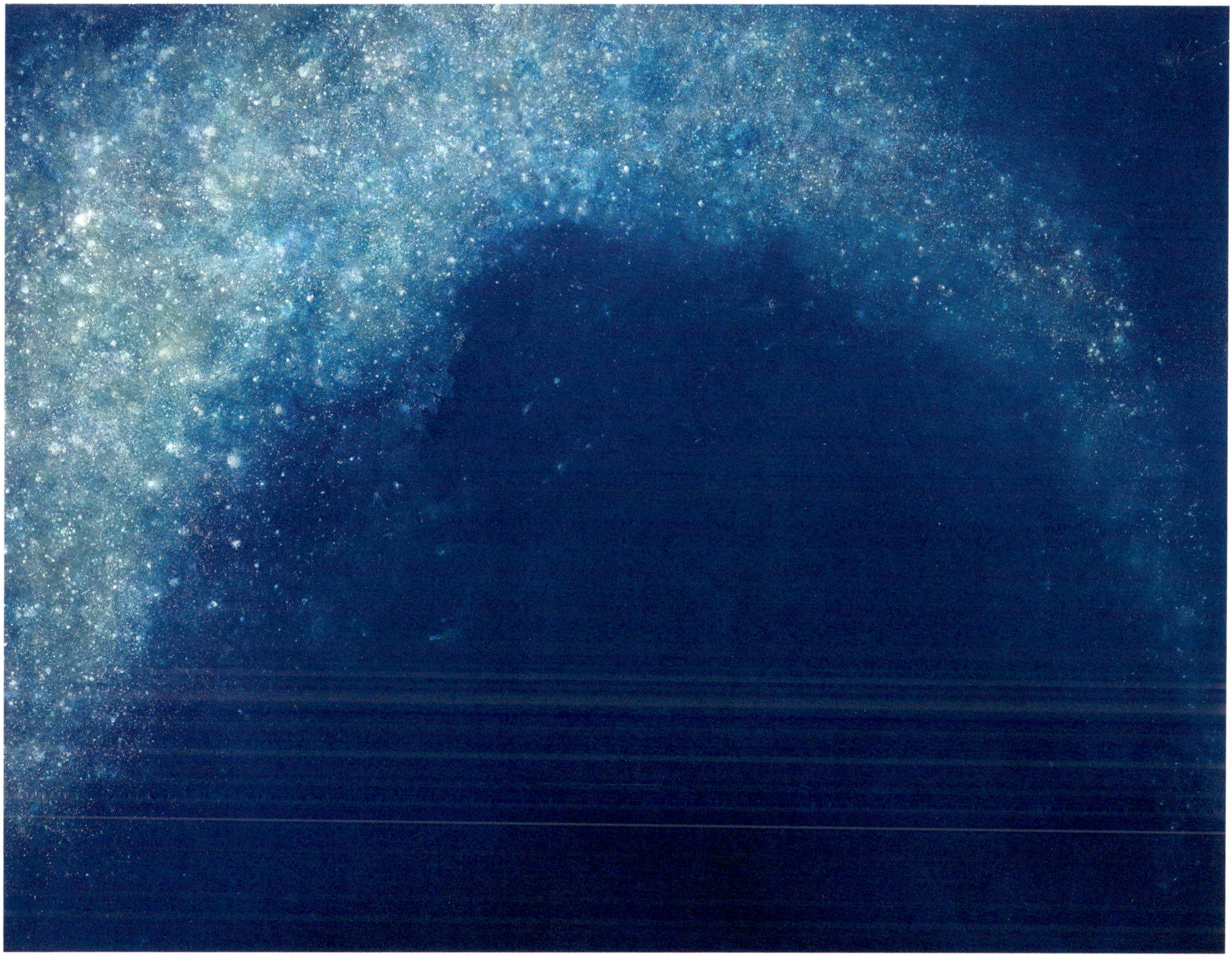

The Inextinguishable, 2013
Oil on canvas
89 ½ × 119 inches (227.3 × 302.3 cm)

George Condo's art manages the clever feat of appearing contemporary while drawing from 600 years of art history. Not quite abstract and never exactly polished, his paintings, drawings, and sculptures have an ethereal, vaguely surreal quality that disconcerts the viewer as much as it charms.

Condo was born in Concord, New Hampshire, in 1957, and came of age as an artist amidst a fetishization of all things new and novel in mid-1980s New York, where he worked for Andy Warhol and was friends with au courant painters like Keith Haring and Jean-Michel Basquiat. Condo's early work drew from old masters like Tiepolo and Caravaggio, but rather than producing derivative variations on the lush colors and rich historicism of these works, or those of Rembrandt and Francisco Goya, Condo translated models of portraiture, iconography, and narrative into a contemporary vernacular.

Despite (or perhaps because of) how different his artwork was from that of his peers, Condo managed to develop a devoted following in America and Europe. In the last three decades, he has had solo shows at the New Museum in New York, the Hayward Gallery in London, and the Berggruen Museum in Berlin. Condo's work is also in the permanent collections of The Metropolitan Museum of Art in New York, the Corcoran Gallery of Art in Washington D.C., the Tate Gallery in London, and the Astrup Fearnley Museum of Modern Art in Oslo

Eventually Condo moved past old masters and medieval iconography and toward a more modern series of influences. In works from the last decade, the influence of painters like Paul Cezanne and Pablo Picasso are hard to miss. Take *The White Album*, a 2015 oil and graphite on linen work that's just over six feet tall. Here, Condo has drawn from twentieth-century abstraction—the work has clear parallels with Paul Klee and even Georges Braque—but he's also infused the canvas with decidedly timely flourishes: interspersed among various lines and shapes, one can find Condo's trademark eyes and teeth figured in a mock-primitive style, while even the color palette—a combination of vivid blues, electric greens, and pale yellows—pulsates with a quasi-avant-garde vitality. It's a painting that, like all of Condo's art, uses history as a tool rather than a crutch. J. T.

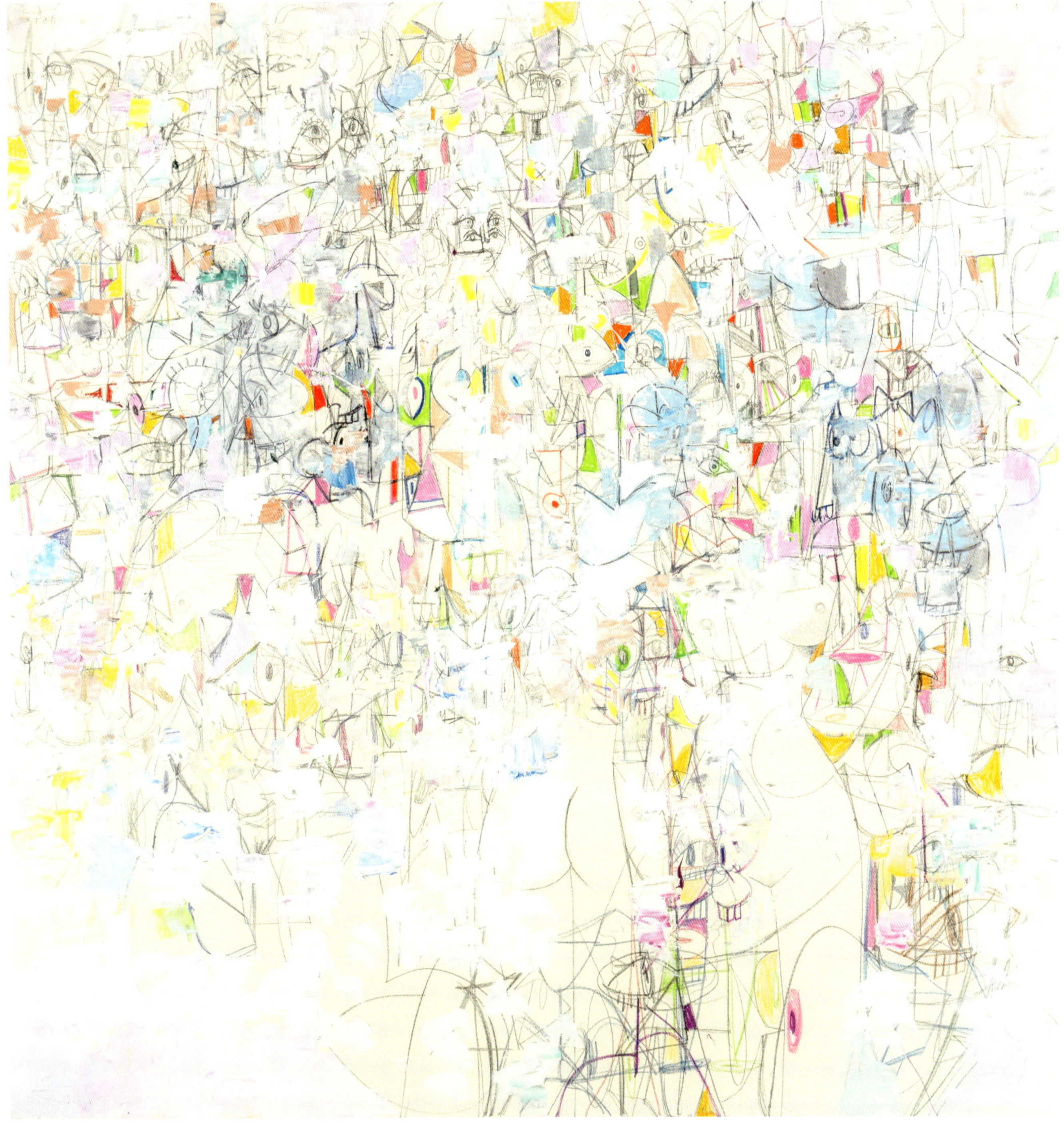

The White Album, 2015
Oil and graphite on linen
77 × 75 inches (195.6 × 190.5 cm)

AARON CURRY

b. 1972, San Antonio, TX

Aaron Curry was born in San Antonio in 1972. A fateful adolescent encounter with Pablo Picasso's late painting convinced Curry to become an artist: he received a BFA from the School of the Art Institute of Chicago in 2002 and three years later earned an MFA from the Art Center College of Design where teachers Mike Kelley and Richard Hawkins became major influences. Inclusion in the New Museum's influential 2007 *Unmonumental* exhibition and a solo show at the Hammer Museum the next year cemented Curry's status; in 2013, he completed a major public sculpture commission at Lincoln Center in New York.

Curry's work gravitates around the possibilities of relief sculpture as a conduit between both dimensionalities and cultural registers. Channeling Alexander Calder, Tony Smith, Joan Miró, postwar Picasso, Richard Serra, and even Francis Bacon, Curry explores biomorphic forms that grope for their own location in space and volume. Fluid shapes sag while rectilinear supports structure and hold. Yet the aesthetics of digital technology and 1980s advertising infect Curry's ensembles, rendering them vivacious in their pastel tones and charming in their unfettered expressivity.

The sensibility of the graphic line saturates his oeuvre: Curry often works from computer designs or sketches before moving to three dimensions. Curry's recent paintings also exhibit these concerns, yet more aggressively pursue the dialectics of hand, mouse, canvas, and screen.

With *Vvirgins* (2011), Curry very clearly exemplifies his unique approach to sculpture. Comprised of painted aluminum shapes slotted together to intersect at right angles (without screws or clips) the work consists of two elements. The larger element is a three-legged figure with a square panel on top. When viewed from above, the sculpture recalls a symmetrical cross, but from other vantage points, one might see an animal-like figure or some sort of gate structure. The second component is tall and narrow, with the top reminiscent of a human head with a long neck. With Curry's flat silhouettes, it is impossible to predict what the forms will look like from any particular viewpoint; his process ensures that when seen from different angles, the sculptures completely change.
J. H.

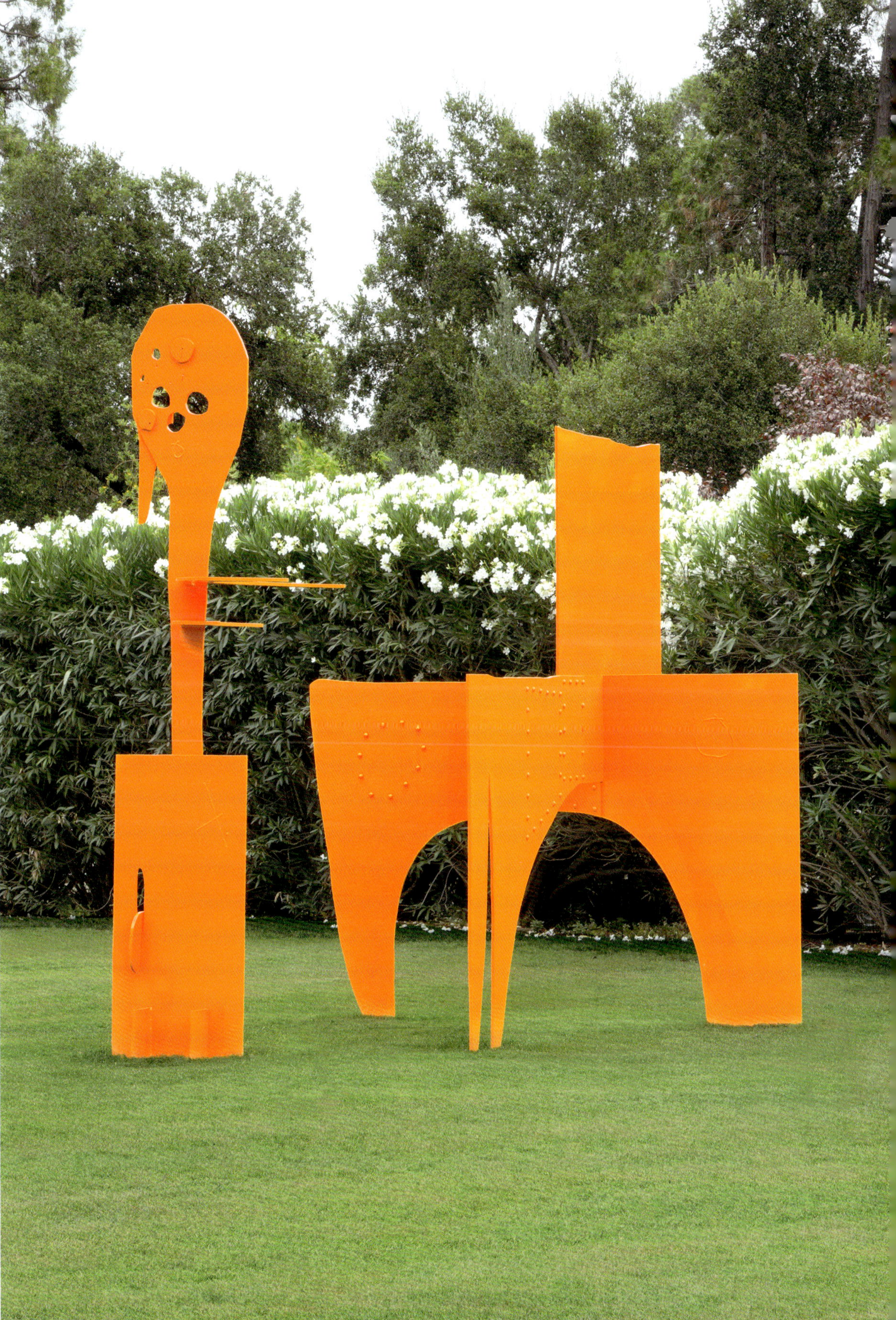

VVirgins, 2011
Painted aluminum
119 × 107½ × 119 inches
(302.3 × 273.1 × 302.3 cm) overall
Component 1 of 2: 102 × 107½ × 92 inches
(259.1 × 273.1 × 233.7 cm)
Component 2 of 2: 119 × 34 × 36 inches
(302.3 × 86.4 × 91.4 cm)

For Latifa Echakhch, an object's identity isn't as important as what it means to dispose of it; only through its absence can its social, cultural, and physical meaning be fully articulated.

This is evident in early work like *Frames* (begun in 2000), in which she unwound the threads of Islamic prayer rugs until only the frames were left. In these works, Echakhch had eliminated the prayer rug but its symbolism, power, and resonance remained. She removed the object, in other words, and in doing so revealed its theoretical constructs.

Echakhch was born in 1974 in El Khnansa, Morocco, and emigrated to France with her family at the age of three. She graduated in 1997 from the Ecole Supérieure d'Art in Grenoble with an advanced diploma from the Paris Cergy National School of Art 1999, and with a Post Diplôme from the School of Fine Arts in Lyon in 2002. Her work has been shown at the Tate Modern in London, the Swiss Institute in New York, and the Hammer Museum in Los Angeles, and she won the prestigious Marcel Duchamp prize in 2013. Today, she lives and works in Martigny, Switzerland.

Perhaps because of Echakhch's childhood and position as a cultural outsider, there's an elegiac quality to much of her work; the aforementioned evisceration of meaning might bring clarity, but it's still an act of removal, a demonstration of violent elimination. This is profoundly conspicuous in her large-scale installation *Tannhäuser* from 2013, which was part of a larger exhibition at Galerie Eva Presenhuber in Zurich called *The Scene Takes Place*. The installation, which includes a wooden floor, three harps, assorted stage lights, and the shells of stage scenery, are recreations of decor for a performance of Wagner's *Tannhäuser* at the Bayreuth Festival in 1955. Here again, Echakhch has created a relic, the literal embodiment of spectacle stripped of meaning. Without singers or viewers, the opera—a profound symbol of German cultural potency—becomes something almost archeological. It's an installation that forcefully underscores the power of objecthood and discursive space. J. T.

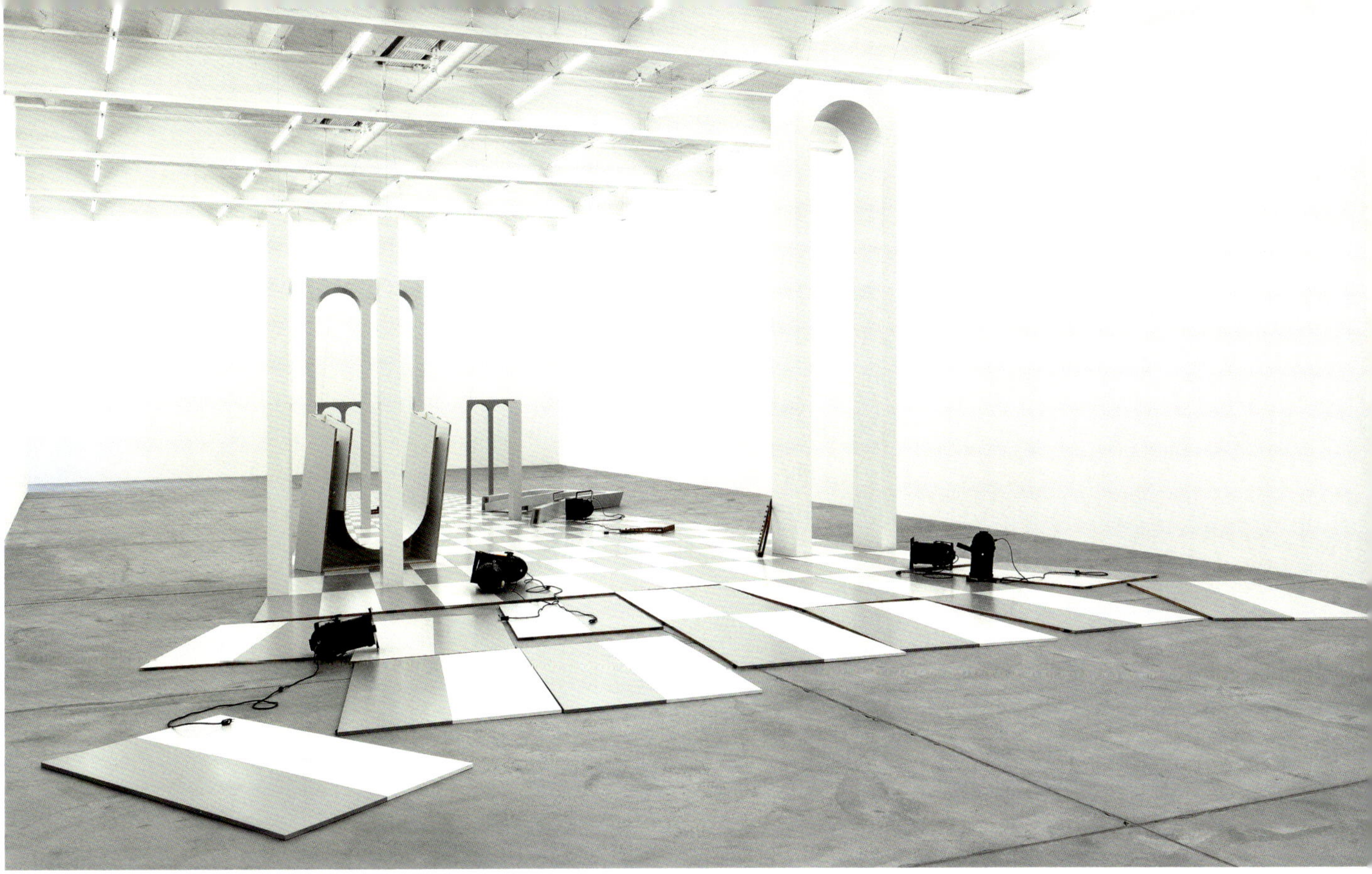

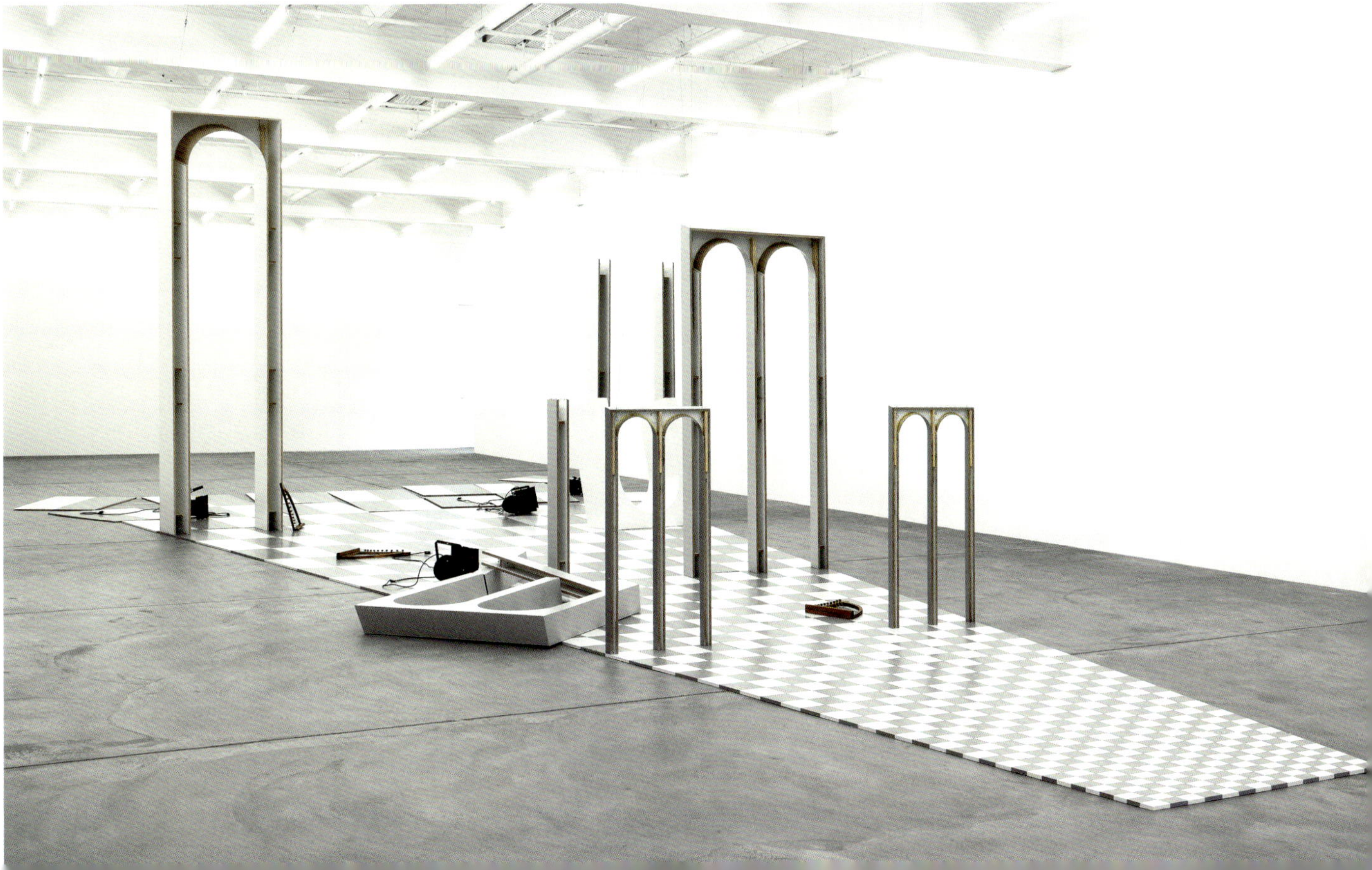

Tannhäuser, 2013
Installation: backdrop of opera decors including wooden floor, 6 MDF modules, 6 spotlights, and 3 harps
158 1/8 × 662 5/8 × 313 inches
(401.5 × 1683 × 797 cm) overall

Branches became black, sky turn to a deep orange. Original shapes disappear in a blurred disorder., 2014
Ink on canvas
78 ¾ × 59 × 1 inches (200 × 150 × 2.5 cm)

ECHAKHCH

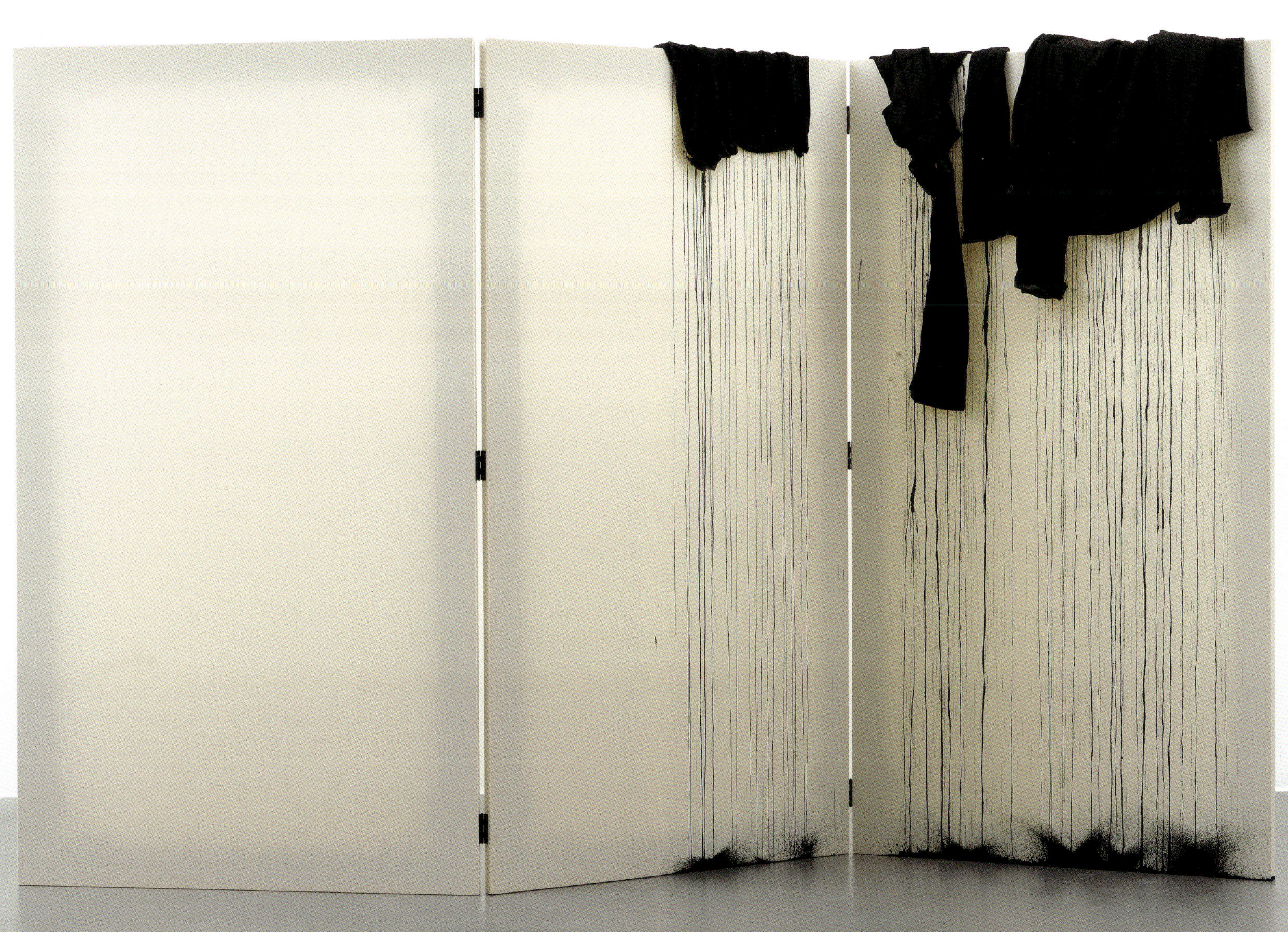

Screen Shot M.K., 2015
Wood, aluminum frames, canvas, tack clothes, and black India ink
68 1/8 × 118 1/8 × 1 inches (173 × 37.5 × 2.5 cm)

ROE ETHRIDGE b. 1969, Miami, FL

Sacrifice Your Body, 2013
C-print
$41\frac{3}{4} \times 51\frac{7}{8}$ inches (106×131.8 cm)
Edition 5 of 5, 2 AP

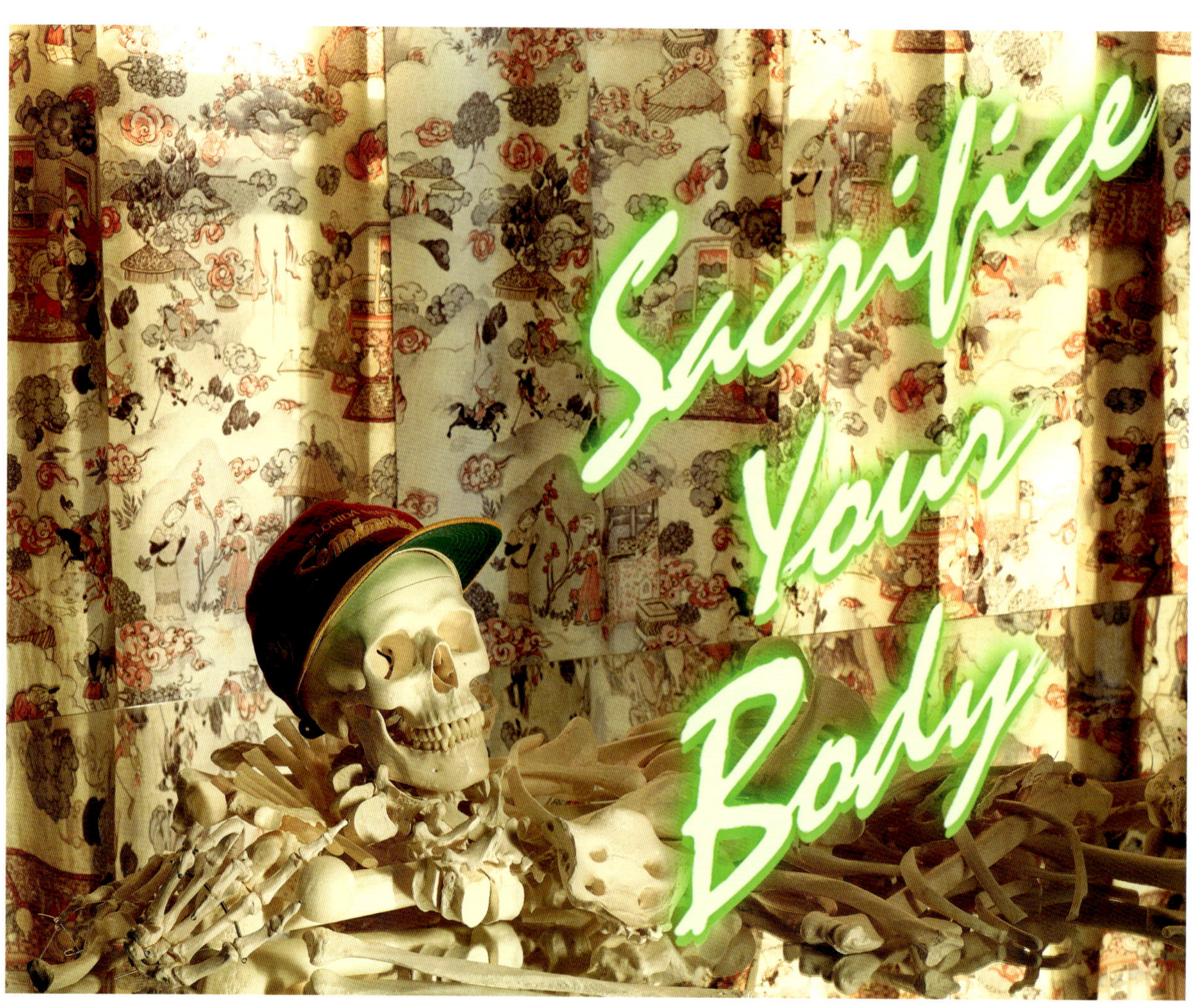

Born in Miami in 1969, Roe Ethridge was raised in Atlanta and received his BFA in photography from the Atlanta College of Art in 1995. The artist's early influences ranged from the straightforward objective-style photography of the Düsseldorf School to an upended Warholian sense of getting it "exactly wrong." After moving to New York City in 1997, Ethridge began a secondary career in commercial photography, and the disparate contexts for his photographs began to blur.

Ethridge has garnered attention since the late 1990s for works that address the ubiquity of photography in contemporary culture, collapse distinctions between art and commercialism, and explore the discord between high and low.

Ethridge's oeuvre employs a varied list of subjects including Chanel perfume, the moon, Bonne Maman jam jars, strip mall signage, footballs, fashion models, surfers, sunsets, and construction workers. His photographs comprise a systematic study in typologies associated with the medium's history—weaving together diverse genres in order to both dismantle and connect them. In approaching his editorial, fashion, and advertising assignments as a "rental atelier," Ethridge moves naturally between commercial and personal projects, transferring and alternating images between magazines and exhibitions. The accumulation of seemingly disconnected images in Ethridge's work loosely follow serial themes or stand alone as single images—exposing photographic typologies as a kind of orderly chaos.

Sacrifice Your Body (2013) belongs to a series of the same title centered around the artist's relationship with his mother and his suburban Florida upbringing. Here, a jumbled skeleton wearing a Florida State Seminoles hat stretches out in a supine pose before a mirrored surface and a backdrop of domestic drapery. Superimposed across the scene in large neon green script, the photograph's title makes reference to the words shouted by mothers to their football player sons on the field during Ethridge's high school years. In Ethridge's punchline, the figure appears to have literally sacrificed his body for the sport.

In *Celine Bracelet for Gentlewoman* (2014), a large, chunky bracelet from luxury brand Céline lies amongst artificial fruit, a lighter, a lipstick-stained disposable coffee cup, and a marble background. Presumably an outtake from an advertising shoot, the image embodies both still life and documentary photographic traditions in its embrace of chance and the intermingling of fantasy and imperfection.
C. R.

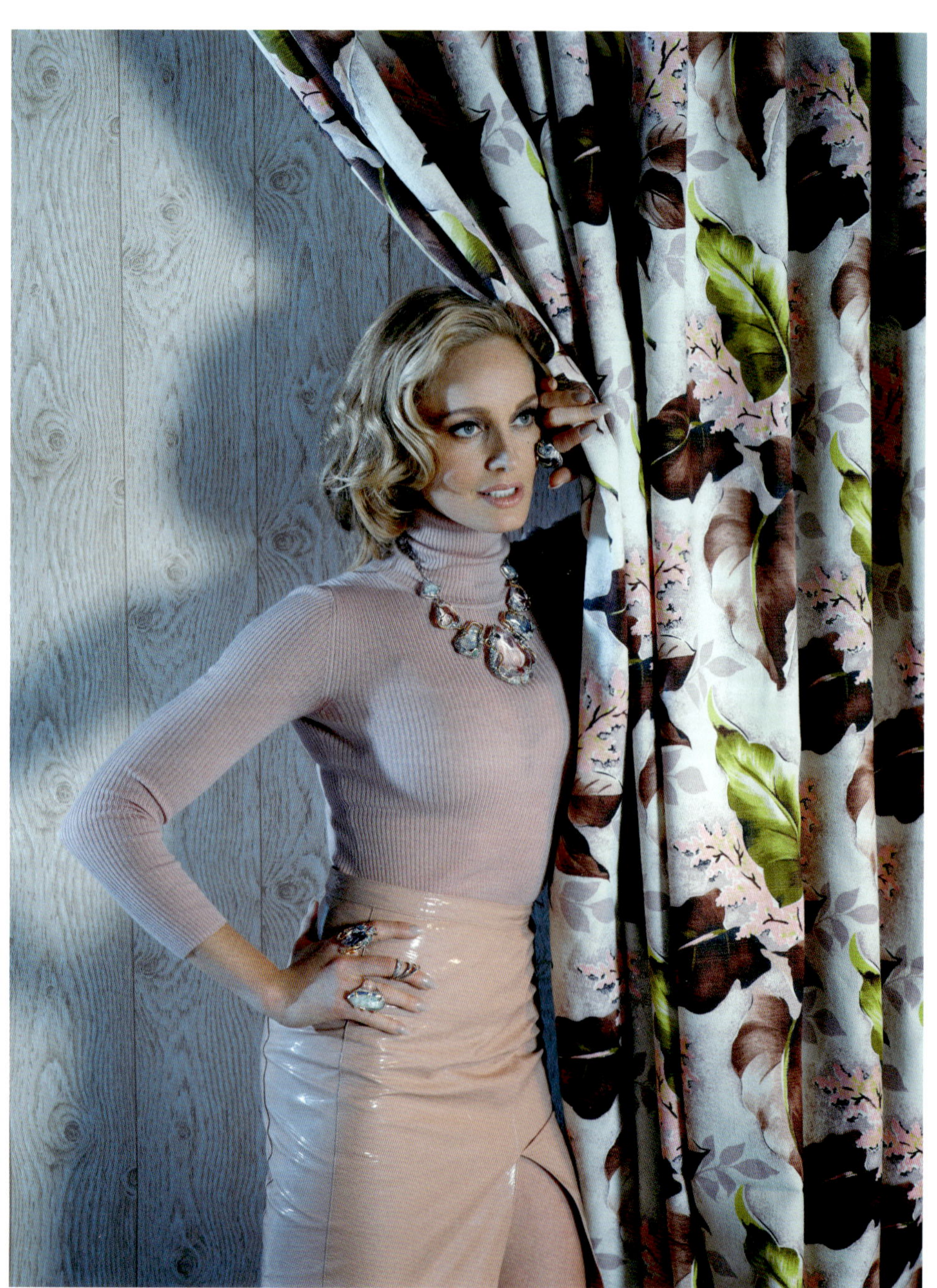

Untitled (Alexis Bittar), 2013
C-print
55⅛ × 41⅝ inches (140 × 105.7 cm)
Edition 5 of 5, 2 AP

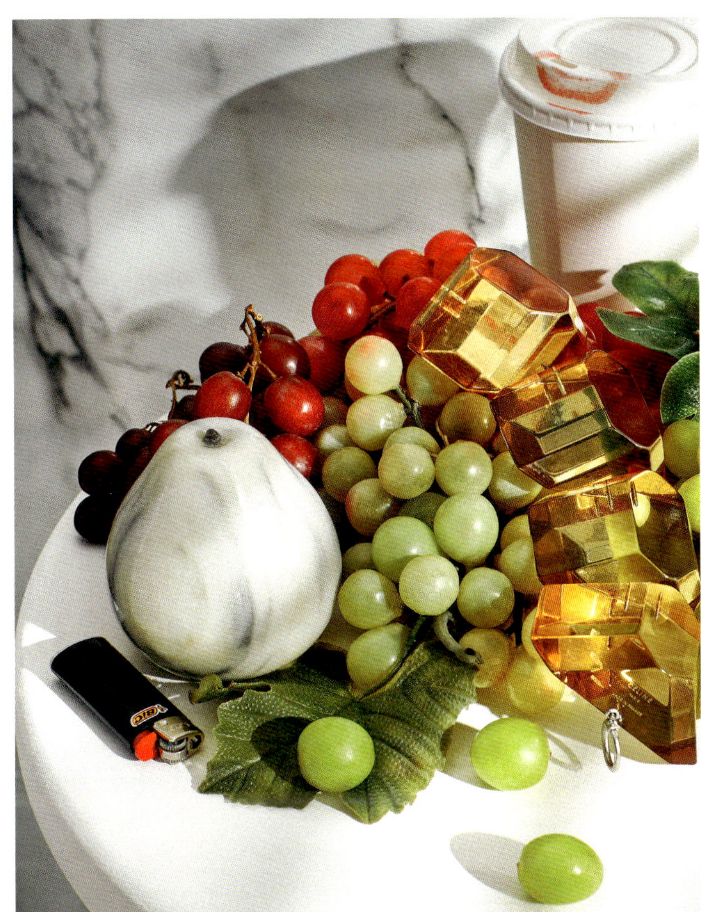

Celine Bracelet for Gentlewoman, 2014
C-print
43¾ × 34¾ inches (111.1 × 88.3 cm)
Edition 2 of 5, 2 AP

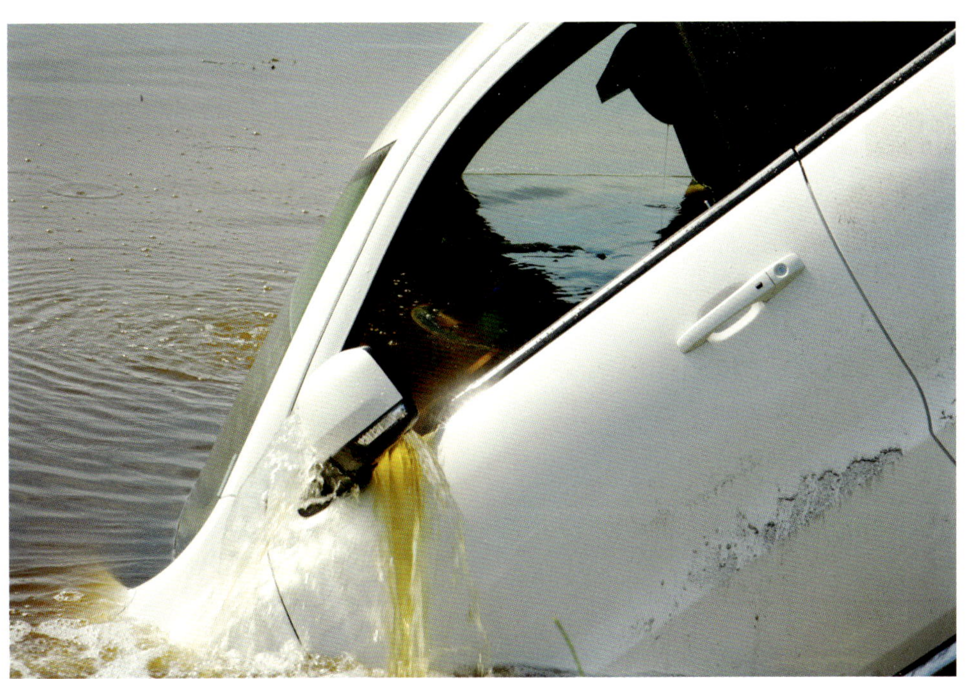

Durango in the Canal, Belle Glade, FL, 2011
C-print
51⅞ × 76⅞ inches (131.8 × 195.3 cm)
Edition 3 of 5, 2 AP

MATIAS FALDBAKKEN

b. 1973, Hobro, Denmark

Poster Sculpture #02, 2010
6000 color posters bound with metal ribbon
78¾ × 27½ × 23⅝ inches (200 × 70 × 60 cm)

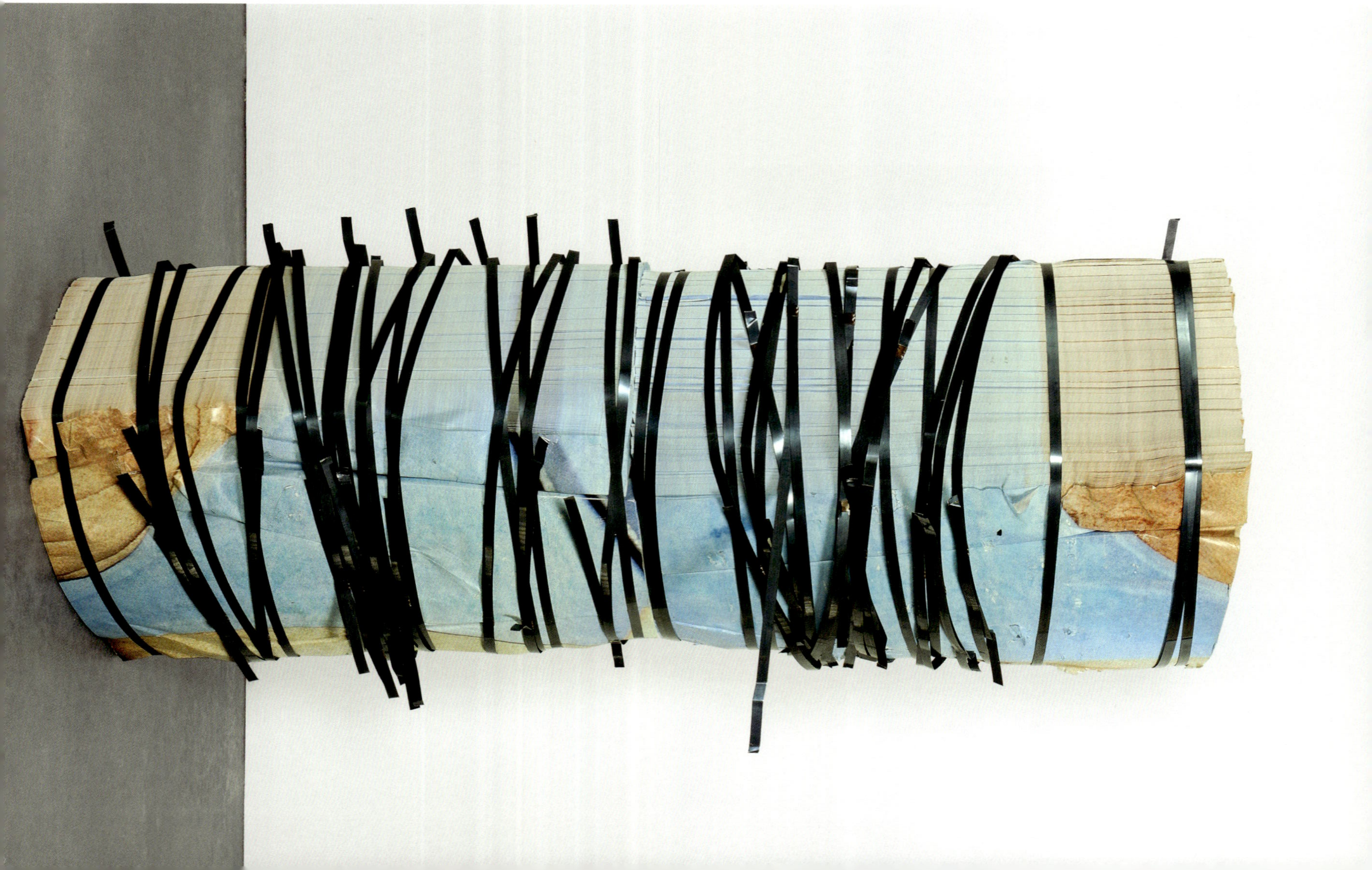

After graduating from the Academy of Fine Art in Bergen, Norway, in 1998, Matias Faldbakken became disillusioned with both the art market and the art world in general. Instead of making art, he began to write. His first book, *The Cocka Hola Company (Scandinavian Misanthropy I)*, debuted in 2001 and pilloried Scandinavian social mores. In a review in Germany's *FAZ*, one critic wrote that "…evidently whoever starts reading it becomes more and more captivated by the affronts to humanity." Faldbakken completed his Scandinavian Misanthropy trilogy in 2008.

Meanwhile, Faldbakken, who also has an MFA from the Academy of Fine Art, Städelschule in Frankfurt, was slowly developing an artistic practice that echoed the anarcho-irreverence of his literature. The Nordic Institute of Contemporary Art in Helsinki gave him his first solo exhibition in 2001, and in 2005 he was chosen to represent Norway at the Venice Biennial.

While Faldbakken's artistic output defies easy classification, it contains a persistent preoccupation with what it means to designate an object a "work of art." This question has been manifested through appropriation—garbage bags scribbled on and presented as fine art—and through videos, such as his POV film of a motorcycle rider speeding through Stockholm.

Faldbakken's ongoing formal/philosophical interrogation is also apparent in the newsprint, ink, and tape work entitled *SEE YOU ON THE FRONT PAGE OF THE LAST NEWSPAPER THOSE MOTHERFUCKERS EVER PRINT #6 (panel 2)* from 2014. The piece was part of a solo exhibition at Paula Cooper Gallery in New York, in which stacks of newspaper, printed by Faldbakken himself, were piled on the floor of the gallery for visitors to take. The same newspapers (including the Marciano Collection's *See You*,) were also for sale on the walls where they were exhibited in frames, with only a few pen marks to distinguish them from their free counterparts. In this manner, Faldbakken highlighted both the precarity of the printed word in digital society (newspaper being currently available but imminently a relic) and also, by only lightly delineating the boundary between free goods and expensive art, called the very essence of artistic value into question. J. T.

Untitled (Canvas #71), 2013
Marker pen on Belgian linen
and wooden stretchers
60 × 60 inches (152.5 × 152.5 cm)

SEE YOU ON THE FRONT PAGE OF THE LAST NEWSPAPER THOSE MOTHERFUCKERS EVER PRINT #6 (panel 2), 2014
Newsprint, India ink, tape, and wooden frame
62 × 43½ inches (157.5 × 110.5 cm)

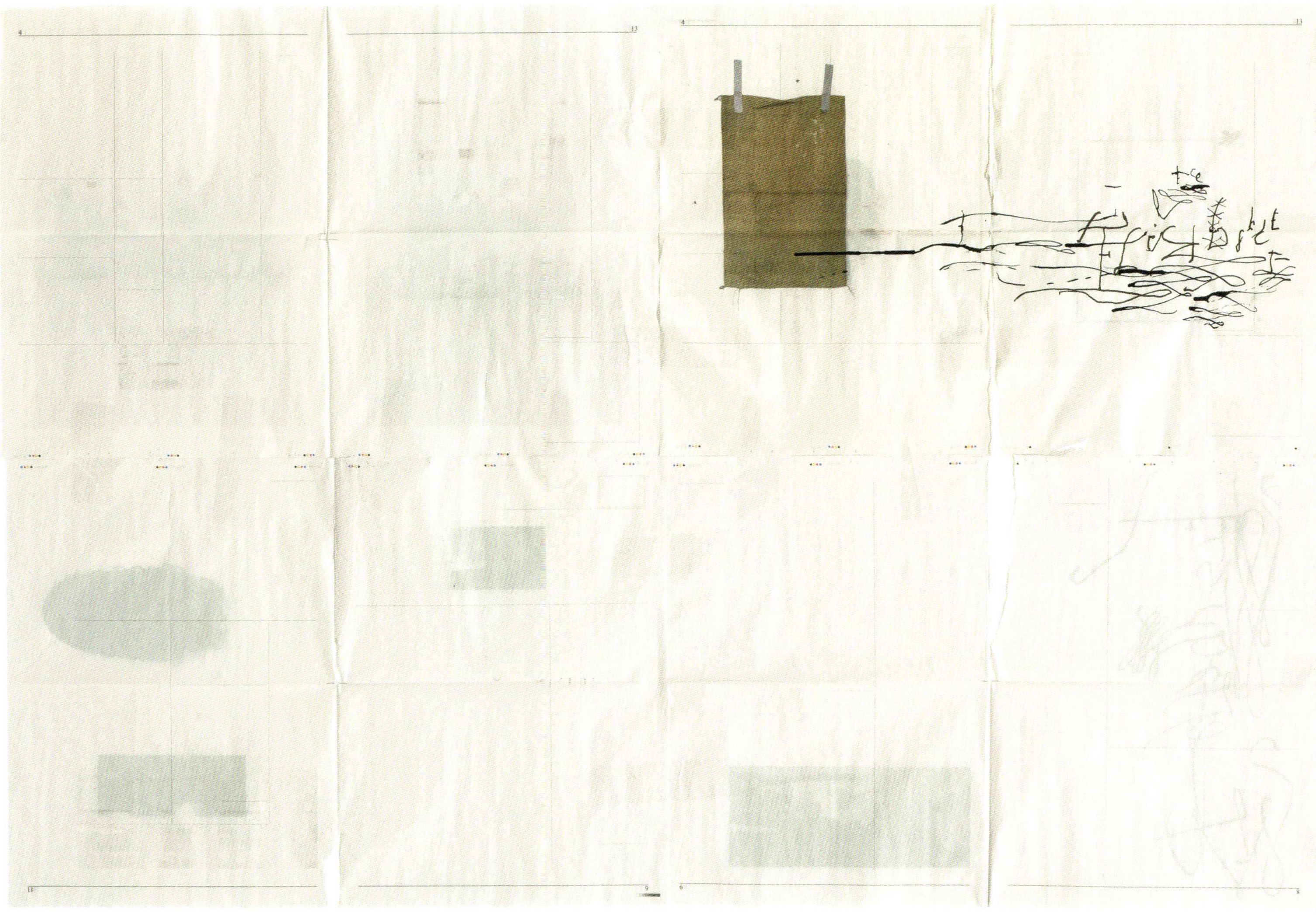

URS **FISCHER** b. 1973, Zürich, Switzerland

For Urs Fischer, material, beauty, and methodology are all beside the point; his only concerns are the experiences of looking at and grappling with art. For the viewer, this can be remarkably liberating: gone are preoccupations with process, art historical precedent, or overwrought theoretical underpinnings that can boggle or unnerve. In their stead is the thrill of simply engaging the object.

Fischer was born in 1973 in Zürich, Switzerland, and studied photography at the Schule für Gestaltung in Zürich. In 1993, he dropped out and moved to Amsterdam after receiving a grant to study at the city's professional arts program, De Ateliers. In 1996, he was given his first solo show in a gallery in Zürich, and by 2000 he had staged the exhibition *Without a Fist—Like a Bird* at the Institute for Contemporary Art in London. His work has since been the subject of major museum retrospectives at the New Museum in New York, the Kunsthaus Zürich, and the Centre Georges Pompidou in Paris. Fischer currently lives and works in New York.

Because Fischer's artwork is so engrossed in its own objecthood, describing its unifying themes or aesthetic is virtually impossible. He has created giant brass teddy bears fused with desk lamps, an alpine-style house made of bread loaves, and true-to-life wax candle replicas of friends, which he lit and melted. In 2007, he cut a massive hole into the ground of his New York gallery and allowed visitors climb into it, and at the 2006 Whitney Biennial he removed large chunks of sheetrock in order to highlight a painting by his friend, the artist Rudolf Stingel.

More than anything, Fischer's art is canny. He uses scale and monumentality to great effect, particularly in his overpainted photo series of 2014. In *Untitled*, a piece from this series, Fischer heavily painted over the surface of a photograph, scanned it, enlarged it, and screen-printed it onto a ten-foot wide aluminum panel. The work has a remarkable impact—viewers are simultaneously compelled by the hyper-detailed magnification of the brushstrokes and repelled by the violence with which they obscure the image. That push and pull is, to Fischer, all that matters. J. T.

2014
Aluminum panel, aramid honeycomb, two-component polyurethane adhesive, two-component epoxy primer, galvanized steel rivet nuts, acrylic primer, gesso, acrylic ink, acrylic silkscreen medium, and acrylic paint
96 × 120 × 7/8 inches (243.8 × 304.8 × 2.2 cm)

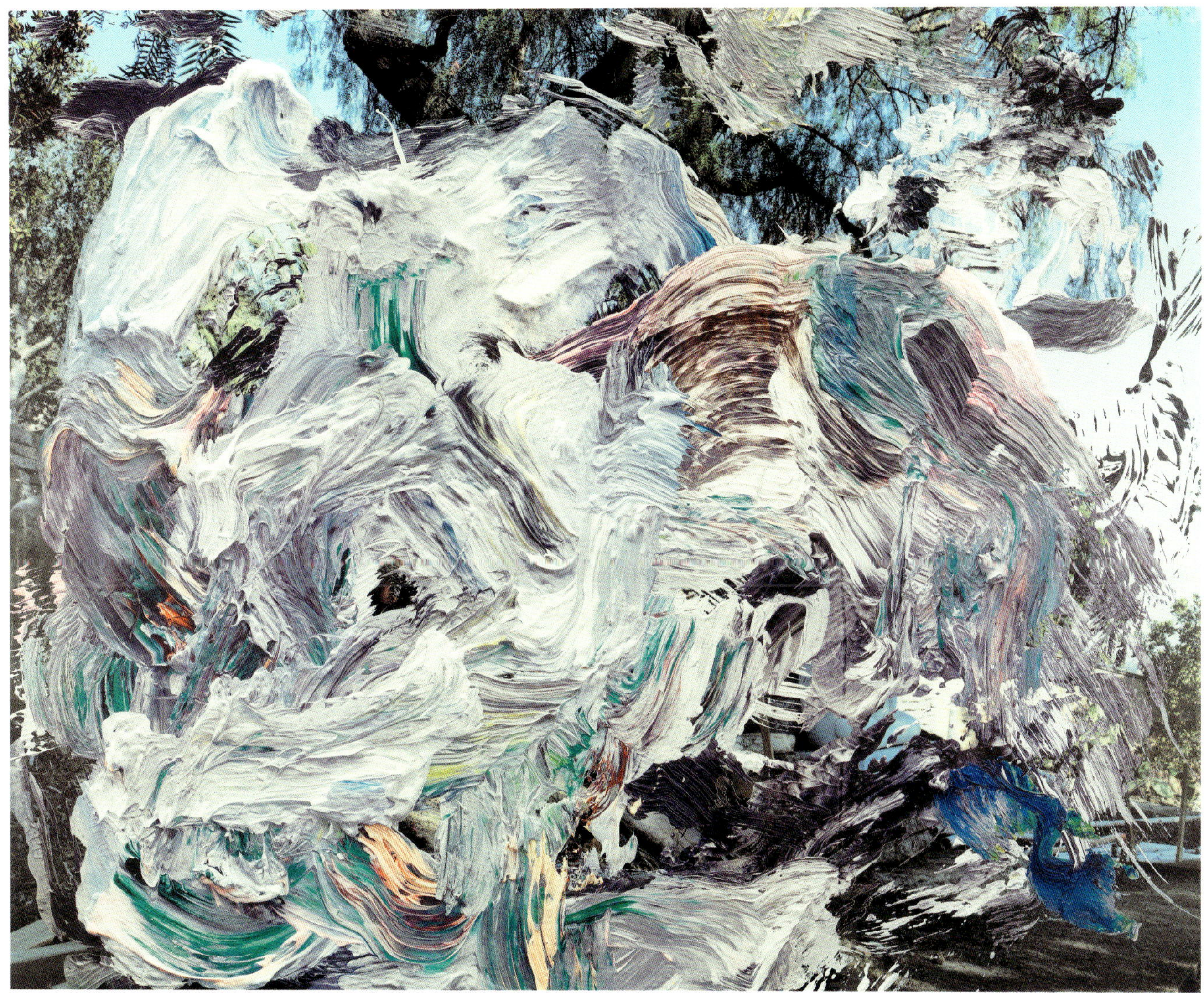

CYPRIEN GAILLARD b. 1980, Paris, France

Unifying these efforts is a probing, almost vagrant approach to social history, as Gaillard dips in and out of the cultures he encounters, prying up facets that many people would rather be left alone.

Cyprien Gaillard came of age in the early 2000s making videos of himself and his friends engaging in various forms of (usually mild) vandalism. Since becoming recognized as an artist, however, Gaillard has largely resisted the urge to present a more dignified presence. Instead, his art (and not coincidentally, his life) still thrives on a rootless exploration of cultures, history, and his own biography.

Gaillard was born in Paris in 1980 and graduated from the École cantonale d'art de Lausanne in Switzerland in 2005. The speed with which he was embraced by the international art world was almost breathtaking: a year after he graduated, his work was included in eight exhibitions around the world, including *Abstraction / Surface*, a group show at the Centre Georges Pompidou in Paris. Since then, he's had solo exhibitions at MoMA PS1 in New York, the Tate Modern in London, the Hamburger Bahnhof in Berlin, the Hammer Museum in Los Angeles, and the Kunsthalle Basel in Switzerland.

Gaillard quickly moved from videos to other mediums. He has experimented with photography, sculpture, land art, and drawing and has created, among other things, room-sized installations of modified *National Geographic* magazines in glass display cases, giant bronze ducks, and towering stone obelisks.

This is in evidence in *Untitled* (2012), which depicts a screen print of the Cleveland Indians mascot "Chief Wahoo," an image that has been condemned as a racist caricature; Native American advocacy groups have been protesting (and attempting through legislative means) to have the logo removed since the 1970s without success. By superimposing the logo over a landscape, Gaillard has imbued Chief Wahoo's leer with tragic overtones: the land is gone and only an insult is left.

Lord Howe Stubtail (2013) echoes a similar theme. Ostensibly a found object, a steel shovel from a construction-parts graveyard near Joshua Tree, California, is taken out of context and embellished with lovely iridescent white onyx. The modified shovel becomes a totem or relic from a world that's all but lost. J. T.

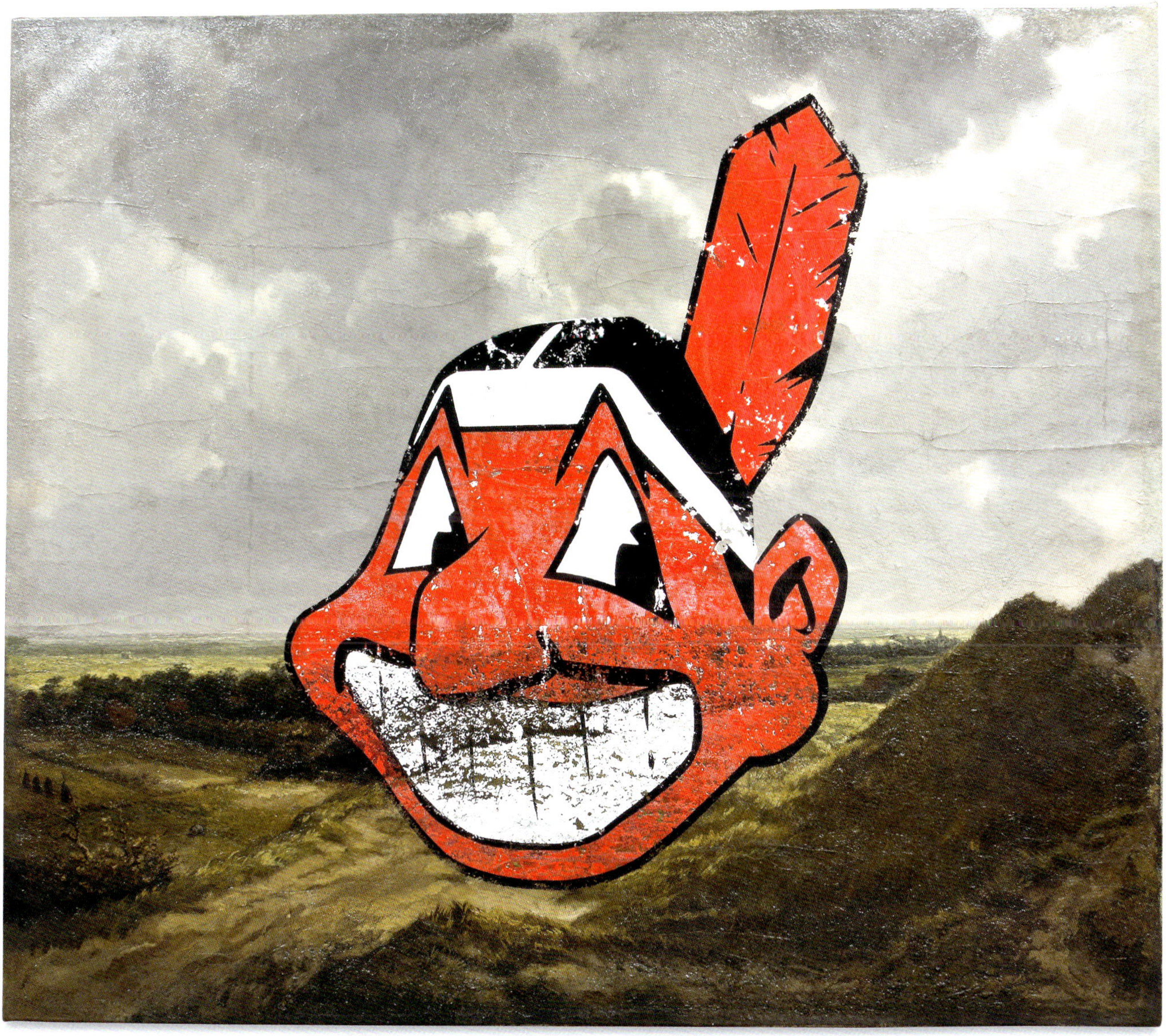

Untitled, 2012
Screen print on oil on canvas
51⅛ × 59 inches (130 × 150 cm)

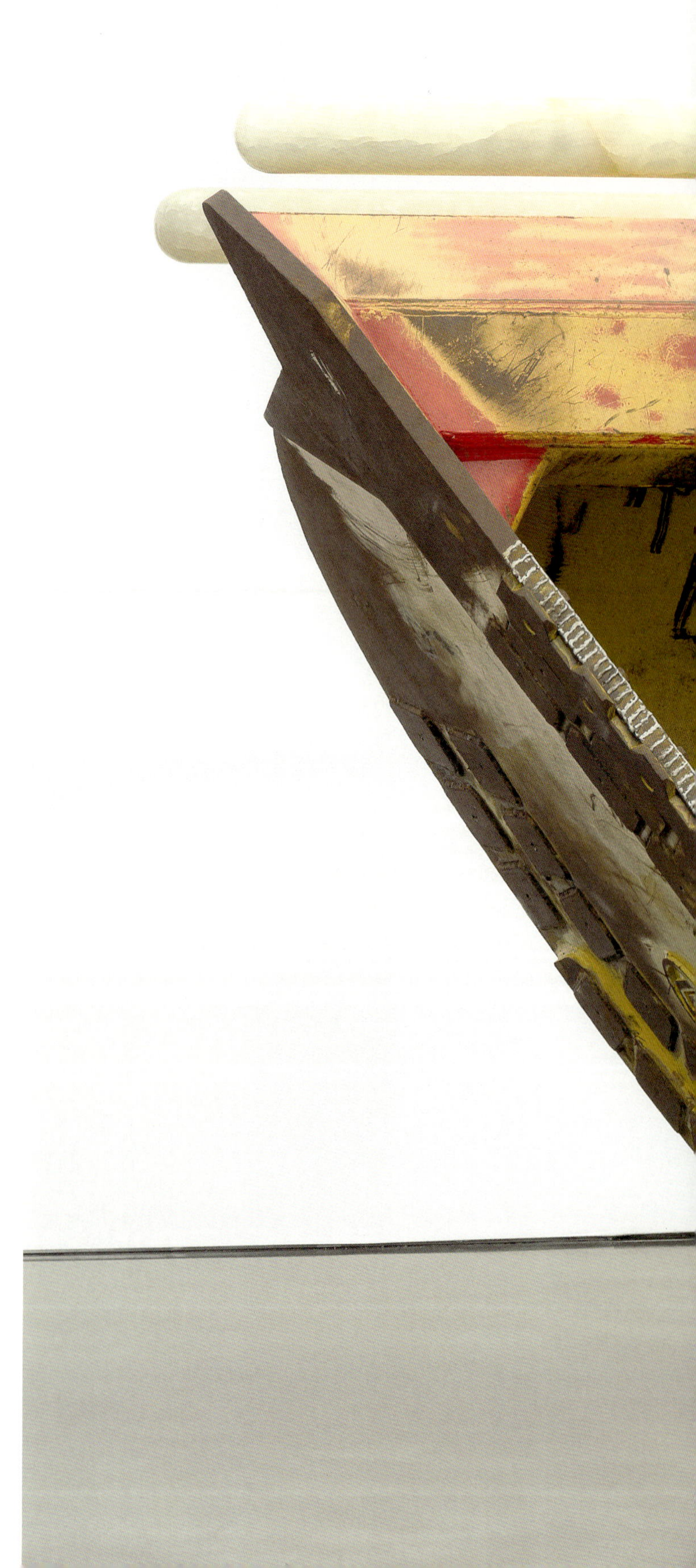

Lord Howe Stubtail, 2013
Excavator head and white onyx
98 × 132 × 87 inches (248.9 × 335.3 × 221 cm)

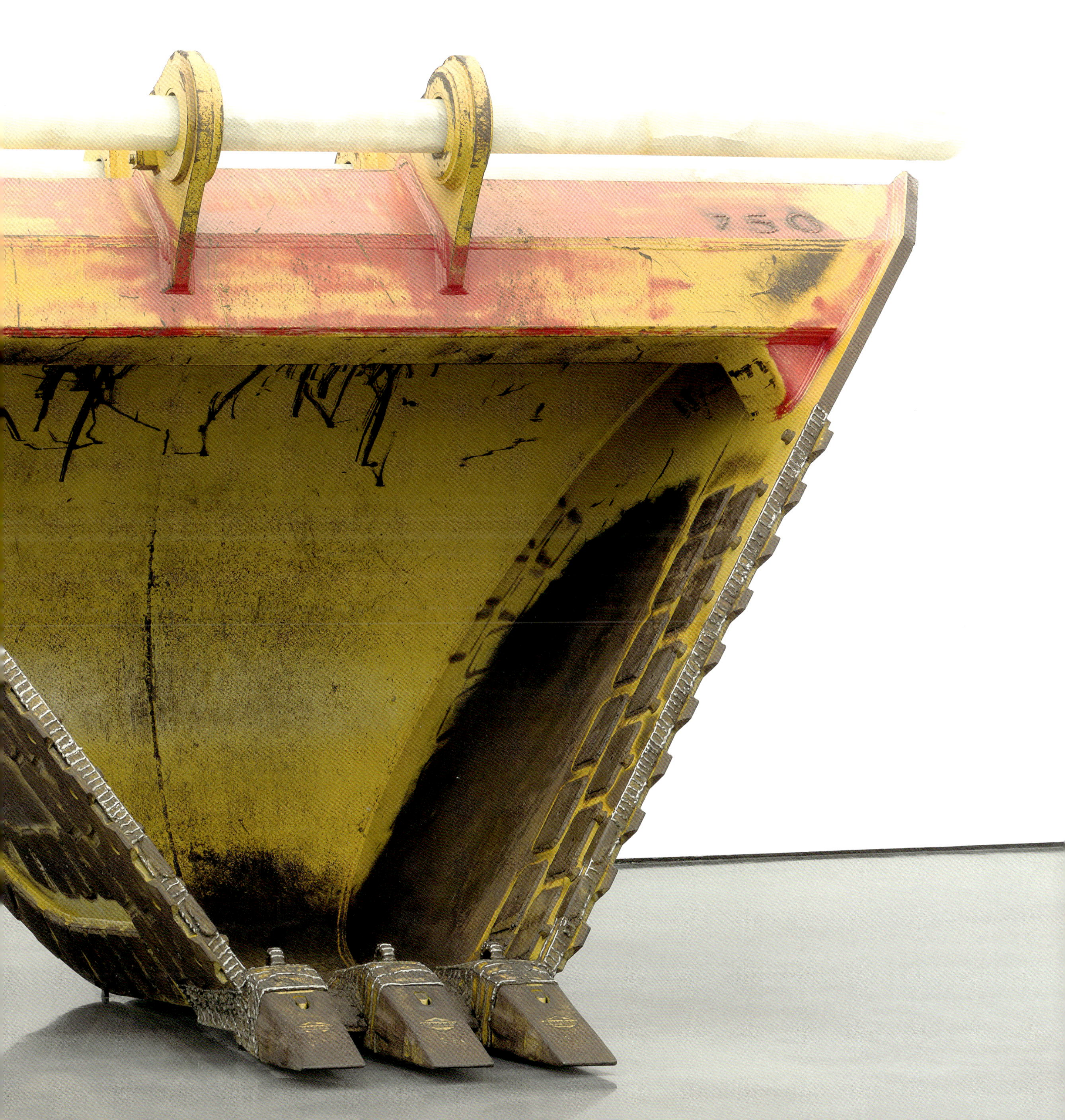
750

MARK GROTJAHN

b. 1968, Pasadena, CA

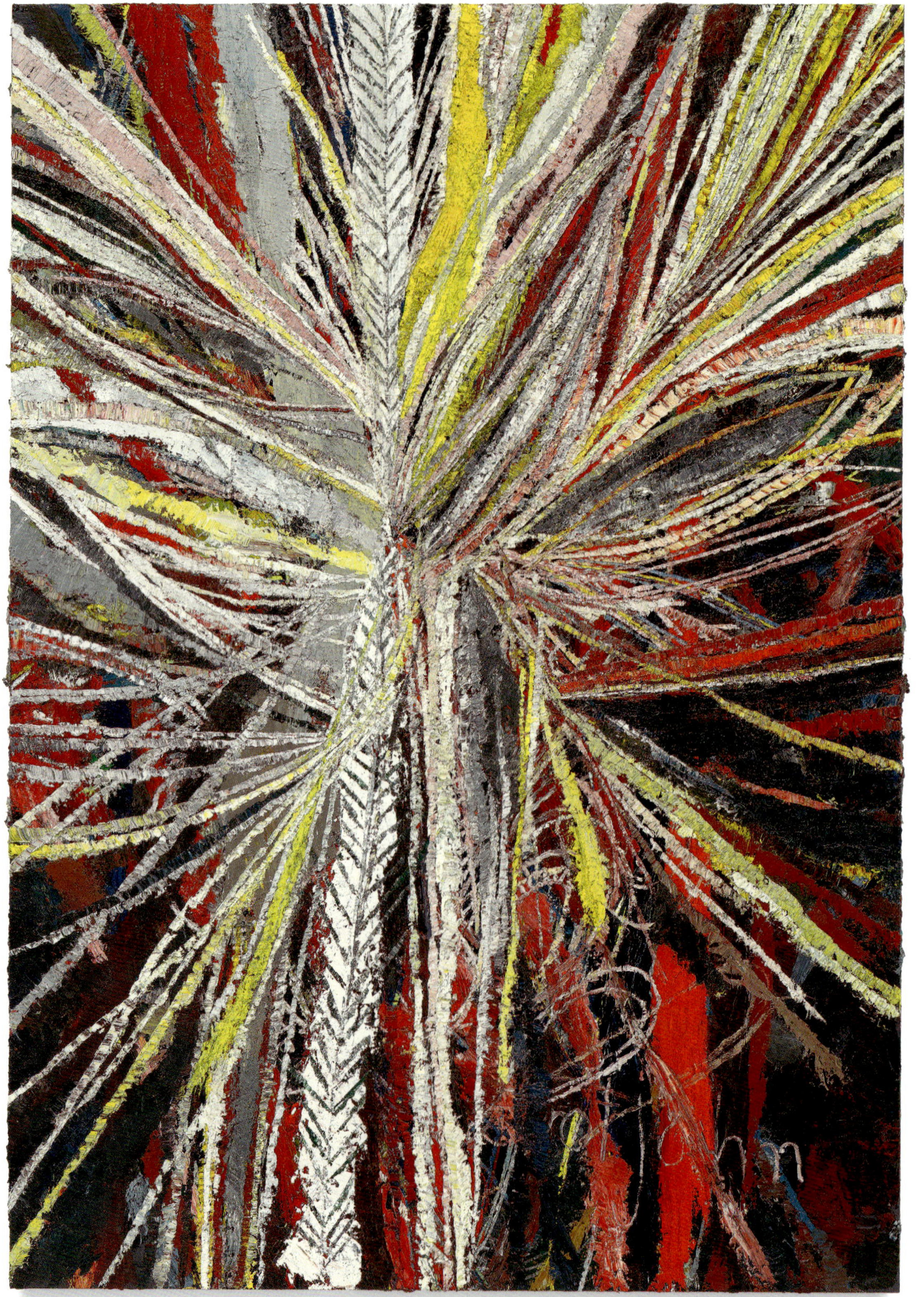

Untitled (Hidden Tea, Face 41.30), 2010
Oil on cardboard mounted on linen
101¼ × 72½ inches (257.2 × 184.2 cm)

Born in 1968 in Pasadena, California, Mark Grotjahn initially struggled to achieve the commercial and critical popularity he enjoys today. He attended the Skowhegan School of Painting and Sculpture in Maine before earning a BFA from the University of Colorado Boulder and an MFA from the University of California, Berkeley. After moving to Los Angeles, Grotjahn and his Cal classmate Brent Petersen opened Room 702, a gallery dedicated to solo presentations by emerging artists. After the gallery's closure in 1998, two early one-man shows at Blum and Poe, and even a stint as a professional poker player, Grotjahn eventually assumed a prominent position in contemporary painting following the success of his famous Butterfly series, begun around 1997. In 2014, Grotjahn joined the board of The Museum of Contemporary Art, Los Angeles—the youngest artist to do so. He continues to work and live in Los Angeles.

Although the influences of geometric abstraction and Primitivist or Expressionist figuration resonate in Grotjahn's work, his career-long interest in strict organizational principles and a generous play of color belie any sense of historical pastiche.

The aforementioned Butterfly paintings carefully delineate a series of vanishing points that direct intense polychromatic vectors to an implied horizon line. In contrast, his Mask sculptures from 2002 onwards are painted cast-bronze versions of cardboard faces Grotjahn would craft from materials such as beer cartons and toilet-paper tubes. Yet Grotjahn has also engaged more conceptual interests: in the mid-1990s, he copied signage from low-end establishments in California neighborhoods before trading the often-improved simulacrum for the original advertisement, which he then exhibited *en masse*.

A recent work from Grotjahn's Face paintings demonstrates both his sense of play and canny formal vision. *Untitled (Non-Indian #1 Face 45.56)* from 2015 features a strident vertical axis from which sharp diamond-shaped forms of lush turquoise, gold, and red project. Yet a manically scrawled pair of eyes prowl the painting's lower half, transforming *Untitled* into a somehow studied talisman that combines comic books and Mark Rothko. Sweeping strokes suggest painterly chaos, but Grotjahn's reserved geometry maintains rhythmic cohesion and stability. Pleasure and rigor meet in equal measure. J. H.

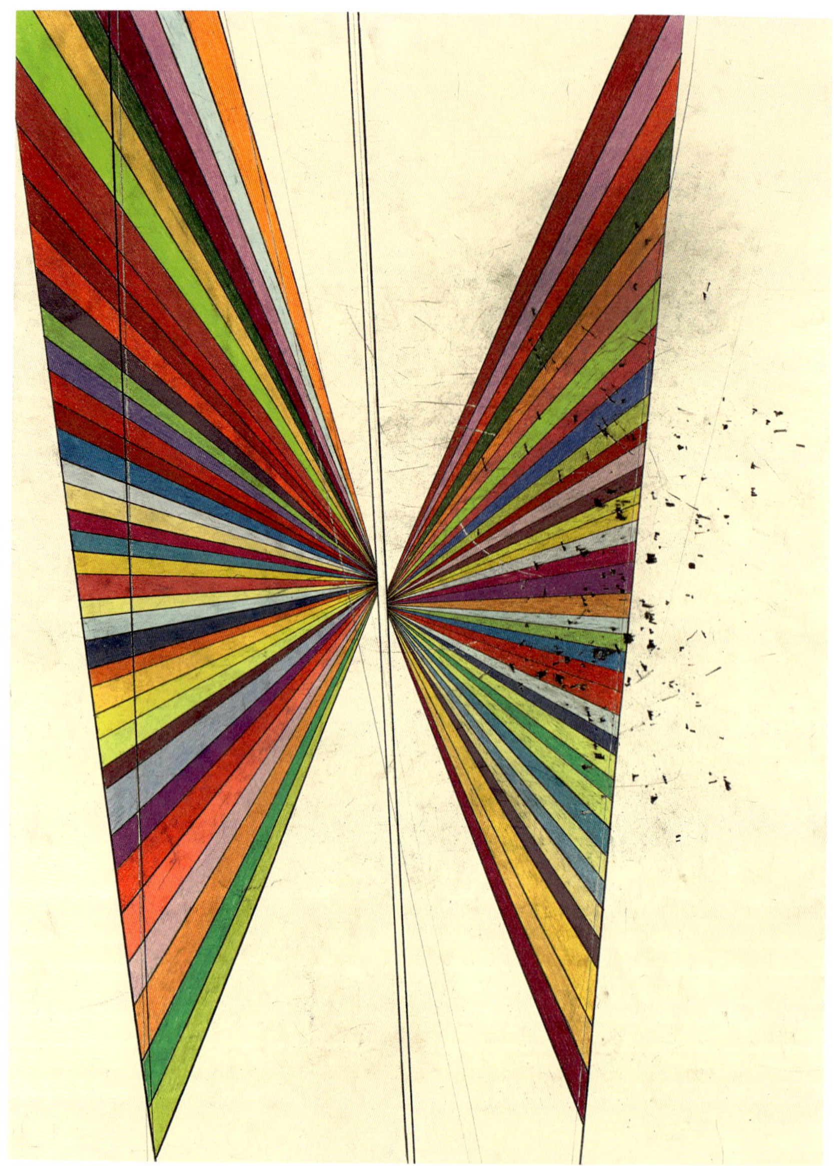

Untitled (2 Wings), 2004
Colored pencil on paper
30 × 22 inches (76.2 × 55.9 cm)

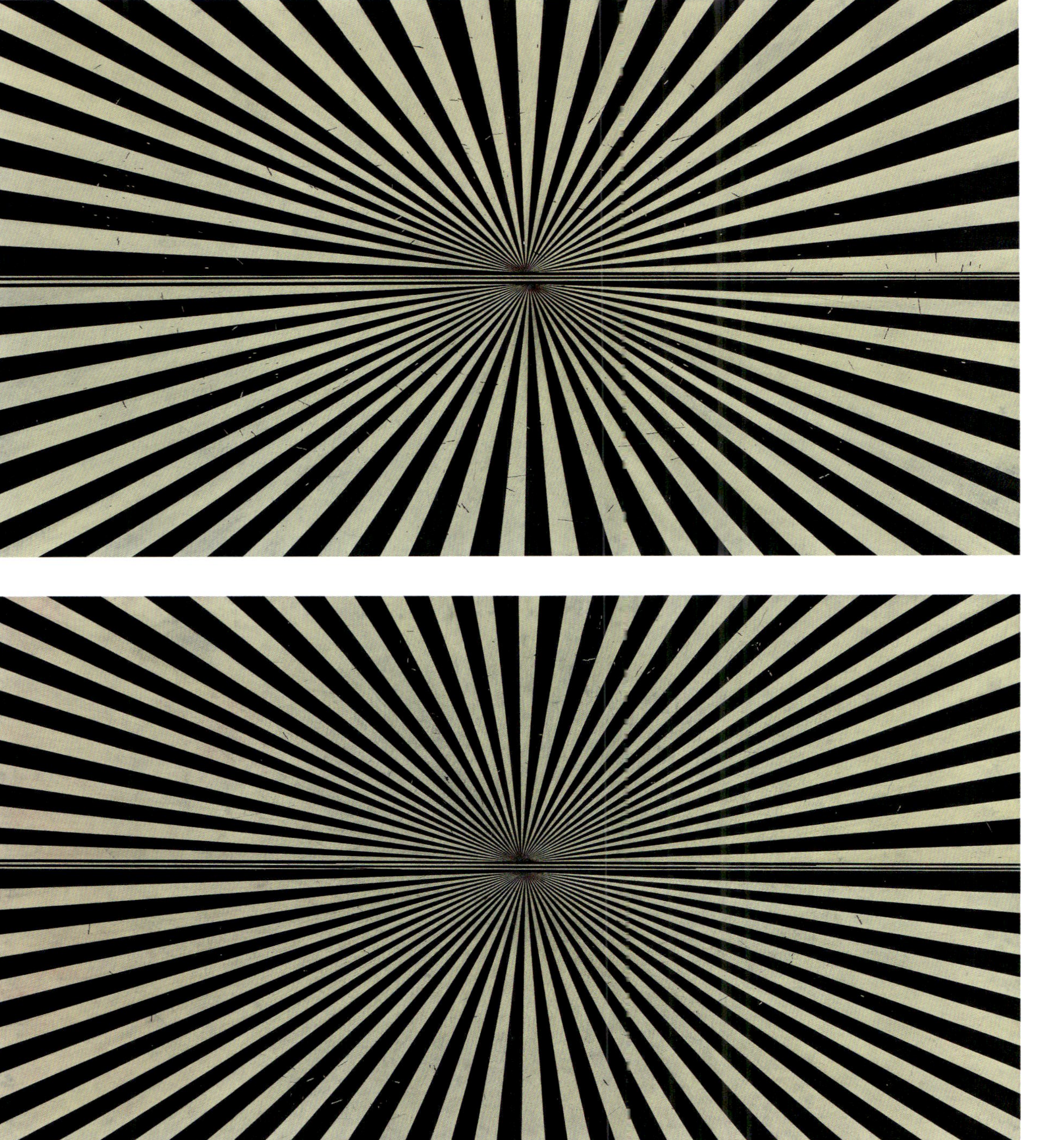

Untitled (Creamsicle Drawing in Two Parts: L: $85\frac{10}{16} \times 47\frac{5}{8}$ R: $85\frac{1}{2} \times 47\frac{1}{2}$ DO NOT SEPERATE 41.12), 2010
Color pencil on paper
Left: $85\frac{10}{16} \times 47\frac{5}{8}$ inches (217.5×121 cm)
Right: $85\frac{1}{2} \times 47\frac{1}{2}$ inches (217.2×120.7 cm)

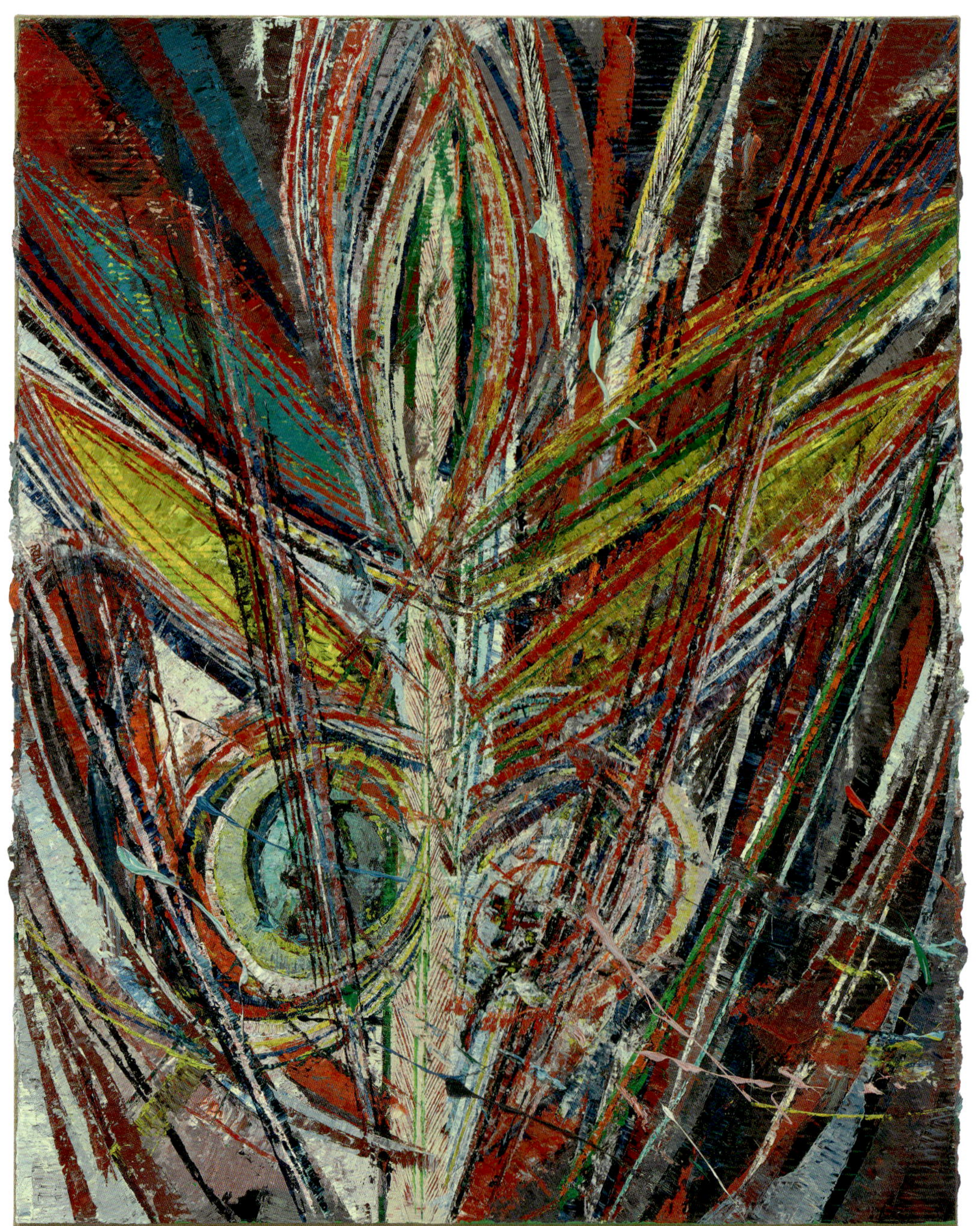

Untitled (Non-Indian #1 Face 45.56), 2015
Oil on cardboard mounted on linen
50½ × 40½ inches (128.3 × 102.9 cm)

Untitled (Four Green Red Eyes Feather Lower Middle Right Face 41.45), 2010
Oil on cardboard mounted on linen
32 3/8 × 23 inches (82.2 × 58.4 cm)

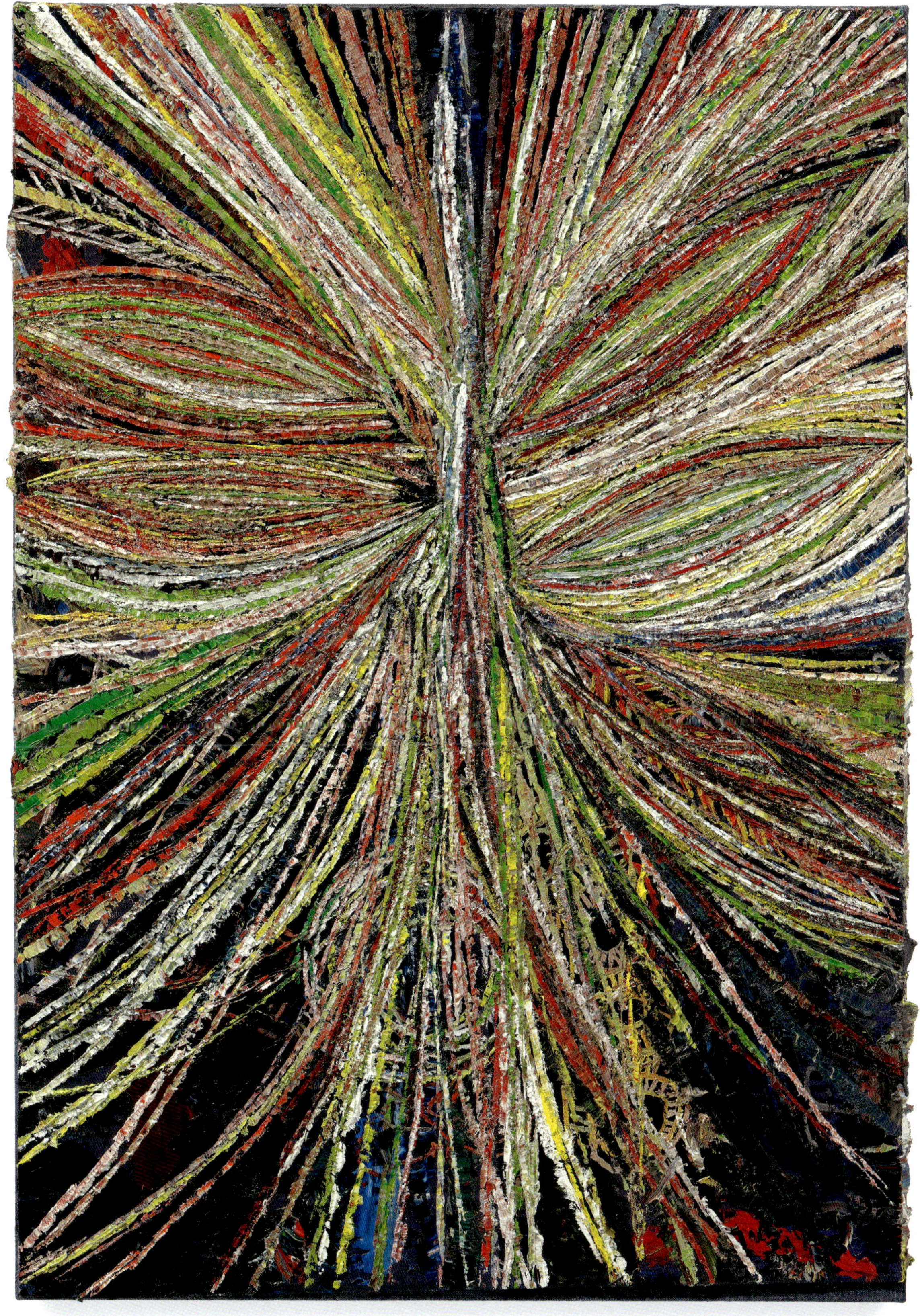

WADE GUYTON

b. 1972, Hammond, IN

Wade Guyton has redefined what it means to put paint to canvas. Whereas Abstract Expressionism took a step back from the easel—paint was flung or dripped onto a surface—Guyton has gone a step further, using inkjet printers, copy machines, and desktop computers as intermediaries between himself and the finished artwork.

Born in 1972 in Hammond, Indiana, Guyton received his BA from the University of Tennessee, then moved to New York to study with the sculptor Robert Morris at Hunter College's MFA program. Since graduating in 1998, Guyton's art has been exhibited globally, most notably at solo shows at New York's Whitney Museum of American Art and the Kunsthalle in Zurich.

While Guyton's work is closely associated with painting, he considers himself a post-Conceptual artist, and in fact several of his notable projects—including twisted, deconstructed metal office chairs—are sculptures rather than canvases. Regardless of the medium, Guyton's practice grapples and plays with questions of forms, motifs, and patterns. Nowhere is this more profoundly in evident than in his inkjet paintings.

When considering these paintings, it's necessary to start with a question: If a shape like the x in *Untitled* (2007) is designed by a computer and painted by a printer, is it, in its own way, a unique work? It's an inquiry that gets to the heart of the supposed perfection of technological and mechanical reproduction, and more to the point, it's a question that, through his inkjet paintings, Guyton sets out to answer.

Take a work like *Untitled* (2008), a fifty-foot-long ribbon of green and orange stripes. In theory, these stripes should be represented in an unbroken line. But ink runs out (note the gradual fading), linen creases, and printers jam. The computer, therefore, understood its output to be technically perfect, and yet the same forces that affected Jackson Pollock's splash paintings—chance and physics— managed to work their way into Guyton's work, too. Technology, in other words, is just a different kind of paintbrush in Guyton's hands: still under the control of the artist and still infused with chance, trial, and luck. J. T.

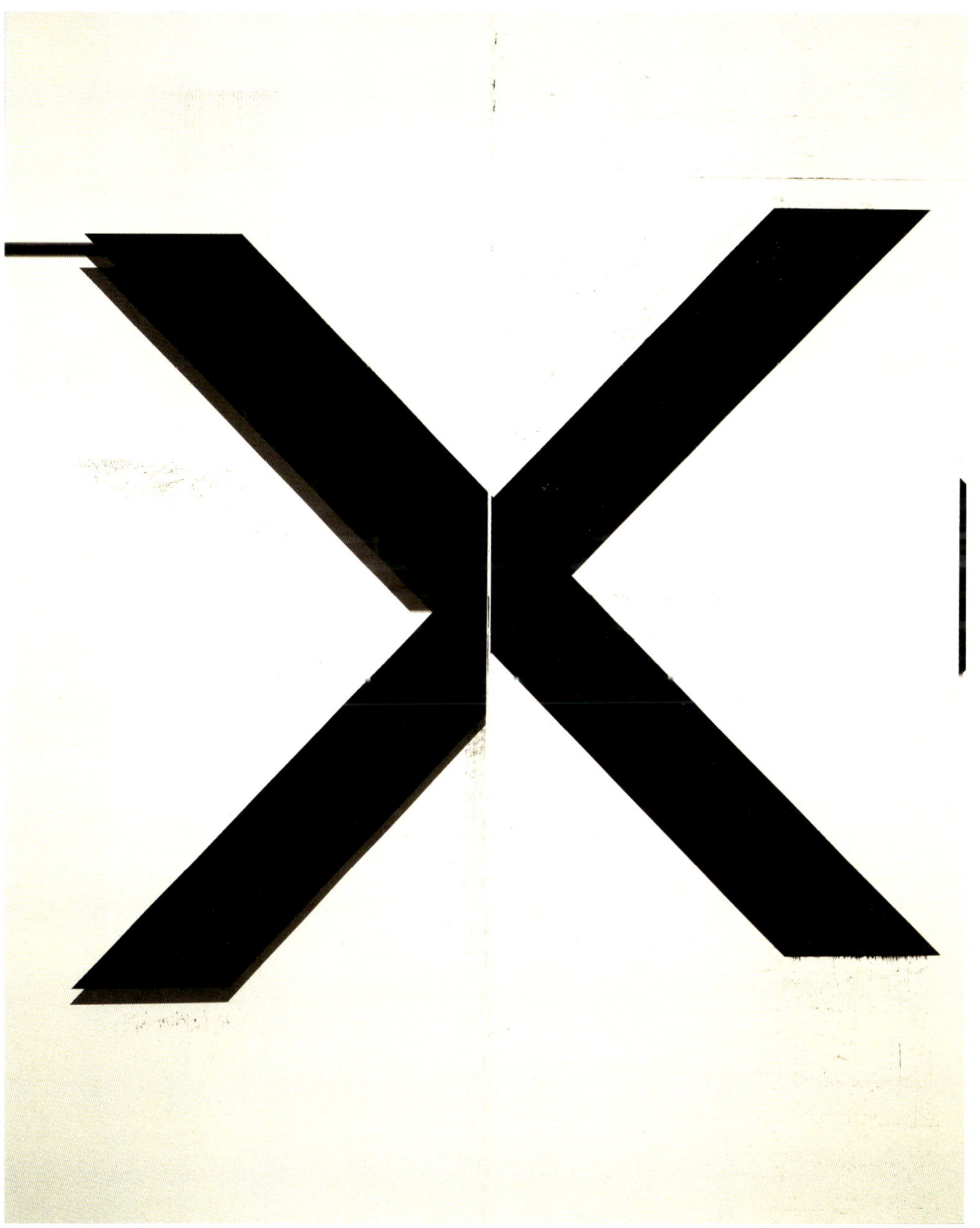

Untitled, 2007
Epson UltraChrome inkjet on linen
84 × 69 inches (213.4 × 175.3 cm)

Untitled, 2009
Epson UltraChrome inkjet on linen
84 × 69 inches (213.4 × 175.3 cm)

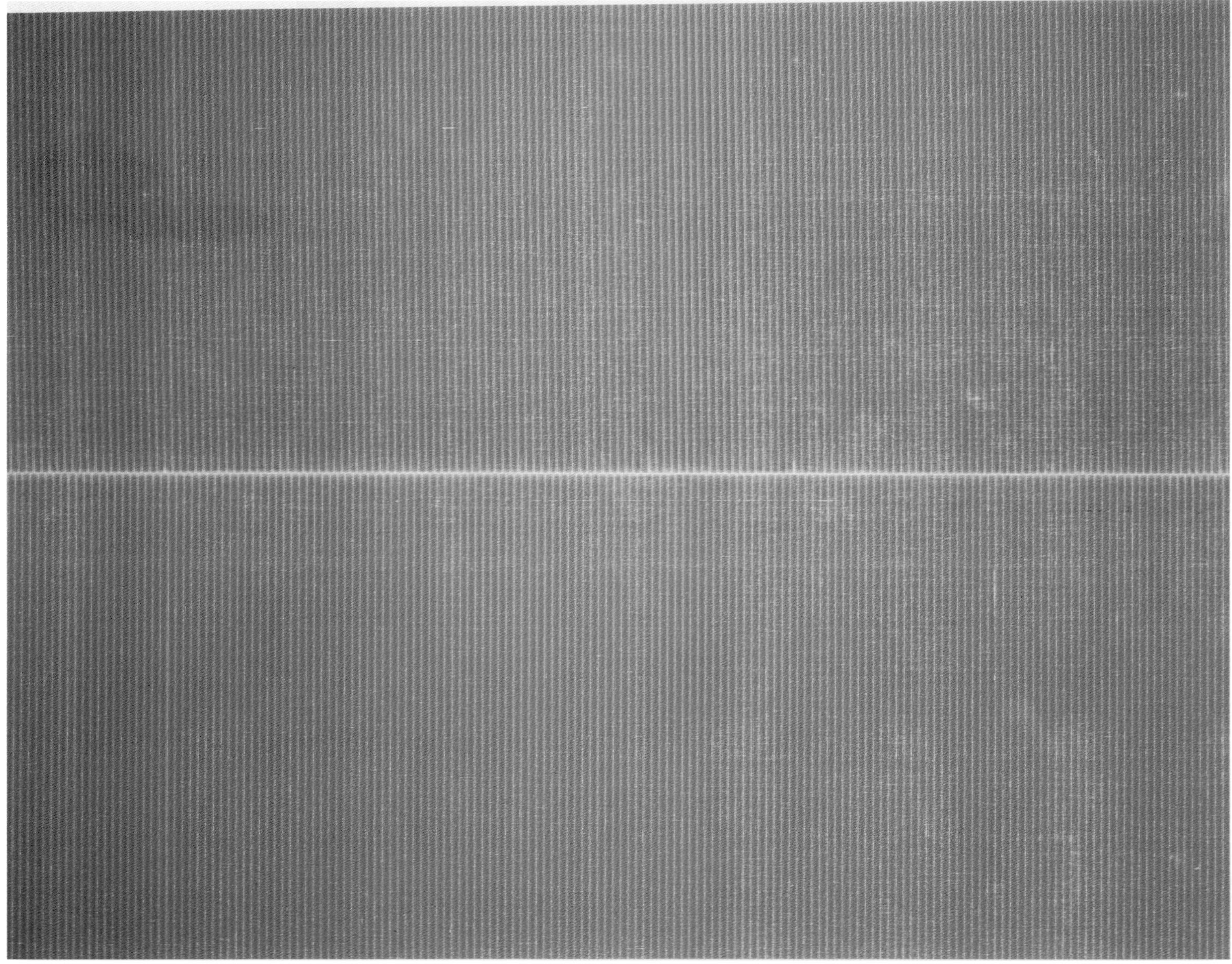

Untitled, 2008
Epson UltraChrome inkjet on linen
93 × 55 inches (236.2 × 139.7 cm)

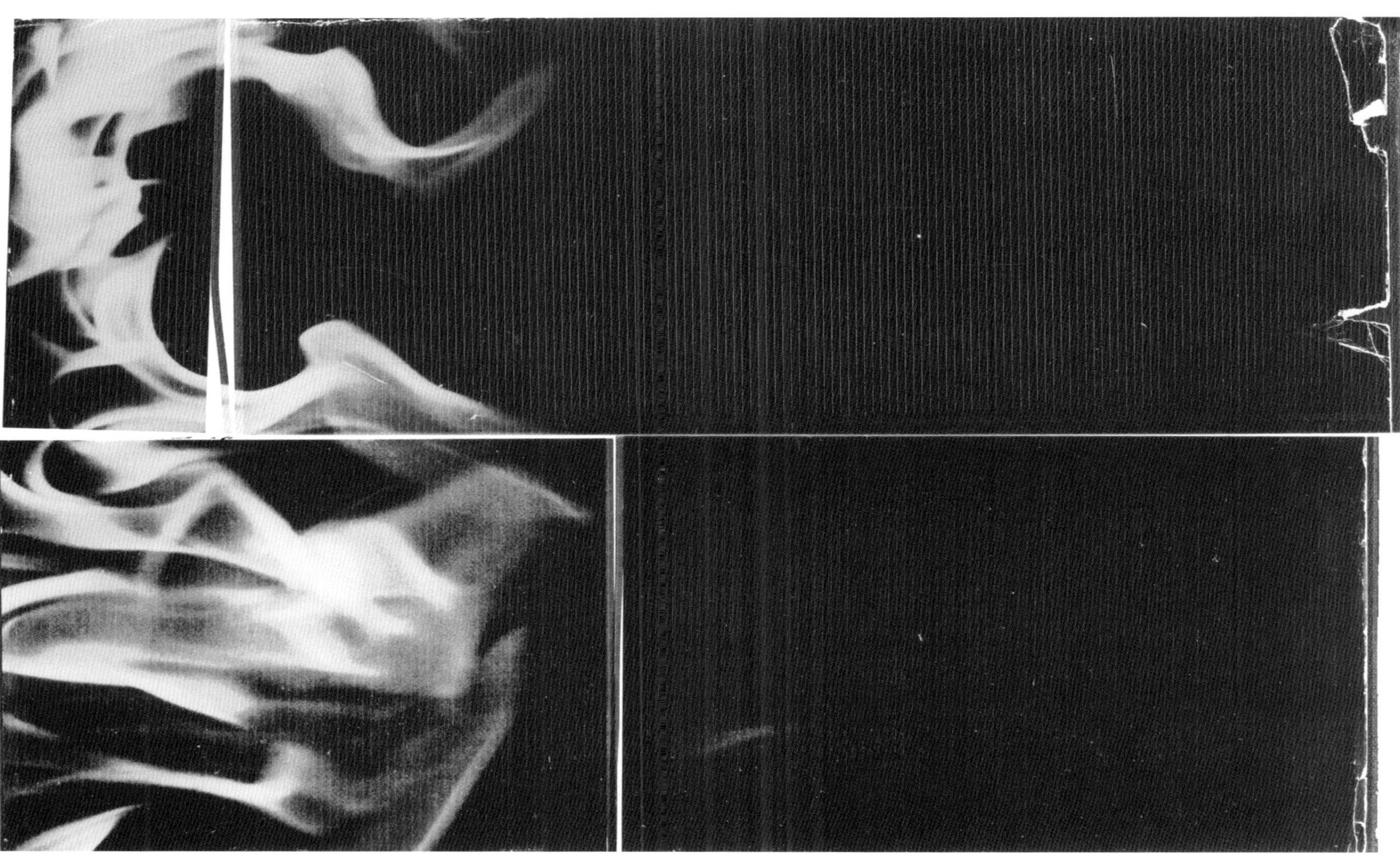

Untitled, 2012
Epson UltraChrome inkjet on linen
108 ¼ × 600 inches (275 × 1524 cm)

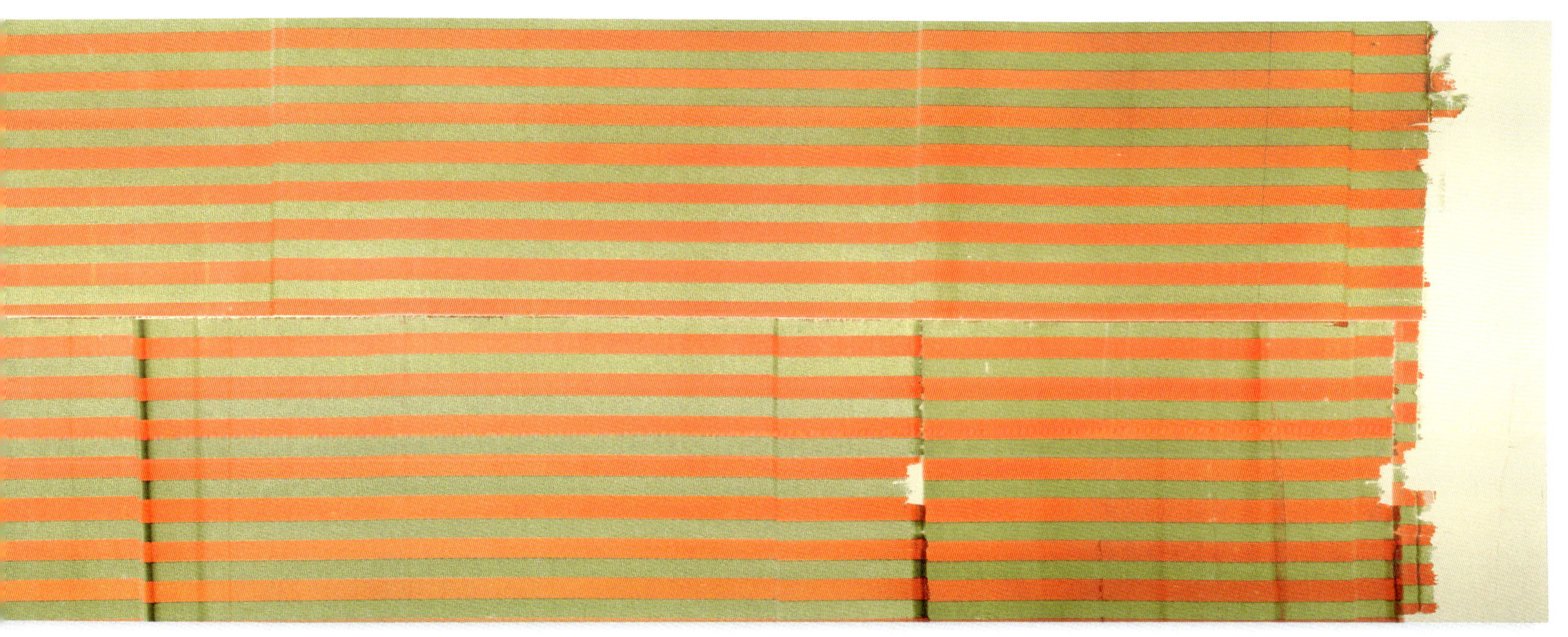

DAVID **HAMMONS** b. 1943, Springfield, IL

The city and its detritus—including grease, chicken wings, bottle caps, and hair—would become major sources for his practice, one that crisscrosses the boundaries of art and life, high and low, and the sacred and profane. His works in performance, installation, sculpture, and printmaking fuse neo-avant-garde and Post-Minimal tendencies with the language and material of African American life.

David Hammons's work forces viewers to confront negative, rejected, and stereotyped signs and symbols, which the artist re-tools through his practice of synthesizing wordplay with an endlessly creative transgression of artistic boundaries. For nearly fifty years, Hammons's work has devoted powerful attention to black experience and articulated a trenchant polemic against social and cultural exclusion.

Hammons was born in Springfield, Illinois, and moved to Los Angeles in 1963, studying at Chouinard Art Institute (now CalArts) and the Otis Art Institute (now Otis College of Art and Design). While in L.A., he was part of an important community of black artists, including key figures such as Charles White, Noah Purifoy, and Betye Saar. In 1974, Hammons settled in New York City, where he lives and works to this day.

More recently, Hammons has given playful and critical attention to the art market. In his tarp works, such as *Untitled* (2010) and *Untitled* (2012), the viewer's appreciation of a generic Abstract Expressionist painting is disrupted by soiled, crinkled, and torn industrial tarps. The tarps' holes reveal only mere glimpses of the painting it conceals, pulling the viewer into a spectatorial game that does not deliver what she may at first expect. With his wife, Chie Hammons, the artist also transformed a series of fox, mink, sable, and chinchilla fur coats into paintings, such as his *Untitled* (2007). The fox fur is defaced with swaths of colorful acrylic and spray paint. The painterly marks on one hand evoke signature gestures, a hallmark of the modern painting masterpiece. Yet these marks, on their chosen canvas, equally luxurious and coveted, disturb the easy imprimatur of value.

Hammons is the recipient of several major awards including the Prix de Rome and a MacArthur Foundation Fellowship. Most recently, he organized a retrospective of his work at the Mnuchin Gallery in 2016. His work has also been exhibited at the Centre for Contemporary Art, Warsaw; PS1, New York; The Studio Museum in Harlem; Williams College Museum of Art; and the Illinois State Museum; among many other venues. J. A.

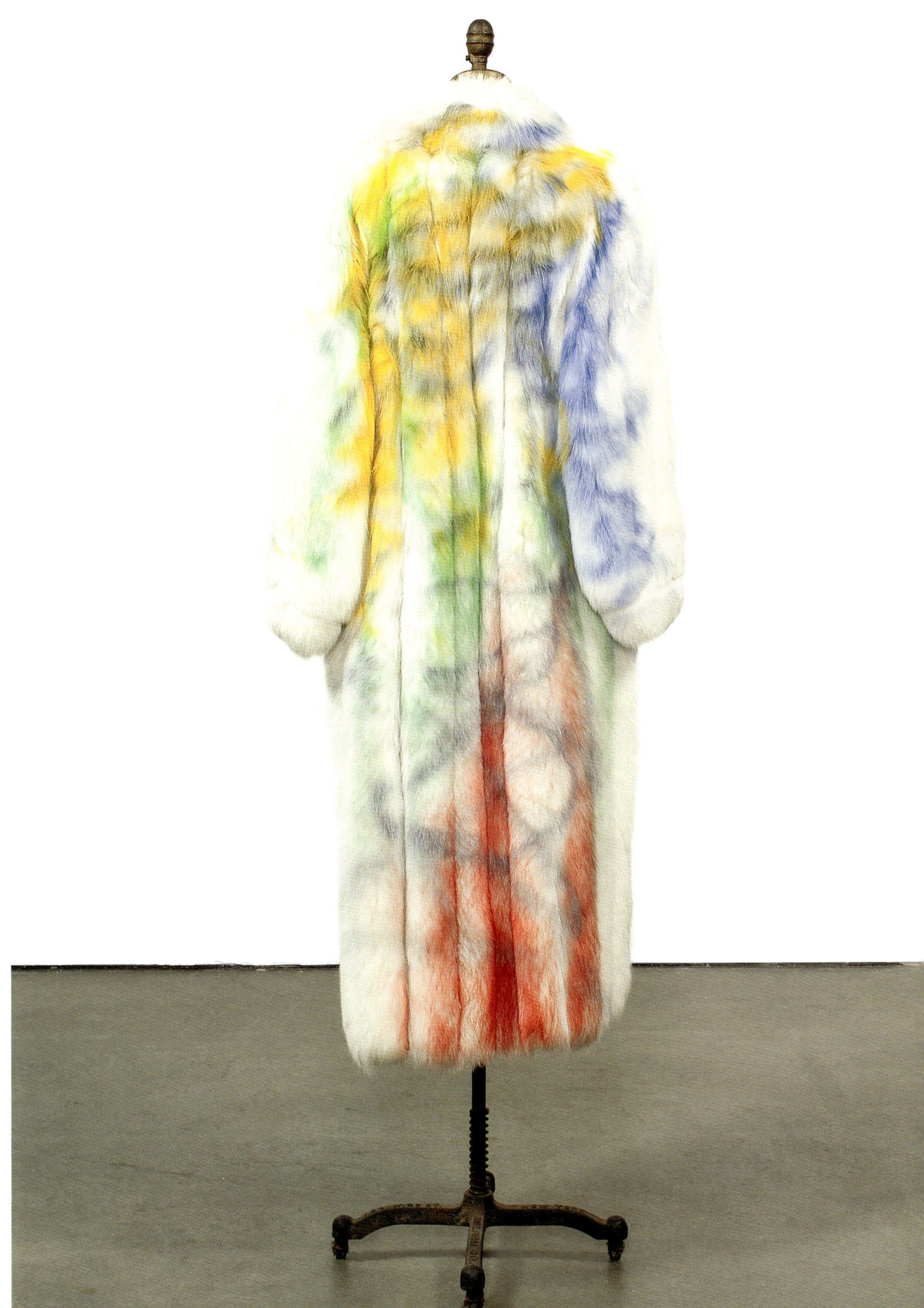

Untitled, 2007
Fox fur coat with acrylic and spray paint
72 × 26 × 14 inches (182.9 × 66 × 35.6 cm)

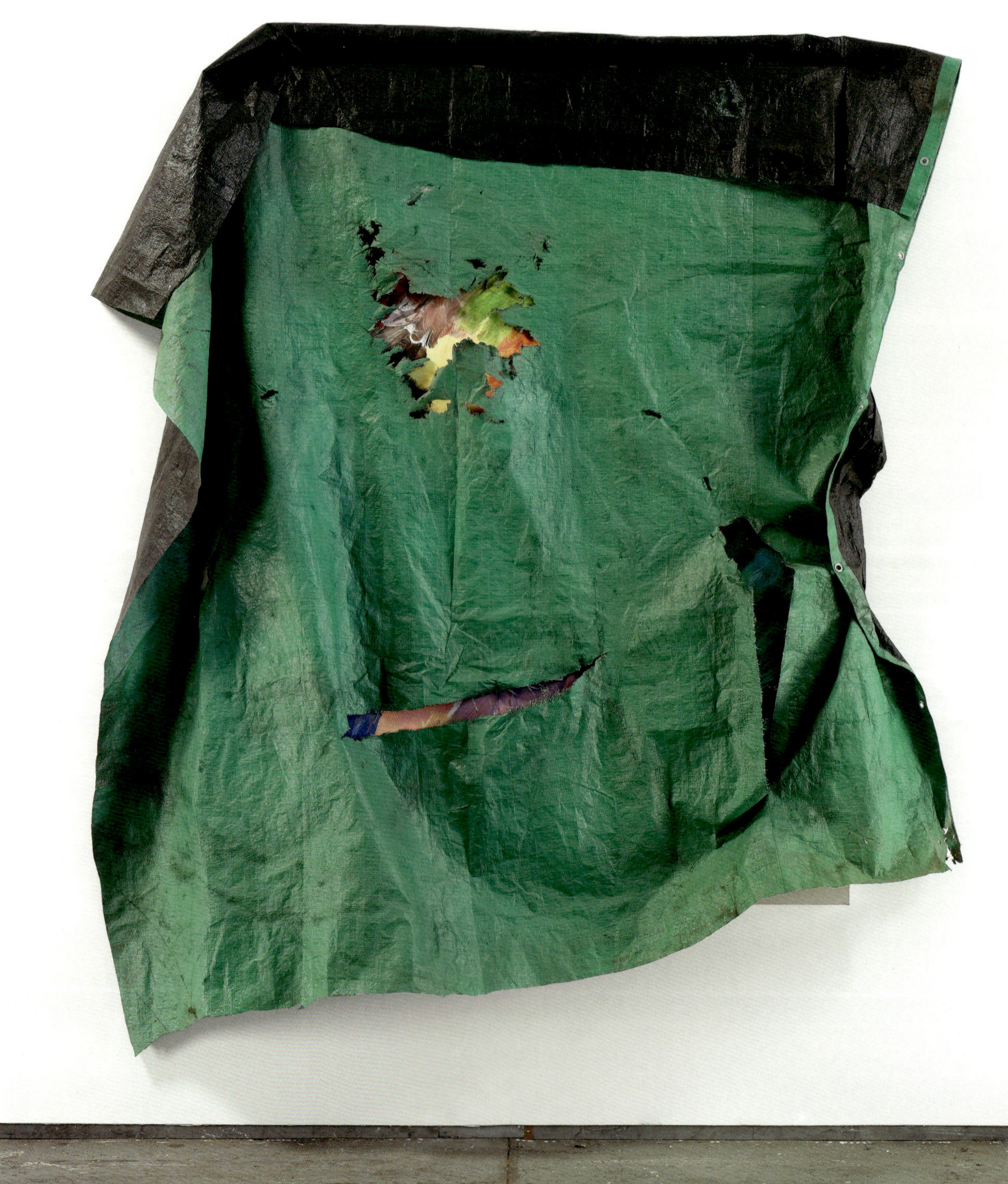

Untitled, 2010
Acrylic on canvas and tarp
103 × 80 inches (261.6 × 203.2 cm)

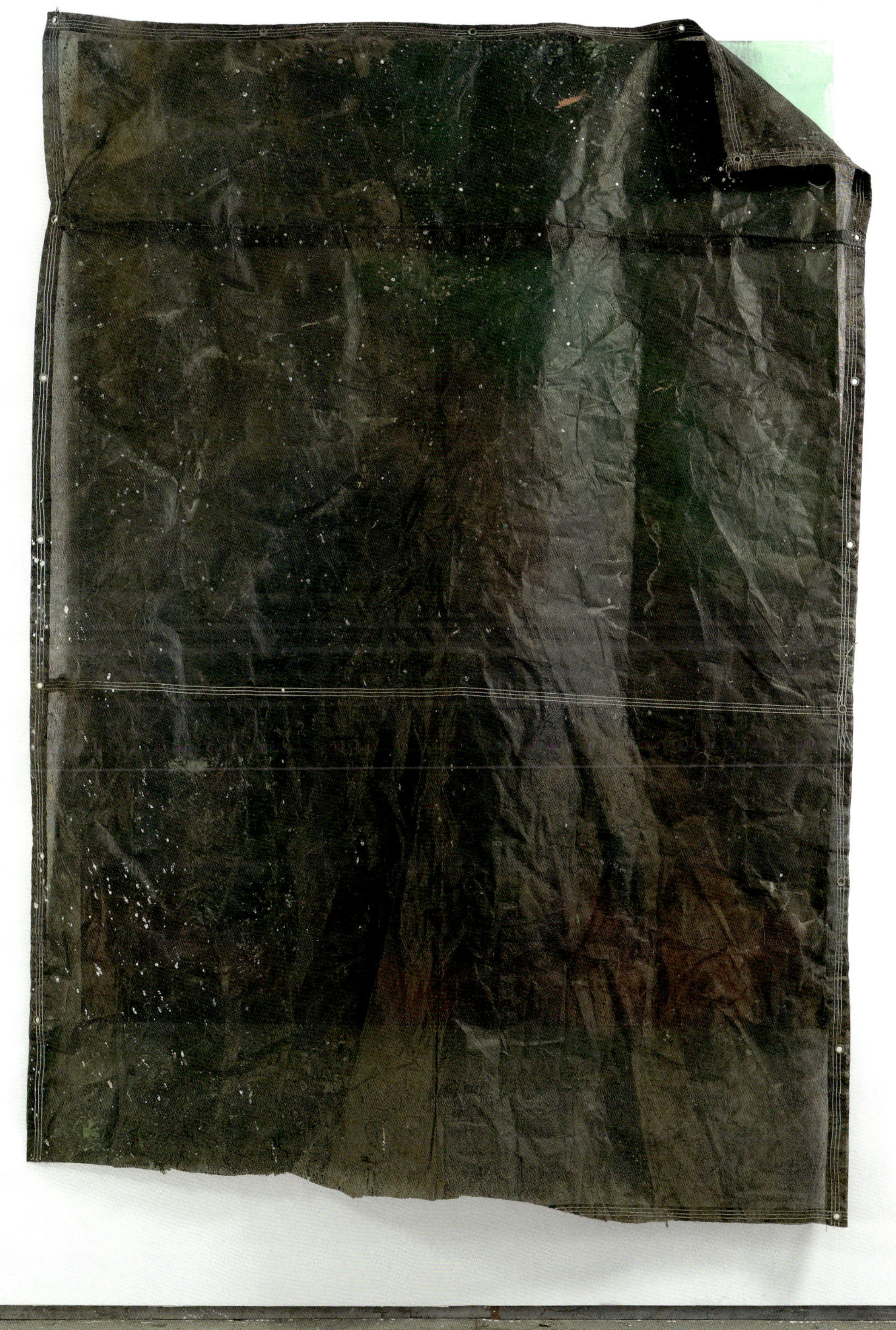

Untitled, 2012
Acrylic on canvas and tarp
130 × 93 inches (330.2 × 236.2 cm)

THOMAS HOUSEAGO

b. 1972, Leeds, England

Dancer II, 2010
Bronze and latex paint
Figure: 81 × 47 × 41 inches
(205.7 × 119.4 × 104.1 cm)
Base: 12 × 50 × 44 inches
(30.5 × 127 × 111.8 cm)
Edition 2 of 3, 1 AP + 1 FC

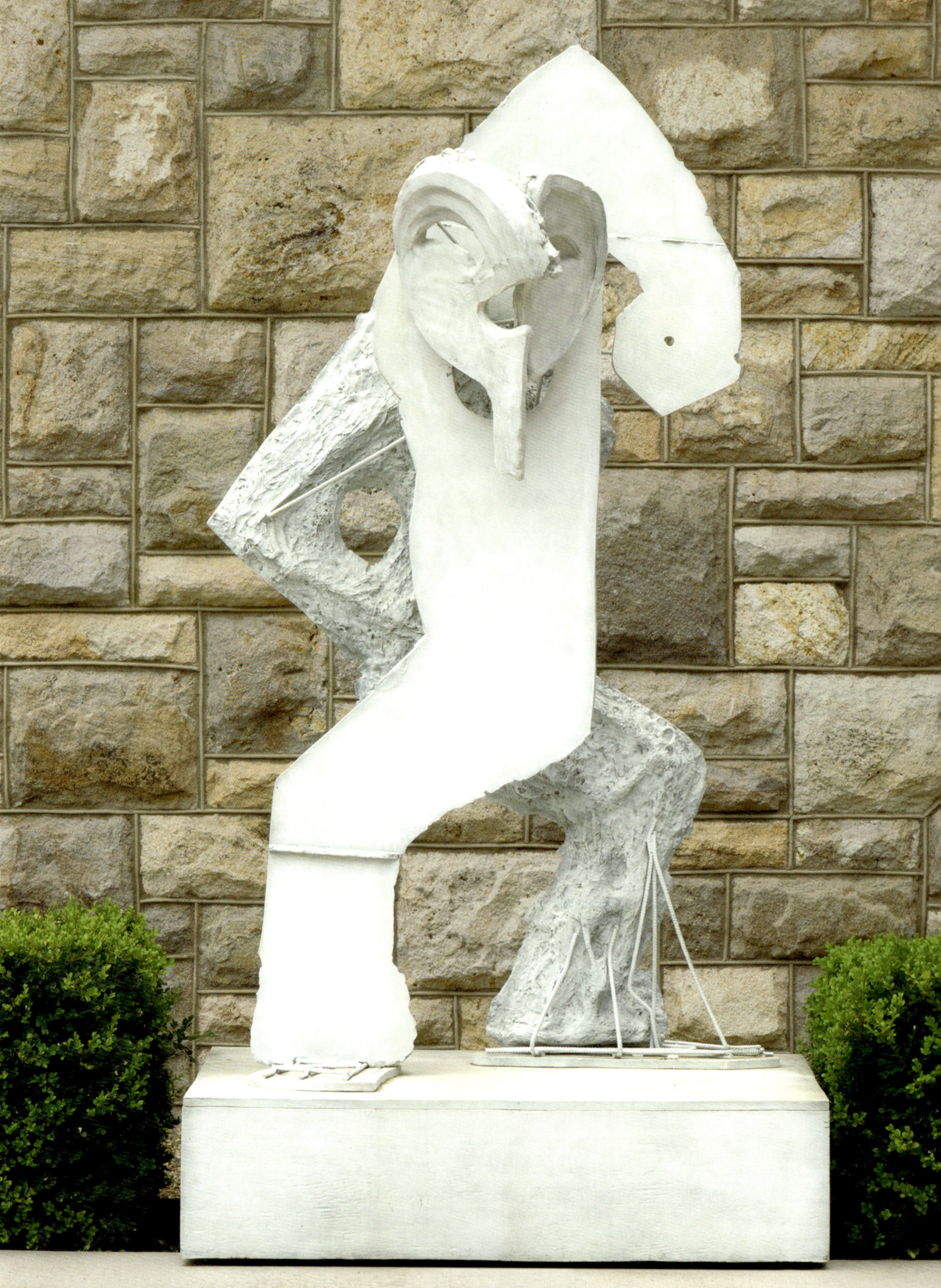

Thomas Houseago was born in Leeds, England, in 1972. In high school the artist earned a scholarship to attend a local arts college for a year, before transferring to St. Martin's School of Art in London in 1991. He continued his studies at De Ateliers in Amsterdam from 1994 to 1996, where he worked with important mentors such as Marlene Dumas and Luc Tuymans. A meeting with Los Angeles dealer David Kordansky in 2006 led to patronage by the collectors Donald and Mera Rubell. Houseago's career skyrocketed from that point on, including a critically lauded appearance in the 2010 Whitney Biennial. He still works and lives in Los Angeles today.

Although Houseago's work joins a broader revival in figurative, Expressionist sculpture, it has become distinctive for its loose, forceful hand and utilization of untreated plaster. Houseago's sculptures are often anthropomorphic creatures in states of duress: they crouch, crawl, hunch, and otherwise agonize in their physicality.

Frequently occupying large-scale dimensions, Houseago's figures loom over the viewer, yet evidence of process renders them vulnerable and almost tragicomic. Graphic lines complete suggestions of volume and metal rods emerge like bones in fleshy limbs. This eccentric composition matches an equally diverse set of influences: Houseago consistently looks to sources ranging from the Flintstones to Pablo Picasso's "Boisgeloup" period.

Even though Houseago staked his claim on his rough treatment of plaster, works in more presentational materials retain the sculptor's interest in formal precariousness and sympathetic characterization. In *Striding Figure (Rome I)* from 2013, a vaguely humanoid being walks forward. Its head forms a cadaverous skull, and its face has been reduced to curving, hollow lines. Although the creature moves in space, Houseago refuses the standard technique of contrapposto: weight does not shift and it looks as if the figure may topple over. Houseago's coarse modeling furthermore draws the eye into the work's sheer materiality. In these multiple investments, *Striding Figure* makes a peculiar demand on the viewer's empathy. J. H.

Death Mask I, 2011
Tuf-cal, hemp, and iron rebar
67 × 46 × 9 inches (170.2 × 116.8 × 22.9 cm)

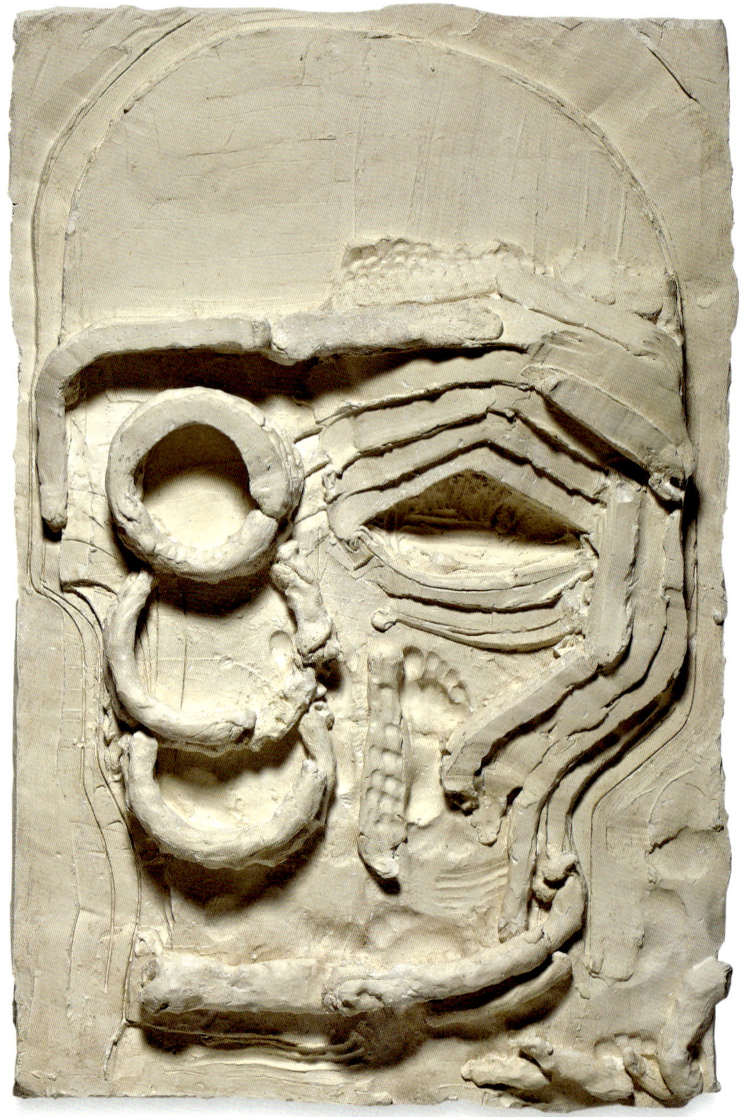

Striding Figure (Rome I), 2013
Bronze
155 × 67 × 94 inches (393.7 × 170.2 × 238.8 cm)
Edition 1 of 3, 2 AP

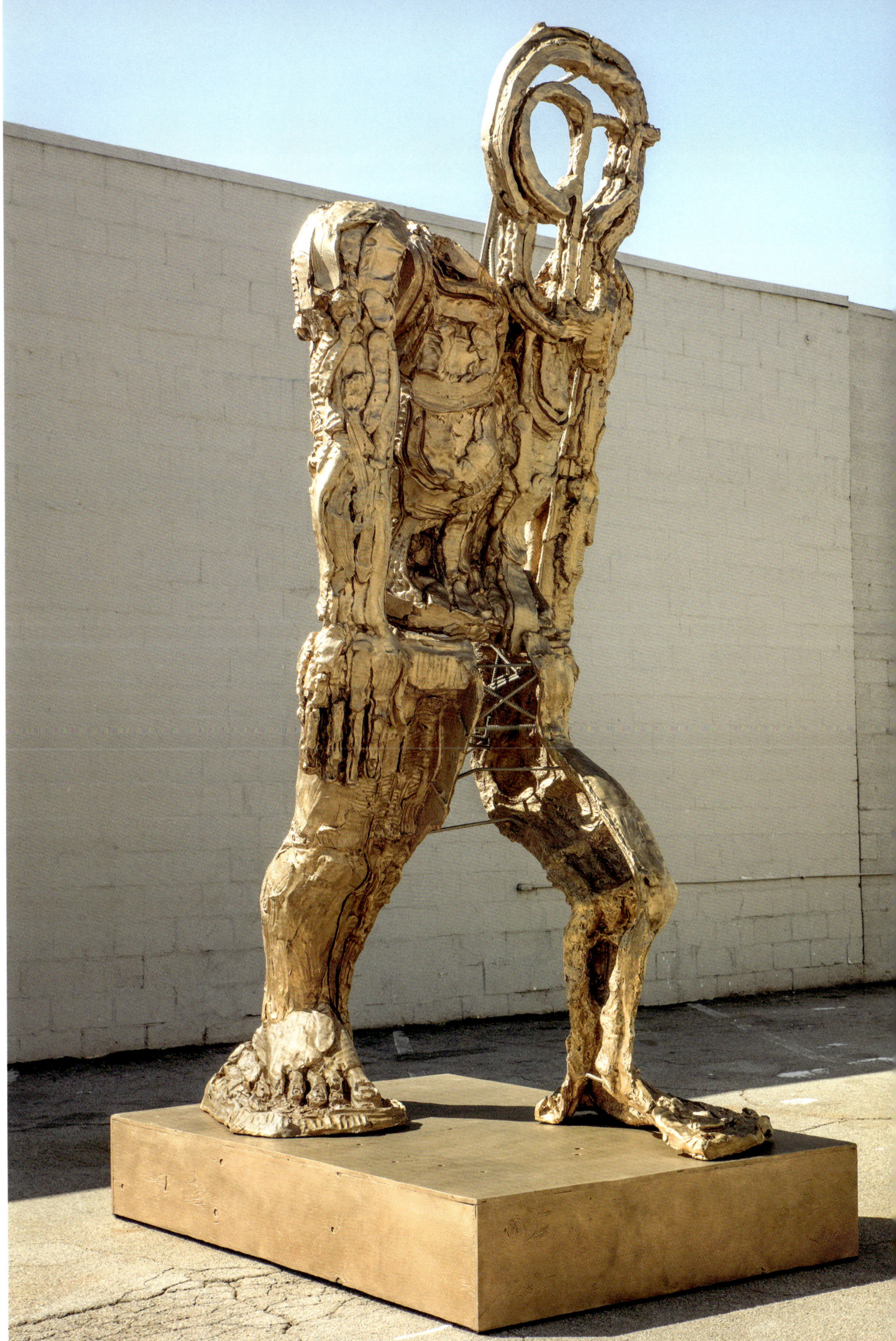

ZHANG HUAN

b. 1965, Anyang City, He Nan Province, China

As Zhang Huan came of age in China in the 1990s, his art—a combination of performance, sculpture, photography, and painting—fearlessly addressed social issues like poverty and inequality, racism and the state, and freedom of expression in a country with a notoriously low tolerance for dissent.

Huan was born in 1965 in Anyang City, He Nan Province, a part of eastern China between Shanghai and Beijing. He got his BA in 1988 from He Nan University in nearby Kai Feng, and his MA from the Central Academy of Fine Arts in Beijing in 1993, after which he joined a loose collective of artists living in a run-down neighborhood in outer Beijing.

As China opened up both culturally and politically in the 1990s, Huan was one of the first mainland artists to achieve international acclaim. Soon after graduating from the Academy of Fine Arts, he was included in the *Configura 2* exhibition in Erfurt, Germany. Since then he has exhibited at the Royal Academy of Arts in London, the Venice Biennale, the Whitney Biennial, and the Storm King Art Center in Mountainville, New York. In 2014, he was awarded France's Legion of Honor. Today he lives in Shanghai and New York City.

Much of Huan's early work was performance-based. In one piece he sat in a soiled public bathroom, coated himself with honey and fish oil, and then tried to endure the flies that flocked to his body. In another piece, he was suspended naked in a white room while doctors drew 250 milliliters of his blood onto a hot plate, which then diffused the fluid into the room's atmosphere. These and other artworks addressed the role of the body—and by extension the human condition—in contemporary communist China.

Similarly, works like *Grand Canal* (2009), while less physically rigorous, address like-minded subject matter. Created using the incense-ash byproduct of Buddhist temple ceremonies, this work recreates, in striking detail, a historical photograph of thousands of laborers who built the Grand Canal from Beijing to Hangzhou. From afar, this monumental artwork could be an actual photograph—up close, the ash figures are ever-so-slightly blurred, their likenesses and forms rendered hazy by the inexorable march of time and China's headlong rush towards modernization. Huan has not only eulogized a forgotten class of people, he's captured the history and texture of his own cultural experience. J. T.

The Creation of the World No. 3, 2011
Ash on linen
23⅞ × 31½ inches (60.6 × 80 cm)

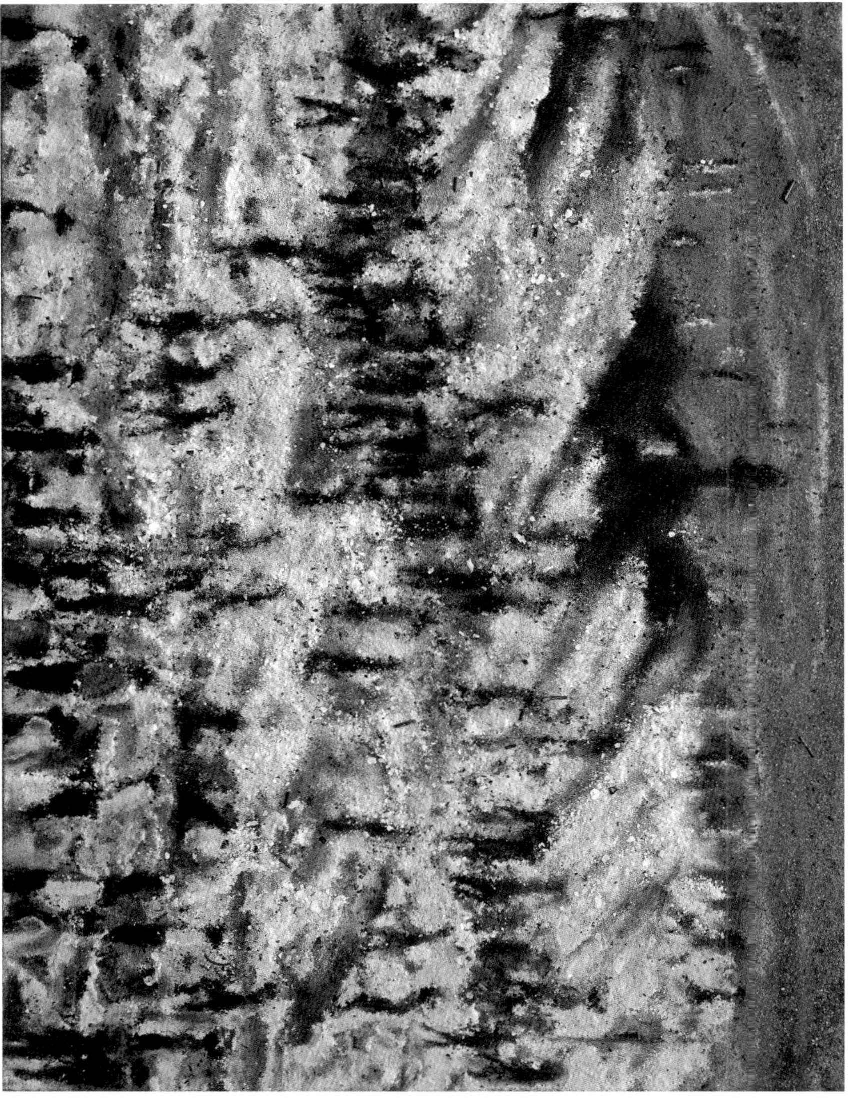

The Creation of the World No. 2, 2011
Ash on linen
24¼ × 36½ inches (61.6 × 92.7 cm)

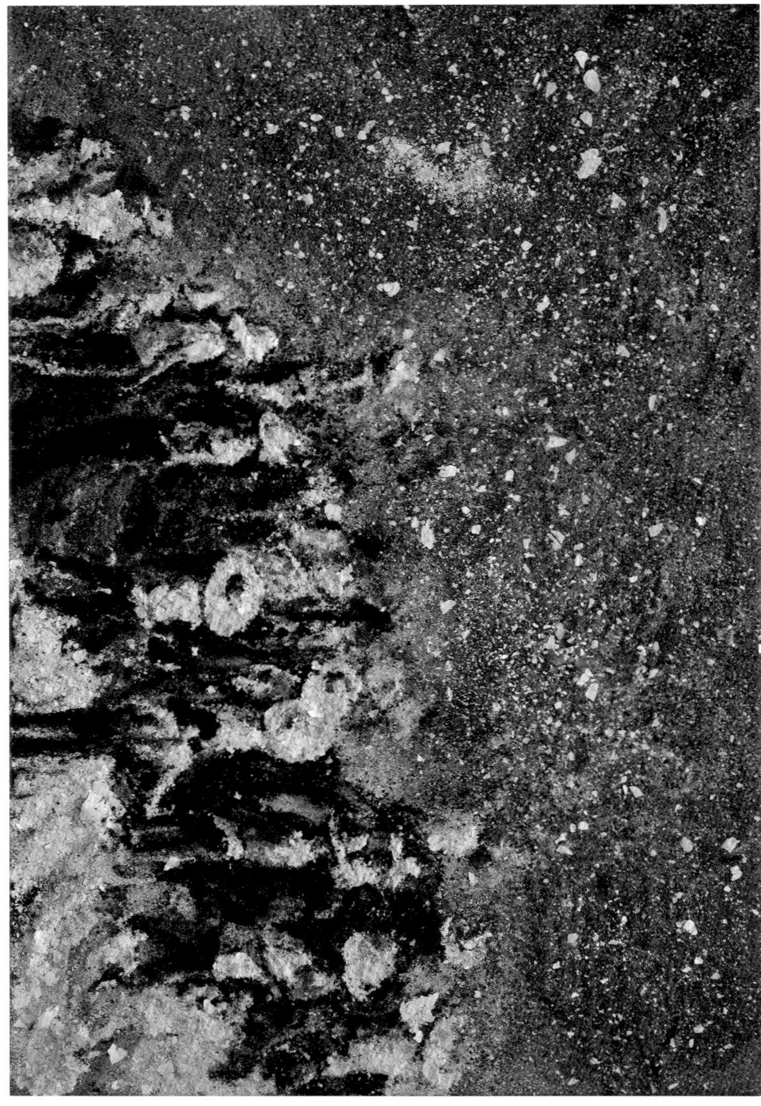

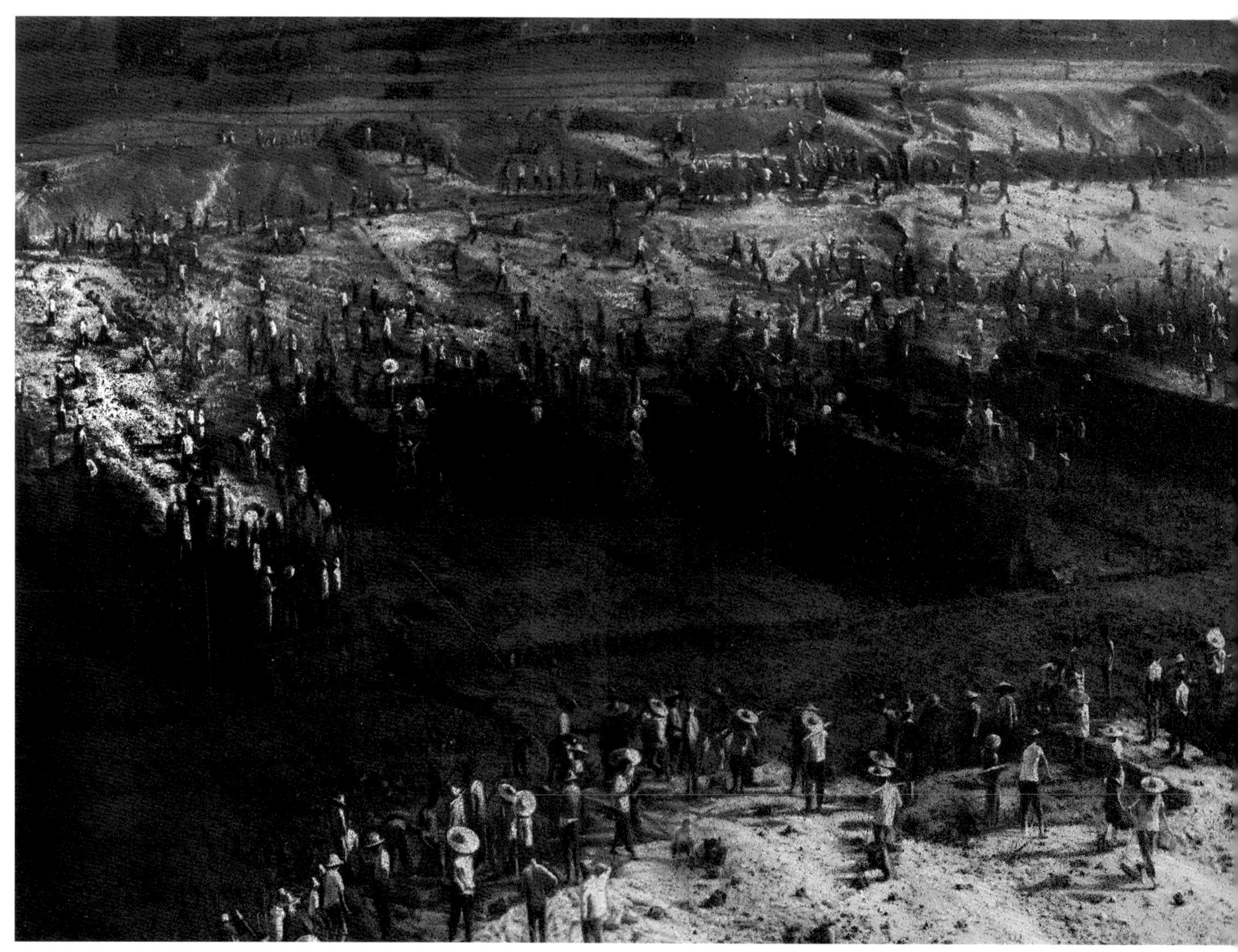

Grand Canal, 2009
Ash on linen
157 × 472 7/16 inches (400 × 1200 cm)

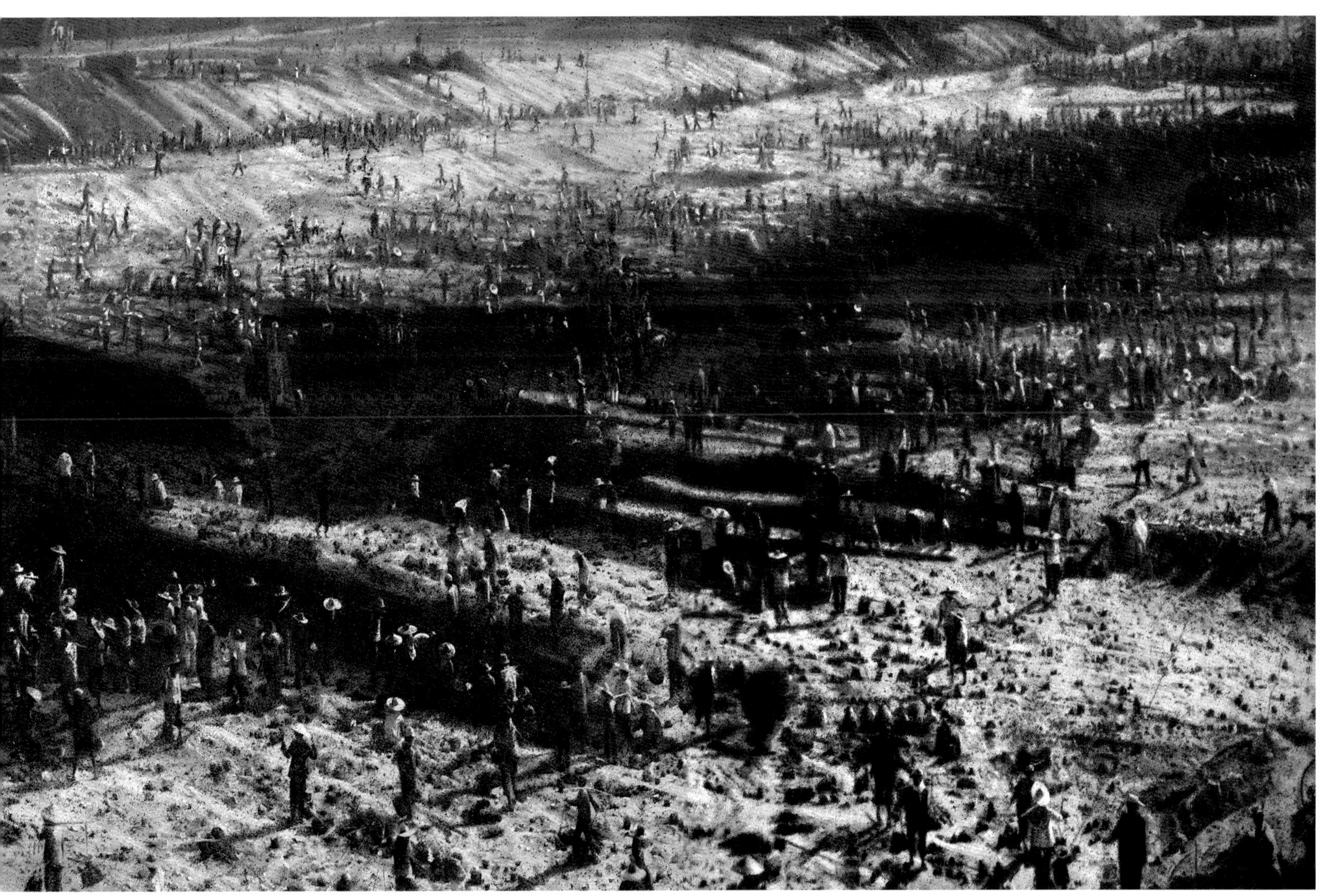

JACQUELINE HUMPHRIES

b. 1960, New Orleans, LA

Paintings are intrinsically static objects, and yet Jacqueline Humphries's canvases practically hum with energy. Some of Humphries's paintings reflect light, others distort it, and still others literally create it (thanks to fluorescent paint that comes alive underneath a black light). It's an artistic output that utilizes materials to novel effect, using brushstrokes and the destruction of those brushstrokes (Humphries occasionally takes a chisel to her canvases) to create an abstract rush of color and shapes so kinetic that the work transcends painting altogether.

Humphries was born in New Orleans in 1960 and graduated from Parsons School of Design in New York in 1985 and the Whitney Museum's Independent Study Program a year later. In the subsequent thirty years, she's been the recipient of numerous awards and solo exhibitions, and her art is featured in the permanent collection of museums around the globe. Today, she lives and works in New York.

Various attempts have been made to situate Humphries's painting in the grand scheme of art history; that these attempts have failed (at least, for the most part) is a testament to the relentless newness of her oeuvre. Works from twenty years ago could have been painted yesterday, and each successive series is an advancement from the last.

Take *Untitled* (2015), one of her black light paintings from a series Humphries initiated in 2005. Seen under natural light, the painting's dots, grids, and gradations look like mere abstractions; under ultraviolet light however, the painting pulsates, its amorphous shapes transformed into a display that closely mimics a computer screen at night.

Humphries's silver paintings take a radically different form. Begun a year after her black light works, this series is created by layering pigment on canvas, coating it in silver paint, and then scratching at the surface to reveal an underlayer. Whereas the black light paintings dazzle the viewer, her silver paintings unsettle with their kinetic complexity. The eye, disoriented by the semi-refractory paint, discordant scratches, and faint, seemingly random coloration, is never quite able to grasp the painting in its totality. J. T.

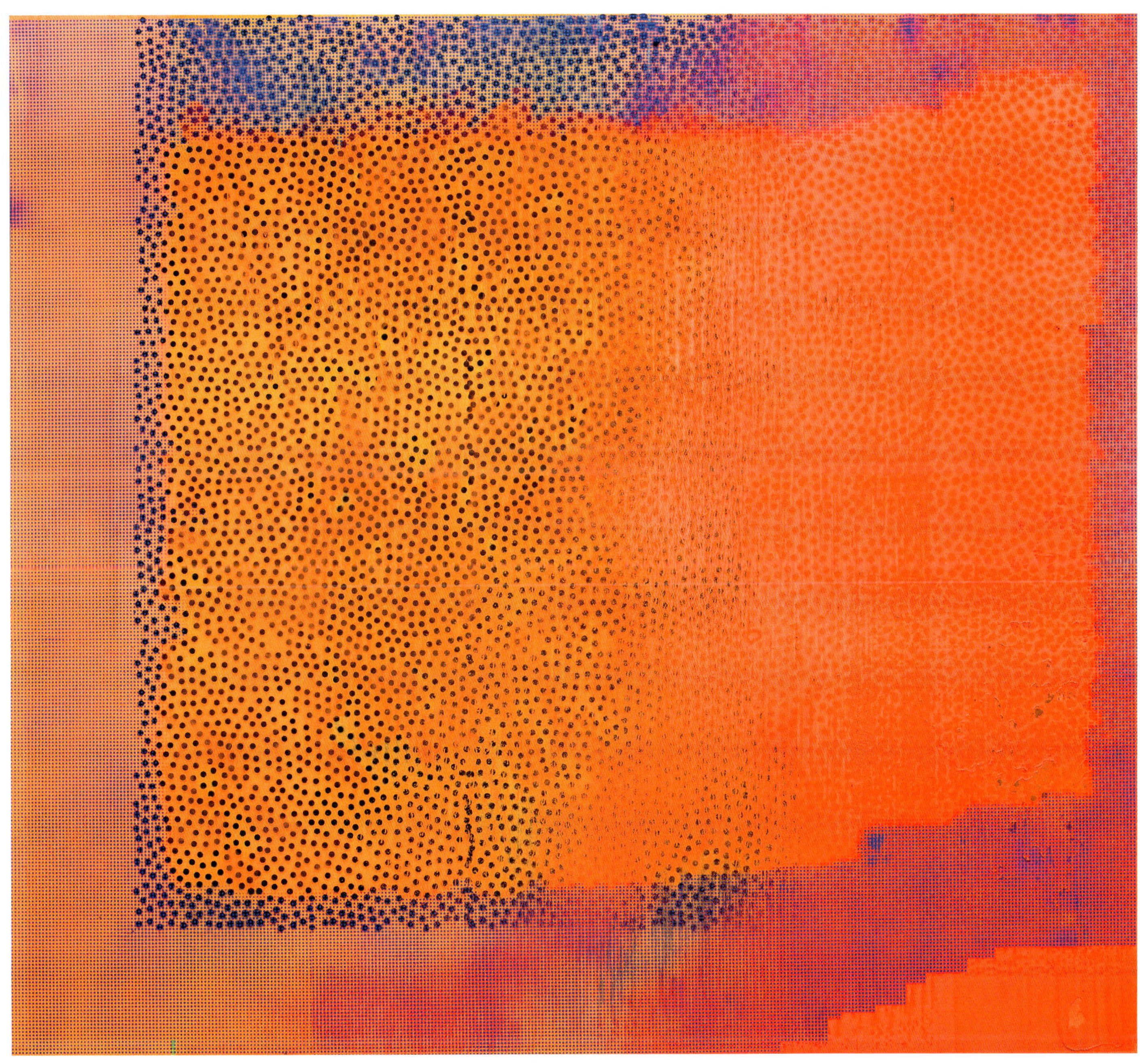

Untitled, 2015
Oil and enamel on linen
114 × 127 inches (289.6 × 322.6 cm)

ALEX ISRAEL

b. 1982, Los Angeles, CA

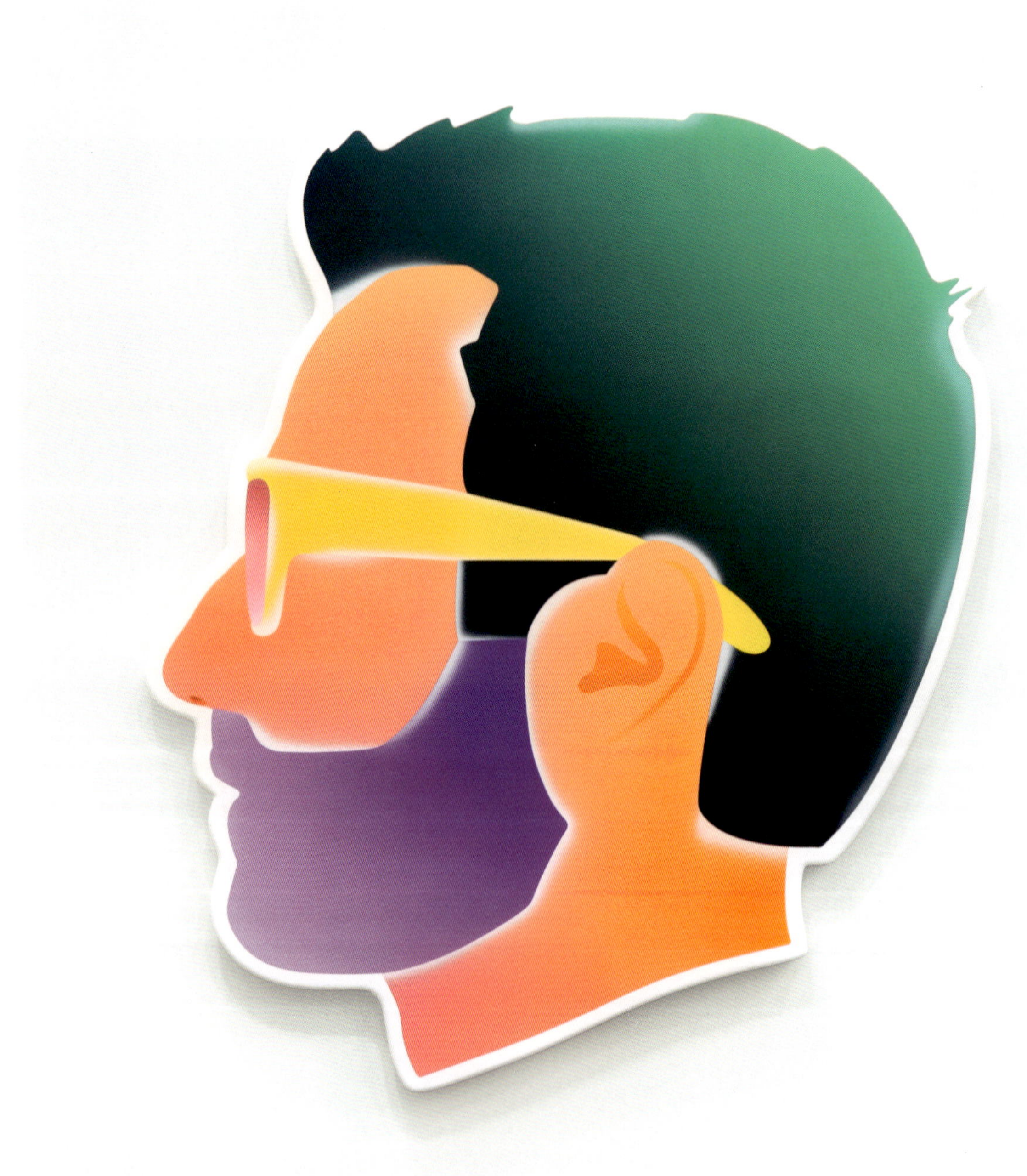

Self-Portrait, 2012
Acrylic and bondo on fiberglass
60 × 69 × 3 inches (152.4 × 175.3 × 7.6 cm)

By exploiting the universally alluring yet elusive aura of Los Angeles in his multifaceted practice, which includes painting, sculpture, installation, film, and performance, Alex Israel invokes his hometown's spirit and essence—both real and perceived—and explores the myths of Hollywood and the cult of celebrity, while simultaneously positing the City of Angels as central to understanding the American dream.

By confronting the representations and clichés of his city, Israel effectively blends, and often blurs, the line between homage and parody, surface and depth, cynicism and hope, seduction and naivete.

Born in Los Angeles in 1982, Israel received his BA in 2003 from Yale University and his MFA in 2010 from the University of Southern California's Roski School of Fine Arts. He worked for a time as an assistant to the late Los Angeles artist Jason Rhoades and now has works in numerous international collections, including those of The Museum of Modern Art in New York, the Centre Georges Pompidou in Paris, and the Moderna Museet in Stockholm.

Israel works not in a traditional artist's studio, but rather in the former scenic art department at Warner Bros. Studios in Burbank, California. There Israel developed a series of paintings entitled *Flats*, including *Untitled (Flat)* (2012), shaped stucco panels that originated from the artist's most significant work to date, a digital talk show entitled *As It Lays* (2012), a performance piece that features a signature sunglasses-clad Israel asking his celebrity guests, in deadpan, a series of random, banal lifestyle questions. Borrowing from the term used on actual television and film sets, the *Flats* served as literal backdrops for *As It Lays*. Stucco, in fact is one of the artist's favorite materials because it "implies a certain hollowness to things." Israel and his assistant, Andrew Pike (Warner Bros.' last remaining fulltime scenic painter), skillfully transform the material into a seamless and seductive symbol of the Hollywood dream machine.

The wall-based mural *Valet Parking* (2013) (see front endsheet), presents a portrait of Los Angeles—the local flora and fauna, as well as the newspaper dispensers, parking meters, and valet signs one encounters while driving around the city. Riffing on the significant history of mural painting in Southern California, Israel reminds us that, after all, "L.A. is all about finding a good parking spot." J.G.M.

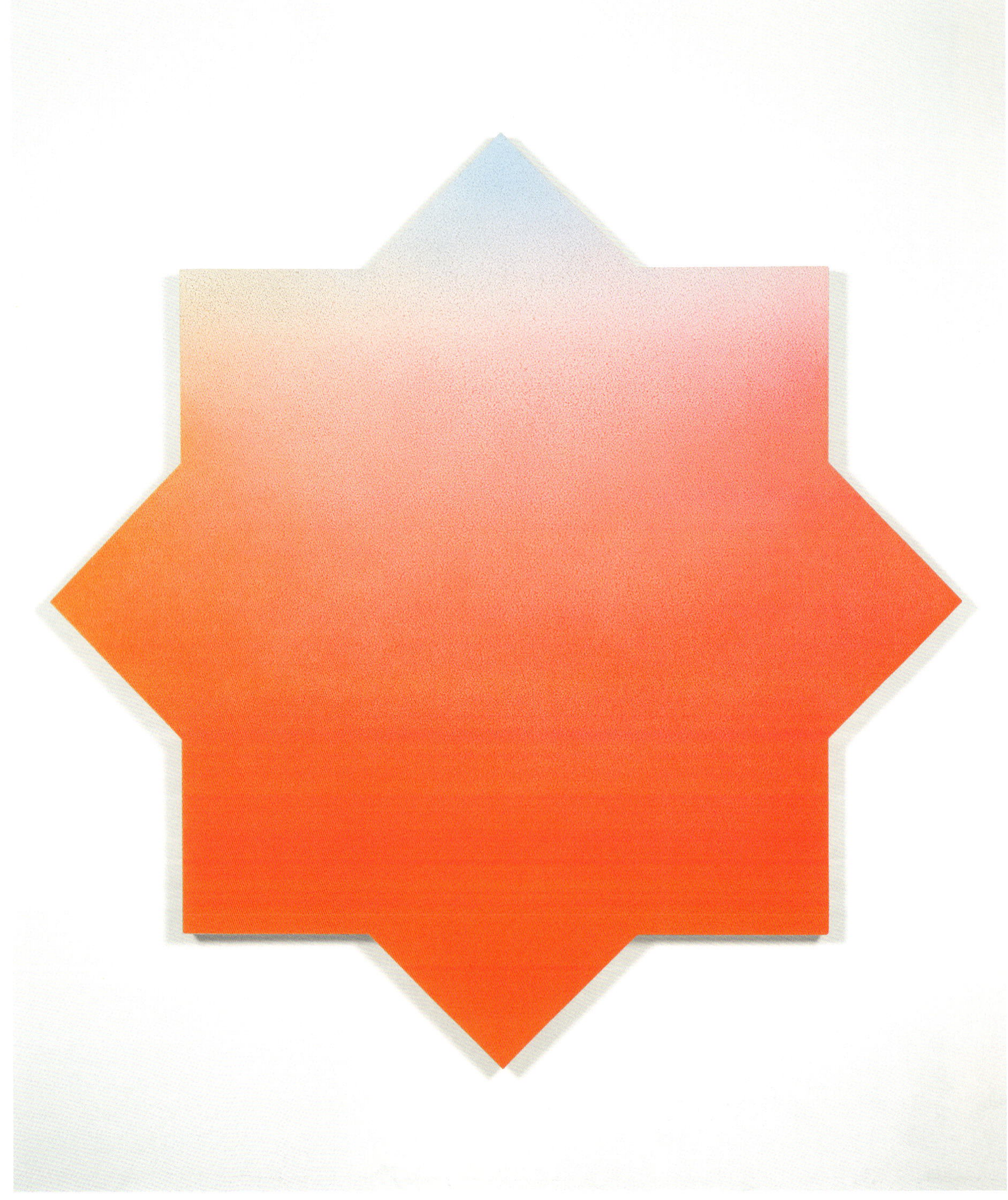

Untitled (Flat), 2012
Acrylic on stucco, wood,
and aluminum frame
84 × 84 inches (213.4 × 213.4 cm)

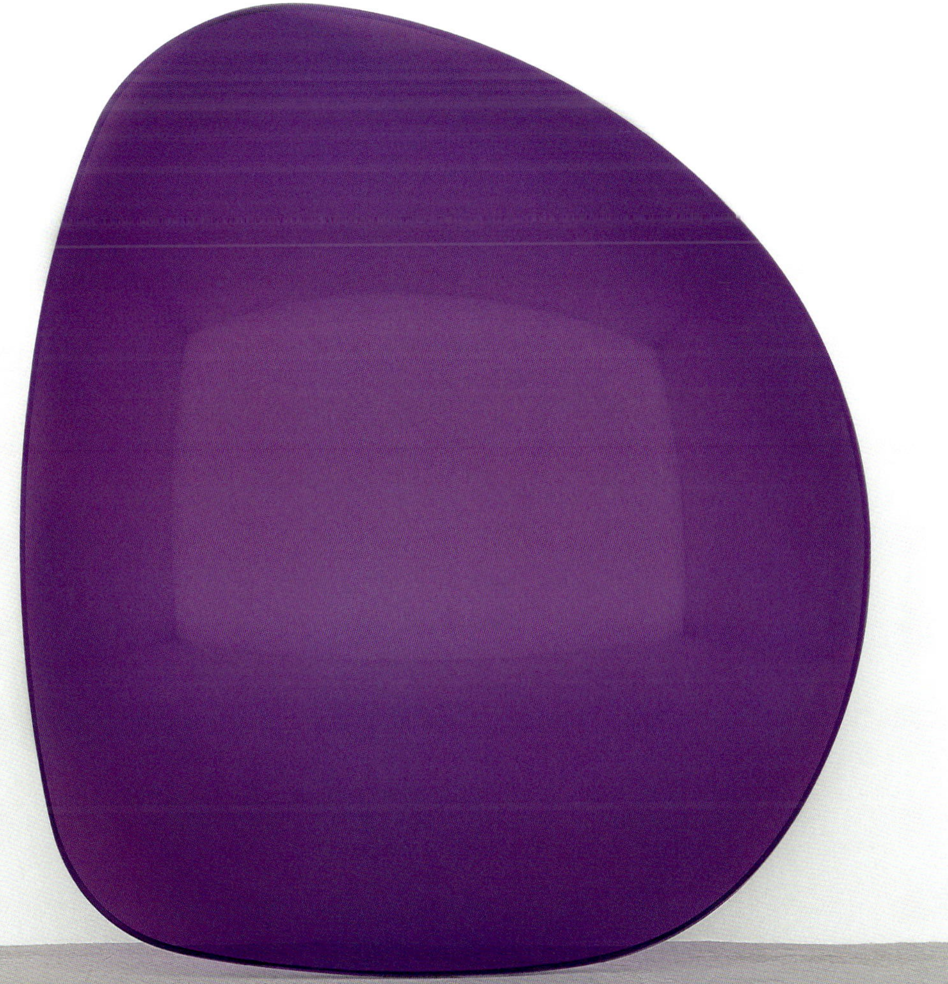

Lens (Purple), 2015
UV protective plastic lens
84 × 96 × 14 1/8 inches
(213.4 × 243.8 × 35.9 cm)
Edition 1 of 4, 1 AP

SERGEJ JENSEN

b. 1973, Maglegaard, Denmark

What makes a painting a painting? A traditional argument would posit that a painting is a work of art that has been made by putting pigment on canvas. In Sergej Jensen's practice, however, a painting isn't as much an object as it is a concept: If an artwork is concerned with color, form, and texture, it is, in his telling, a painting—regardless of what materials were used to create it. Given that logic, it shouldn't be too much of a surprise to learn that much of Jensen's paintings are made with fabric rather than paint—he'll patch, sew, and collage material to create his subtle works of art, only occasionally adding acrylic or oil paint to the finished products.

The point, ultimately, is that sometimes linen or silk or burlap can create the texture and color and intended effect that Jensen needs; in this manner of transcending material concerns, Jensen has created a practice that not only exemplifies painting, but arguably goes a long way to furthering the medium as a whole.

Jensen was born in Maglegaard, Denmark, in 1973. He studied at the Städelschule, Staatliche Hochschule für Bildende Künste in Frankfurt, the city in which he had his first show in 1997. Since then, his art has been exhibited in dozens of museums and art spaces including MoMA PS1 in New York, the KW Institute for Contemporary Art in Berlin, and the Hammer Museum in Los Angeles. Jensen's oeuvre includes musical performance, installation, and sculpture, and for many years he has collaborated on performances with Claus Richter, Oliver Husain, and Michaela Meise under the name "Da Group."

It is through his paintings, though, that Jensen's preoccupation with formal and aesthetic concerns takes flight. For example, *Green Digital Snake* (2010), created out of cashmere and acrylic, exemplifies Jensen's untraditional attitude towards painting and how the work's value resides more in the process of its creation than in the finished product. Here Jensen has draped gray cashmere scarves over the stretcher bars as if they were canvas, creating a moiré effect with the weave's pattern. Jensen often draws the viewer's attention to many of the minor details of his paintings, such as frayed edges, hushed palettes, and gestural marks (such as the subtle green line of acrylic paint in *Green Digital Snake*), which often serve as the source for works' titles. Though infused with depth, detail, and nuance, only one identifiable gesture on the surface appears to be an actual act of painting. J. T.

Green Digital Snake, 2010
Acrylic on sewn cashmere silk
63 × 74 13/16 inches (160 × 190 cm)

Untitled, 2009
Various sewn fabrics
$96\frac{7}{16} \times 74\frac{13}{16}$ inches (245 × 190 cm)

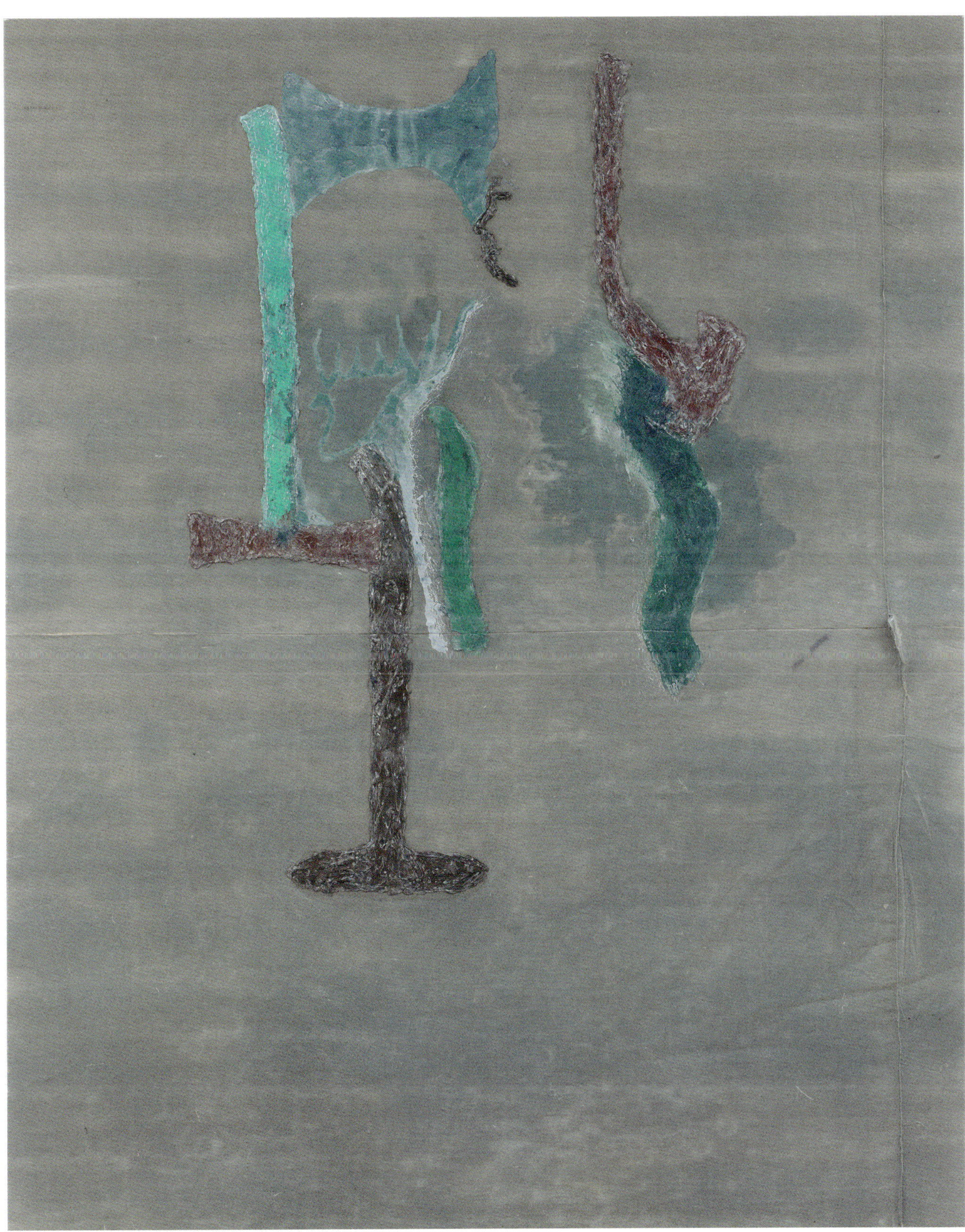

No Title, 2012
Acrylic on sewn linen
141¾ × 116⅛ inches (360 × 295 cm)

RASHID **JOHNSON** b. 1977, Chicago IL

Though he plays with medium, style, and format toward various ends, a unified concern runs through every one of Rashid Johnson's artworks: the experience of black people in America. Far from limiting his practice, this central theme, which Johnson applies to both current and historical contexts, has infused his art with a ringing, pulsating energy imbued with an almost desperate urgency.

This is evident in the rapid pace with which Johnson came onto the art scene. Born in 1977 in Chicago, Johnson graduated with a BA from Columbia College Chicago in 2000 and received an MFA from the Art Institute of Chicago in 2004. Before he had even graduated, he was making a name for himself as the youngest artist in the seminal *Freestyle* exhibition at The Studio Museum in Harlem in 2001. By 2004, Johnson had been included in exhibitions at the Corcoran Gallery of Art in Washington D.C., the Whitney Museum of American Art in New York, and the Walker Art Center in Minneapolis. His work continues to be exhibited globally, including solo shows at the Grand Palais in Paris, the Drawing Center in New York, and the Museum of Contemporary Art in Chicago.

Much of Johnson's work incorporates autobiographical elements. This is especially true in his sculptures. The wall-mounted *The Long Dream* (2014), for example, constructed from red oak flooring and topped with books, plants, and shea butter (among other ephemera), displays the banal albeit resonant objects from his everyday life. The books and plants serve as a stark rejoinder to the racist stereotype of an "angry black male," while the shea butter—a product of African Shea trees—speaks to a phenomenon Johnson has described as African Americans "coating themselves in the theater of Africanism."

Other works have a more universal application—most notably his ongoing Anxious Men series. To make *Untitled Anxious Men* (2015), Johnson covered white ceramic tiles with a heavy black soap and wax, then scored the substance to create semi-abstract faces. Beyond its formal novelty (dancing between drawing and painting), the work is a literal and figurative manifestation of contemporary black anxiety in the face of police brutality, endemic social racism, and the casual indifference of political and cultural leaders.
J. T.

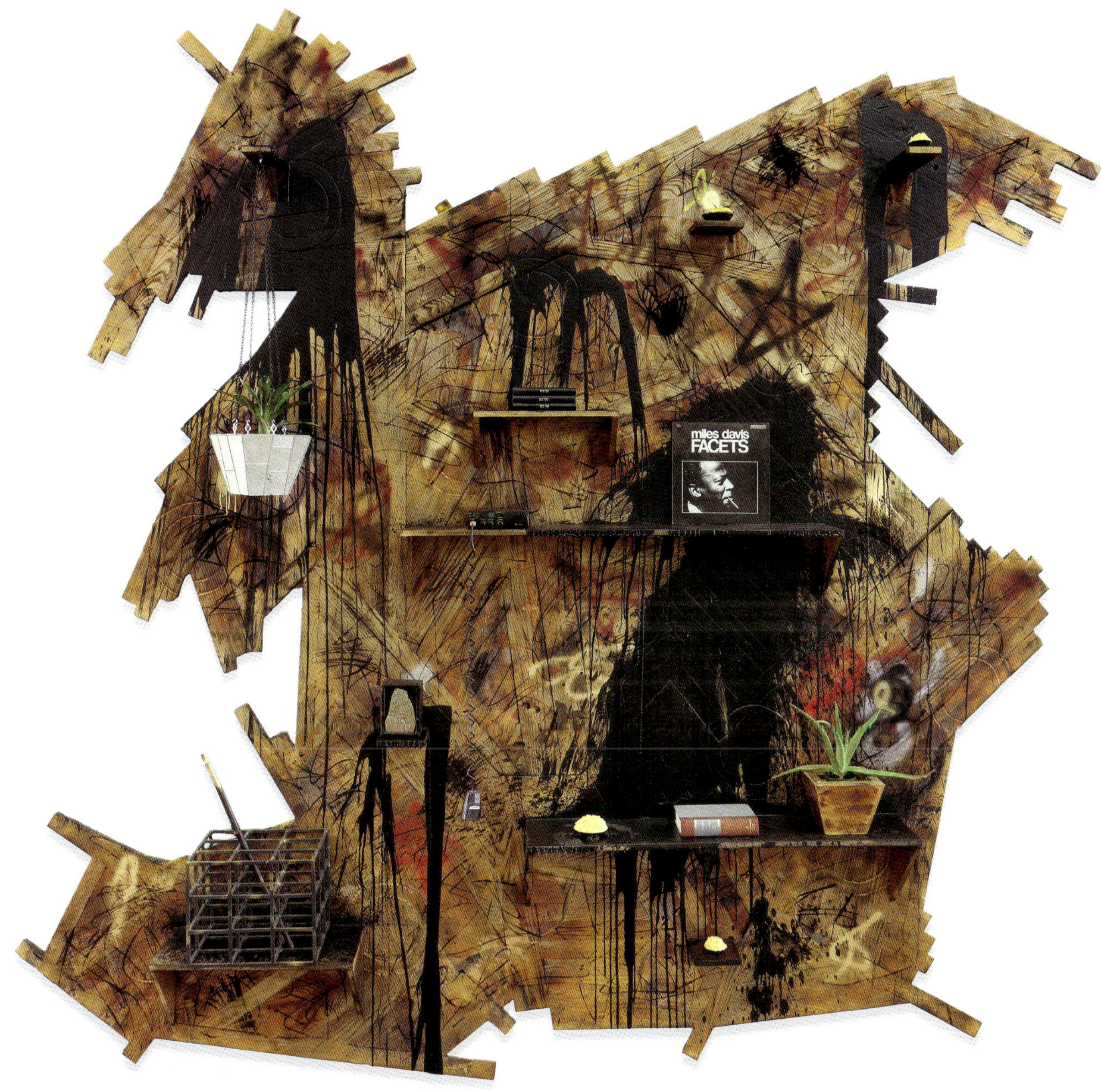

The Long Dream, 2014
Burned red oak flooring, black soap, wax, spray enamel, vinyl, steel, bamboo, shea butter, books, plants, and mirrored planter
133⅞ × 140¼ × 16¼ inches
(340 × 356.2 × 41.3 cm)

Untitled Anxious Men, 2015
White ceramic tile, black soap, and wax
73 × 94½ × 3 inches (185.4 × 240 × 7.6 cm)

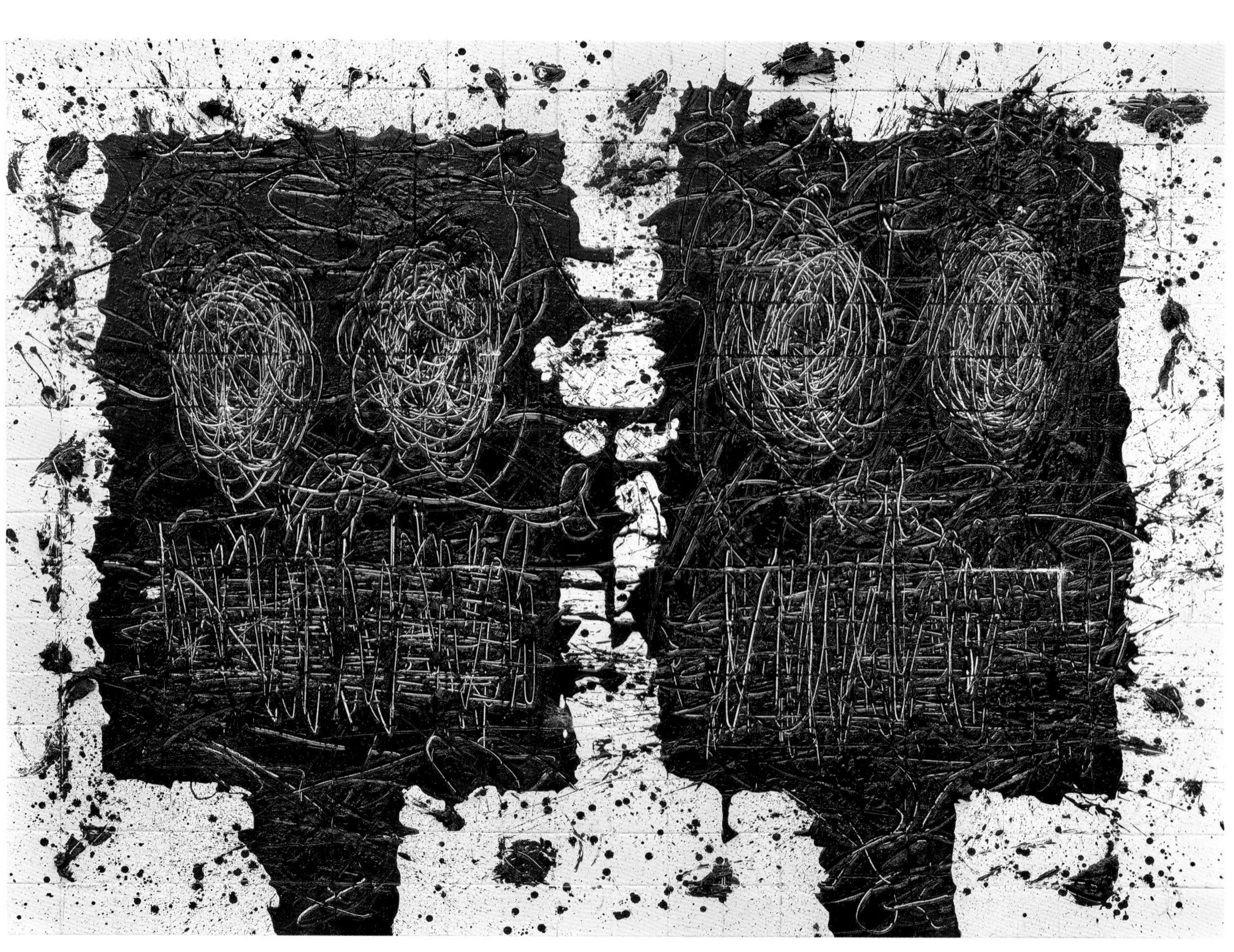

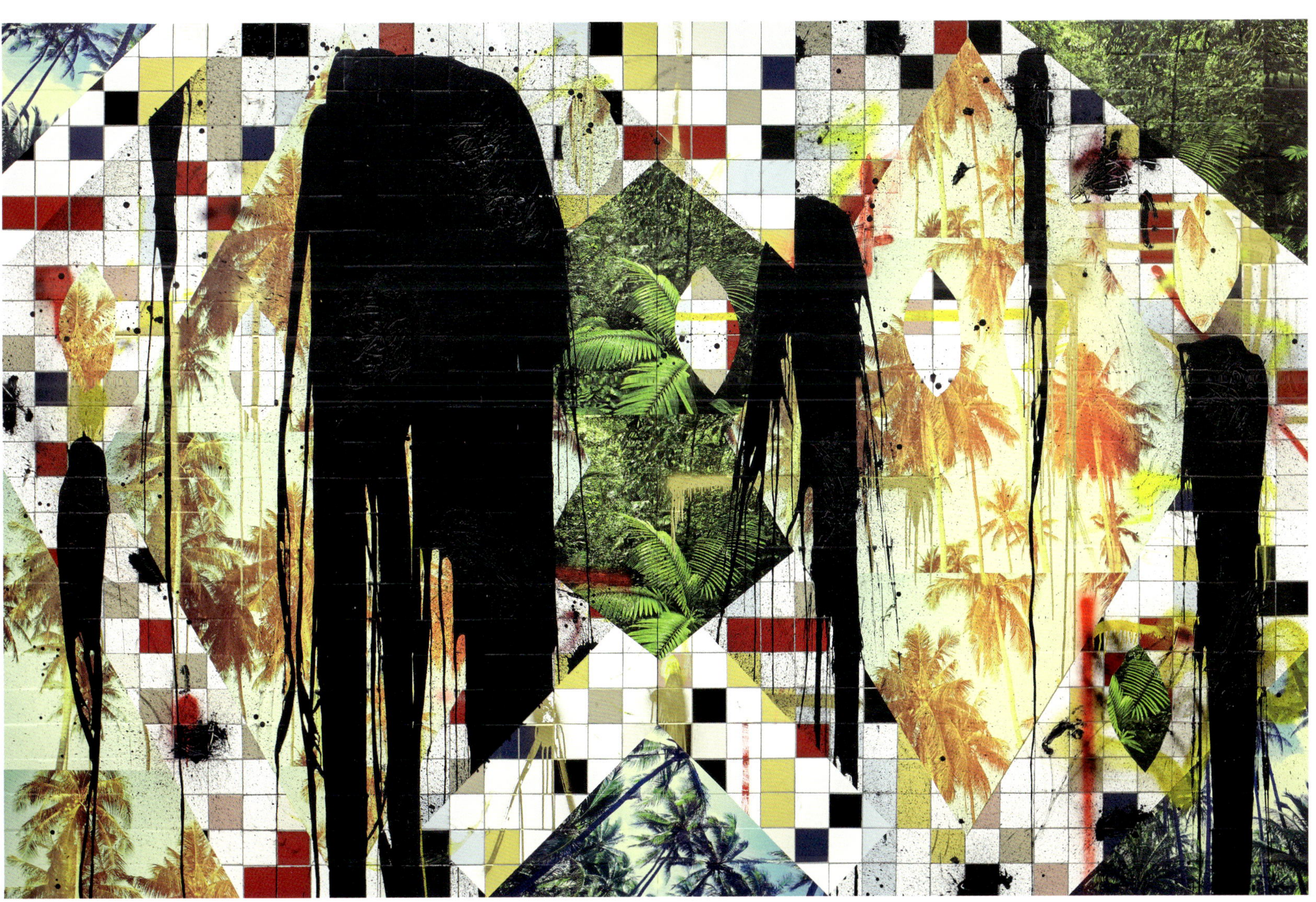

Untitled Escape Collage, 2016
Ceramic tile, black soap, wax, vinyl,
and spray enamel
95 × 142 × 2½ inches (241.3 × 360.7 × 6.4 cm)

WYATT KAHN

b. 1983, New York, NY

Wyatt Kahn was born in 1983 in New York, where he currently lives and works. He received his BFA from the School of the Art Institute of Chicago before returning to New York to complete his graduate studies at Hunter College, where he earned an MFA in 2012. His career picked up almost immediately, with a solo exhibition at Hannah Barry Gallery in London in 2012 and a two-person exhibition with Bob Zoell at Rachel Uffner Gallery in New York in 2013. Kahn has since gained critical visibility with solo exhibitions at LA><ART in Los Angeles, the Contemporary Art Museum in St. Louis, Missouri, and the Museo di Arte Moderna e Contemporanea di Trento e Roverto in Trento, Italy. Commissioned by Performa to develop a piece for its biennial, he premiered his puppet show, *Work*, at the Swedish Cottage Marionette Theater in New York in November 2015.

Kahn has become most famous for his monochromatic, shaped paintings, such as *Maltese* (2012), which explore sculptural and volumetric concerns through their construction. Gaps between the panels reveal the architectural support—the wall behind—and also trace the outlines of abstract compositions. His most recent works hover between the abstract and the figural, depicting everyday objects in three representational systems through idiosyncratic, hand-drawn designs on the canvas.

In Kahn's more recent work, the artist forays into pictorial representation, with forays into pictorial representation, with composition and design speaking to the theme of rain and the object of the umbrella. Handwritten text evokes the sound of raindrops, pictographic symbols metonymically represent the painting overall, and a third pattern abstracts the shape of the umbrella into a simplified form. Through each hand-drawn motif, Kahn explores the essential and imagined properties of objects with a subtle humor that tickles the tenants of abstractions. J. H.

Assembled from multiple wooden panels, each skillfully outfitted with several layers of unprimed canvas, these works literalize the fragmentation of the picture plane inaugurated in Cubist and Constructivist art while working within the legacy of Minimal abstraction.

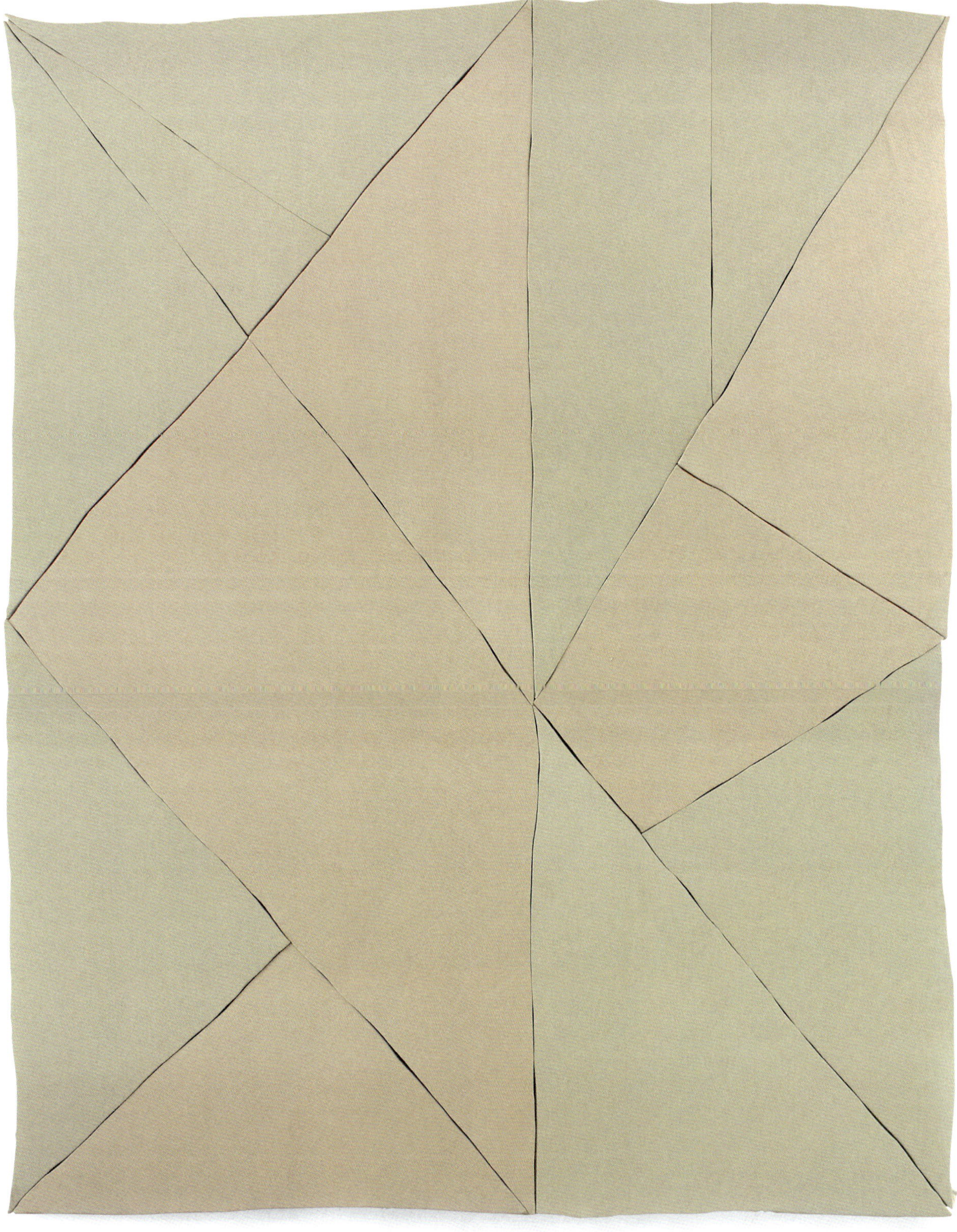

Maltese, 2012
Canvas on panel on panel
78 × 63 inches (198.1 × 160 cm)

MIKE KELLEY b. 1954, Detroit, MI–d. 2012

The work of Mike Kelley disgorges the artist's obsessions with themes of psychology, trauma, sexual desire, philosophy, and kitsch into the public sphere. As he remarked, "I make art in order to give other people my problems." Through performance, installation, painting, film, and sculpture, Kelley hearkened a punk attitude that unabashedly critiqued American culture's attitudes toward family, religion, sexuality, art history, and education.

Calling attention to repressed memories, generic high school activities, and awkward pubescent experiences, Kelley bluntly dissected American culture and ritual, forcing the viewer to consider the long-lasting subtexts and implications of these institutionalized acts and expectations.

Born in Detroit in 1954 to a working-class Catholic family, Kelley attended the University of Michigan in Ann Arbor, where he founded the "anti-rock" band Destroy All Monsters with Jim Shaw, Cary Loren, and Lynn Rovner. Kelley and Shaw both moved to Southern California in 1976 to attend graduate school at the California Institute of the Arts. It was there that Kelley befriended and collaborated with fellow student Tony Oursler and collaborated on performance/video works with Paul McCarthy.

In the late 1970s and into the mid 1980s, Kelley's multimedia works imparted dread and adolescent abjection onto the viewer. Some of his most celebrated and well-known works were made from stuffed-animals he found in thrift stores. In this spirit of using found non-art objects, Kelley mined American history textbooks he found at yard sales for *Reconstructed History* (1989) in which he defaced and sullied the text's illustrations with lewd doodles and notations to question the way history books communicate the stories of our predecessors.

In the years before his death, Kelley concentrated on his *Kandors* project (1999–2011), a reference to the *Superman* comic's fictional city of Kandor, which was shrunken and bottled before the destruction of the planet Krypton. Kelley created twenty unique *Kandors,* including *Kandor 18B* (2010), in which he continues his recurring theme of trauma, using the story of Superman and Kandor as a metaphor for loss and memory.

Mike Kelley received the Skowhegan Medal in Mixed Media and two grants from the National Endowment for the Arts in 1997. Major solo exhibitions include Whitney Museum of American Art, New York; Los Angeles County Museum of Art; Hirshhorn Museum and Sculpture Garden, Washington, DC; Tate Liverpool, London; Centre Georges Pompidou, Paris; and Kunsthalle, Basel; among others. Kelley lived and worked in Los Angeles, where he passed away in February 2012. L.C.

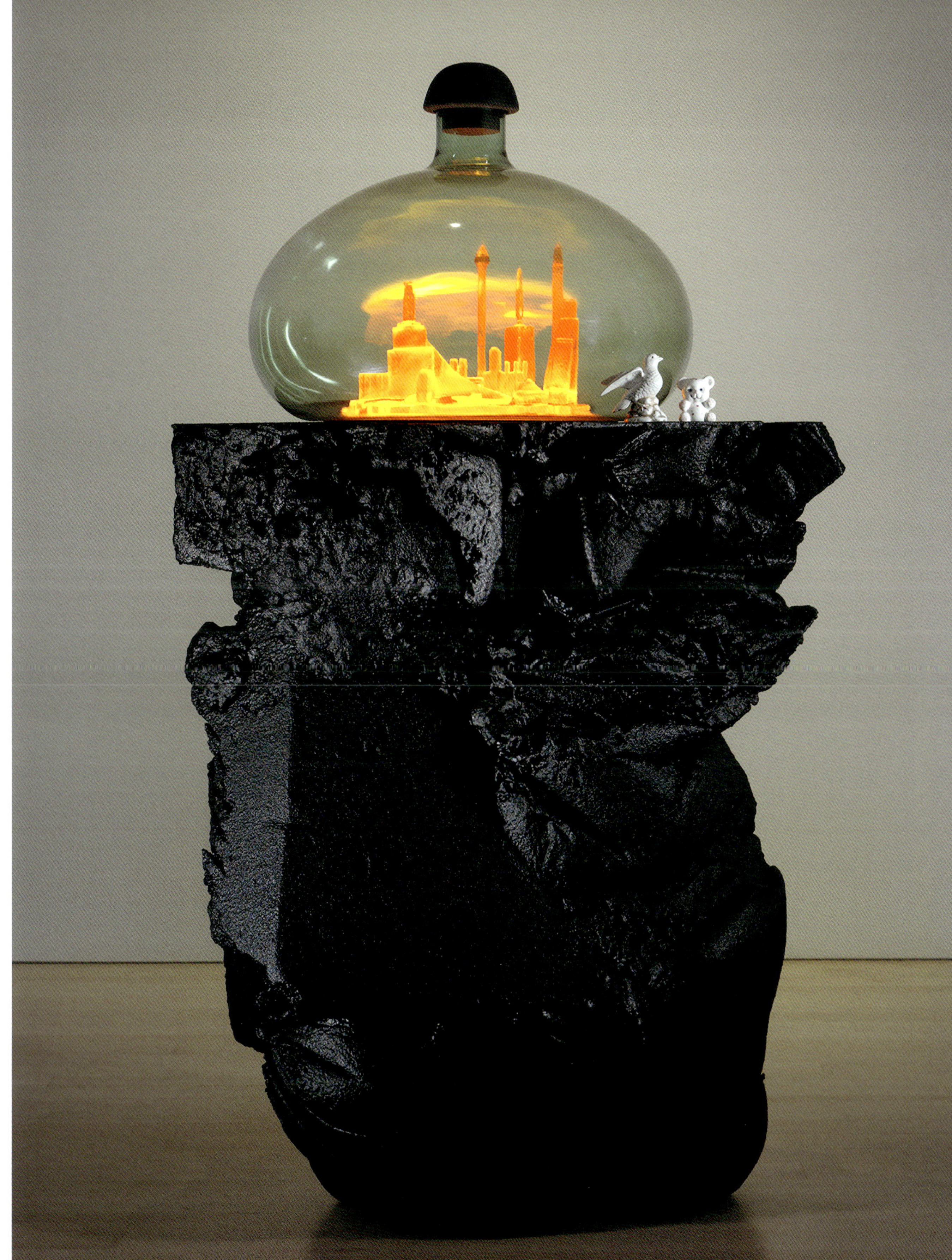

Kandor 18B, 2010
Foam coated with Elastomer, blown glass with water-based resin coating, tinted Urethane resin, wood, found objects, and lighting fixture
87 × 36 × 48 inches (221 × 91.4 × 121.9 cm)

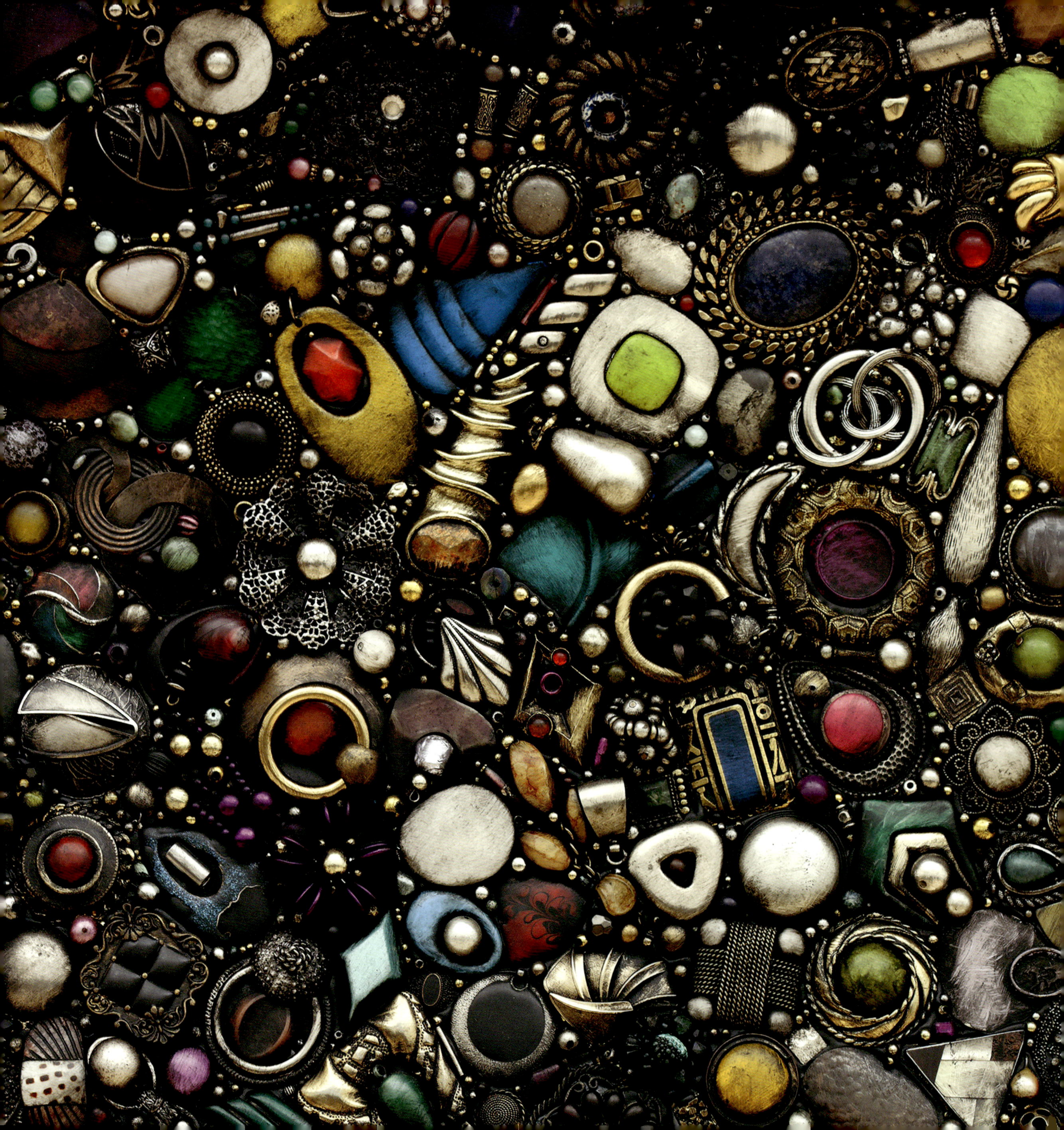

Memory Ware #60, 2010
Foam, tinted resin, found jewelry,
coffee pot, and plastic toys
47 × 81 × 12 ½ inches (119.4 × 205.7 × 31.8 cm)

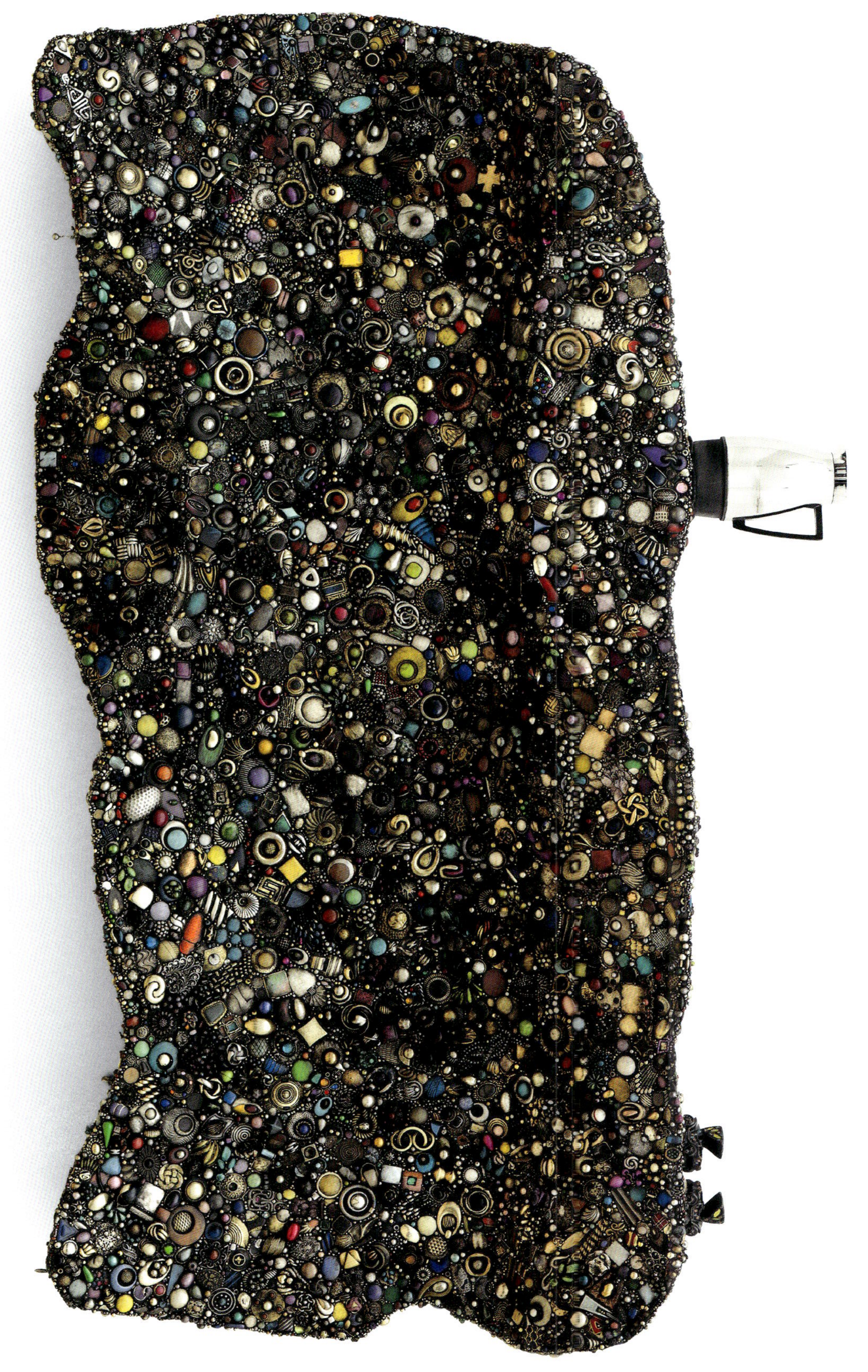

Repressed Spatial Relationships Rendered as Fluid, No. 3: Reconfiguration of Wayne High School into the Ritual Presentation of the Educational Complex, 2002
Aluminum, steel, ceramic, and cloth
Mobile: 42 × 63 × 42 inches
(106.7 × 160 × 106.7 cm)
Frame: 48 ¾ × 67 ¾ × 2 inches
(123.8 × 172.1 × 5.1 cm)

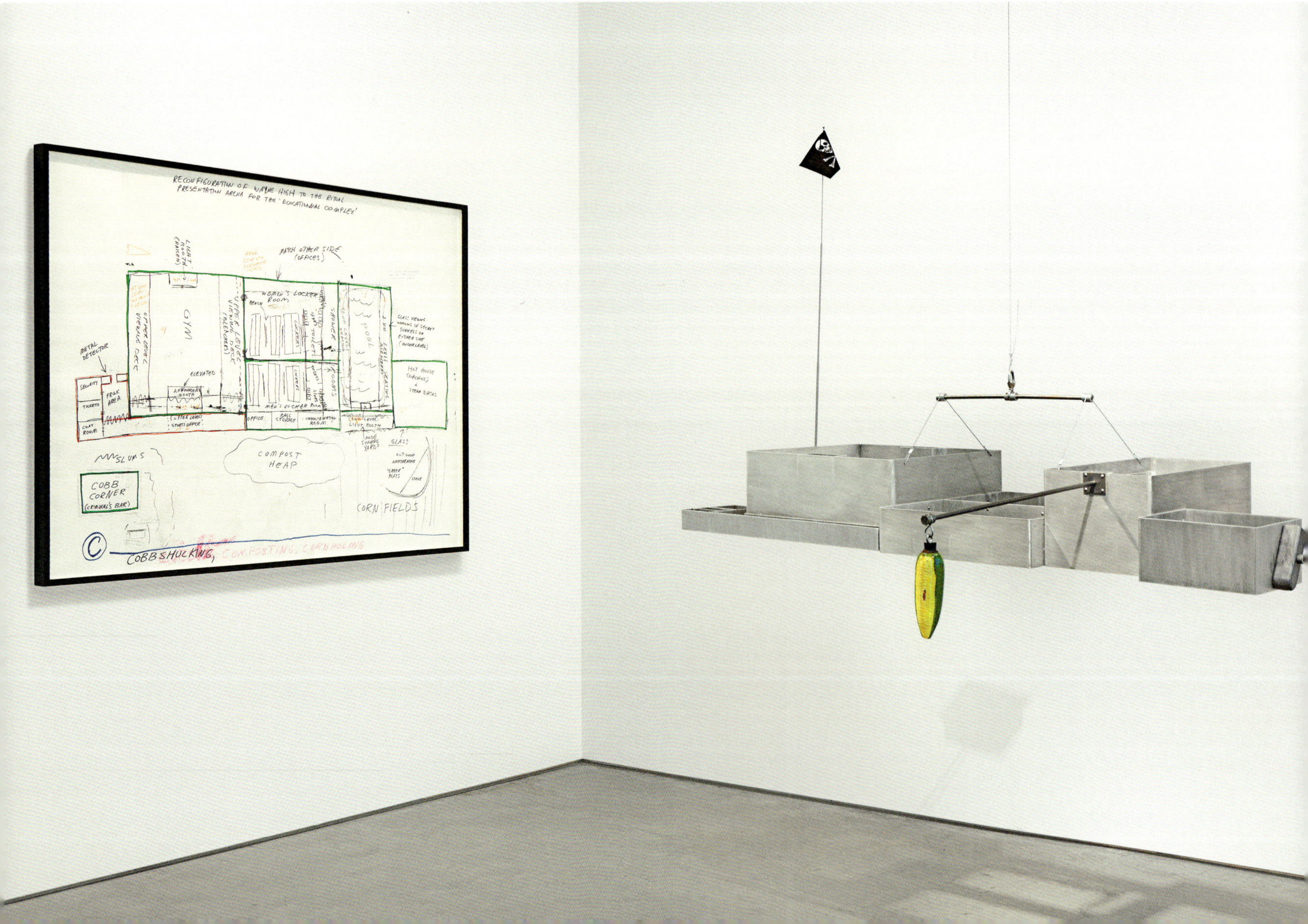

Reconstructed History, 1989 (detail)
17 gelatin silver prints
10 × 8 inches (25.4 × 20.3 cm) each

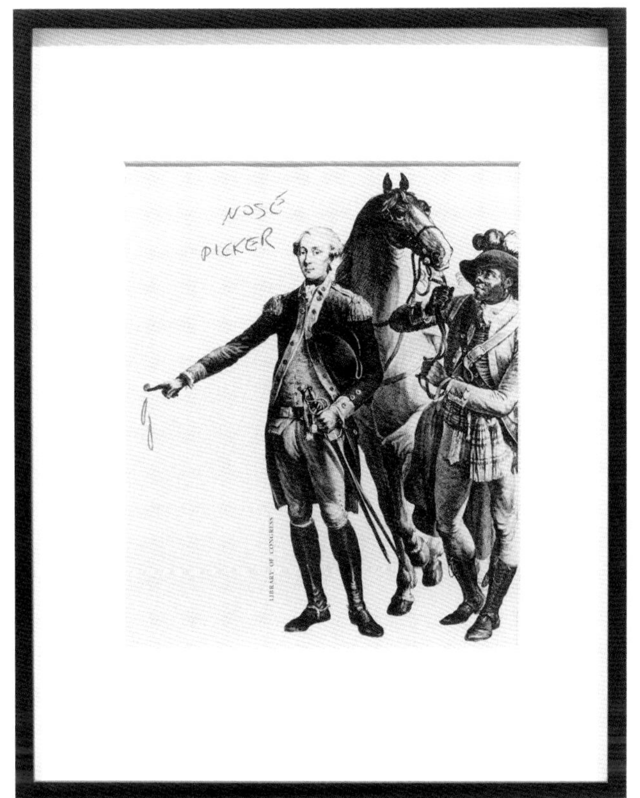

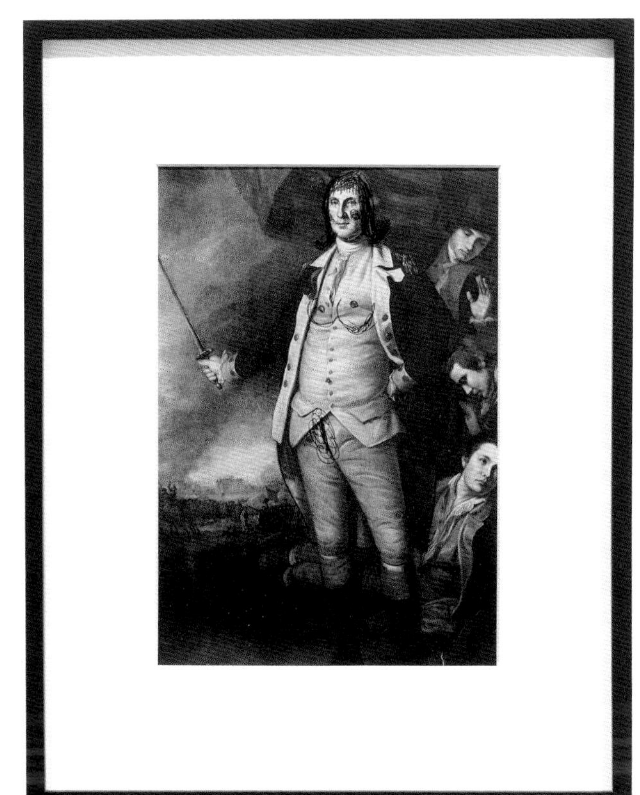

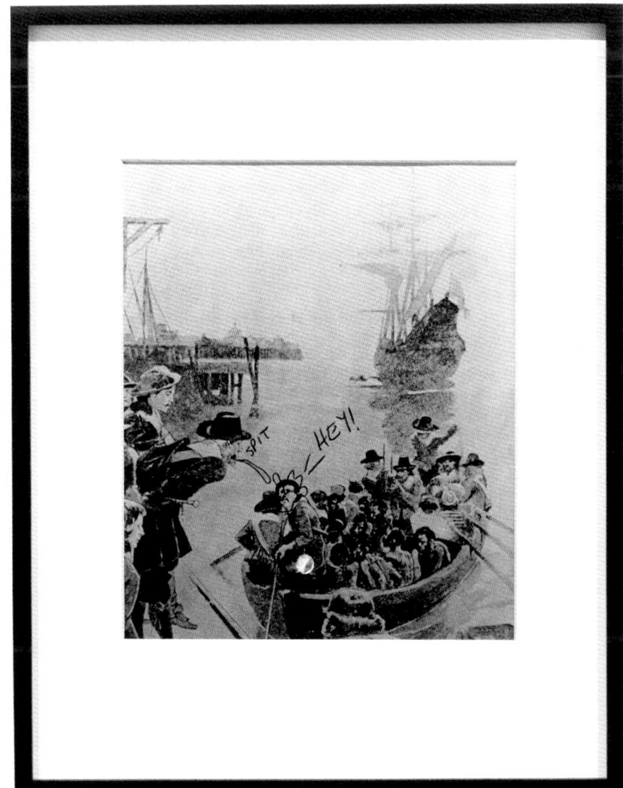

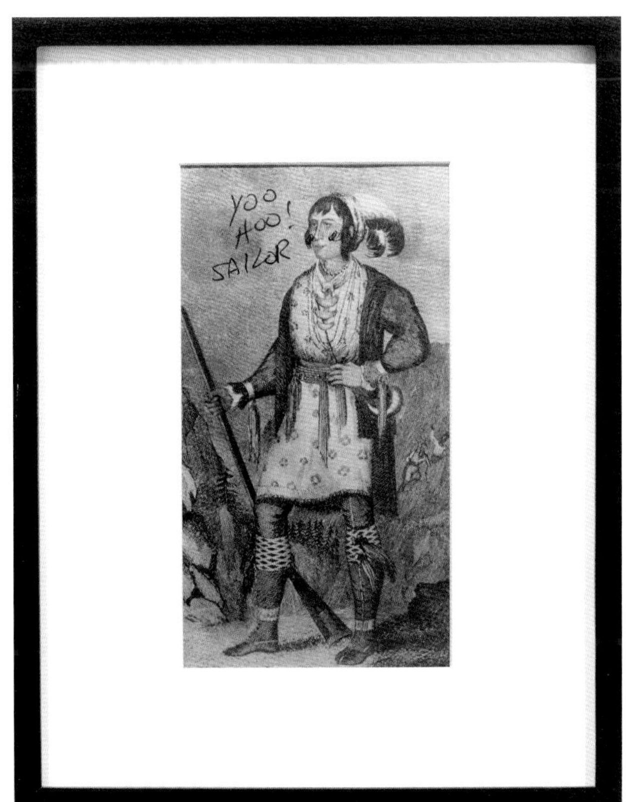

FRIEDRICH **KUNATH** b. 1974, Chemnitz, Germany

The argument can be made that all art is, in its various and sundry ways, a reaction to or a manifestation of the human condition. That argument becomes practically airtight when confronted with the work of Friedrich Kunath, whose maudlin, cynical, and (occasionally) upbeat oeuvre is an exploration of what it means to have an inner life as a person lives, loves, procreates, and dies.

Kunath was born in 1974 in Chemnitz (at the time called Karl-Marx Stadt) in East Germany. He received the Peter Mertes Stipendium scholarship at the Kunstvereinin Bonn in 2001, and then graduated from the work scholarship program of the Jürgen Ponto-Stiftung in Frankfurt am Main in 2005. Throughout his education, he made and showed art; his earliest exhibition, *The Easiest Thing to Grow in a Garden is Tired,* was at a small gallery in Braunschweig, Germany, in 1994. Over the subsequent decade he continued to exhibit—mostly in galleries in Germany—and his art slowly gained recognition on an international level. In 2004, he was included in the Tate Liverpool's *Rhinegold: Art from Cologne*; since then, he has had solo shows at the Aspen Museum of Art, the Hammer Museum in Los Angeles, Modern Art Oxford in England, and the Centre d'art contemporain d'Ivry–le Crédac in Ivry-sur-Seine, France. Today, Kunath lives and works in Los Angeles and is a resident professor at the Art Center College of Design in Pasadena.

Kunath's practice includes sculpture, installation, video art, drawing, and painting, though it's in the latter two mediums where his aesthetic—lush colors, figural people and animals, unresolved, vaguely surreal imagery—is most pronounced. In his large oil, acrylic, and silkscreen painting *Someday You Will Find Me Carpeting the Landslide (Fence Version)* (2012), all of these elements are in play. The title is presumably a play on the often-misheard lyrics from Oasis's song *Champagne Supernova* ("Someday you will find me / Caught beneath the landslide"), while the imagery, which includes a gramophone, a torsoless figure, a person on horseback, and other objects interwoven into a verdant landscape, is obscured behind a trompe l'oeil chain-link fence. It's a painting, in other words, rife with misunderstanding, ambiguity, and, most wrenchingly, the profound absence of resolution.

J. T.

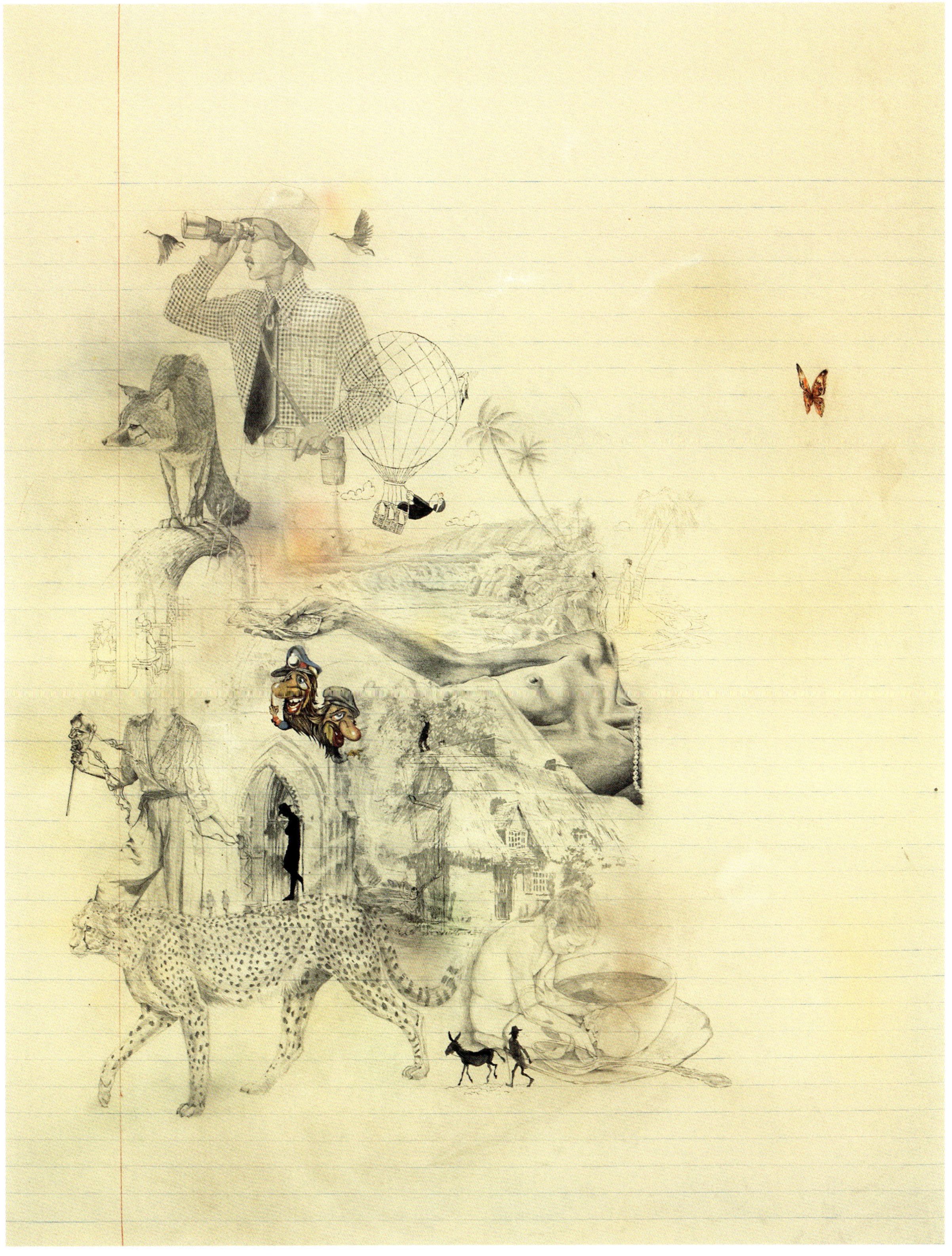

Life's a beach, and then you die, 2011
India ink, pencil, watercolor, acrylic,
and lacquer on canvas
$97\frac{1}{4} \times 76$ inches (247×193 cm)

Not in Cologne anymore, 2010
Watercolor, lacquer, and acrylic on canvas
76 × 97½ inches (193 × 247.7 cm)

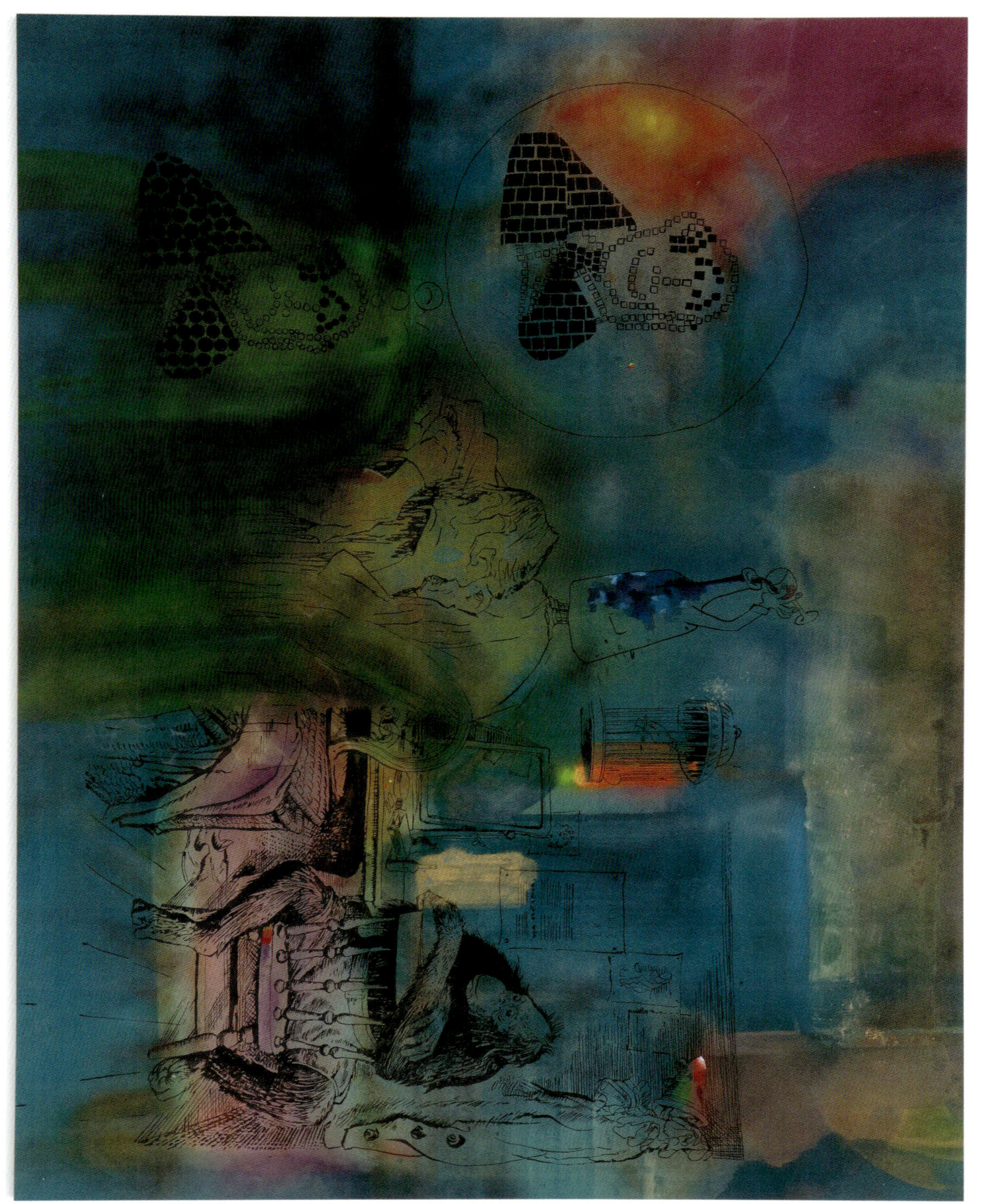

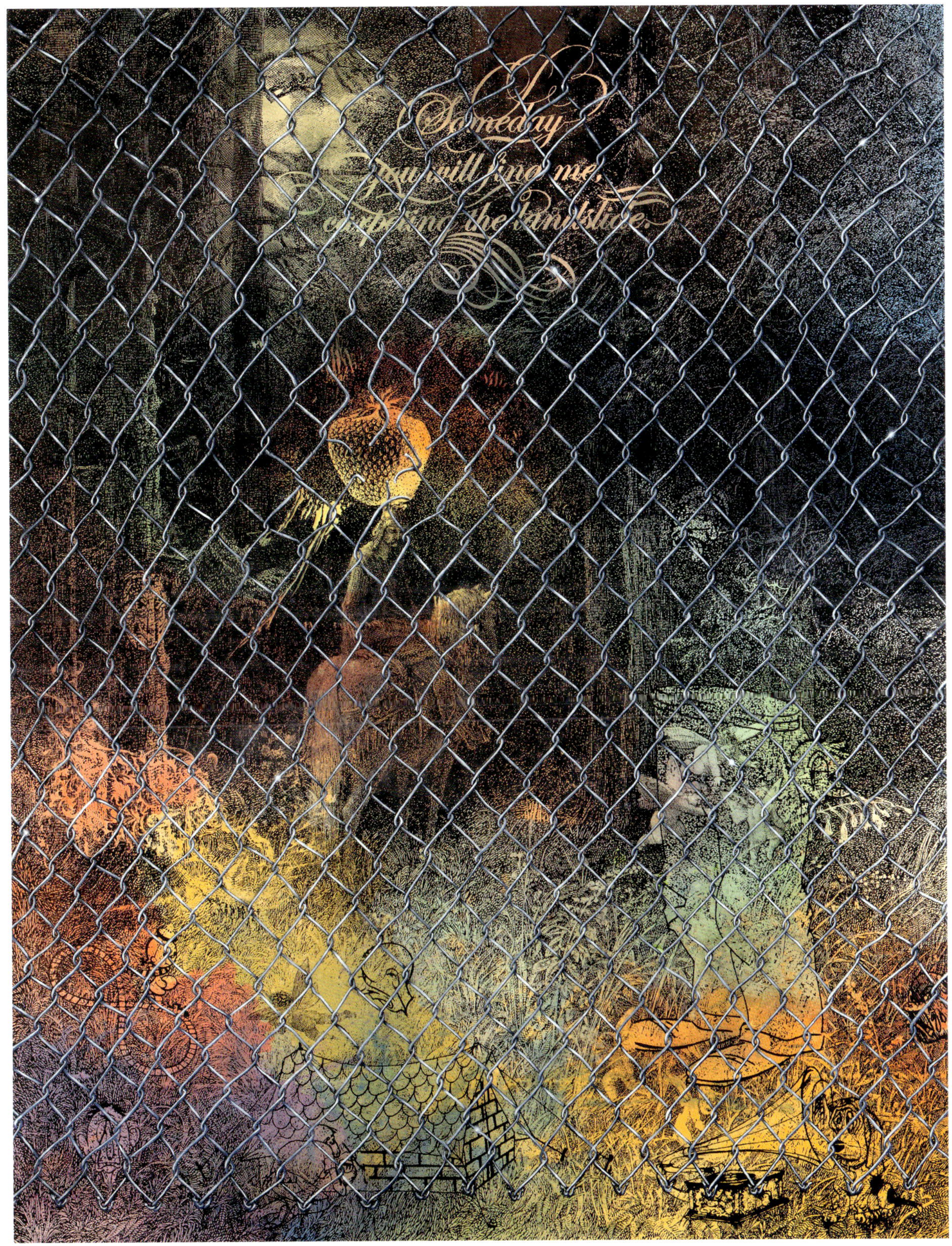

Someday You Will Find Me Carpeting the Landslide (Fence Version), 2012
Oil, acrylic, and silkscreen on canvas
96 ½ × 75 inches (245.1 × 190.5 cm)

YAYOI **KUSAMA**

b. 1929, Nagano Prefecture, Japan

Infinity Nets QHZA, 2006
Acrylic on canvas
76½ × 76½ inches (194 × 194 cm)

Born in Japan in 1929, artist and writer Yayoi Kusama moved to New York City in the late 1950s to be part of the postwar avant-garde scene. There she created the first of her Infinity Net paintings—large bespeckled canvases covered in repetitive loops of paint that seem to extend beyond the picture plane indefinitely—for which she is best known. This imagery has become a touchstone of her oeuvre: "I was under the spell of the polka dot nets. Bring on Picasso, bring on Matisse, bring on anybody! I would stand up to them all with a single polka dot!"

Her Infinity Net paintings of the recent two decades preserve this zest, as evidenced in *Infinity Nets QHZA* (2006). Kusama has described these works as manifestations of the recurring hallucinations she has experienced since childhood.

Her obsession with the pattern, she says, is a means of self-obliteration, a concept Kusama defines as becoming one with the surroundings, dissolving the boundaries of the Self, and disappearing into an all-embracing emptiness.

She has developed striking bodies of work in different media that invite visitors to lose themselves in the infinite nets, mirrored rooms, and the thousands of polka dots with which she covers the world.

Another recurring motif in her work is the flower—from her earliest paintings to her collages made in the 1970s and self-portraits. In recent years, Kusama has produced series of large-scale flower sculptures cast in highly durable fiberglass-reinforced plastic and metal. *Flowers That Bloom Tomorrow M* (2011), for example, is brilliantly hued in psychedelic fashion and finished with her compulsive polka dot pattern.

Kusama's work is in numerous collections including The Museum of Modern Art, the Los Angeles County Museum of Art, Walker Art Center, Tate Modern, Stedelijk Museum, Centre Georges Pompidou, and the National Museum of Modern Art, Tokyo. Major exhibitions of her work include those organized by the Los Angeles County Museum of Art; The Museum of Modern Art; Le Consortium, Dijon, France; National Museum of Modern Art, Tokyo; and the Museum Boijmans Van Beuningen, Rotterdam, among others. L. C.

The Night, 1985
Acrylic on canvas
Triptych: 76 1⁄3 × 51 1⁄5 inches
(194 × 130 cm) each
76 1⁄3 × 153 1⁄2 inches (194 × 390 cm) overall

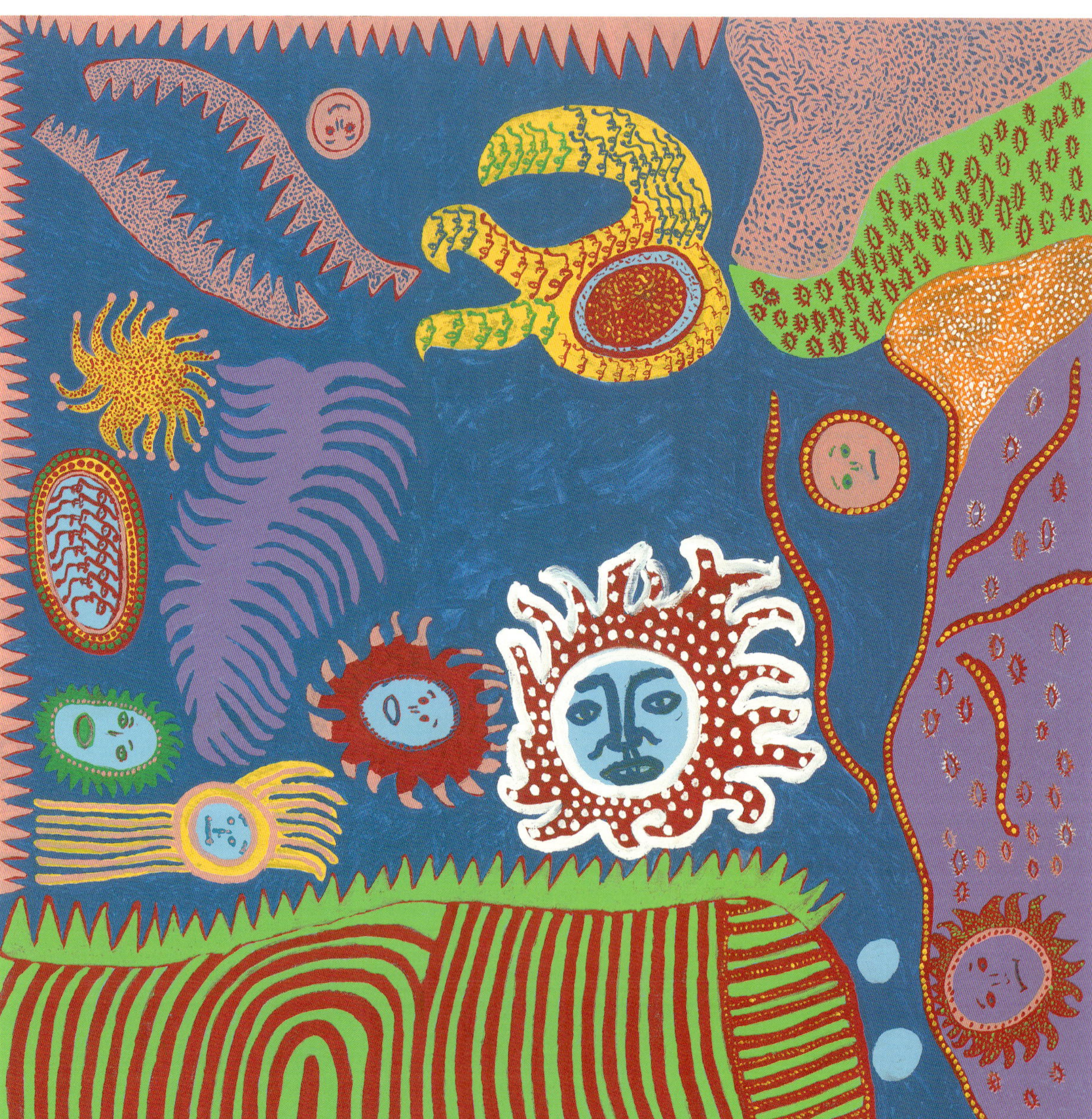

MYSTERY OF THE UNIVERSE, 2013
Acrylic on canvas
76⅜ × 76⅜ inches (194 × 194 cm)

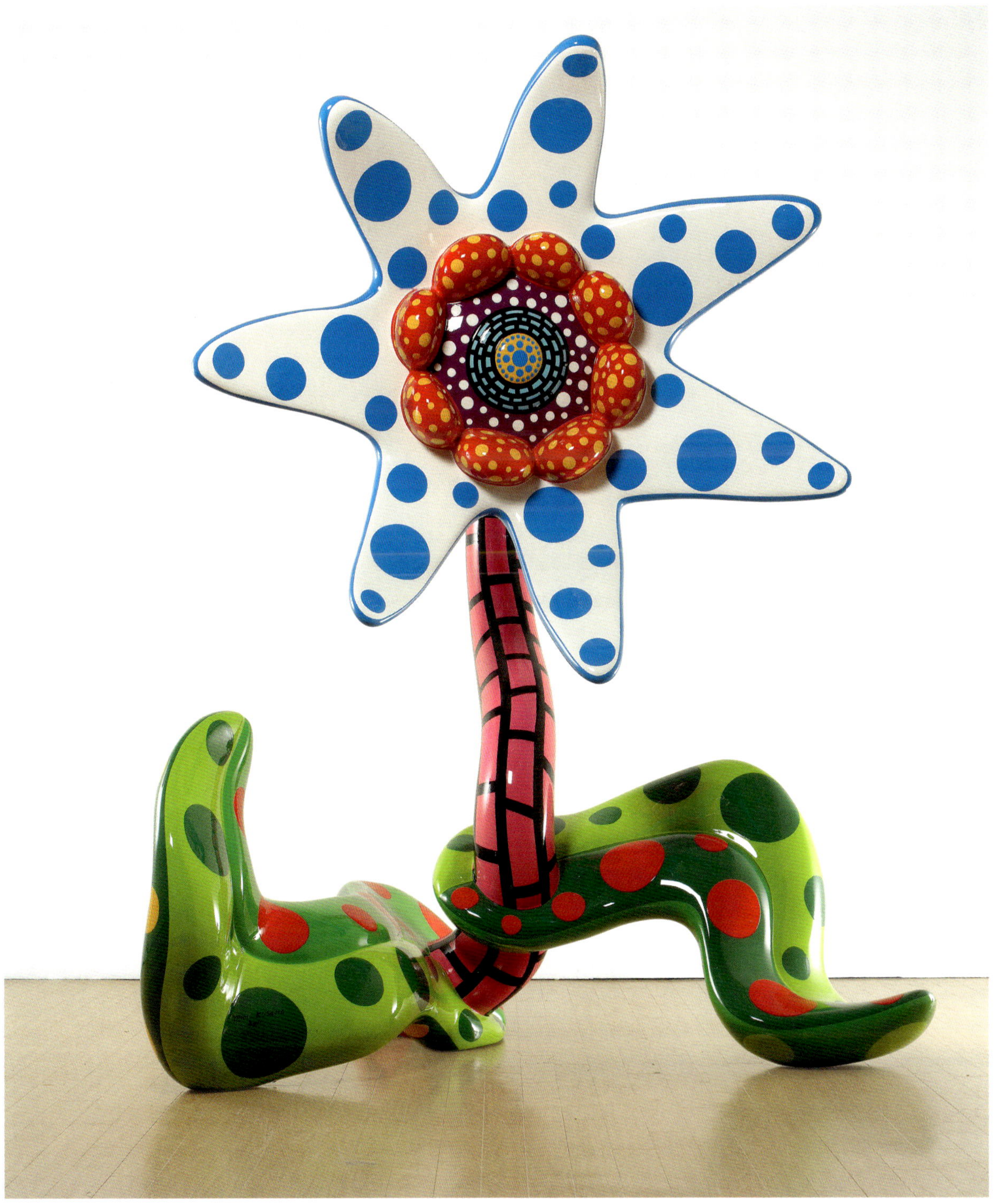

Flowers That Bloom Tomorrow M, 2011
Fiberglass reinforced plastic, metal, and urethane paint
112¼ × 92½ × 42½ inches
(285 × 235 × 108 cm)

LOUISE **LAWLER** b. 1947, Bronxville, NY

The ever-changing lives of art objects have been the focus of Louise Lawler's art practice since the 1970s. Lawler is most well known for her photographs of other artists' works in a wide range of settings that map the world of art—from the commercial gallery, the museum, and the storage room to the corporate office lobby and collector's bedroom.

As artworks move from one place to another, the photographs beg simple yet deceptively critical questions: "Who arranged these artworks?" "What are these artworks doing?" "Why are these artworks here?" Extending the claims made by artists associated with feminism and institutional critique, Lawler's practice argues that the work of art's external situation, or context, shapes its role and meaning.

By paying attention to the conditions of art's display, Lawler has sustained an unrelenting analysis of art's system of distribution, presentation, and reception.

In recent works, Lawler has thrown context into even sharper relief. Whereas in *Soup and Mirror* (2001/2005) Lawler keys our attention to the auction house label and the setting in which artworks by Andy Warhol and Roy Lichtenstein are perhaps best identified by their monikers, in *Pollyanna (adjusted to fit)* (2007/2008/2012) Lawler unleashes context to transform an artwork of her own. Printed on vinyl adhesive, *Pollyannna (adjusted to fit)* stretches her 2007 photograph of the same name. The image is distorted to conform to the proportions of the gallery wall that supports the work. Beholding the oversize image of Takashi Murakami and Andy Warhol's art objects, the viewer has little choice but to acknowledge the literal space she and the image inhabit.

Louise Lawler's extensive record of solo exhibitions includes venues such as Museum Ludwig, Cologne; Albertinum, Dresden; Wexner Center for the Arts, Ohio; and the Museum für Gegenwartkunst, Basel. She has participated in numerous group exhibitions and biennials including Manifesta, the Whitney Biennial, Shanghai Biennale, and the Sydney Biennale. J. A.

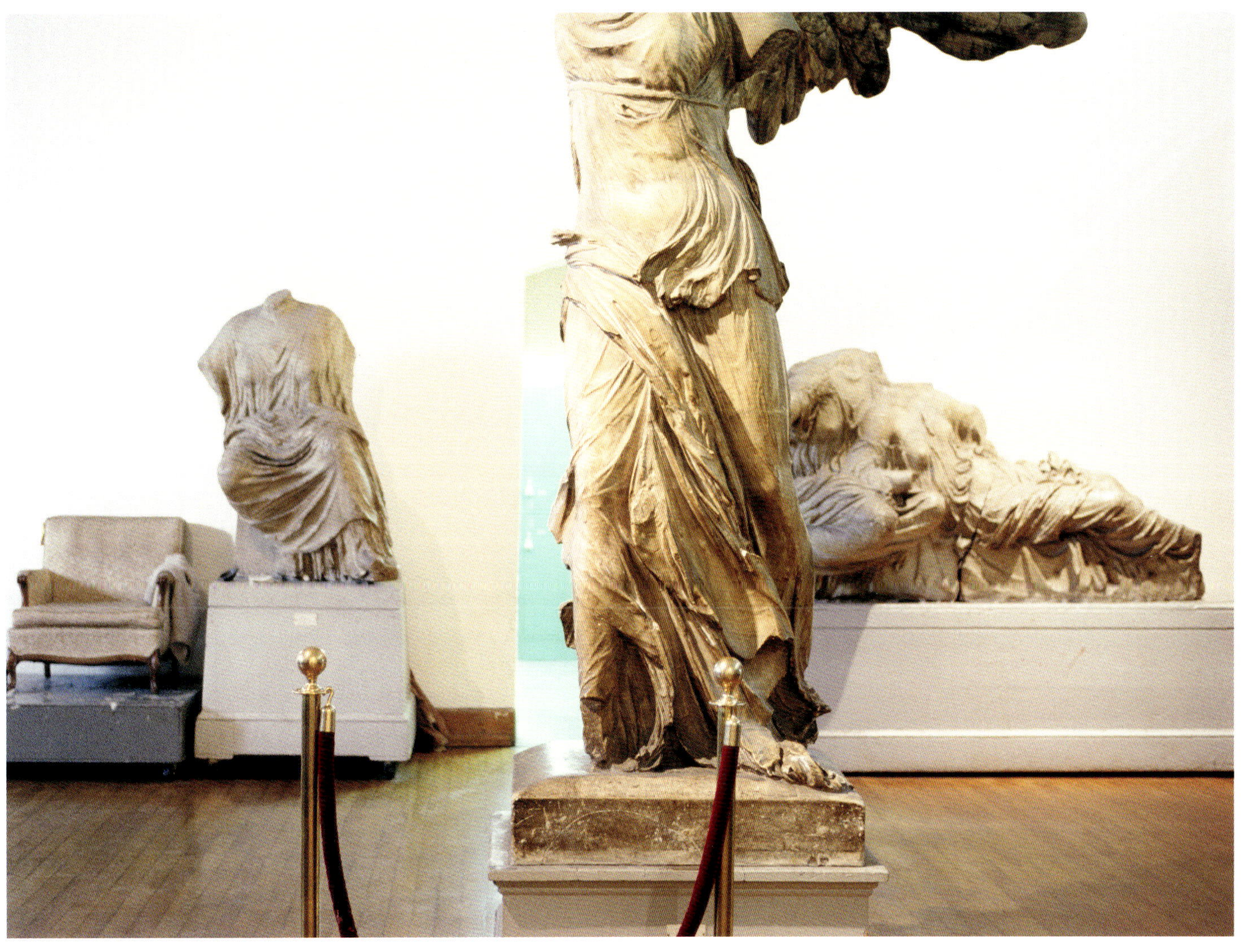

A.C.A.D.E.M.Y., 1987
Cibachrome mounted to Plexiglas
on museum box
29 × 39½ inches (73.7 × 100.3 cm)
Edition 4 of 5

LAWLER

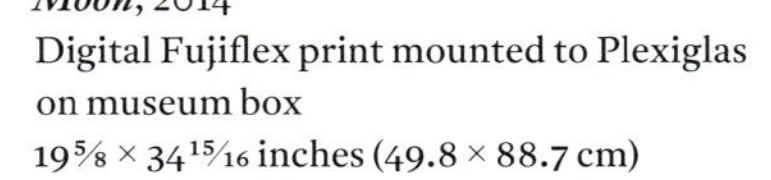

Moon, 2014
Digital Fujiflex print mounted to Plexiglas on museum box
19⅝ × 34¹⁵⁄₁₆ inches (49.8 × 88.7 cm)
Edition 3 of 5, 1 AP

Soup and Mirror, 2001/2005
Cibachrome laminated on aluminum museum box
19¾ × 15¾ inches (50.2 × 40 cm)
Edition 2 of 5

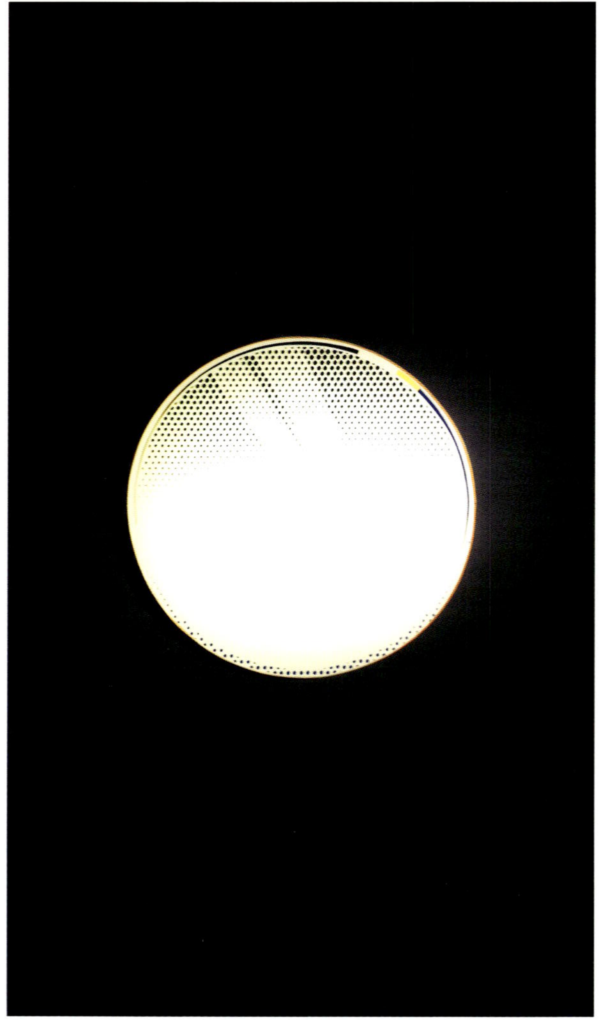

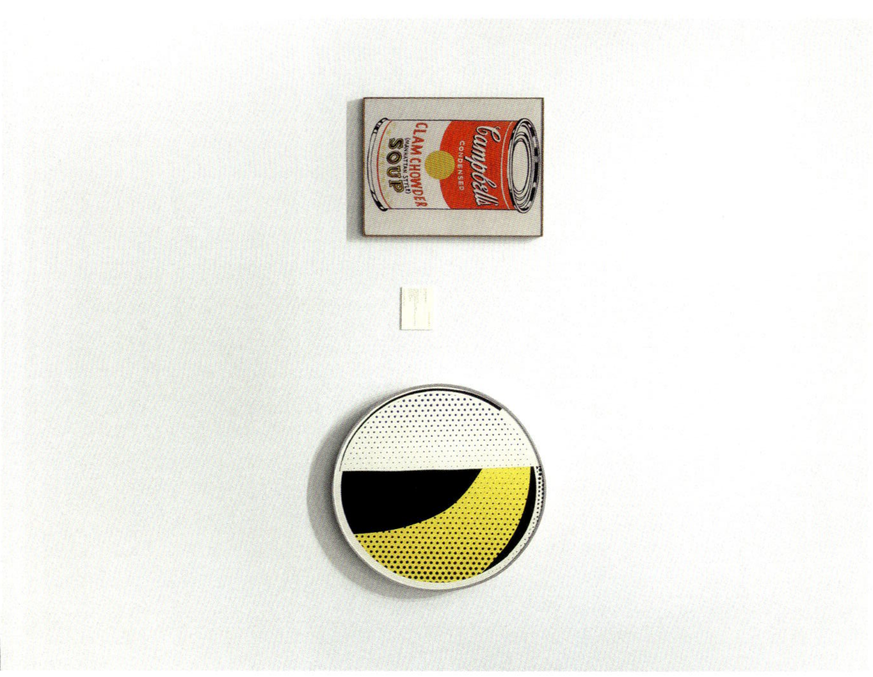

Pollyanna (adjusted to fit), 2007/2008/2012
Adhesive wall material
Variable dimensions constrained to match aspect ratio of wall

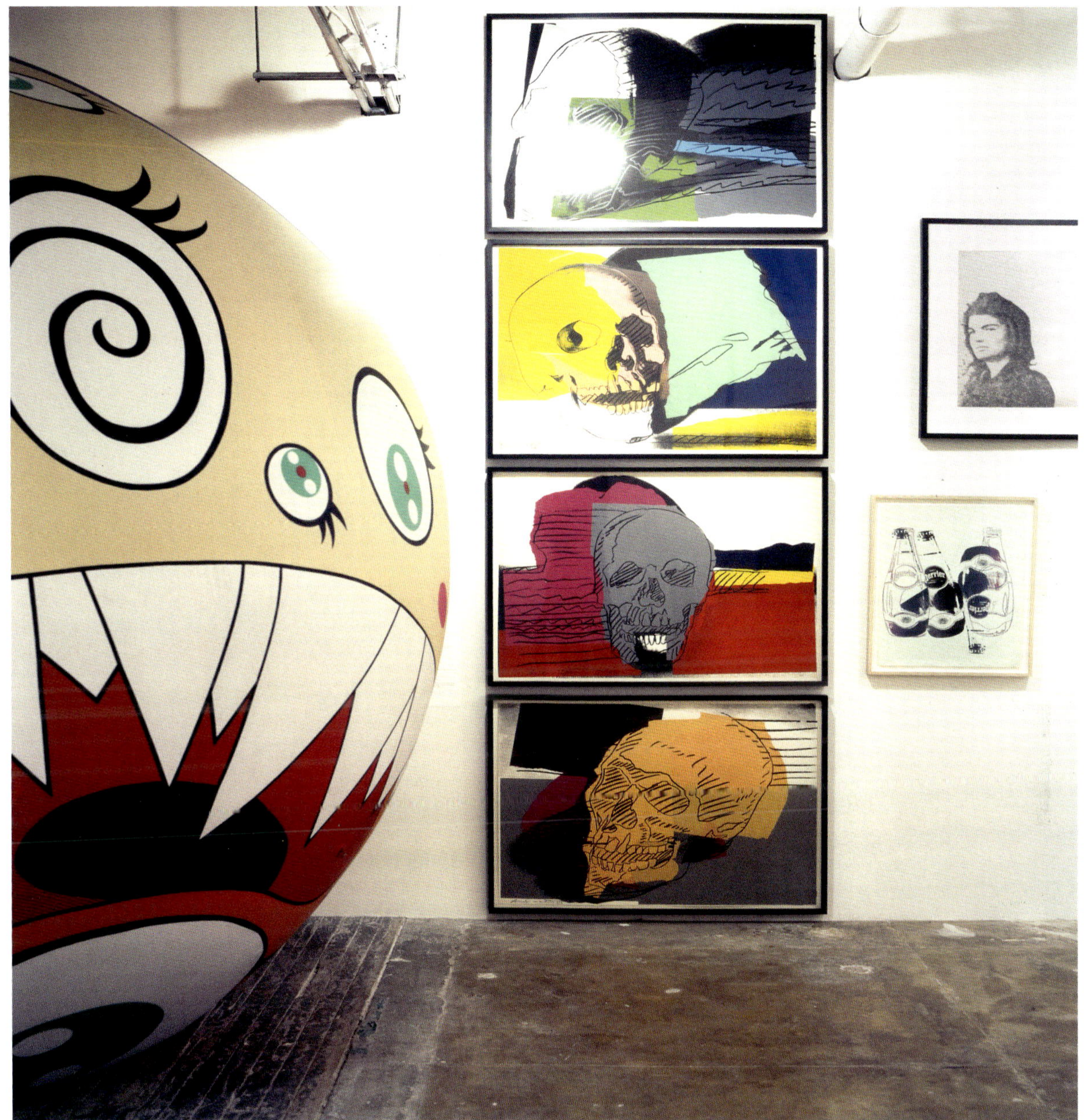

MARK LECKEY b. 1964 Birkenhead, England

The flood of recent accolades which have been heaped on Mark Leckey—solo shows at MoMA PS1 in New York and the Walker Art Gallery in Liverpool, for instance—isn't because his art is any better than it was twenty years ago. Rather, it's proof that the art world has (finally) caught up with him.

Leckey has been creating exuberant and challenging videos and installations since the early 1990s. After briefly (and unsuccessfully) being lumped in with other "Young British Artists" like Damien Hirst, Leckey spent almost a decade creating art on his own terms. Today, his art from that period is being recognized as a practice that was so ahead of its time that it represents, in a sense, a keen vision of the present.

This is nowhere more clear than in the whimsical, exhilarating 1999 video *Fiorucci Made Me Hardcore*, a music video-style mash-up of dance styles, music, and subcultures as they evolved from the 1970s through the 1990s.

Born in England's northwest in 1964, Leckey received a BA from Newcastle Polytechnic in Newcastle, England, in 1990. He soon moved to London, then spent several years traveling around the United States, before finally moved back to the U.K. in the late 1990s, at which point his star began to rise. He was included in a group show at London's Institute of Contemporary Art in 1999, and in 2008 Leckey won the prestigious Turner Prize, awarded annually to a British artist under fifty. His art is in the permanent collections of the Centre Georges Pompidou in Paris, the Solomon R. Guggenheim Museum in New York, the Tate Gallery in London, and The Museum of Contemporary Art in Los Angeles.

Leckey is motivated by the intersections of high art and low objects and how history, technology, and culture can infiltrate aesthetics. This is profoundly evinced in his 2012 work *Transformer (RGB)*, an animated LED board that depicts Pinocchio's transition from boy to donkey. In Leckey's hands, the trauma of this transformation is obscured—the violence of Pinocchio's shifting state is aestheticized and digitized to the extent that viewers are ultimately forced to strain their eyes in order to see past the pure glittering forms. J. T.

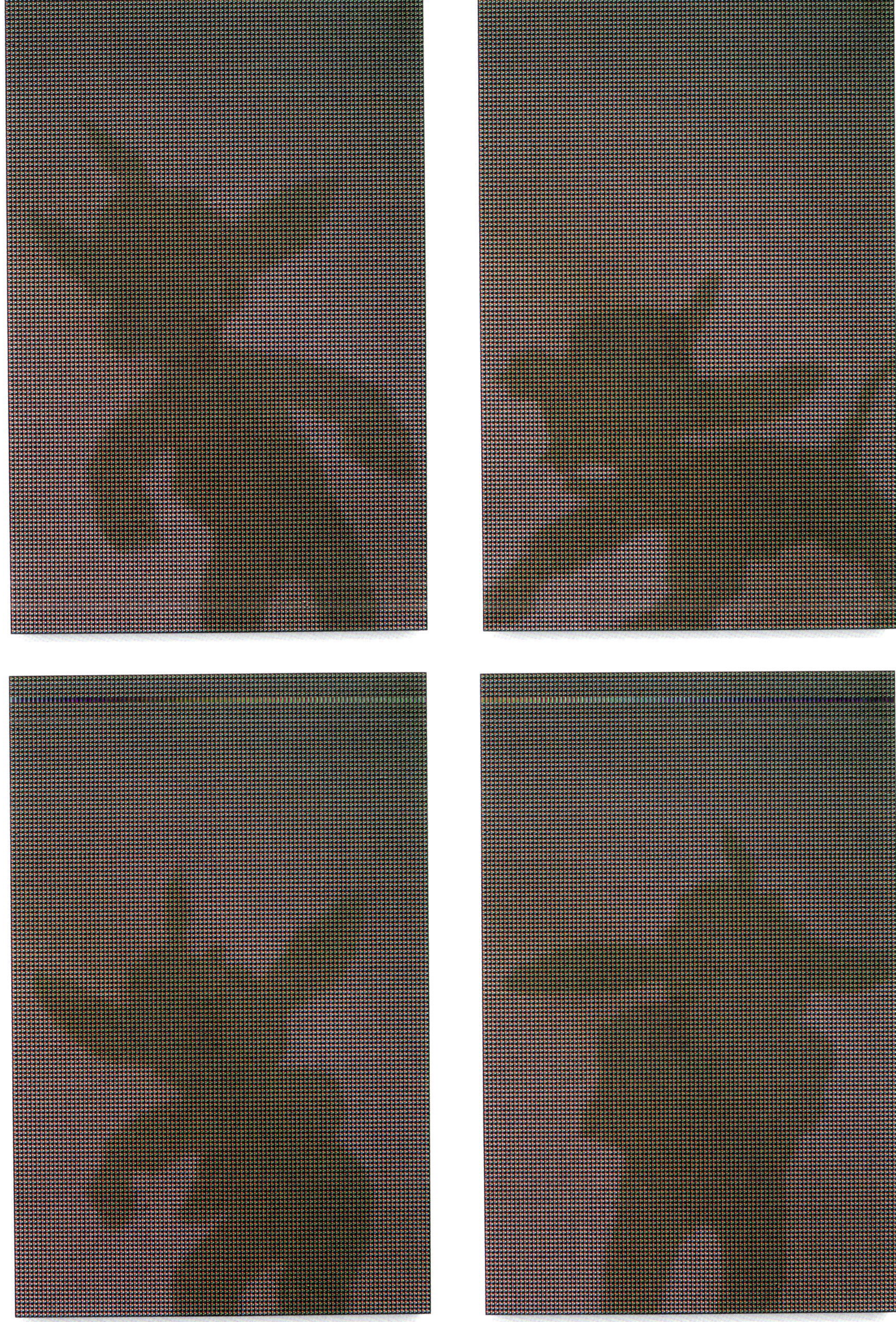

Transformer (RGB), 2012
LED screen
$57 \times 44\frac{1}{2} \times 3\frac{1}{2}$ inches ($144.8 \times 113 \times 8.9$ cm)

SHERRIE **LEVINE** b. 1947, Hazelton, PA

Born in Hazleton, Pennsylvania, in 1947, Sherrie Levine originally trained in painting and printmaking and received both her BA (1969) and MFA (1973) from the University of Wisconsin, Madison. Levine first came to prominence in 1977 with her inclusion in the *Pictures* exhibition, organized by curator and critic Douglas Crimp at Artists Space in New York. Over the course of the 1970s and 1980s, Levine, Sarah Charlesworth, Louise Lawler, Richard Prince, and others—artists of the so-called Pictures Generation—appropriated images from visual culture in order to address problems of representation and the growing dominance of images in contemporary life.

The appropriation strategies utilized by Levine and her peers worked to cause monumental shifts in the historical developments of postmodern art, feminism, and photographic practice.

Throughout her career Levine has countered established notions of authorship and authenticity, most directly by re-photographing or re-fabricating work by male artists, including canonical modernist photographers such as Eliot Porter, August Sander, and Edward Weston. She calls attention to long traditions of "master" photographers appropriating the world and cultures around them through their medium—and her work asks us to not reject this history but to identify and question it. In 1981, Levine's first solo exhibition, held at the newly opened New York gallery Metro Pictures, comprised re-photographed images from Walker Evans's Depression-era series created for the Farm Security Administration. Titled *After Walker Evans*, the project generated controversy in its faithful re-presentation of Evans's work and went on to become a hallmark of feminist activity and postmodern art history.

Levine revisits Evans's photographic oeuvre and expands upon her previous works in *African Masks After Walker Evans: 1–24* (2014). Evans was commissioned to make the original photographs in 1935 by The Museum of Modern Art for *African Negro Art*—an exhibition that aimed to broaden awareness of African art and illustrate its influence on artists working in Europe and the United States. Though first intended as educational tools, Evans's photographs came to be regarded as important art objects on their own. Levine's photographs of these images raise important questions surrounding the identity and authority of the artist and highlight issues of originality, desire, and commodification. C. R.

Dada, 2008
Cast bronze
39 × 70 × 12 inches (99.1 × 177.8 × 30.5 cm)
Edition of 12, 3 APs
Edition AP 1

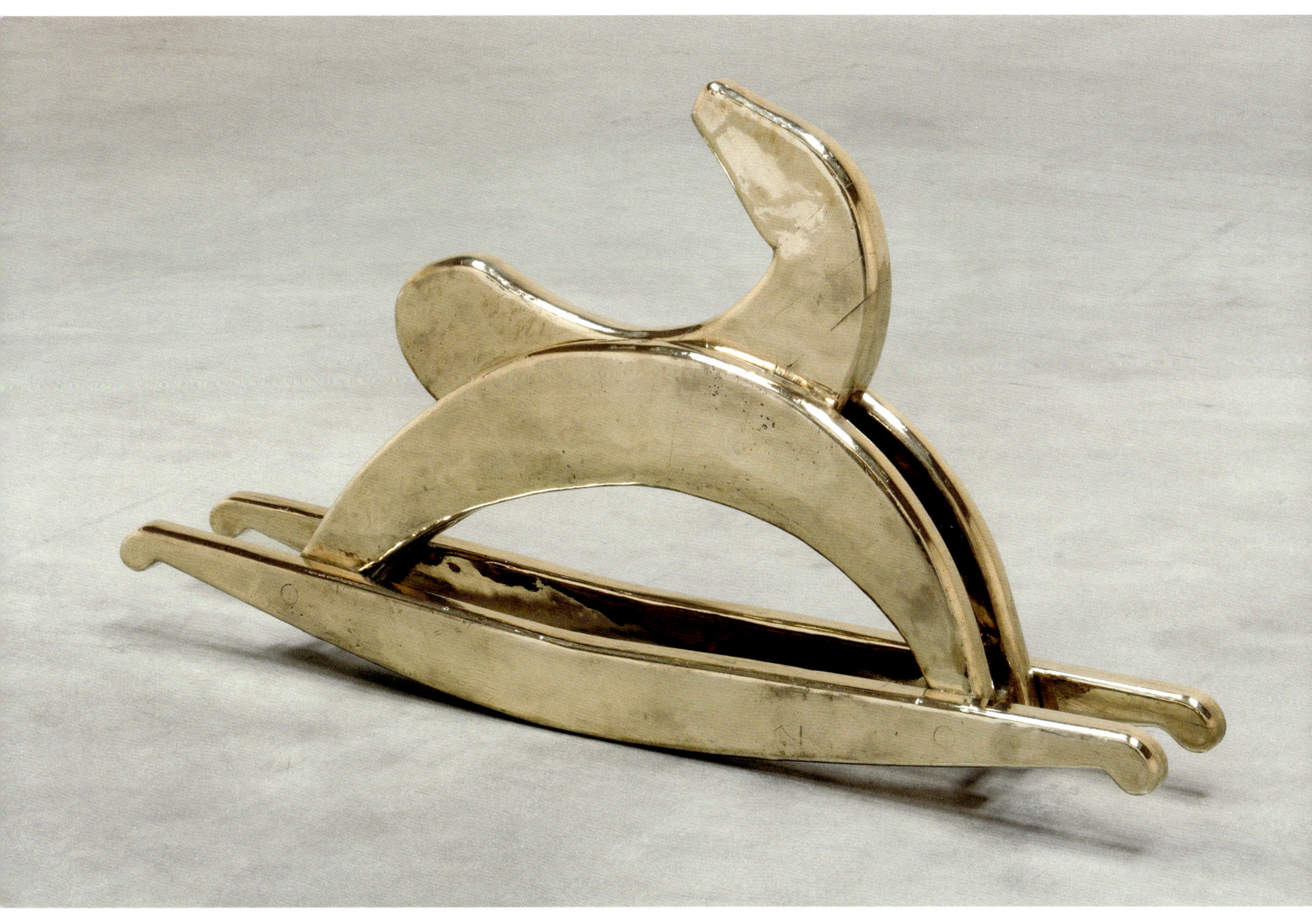

African Masks After Walker Evans:
1–24, 2014
24 Giclée inkjet prints
19 1/8 × 13 inches (48.6 × 33 cm) each

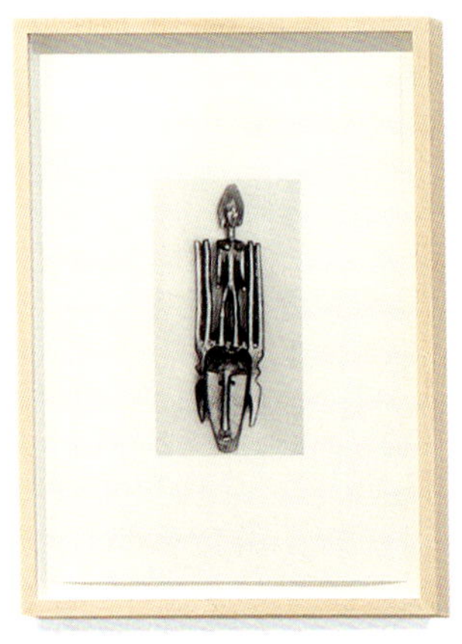
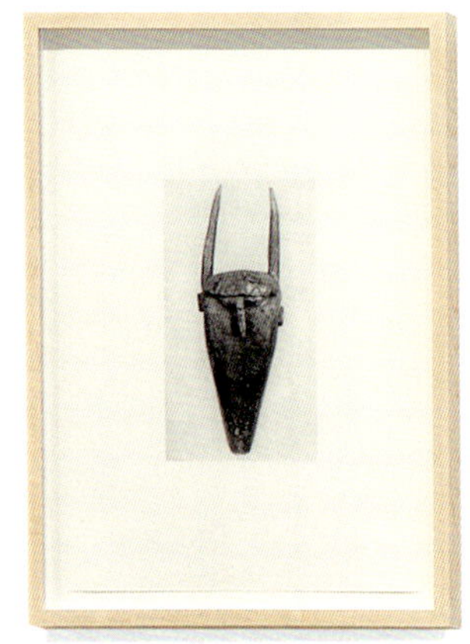
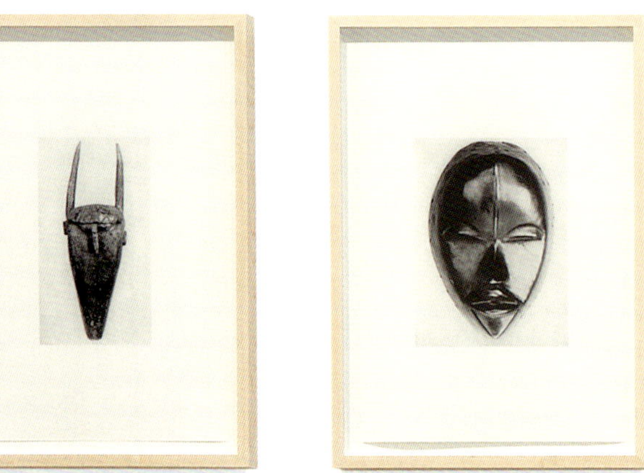
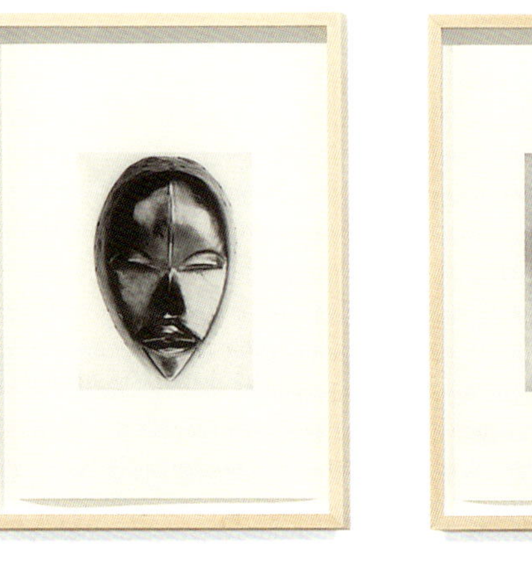
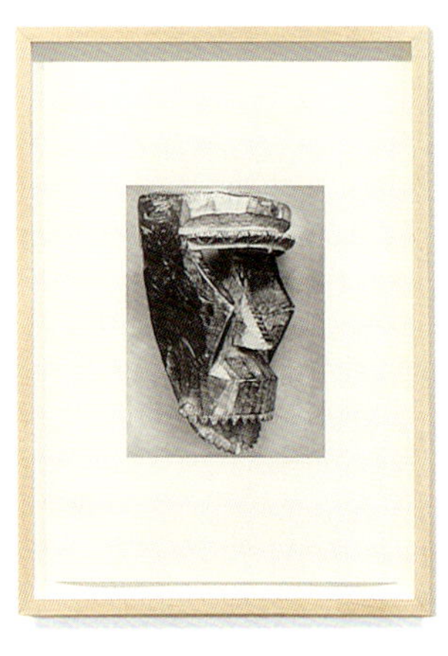
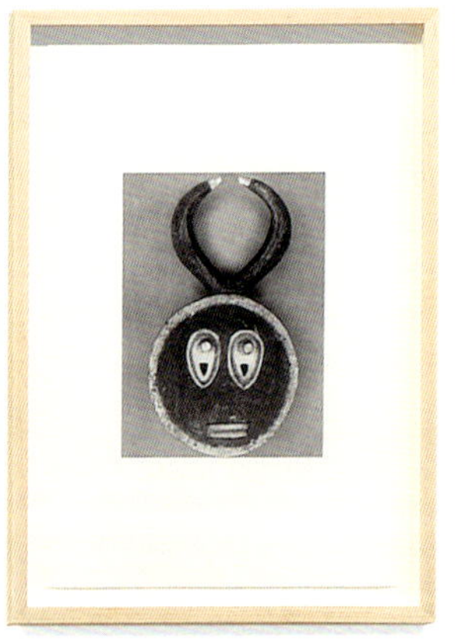
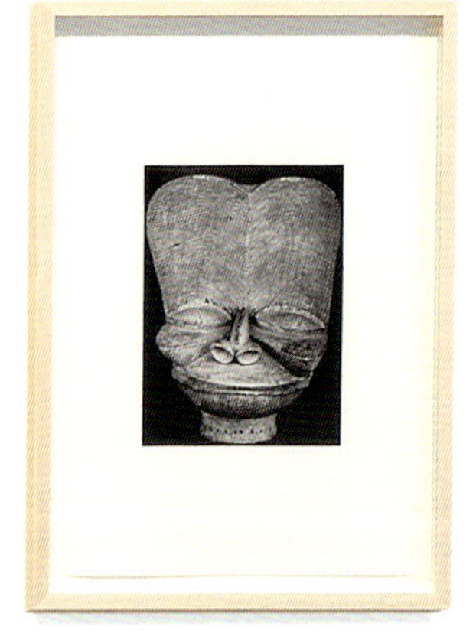
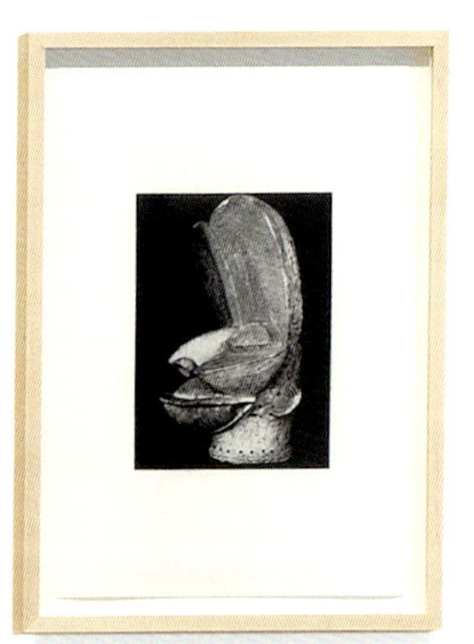
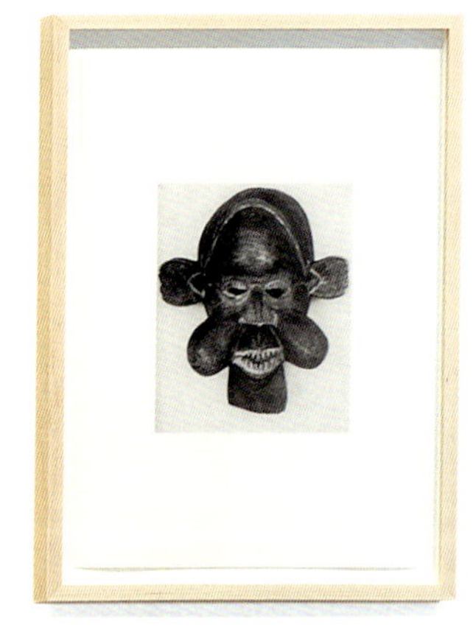
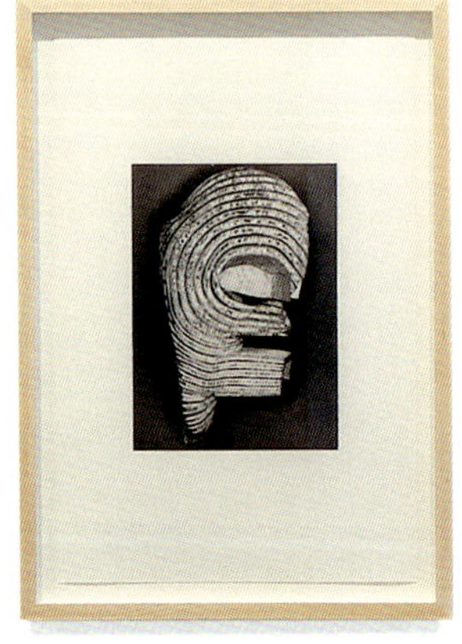
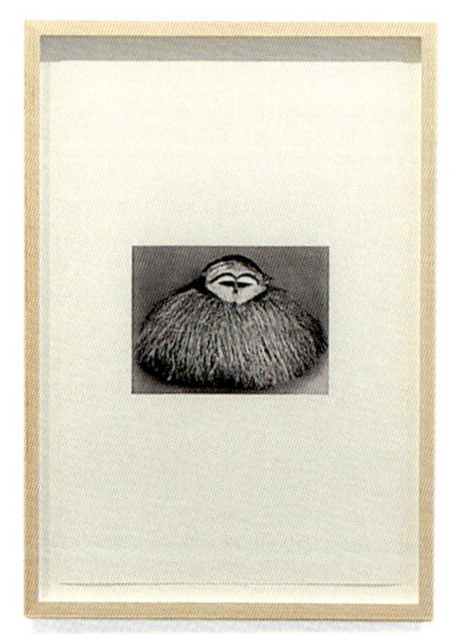
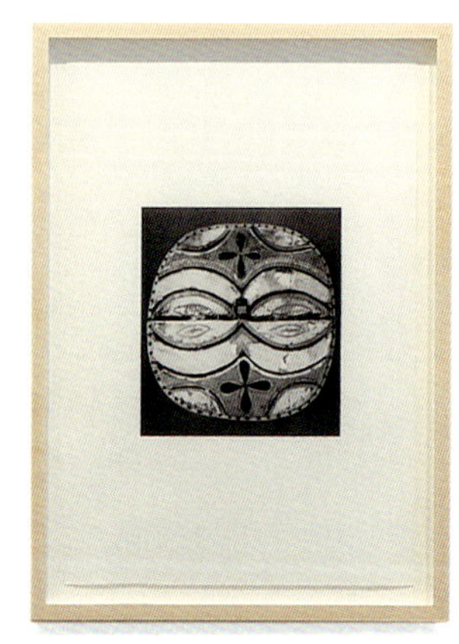
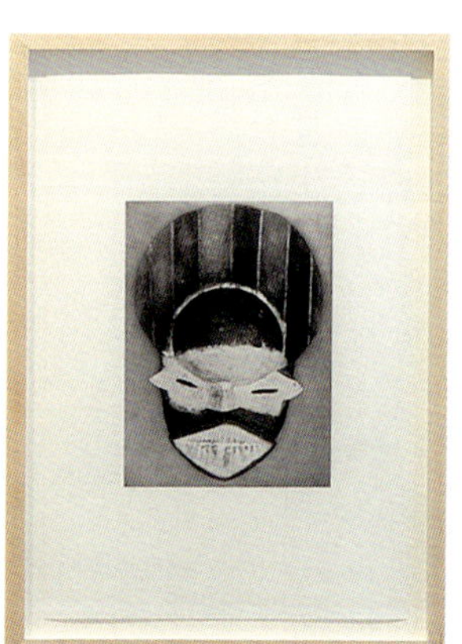

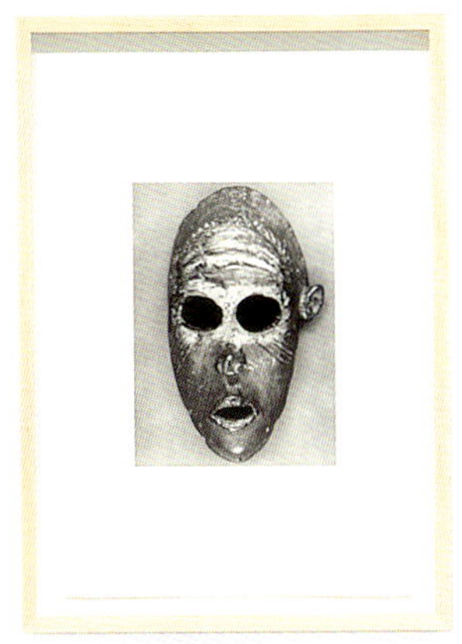
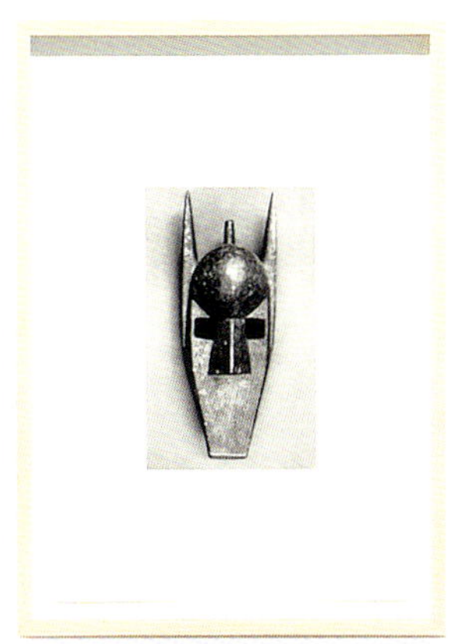
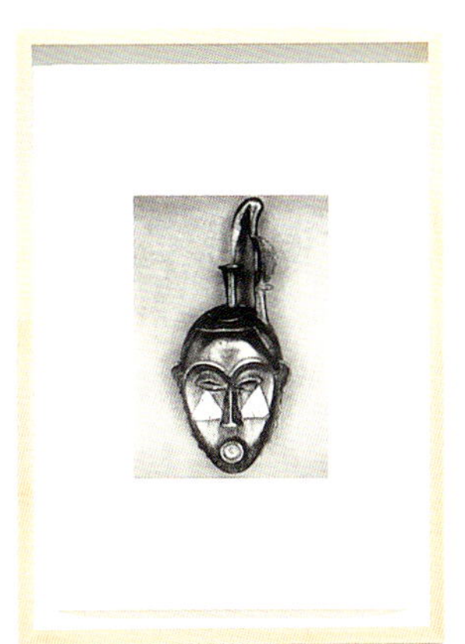
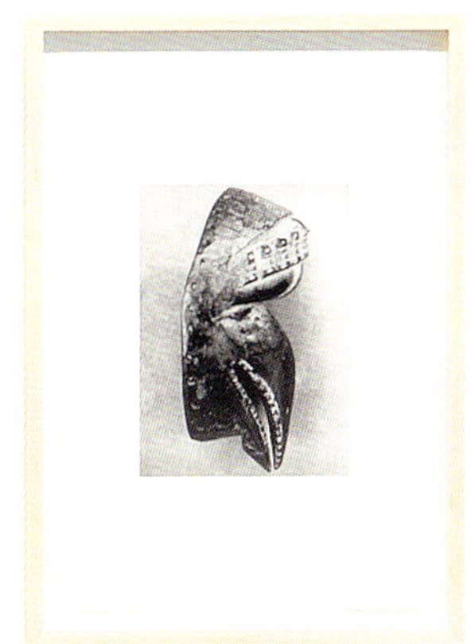
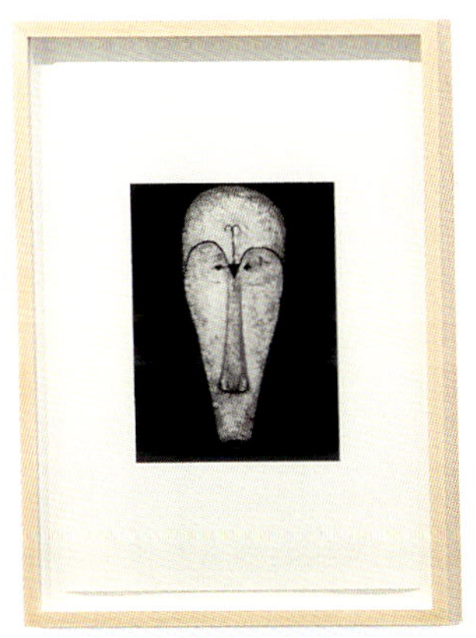
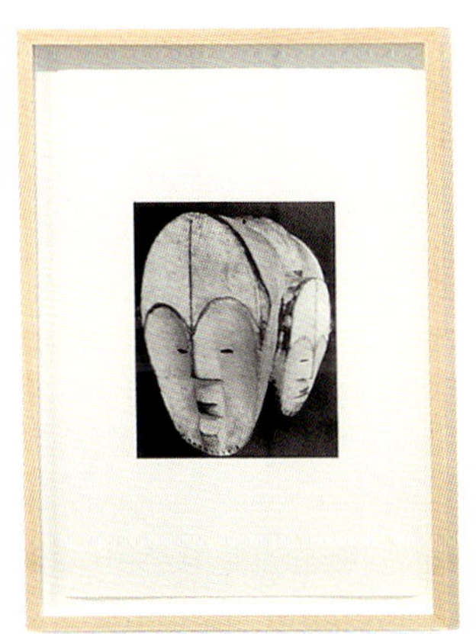
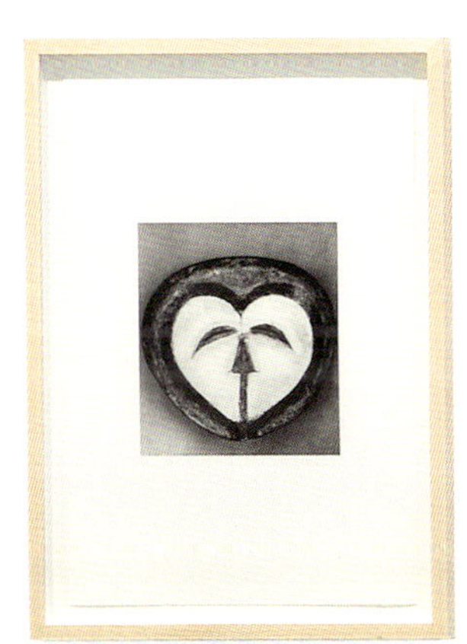
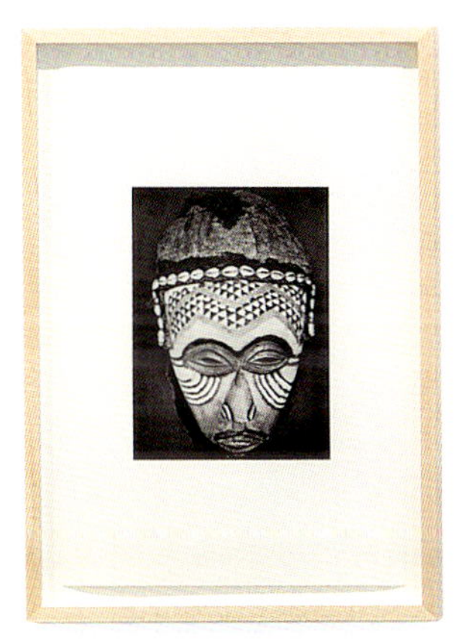
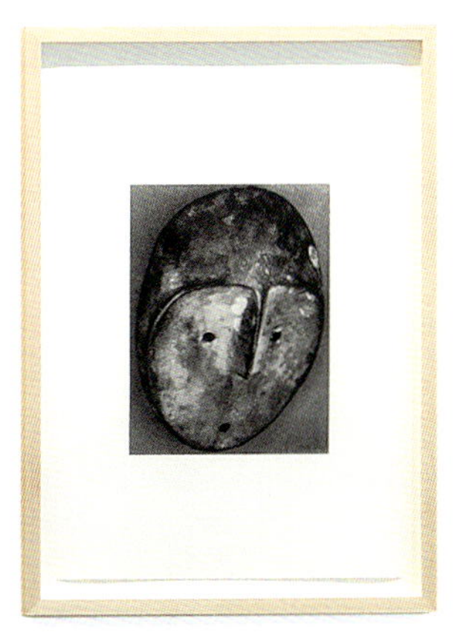
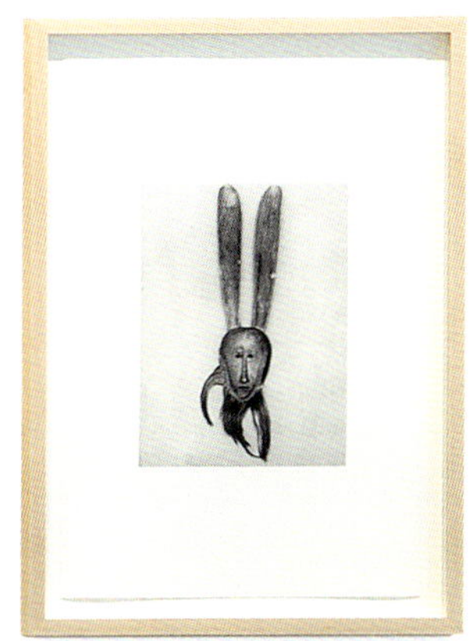
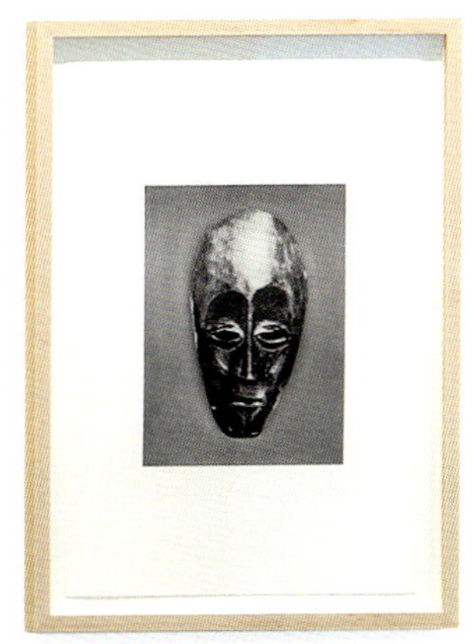
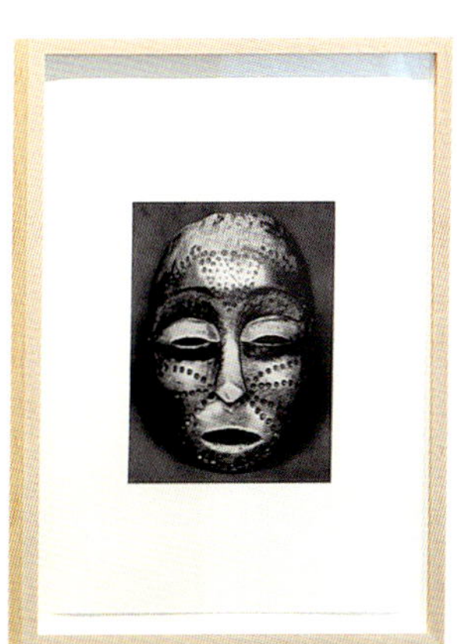

Black Moonlight After Man Ray: 8, 2016
Oil on plywood
20 × 16 × ½ inches (50.8 × 40.6 × 1.3 cm)

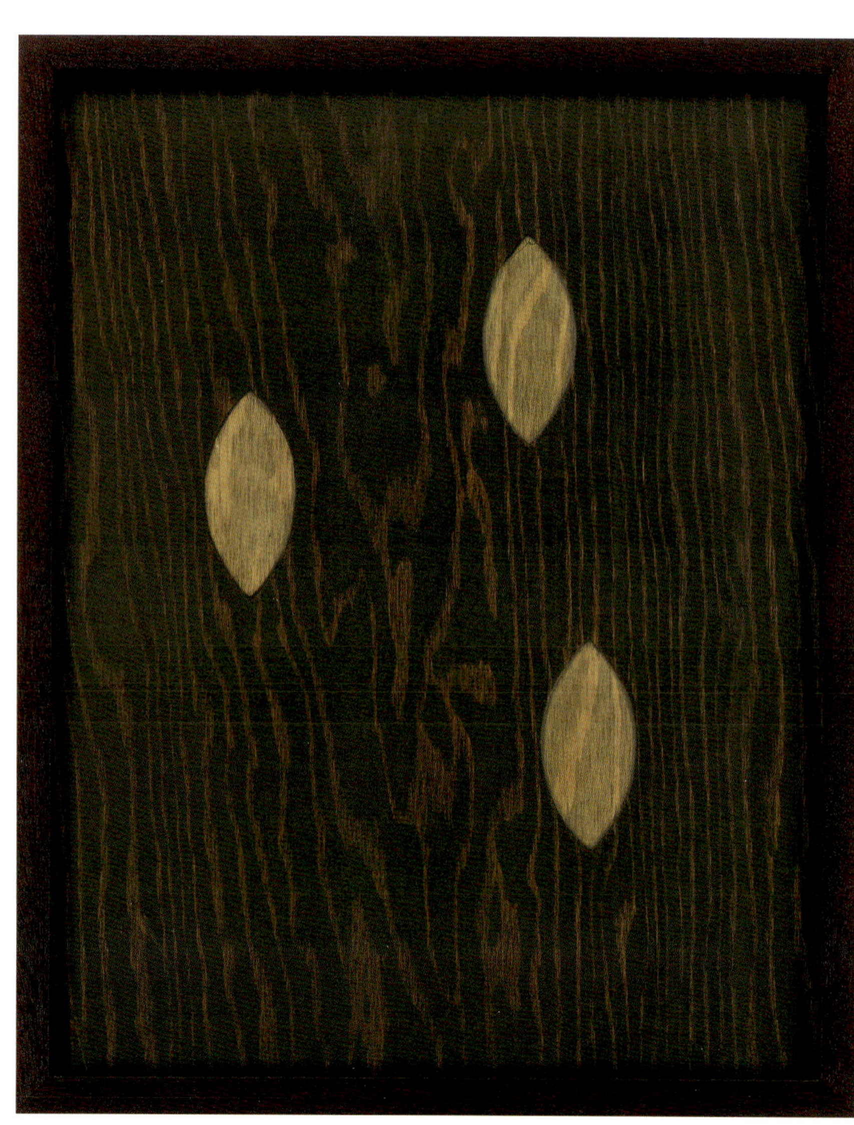

Red, Yellow, Blue Mirrors: 1-3, Suite IV, 2014
Red, yellow, and blue mirrored glass,
wooden frame
3 panels: 21⅛ × 17⅛ inches
(53.7 × 43.5 cm) each

GLENN LIGON

b. 1960, The Bronx, NY

Figure #76, 2011
Acrylic and coal dust on canvas
60 × 48 inches (152.4 × 121.9 cm)

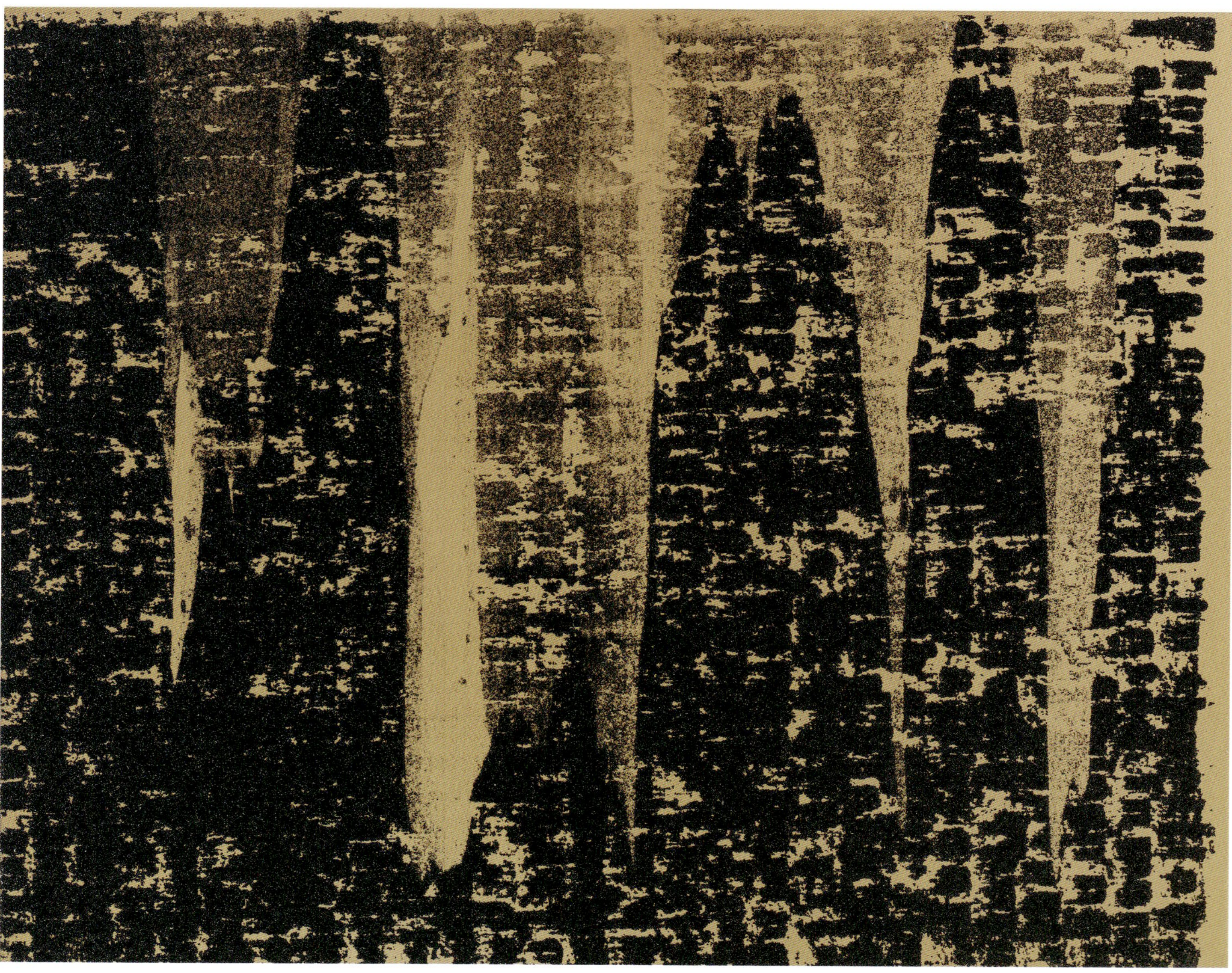

Rendered in a viscous mix of oil stick and gesso, Glenn Ligon's text painting *Stranger #43* (2011) starts with a dramatic scene: "From all available evidence no black man had ever set foot in this tiny Swiss village before I came." The painting's words are appropriated from writer James Baldwin's 1953 essay, "Stranger in the Village." Baldwin opens with a stark encounter of oppositions: American and Swiss, black and European, self and other.

In the text's painted form, Ligon inherits and extends the lessons of Baldwin's powerful social and political thought by casting additional attention to corresponding artistic problems: text and painting, lightness and darkness, expression versus appropriation, legibility and illegibility.

Like Baldwin, as well as the other fellow artists, writers, musicians, and comedians Ligon has engaged, duality, difference, and inextricable forms of relation lie at the heart of the artist's nearly thirty-year examination of identity and American society.

Ligon was born in The Bronx, New York, in 1960 and originally trained as a painter. His emergence within the milieu of late 1980s/early 1990s New York City—a moment marked by the struggles over art, identity politics, and a nation's slow and deadly response to the HIV/AIDS crisis—encouraged his unique synthesis of critical and conceptual tendencies, such as appropriation and text, with painterly modes of expression and materiality. While he is perhaps best known for his text paintings, his practice spans other media, including photography, sculpture, installation, and, most recently, neon light, such as his work *Double America 2* (2014). Here, Ligon inverts the neon fixtures relationship between light and dark by painting the tubes outward facing half. Ligon's painterly gesture forces the neon light to emanate from a dark black ground, a poetic and critical inversion also echoed in the flipping of the neon's text, "AMERICA."

The recipient of numerous awards, including the United States Artists Fellowship, Joyce Alexander Wein Artist Prize, Skowhegan Medal for Painting, and the John Simon Guggenheim Memorial Foundation Fellowship, Ligon has had solo shows at the Tate Liverpool, Whitney Museum of American Art; and The Studio Museum in Harlem, among other venues. He has also participated in Documenta as well as the Whitney, Sydney, and Venice biennials. J. A.

Stranger #43, 2011
Oil stick and gesso on canvas
96 × 72 inches (243.8 × 182.9 cm)

Stranger #78, 2015
Oil stick and gesso on canvas
96 × 72 inches (243.8 × 182.9 cm)

Double America 2, 2014
Neon and paint
48 × 145 × 3 inches (121.9 × 368.3 × 7.6 cm)
Edition 2 of 3, 2 AP

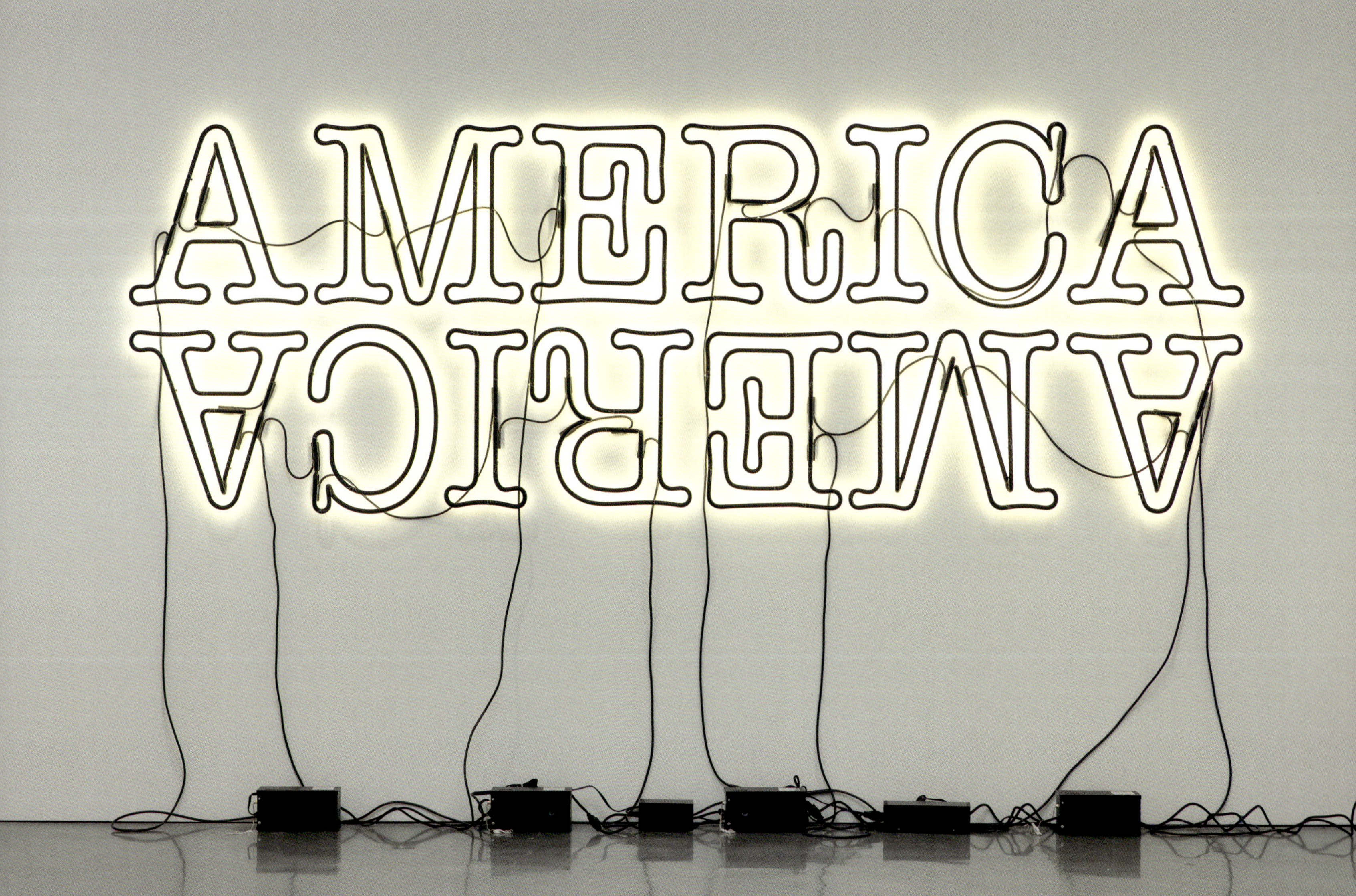

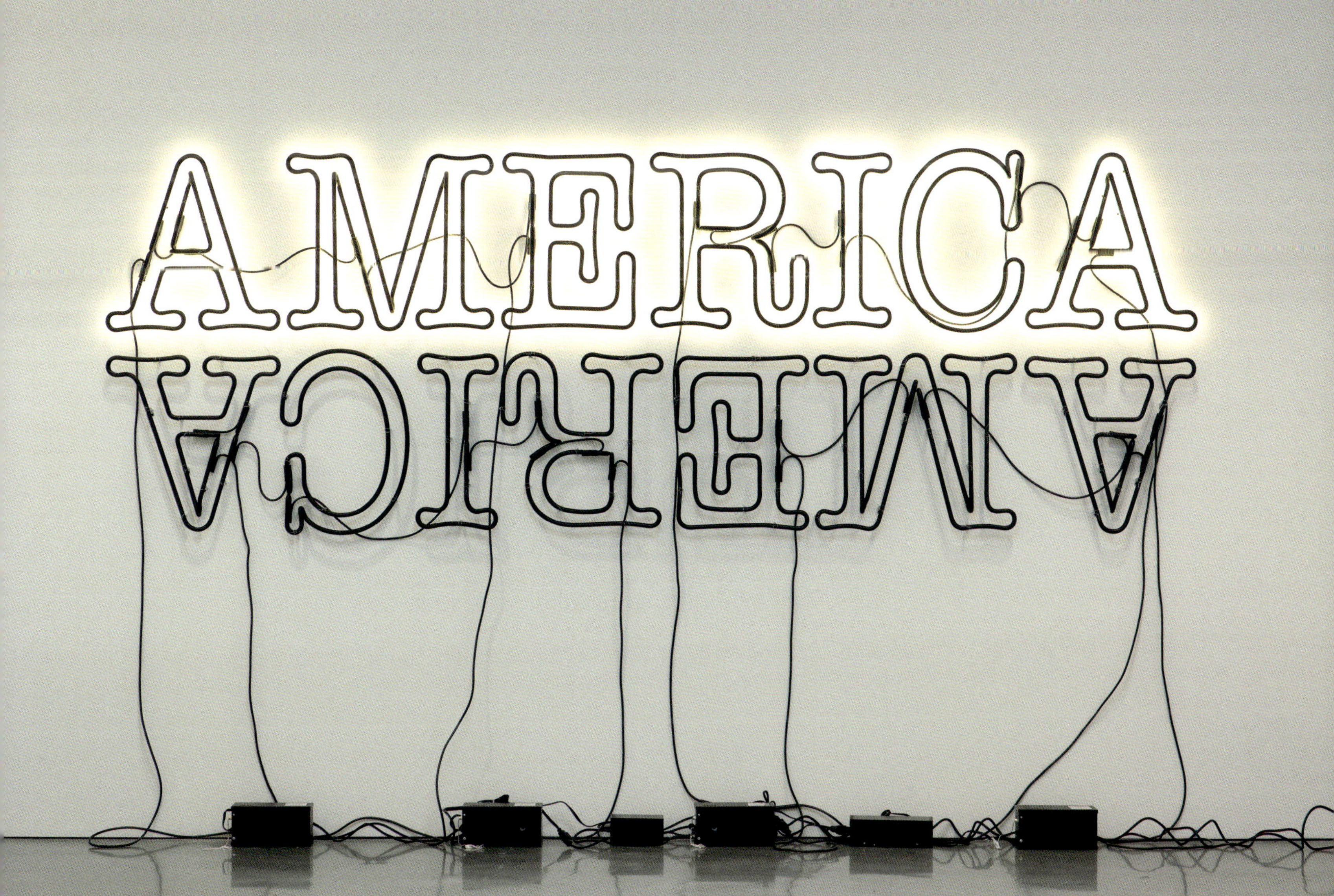
AMERICA

NATE LOWMAN

b. 1979, Las Vegas, NV

Despite his immediate associations with New York's downtown scene, Nate Lowman was born in Las Vegas in 1979 and grew up in Idyllwild, California, about two hours from Los Angeles. He moved to New York to attend New York University, where he earned a BS in 2001. Lowman's upward trajectory was furthermore secured by a buzzy appearance in MoMA PS1's 2005 *Greater New York* exhibition. A number of high-profile occasions followed, including a 2013 solo show at the Brant Foundation. He continues to live and work in New York and retains a side career as a DJ and curator.

Lowman, along with fellow New Yorkers Dan Colen, Ryan McGinley, and the late Dash Snow, is often considered the inheritor of an American Pop legacy that begins with the excessive commercialism of Andy Warhol and extends to the corrosive critique of figures such as Cady Noland and Richard Prince.

Lowman's work tends to fixate on kitschy or seedy images of the American imaginary, such as the ubiquitous smiley face of take-out food apparel or even the very Ford Bronco in which O.J. Simpson fled from the police in 1994. Lowman multiplies and recontextualizes these motifs until they form part of larger narratives that often include bawdy jokes, references to Lowman's sheer monetary success, and even his self-doubt in his ability as an artist. Yet Lowman practices a fluency in the painterly hand that always imbues these cheeky gestures with a degree of irony and humility.

Lowman's irreverent yet strangely moving approach appears in his oil and alkyd 2013 work *ItsSoWonderful Happy Endings Painting*. The piece is a compendium of crudely painted smiley faces in the form of cats, peace signs, the McDonald's logo, dollar bills, and other exhausted signifiers of popular culture. Lowman's approach appears narratively and formally arbitrary, yet the barrage of pleasant affects hints at something darker in its aggressive cheerfulness. The insertion of a grinning pentagram, a bong, and the scrawled word "SHIT" disturb the veneer of good feeling for a crazed, narcotic sense of repetition and imagistic saturation. J. H.

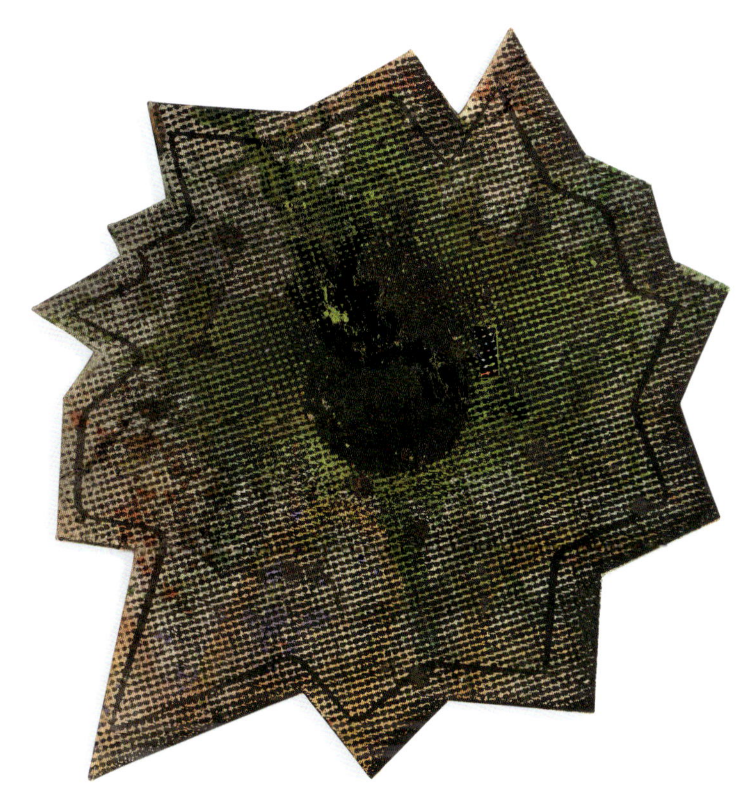

Dropcloth Escalade with Paper, 2012
Acrylic, silkscreen ink, and paper on canvas
69 × 56 × 1 ¼ inches (175.3 × 142.2 × 3.2 cm)

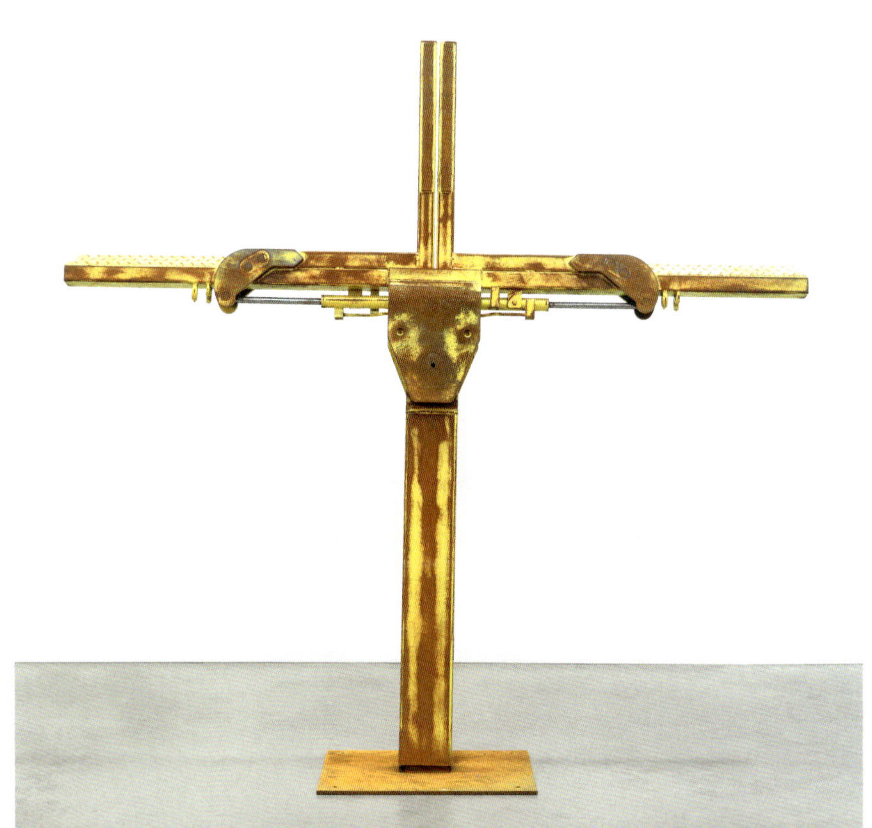

Yellow Outdoor Sculpture, 2015
Corten steel and enamel
84 × 84 × 25 inches (213.4 × 213.4 × 63.5 cm)

ItsSoWonderful Happy Endings Painting,
2013
Oil and alkyd on canvas
$84\frac{1}{8} \times 120\frac{1}{8} \times 1\frac{1}{2}$ inches
(213.7 × 305.1 × 3.8 cm)

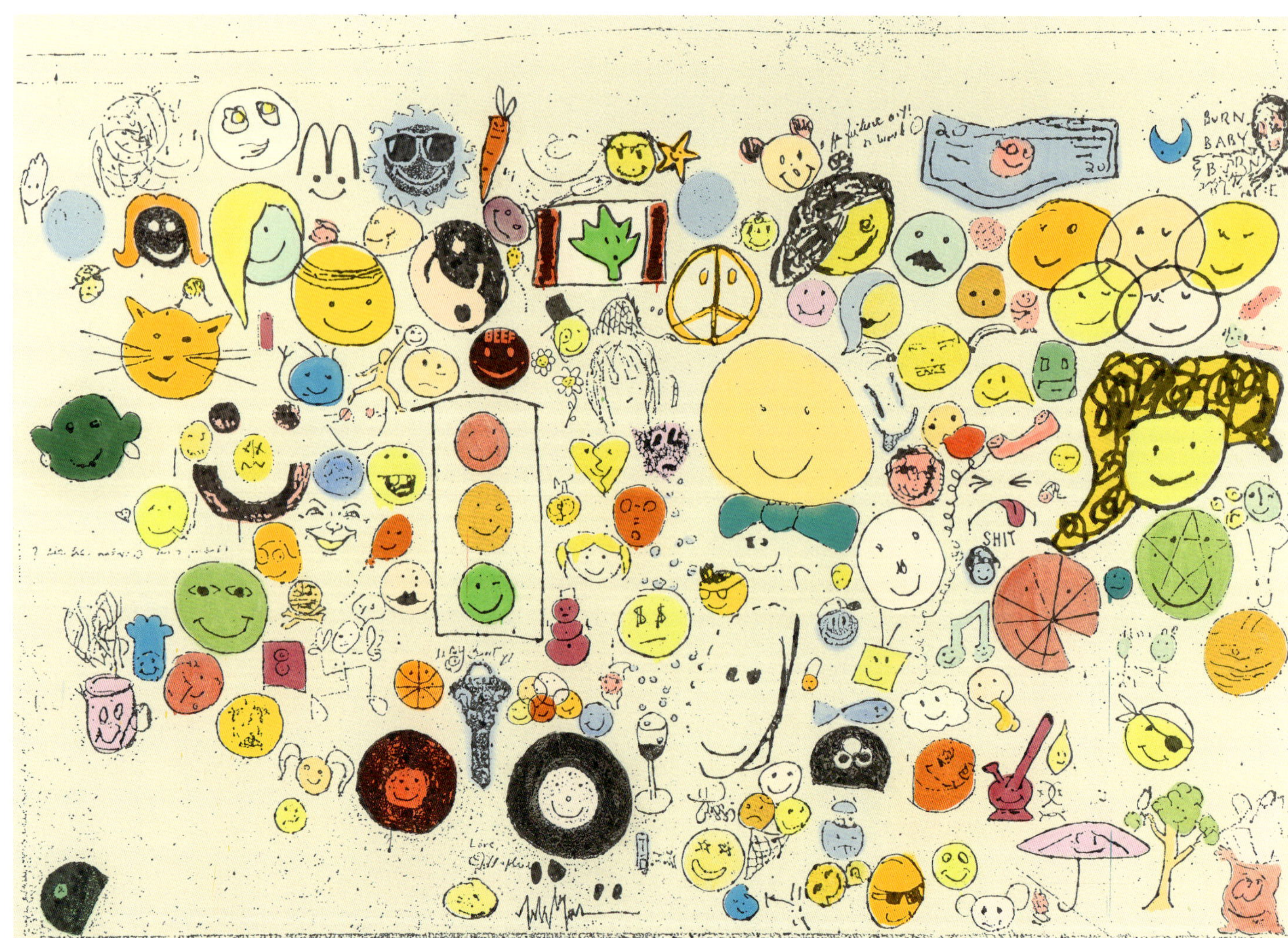

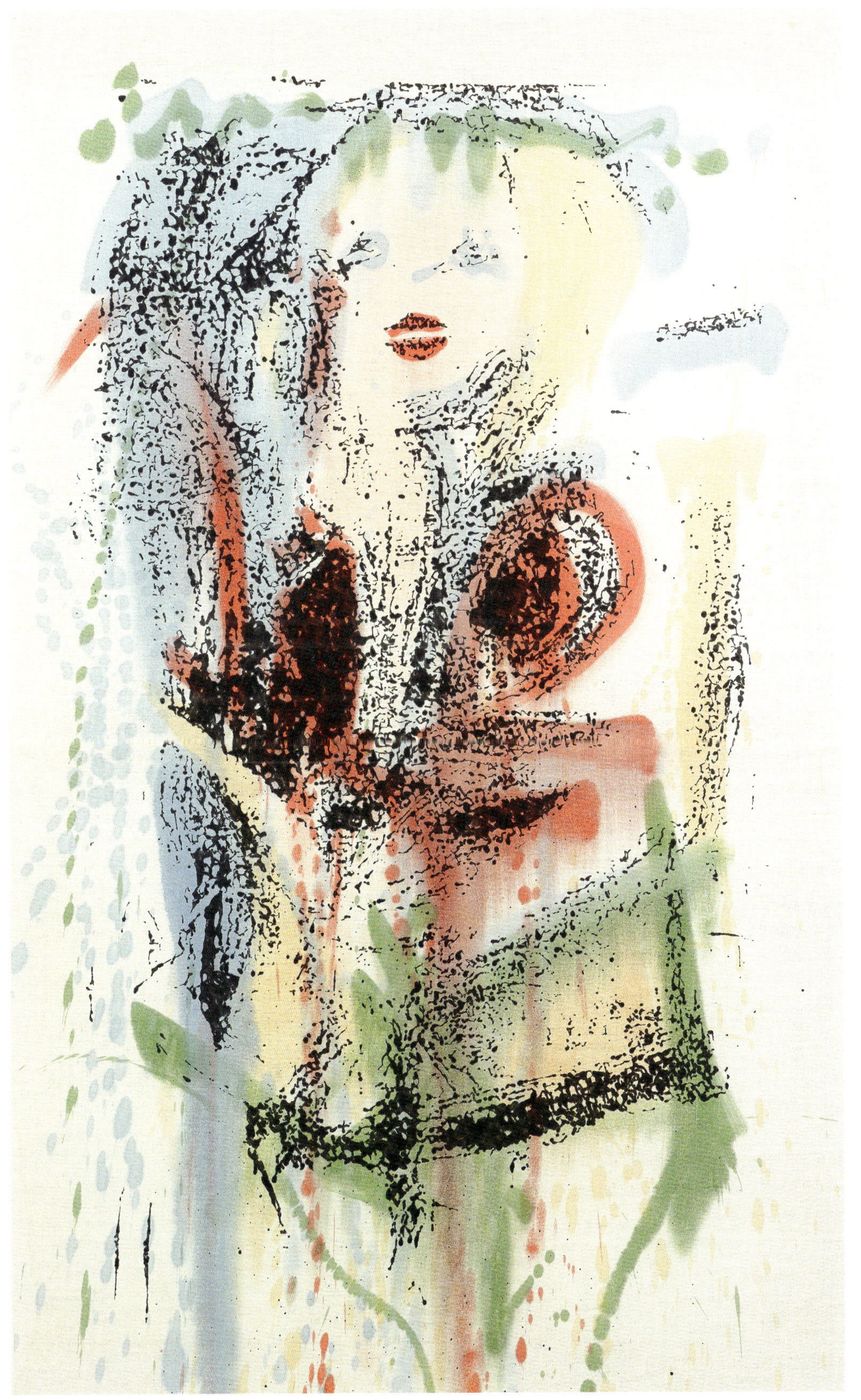

Marilyn's Name, 2013
Oil and alkyd on linen
84 × 52 × 1½ inches (213.4 × 132.1 × 3.8 cm)

GOSHKA **MACUGA** b. 1967, Warsaw, Poland

Goshka Macuga's work mines the conditions that underlie art's figures, communities, and institutions. Born in Warsaw, Poland, in 1967, Macuga graduated from Central St. Martins College of Art and Design in London, where she continues to live and work. Macuga is known for a research-based practice in which she dives into the depths of the archive and enlists expert collaborators.

Since 2009, her research has led to the creation of monumental tapestries, which weave together people, events, and sites to stage provocative questions about the social, political, and economic role of art, artists, and the art world.

A key example of Macuga's work is *Of what is, that it is; of what is not, that it is not 2* (2012). Made for Documenta 13, *Of what is* responded to a special invitation by the exhibition's organizers. Unlike previous iterations, the 13th Documenta held exhibitions in locations outside Kassel, including Banff, Cairo, and Kabul. Macuga completed extensive research in Kassel and Kabul to investigate the ramifications of the exhibition's conjuncture of disparate geographies and contexts.

Macuga's contribution was a tapestry in two parts. Each tapestry depicts a photocollage of actual images Macuga captured, edited, and reconfigured into complete tableaus. In both tapestries one sees figures and events associated with Documenta alongside others that interrupt both the spectacle and smooth operations of one of contemporary art's banner occasions. In tapestry 2, for example, Occupy protesters and their encampments are scattered among mingling artists, curators, and press, including Macuga herself receiving the Arnold-Bode-Preis.

Further underlining the exhibition's multiple geographic coordinates, the diptych was installed separately—the second tapestry depicting Kassel was installed in Kabul and the first tapestry depicting Kabul was displayed in Kassel. Both were hung in semicircular spaces designed by the artist. The tapestries' scale and architectural installation transformed the viewer's space, making one both a spectator and participant in Macuga's critically revisionary and imaginative scene.

In addition to Documenta, she has participated in the Venice Biennale, the Berlin Biennial, and was nominated for the Turner Prize in 2008. Macuga has had solo exhibitions at the New Museum, New York; the Museum of Contemporary Art, Chicago; and Whitechapel Art Gallery, London; among other venues.
J. A.

International Institute of Intellectual Co-operation, Configuration 15, End of Men: Madame Blavatsky, Mary Shelley, Guerilla Girls, Ada Lovelace, Donna Haraway, Olympe de Gouges, 2016
Bronze
150 × 125 × 125 inches (381 × 317.5 × 317.5 cm)

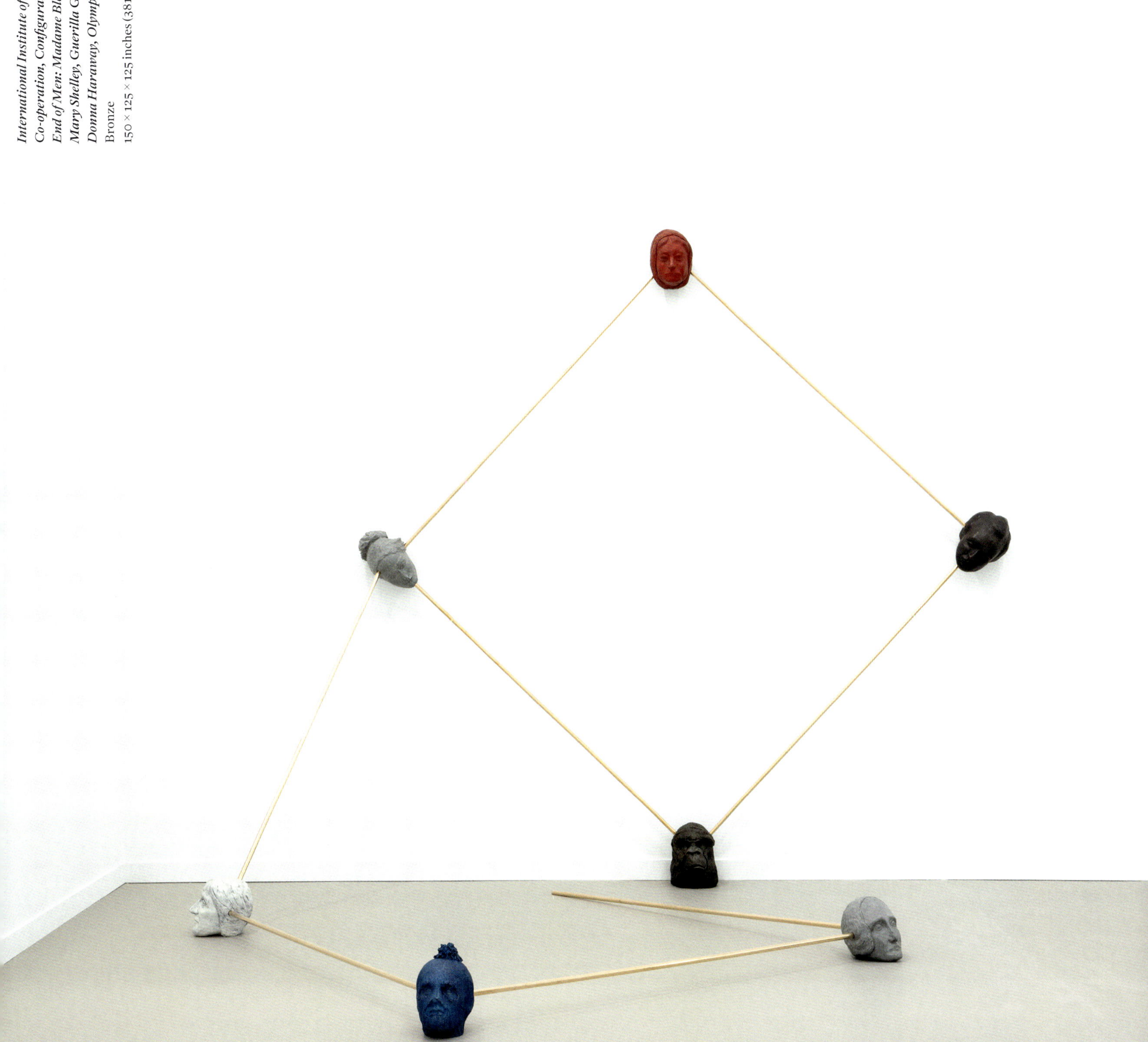

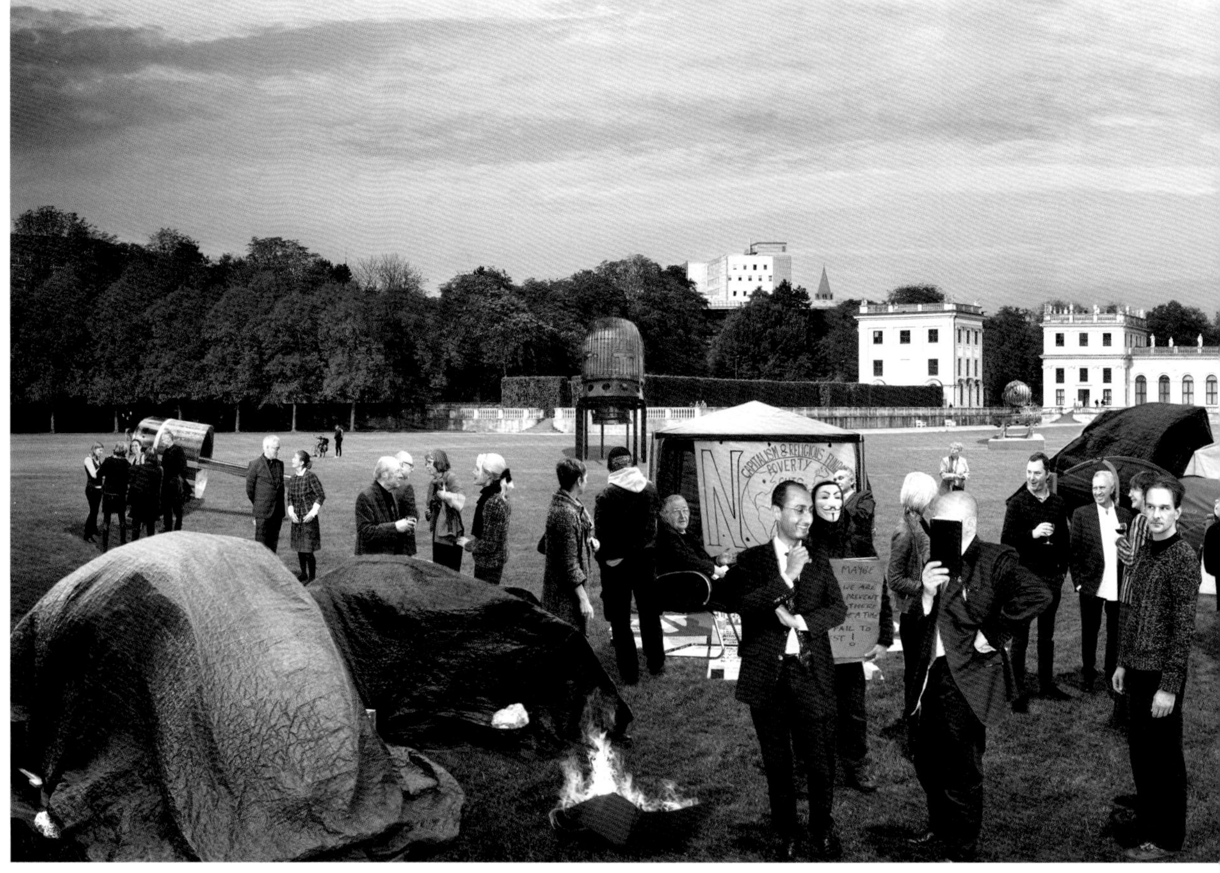

Of what is, that it is; of what is not, that it is not 2, 2012
Wool tapestry
129 7/8 × 435 5/8 inches (330 × 1106 cm)
Edition 2 of 3, 1 AP

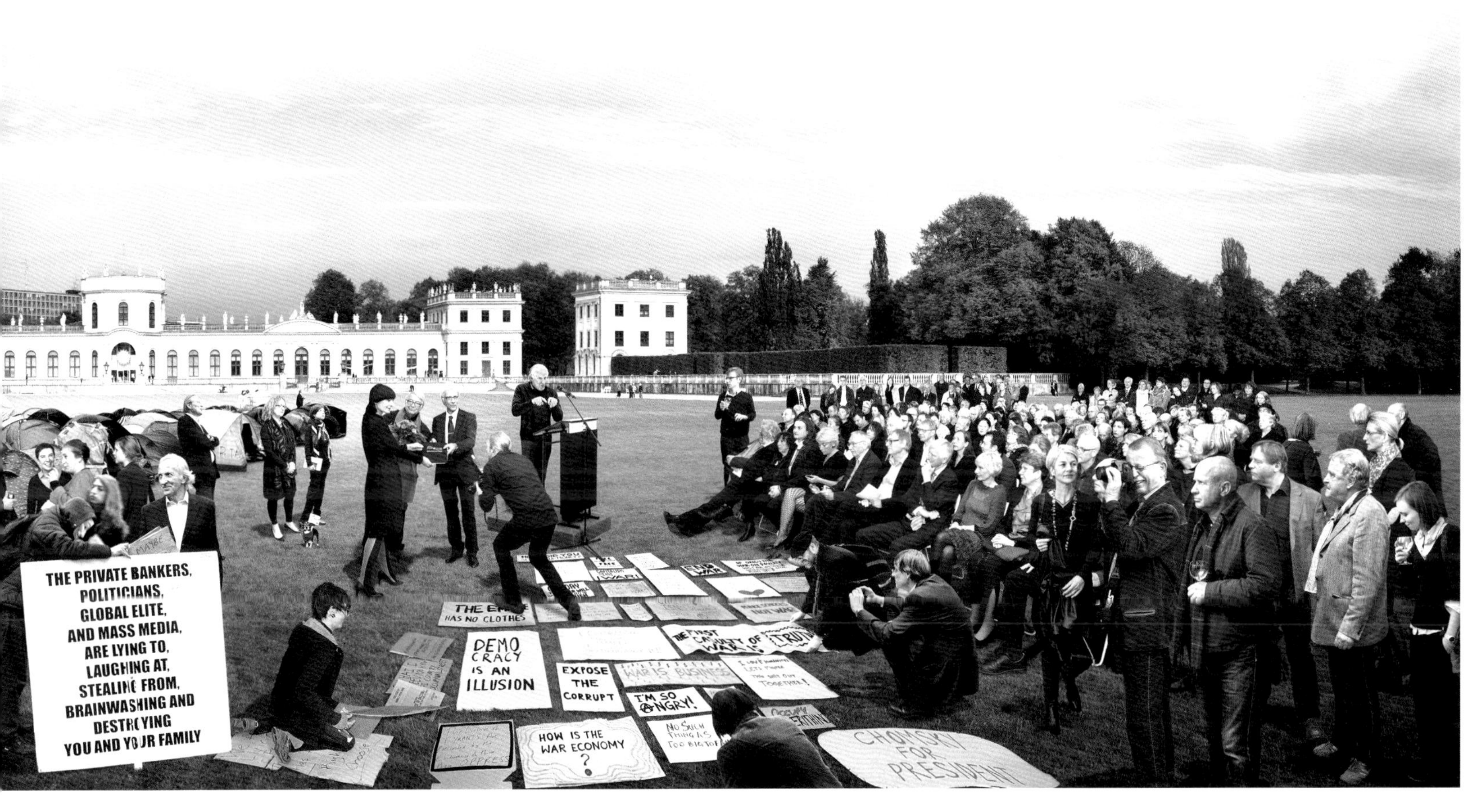
THE PRIVATE BANKERS, POLITICIANS, GLOBAL ELITE, AND MASS MEDIA, ARE LYING TO, LAUGHING AT, STEALING FROM, BRAINWASHING AND DESTROYING YOU AND YOUR FAMILY
END WAR
HAS NO CLOTHES
DEMO CRACY IS AN ILLUSION
THE FIRST CASUALTY OF WAR IS TRUTH
EXPOSE THE CORRUPT
WAR IS BUSINESS
I'M SO ANGRY!
HOW IS THE WAR ECONOMY ?
NO SUCH THING AS TOO BIG TO
CHOMSKY FOR PRESIDENT

CHRISTIAN MARCLAY

b. 1955, San Rafael, CA

For more than thirty years, Christian Marclay has explored the connections between sound and art and, in doing so, has succeeded in transforming music into a tangible, physical form that can be visually represented.

Born in San Rafael, California, to a Swiss father and an American mother, Marclay was raised in Geneva, Switzerland. Originally a sculpture major, his first experimentations with sound began as a student at the Massachusetts College of Art (MassArt) in the late 1970s, where he performed in the Duchampian punk duo "The Bachelors" as one of the first musicians to employ the turntable as a musical instrument.

Interested in themes such as improvisation, music-making rituals and Dadaism, Marclay's early work takes the form of manipulated and reassembled thrift-store found records, which could be played to produce continuous loops and skips. Some of Marclay's best-known works are spliced together audio/visual collages. For example, in Marclay's film *Telephones* (1995), which is included in the Marciano Collection, a sequence of various movie clips are presented where actors are speaking on the telephone. Marclay leads the viewer/listener to a certain awareness of the limitations of the media; for though the actors in the clips cannot see each other, they frequently remark, "I see."

Some of Marclay's pieces make no sound at all. Instead, the artist evokes sound through allusion. His recent *Action* series, including *Actions: Whipp Shlump Sloosh Slutch No. 4* (2014), illustrate this point; while the painting as an object is silent, the viewer can conjure the evocative descriptive words of sounds spelled out and painted on the canvas. For his 2008 series of cyanotypes, Marclay experimented with music cassette tapes, using the hard-lined, geometric shapes of the plastic cases and the spools of unwound tapes to leave traces of the music the cassettes once played. He appropriated the titles for each work in the series after the specific cassette tapes that are depicted in the photograph, such as *All Over (Kenny Rogers, Rod Stewart, Jody Watley and Others)* (2008).

Marclay's work is in numerous institutional collections, and his work has been widely shown internationally, with solo exhibitions at Walker Art Center, Minneapolis; Tate Modern, London; San Francisco Museum of Modern Art; Kunsthaus Zurich, Zurich; and Whitney Museum of American Art, New York (1997). Marclay won the Golden Lion at the 2011 Venice Biennial for his work *The Clock* (2010). L. C

Surround Sounds, 2014–15
Four silent synchronized projected animations
13:40 min. (loop) each
Edition 5 of 5, 2 AP

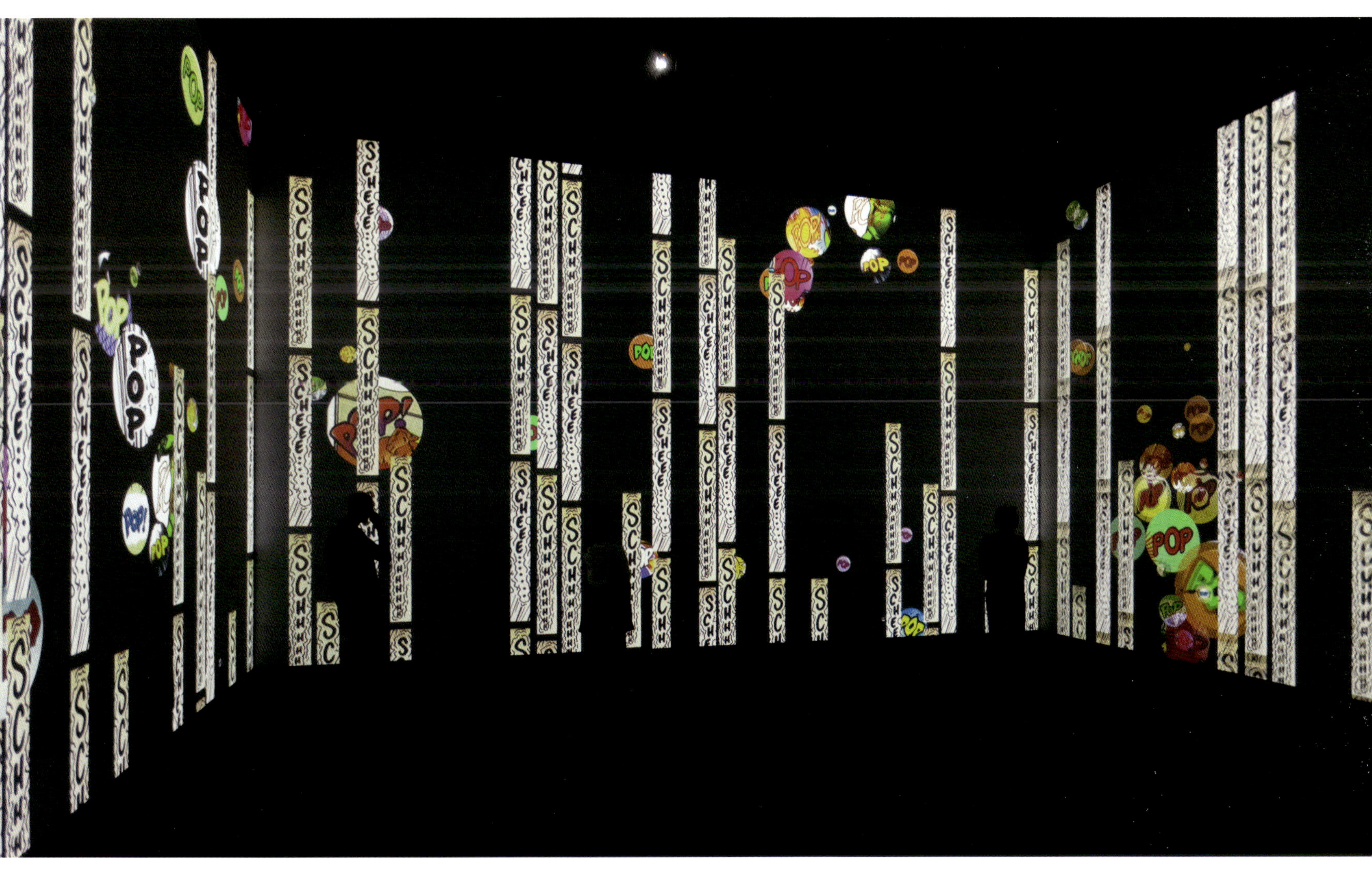

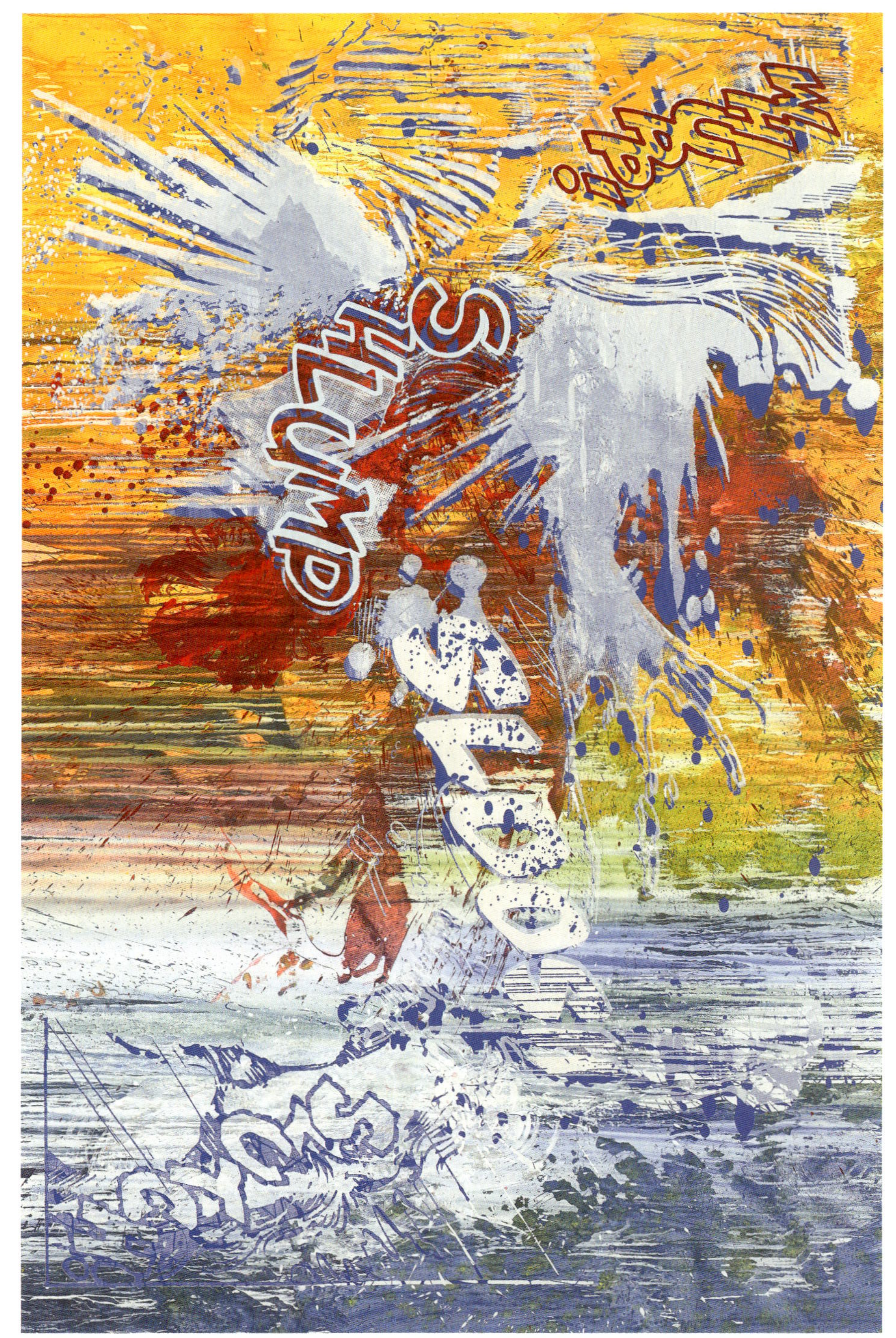

Actions: Whupp Shlump Sloosh Slutch (No. 4), 2014
Screen print and acrylic on canvas
$60\frac{1}{16} \times 94\frac{11}{16}$ inches (152.5 × 240.5 cm)

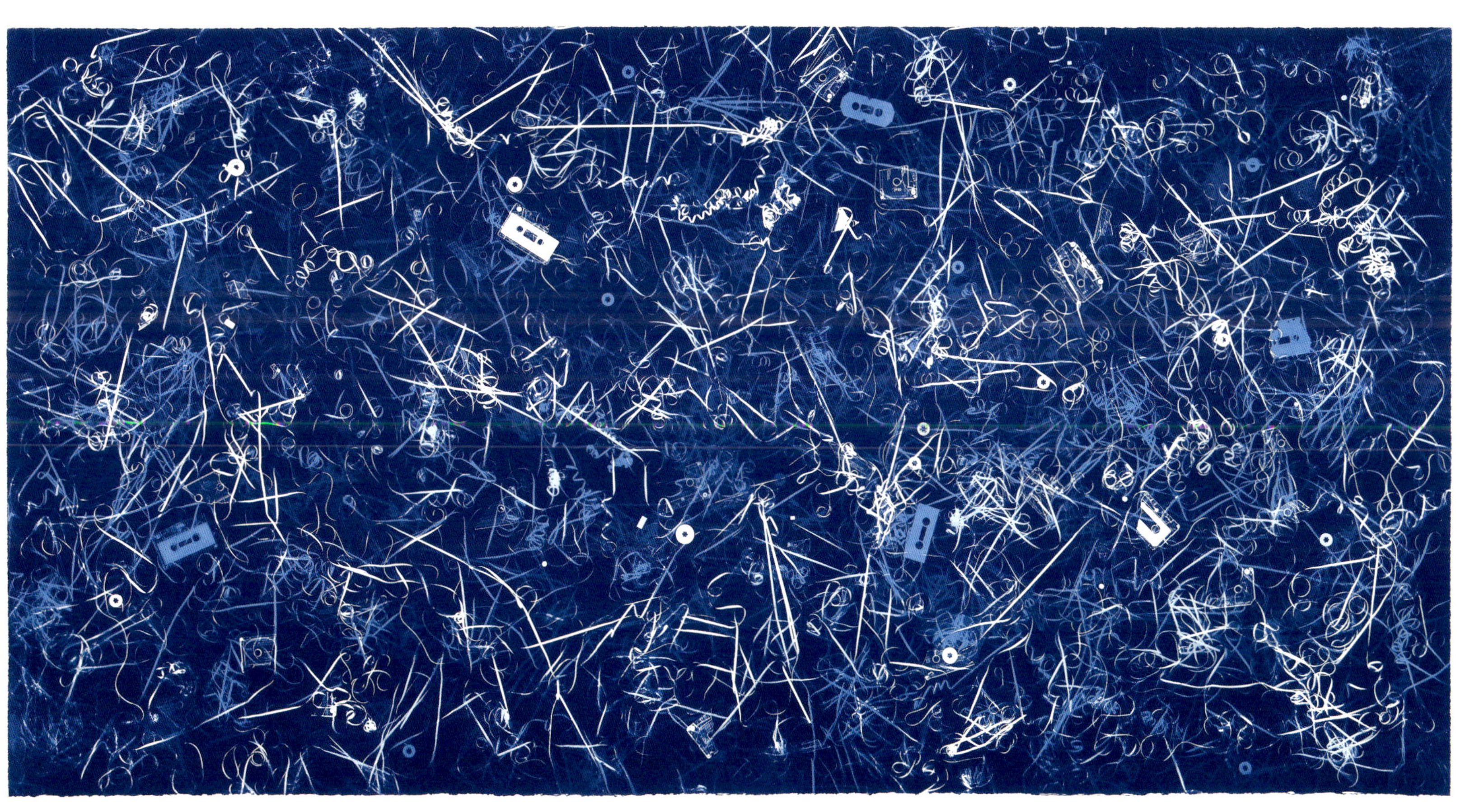

All Over (Kenny Rogers, Rod Stewart, Jody Watley and Others), 2008
Cyanotype
$51\frac{1}{2} \times 100\frac{1}{8}$ inches (130.8 × 254.3 cm)

PAUL MCCARTHY b. 1945, Salt Lake City, UT

Los Angeles–based artist Paul McCarthy unapologetically tackles taboo subjects and condemns polite society through performance, video, installation, freestanding and kinetic sculpture, photography, and drawing. He constantly challenges archetypal American myths, icons and authority, resulting in disturbing depictions of traditionally chaste subjects that are, in all other cases, extoled for their purity.

By conflating real-life, controversial individuals with idolized figures from childhood, ranging from various characters to Santa Claus, the artist forces the viewer to question his or her own dark habits, secret desires, irrational fears, and involuntary biological functions. McCarthy's work can also depict fictional violence and abuse related to family and childhood through a wide-range of tactile vehicles, such as traditional paint, food, and household products, all of which are employed throughout his filmed theatrics.

McCarthy's trademark themes of loss of innocence, human biology and sexuality, and trauma and family dysfunction flourish in series like *White Snow*, in which McCarthy, together with his son, Damon McCarthy, reinterpret the classic children's story, *Snow White*, and examine its multilayered references and inferences. The project began with a series of drawings in 2009 and has evolved to include sculpture, installation, performance, and video. The sculpture *White Snow Head* (2012–13) appears as a mutilated version of the Snow White character. The enormous red bust of the young protagonist features red and blue scarlike indentations from presumed lacerations to the face, evincing McCarthy's predilection for disturbing imagery that assaults the innocence of childhood. Other works from the same series, such as the sketches *White Snow, Part 2, The Trial Effects* (2014), allow the viewer to peruse McCarthy's storyboard of his take on the fairy tale. McCarthy's graphic drawings depict a boy with a butcher knife cutting through his leg, boys revealing their penises, and forceful acts of fellatio—all violations of the wholesome story we have all come to know.

McCarthy was born in Salt Lake City, Utah, in 1945. He completed his BFA at the San Francisco Art Institute and then received his MFA in 1973 from the University of Southern California. A professor at the University of California, Los Angeles, from 1984 to 2003, McCarthy has shown widely including the Whitney Museum of American Art, S.M.A.K. Stedelijk Museum voor Actuele Kunst, Moderna Museet, and Haus der Kunst, Munich, among others. He has also participated several times in the Whitney, Berlin, and Venice biennials. McCarthy lives and works in Los Angeles, California. L. C.

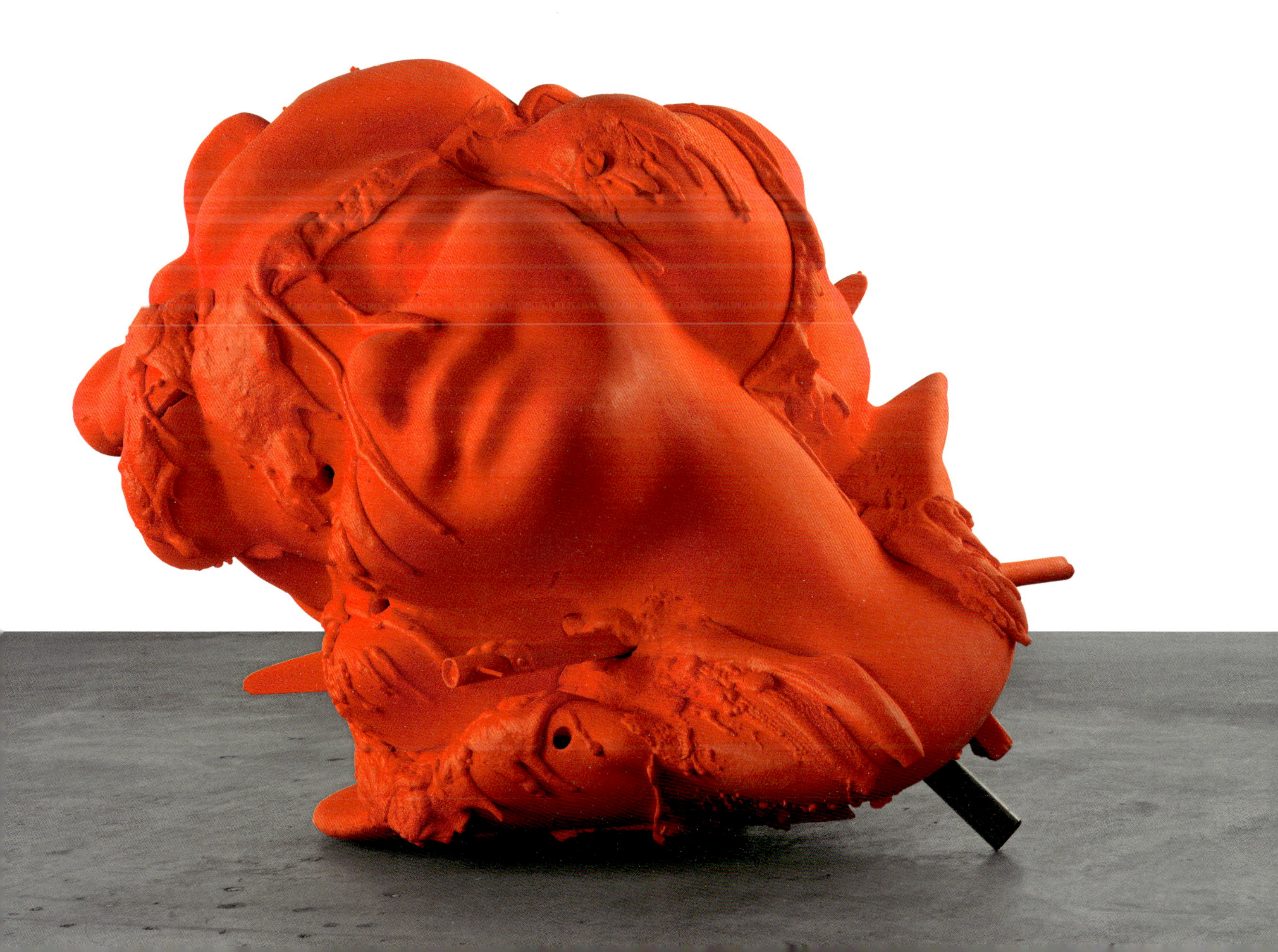

White Snow Head, 2012–13
Silicone (red), fiberglass, and steel
57 × 65 × 58 inches (144.8 × 165.1 × 147.3 cm)

White Snow, Part 2, The Trial Effects, 2014
Group of 18 drawings, pencil on paper
11 × 14 inches (27.9 × 35.6 cm) each
47 × 74 inches (119.4 × 188 cm) overall

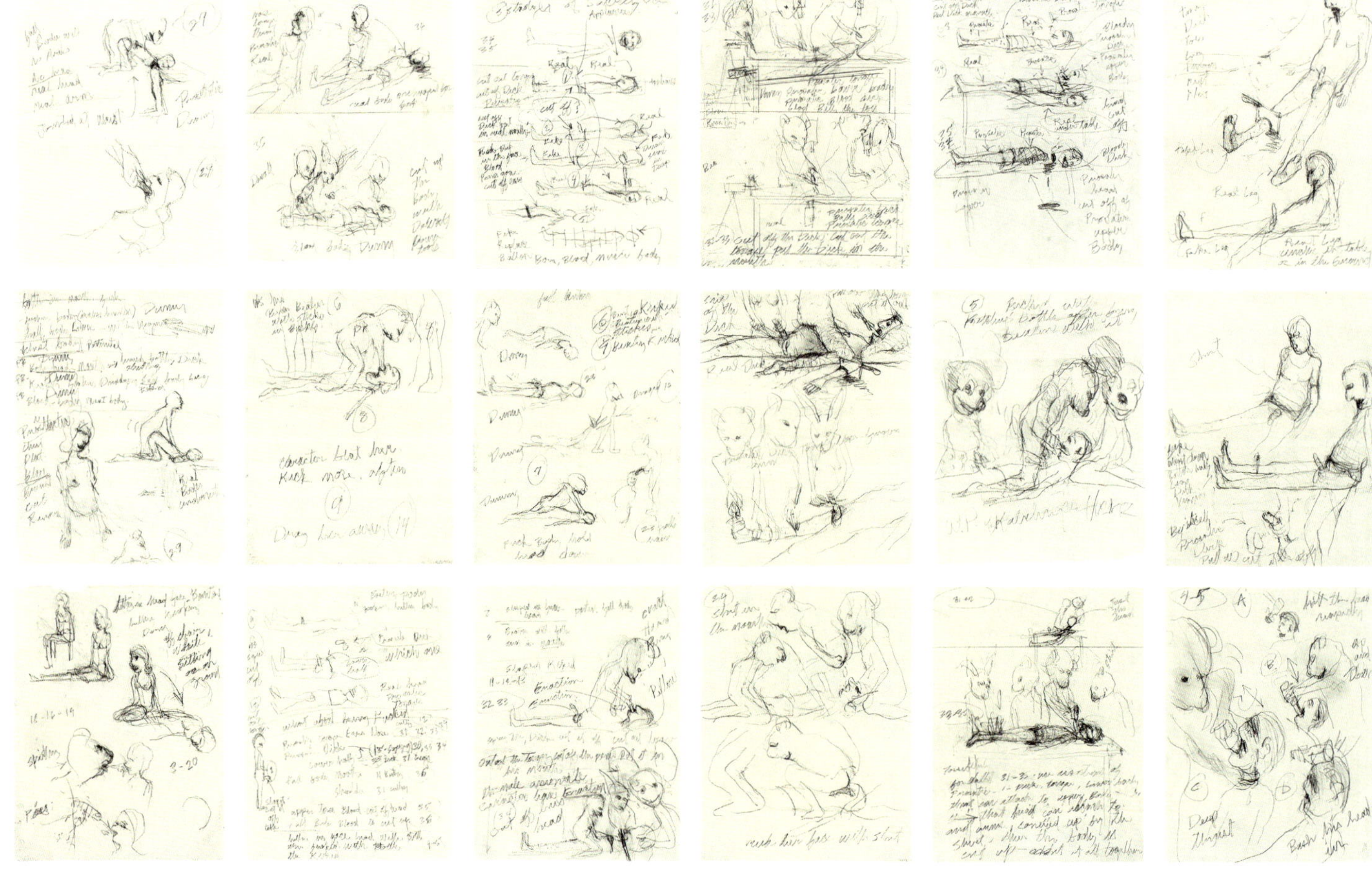

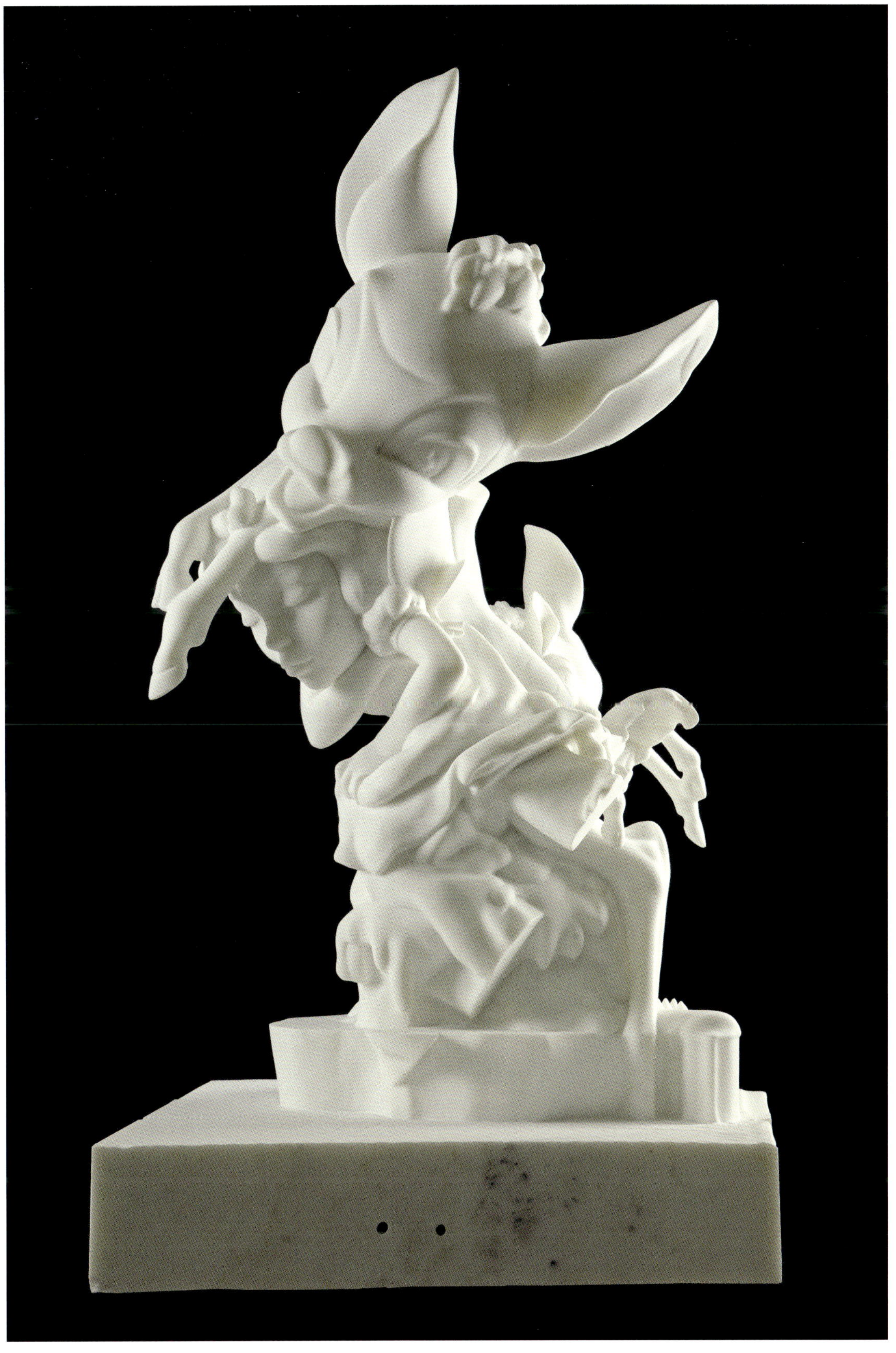

White Snow and Bambi (marble), 2014
Marble
39 3/8 × 24 3/8 × 16 1/2 inches (100 × 62 × 42 cm)

White Snow, Balloon Dog, 2013
Sealed PVC polyvinyl chloride plastic,
fan (cerulean blue)
62 × 33 × 82 inches (157.5 × 83.8 × 208.3 cm)

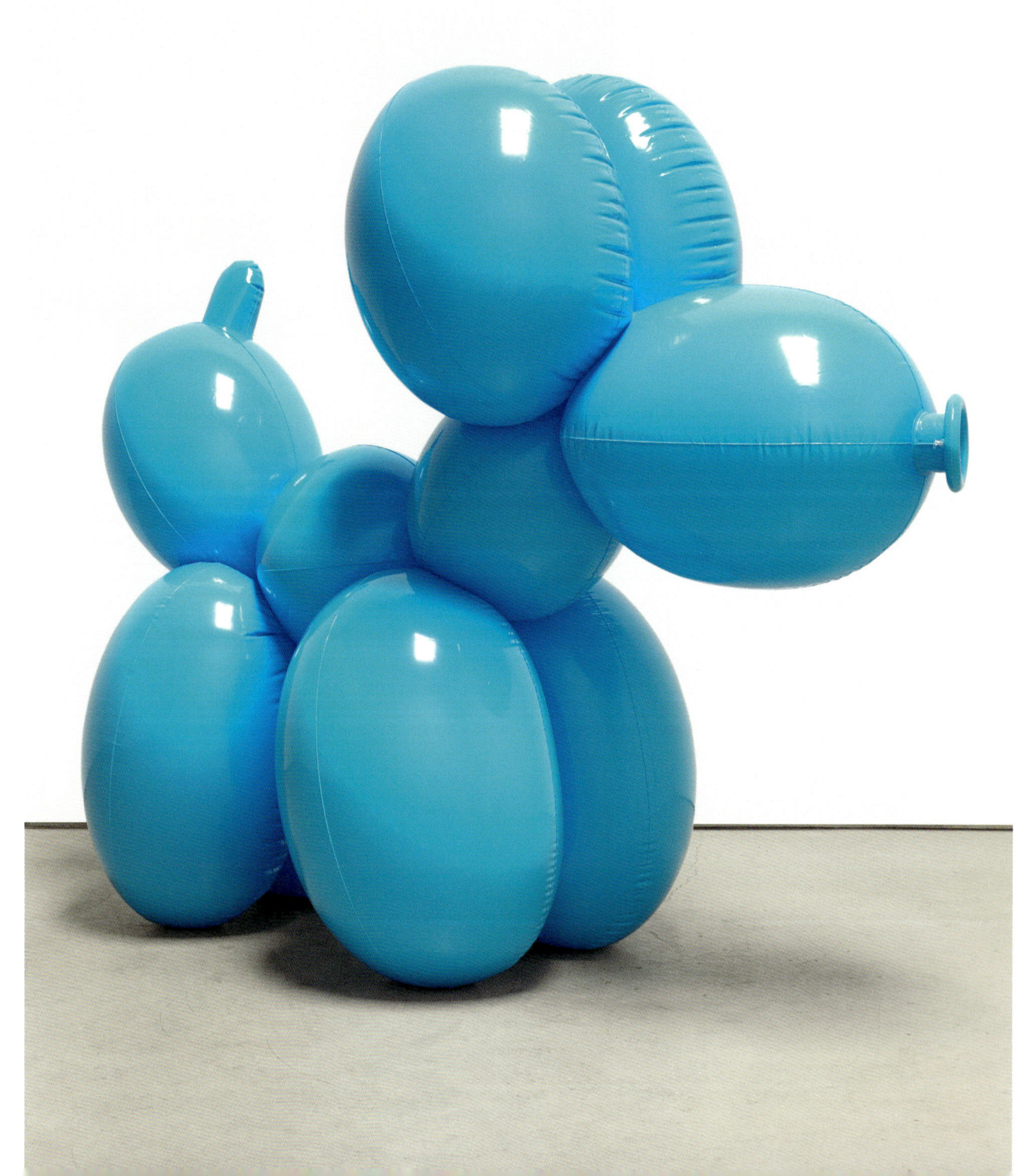

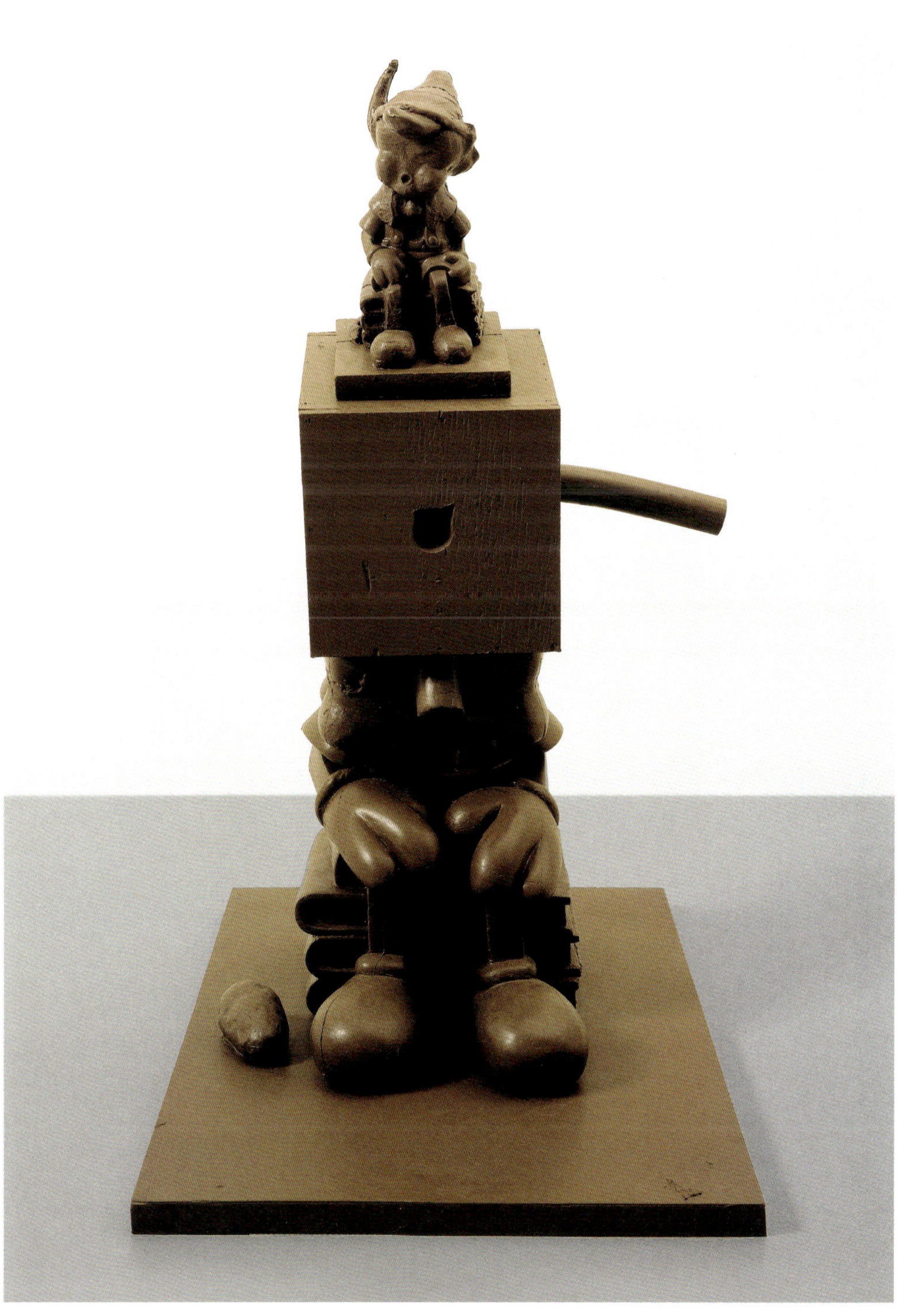

Chocolate Silicone Block Head, 1999–2000
Silicone
35⅞ × 43¼ × 27⅛ inches (91 × 110 × 69 cm)

TAKASHI MURAKAMI

b. 1962, Tokyo, Japan

And then, and then and then and then and then, 1996
Acrylic on canvas laid down on board, in two parts
$39\frac{3}{8} \times 39\frac{3}{8}$ inches (100 × 100 cm) each

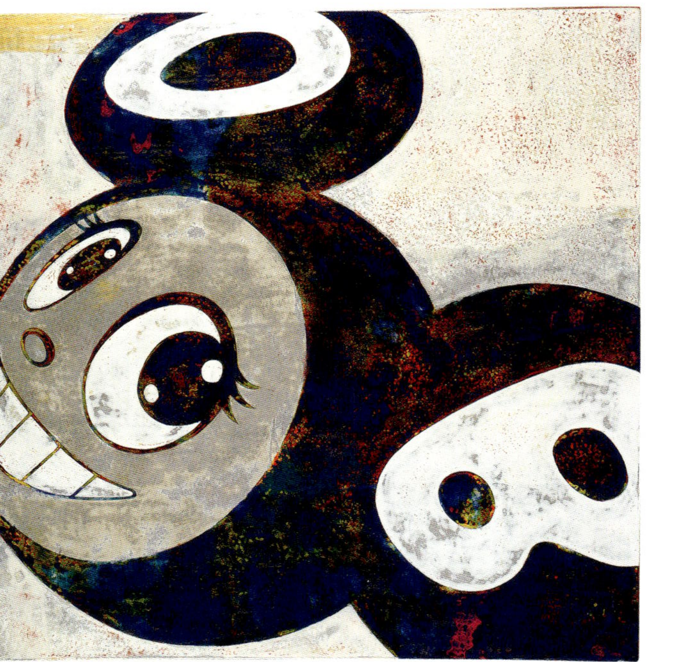

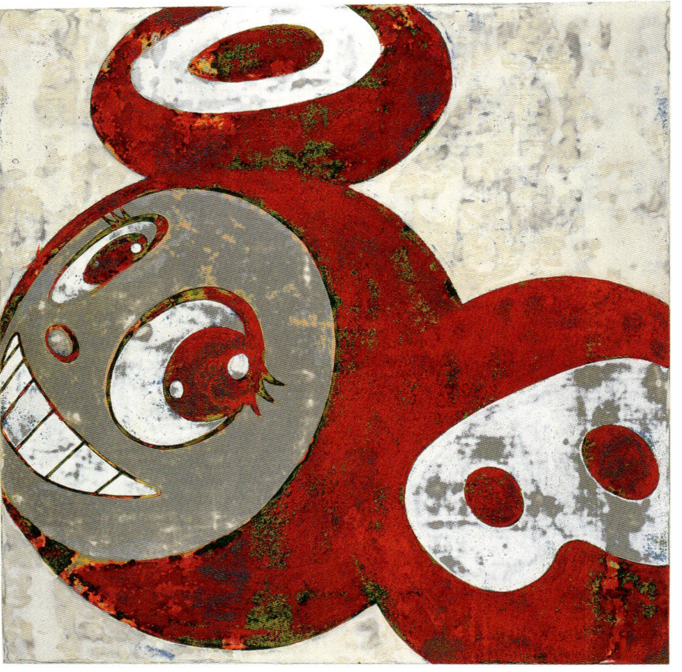

From the beginning of his career, Takashi Murakami has perpetually mixed old and new, East and West. Born in Tokyo in 1962, Murakami received both a BFA (1986) and Ph.D. (2003) from the Tokyo National University of Fine Arts and Music. He was the university's first student to earn a doctorate in *nihon-ga*, a type of painting based on traditional Japanese style. Frustrated with the lack of a reliable art market in postwar Japan, Murakami moved to New York in 1994 for a studio fellowship with the express goal of establishing his career in the West before moving back to Japan. The studios he founded in both New York and Tokyo in the mid-1990s would eventually become Kaikai Kiki, the sprawling company he manages today. High-profile collaborations with figures such as Marc Jacobs, Kanye West, and Pharrell Williams followed, and today Murakami has become one of the most well-known international artists. He continues to work between New York and Tokyo.

Murakami's personal style and aesthetic philosophy can be summarized through the concept he calls "Superflat." It refers not only to Murakami's graphic approach, which emphasizes planarity, bright colors, and cartoonish figuration, but a broader sensibility that confuses any cultural distinction of high and low.

The images of his painting and sculpture easily translate into consumer merchandise such as toys and clothing; he has franchised a number of characters, including the iconic Mr. DOB, a toothy, impish variant on Mickey Mouse that Murakami considers an alter ego. Murakami explicitly borrows from the imagery of Japanese *anime* (animation), *manga* (comic books), and *otaku*, the culture of intense fandom around these two genres. Part of these references is a thematic intertwining of the adorable, the grotesque, and the prurient.

Yet, influenced by the 2011 earthquake and tsunami, which led to a nuclear disaster in Fukushima, Murakami's more recent work has embraced darker themes and a more historicized style. His monumental *100 Arhats* from 2013, for example, exists somewhere between the deliberate composition of Japanese painting and the stylized modeling of *anime*. The arhats, enlightened followers of the Buddha, stand in frontal view in varying dimensions and anatomies, ranging from the cute to the monstrous. A gradient pattern fills the background, while Murakami's strategic yet maximalist colors beguile the eye. J. H.

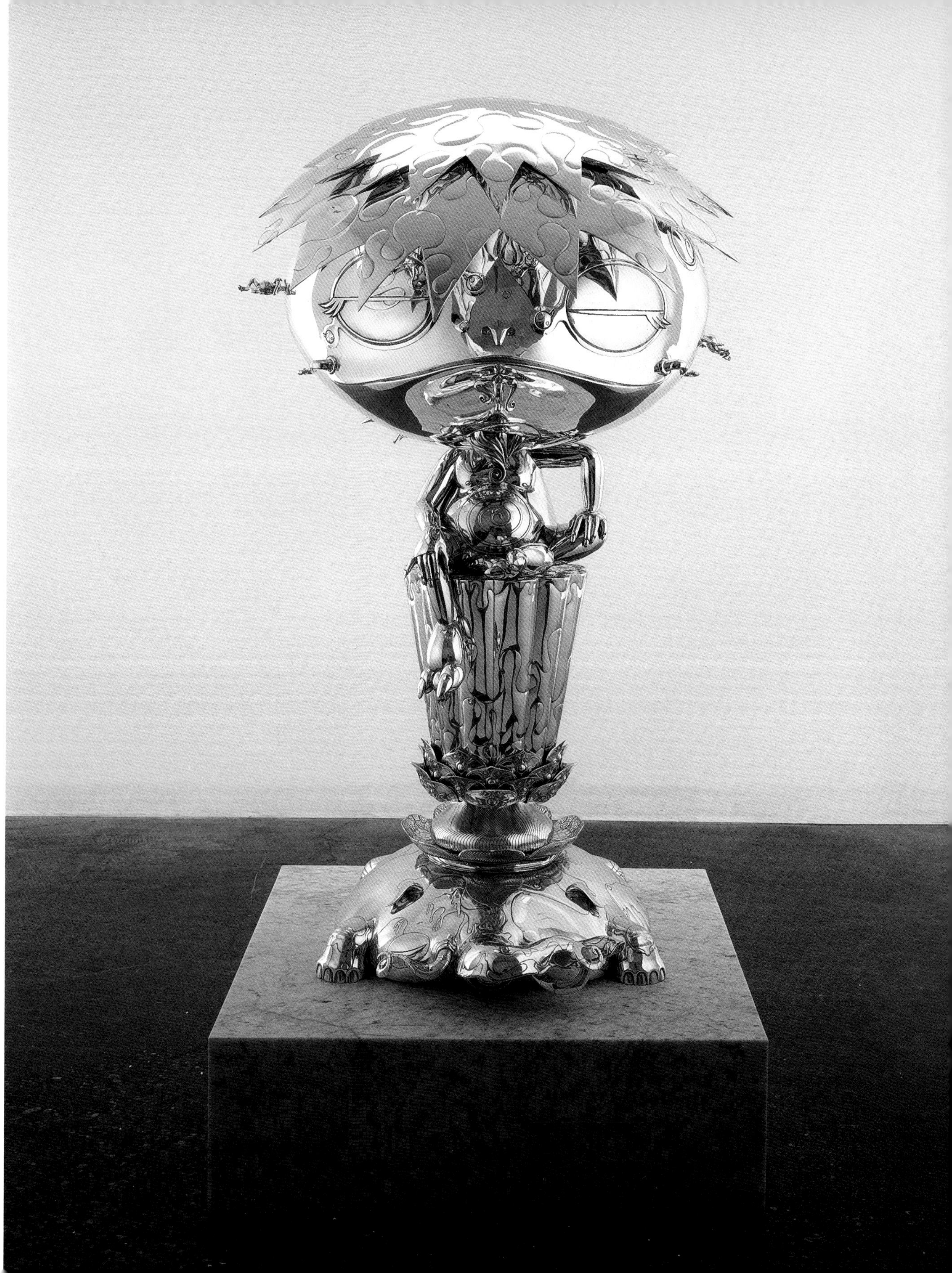

Oval Buddha Silver, 2008
Sterling silver and steel, marble base
Sculpture: $53\frac{5}{8} \times 31\frac{5}{8} \times 30\frac{5}{8}$ inches
(136.4 × 80.5 × 78 cm)
Base: $9\frac{3}{4} \times 31\frac{3}{4} \times 33$ inches
(24.8 × 80.6 × 83.8 cm)
Edition of 10

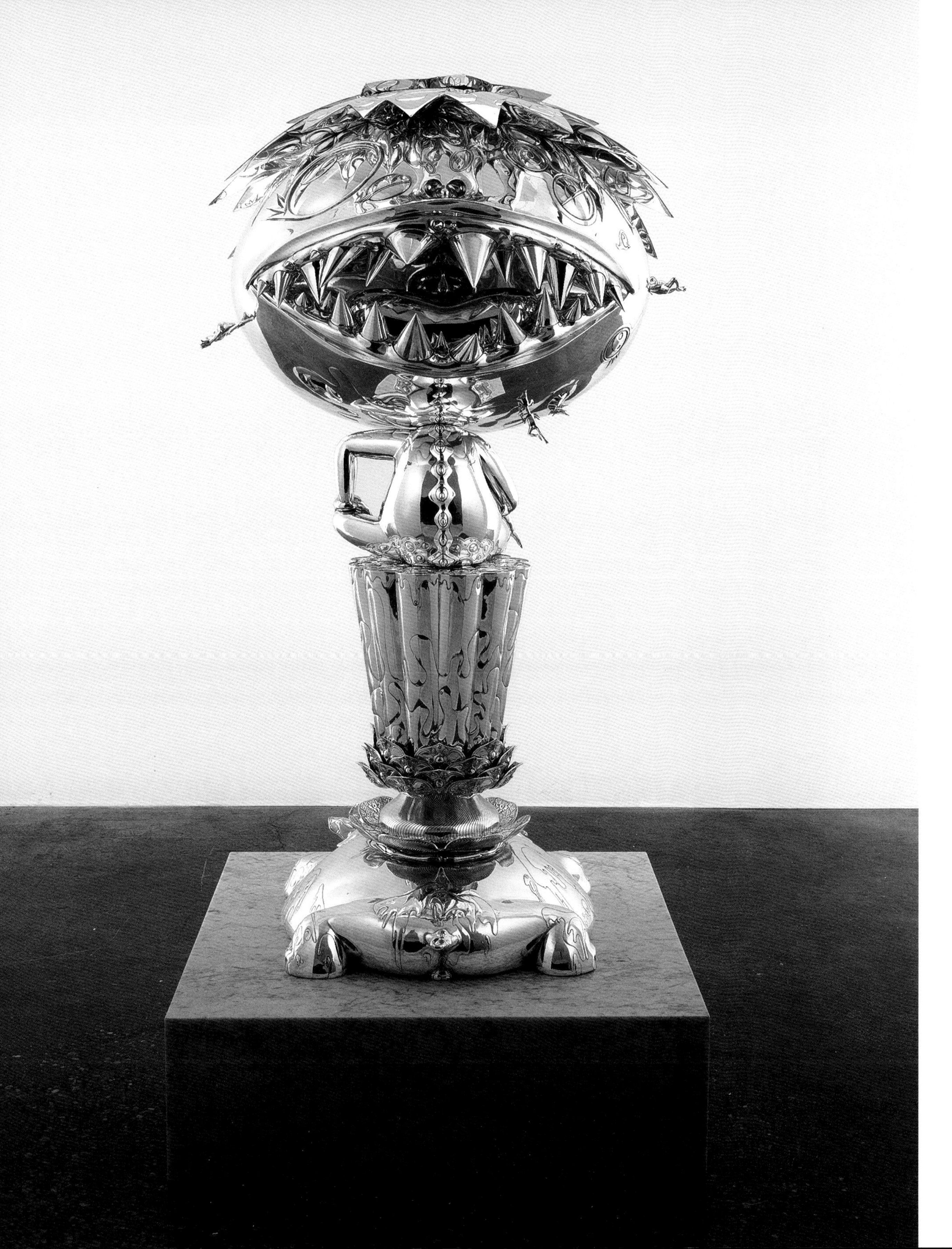

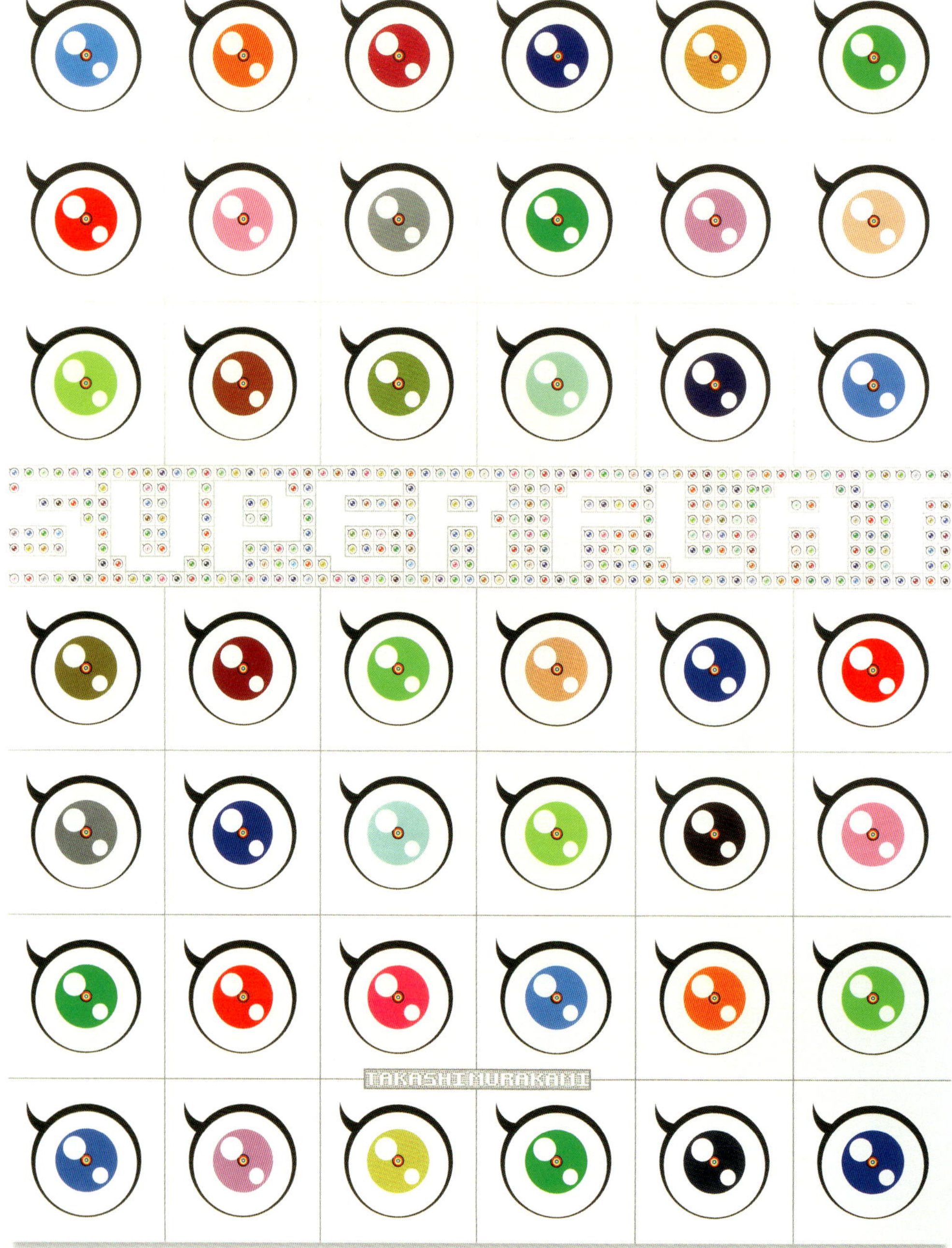

SUPERFLAT, 2009
Acrylic on canvas mounted on board
82 1/3 × 63 × 2 inches (209 × 160 × 5.1 cm)

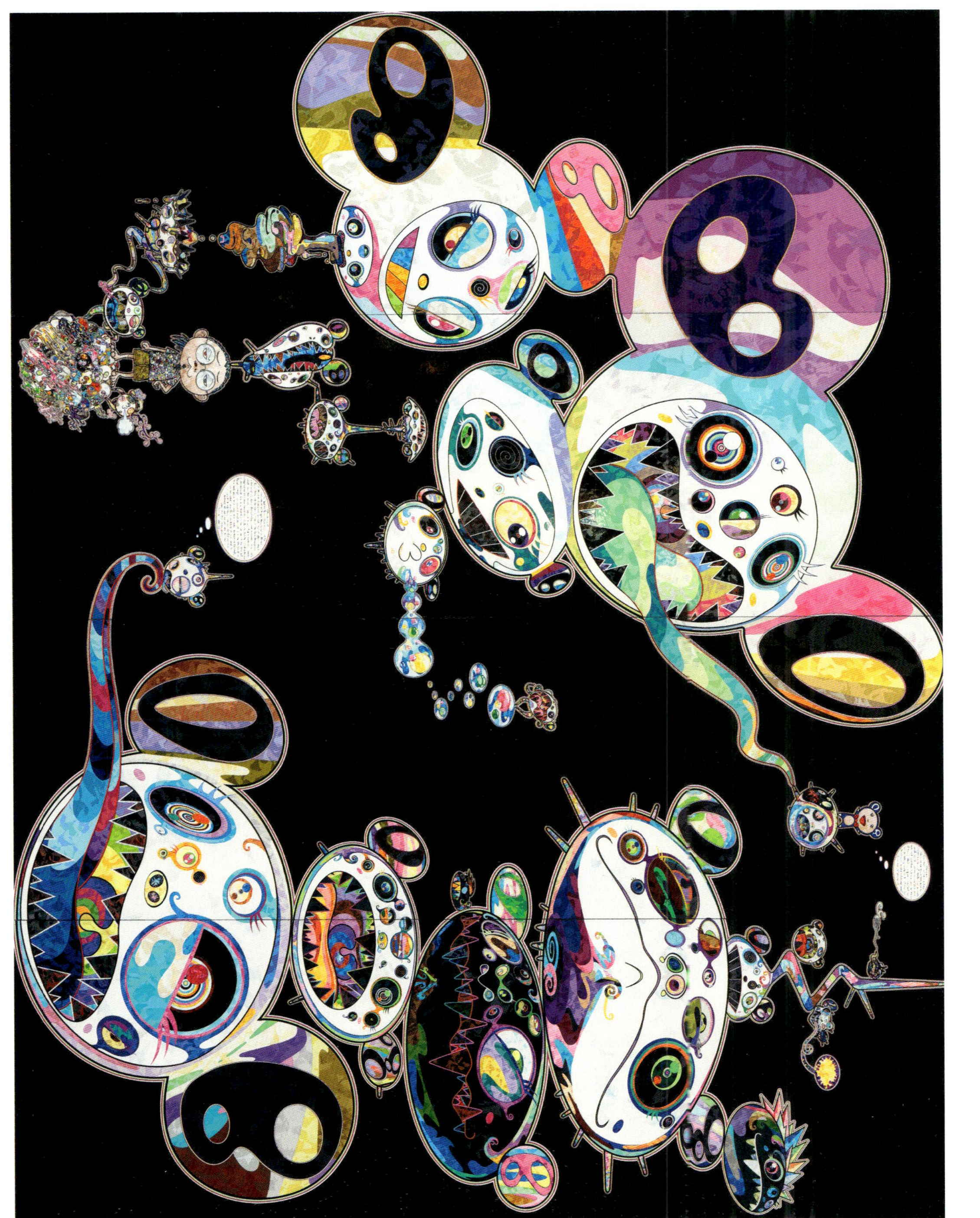

Double Helix Within Dark Matter, 2014
Acrylic on canvas
118 1/8 × 157 1/2 inches (300 × 400 cm)

100 Arhats, 2013
Acrylic, gold, and platinum leaf on canvas
mounted on board
10 panels: 118 1/8 × 393 11/16 inches
(300 × 1000.2 cm) overall

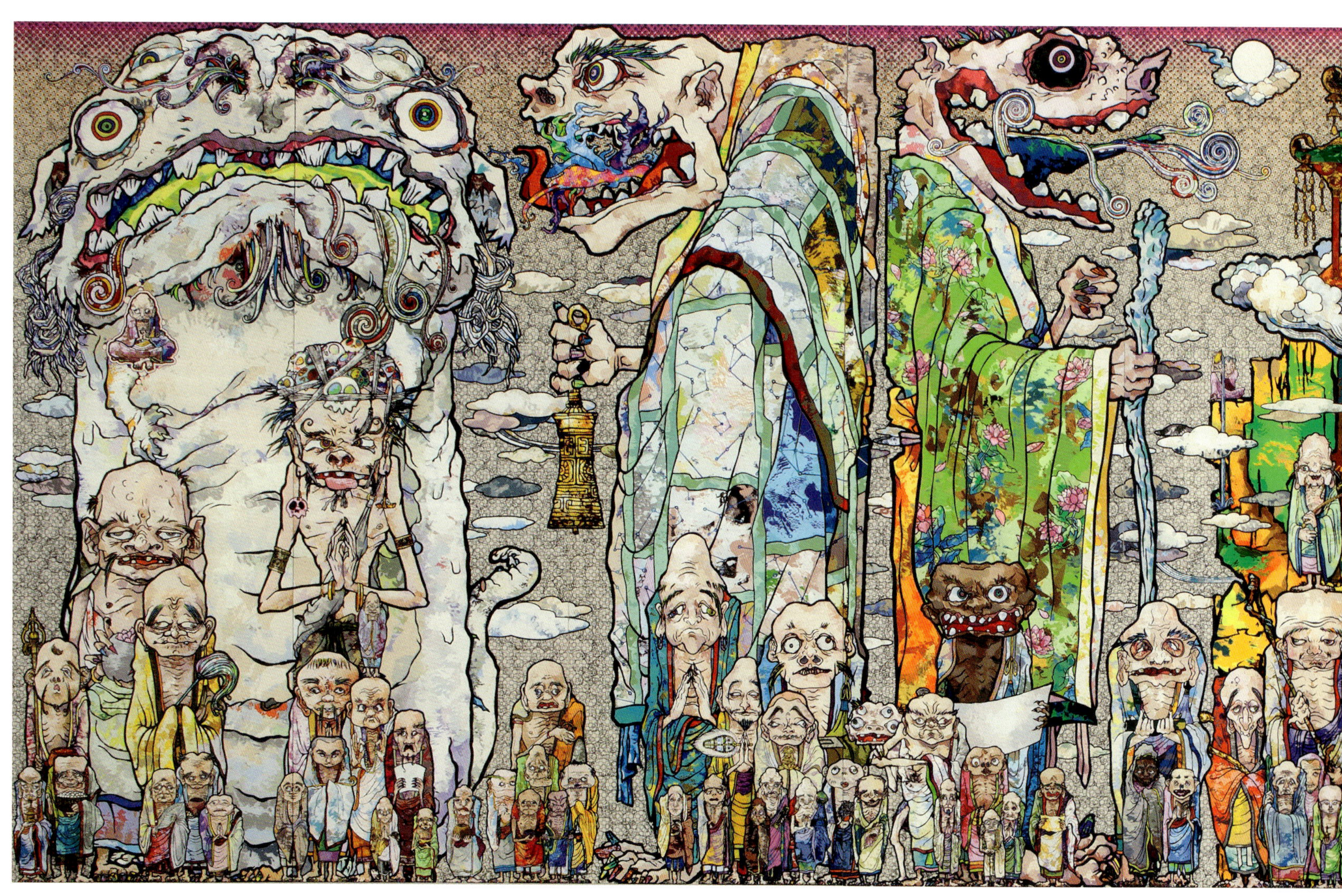

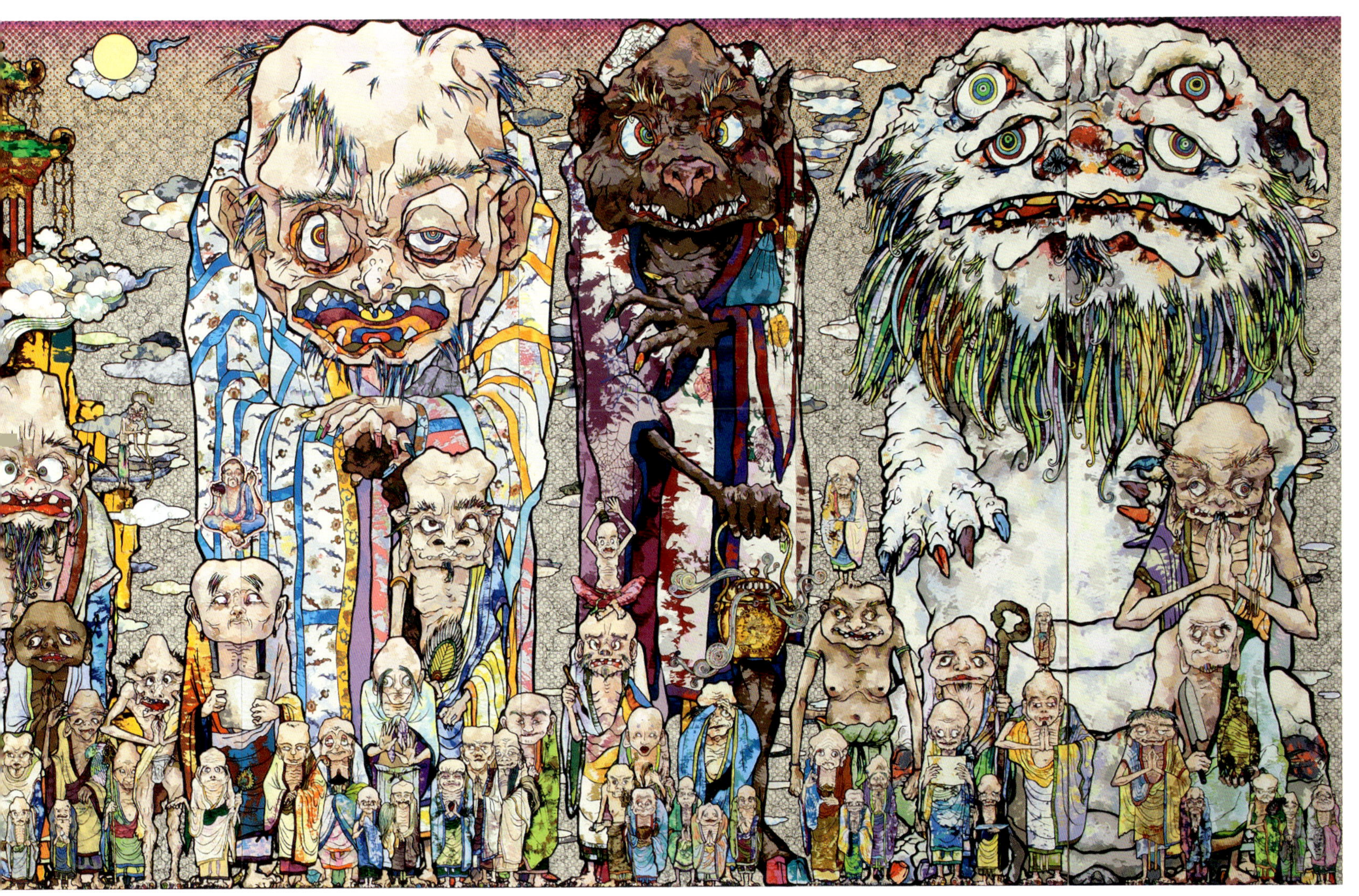

ALBERT **OEHLEN** b. 1954, Krefeld, Germany

Albert Oehlen was born in 1954 in Krefeld, Germany, and attended the Hochschule für Bildende Künste in Hamburg, training under the influential postwar German artist Sigmar Polke. Oehlen developed his practice in Cologne in the 1980s, mentored by figures such as Polke and Jörg Immendorff, while absorbing the influences of punk culture and Maoist politics. Oehlen's first gallerist, Cologne dealer Max Hetzler, fostered a coterie of rebellious and irreverent artists that included Werner Büttner, Georg Herold, and most importantly for Oehlen, Martin Kippenberger. Working closely alongside Kippenberger, Oehlen eventually dedicated himself to a painting practice that continues to this day. From 2000 to 2009, Oehlen also served as professor of painting at the famed Kunstakademie Düsseldorf, and in 2015, he was the subject of a major retrospective at the New Museum in New York. He currently lives and works in Bühlen, Switzerland.

Oehlen's work can be best understood as a critical addendum to the history of twentieth-century painting. Although he is often associated with the Neo-Expressionist and *Neue Wilde* movements of the 1980s, Oehlen has engaged less with the return of painterly figuration then with the legacy of modernist abstraction. Similar to his compatriot Kippenberger, Oehlen embraces a stylistic heterogeneity matched by an iconoclastic approach to subject matter.

Benign objects and blank figures emerge against grounds of clashing color and at times arbitrary delineations of brushwork. Yet Oehlen has also pushed his practice to embrace technologically novel or even amateur techniques: a series from 2008 onwards saw Oehlen only use his fingers to paint while a black-and-white group of paintings from the early 1990s featured primitive drawing software.

The 2008 painting *Angela Molina* exemplifies many of Oehlen's artistic concerns. Named after a successful Spanish actress, the work belongs to a recent series in which Oehlen pasted Spanish street posters directly onto the canvas. A struggle between stubborn abstraction and the figure emerges: smeary passages of earth tones dominate over a pair of eyes, hastily drawn stilettos, and a graphite dog, all of which hang awkwardly on rotated axes. Although the work features inexplicably placed voids and an incongruent chromatic range, Oehlen maintains a balance that both rebukes and invites the eye. J. H.

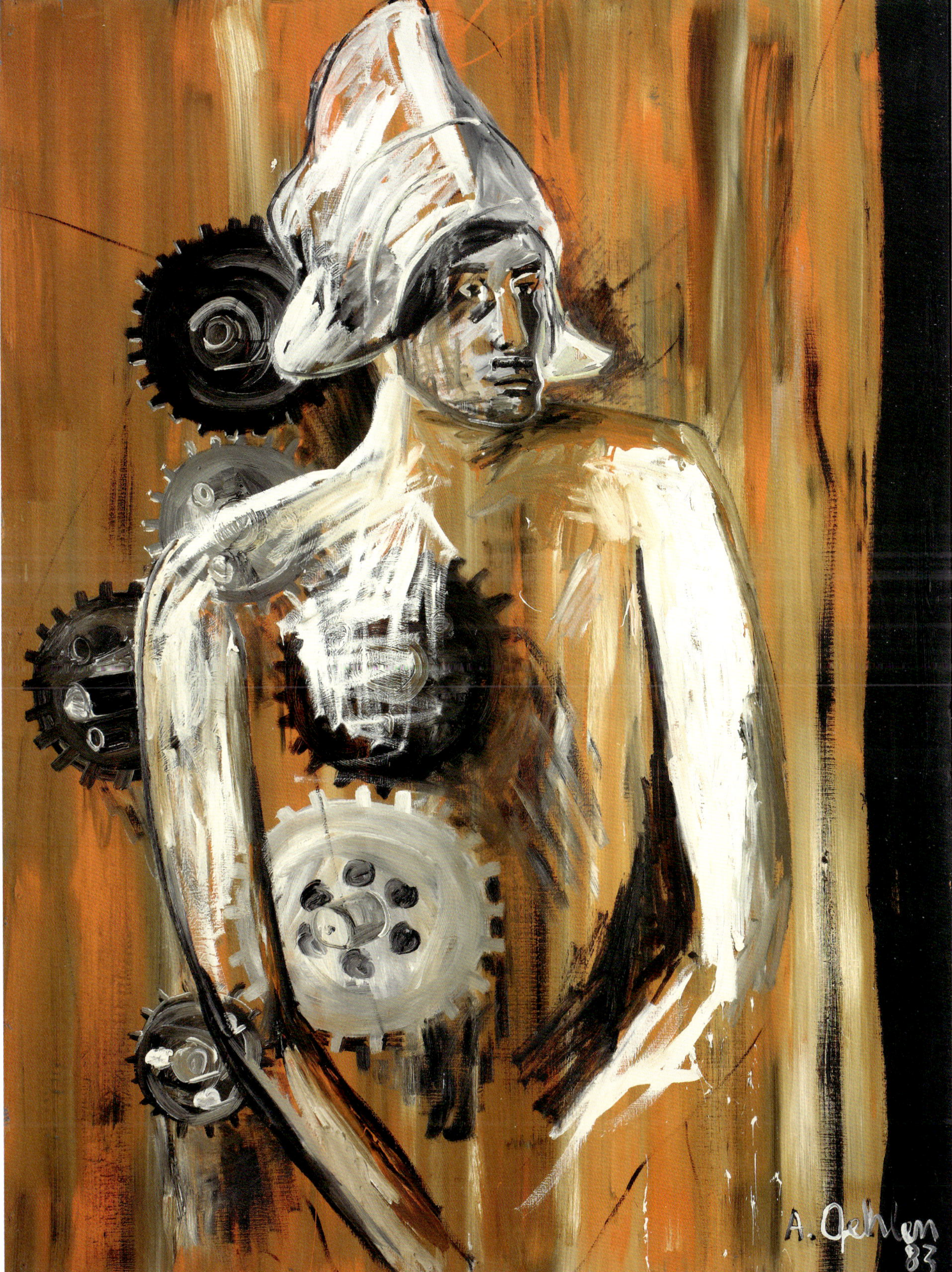

Selbstportrait als Holländerin (Selfportrait as a Dutch woman), 1983
Oil on wood
$76\frac{3}{4} \times 57\frac{7}{8}$ inches (195 × 147 cm)

Treppenhaus alt, 1982
Oil, lacquer, and mirrors on canvas
102 2⁄5 × 70 9⁄10 inches (260 × 180 cm)

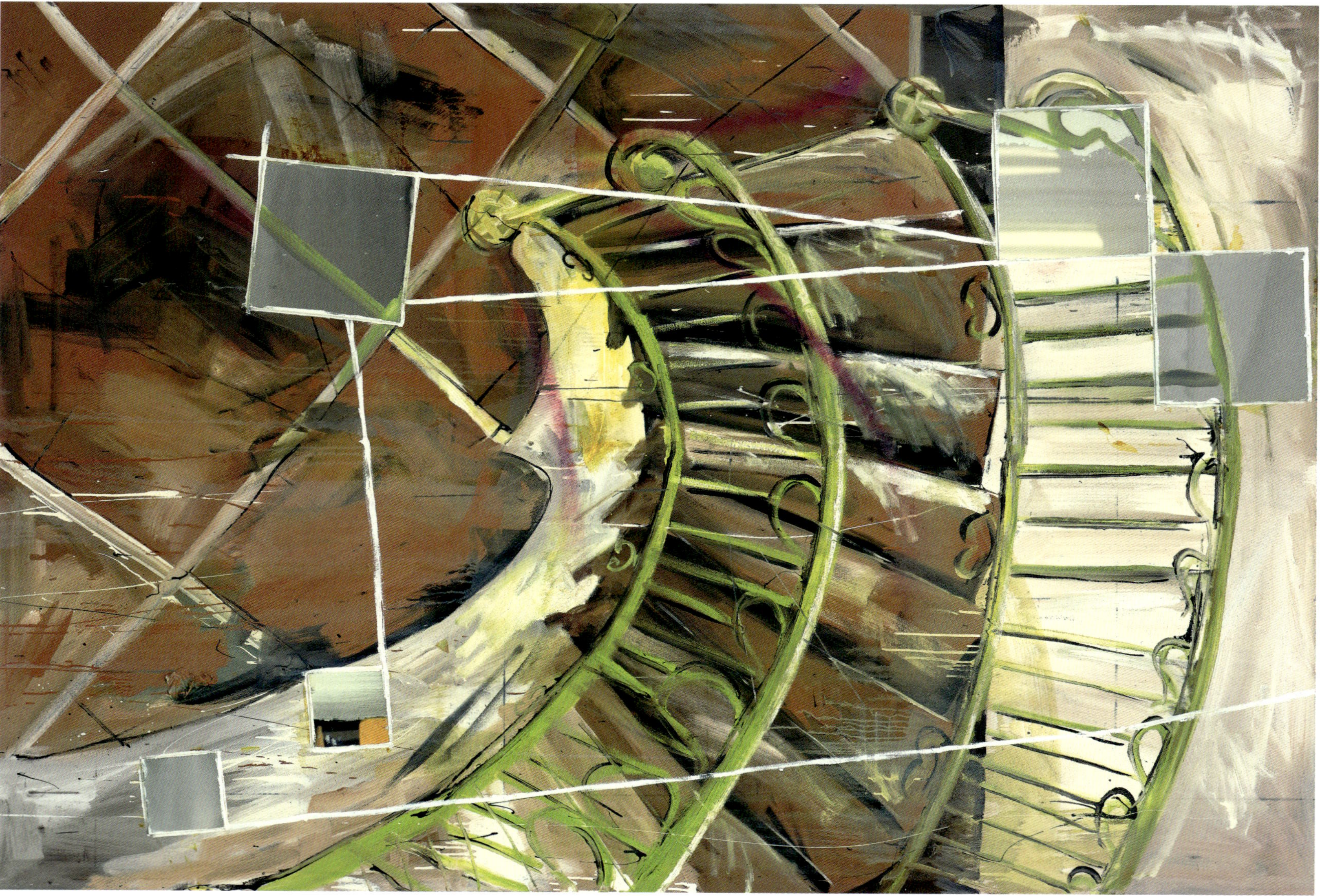

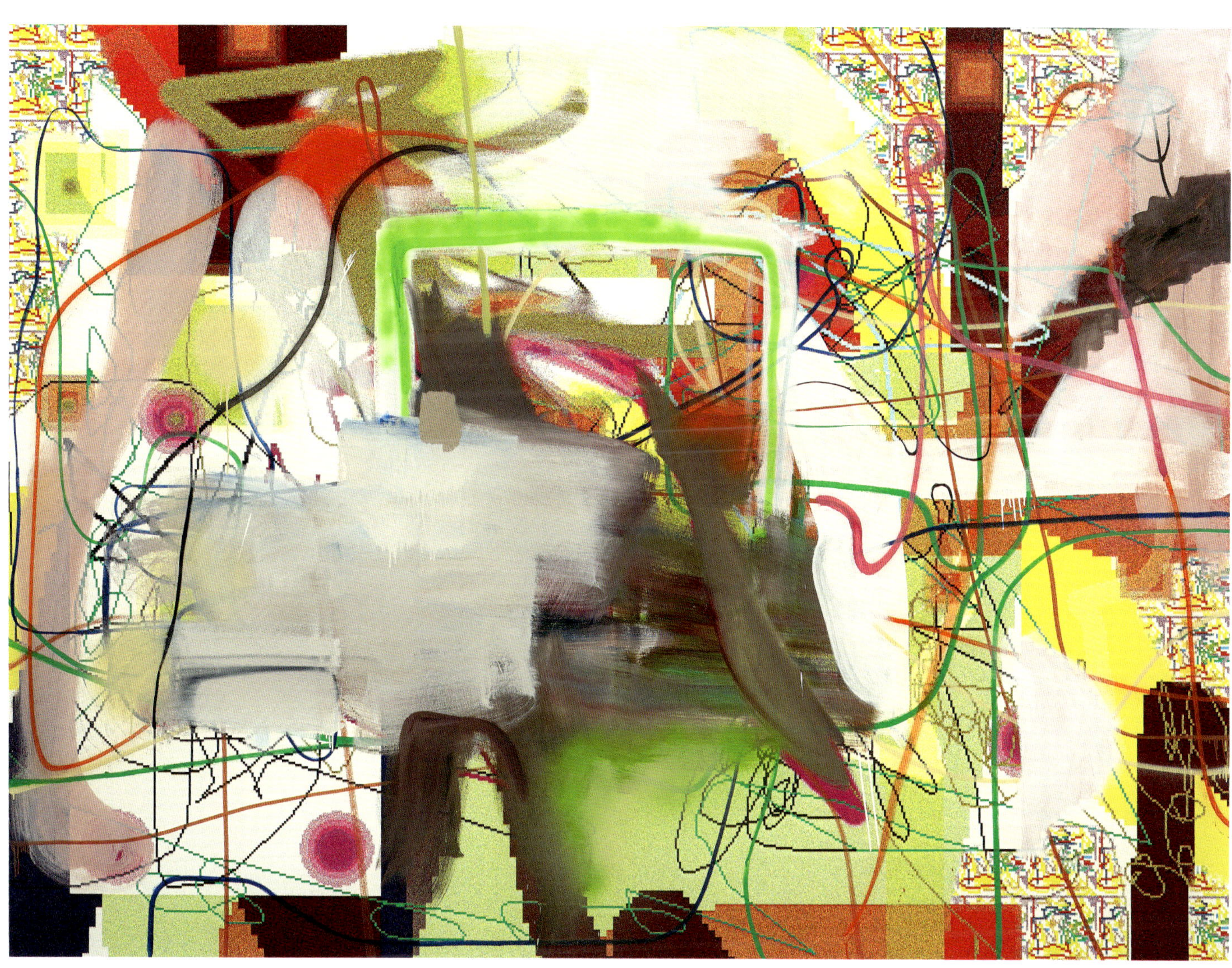

Schnee, 1996
Oil on canvas
85⅞ × 114½ inches (218 × 291 cm)

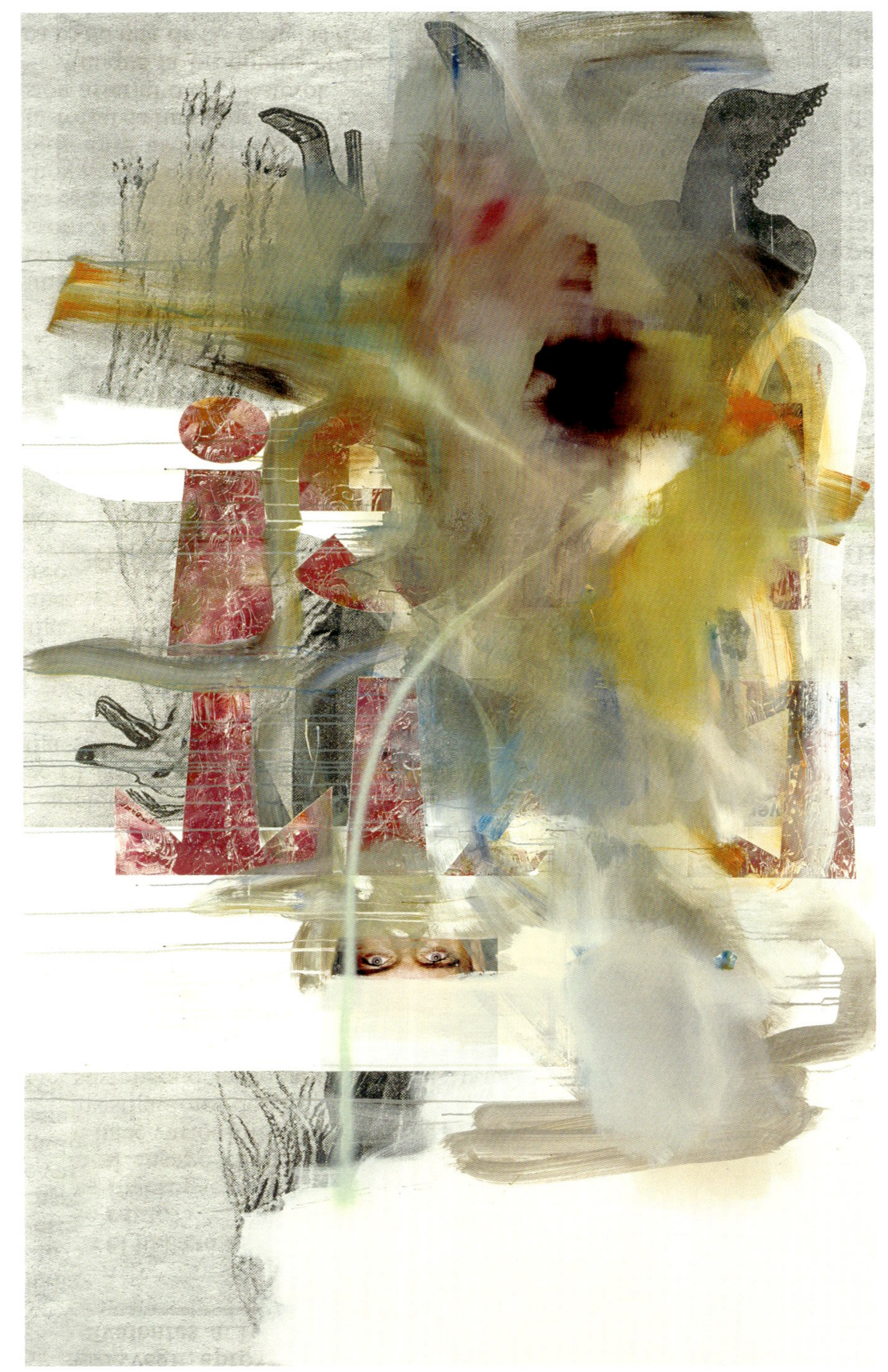

Angela Molina, 2008
Oil and paper on canvas
67 × 110 inches (170 × 280 cm)

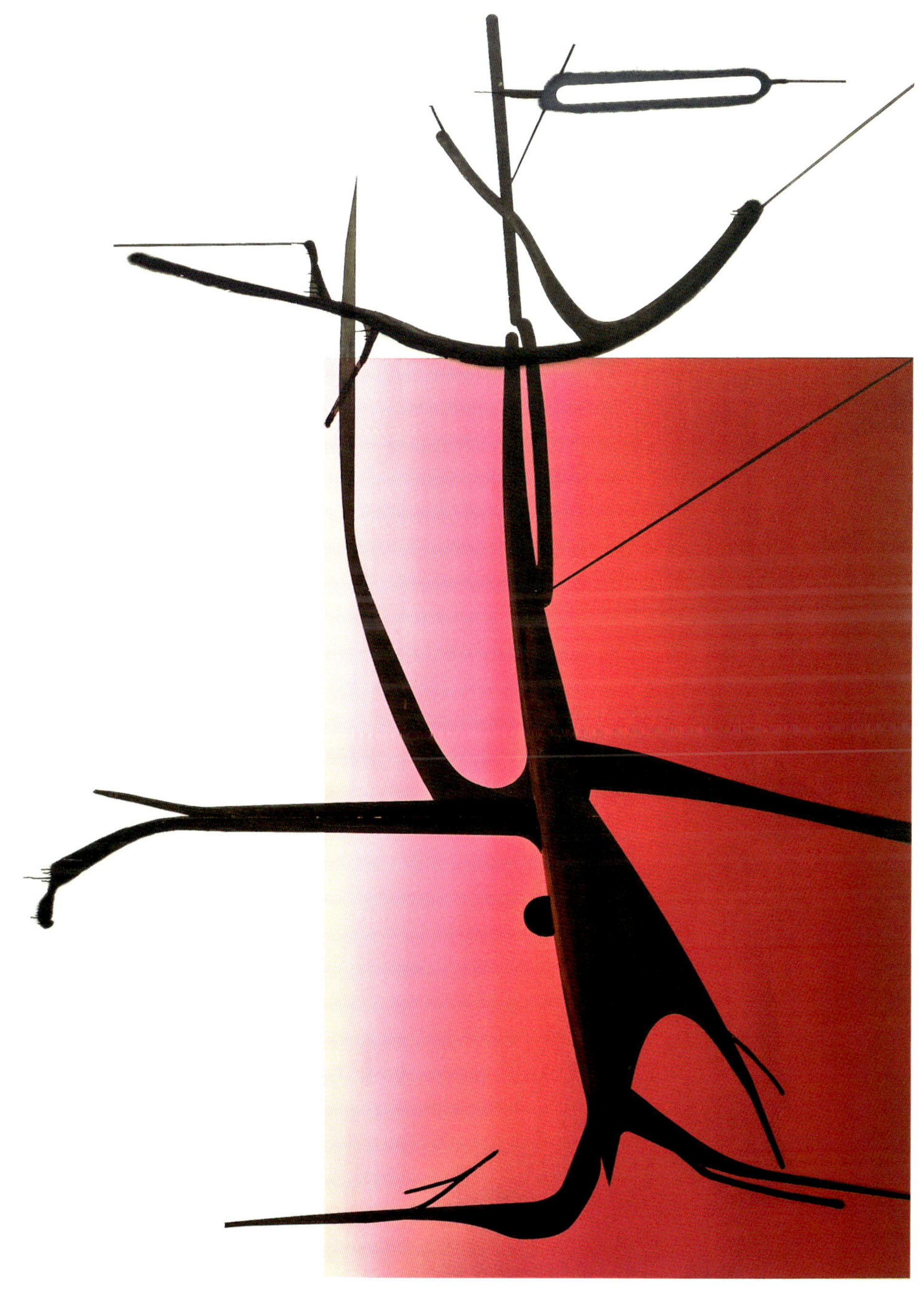

Untitled (Baum) 3, 2014
Oil on dibond
147⅝ × 98 7/16 inches (375 × 250 cm)

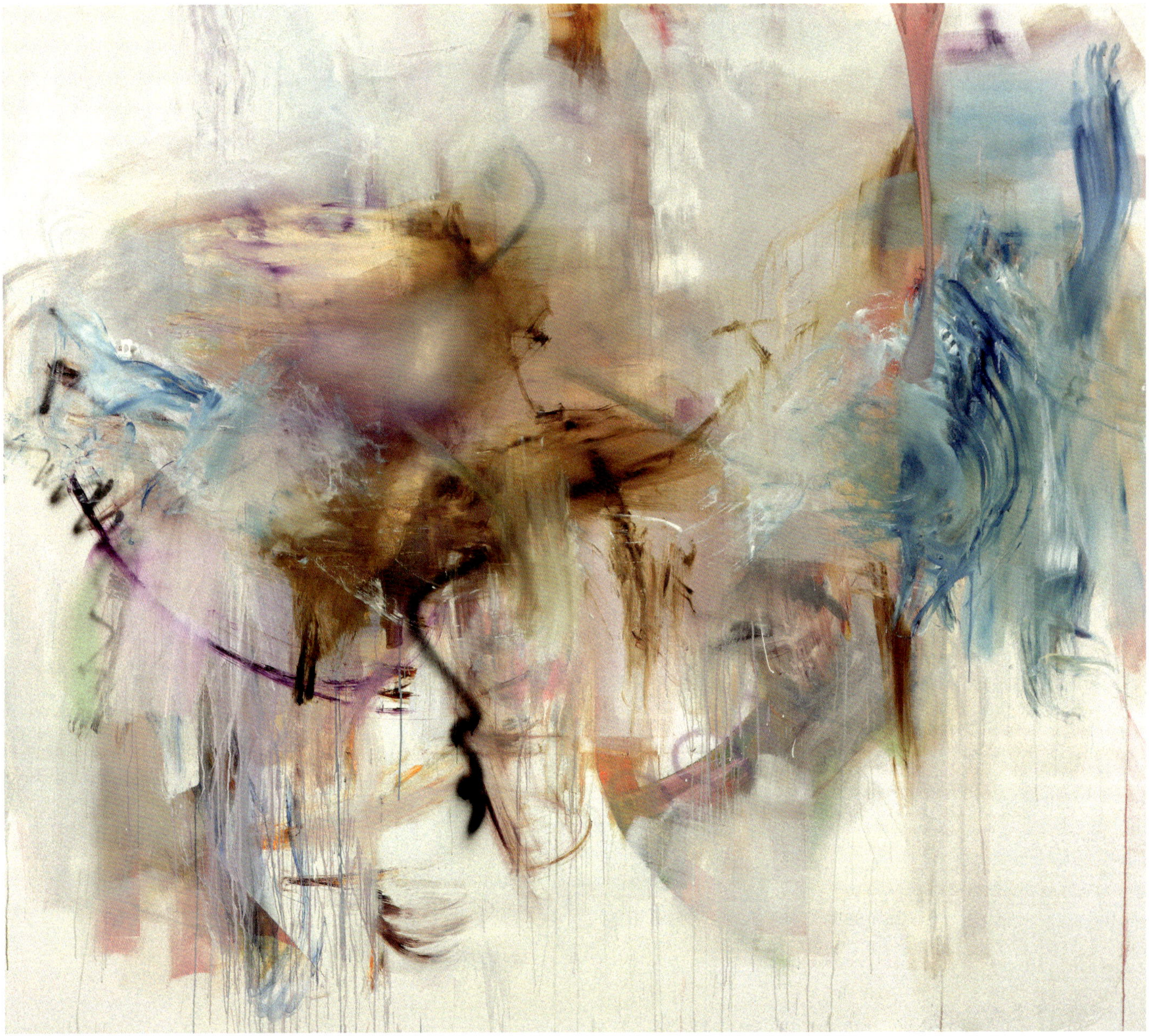

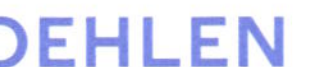

Untitled, 2009
Oil on paper on canvas
78¾ × 90½ inches (200 × 230 cm)

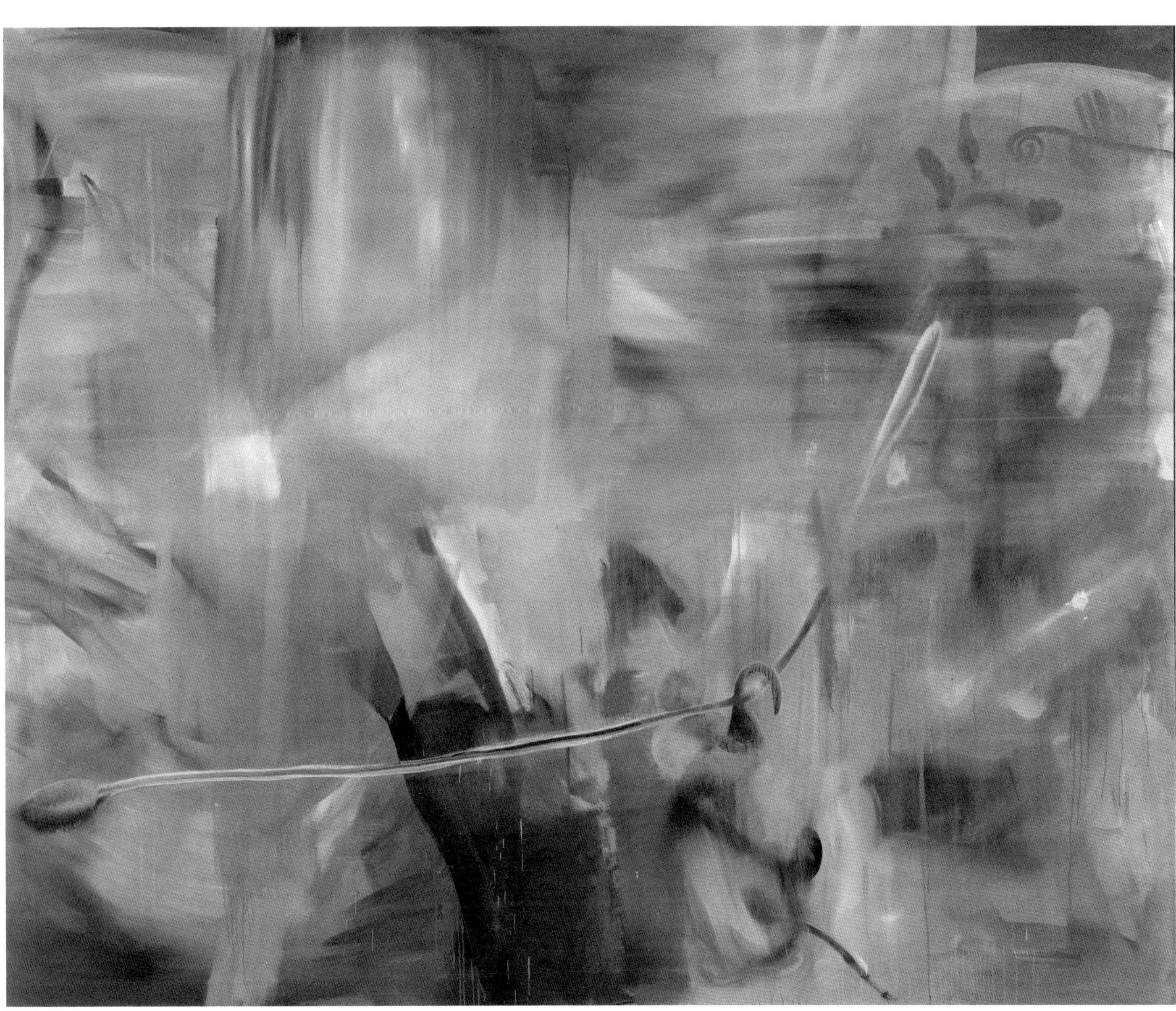

Haken, 2003
Oil on canvas
$86\frac{5}{8} \times 106\frac{1}{4}$ inches (220×270 cm)

CATHERINE OPIE b. 1961, Sandusky, OH

Los Angeles–based artist Catherine Opie has, since the early 1990s, built a body of photographic work focused on the people and spaces around her, namely through projects that investigate the formation of urban and suburban spaces, community, and cultural identity. Born in 1961 in Sandusky, Ohio, she received her BFA in 1985 from the San Francisco Art Institute, where she studied with photographers Larry Sultan and Henry Wessel, and in 1988 completed her MFA at the California Institute of Arts. Opie is currently a professor of photography at the University of California, Los Angeles, where she has taught for the last fifteen years.

Opie first became known for her self-portraits and studio portrait series of friends within the LGBT and S/M leather communities. She went on to photograph vacant urban landscapes in major American cities, including strip malls and freeways in Los Angeles such as *Untitled #1–18, 20–31, 33–42* from the Freeways series, skyways in Minneapolis, and Wall Street city blocks in Manhattan's financial district. Other distinctive series followed including portraits of surfers, high school football players, children, and domestic interiors and outdoor scenes in and around her home.

Over the course of six months in 2011, Opie photographed the Bel-Air residence and interior world of the late actress and activist Elizabeth Taylor. Comprising two series, Closets and Jewels and 700 Nimes Road, the artist took nearly 3,000 images and created an intimate portrait of Taylor through the documentation of her home and belongings. Opie's images capture Taylor's cherished personal items from jewelry, cosmetics, and handbags to her childhood ballet slippers, Oscar statuettes, and framed photographs taken of her with family, friends, royalty, and politicians. In *Untitled #4 (Elizabeth Taylor's closet)* (2012), bright red and pink fabrics drape vertically across the picture, revealing different materials and textures in Taylor's sunlit wardrobe. Halfway through Opie's project, Taylor was hospitalized and passed away shortly afterward. In her serial presentation of objects that held meaning and importance to Taylor, Opie offers a human and touching portrayal of the celebrity's private life. C. R.

Utilizing traditions of portraiture, landscape, and studio photography with formal and technical precision, Opie's unwavering commitment to the sensitive representation of her varied subjects has resulted in powerful and lasting documents of contemporary American life.

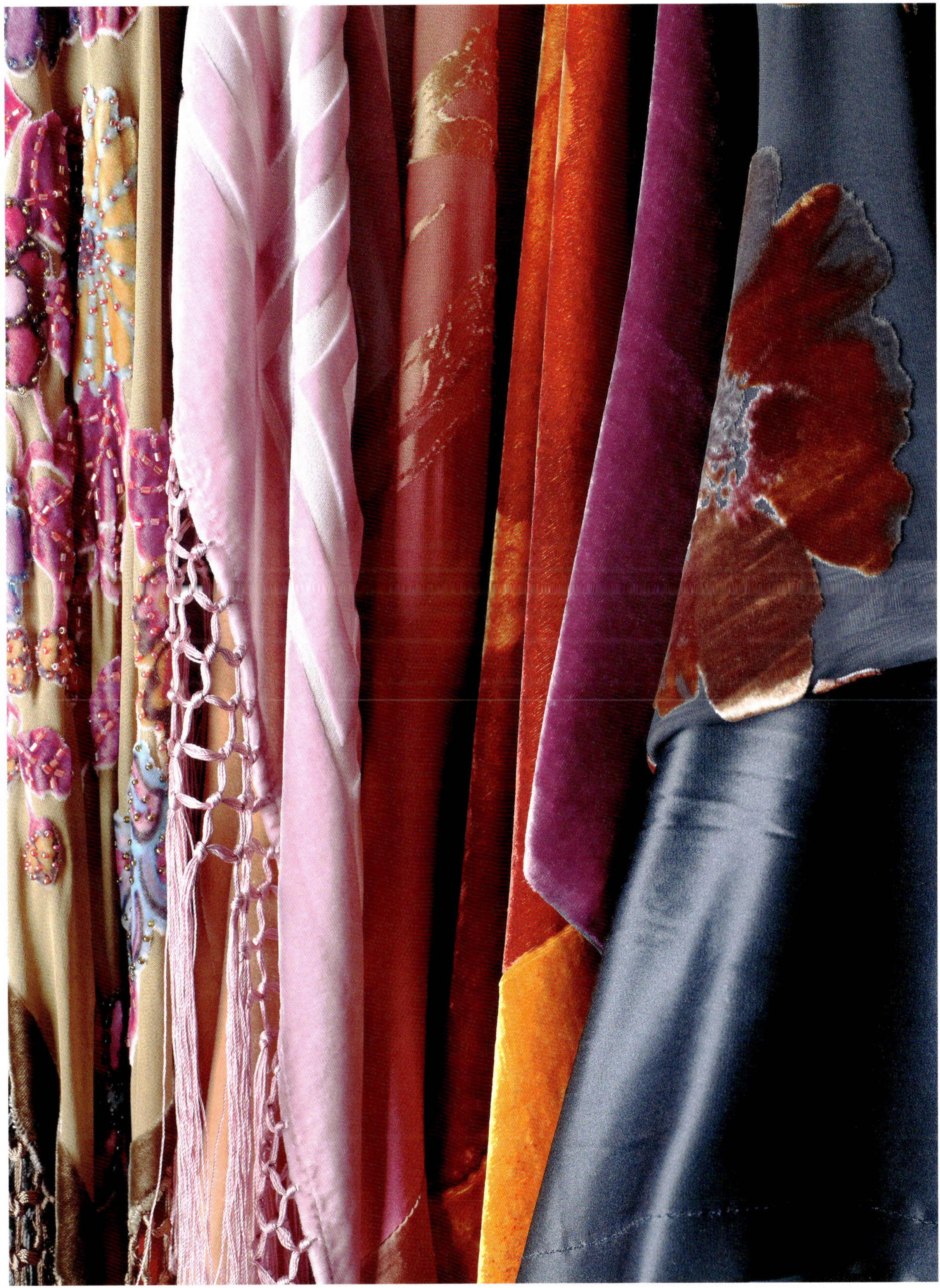

Untitled #4 (Elizabeth Taylor's closet), 2012
Pigment print
40 × 30 inches (101.6 × 76.2 cm)

Untitled #1–18, 20–31, 33–42
from Freeway series, 1994–95
Platinum prints
2 1/4 × 6 3/4 inches (5.7 × 22.2 cm) each
Edition of 5, 2/2 AP

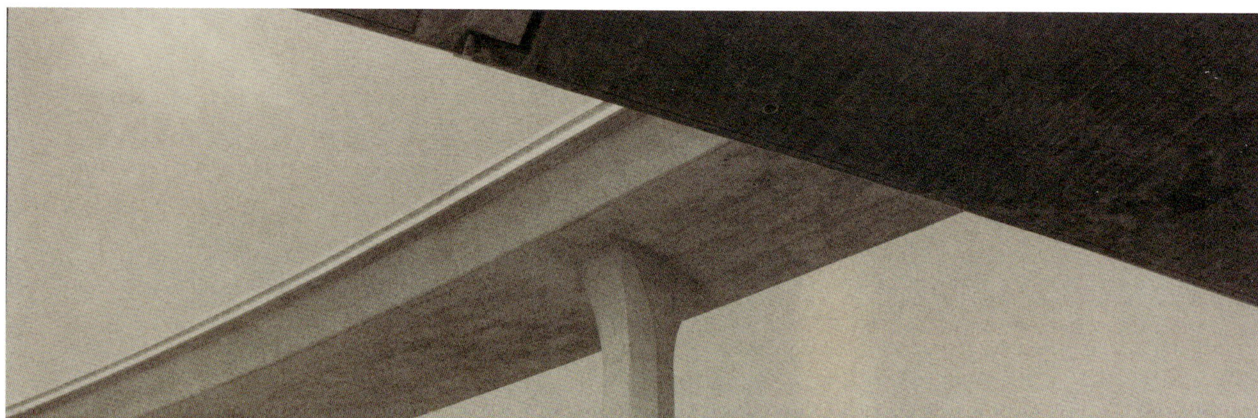

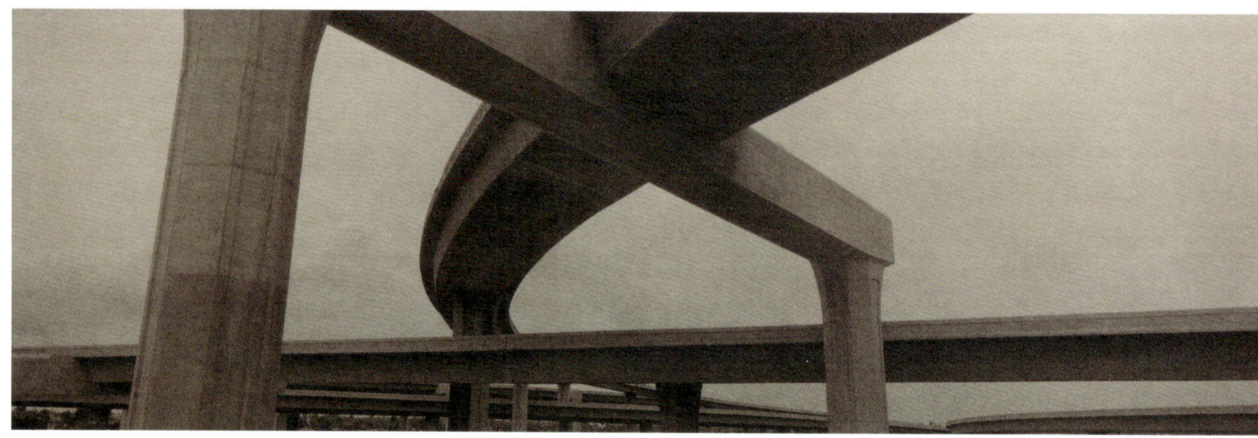

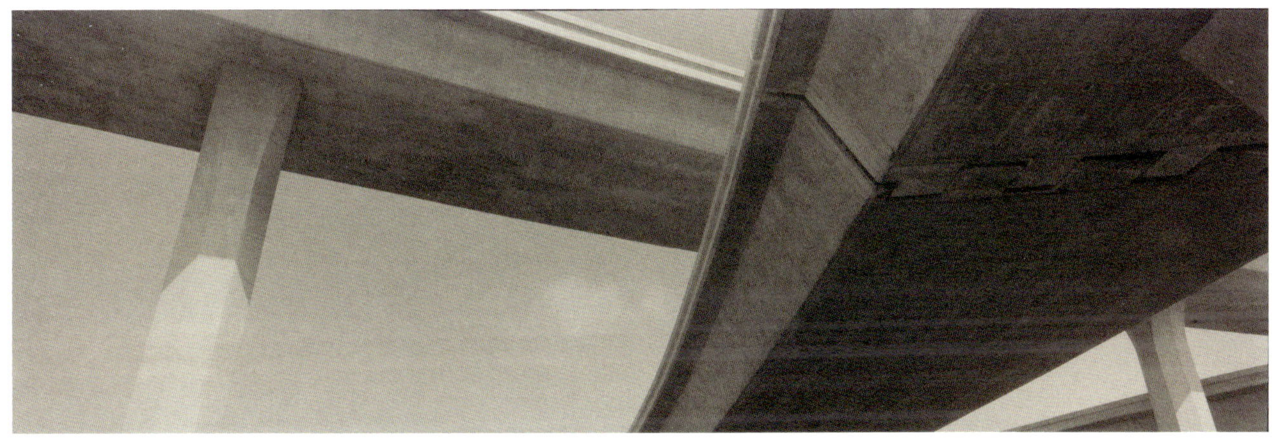

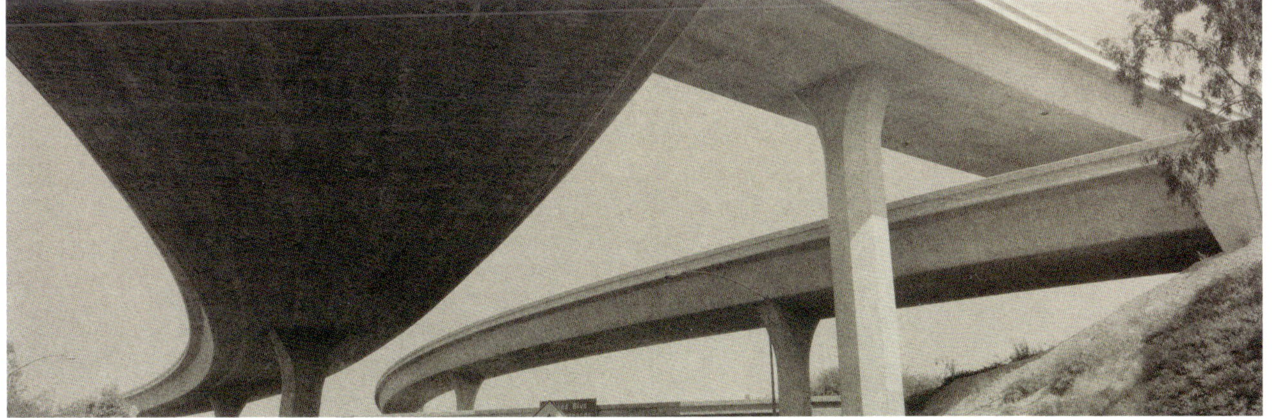

GABRIEL OROZCO b. 1962, Jalapa, Veracruz, Mexico

Roto Spinal, 2005
Acrylic on canvas
79 × 79 inches (200.7 × 200.7 cm)

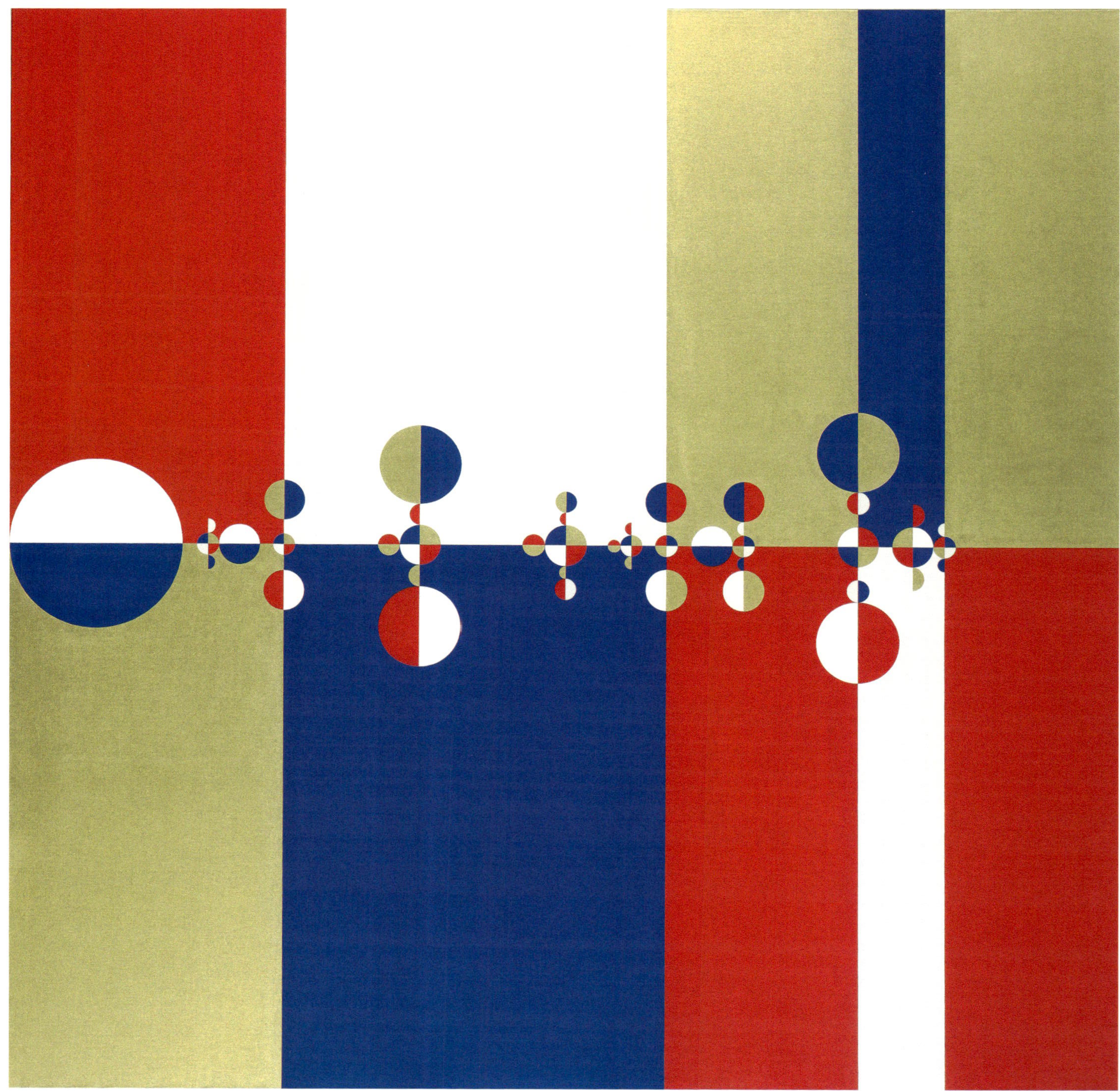

Gabriel Orozco is one of the most renowned Mexican artists working today. His multifaceted approach to art making examines his various interests, which range from complex geometry to politics to mapping urban landscapes to finding beauty in everyday objects, the latter of which he masterfully and subtly alters to reveal new ways of looking at the quotidian, usually with a sense of humor.

Born in 1962 in Jalapa, Veracruz, Mexico, Orozco studied at the Escuela Nacional de Artes Plasticas in Mexico City before continuing his studies at the Círculo de Bellas Artes in Madrid, where he created his first works from found objects as he walked to and from the arts academy. In the 1990s Orozco objected to working from a studio in reaction against the mainstream commercialization of art in the 1980s.

Instead, he created art in the streets, his apartment, or wherever he felt inspired, using objects he found in the street such as used airplane boarding passes or deflated soccer balls. His diverse practice includes sculpture, photography, painting, installation, and video, and he employs these media to blur the line between art and the everyday.

By the mid 2000s, Orozco returned to the studio to work in the traditional medium of painting for his series, Samurai Tree, which he created using computer and drafting software to render geometric circles, rectangles, and permutations of color. The process relied on chance and an organic progression with an uncertain end. In *Roto Spinal* (2005) from this series, for example, Orozco began with a circle at the center of the canvas, as the centrifugal point of the plane. As he moved toward the frame, the circle grew into more circles in different sizes along horizontal and vertical lines. Based on the Samurai move in the game of chess, the sequence of colors jumps from the axis into the shapes. Like all of his Samurai Tree paintings, the end effect of *Roto Spinal* appears as a colorful geometric field. This confrontation between the organic and the mechanical is characteristic of much of Orozco's work.

Widely exhibited, Orozco has participated in numerous international exhibitions including the 1999 Carnegie International, Documenta 11, and the 50th and 51stVenice Biennales. He has had solo exhibitions at Museo Internacional Rufino Tamayo; The Museum of Contemporary Art, Los Angeles; Hirshhorn Museum and Sculpture Garden; Serpentine Gallery, London; Museo Nacional Centre de Arte Reina Sofia; The Museum of Modern Art; Deutsche Guggenheim, Berlin; and the Moderna Museet Stockholm, among others. Today he lives and works in New York, Paris, and Mexico City. L. C.

***Engranaje azul (Blue gear)*, 2010**
Tempera and burnished gold leaf
on sabine wood
$23\frac{1}{4} \times 23\frac{1}{4}$ inches (59×59 cm)

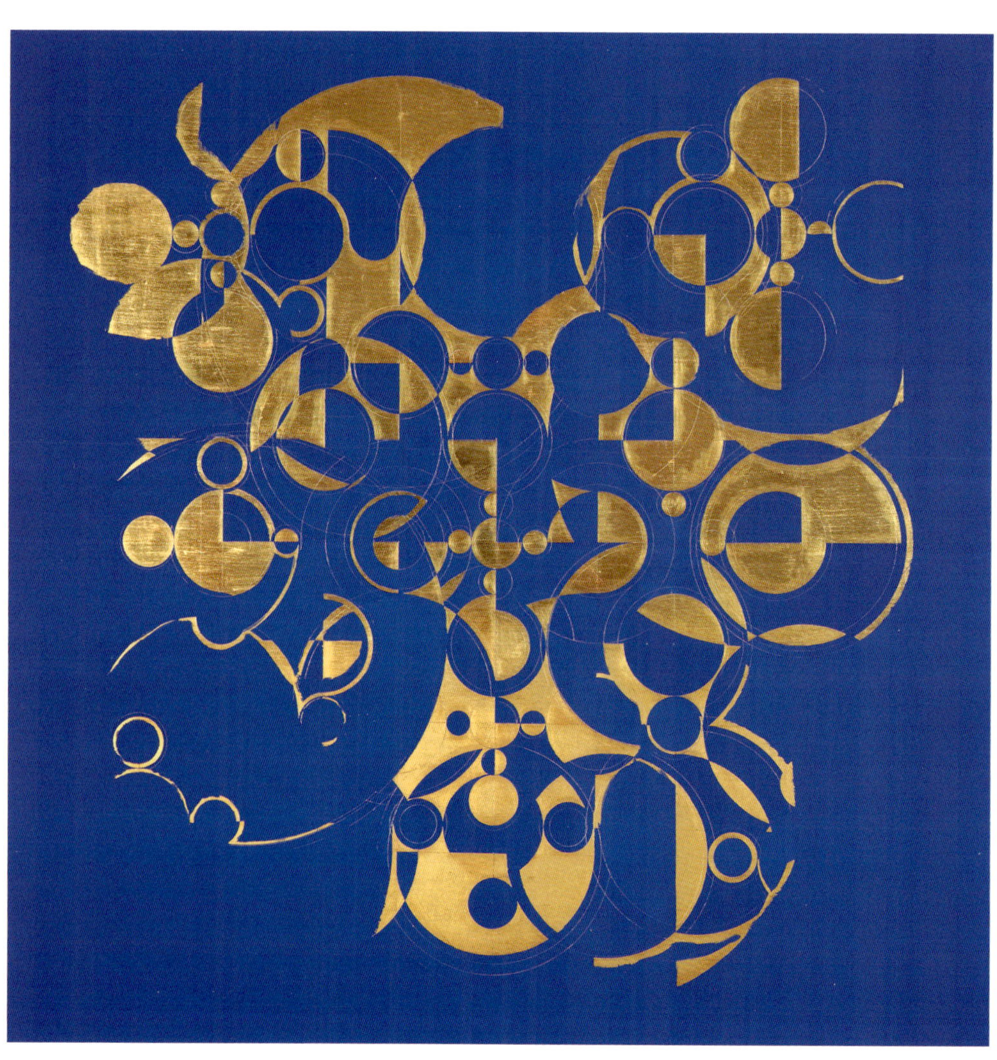

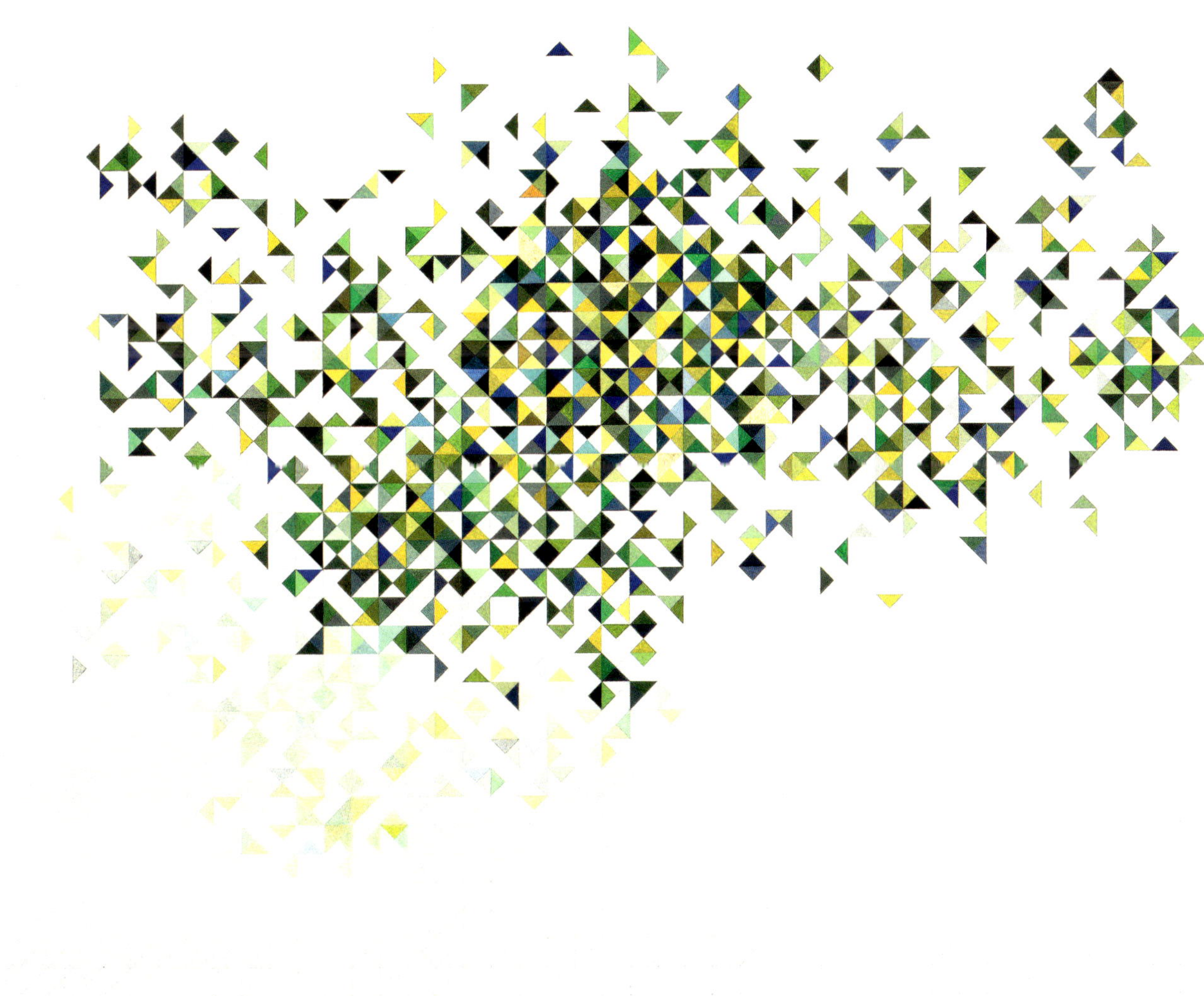

Untitled, 2016
Tempera and burnished gold leaf on linen canvas
78¾ × 78¾ inches (200 × 200 cm)

DAMIÁN ORTEGA

b. 1967, Mexico City, Mexico

Mexican artist Damián Ortega began his career as a political cartoonist and, despite having no formal art education, has become internationally recognized for his work, which explores the economy, culture, and aesthetics with both intellectual rigor and a sense of playfulness. Ortega honed his craft through weekly experimental workshops at his friend Gabriel Orozco's home in Mexico City in the late 1980s and early 1990s. These workshops eventually developed into the Taller de los Viernes (Friday Workshop), which included other Mexican artists such as Gabriel Kuri, Abraham Cruzvillegas, and Dr. Lakra.

By employing wit and humor in his sculptures, installations, performances, and videos, Ortega has been recognized for recombining and disassembling mass-produced, found, and vernacular objects to expose the complex social, economic, and political forces that underlie the current material culture and contemporary landscape.

It is through these materials that Ortega can practice his "mischievous process of transformation and dysfunction."

In *Architecture without Architects* (2010), for example, a living room is dissected and suspended from the ceiling in a cosmological scale. Keeping with his first profession, the exploding installation was inspired by an image Ortega saw in a newspaper article of an interior of a house in New Zealand damaged by an earthquake. In line with his trademark disassembled and suspended objects, in *Building #4* (2009), which is part of a larger series, Ortega pressure-sanded a seven-foot-tall rectangular plinth of red brick and mortar into an irregular hulk. The sculpture appears as a ruin or perhaps a fragment of a dilapidated building. In this way, Ortega alters the viewers' perception and propels them into a new world.

Born in Mexico City, Ortega now lives and works in Mexico City and Berlin. He has presented work in solo exhibitions at the Institute of Contemporary Art, Philadelphia; Kunsthalle Basel; Tate Modern; Museu da Arte Pampulha, Belo Horizonte, Brazil; The Museum of Contemporary Art, Los Angeles; Centre Georges Pompidou; Institute of Contemporary Art, Boston; and Museo Jumex, Mexico City, among others. He has also participated in the 50th Venice Biennale and the 2006 São Paulo Biennial. L. C.

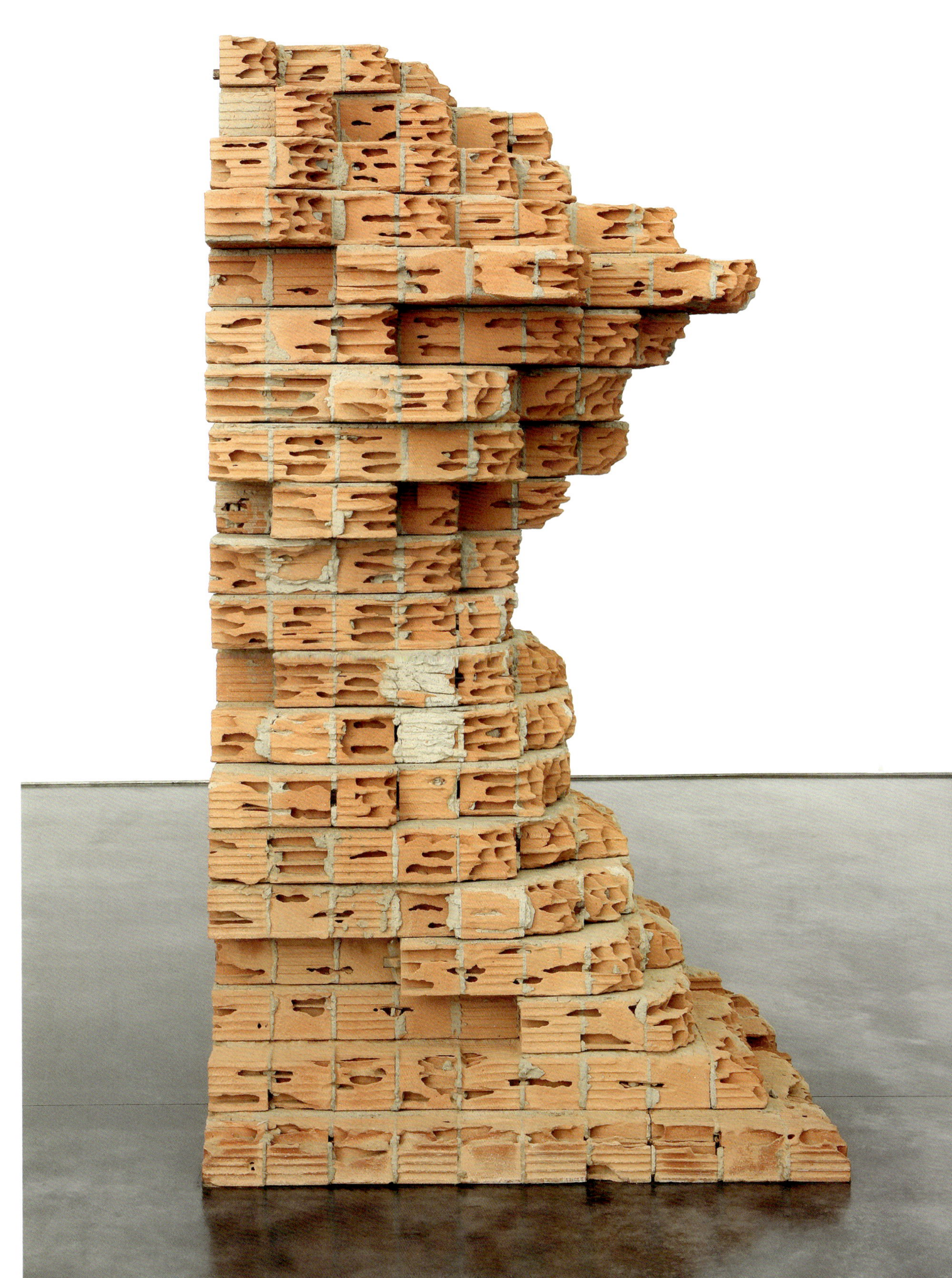

Building #4, 2009
Unique structure, eroded bricks, and
metallic internal support
$84\frac{11}{16} \times 63 \times 51\frac{3}{16}$ inches (215 × 160 × 130 cm)

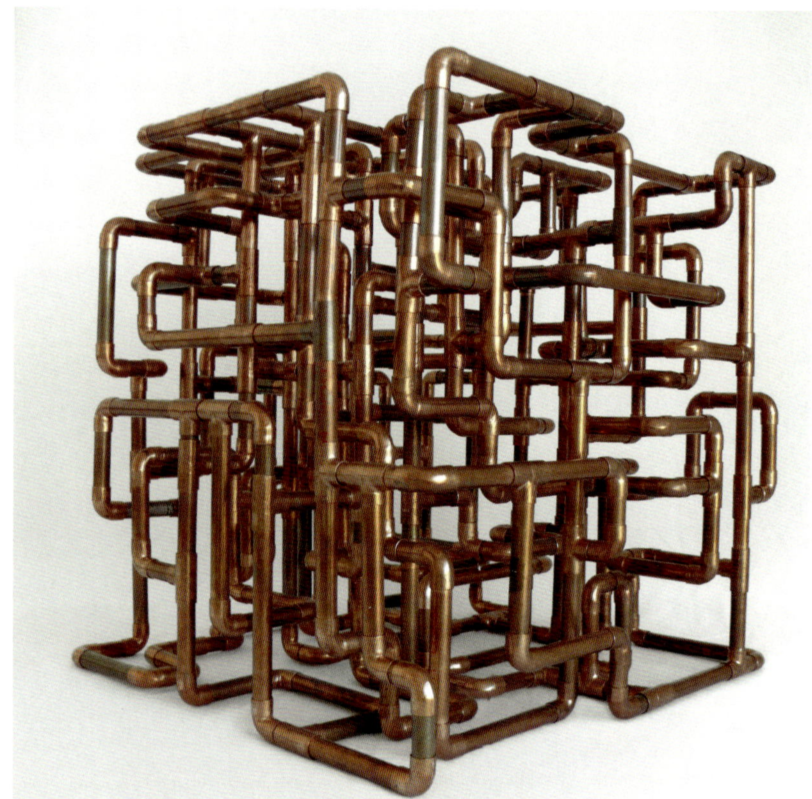

Labyrinth 1, 2015
Copper
$17\frac{3}{4} \times 17\frac{3}{4} \times 17\frac{3}{4}$ inches ($45 \times 45 \times 45$ cm)

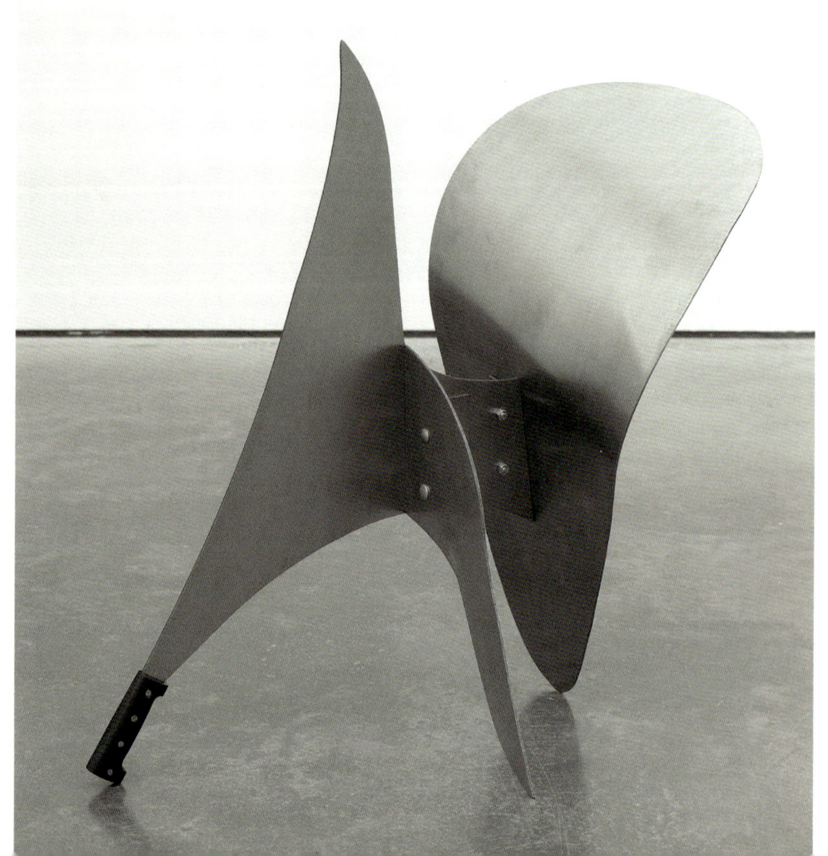

Tool in the expanded field. Dissection in the open space (Alexander Calder tool), 2013
Sheet metal and plastic
$31\frac{1}{2} \times 24\frac{7}{16} \times 19\frac{11}{16}$ inches ($80 \times 62.1 \times 50$ cm)

ORTEGA

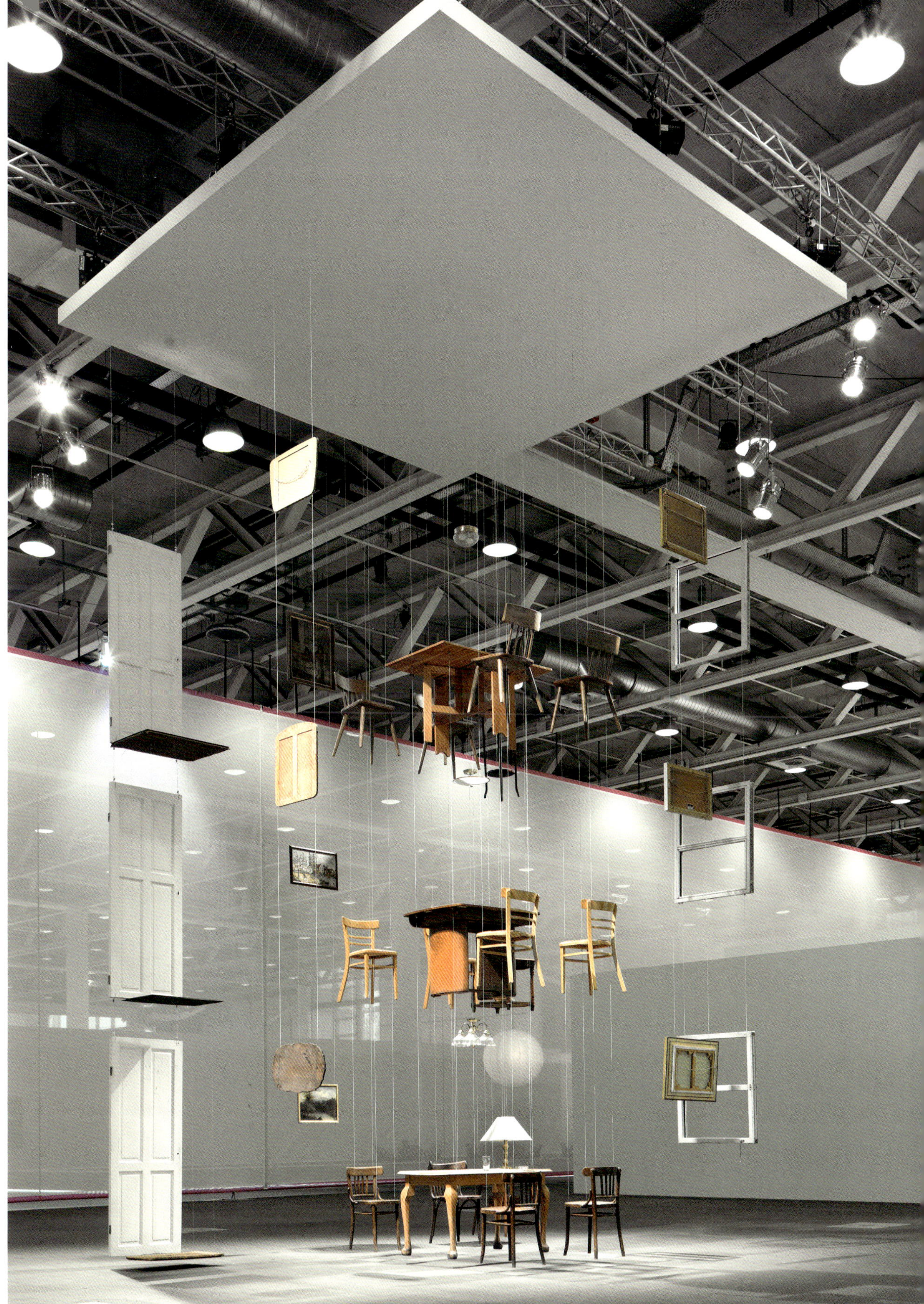

Architecture without Architects, 2010
Mixed media
Dimensions variable

LAURA OWENS b. 1970, Euclid, OH

Laura Owens is a painter's painter. She approaches the practice with full force and unreserved commitment. When many artists are trying to make paintings that look like something else, Owens makes paintings that actually look like paintings and are about painting, as she addresses the multitude of challenges the medium presents seemingly all at once. Her paintings are playful, complex, detailed, layered, and more than anything, confrontational.

Because Owens often employs Photoshop to construct her carefully composed canvases, the paintings also retain a mysterious quality with their screen-printed text, illusive shadows, automated gestures, and sneaky erasures. Collage also plays a large role, as in *Untitled* (2013) where Owens attached bicycle wheels to the canvas. Her paintings always wear many hats—at once abstract and representational, mechanic and organic, heroic and accessible, flat but also full of depth.

Owens allows her paintings to assume different roles other than painting such as in *Untitled* (2015), a group of twenty "clock" paintings whose canvases contain revolving, battery-powered hands of a clock, even though they don't tell the time. Each painting is different: some feature brightly colored grids, while others show amorphous blocks of color or freehand gesture, some are hand-painted and some are embroidered, some have text and others don't, some contain collage elements while others are completely two-dimensional, with one painting often continuing or picking up on a pattern or phrase begun by another. In this particular grouping of clocks, no clock numbers surround the actual clock hands, which are simply raised lines that move and cast their shadows as they tick. Time, this invisible force, is abstracted by turning the clock, the object that represents the passage of time, into a kinetic object that pokes fun at the concept it's meant to convey.

Born in 1970 in Euclid, Ohio, Owens is a graduate of the Rhode Island School of Design and the California Institute of the Arts (CalArts). Solo exhibition venues include Secession, Vienna; Kunstmuseum Bonn; Kunsthalle Zürich; Camden Arts Centre, London; The Museum of Contemporary Art, Los Angeles; Milwaukee Art Museum; and Isabella Stewart Gardner Museum, Boston, among others. J. G. M.

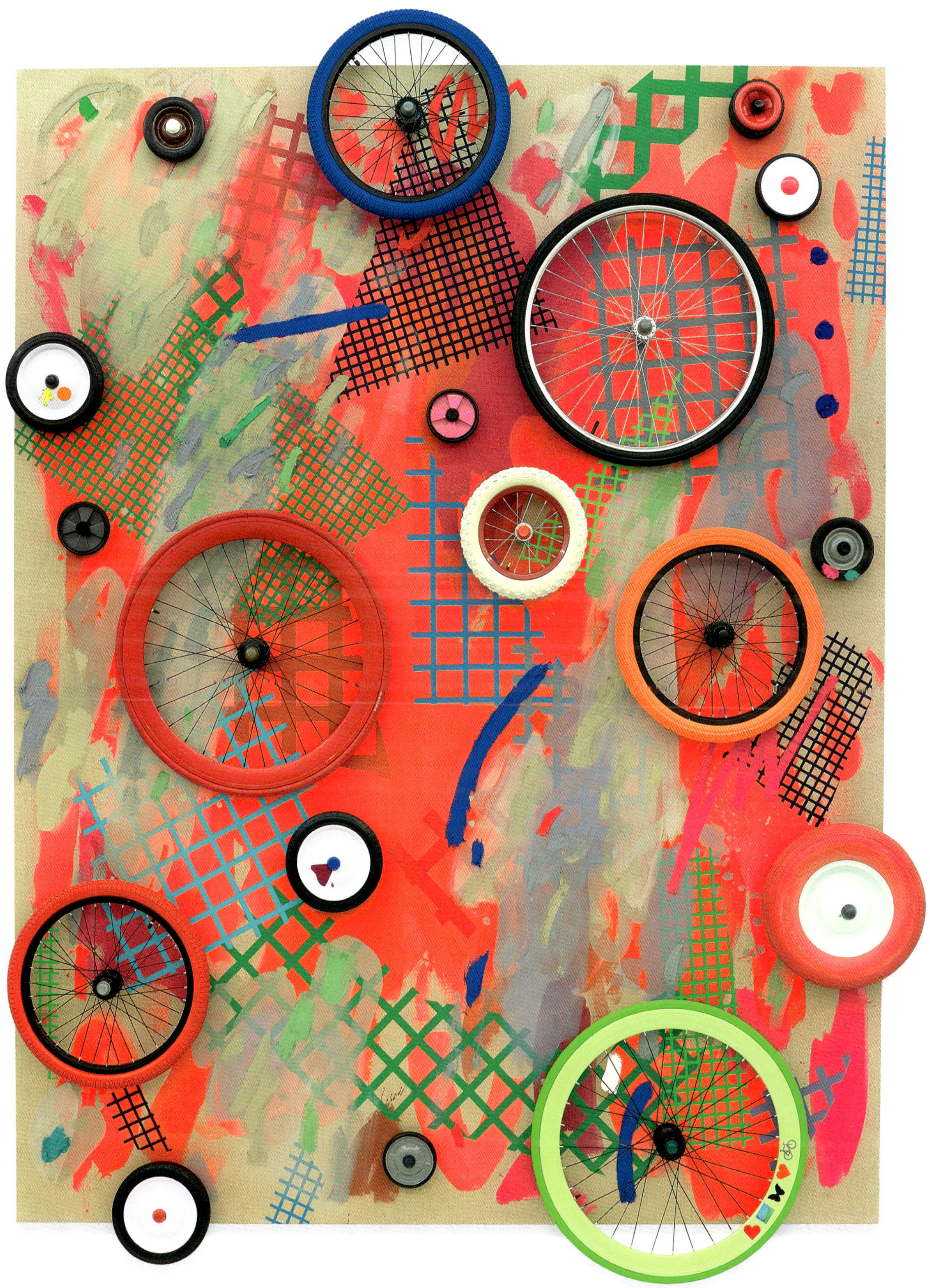

Untitled, 2013
Oil, Flashe, acrylic, and collage on linen
108 × 84 inches (274.3 × 213.4 cm)

Untitled, 2015
Acrylic, oil, Flashe, charcoal, screenprinting ink, pastel, clock motor, mechanical parts, pumice, aquarium rocks, buttons, cardboard, wallpaper, yarn, and collage on linen and hand-dyed linen
20 panels: 26 × 26 inches (66 × 66 cm) each

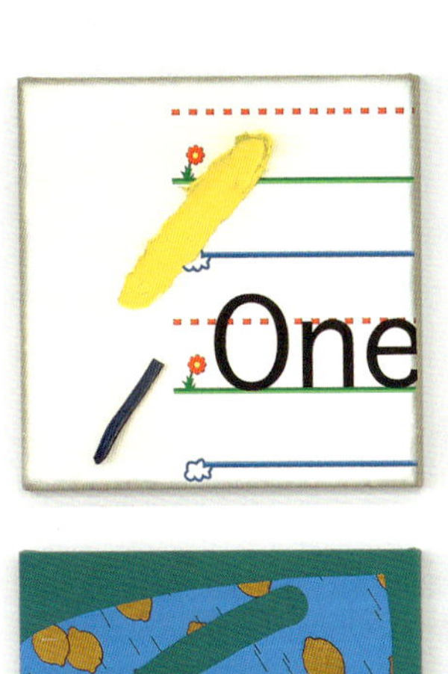

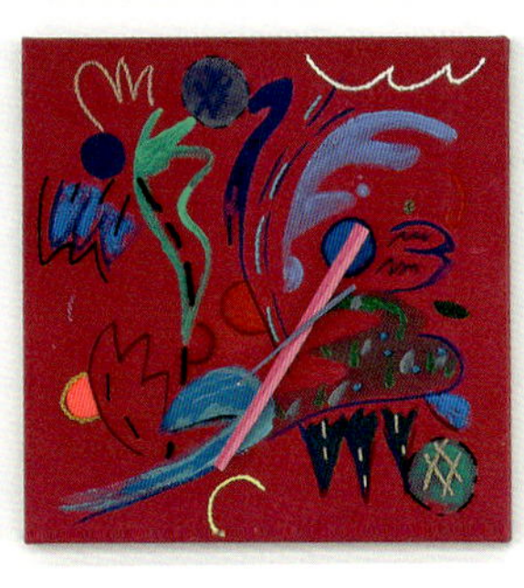
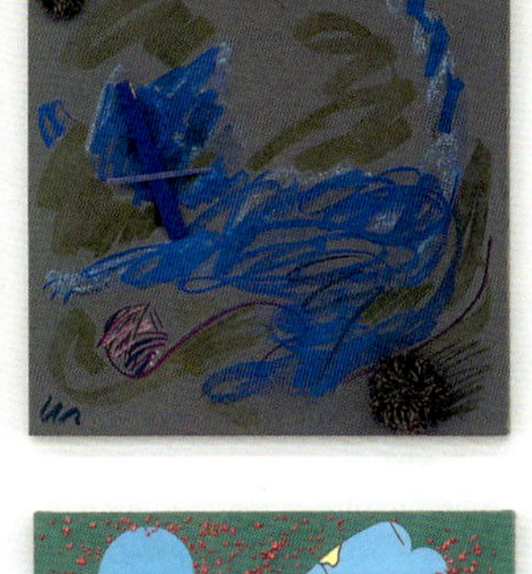
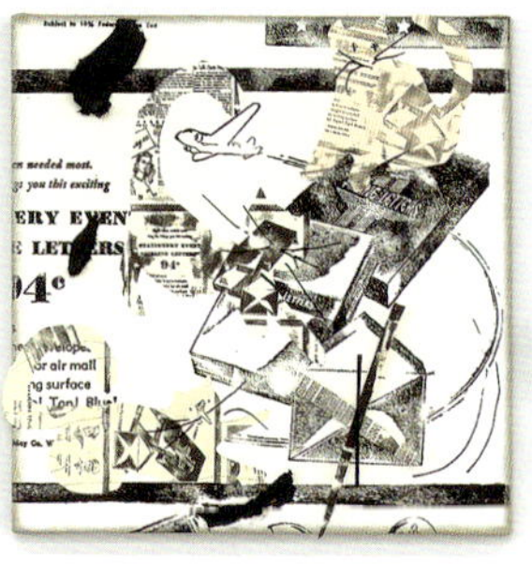
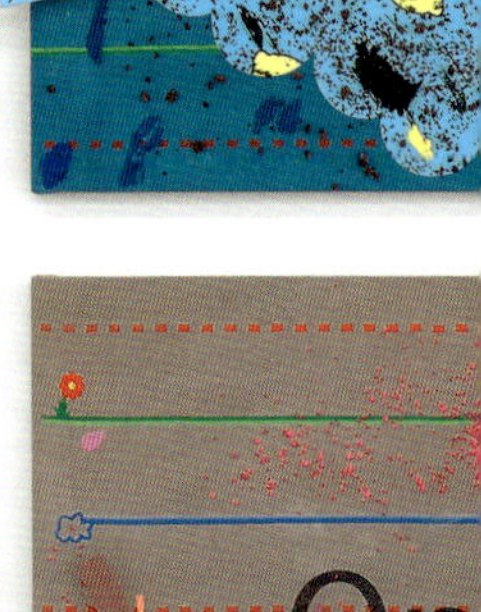
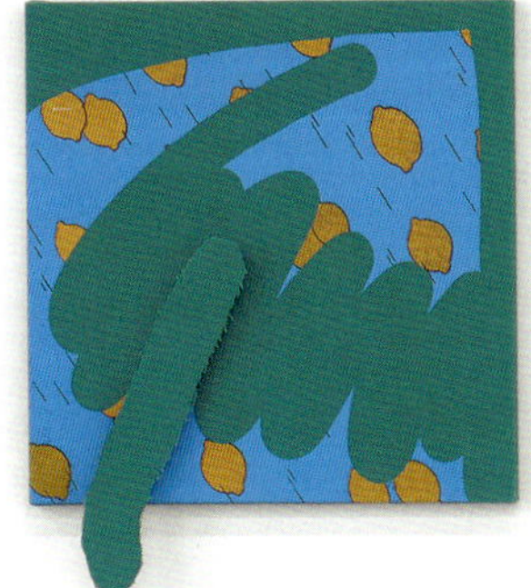
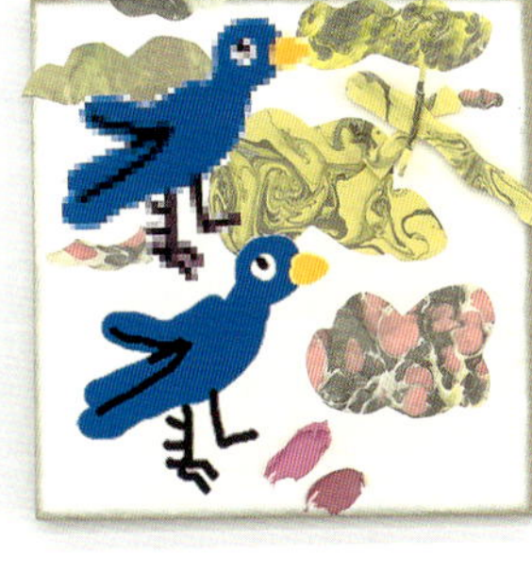
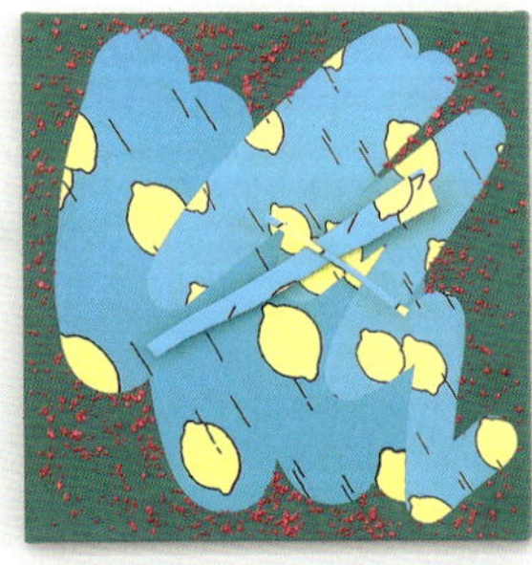
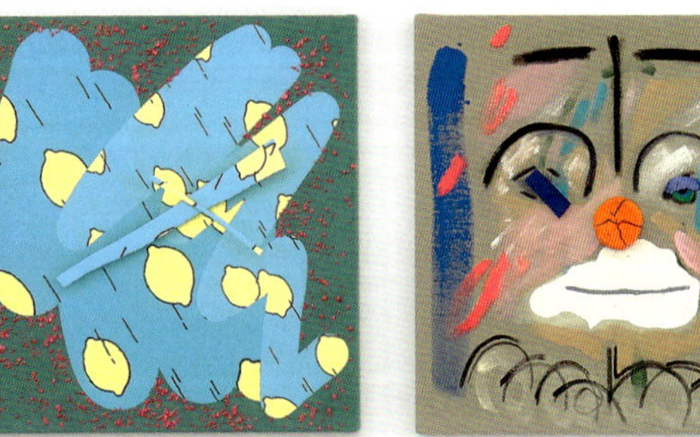
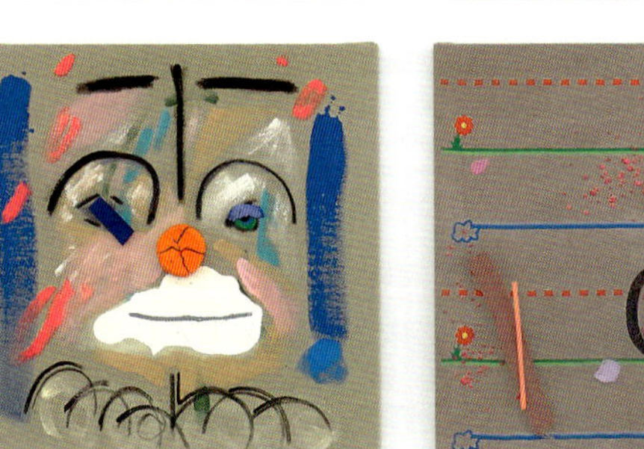

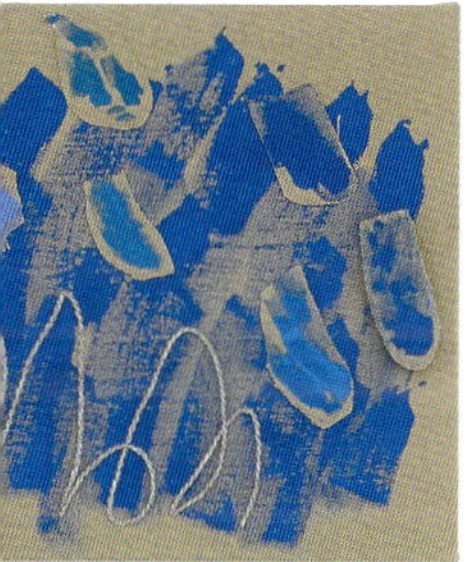
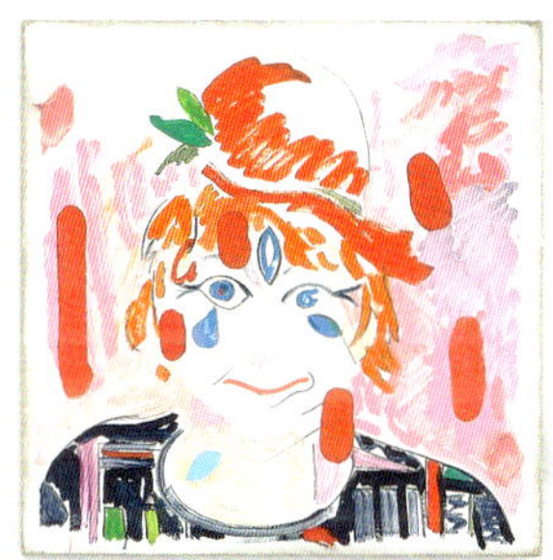
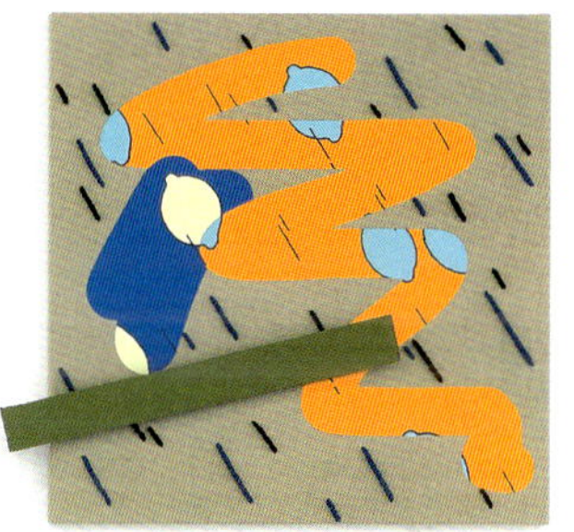
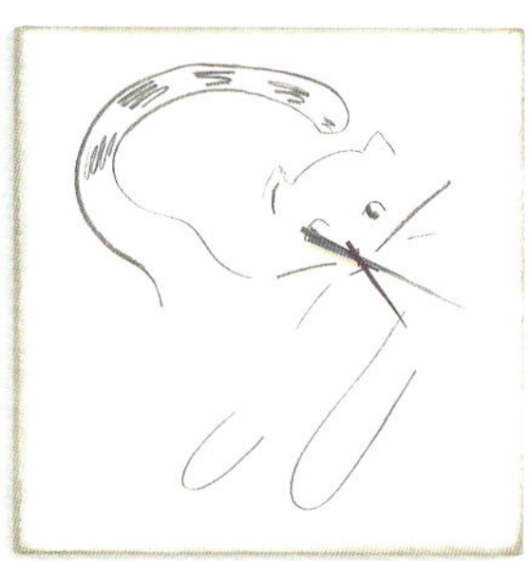
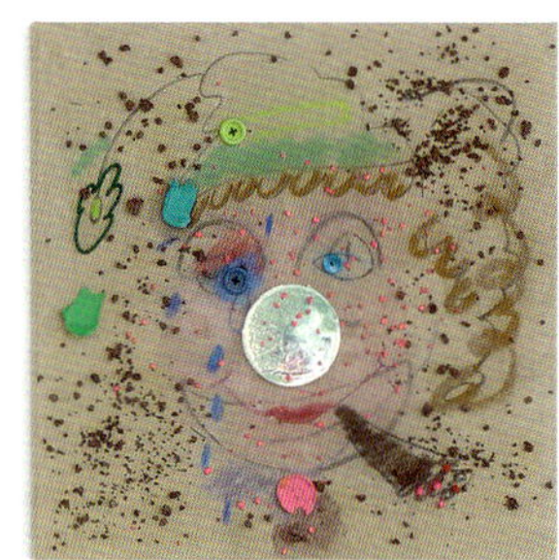
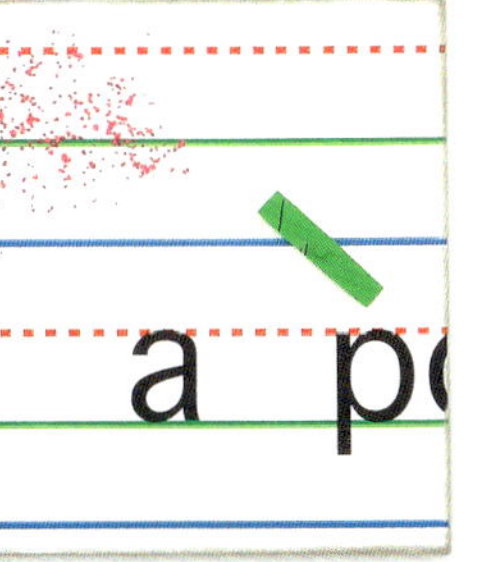
a
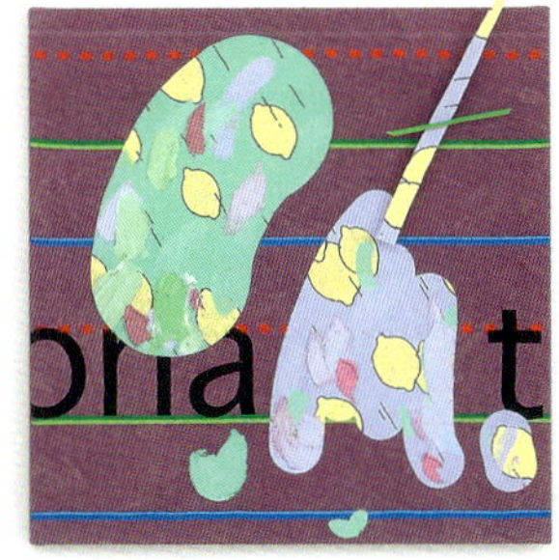
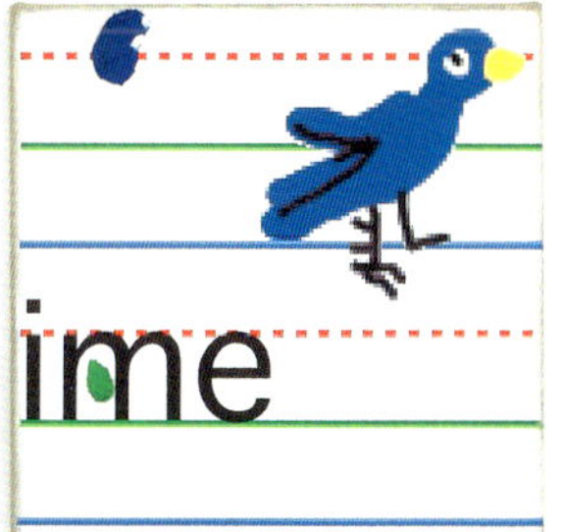
ime
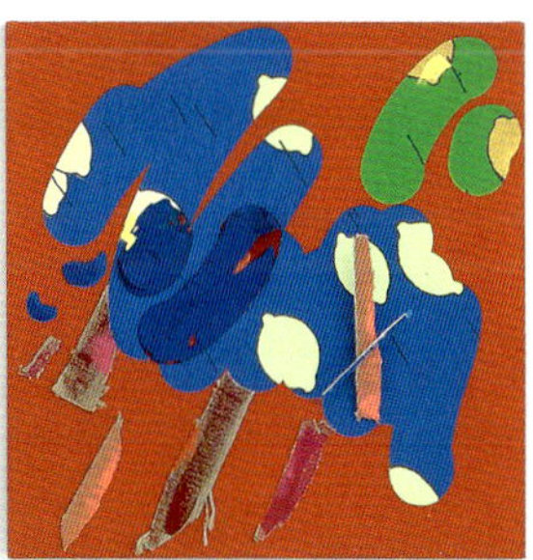
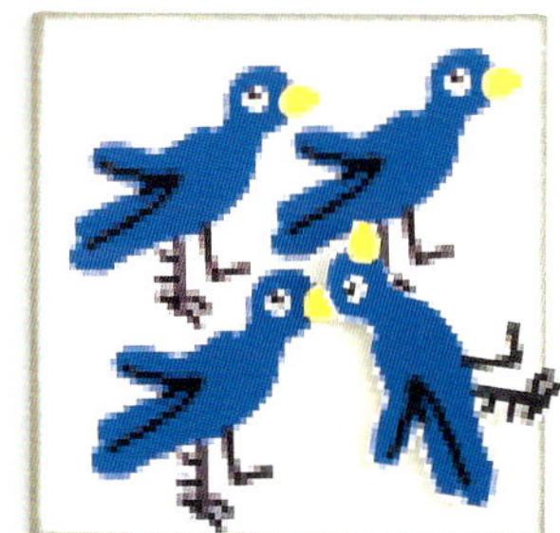

MAI-THU **PERRET** b. 1976, Geneva, Switzerland

Franco-Vietnamese artist Mai-Thu Perret's body of work is largely inspired by an ongoing, open-ended literary initiative she began in 1992 called *The Crystal Frontier*, a group-based narrative that focuses on an imagined, all-female, utopian commune in the New Mexican desert called New Ponderosa Year Zero. Combining fictional elements with a self-imposed conceptual framework, Perret offers a contemporary and mythical response to the mostly male consortiums scattered throughout the early part of the twentieth century, such as Dada, the Bahaus, and Constructivism.

In her work, Perret combines art and design theory with feminist literature, resulting in a symphonic, ever-changing and multidimensional practice that carefully examines subjects ranging from revolutionary politics to contemporary art production to the functionality of objects within specific social systems.

Born in Geneva, Switzerland, where she currently lives and works, Perret received a BA from Cambridge University in England in 1997 and later enrolled in the Whitney's Independent Study Program in New York. She has participated in numerous international group exhibitions and has solo exhibitions at the San Francisco Museum of Modern Art, the Centre d'art contemporain in Geneva, the Nasher Sculpture Center in Dallas, and Le Magasin in Grenoble, France, among others.

In *Migraine I* (2010), Perret examines the relationships between pure formalism and craft and between the material and the spiritual worlds by pressing a graphic, Rorschach-like form in red acrylic paint onto a non-descript grey carpet. The Migraine series borrows its name from the medical condition, which can often result in optical side effects. By transforming common, domestic carpet into a wall support or a canvaslike structure for the abstract forms to live on, Perret asks the viewer to contemplate the age-old relationship between formalism and functionality. The artist's use of psychedelic forms (a direct reference to the human brain's structure and functions) also forces the viewer to consider the connection between traditional abstraction and more contemporary visual phenomena and modes of thinking.

In Perret's practice, ceramics can be viewed as a sculptural metaphor for painting. Her wall-based ceramic works are essentially remnants of paintings past that allude to real objects (usually those found in nature) and abstract concepts (such as grids and geometric forms). Exploring new approaches to an ancient art form, the resulting works ultimately communicate a message of transformation and change.

J. G. M.

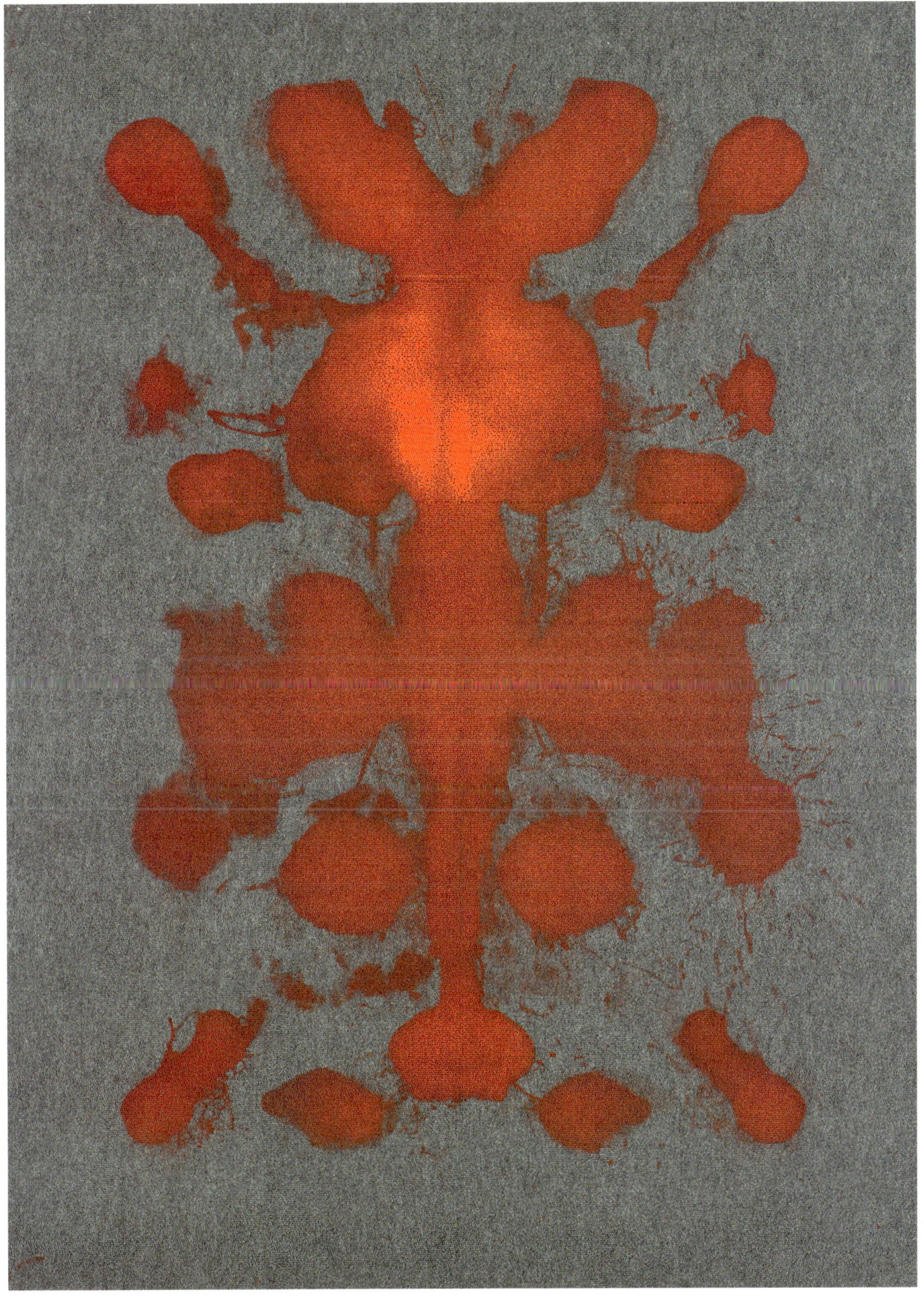

Migraine I, 2010
Acrylic on carpet, mounted on board
96 × 72 inches (243.8 × 182.9 cm)

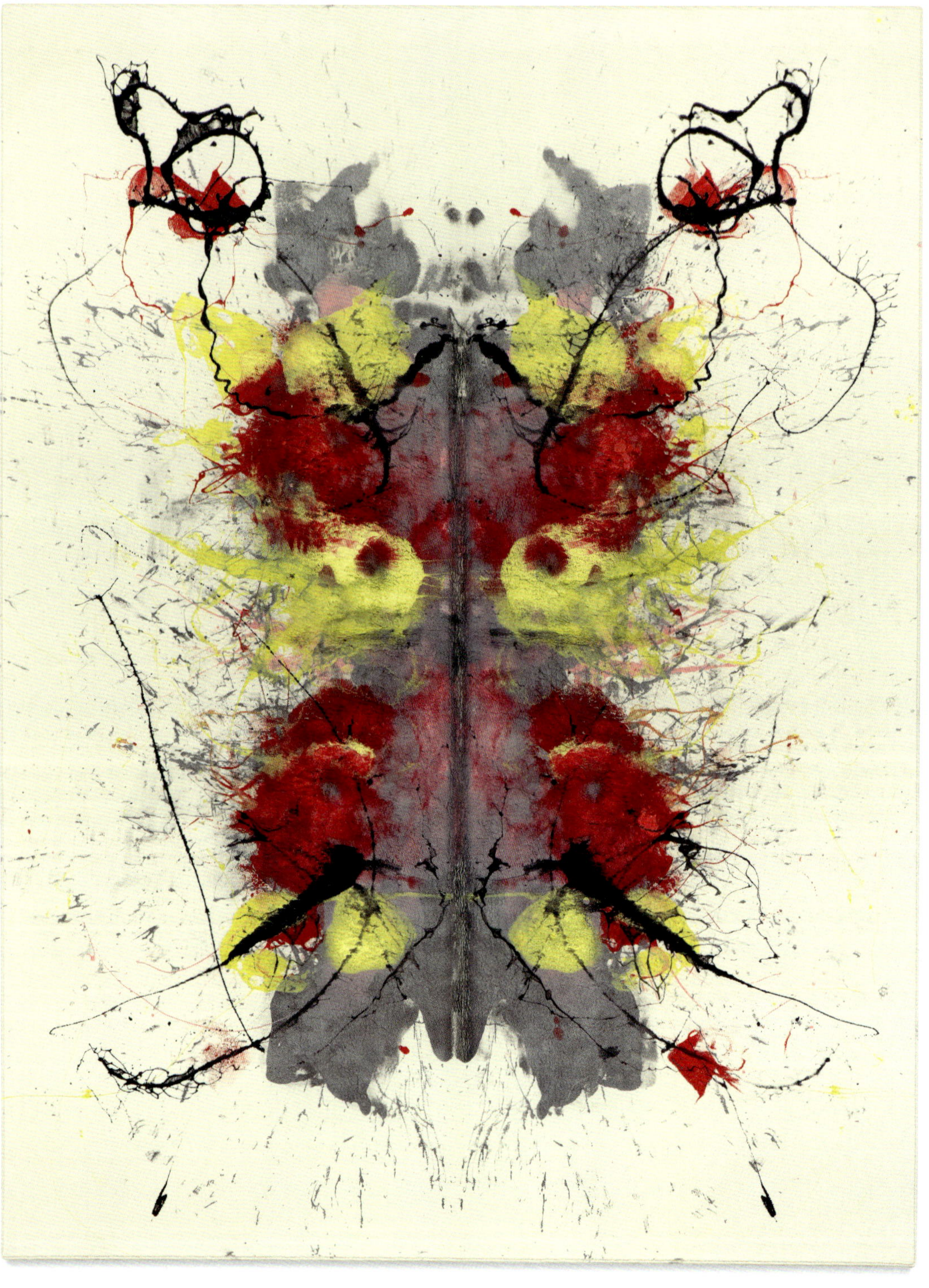

Agoraphobia I, 2016
Acrylic paint on carpet
157½ × 118 × 1 inches
(400.1 × 299.7 × 2.5 cm)

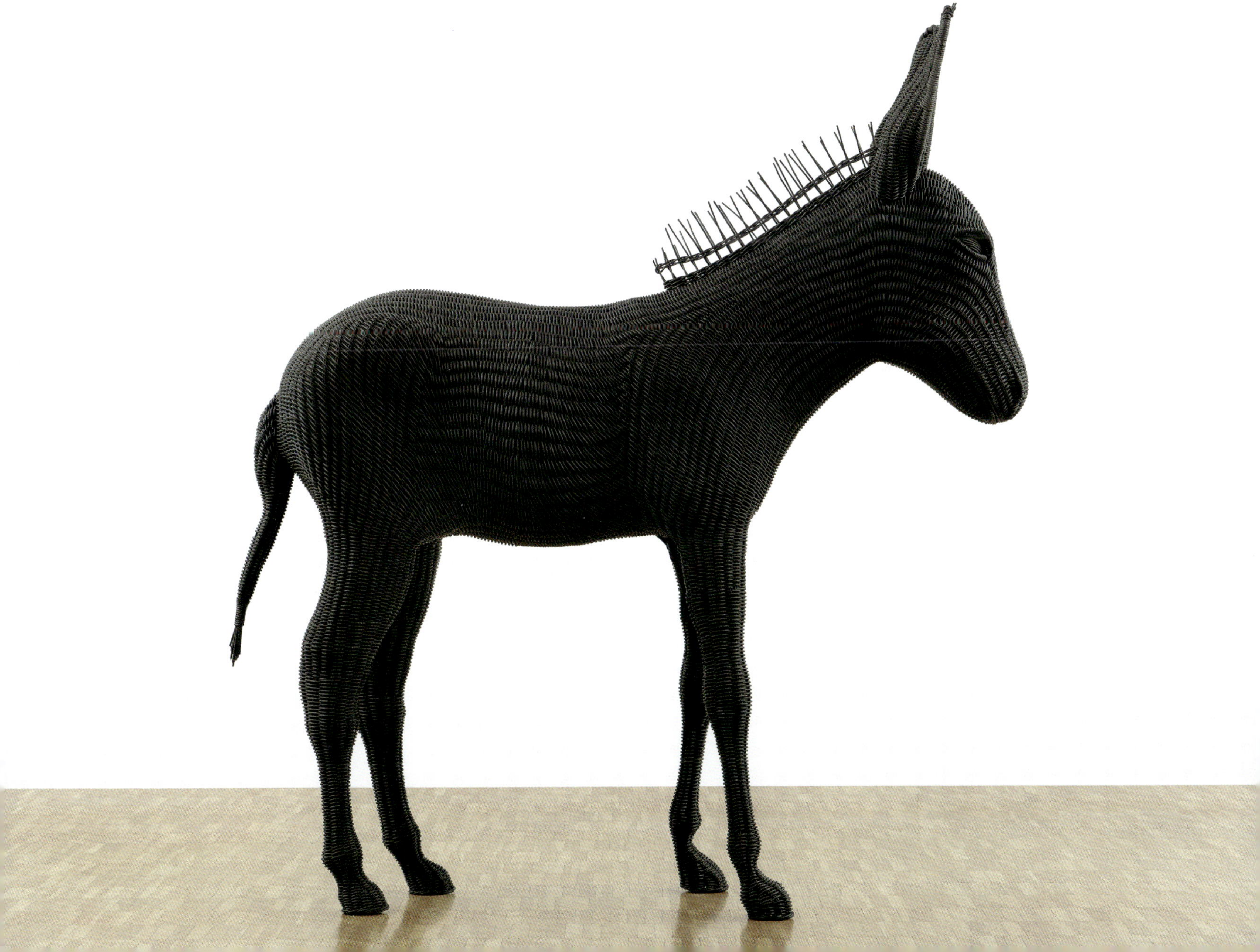

Black Balthazar, 2013
Birch plywood, rattan core,
and water-based paint
48 1/2 × 45 3/8 × 11 7/8 inches
(123 × 115 × 30 cm)

RAYMOND PETTIBON

b. 1957, Tucson, AZ

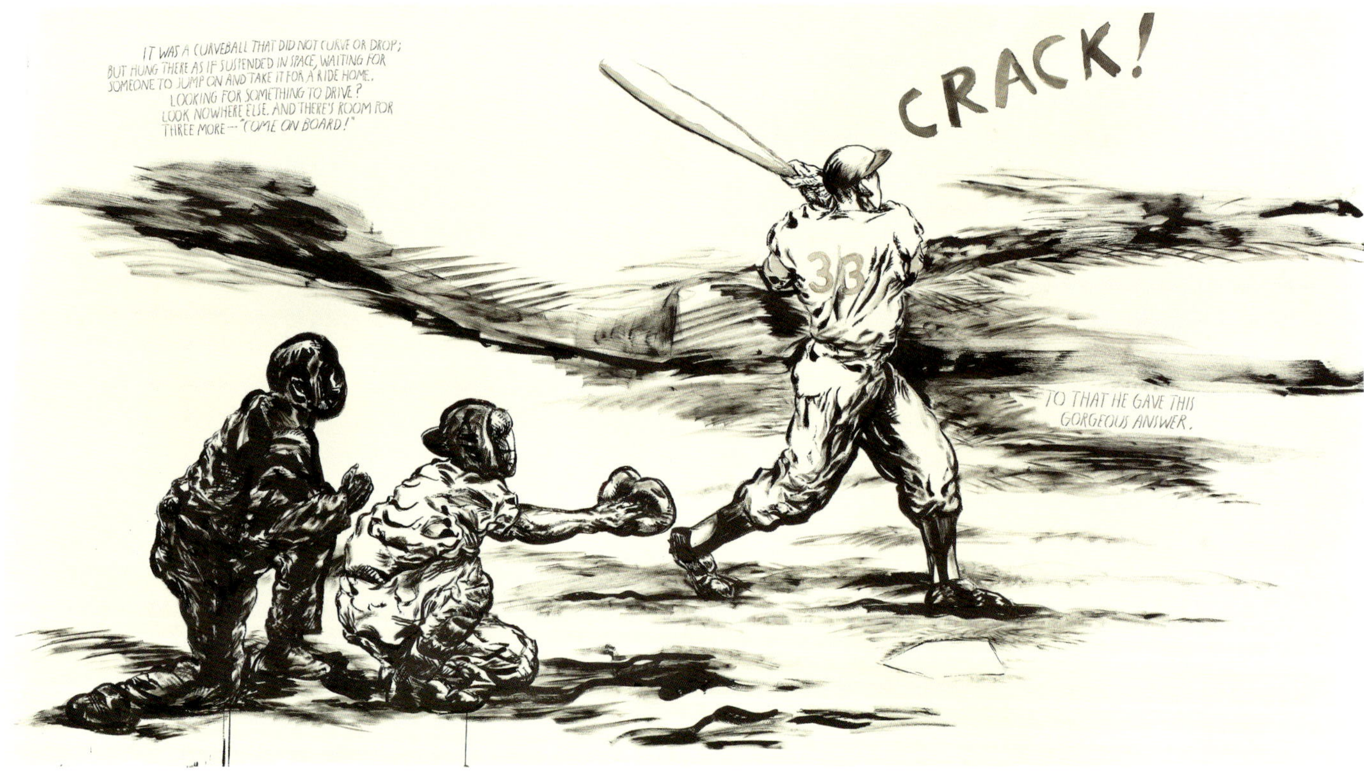

No Title (It was a), 2011
Pen, ink, acrylic, and pastel on paper
51¾ × 94½ inches (131.4 × 240 cm)

Pettibon's style could be considered post-Pop art. He makes videos and paintings, though the majority of his oeuvre is comprised of drawings and watercolors. His subject matter ranges from subverted Americana to political theater to sly, socially topical jokes, and is rendered in a comic book style, with word-bubbles, text, and occasionally multiple panels in a single artwork.

Raymond Pettibon's career began not at an art school or MFA program but in the riotous punk scene of 1970s and 1980s Los Angeles. His brother, Greg Ginn, was a founding member of the band Black Flag, and Pettibon designed its famous four-band logo as well as apparel and fliers. Meanwhile, Pettibon, who was born in Tucson in 1957 and graduated from the University of California, Los Angeles, in 1977, began to exhibit his art at small galleries and group shows. Though he maintained his connection to the music world, most notably by designing the album cover for Sonic Youth's *Goo* in 1990, in 1991 his star had risen to the extent that he was included in the Whitney Biennial. By 1992, when curator Paul Schimmel chose his work for the influential *Helter Skelter* exhibition at The Museum of Contemporary Art in Los Angeles, Pettibon had cemented his reputation as a fine artist of global standing.

In the following decades, Pettibon has been the subject of dozens of solo exhibitions including presentations at the Drawing Center in New York and the Kunstmuseum in Lucerne; his work is in the permanent collections of museums around the world, including The Museum of Modern Art in New York, the Tate Gallery in London, and the Centre Georges Pompidou in Paris. Today, Pettibon lives and works in New York.

The work *No Title (It was a)* (2011), drawn on paper with pen, ink, and acrylic, is an example of Pettibon's trademark style. He depicts an all-American tableau, with a herculean batter, a catcher with his arms outstretched, and an umpire, present but out of the action. Above this there's text: "It was a curveball that did not curve or drop..." The entire artwork could be yet another piece of hagiographic sports memorabilia specific to a certain strain of American nostalgia. Closer inspection, however, reveals that the bat is too big, the ground is uneven, the catcher and pitcher are rumpled and bathed in shadow—even the setting is otherworldly. In Pettibon's hands, thegreat American pastime becomes a sinister site of distortion, reflection, and, perhaps, fear. J. T.

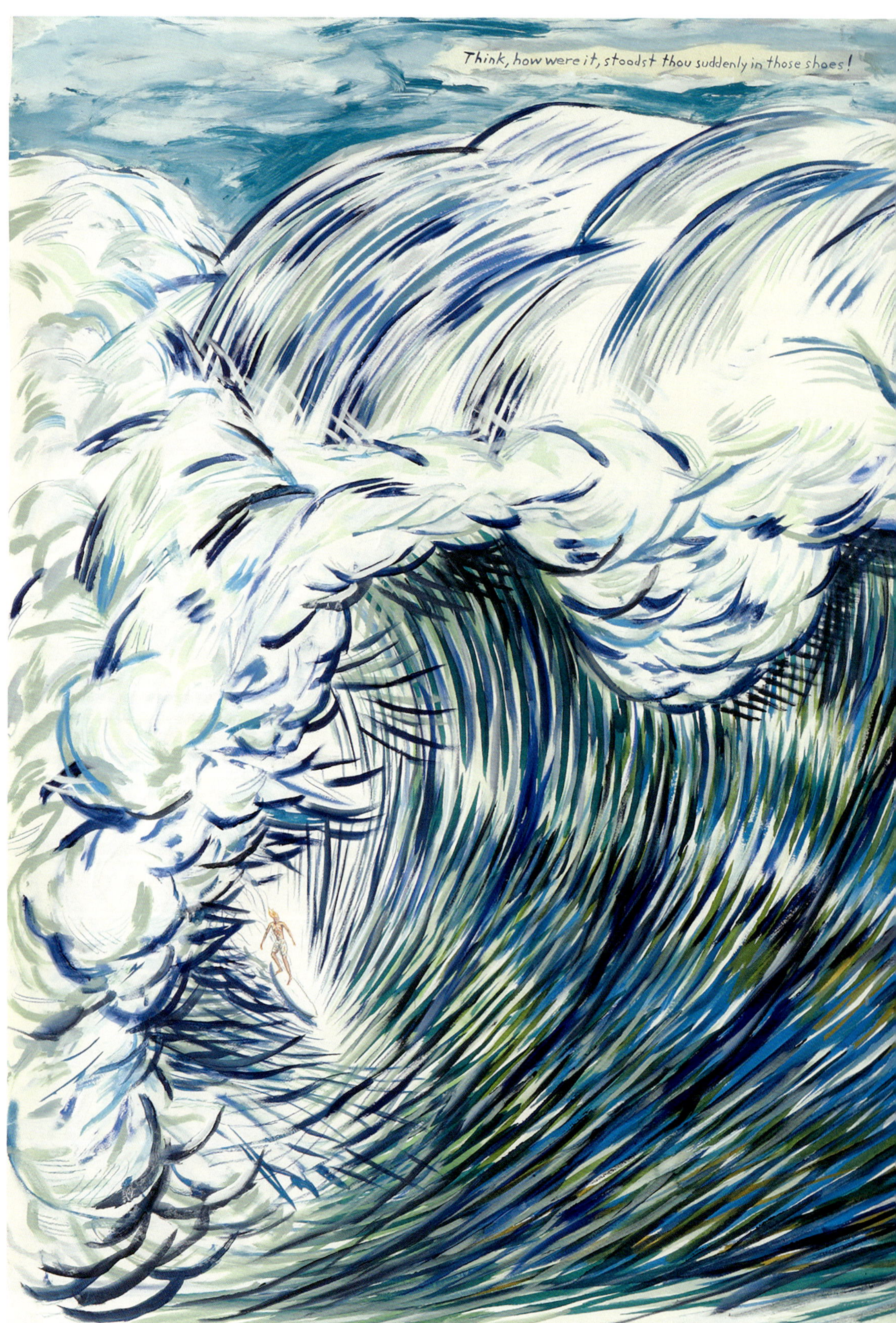

No Title (Think, how were), 2011
Pen, ink, and gouache on paper
51¾ × 86¼ inches (131.4 × 219.1 cm)

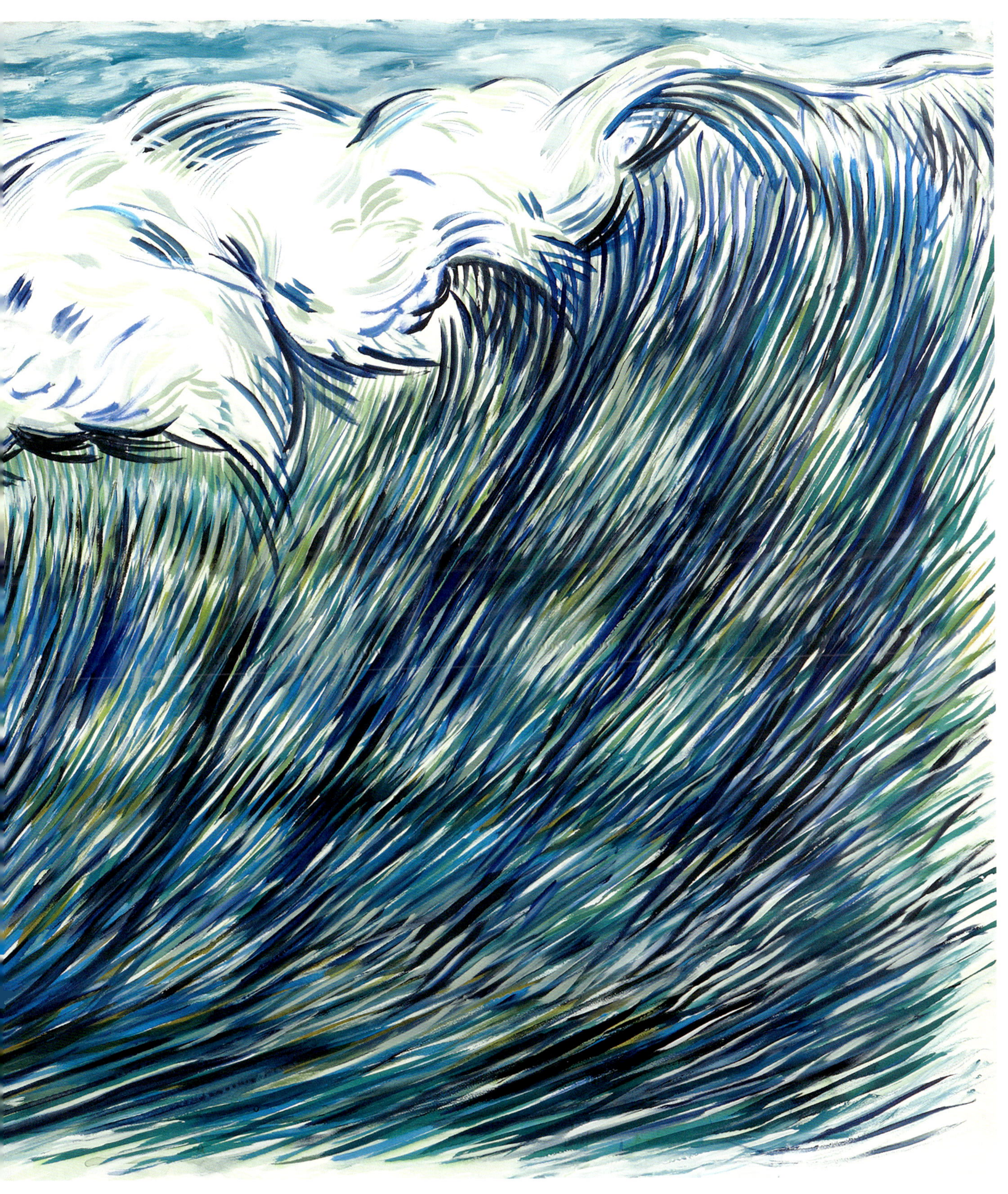

LARI PITTMAN

b. 1952, Los Angeles, CA

Painter Lari Pittman was born in 1952 in Los Angeles and spent many of his formative years moving between the diverse cultures of his hometown and those of Cali and Tumaco, Colombia. In the early 1970s, he attended the University of California, Los Angeles (UCLA), and graduated from the California Institute of Arts with his BFA in 1974 and MFA in 1976. Still based in Los Angeles, Pittman is a professor at UCLA, where he has taught since 1993.

Over the last forty years, Pittman's formally rigorous and intricately layered paintings have addressed topics surrounding American culture and politics, gender, sexuality, identity, and personal experience.

Like his varied cultural, familial, and religious upbringing, his work comprises a constant play of dichotomies. At the same time that his paintings investigate heavy issues such as violence and inequality, they also look at the world with a rare sense of optimism and order.

Employing bold and colorful combinations of abstraction, figuration, and ornamentation with a personalized visual lexicon, Pittman weaves together heterogeneous symbols and images through a democratic system of arrangement. The complex nature of his work is further emphasized through its serial production. The artist creates many paintings simultaneously, drawing physical and conceptual associations between them while also obscuring a clear view of their chronologies.

In the mural-size paintings *Flying Carpet with a Waning Moon Over a Violent Nation* (2013) and *Flying Carpet with Petri Dishes for a Disturbed Nation* (2013), both from the same series, Pittman portrays a dark, traumatized country with an escape plan—the flying carpet. Black bullet holes punctuate the tapestry-like canvases amongst suspended nooses, molecular cultures in petri dishes, guns, ducks, pink triangles, and the view of the waning moon through a sniper's rifle. Throughout his career, Pittman's work has provided a visual reportage of American history and current events—both public and private. In 1985, an intruder shot Pittman in his Los Angeles home. The incident, which resulted in numerous surgeries, certainly informs some of the recurring themes of violence and trauma in his paintings, though his work is not autobiographical. Pittman's recent paintings instead offer a contemporary look at nationhood through traditions of western history painting and various lenses—that of the rifle's telescopic crosshairs or the cylindrical glass of the petri dish. C. R.

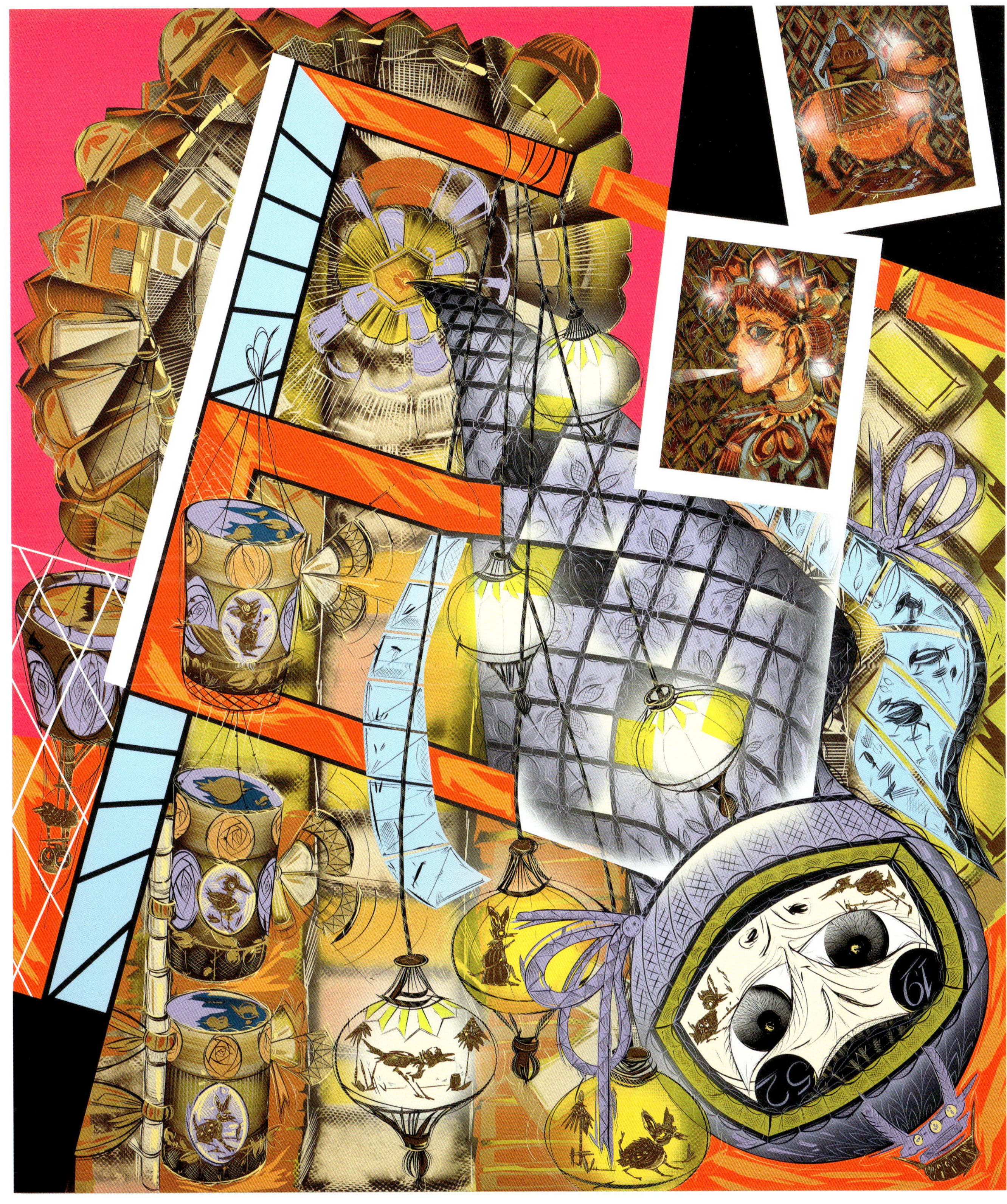

Begat From a Flower, 2011
Acrylic, Cel-Vinyl, and aerosol lacquer on
gessoed canvas over panel
102 × 88 inches (259.1 × 223.5 cm)

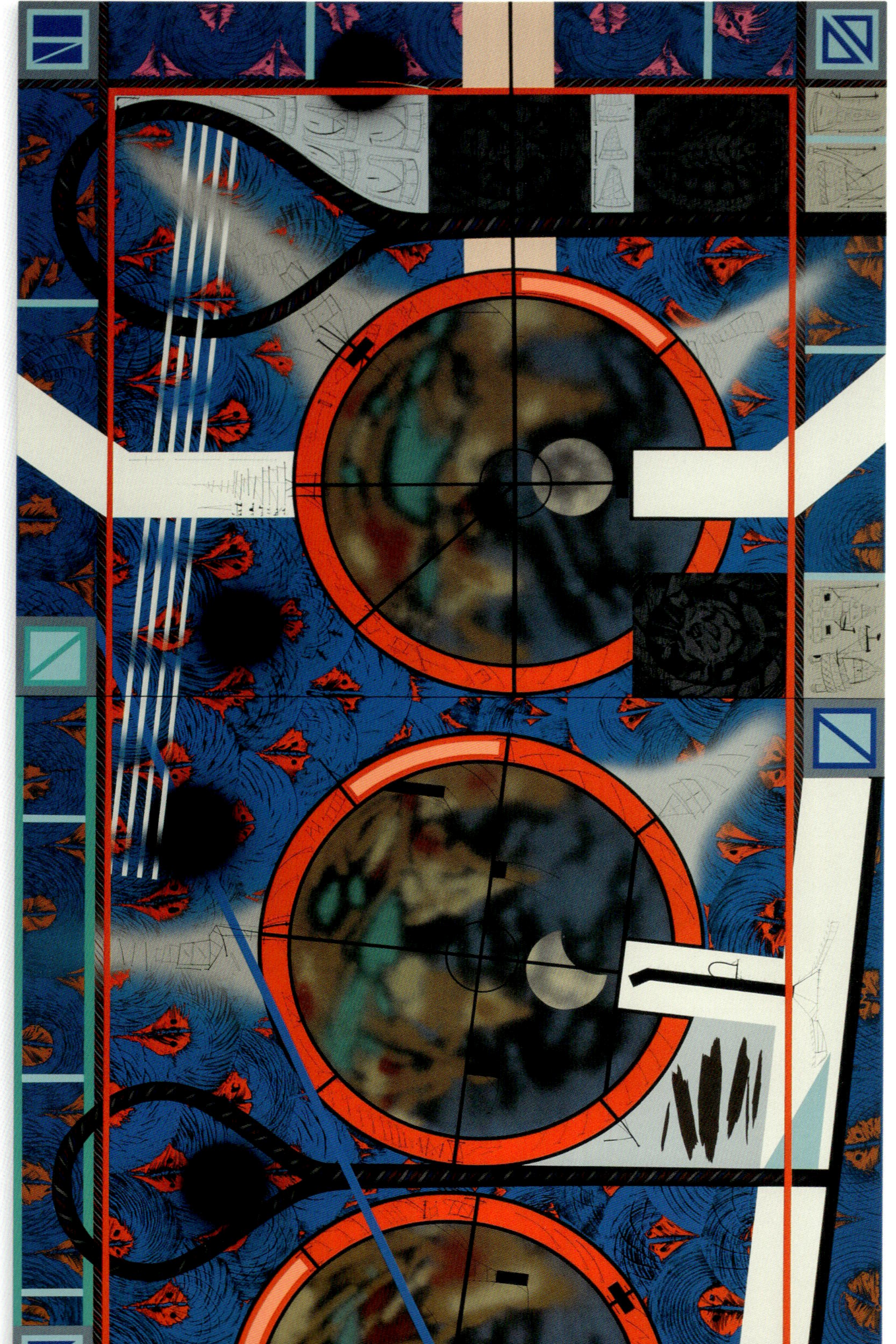

***Flying Carpet with a Waning Moon Over a Violent Nation*, 2013**
Cel-vinyl and spray enamel on canvas over wood panel
108 × 360 ⅜ inches (274.3 × 915.4 cm)

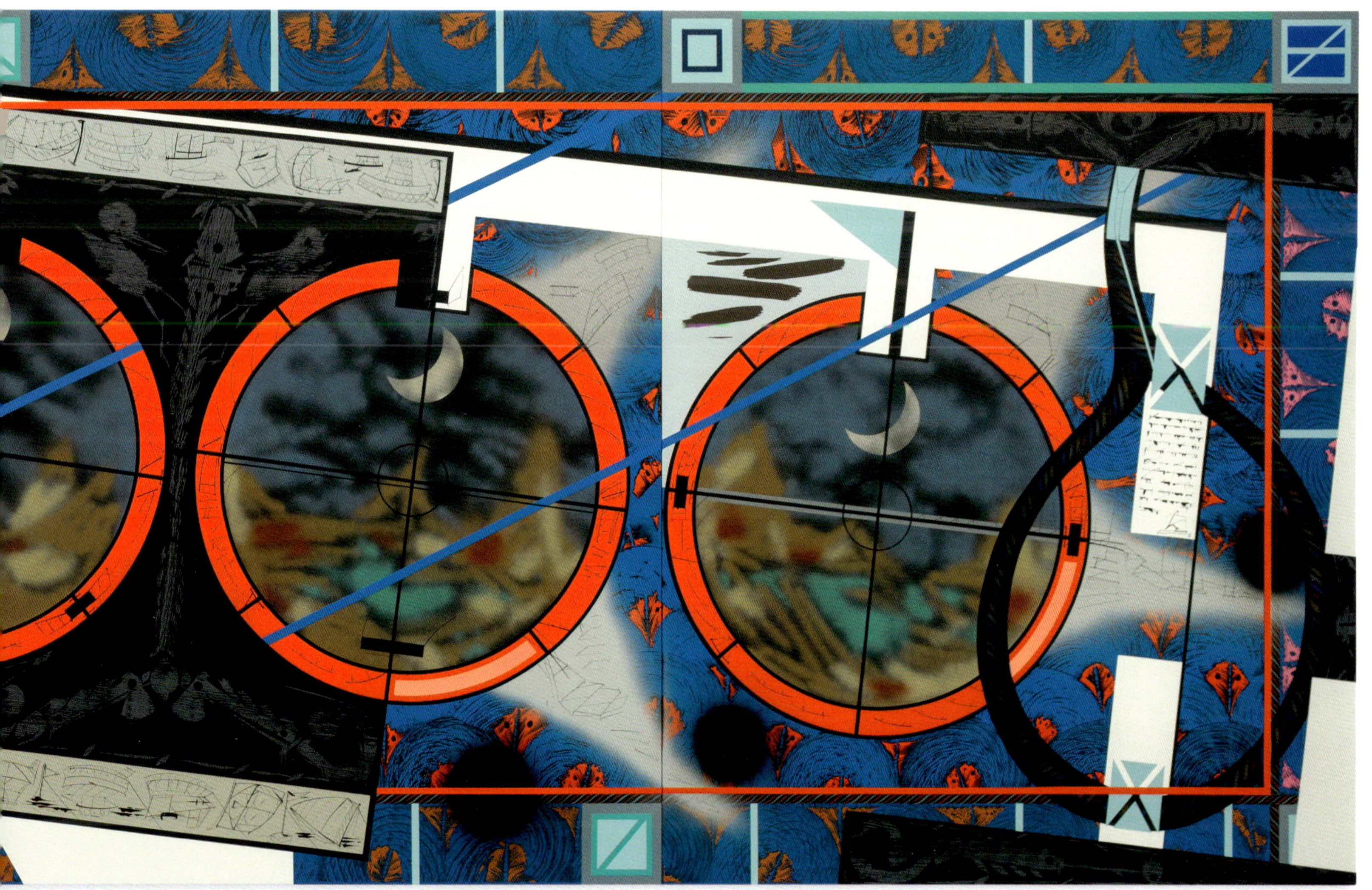

Seth Price's multidisciplinary, post-Conceptual artistic output is a means to address the consumption, communication, and theory that undergirds art, society, and culture. Everything Price produces, in other words, is a byproduct of an intellectual exercise rather than an end in itself.

That, in turn, might explain Price's range—his work spans writing, sculpture, photography, assemblage, sound art, Internet art, drawing, painting, and video. But even if, say, a bunch of cardboard wrapped in printed vinyl and displayed on a wooden pallet (*Printed Waste*, 2016) looks nothing like a gessoed piece of plywood with a hole etched out of its middle (such as Price's early series of screen printed envelope paintings), one thing ties them together: They both, in their own way, are an exploration of what it means to produce and sell artwork in the twenty-first century.

Born in East Jerusalem in 1973, Price graduated from Brown University in 1997 and moved to New York City. By 2002, he was included in the prestigious Whitney Biennial and given his first solo show at Artists Space in downtown New York. Since then, he's exhibited globally, appearing in the Venice Biennale, The Museum of Contemporary Art in Los Angeles, and MoMA PS1 in New York. For years, however, Price was considered an artist's artist, known among a select few without broader recognition; his vacuum-sealed series changed that, pulling Price into the public eye.

The attention paid to Price's vacuum pieces is at least partially due to the fact that they're (arguably) the most tangible, accessible demonstrations of his overall practice. For *Vintage Bomber* from 2008, Price took a cult object infused with a machismo-laden Americana—these jackets were popularized by World War II pilots after all—placed it in a polyurethane bag, and then vacuum-sealed it, thereby both preserving and abstracting the jacket: Its use value was eliminated, its concept, the only thing left. Put differently, through Price's intervention the physical object (in this case a jacket, but it could just as easily be a painting or a piece of rope) is rendered irrelevant; it's up to the viewer to ascribe meaning and, not coincidentally, value. J. T.

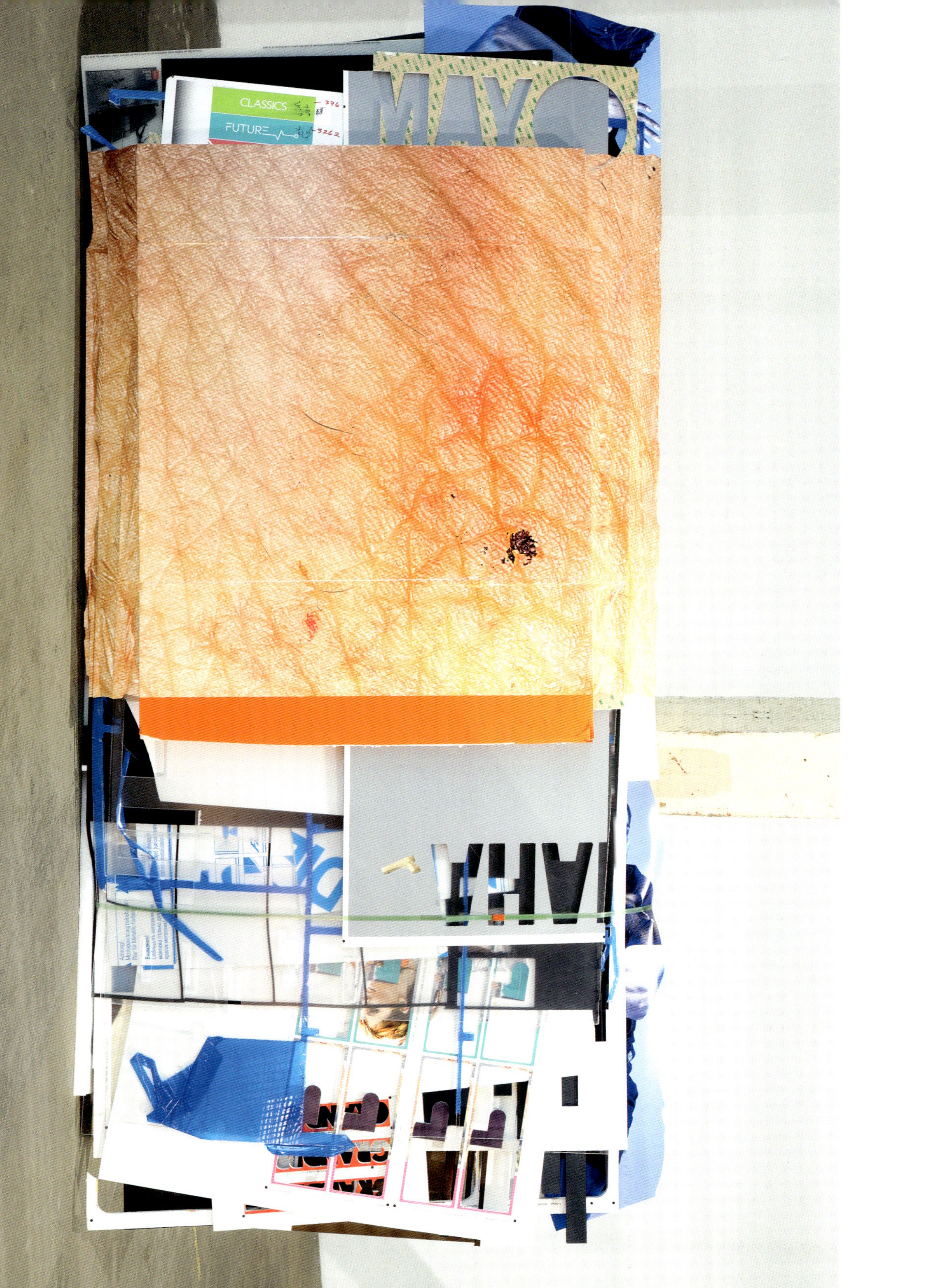

Print Waste, 2016
Printed vinyl wrapped around print-waste from commercial imaging facility, wooden pallet, and cinch straps
53 × 116 × 15 inches (134.6 × 294.6 × 38.1 cm)

Installation view, *Wrok Fmaily Freidns*, 356 S. Mission Rd., January 30–April 10, 2016

PRICE

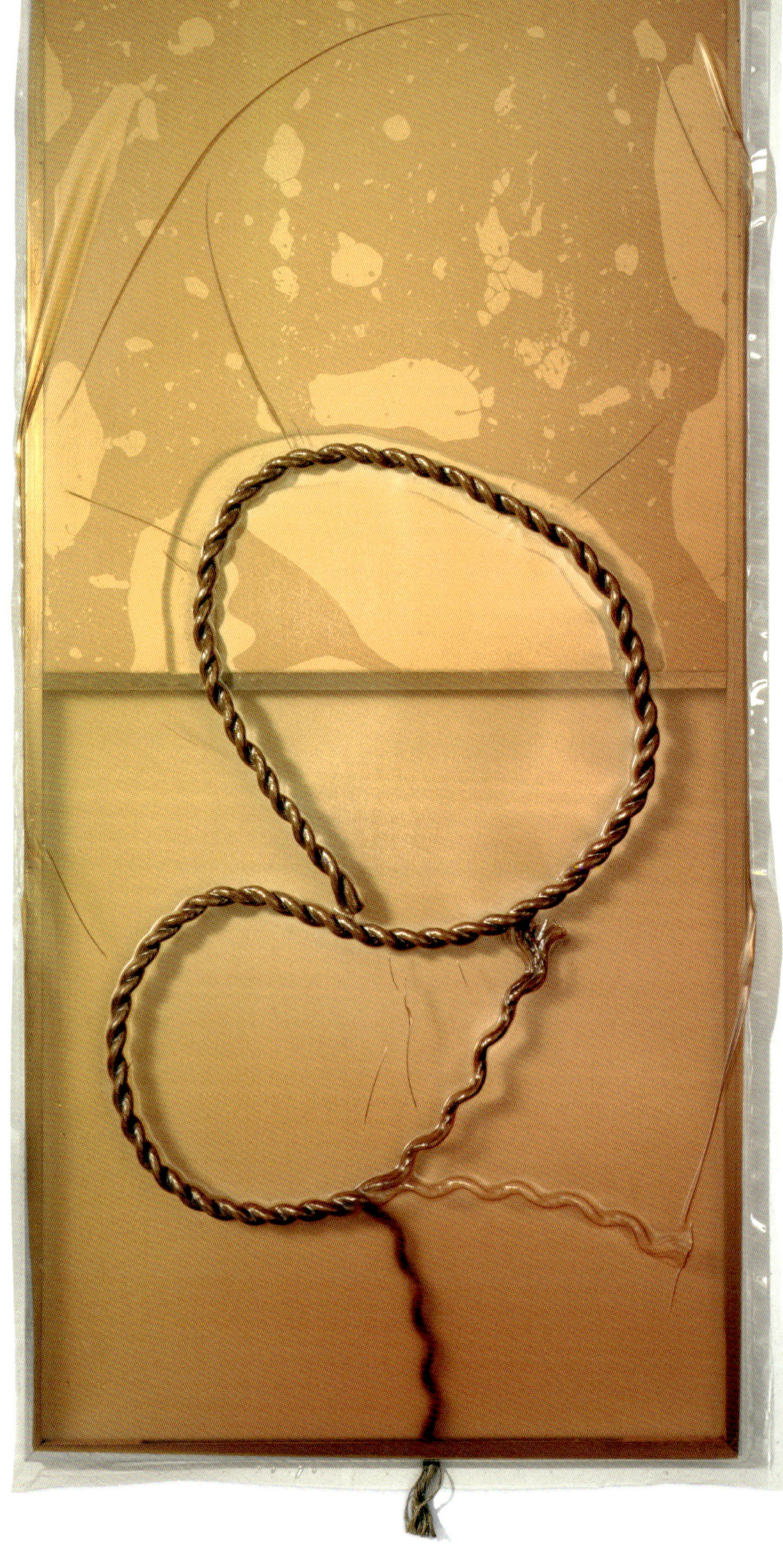

Untitled, 2010
UV-cured inkjet on PETG vacuum-formed over rope
96 × 48 inches (243.8 × 121.9 cm)

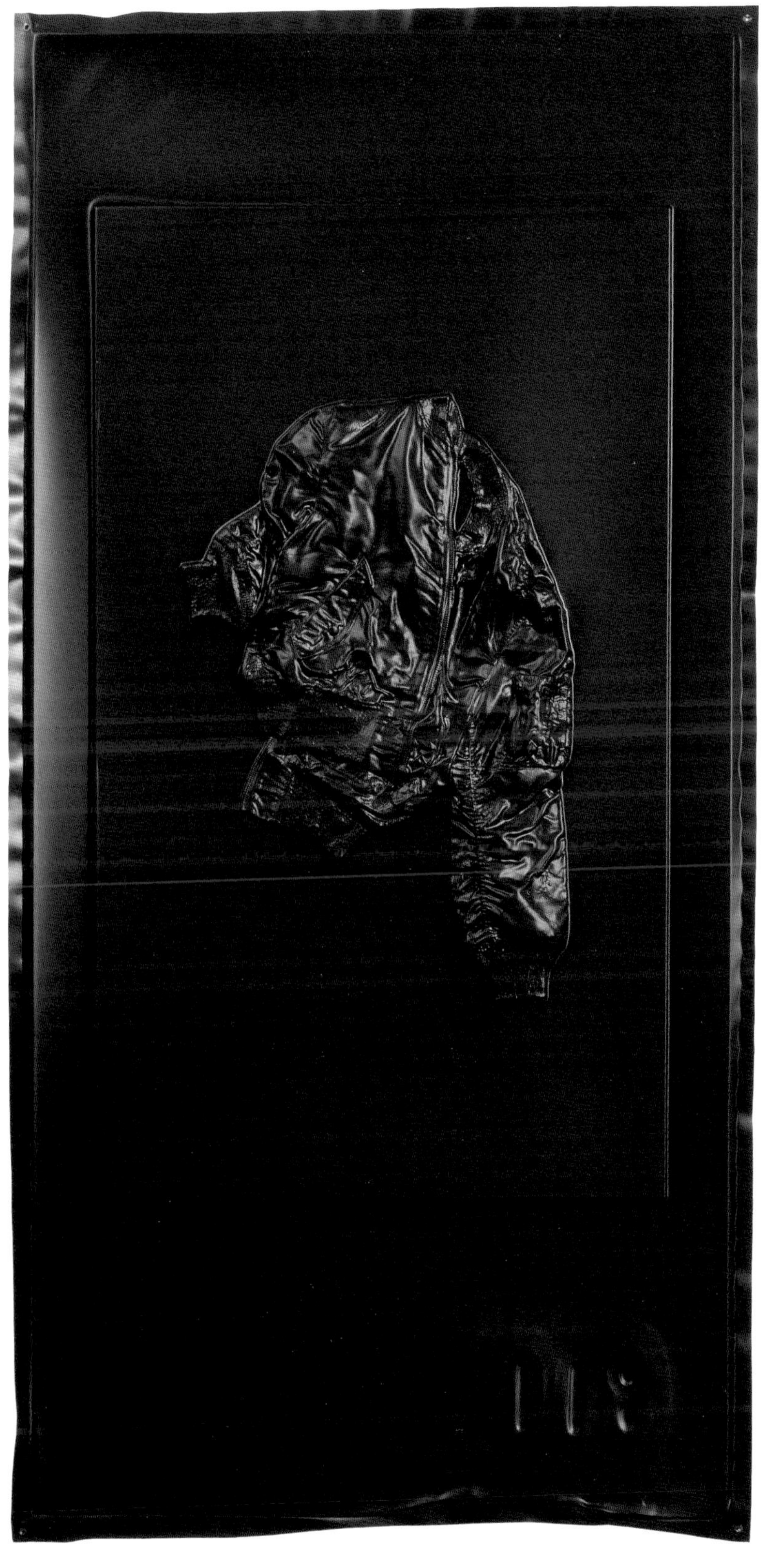

Vintage Bomber, 2008
Vacuum formed high impact polystyrene
96 × 48 inches (243.8 × 121.9 cm)

RICHARD PRINCE
b. 1949, Panama Canal Zone

Born in 1949 in the Panama Canal Zone and raised in a suburb of Boston, Richard Prince moved to New York in 1973. As a young painter in the mid-1970s, Prince worked as an archivist in the periodical library at Time-Life Incorporated. After cutting out magazine articles for staff copywriters, Prince would typologically arrange and photograph the leftover advertising images—ultimately printing, framing, and presenting the images as original art works. Prince has become affiliated with the Pictures Generation—a loose grouping of artists who responded to the expanding visual culture of the 1970s and 1980s through various strategies of appropriation.

For nearly forty years, Prince has continuously utilized appropriation in his work, primarily in series of photographs and paintings, in order to investigate notions of truth, fiction, identity, and desire associated with advertising and media culture. He currently lives and works in upstate New York.

In the aftermath of Pop and Conceptual art, Prince and contemporaries such as Sarah Charlesworth and Sherrie Levine forged new directions in postmodern photographic practice in their serial re-photography approach to the medium. Prince turned his focus to advertising and fashion images as well as representations of identities and subcultures portrayed in the American media. In the early 1980s, Prince created a series of photographic grids he called "gangs," in which he assembled appropriated images into distinct categories of cultural niches and visual motifs such as monster trucks, cowboys, sunsets, and biker "girlfriends." Prince's photographs and paintings have explored similar lines of inquiry and subjects throughout his career but have taken on different forms. Often steeped in controversy for both their content and theftlike production, Prince's practice offers filtered representations of contemporary life and fantasy as seen in public platforms ranging from magazines to social media.

In Prince's early work *Untitled (Four women looking in the same direction)* (1977), the artist collected, cropped, and re-photographed four images of women from advertisements. The repetitive juxtaposition highlights similarities and differences between the anonymous models, while also calling attention to conventions of advertising. In his more recent *Untitled (portrait)* images (2014), Prince uses the iPhone's "screen shot" tool to voyeuristically capture Instagram posts by various users. Included at the bottom of each image is a comment by Prince—his literal mark on images taken from one public space and transferred to another. C. R.

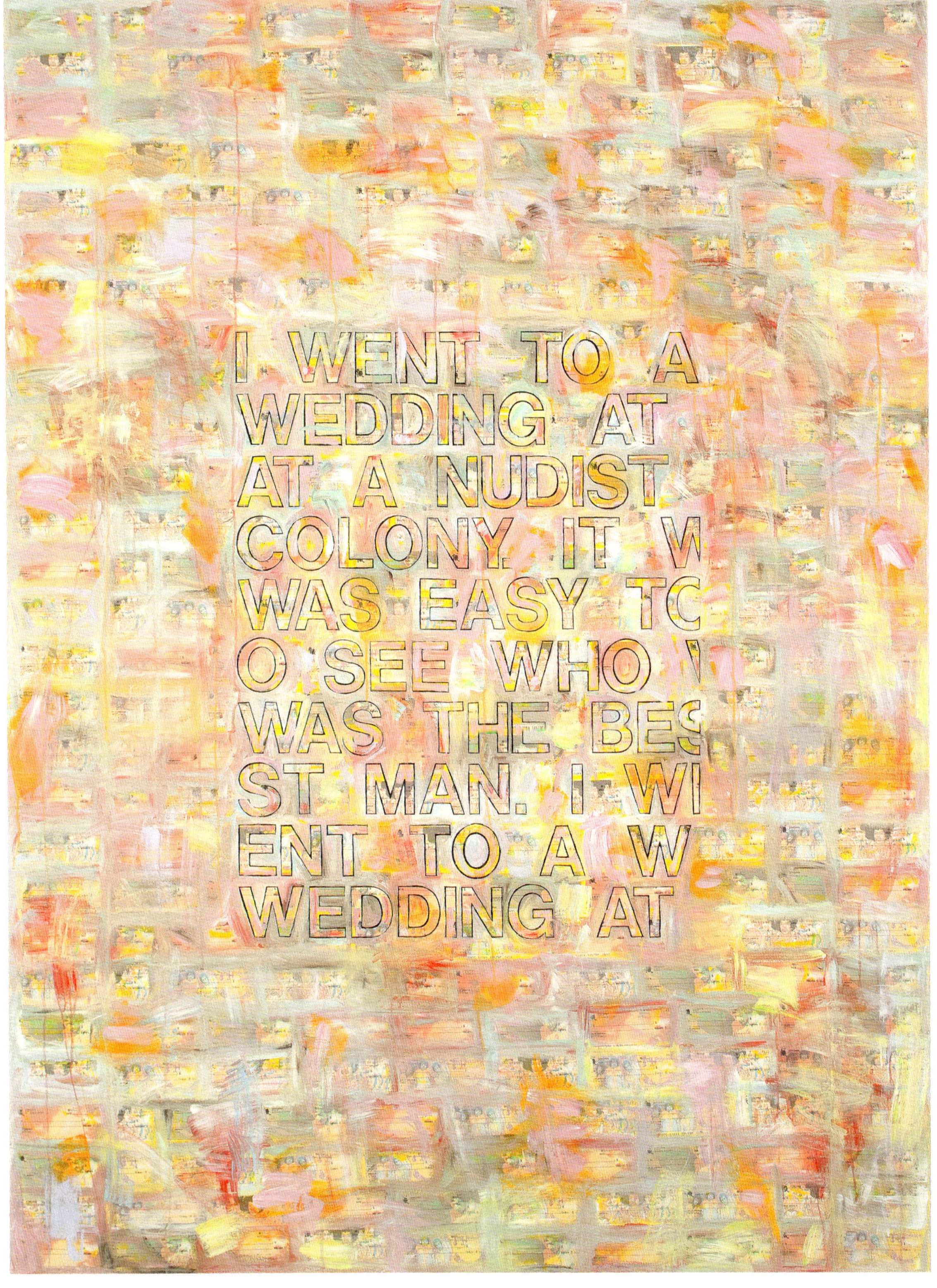

Best Man, 2005
Acrylic and checks on canvas
78 × 58 inches (198.1 × 147.3 cm)

Untitled (Four women looking in the same direction), 1977
4 ektacolor photographs
23¼ × 31 inches (59.1 × 78.7 cm) each framed
Edition 1 of 10, 2 AP

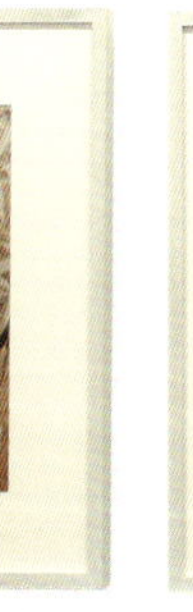

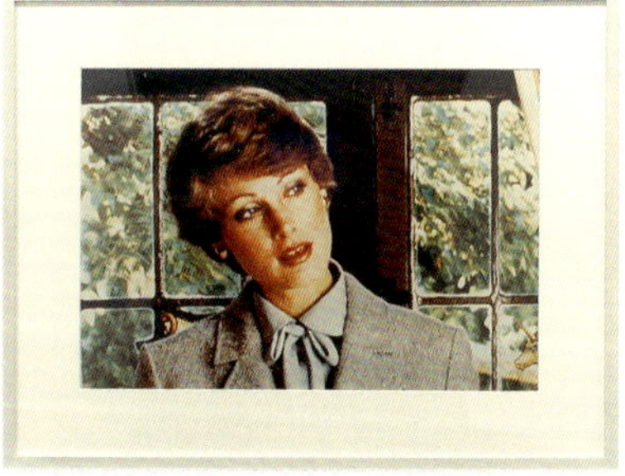

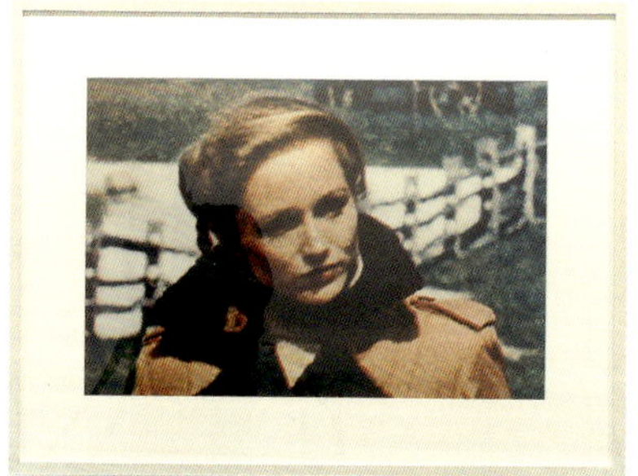

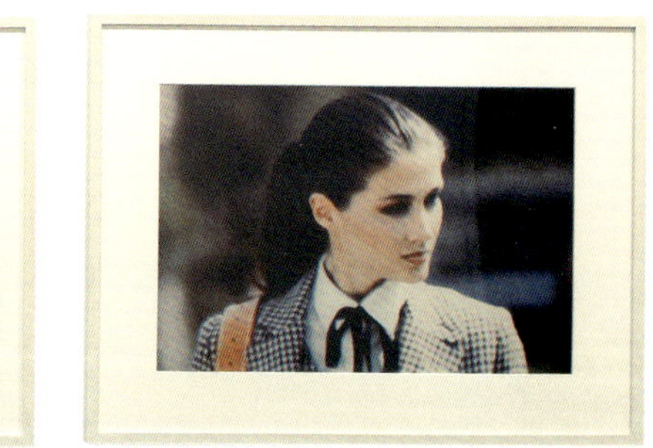

Untitled (portrait), 2014
10 inkjet prints on paper
22 × 17 inches (55.9 × 43.2 cm) each

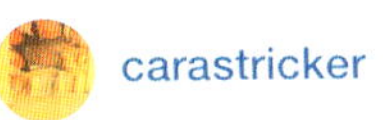

carastricker 13w

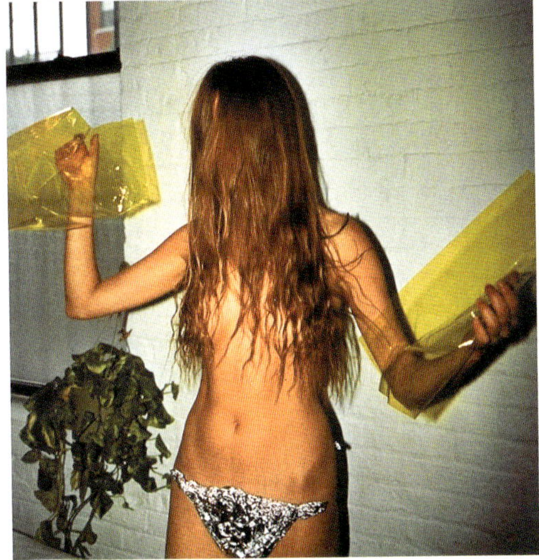

197 likes
jaiegon Hb lol
kawsholland 😌 👌
richardprince4 Tinfoil 👙 ???

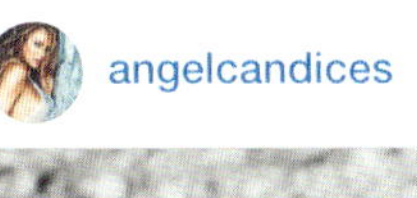

angelcandices 52w

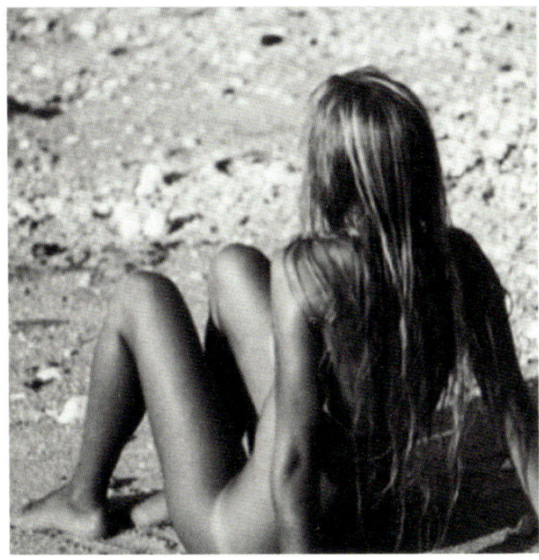

63886 likes
erikaeliseh for those wondering, im pretty sure this is brooke shields from blue lagoon :)
richardprince4 Bikini Medicine. 👙

deborahandersonphotos 1w

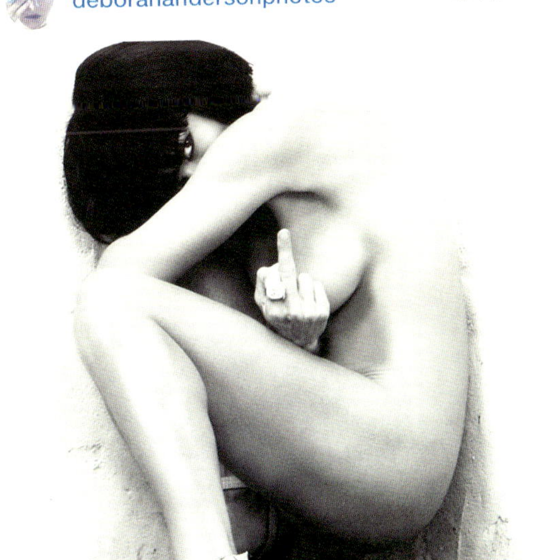

61 likes
deborahandersonphotos
www.deborahanderson.com
richardprince4 Grace&temptation crates that dewlin frat of energy. WAY better ☝

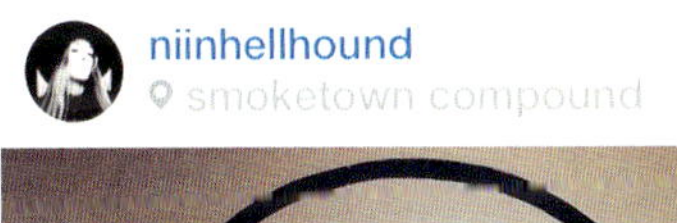

niinhellhound 3w
smoketown compound

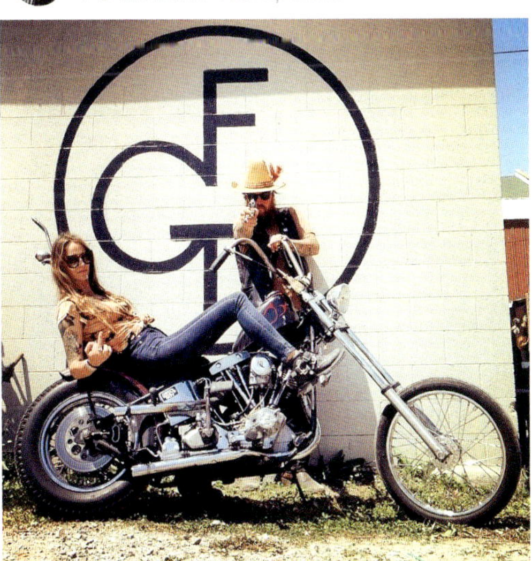

598 likes
kt_lonewolf I fucking love you two
borntobebadvintage FUCKING HELL YEAH
richardprince4 Cowboys And Girlfriends 📷

ROB PRUITT b. 1964, Washington D.C.

Rob Pruitt's signature earnest, childlike innocence is paired, often as not, with a sophisticated dissection of the art world and art theory. Whereas in some artistic practices this synthesis might be off-putting, in Pruitt's hands the two disparate poles form the inextricable and persuasive core of a robust conceptual practice.

Spanning the mediums of painting, sculpture, installation, and performance, Pruitt's twenty-five-year-long career has drawn from a perennially introspective and often outright autobiographical interrogation.

Born in 1964 in Washington, D.C., Pruitt studied at the Corcoran College of the Arts and Design, then transferred to the Parsons School of Design in New York after befriending the Parsons professor Tim Gunn. Post graduation, Pruitt formed an artistic collaboration with Jack Early, most notably creating the series Artworks for Teenage Boys, an exploration of pop culture, gender identity, stereotypes, and art world binaries.

After splitting with Early in the early 1990s, Pruitt took a brief hiatus from the art world and returned in 1998 with the provocative installation *Cocaine Buffet*, a sixteen-foot mirror with a line of cocaine running its length. Participants were invited to (and did) snort the drug, engaging in a performative demonstration of the consumerism, ephemerality, and transactional nature of the gallery system. Pruitt's art soon mellowed somewhat, and he began to paint colorful, glitter-covered pictures of pandas—a glib paean to the slick, corporate embrace of feel-good motifs. He also notably initiated a series of "flea markets," wherein he used his and his friends' unwanted possessions to stage a gallery-sponsored tag sale. Soon enough Pruitt's art began to be exhibited widely, appearing in solo exhibitions in Paris, Rome, Tokyo, and Los Angeles.

Meanwhile, Pruitt's subject matter continues to flirt with his own relationship to art and art creation, while simultaneously tackling broader conceptual issues. His Suicide Paintings are a case in point. In *Suicide Painting XLVI* from 2014, a pastel-neon gradient fades from a light peach into a blue that is nearly black. The operation of "suicide" in this series can be understood in the same personal/conceptual binary at work throughout the rest of Pruitt's practice. Unlike, the Panda paintings, however, here Pruitt has effaced figuration altogether, electing instead to destroy the meaning, content, and message of his very personal work: three suicides for the price of one. J. T.

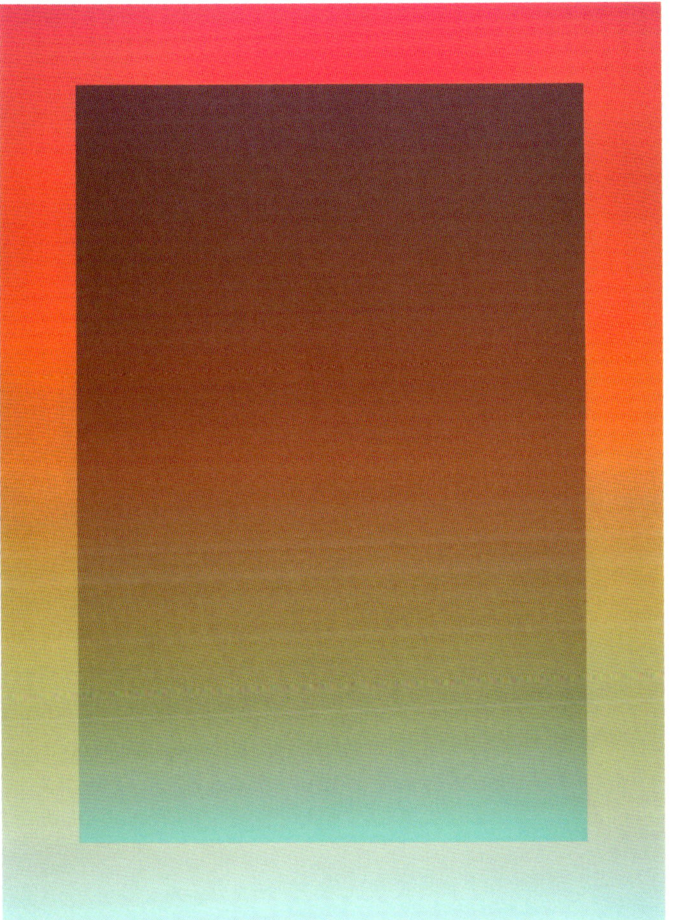

Suicide Painting XVIII, 2014
Acrylic on linen
108 × 81 inches (274.3 × 205.7 cm)

Suicide Painting XLVI, 2014
Acrylic on linen
108 × 81 inches (274.3 × 205.7 cm)

UGO RONDINONE b. 1964, Brunnen, Switzerland

While it's difficult to describe Rondinone's oeuvre in sweeping terms, certain theoretical and aesthetic cues emerge. He consistently returns to the boundaries between humor and subversion, nature and artifice, and scale in relation to power.

If there is a constant in Ugo Rondinone's work, it's that whatever he makes bears little or no resemblance to what he was making before. Rondinone has made full-size labyrinths, seven-foot-high monolithic stone figures, blazing rainbow neon signs, tiny bronze horses, and installations with scores of (living) sad clowns. Rondinone's work has been described as sound art, landscape art, conceptual art, abstract art, and merely commercial art, but it has never—at least not yet—been described as tedious.

Rondinone was born in 1964 to Italian parents in Switzerland and studied at Vienna's Hochschule für Angewandte Kunst, graduating in 1990. His first solo exhibition was in 1985, when the Galerie Marlene Frei in Zurich gave him a show in its inaugural year. In 1998, Rondinone moved to New York, where he still lives and works. Rondinone's art has been exhibited at MoMA PS1 in New York, the Centre Georges Pompidou in Paris, and the Kunsthistorisches Museum in Vienna; in 2007, he represented Switzerland in the Venice Biennale.

This is evidenced in his white cast-aluminum *air/gets/into/everything/even/nothing* (2006), a seventeen-foot-tall sculpture (its title is a short poem by Rondinone), made by creating a rubber cast of a 2,000-year-old olive tree from the countryside outside of Naples, where his parents were born. Once cast into metal, the tree's shape became, in Rondinone's words, "a memoriam of condensed time." The tree's age, in other words, is encased in an ageless medium; Rondinone captures and preserves the wonder of nature only by removing it from nature altogether.

Another work, *the interested + the gleeful* (2013), consisting of two bluestone and steel sculptures on a granite slab, seems to have little in common with the cast aluminum tree. Primitive but distinctly figurative, they have the air of simple pre-historic totems. And yet these sculptures too are vessels for Rondinone's theoretical preoccupations: naturalistic and yet altered, the sculptures are cyphers, both timeless and distinctly of our time. J. T.

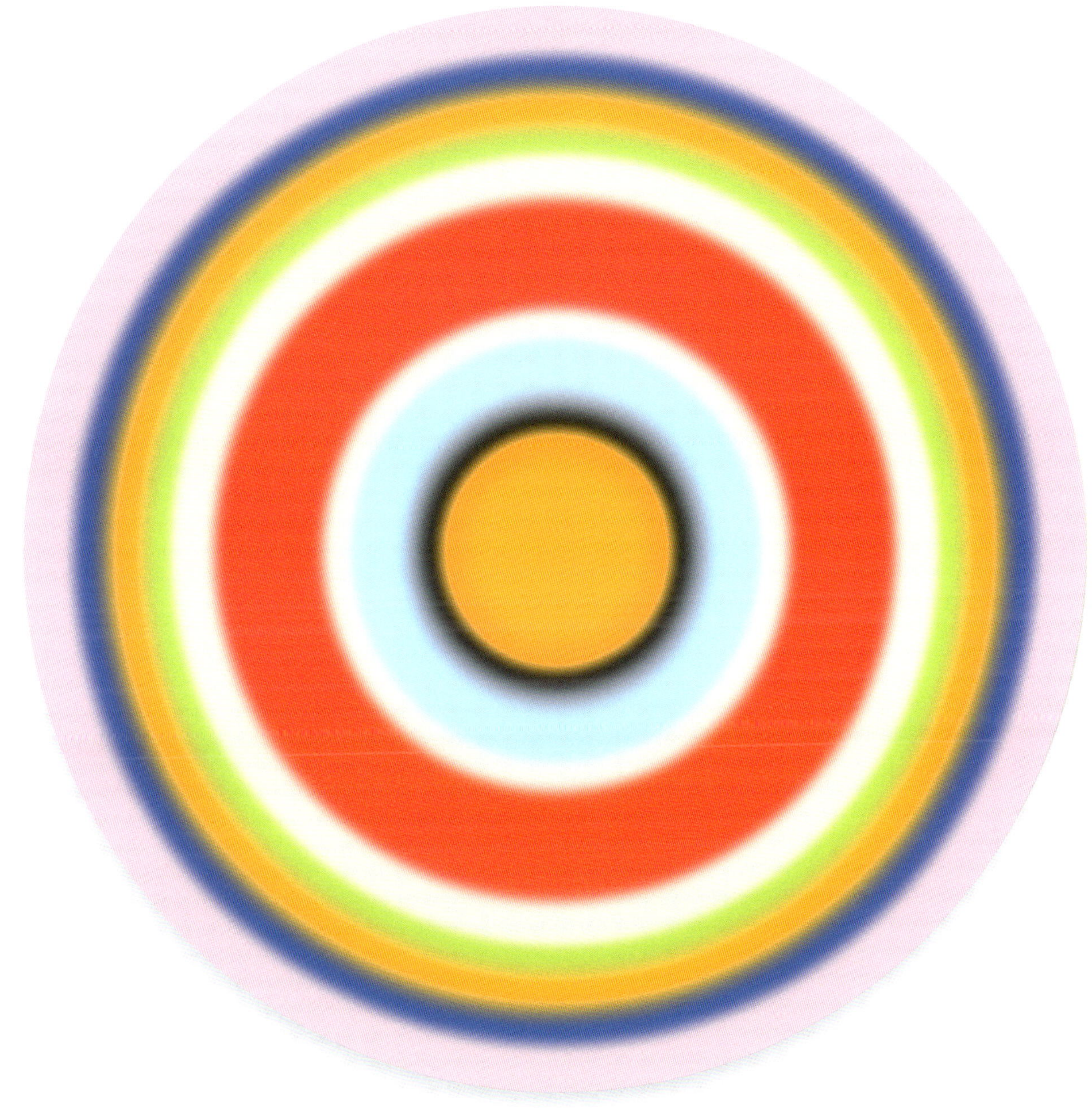

No. 172 ACHTZEHNTERJANUARZ-WEITAUSENDUNDNULL, 2000
Acrylic on canvas with Plexiglas plaque
106¼ × 106¼ inches (269.9 × 269.9 cm)

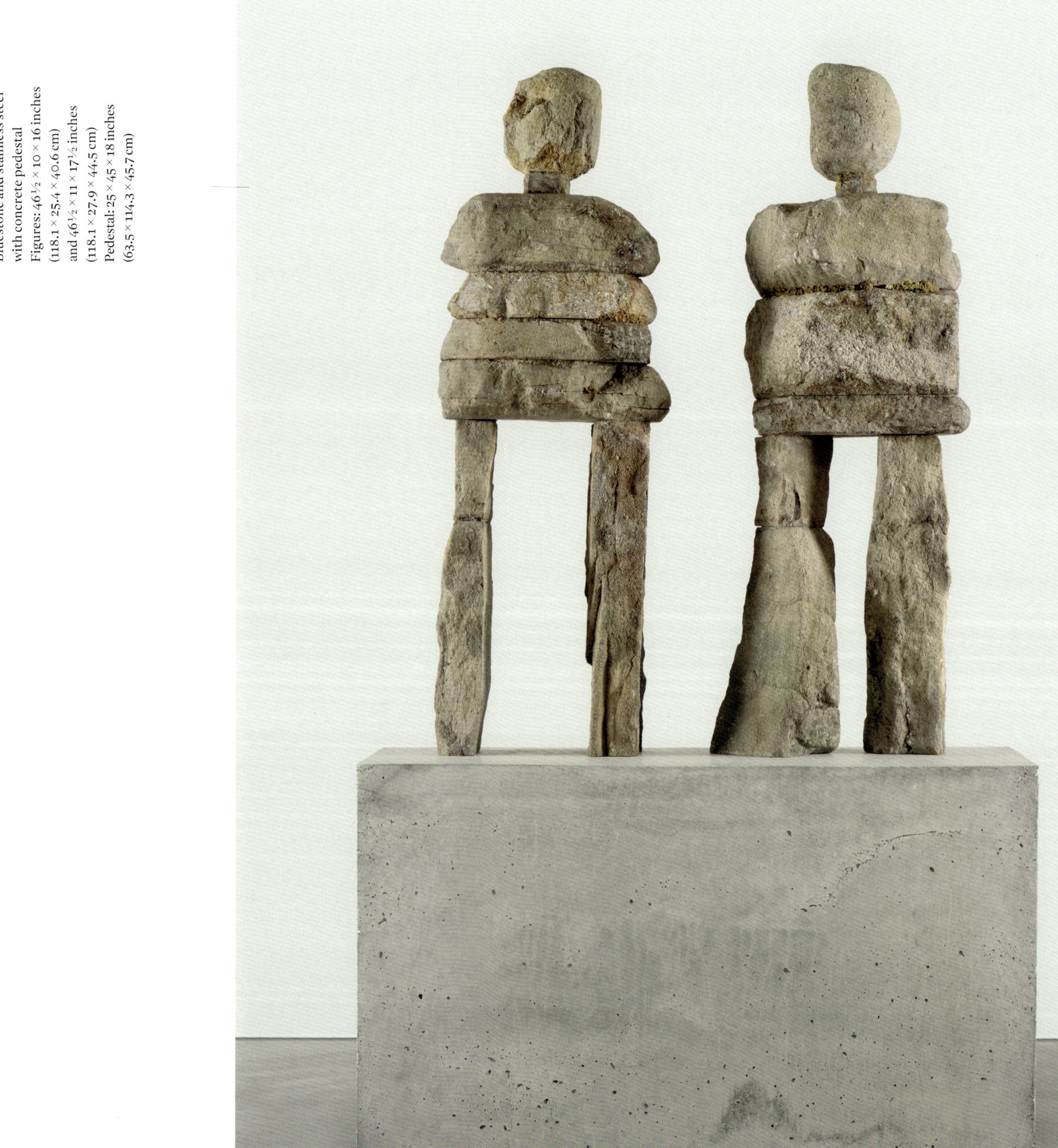

the interested + the gleeful, 2013
Bluestone and stainless steel
with concrete pedestal
Figures: 46½ × 10 × 16 inches
(118.1 × 25.4 × 40.6 cm)
and 46½ × 11 × 17½ inches
(118.1 × 27.9 × 44.5 cm)
Pedestal: 25 × 45 × 18 inches
(63.5 × 114.3 × 45.7 cm)

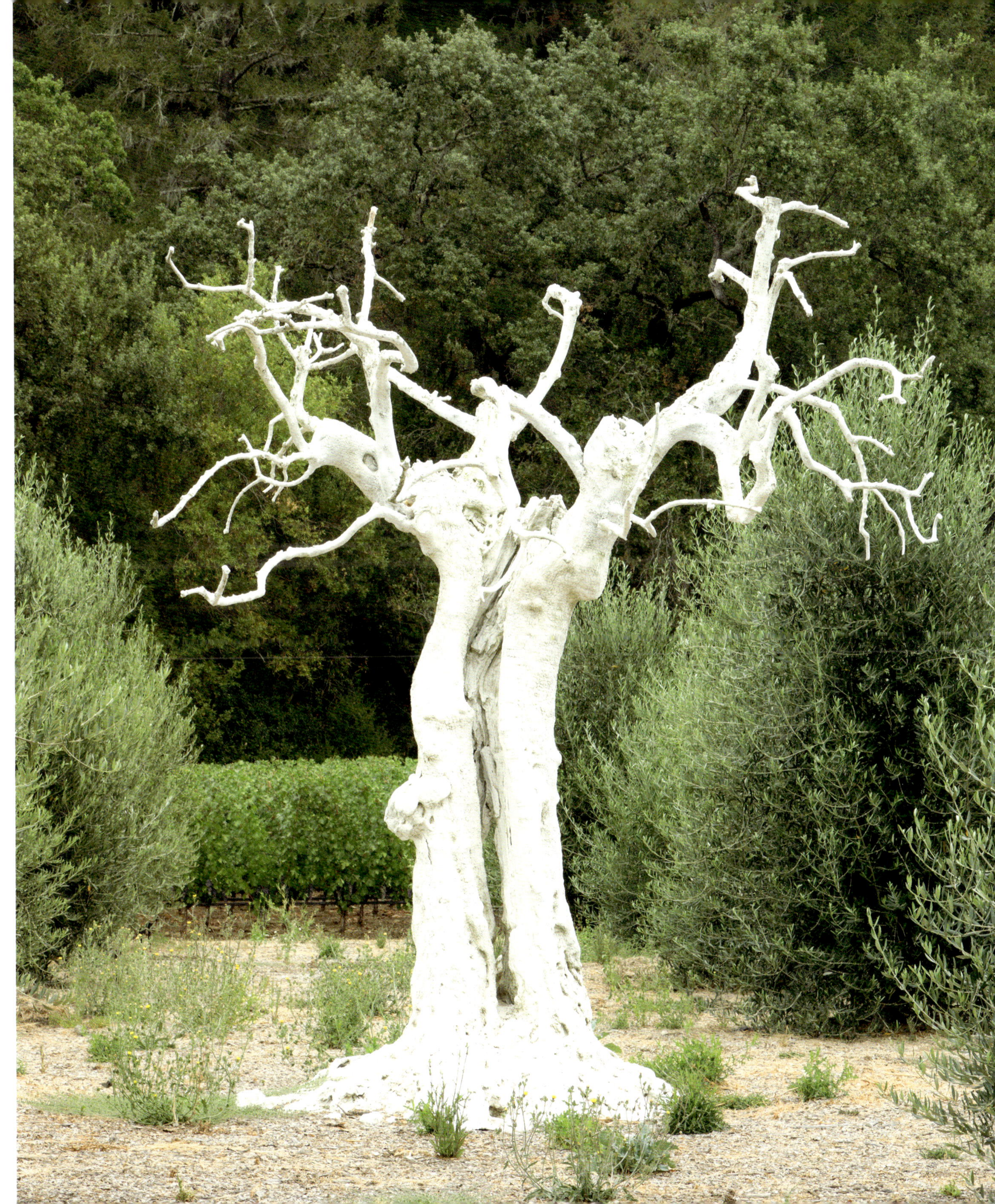

air/gets/into/everything/even/nothing, 2006
Cast aluminum, white enamel
159 1/2 × 147 5/8 × 133 7/8 inches
(405 × 375 × 340 cm)

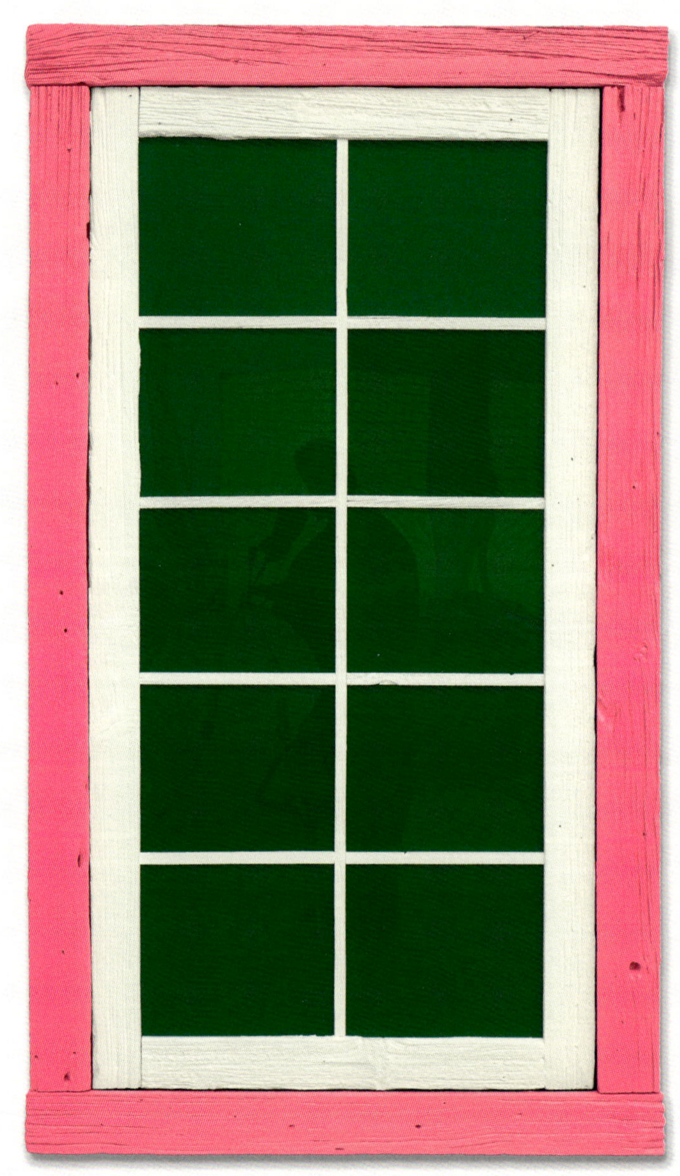

The Blank, 2014
Wood, acrylic paint, and Plexiglas
77⅛ × 44⅛ × 2 inches (196 × 122 × 5 cm)

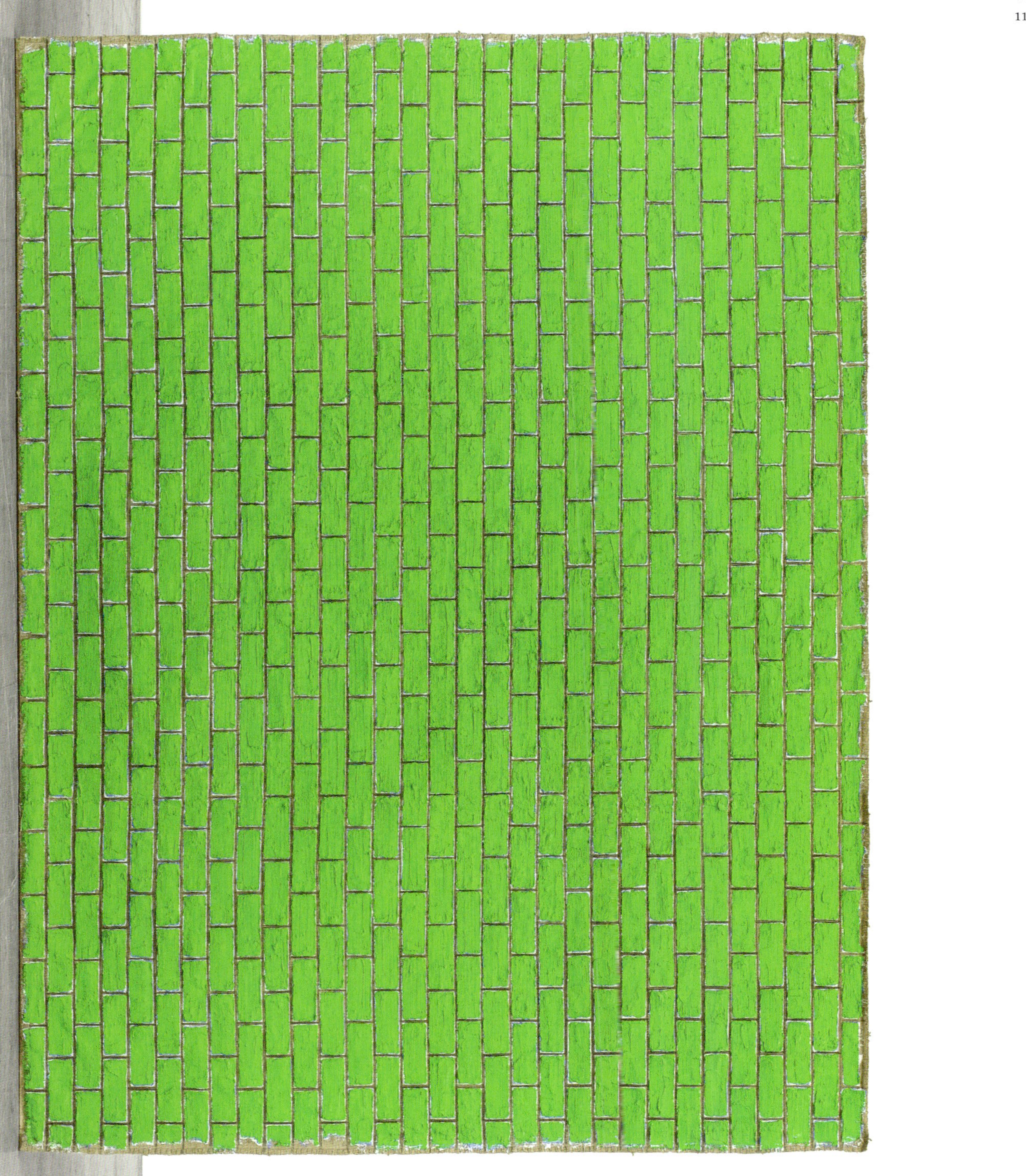

achterseptemberzweitausendunddreizehn,
2015
Oil on burlap, wood
119 ¾ × 161 ⅝ inches (304.2 × 410.5 cm)

STERLING RUBY

b. 1972, Bitburg, Germany

SP 93, 2010
Spray paint on canvas
125 × 185 inches (317.5 × 469.9 cm)

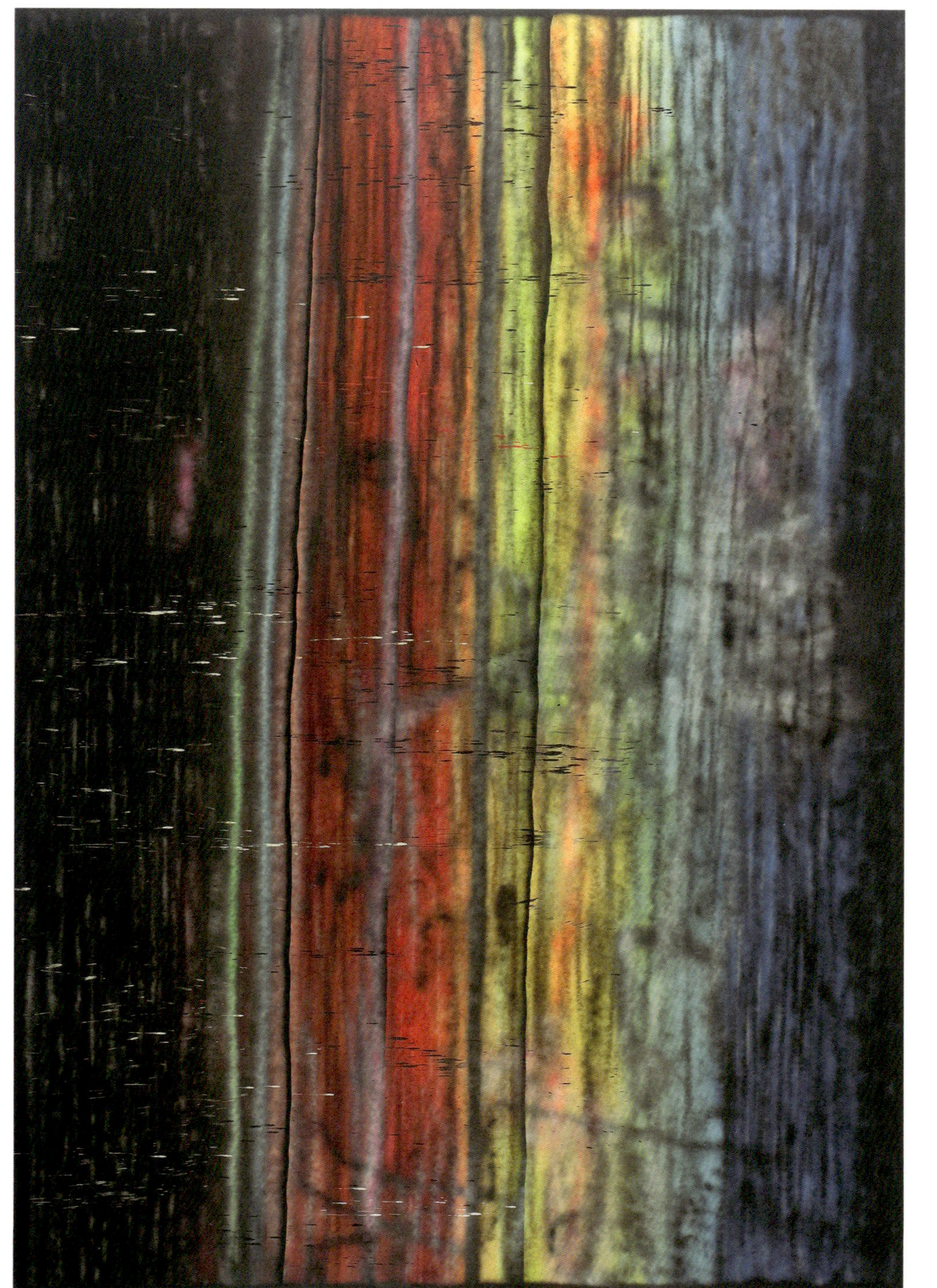

Sterling Ruby has flirted with so many styles, materials, mediums, and methods of creating art that tracking an overarching aesthetic or theoretical concern in his budding and prolific career is challenging. Yet it's a testament to Ruby's ability to make his art stick—in the minds of critics, viewers, and collectors alike—that works from all of his many phases are instantly recognizable. His rough, giant clay basins, his elongated urethane stalactites, his spray-painted canvases—not one is like the other, and each is distinctly a product of Ruby's febrile practice.

Ruby was born in 1972 to an American father and a Dutch mother on the Bitburg Army base in Bitburg, Germany. After getting a BA from the Pennsylvania School of Art and Design in 1996, he graduated with a BFA from the Art Institute of Chicago in 2002. He then moved to Los Angeles (where he still lives and works), and studied under artists Paul McCarthy, Chris Burden, and Mike Kelley at the Art Center College of Design in Pasadena. Ruby's work has been exhibited in dozens of solo exhibitions around the globe, including a 2008 show at The Museum of Contemporary Art, Los Angeles, and his art is in the permanent collections of New York's Solomon R. Guggenheim Museum, Whitney Museum of American Art, The Museum of Modern Art, Centre Georges Pompidou in Paris, and the Tate in London.

There have been various attempts to contextualize Ruby's art through the guise of psychoanalysis; the word "repression" comes up a lot when discussing his work, which is perhaps a result of the fact that Ruby often creates objects on an immense scale—how better to describe monumentality than as a reaction to its own limits?

Still, there might be some merit to that analysis, simply because Ruby's work—large and small—does have the unmistakable tinge of violence. It's occasionally explicit, like his 2013 work *Big Yellow Mama*, a massive powder-coated aluminum reproduction of an electric chair. It's also evident in more subtle ways; *SP 88*, a giant spray paint on canvas work from 2010, has the makings of a Rothkoesque series of pleasing colors, which Ruby has carefully and comprehensively ruined with black, barlike lines that deface the canvas, inch by inch. J. T.

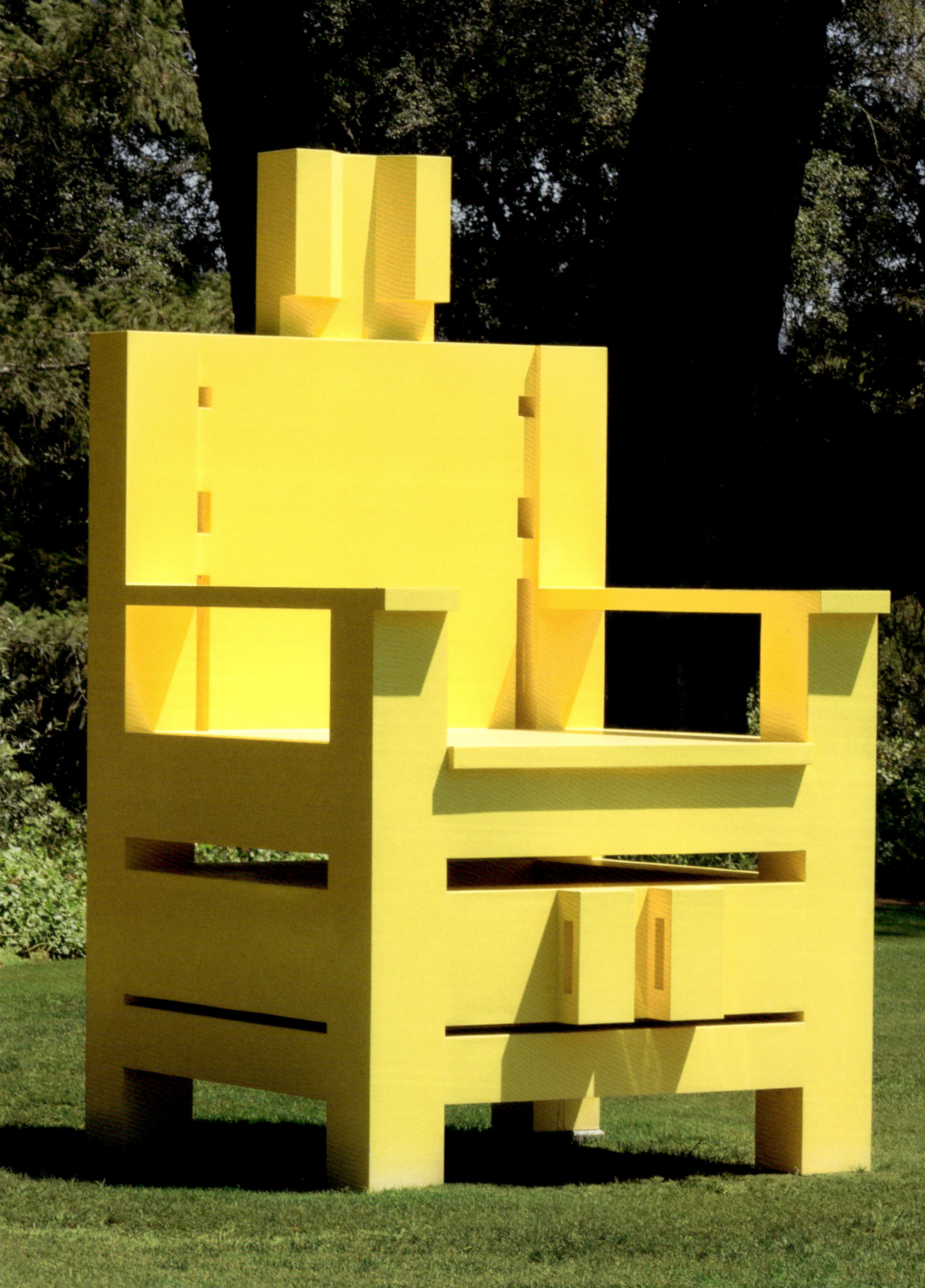

Big Yellow Mama, 2013
Powder-coated aluminum
96 × 56 × 56 inches (243.8 × 142.2 × 142.2 cm)
Edition of 3, 1 AP

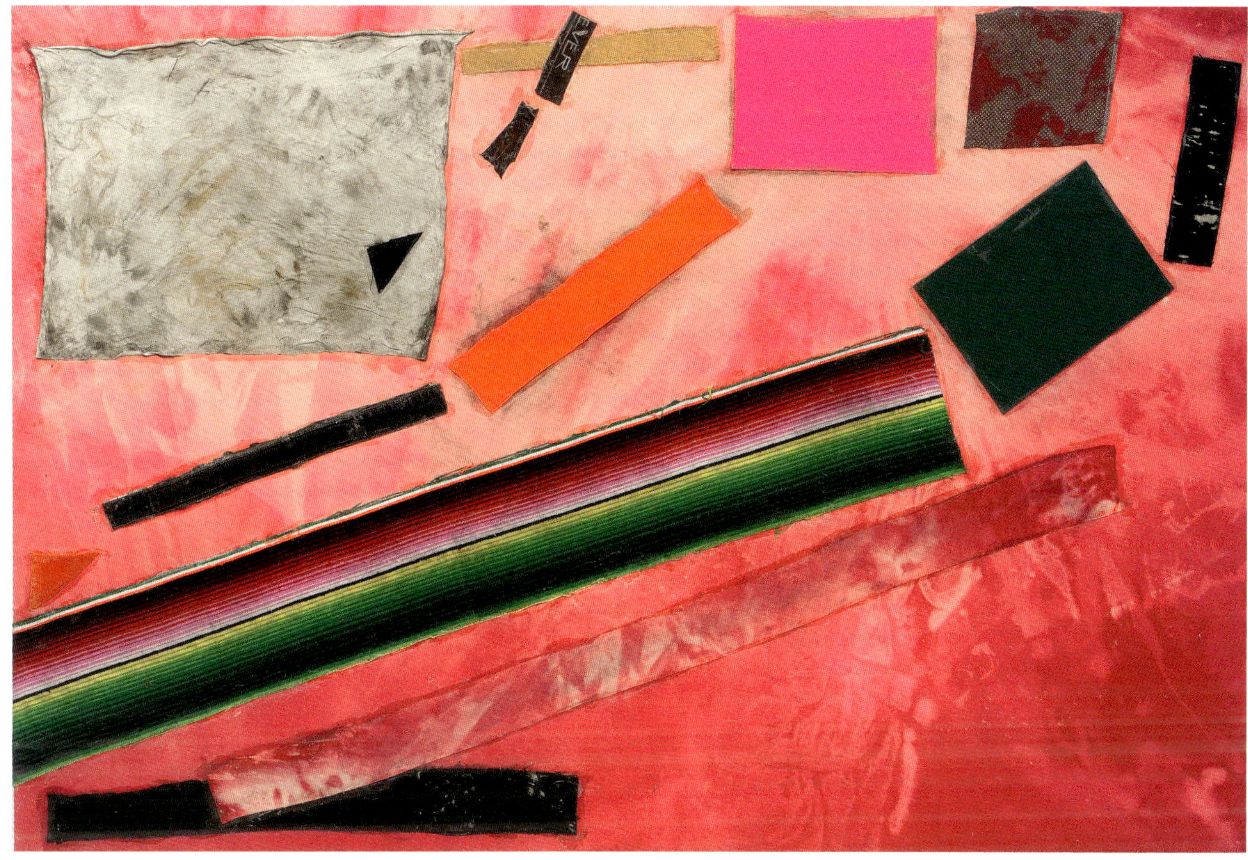

BC (3454), 2011
Collage, paint, bleach, glue,
and fabric on wood
48 × 72 × 2 inches (121.9 × 182.9 × 5.1 cm)

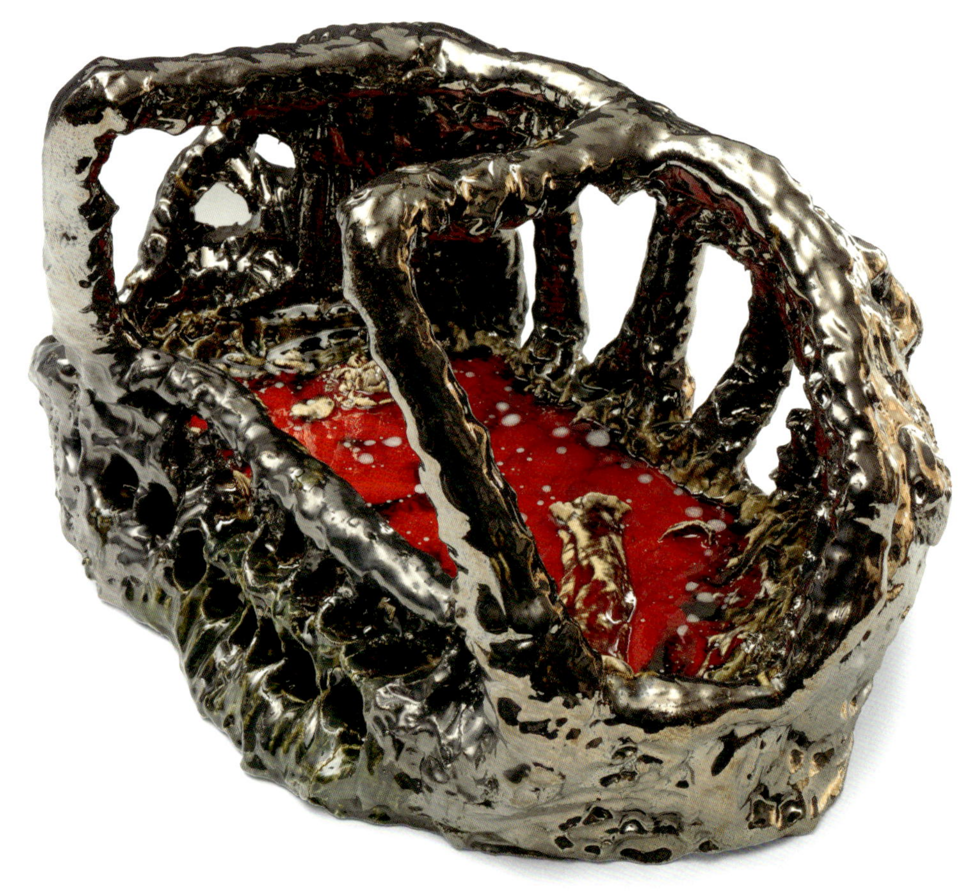

Modern Brass/Ketamine User, 2012
Ceramic
15 × 24½ × 15 inches (38.1 × 62.2 × 38.1 cm)

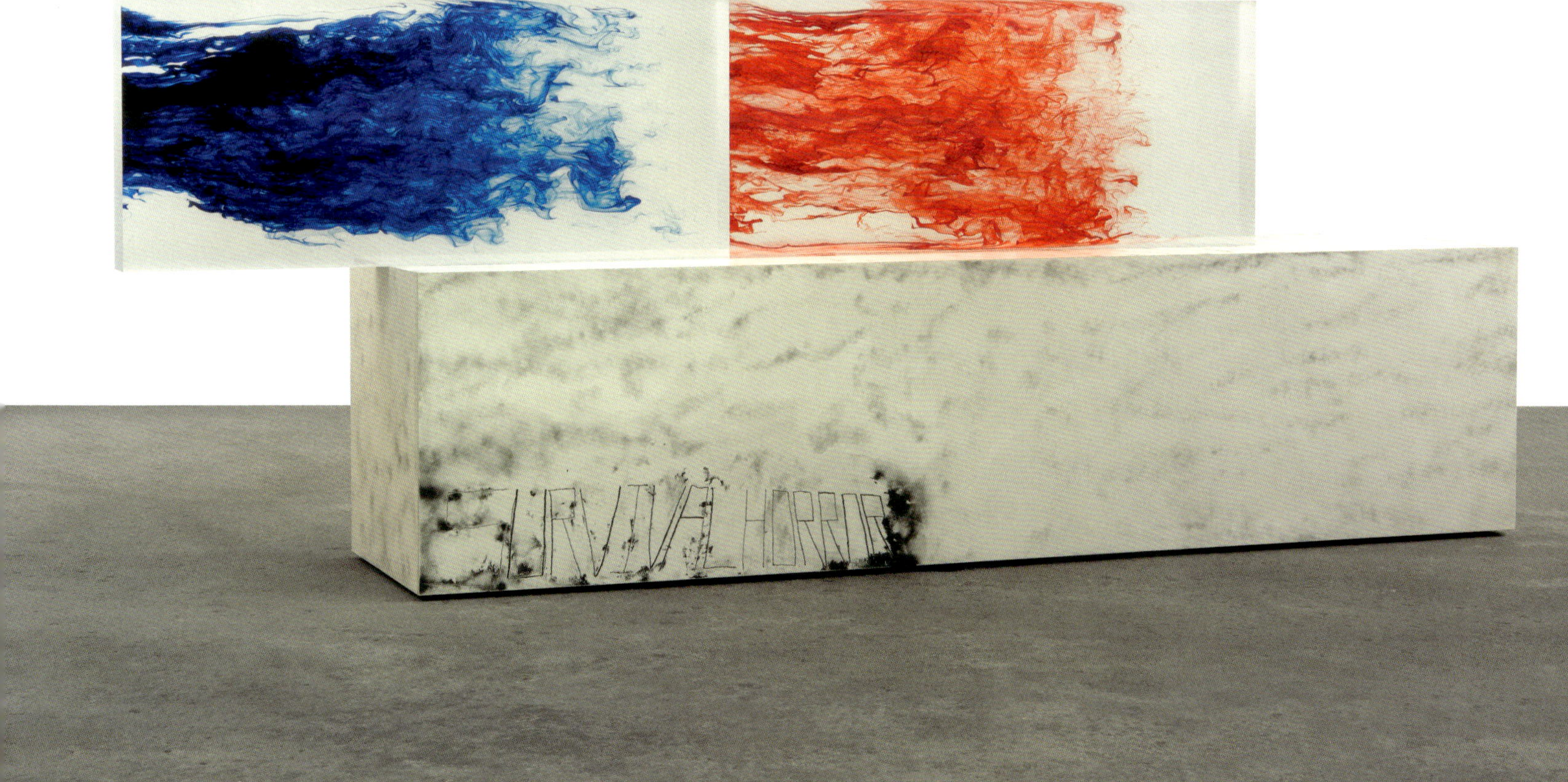

ACTS/SURVIVAL HORROR, 2015
Clear urethane blocks, dye, wood,
and formica
66 ¼ × 174 ½ × 35 inches
(168.3 × 445.8 × 88.9 cm) overall

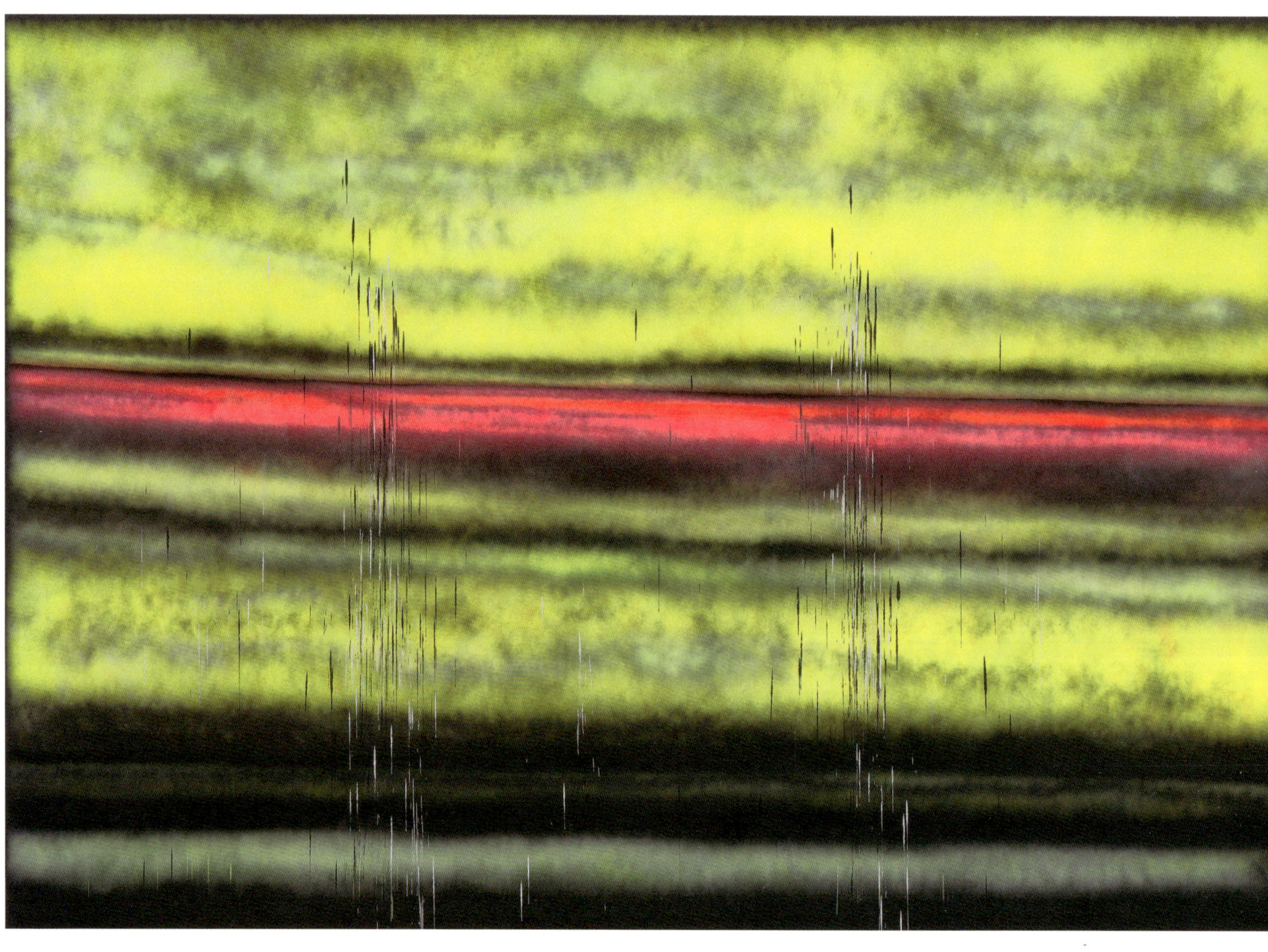

SP308, 2015
Spray paint on synthetic canvas
Diptych: 100 × 144 × 2 in.
(254 × 365.8 × 5.1 cm) each

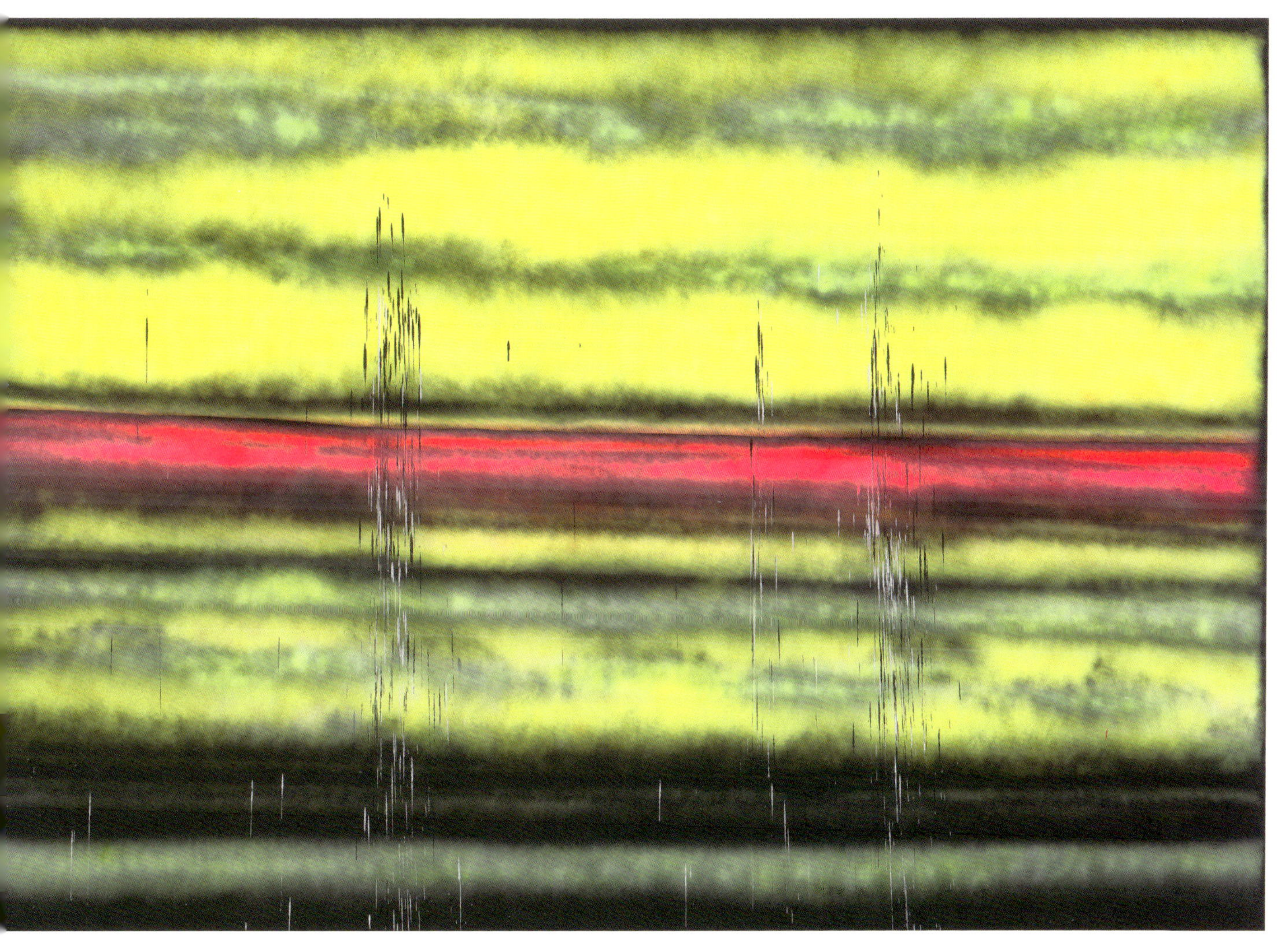

ANALIA SABAN

b. 1980, Buenos Aires, Argentina

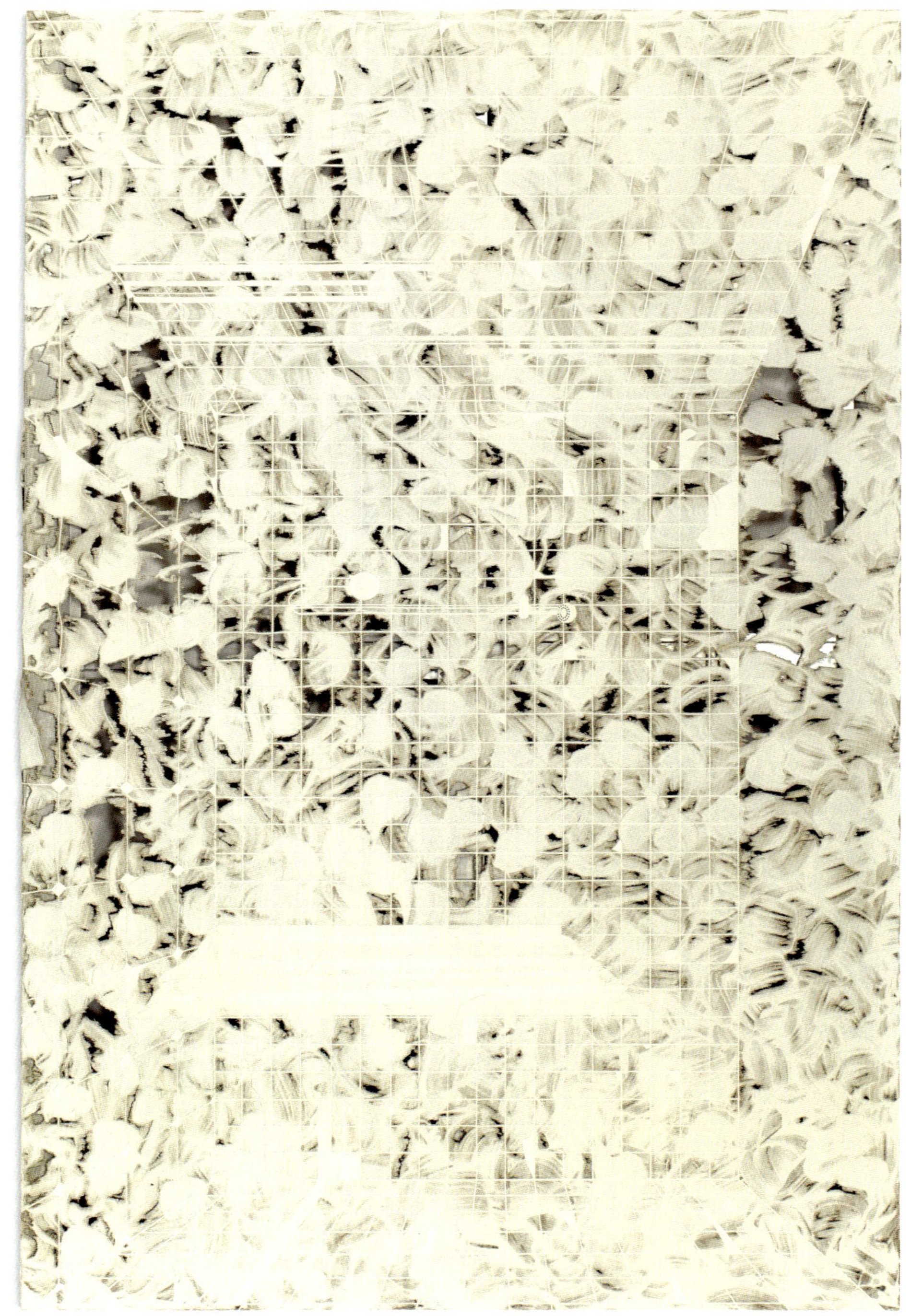

Erosion (Changing Room #2), 2012
Laser sculpted acrylic paint on canvas
38 × 58 × 2 inches (96.5 × 147.3 × 5.1 cm)

There's a certain irony to the fact that Analia Saban's practice revolves around the materiality of objects and yet is beholden to none. Paintings, in Saban's hands, are unravelled and repurposed; marble is broken and draped; ink is dumped into plastic bags; newspapers are etched with lasers. Traditional media—e.g. paint, ink, and pencil on canvas and paper—are, to Saban, both the tools and the subjects of her work.

Saban was born in 1980 in Buenos Aires and received a BFA from Loyola University in New Orleans in 2001. While attending the University of California, Los Angeles (receiving her MFA in 2005), Saban met key mentor John Baldessari, who advised her artistic practice and provided her with a studio space in Santa Monica. Unlike some of her peers, Saban's rise to global recognition has been unhurried. After a first solo show at Kim Light Gallery in Los Angeles, her next solo show wasn't for another two years; but since then, her work has been exhibited in London, Berlin, Buenos Aires, Paris, and New York, and has entered the permanent collections of the Hammer Museum in Los Angeles, the Hessel Museum at Bard College in Annandale-on-Hudson, New York, and the Centre Georges Pompidou in Paris. Saban lives and works in Los Angeles.

Saban's *Draped Marble (Fior di Pesco)* from 2015 particularly embodies her interrogation of medium specificity. A broken slab of marble mounted on steel and draped over a wooden sawhorse, the sculpture operates on multiple planes. First, marble is most commonly used as a material into which artists carve, effectively transforming a stone to an artwork; Saban turns this process on its head by "draping" it, thereby emphasizing its physical composition through her artistic intervention rather than effacing the material in service of her objectives. Second, by draping the marble Saban exposes the minerals in the stone, which can be used as pigment for paint. The draped marble thus does double duty: highlighting the medium while simultaneously combining it, if only by inference, with something else entirely. J. T.

Outburst (Living Room), 2014
8 graphite on laser sculpted papers
28¼ × 47¼ × 2 inches (71.8 × 120 × 5 cm)
each framed

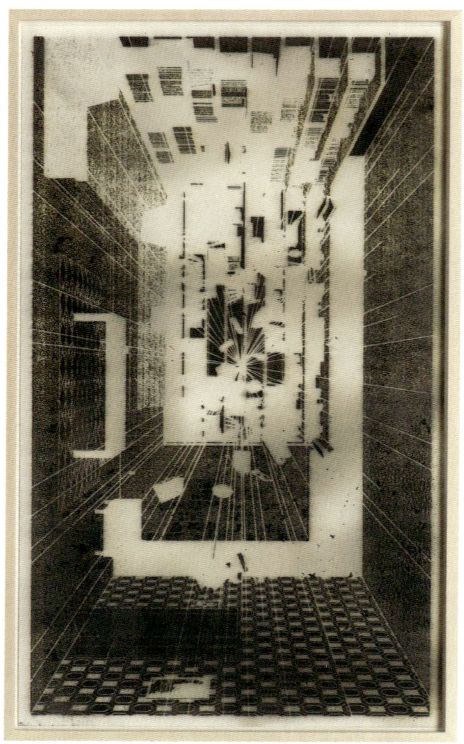

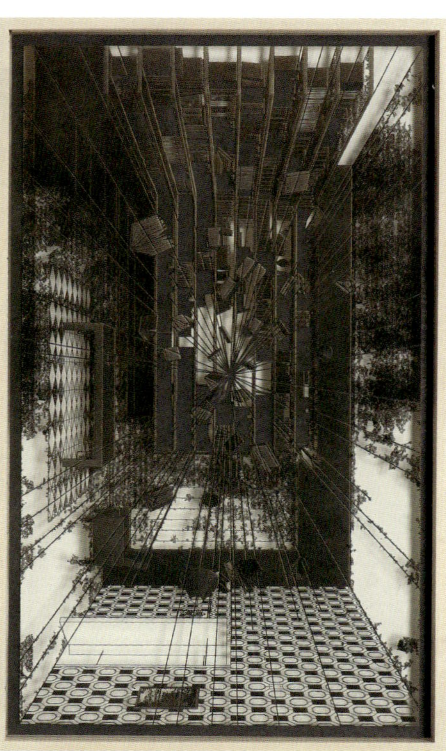

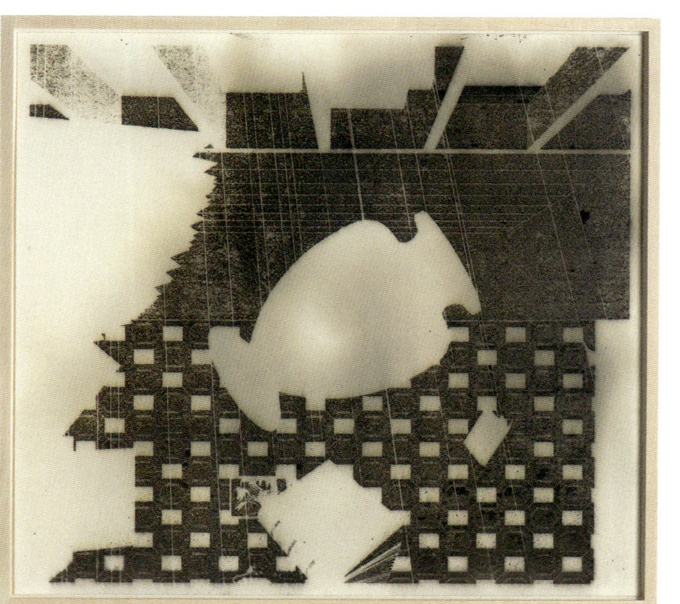

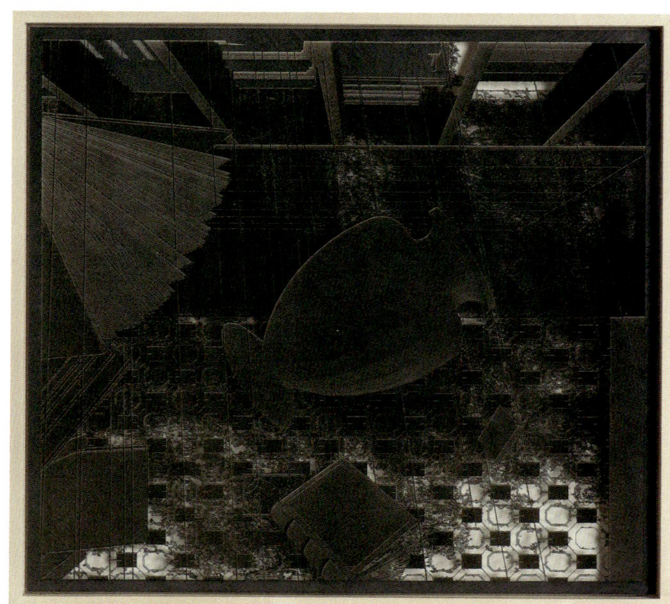

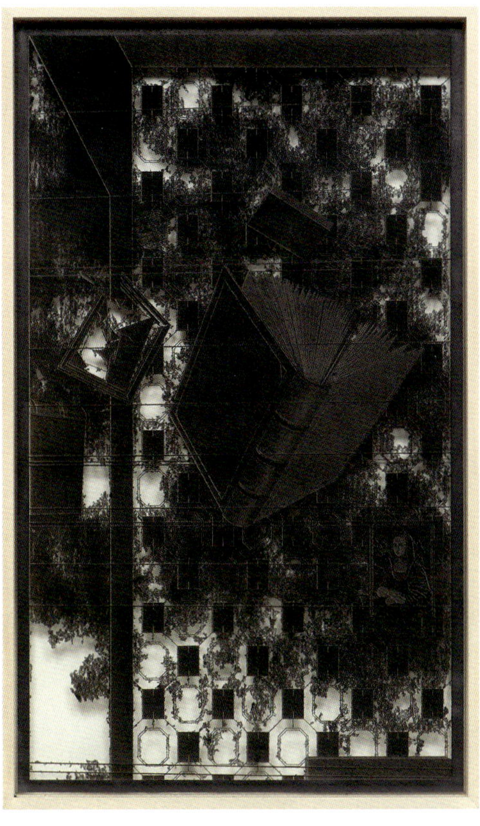
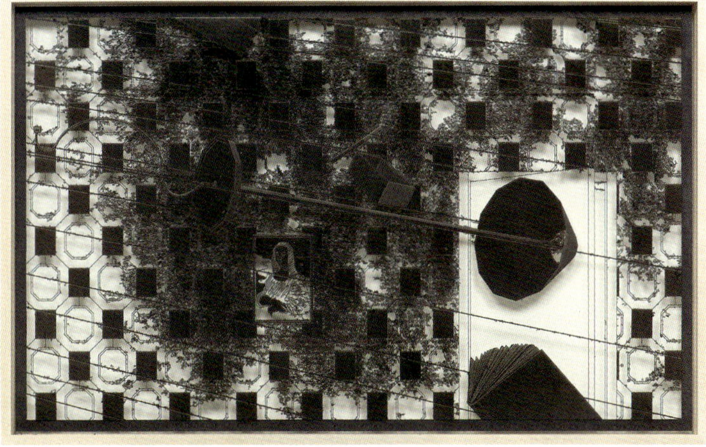
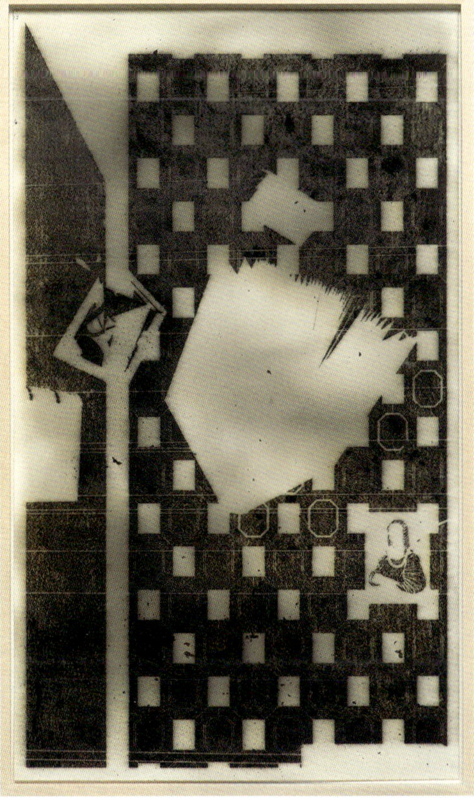
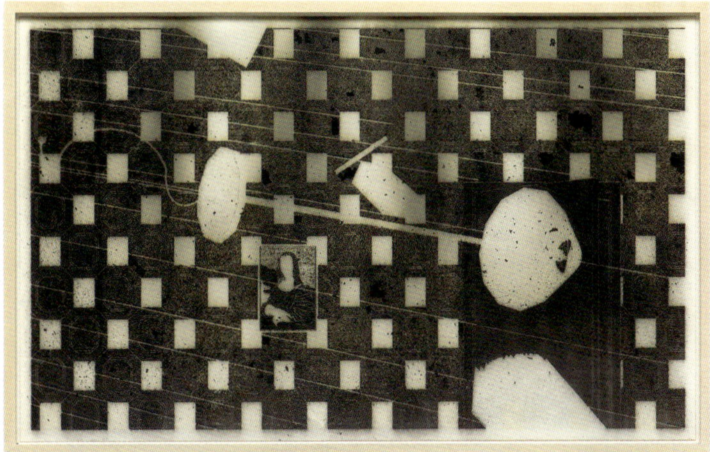

Cane Back Chair (with Back Weaving Rubbing), 2014
Linen and oil stick on chair
38½ × 18½ × 18 inches (97.8 × 47 × 45.7 cm)

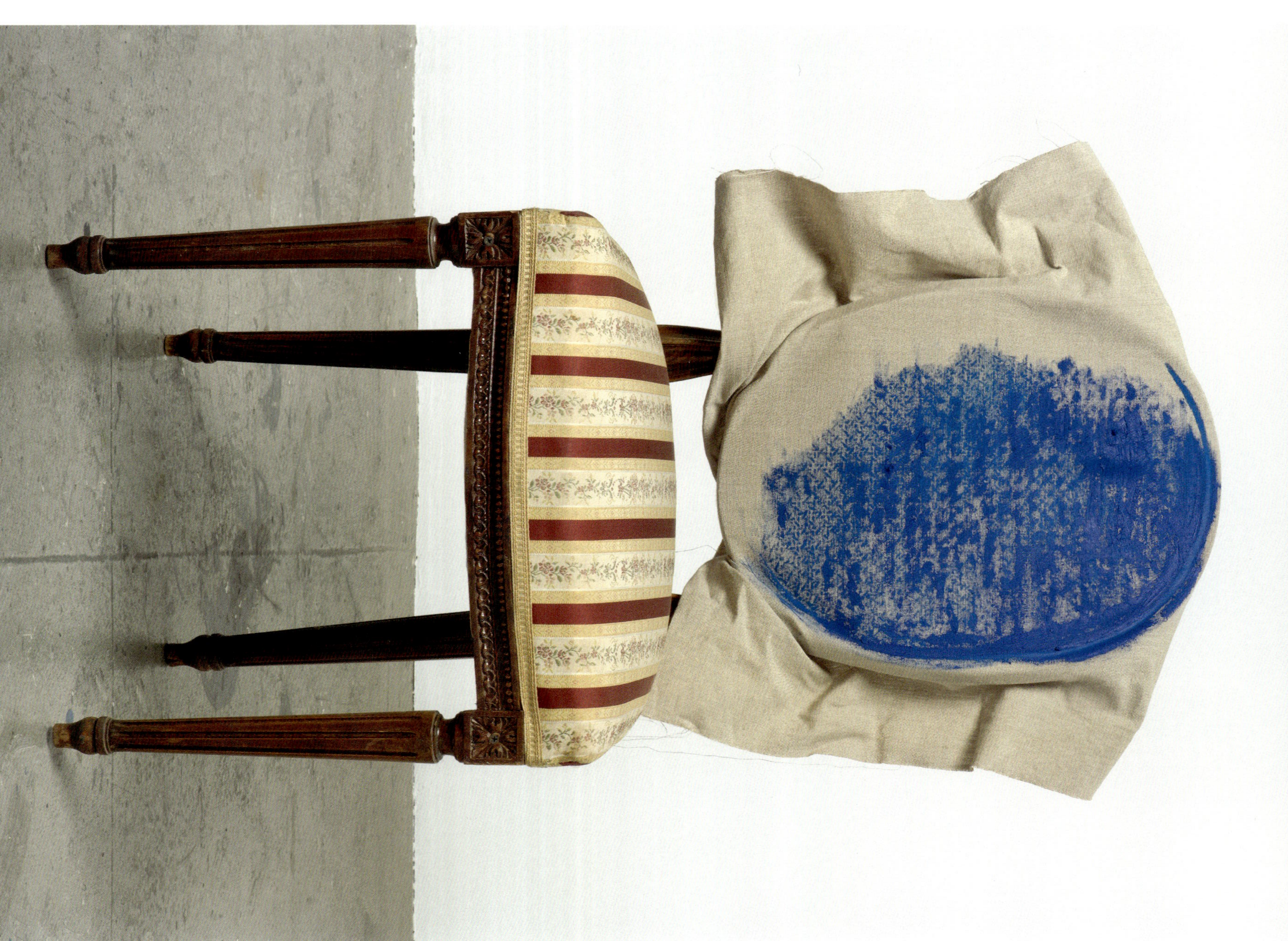

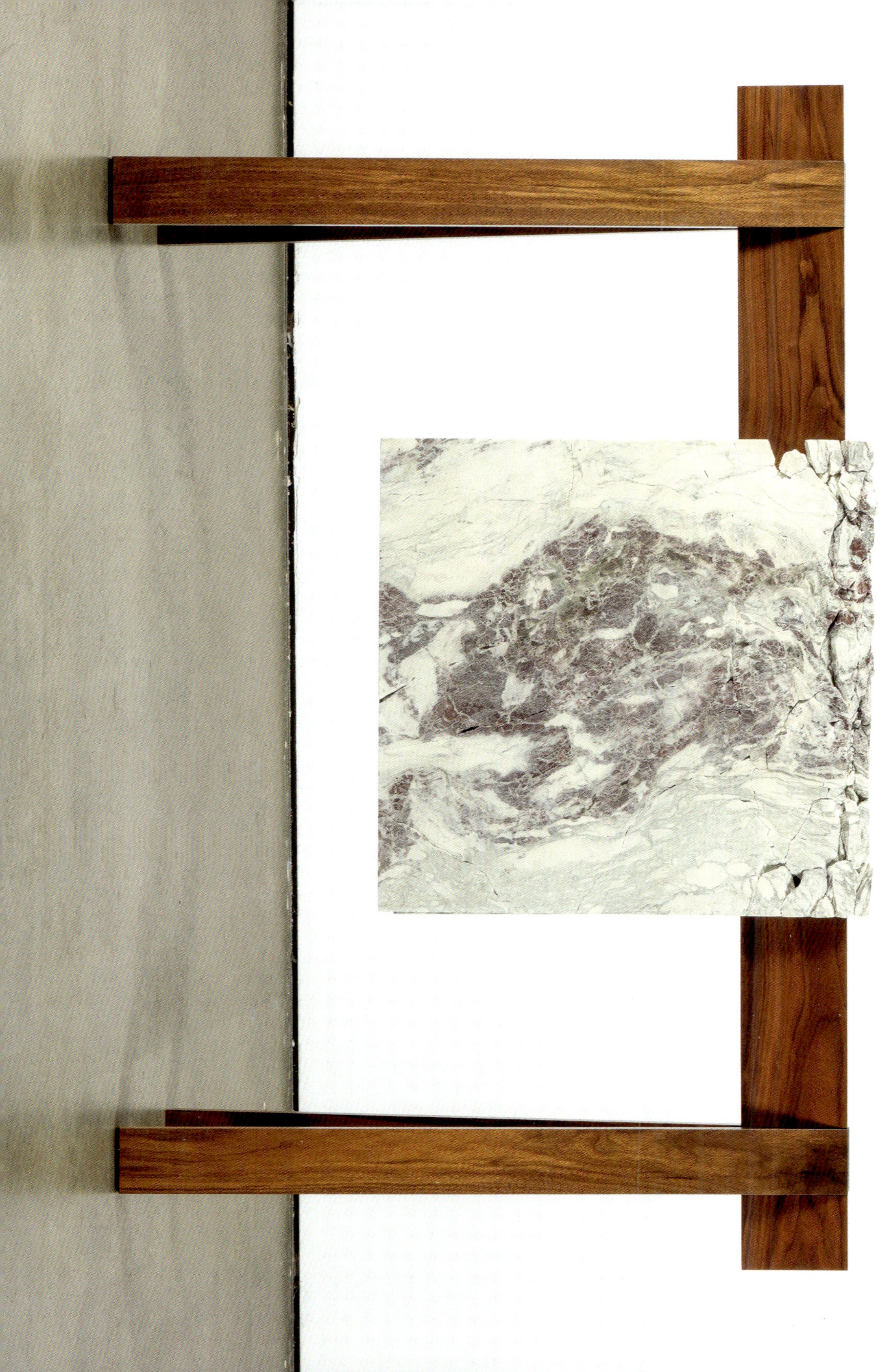

Draped Marble (Fior di Pesco), 2015
Marble mounted on steel on wooden sawhorses
39 × 62½ × 16½ inches
(99.1 × 158.8 × 41.9 cm)

In an age where all objects, no matter how large, small, old, or intricate, can be digitized and put online, their two-dimensional images visible to anyone with a computer and an internet connection (beds for sale on Amazon, dogs available on Petfinder, even cities flattened out on Google Maps),

Paul Sietsema's art forces its viewers to reconsider the material dimensionality of an object's representation. Working in a range of mediums, most notably film, drawing, and painting, Sietsema's conceptual art plays with history, materiality, and medium, creating uncanny images that ultimately disorient and intrigue.

Sietsema was born in Los Angeles in 1968, graduated with a BA from University of California, Berkeley, in 1992, then attended the University of California, Los Angeles's New Genres MFA program, studying with giants of the Los Angeles art scene, including Paul McCarthy and Chris Burden. Just four years after he graduated in 1999, Sietsema was given a solo show, *Empire*, at the Whitney Museum of American Art in New York. He's since had exhibitions at The Museum of Modern Art in New York, the Wexner Center for the Arts in Columbus, and the Museo Nacional Centro de Arte Reina Sofía in Madrid. His work is in the permanent collections of more than a dozen public institutions, including the Hammer Museum in Los Angeles, the Tate Modern in London, and the Walker Art Center in Minneapolis.

Sietsema's video art could be considered the foundation of the rest of his work. After collecting and/or making sculptures, drawings, and paintings, he films those objects, creating what appeared to be a slideshow that he then projects on gallery walls. Stripped of context and converted from three dimensions into flat projections, his objects become wholly transformed.

The reverse of this phenomenon, which can be found in his more recent work, also holds. For *Painted coins* (2014), Sietsema dipped coins into paint, laid them out on newspaper, photographed the tableau, and then painstakingly recreated it with ink and enamel. Here was the same decontextualization of objects that was operative in his videos, except that instead of using a camera to flatten the objects he used paint and pen to re-materialize them. The work is a prescient (not to say poignant) commentary on function and form, the *tromp l'oeil* coins calling both the objectivity of the viewer and the veracity of the subject into question. J. T.

Painted coins, 2014
Ink and enamel on paper in artist's frame
32 × 34½ inches (81 × 88 cm)

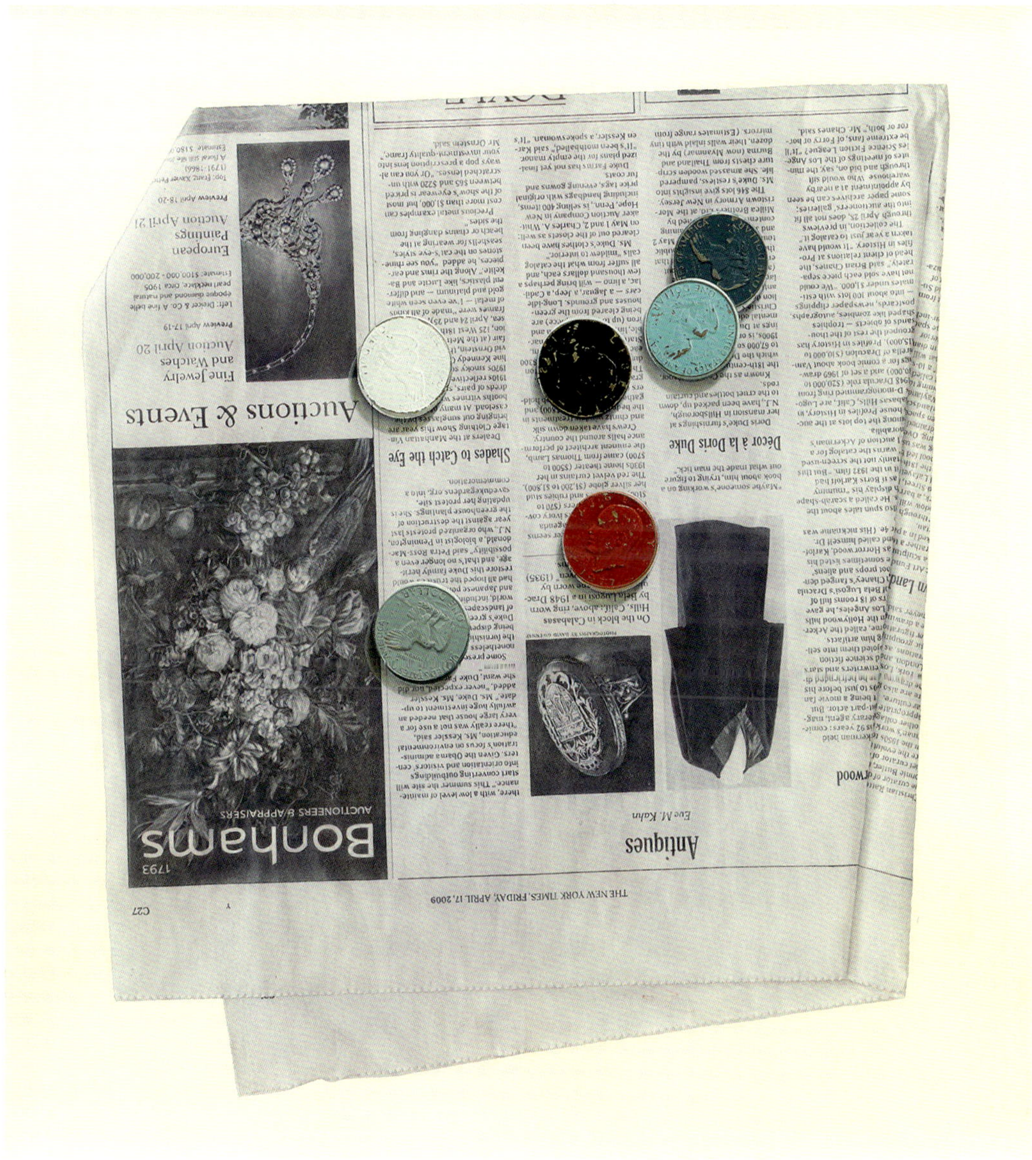

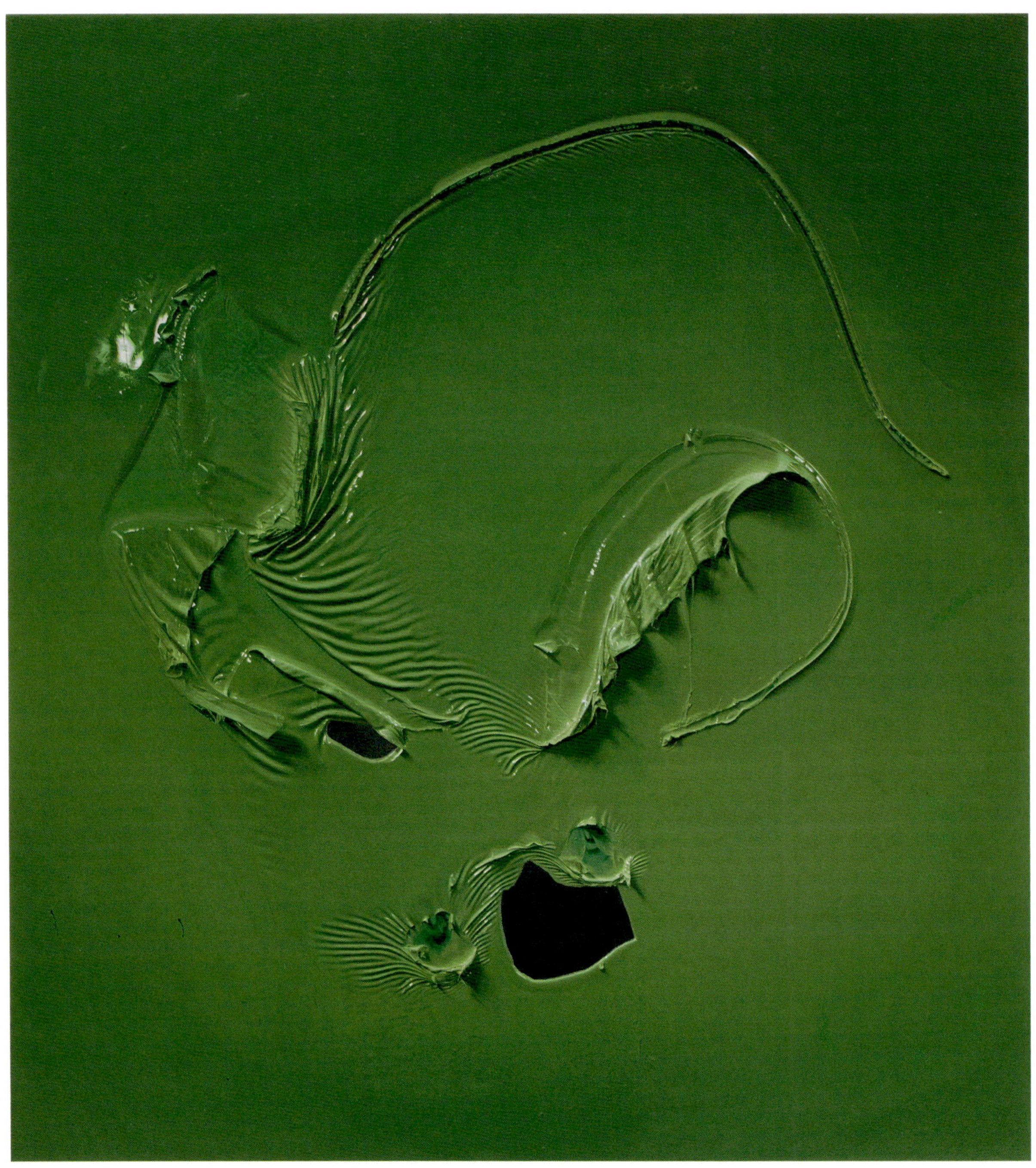

Green painting, 2016
Enamel on linen
51½ × 47⅞ inches (131 × 122 cm)

Painter's Mussel 4, 2011
Ink on paper in artist's frame
72¼ × 71½ in. (183.5 × 181.6 cm)

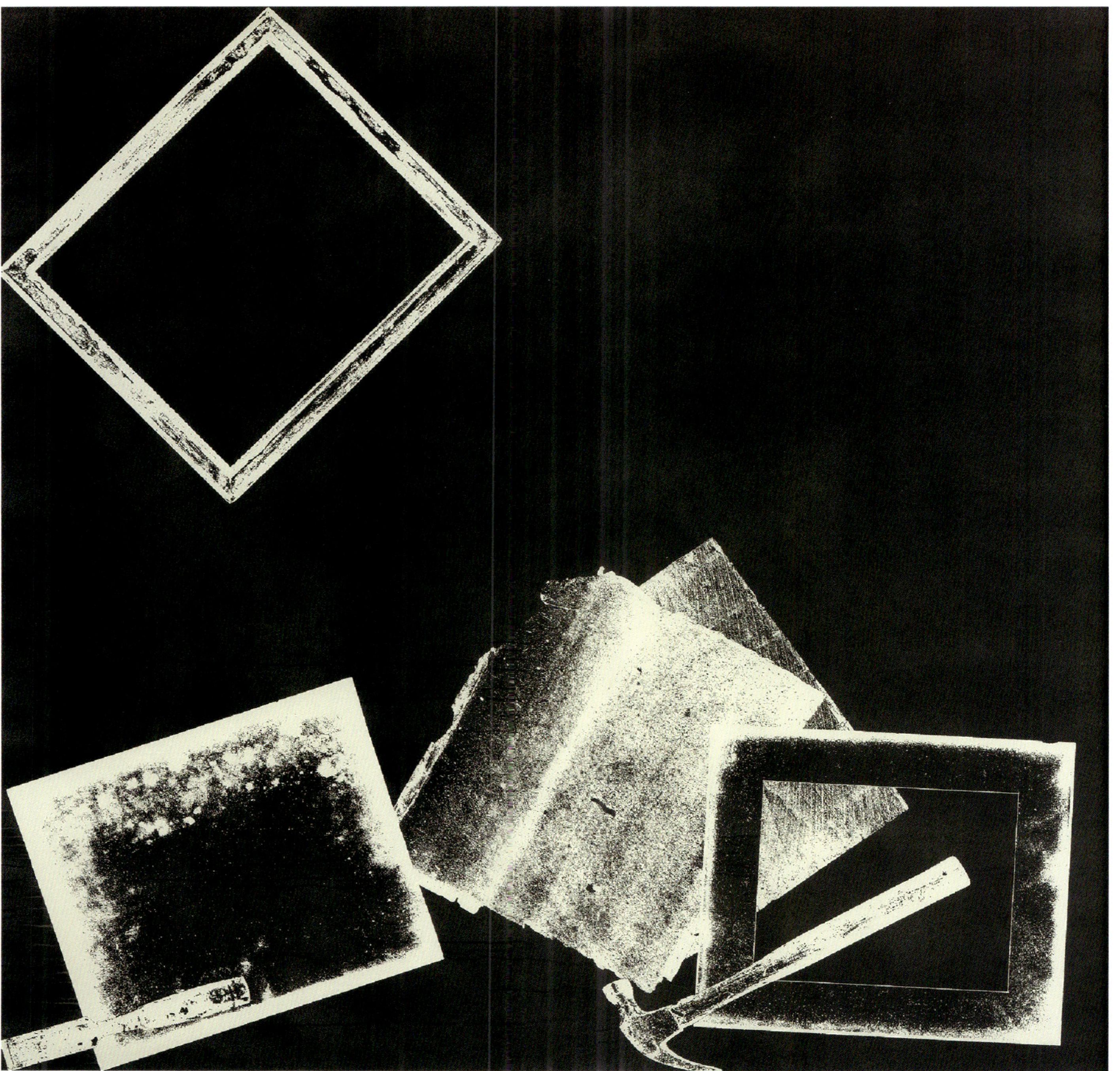

RUDOLF STINGEL b. 1956, Merano, Italy

First recognized in the late 1980s for his sublime, silvery monochromatic paintings, Rudolf Stingel's conceptual painting practice and site-specific installations aim to question the conventions of the traditional mode of painting by using an array of techniques, textures, and materials to redefine the medium.

Born in 1956 in Merano, Italy, Stingel continues to live and work in Merano, as well as New York City. In 1989, Stingel produced a series of silkscreens presented as an instructional manual, *Instructions* (1989), published in several languages, on how to create silver paintings in his own, distinct style. Through parody, Stingel undermined the mystique of artistic production by giving the public a step-by-step guide to mimic his own complex and untraditional methods of paint application.

Since then, Stingel has further expanded the boundaries of painting in a series of installations where he covered entire walls and floors of exhibition spaces with monochrome or patterned carpets, transforming the architecture and space itself into a sort of painting. He has also applied silver panels made from aluminum-coated insulation material called Celotex onto the walls of galleries, on which visitors could write or imprint. These large Celotex walls were then broken up, resulting in separate works, such as *Untitled* (2001) from Stingel's very first Celotex installation at the Museo di Arte Moderna e Contemporanea in Trento, Italy, in 2001. In effect, Stingel raises questions of artistic authorship and autonomy while also calling attention to the passage of time.

Moving from abstraction to figuration, Stingel produced his first self-portraits and portraits in the mid 2000s, executed in a photorealistic style. In the self-referential *Untitled* (2010), for example, Stingel represents himself as a melancholic young man. Made by repeatedly painting from the same black-and-white photograph and executed in grayscale, Stingel decidedly shifted from challenging the constraints of painting to questioning the role of the artist himself. As he stated, "The only activity in these paintings is self-doubt."

Stingel's work has been exhibited in at the Museo di Arte Moderna e Contemporanea, Palazzo delle Arbere in Italy; Museum für Moderne Kunst in Frankfurt; the Walker Art Center; Museum of Contemporary Art, Chicago; The Whitney Museum of American Art, New York and Neue National Galerie, Berlin. His work is included in the collections of The Museum of Modern Art, New York; The Art Institute of Chicago; Museum of Contemporary Art Chicago; The New Museum of Contemporary Art, New York among many others. L. C.

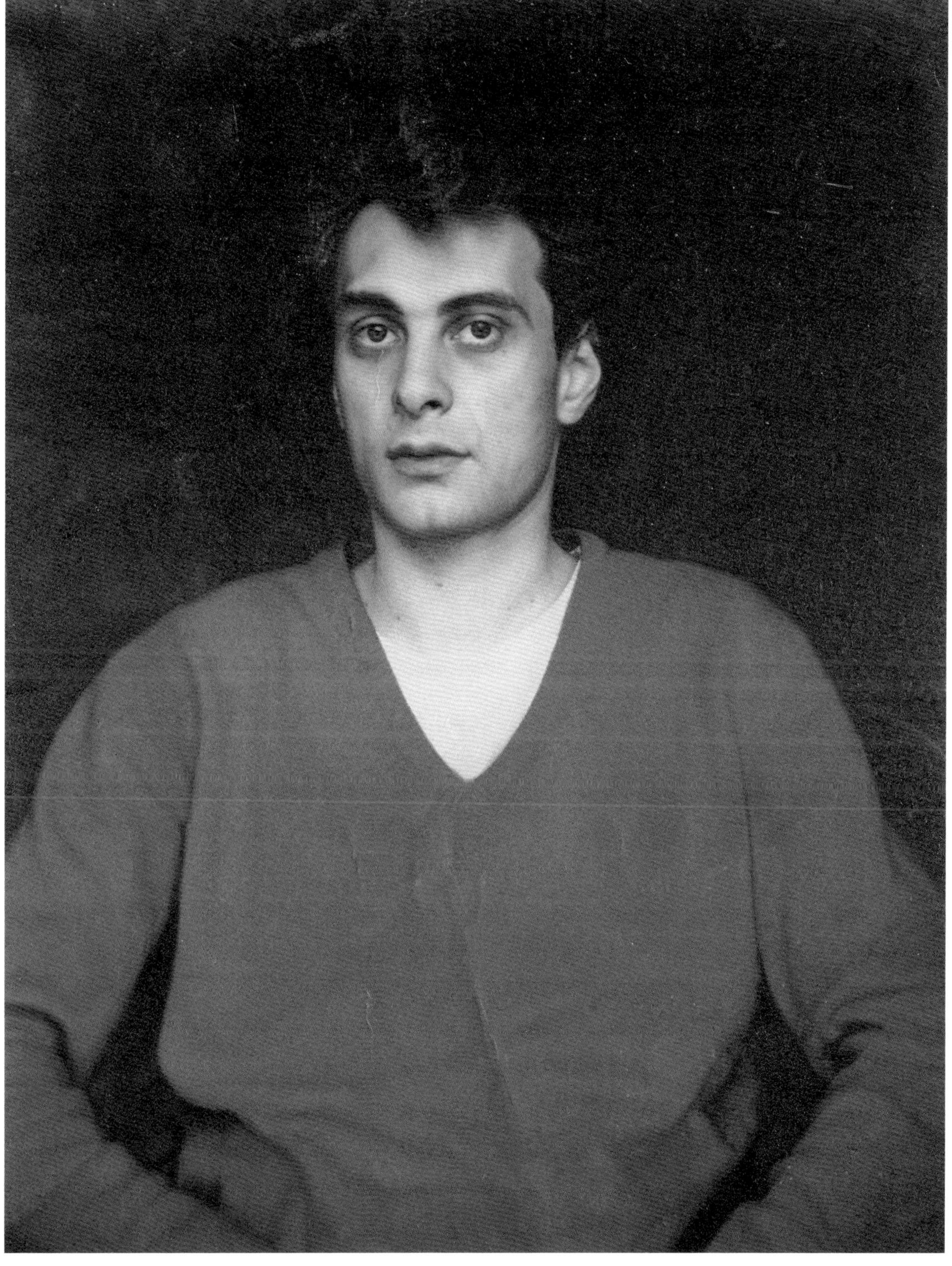

Untitled, 2010
Oil on canvas
131 × 102 inches (332.7 × 259.1 cm)

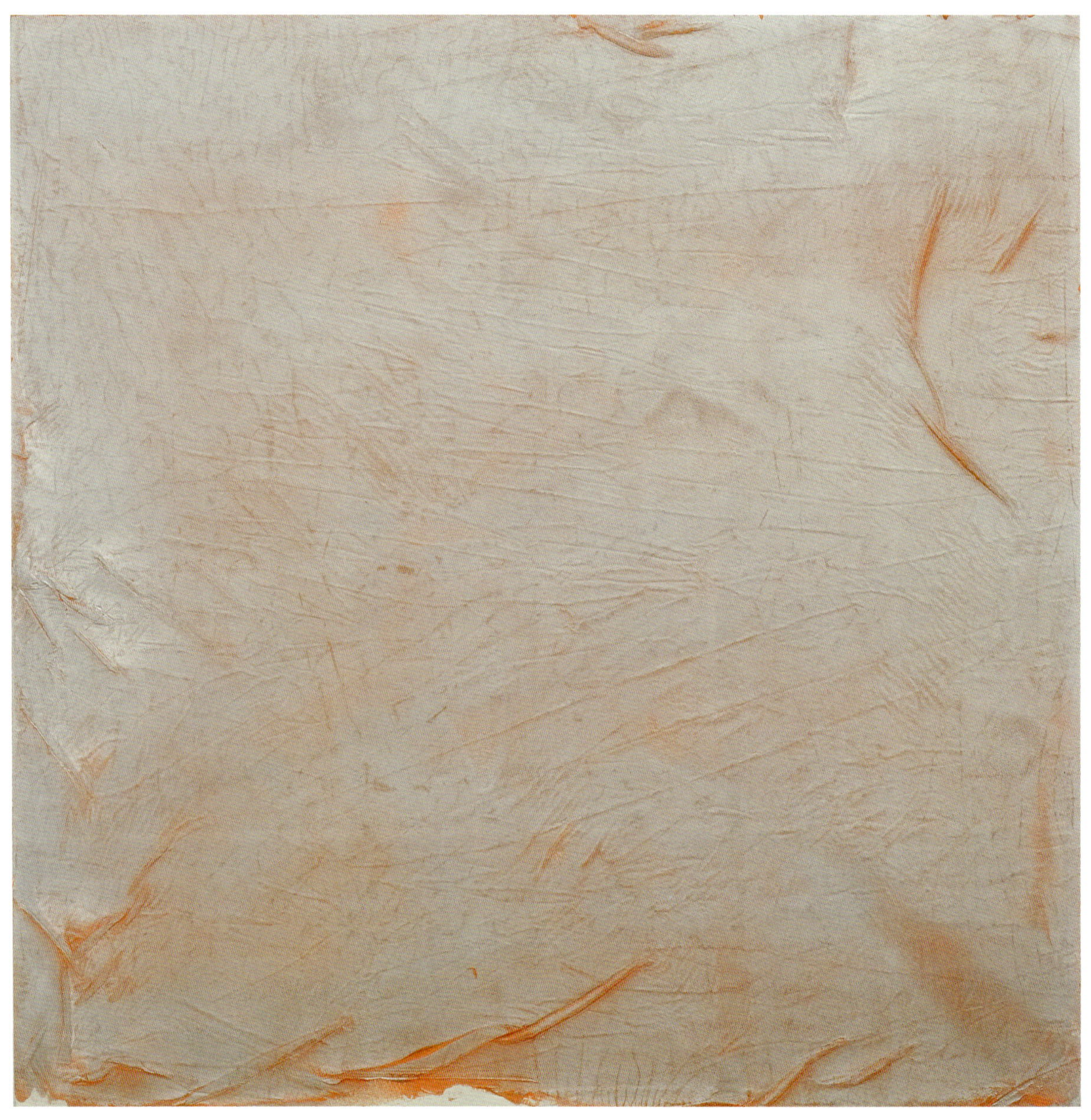

Untitled, 1993
Oil and enamel on canvas
40 × 40 × $1\frac{5}{8}$ inches (101.6 × 101.6 × 4.1 cm)

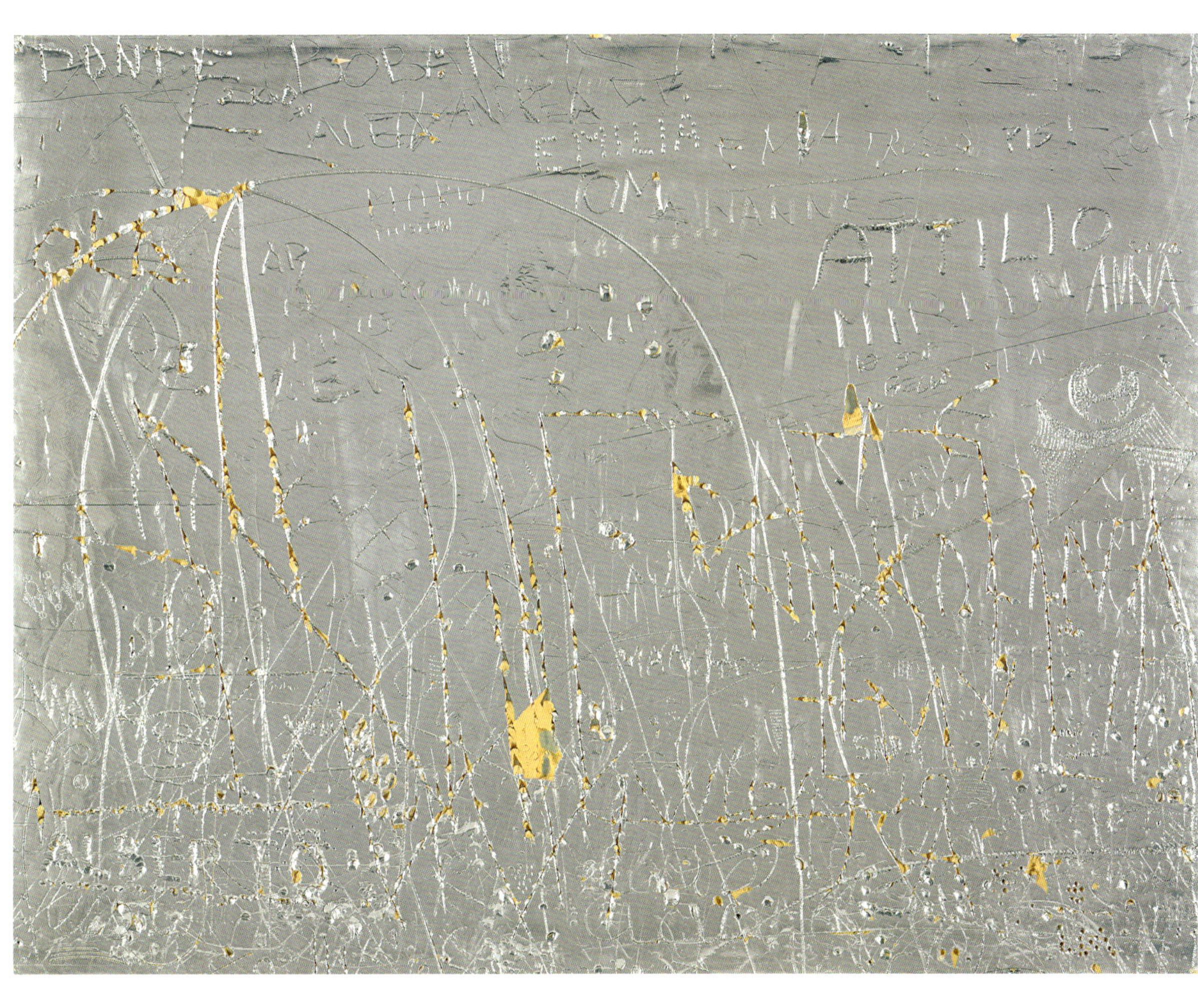

Untitled, 2001
Celotex
48 × 60 inches (121.9 × 152.4 cm)

Untitled, 2011
Oil and enamel on canvas mounted on linen
Triptych: 80 × 63 inches
(203.2 × 160 cm) each
80 × 191 inches (203.2 × 485.1 cm) overall

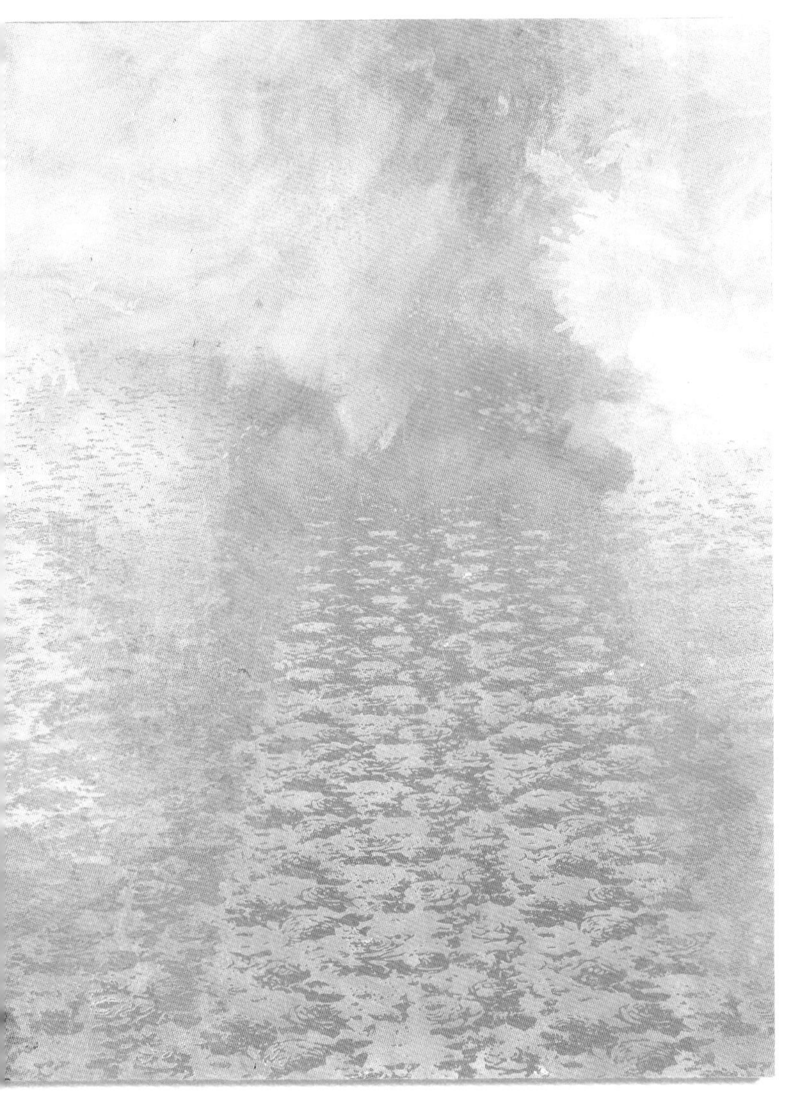

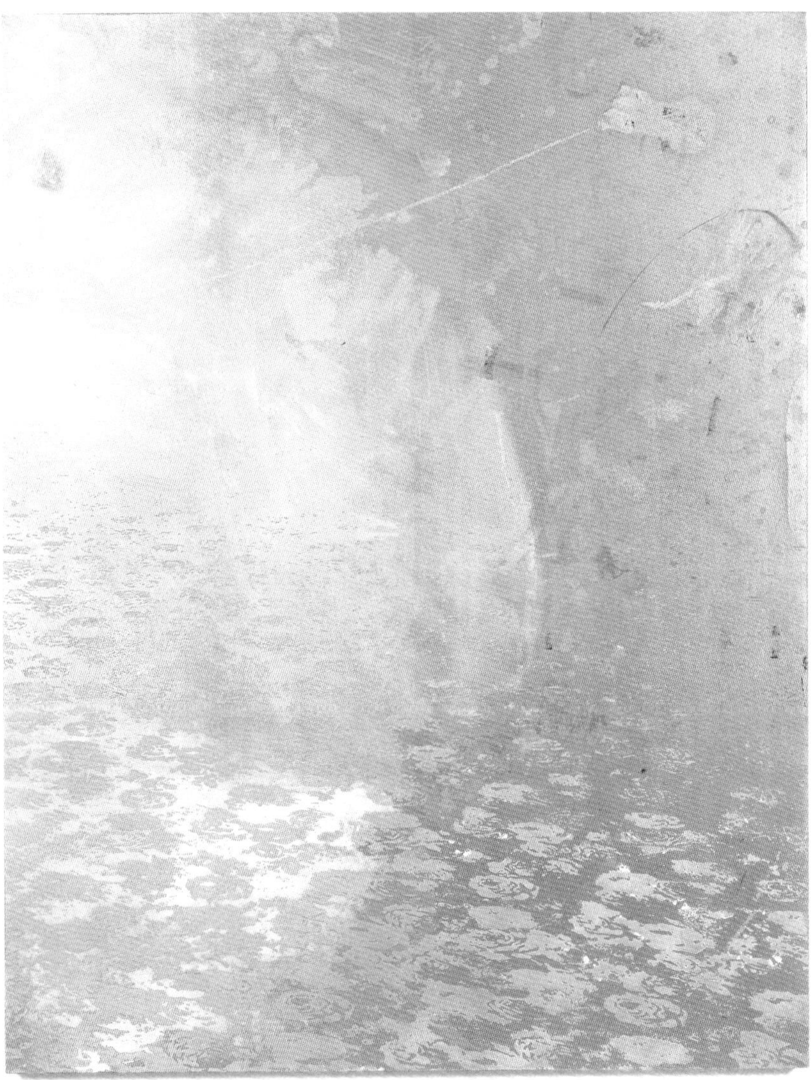

RIRKRIT TIRAVANIJA

b. 1961, Buenos Aires, Argentina

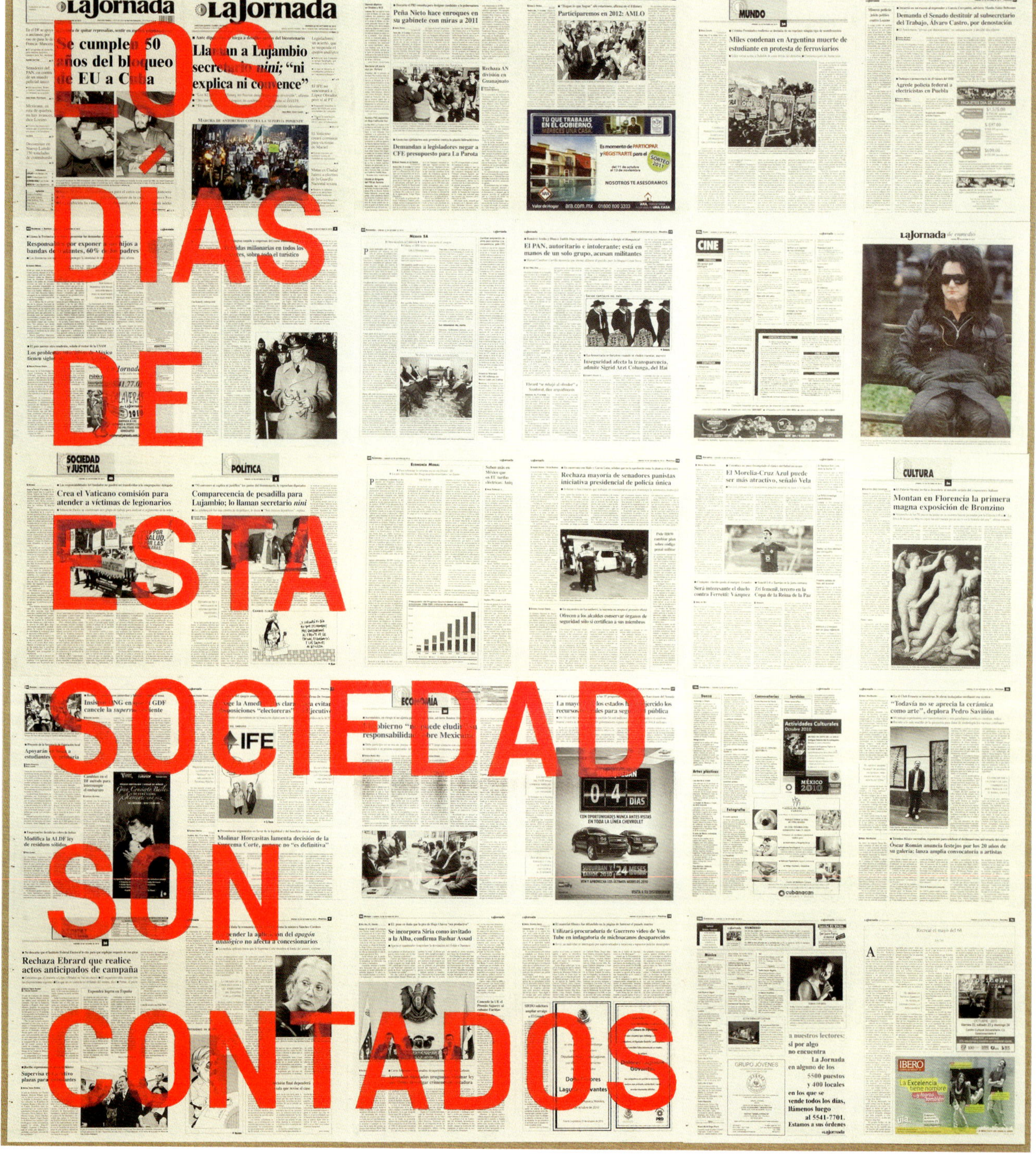

Untitled (Los días de esta sociedad son contados/18 de diciembre de 2009), 2011
Acrylic and newspaper on linen
75 1/3 × 68 inches (191.3 × 172.8 cm)

From the outset of his career, Rirkrit Tiravanija has produced socially engaged conceptual works that invite the public to be a part of the art-making process. Tiravanija's practice veers away from traditional media and undermines the conventional "white cube" presentation of artwork. In one of his best-known series, starting with *pad thai* at Paula Allen Gallery in New York in 1990, Tiravanija prepared, cooked, and served home-style Thai curry to exhibition visitors.

He is regarded as one of the pioneering artists of relational aesthetics, a term coined by French art theorist Nicolas Bourriaud to describe "a set of artistic practices which take as their theoretical and practical point of departure the whole of human relations and their social context, rather than an independent or private space." His work seeks conviviality, prioritizing participation above all else.

Tiravanija was born in Buenos Aires, Argentina, and grew up in Thailand, Ethiopia, and Canada. He studied at the Ontario College of Art in Toronto, Banff Center School of Fine Arts, and the School of the Art Institute of Chicago. Later, he participated in the Whitney Independent Studies Program in New York. Presently, he lives and works in New York, Berlin, and Chiang Mai, Thailand.

His nomadic upbringing and lifestyle seem to come through in the multicultural aspects of his work, as evidenced in a series of provocative text-based works in which Tiravanija stencils punchy slogans in capital letters over deliberately chosen pages of newspapers. In *Untitled (Los días de esta sociedad son contados/18 de diciembre de 2009)*, which translates in English to "The Days of Our Society Are Numbered," he stenciled a Spanish translation of a quote by the French Marxist theorist Guy Debord over a grid of the Mexican newspaper *La Jornada*. The headlines of the newspaper, dated October 22, 2009, deal with corruption within the Mexican government and the fiftieth anniversary of the Cuban embargo. The effect of the juxtaposition of the newspaper and text that ominously suggests society's impending collapse is characteristic of Tiravanija's work, which asks the viewer to critically engage with and confront global political issues. This series articulates his long-standing engagement with issues of propaganda: "I am interested in constructing a condition in which people find themselves implicated." L. C.

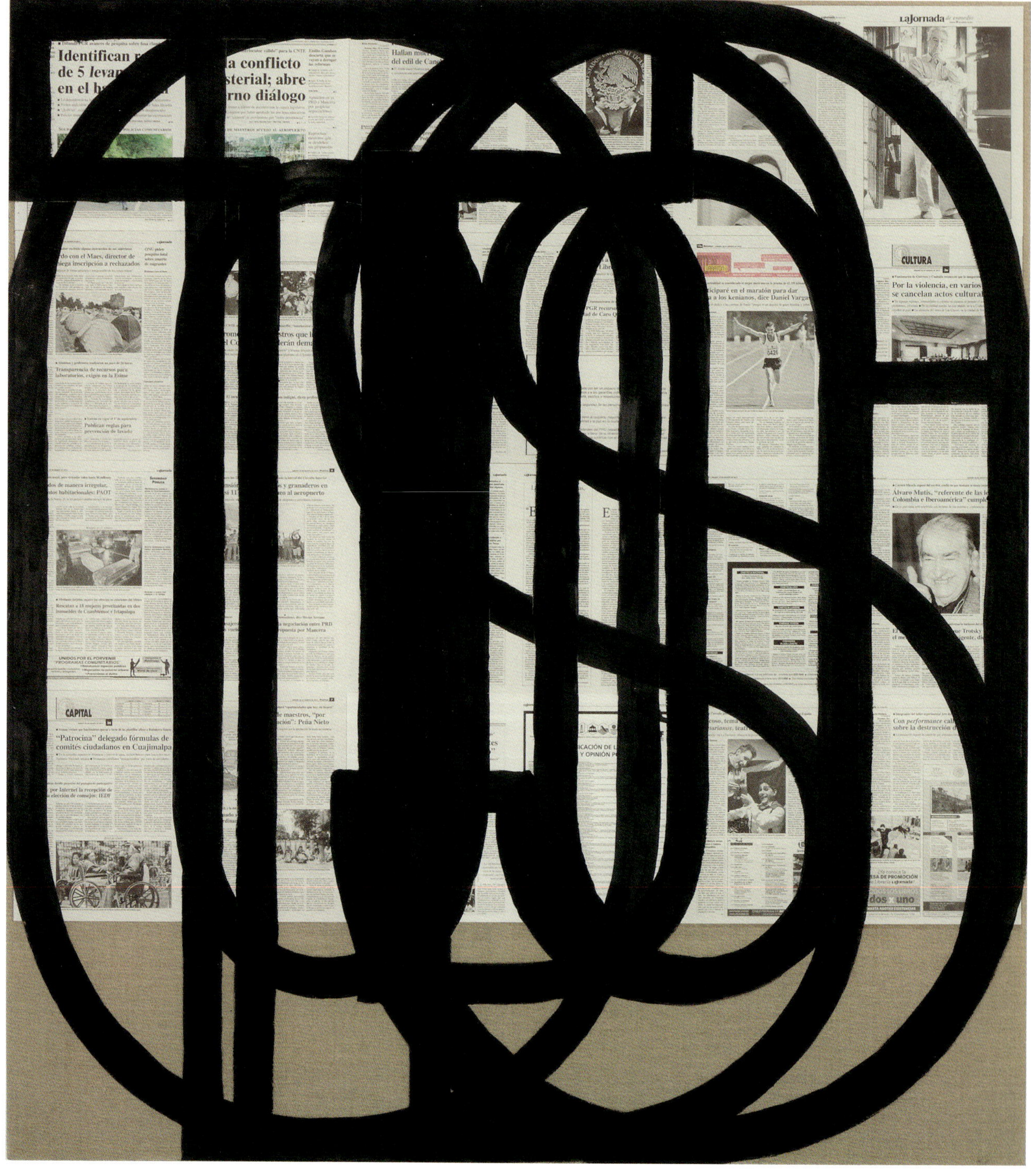

Untitled (Todos juntos / jueves 5 y viernes 6 de septiembre de 2013), 2013
Encaustic and newspaper on linen
Set of 2
75 1/3 × 68 inches (191.3 × 172.8 cm) each

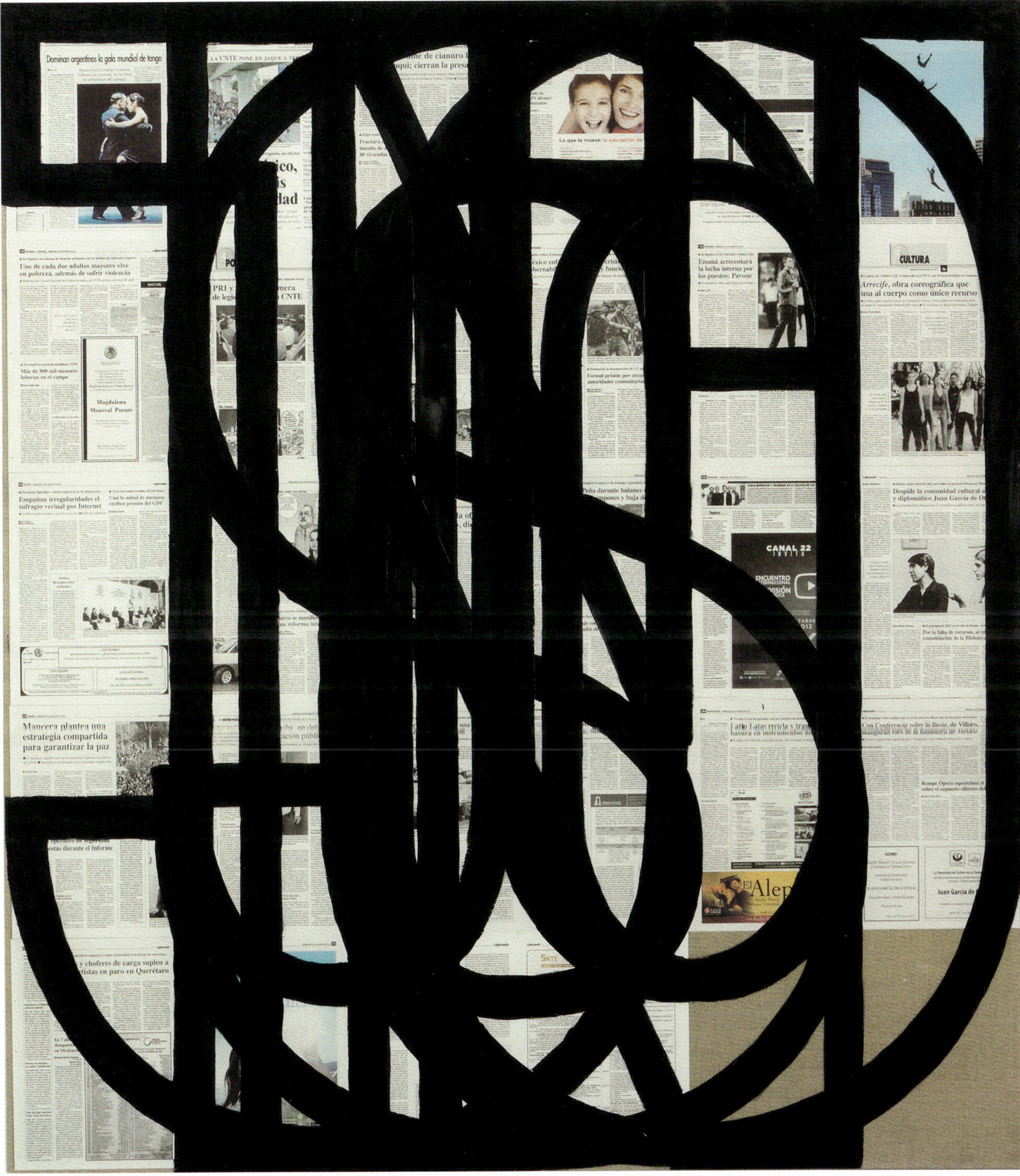
Dominan argentinos la gala mundial de tango
Uno de cada dos adultos mayores vive en pobreza, además de sufrir violencia
Más de 900 mil menores laboran en el campo
Magdalena Monreal Puente
Empañan irregularidades el sufragio vecinal por Internet
Mancera plantea una estrategia compartida para garantizar la paz
Ensenada acrecentará la lucha interna por los puestos: Pavone
CULTURA
Arrecife, obra coreográfica que usa al cuerpo como único recurso
CANAL 22

Ryan Trecartin was once considered (merely) a product of his time. Subsequently he was described as representative of his time, and finally, after more than a decade of universally acclaimed exhibitions, he is understood as actually having created the zeitgeist with which he is associated.

Trecartin's art—much of made in collaboration with the artist Lizzie Fitch (b. 1981, Bloomington, Indiana)—encompasses sculpture, installation, and digital prints, but video is at the heart of almost everything he makes: frenetic, high-octane, and pulsing with colors, screams, and disjointed, piercing soundtracks, Trecartin's videos depict an anarchic post-racial, post-sexual teenage existence, glinting with a distinctly suburban American dystopic sheen.

The videos, at least superficially, can be seen as an outgrowth of Trecartin's life. Born in 1981 in Webster, Texas, Trecartin spent most of his childhood in Ohio and then graduated with a BFA from the Rhode Island School of Design in 2004. His senior thesis, the forty-one-minute movie, *A Family Finds Entertainment*, featured Trecartin himself in costumes and costumey makeup and co-starred many of his friends. This work and others that followed led to several solo gallery exhibitions and inclusion in the 2006 Whitney Biennial. By 2009, Trecartin had mounted solo shows at the Hammer Museum in Los Angeles, the Wexner Center in Columbus, and the Kunsthalle Wien in Vienna. A major exhibition of Trecartin's art, *Ryan Trecartin: Any Ever*, traveled from MoMA PS1 in New York to KW Institute for Contemporary Art, Berlin; Museum of Contemporary Art, North Miami, FL; Istanbul Modern, Istanbul; The Museum of Contemporary Art, Los Angeles; and The Power Plant, Toronto.

Crucially, Trecartin extends the theatrical components of his movies into environments that transform his art into a sort of immersive theater. At MoMA PS1, for instance, he filled each of the exhibition's seven galleries with props and decoration that amounted to ecstatic and unnerving stage sets, all coordinated to work in conjunction with a specific movie. Similarly, *Ledge* (2014), a work by Trecartin and Fitch filmed in the Marciano Art Foundation prior to renovation, operates with a similar element of stagecraft. A six-channel HD video shows a forty-nine-minute parade of Trecartin and friends in zombie drag; it is projected on six screens underneath a voluminous tent, evoking the American pastiche Trecartin loves to penetrate. Campfire stories, cheesy horror movies, and teenage melodrama all fall prey to his distinct, cackling voice and piercing vision. J. T.

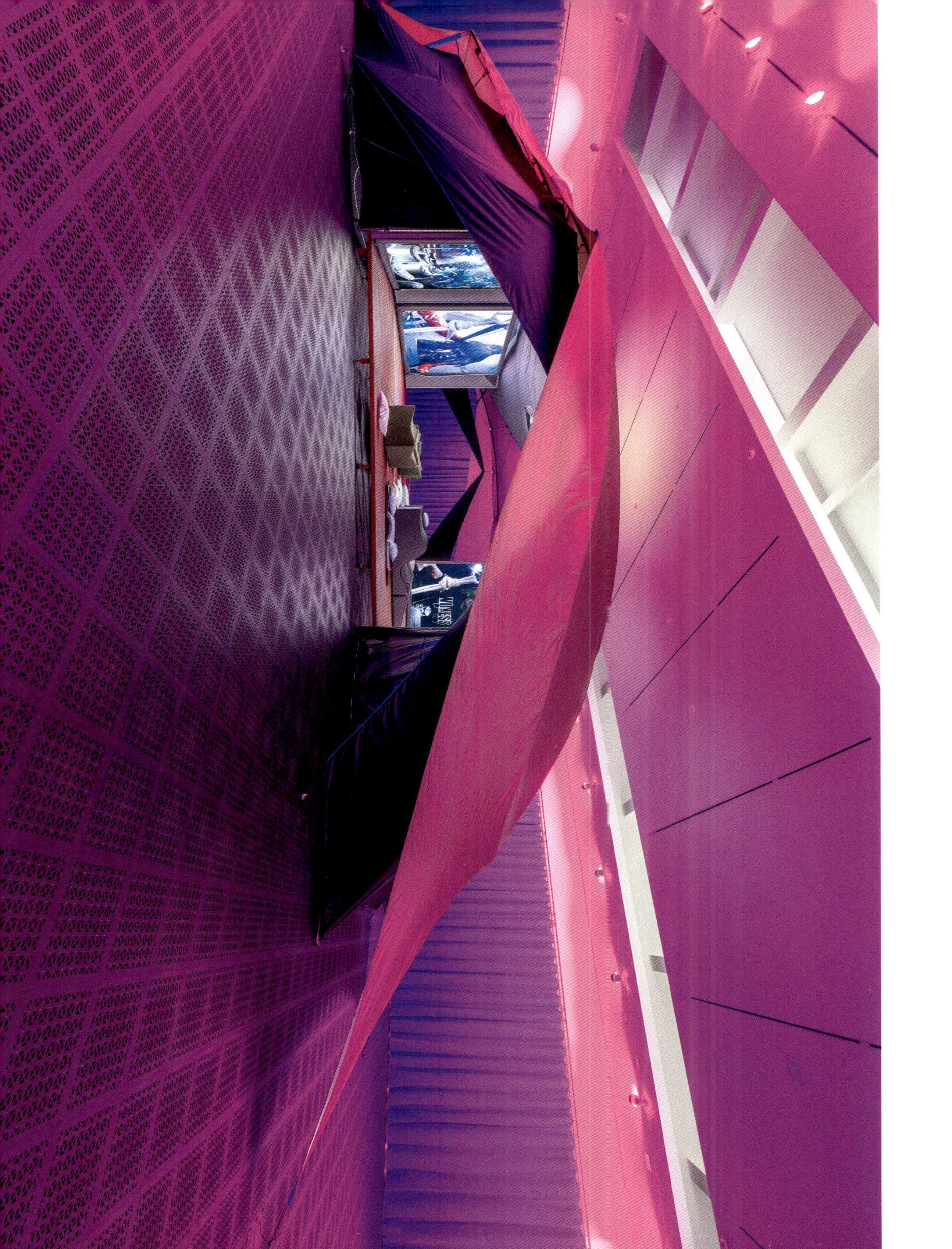

Ryan Trecartin / Lizzie Fitch
Ledge, 2014
Unique sculptural theater with 6-channel HD Video and 5.1 soundtrack, 3D animations with Rhett LaRue
49:24 min.
Aluminum, ambient audiofiles, amps, anodizing pigment, cuben fiber, ethernet switches, foam, glue, grommets, mac mini, media players, no-see-um mesh fabric, paint, plastic, powdercoat, projectors, snaps, spacer mesh, speakers, staples, steel, rear projection fabric, reflective tape, rip-stop nylon fabric, rope, rubber, tape, thread, tubular webbing, various hardware, webbing, wireless programmable lights, wireless router, wood, and zippers
Dimensions variable

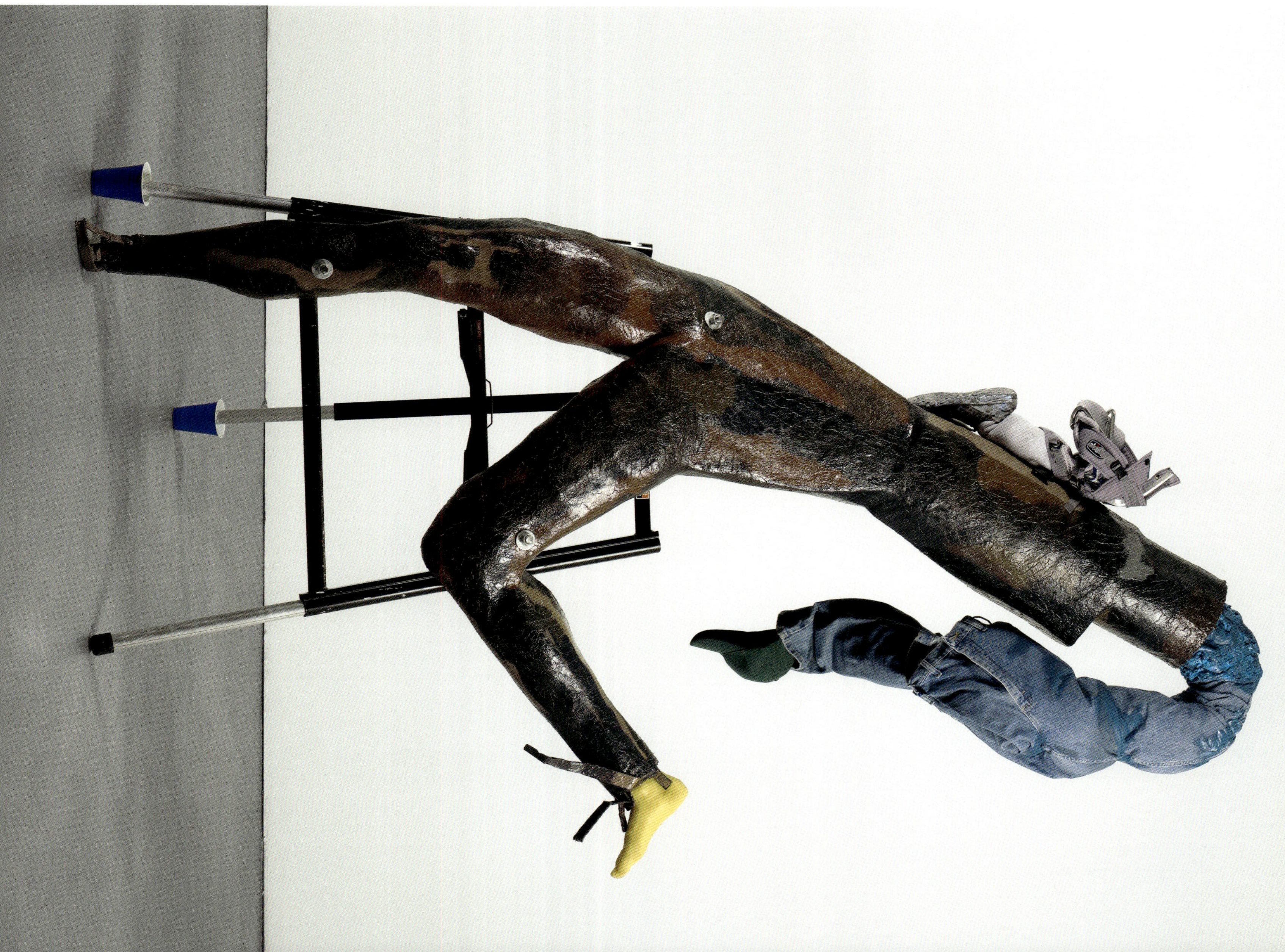

Ryan Trecartin/Lizzie Fitch
Drop Cause, 2013
Acrylic paint, aluminum, baby carrier, baseball cap, blue Solo cups, bolts, Bronco scaffold, carabineers, cardboard, epoxy, fiberglass, foam, gel medium, jeans, metal rod, paper, pigment, plastic, screws, silicone, socks, staples, stuffing, Vibram shoes, washers, and zip ties
92 × 60 × 46 inches
(233.7 × 152.4 × 116.8 cm)

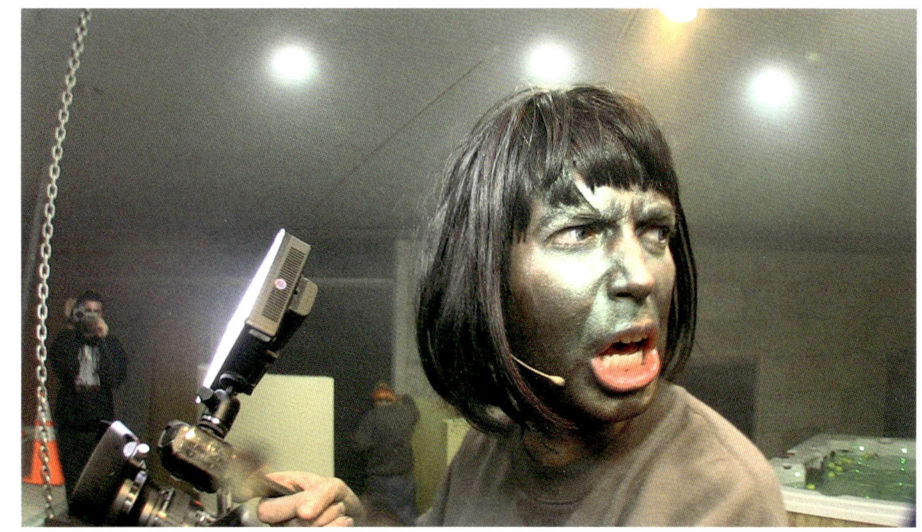

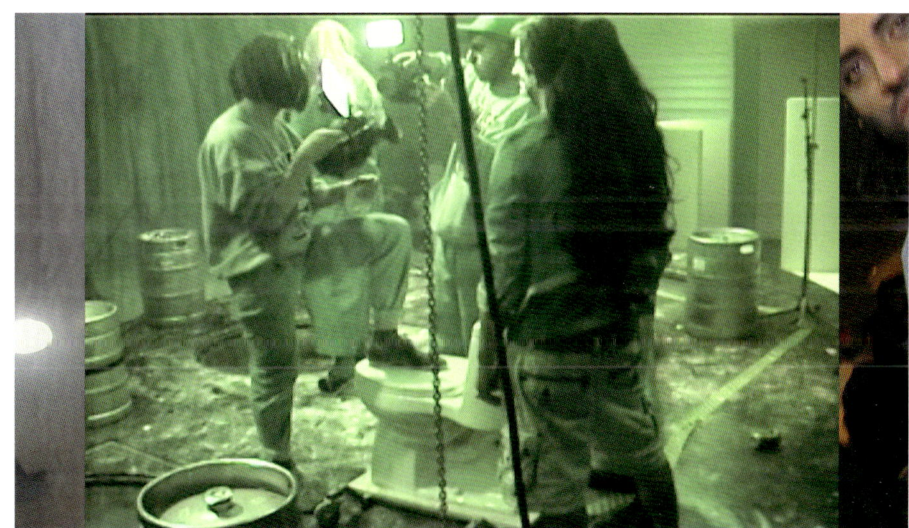

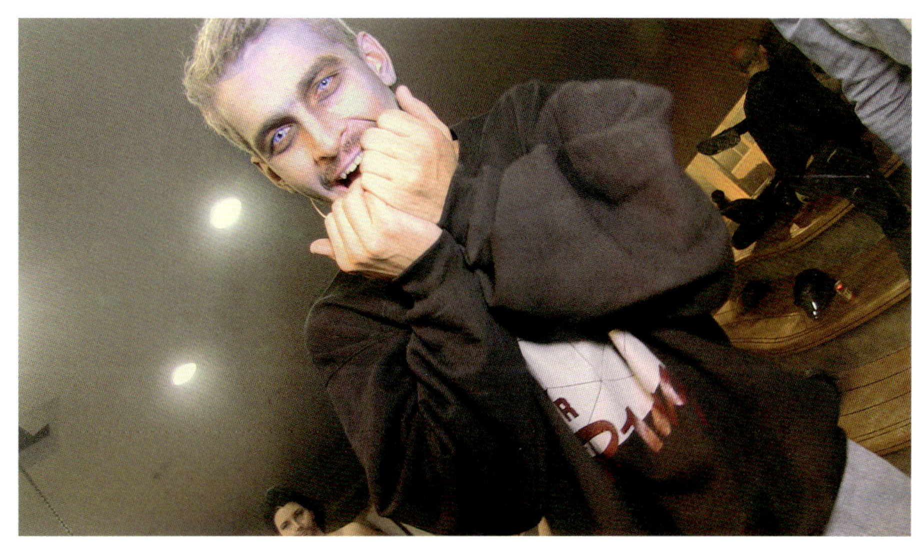

Comma Boat, 2013
Three-channel HD video
33 min., 2 sec.
Edition 2 of 6, 2 AP

OSCAR TUAZON

b. 1975, Seattle, WA

When Oscar Tuazon graduated high school, instead of attending a traditional four-year college he enrolled in an elite, two-year college in the California desert where around twenty-five young men tend livestock, irrigate alfalfa fields, ride horses, and read high theory. While the school is one of the most exclusive colleges in America—well under ten percent of applicants are admitted—very few people outside of academia have heard of it. Yet there are traces of Tuazon's education at Deep Springs in virtually every piece of art he creates.

His sculptures—raw, architectural interventions—bear the mark of someone who knows how to build a structure, and more importantly, understands the social and cultural ramifications of constructing something—anything—in the throes of late-capitalist society.

Tuazon was born in 1975 outside of Seattle. After graduating Deep Springs in 1994, he moved to New York to study at Cooper Union and then enrolled in the legendary Independent Study Program at the Whitney Museum American Art. He returned to Cooper Union and graduated from the school's urban studies program in 2003. Tuazon then studied with the pioneering video, architectural, and Conceptual artist Vito Acconci, after which he moved to live and work in Paris. Today, Tuazon lives in Los Angeles.

Tuazon has had solo shows at the Museum Ludwig in Cologne, Artists Space in New York, the Institute of Contemporary Arts in London, and the Schinkel Pavillon in Berlin; he was also included in the 2012 Whitney Biennial and the 2011 Venice Biennale and has participated in group shows at the Palais de Tokyo in Paris and the Museum of Contemporary Art in Chicago, among others.

His sculpture easily lends itself to public spaces, primarily because the majority of his works double as monuments. This is certainly the case with *People* (2012). Created out of a sugar maple tree and a concrete wall, the sculpture is a relic reminiscent of an abandoned inner-city neighborhood. The tree is dead, the basketball hoop is net-less, the lights affixed to the tree are permanently turned off; the only thing that functions as it should is a bunkerlike, polished concrete wall that cleaves the artwork in half. The use of such a structure is nebulous and yet it bears all the familiar semiotics of very real, very alienating, and very familiar urban fabric that's never too far away.
J. T.

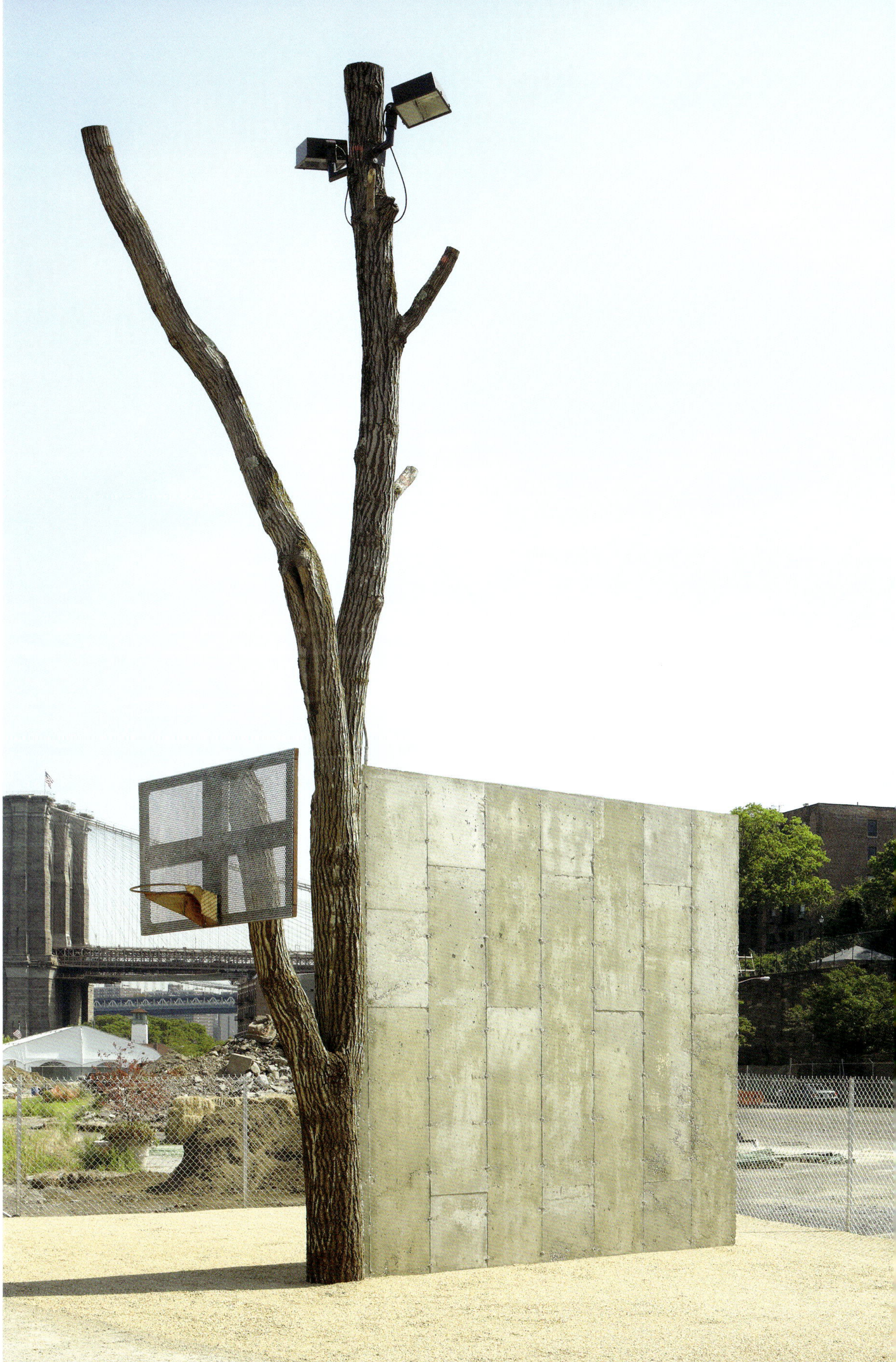

People, 2012
Sugar maple tree, metal basketball
backboard and hoop, and concrete wall
Dimensions variable

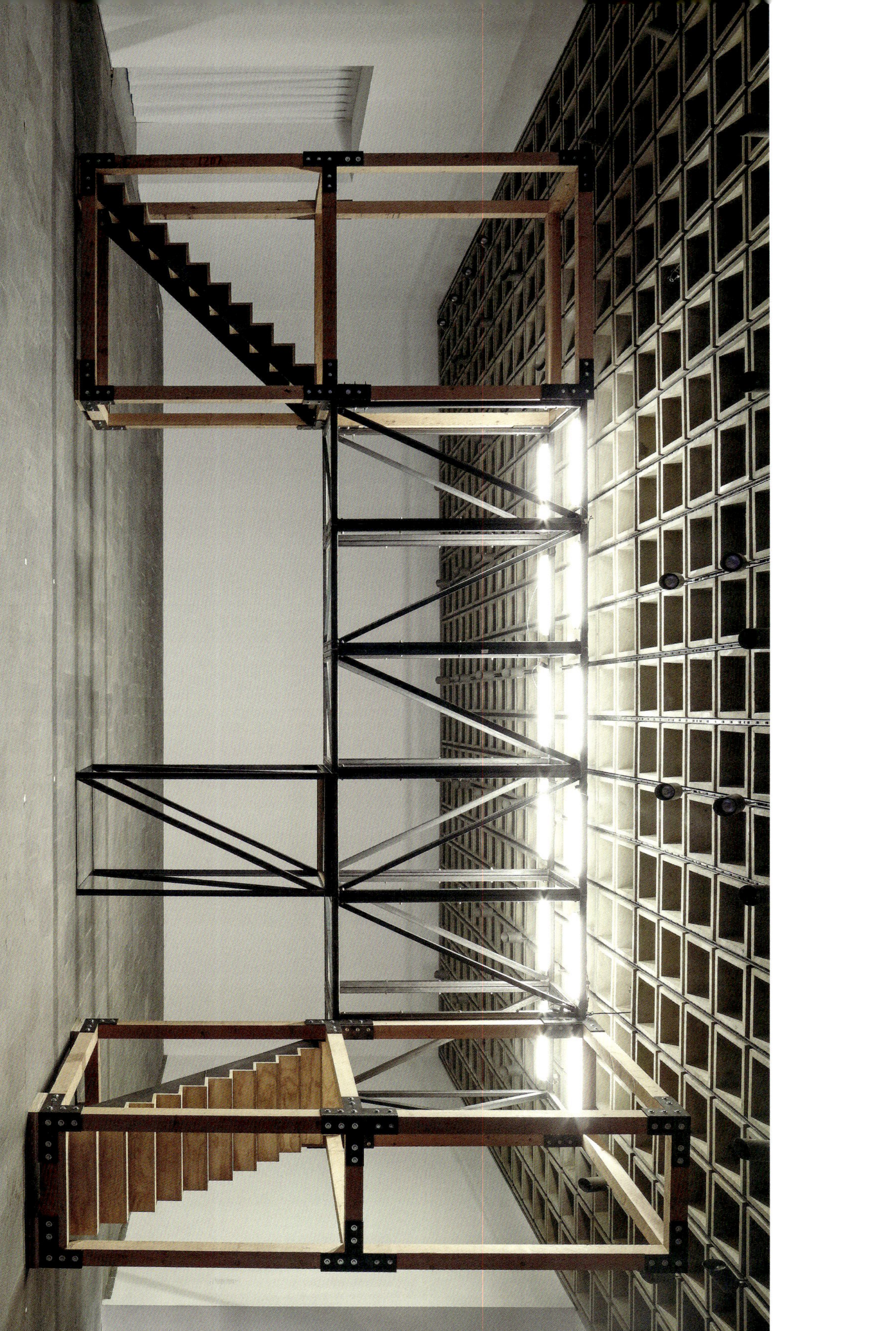

For Hire, 2011–12
Galvanized steel, acrylic, Douglas fir, glass,
plastic fluorescent lights, and tile
Dimensions variable

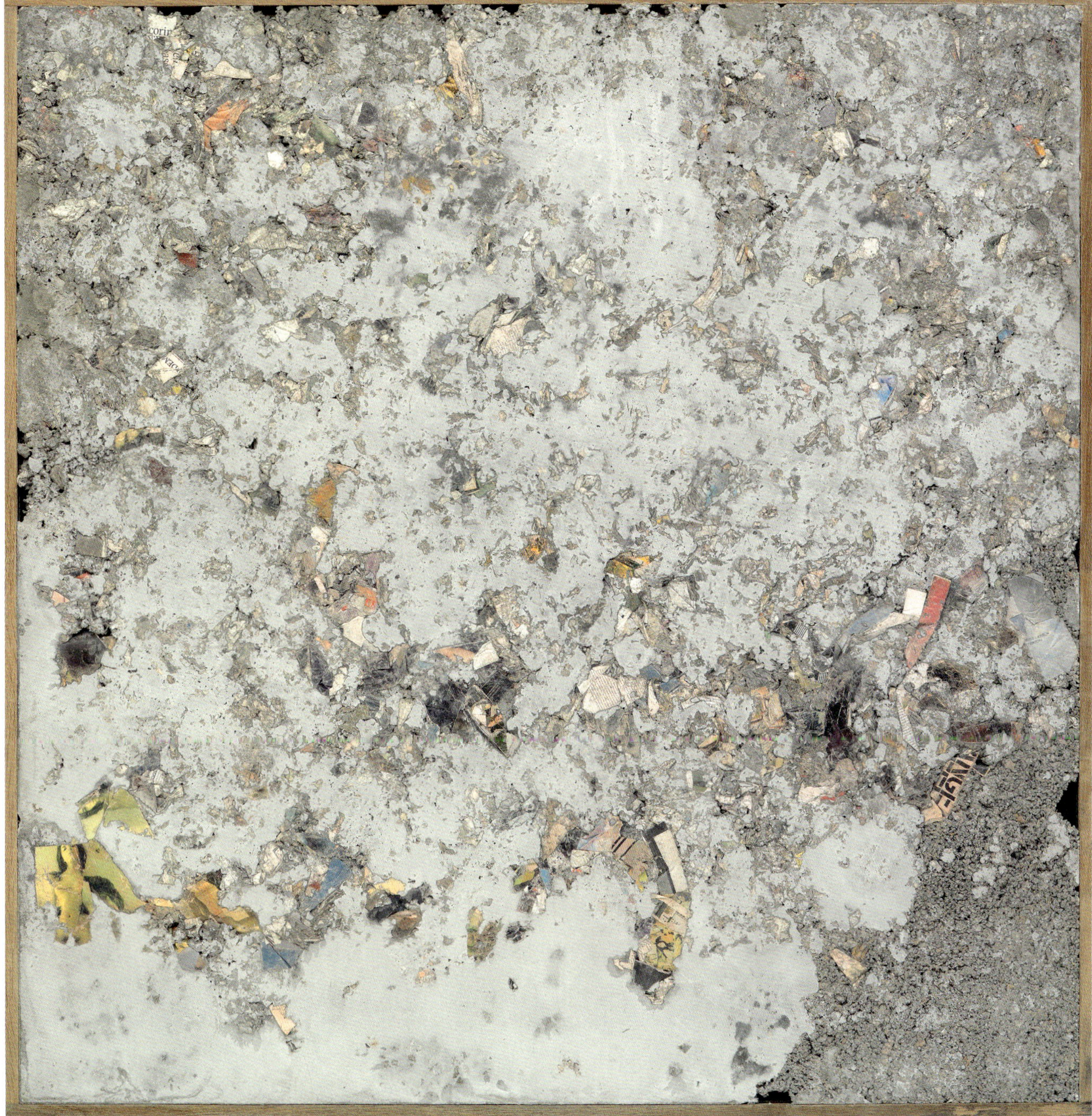

Playboy Papercrate, 2012/2013
Concrete
65 × 65 × 4¾ inches (165 × 165 × 12 cm)

KAARI **UPSON** b. 1972, San Bernardino, CA

The psychological entanglement of the artist and her subject is not a novel idea, and yet Kaari Upson has pushed this concept far beyond its traditional confines. After graduating from CalArts in 2007, Upson revisited a box of items scavenged from the abandoned home of her parents' former neighbor in San Bernardino. When the house partially burned down, Upson photographed the space and collected handwritten journals, legal documents, photographs, and other personal items left behind by the former owner.

Though she had never met him, Upson formed a fictional identity, whom she named "Larry," constructed through the loose analysis of his personal items as well as the artist's own memories, fantasies, dreams, and experiences. The conflation of the two identities marked the beginning of The Larry Project—an exploration of memory, representation, and how they intertwine—which would dictate Upson's artistic practice for the next several years.

Many of Larry's belongings revealed a man who strongly embraced the clichés of Southern California in the 1970s and 1980s, and his journals described his fears and frustrations, as well as his own quest for self-discovery and enlightenment. At odds with his private ideas, however, were accompanying photographs that depicted a man who advertised himself as slick, sexy, and successful. When Upson lost the handwritten journals, and the house was completely razed, she had only her memories and remaining objects to rely on and soon realized these gaps were crucial to the project.

The Larry Project resulted in numerous works, including drawings, sculptures, installations, videos, and performances—all functioning as a sort of residue that points both to Larry's absence and the artist's goal to re-enter his life. The transformation of subject from physical being to one of memory and representation can be traced through the numerous incarnations of the Larry "doll" that Upson first created in 2007. Upson first made charcoal casts of the dismembered Larry doll in 2009, purposefully employing ashes—a material that references Larry's house as well a summation of his life. Later came a series of wall-mounted charcoal tablets, such as *Charcoal Sheet 1 (Position 1)* (2012), whose smooth surfaces are crumpled and dented by impressions and gestures made with various human body parts, recording both a performative act and sustaining a gesture. Ultimately, Upson strives to know the self not only through the other, but also through life, death, and re-birth. J. G. M.

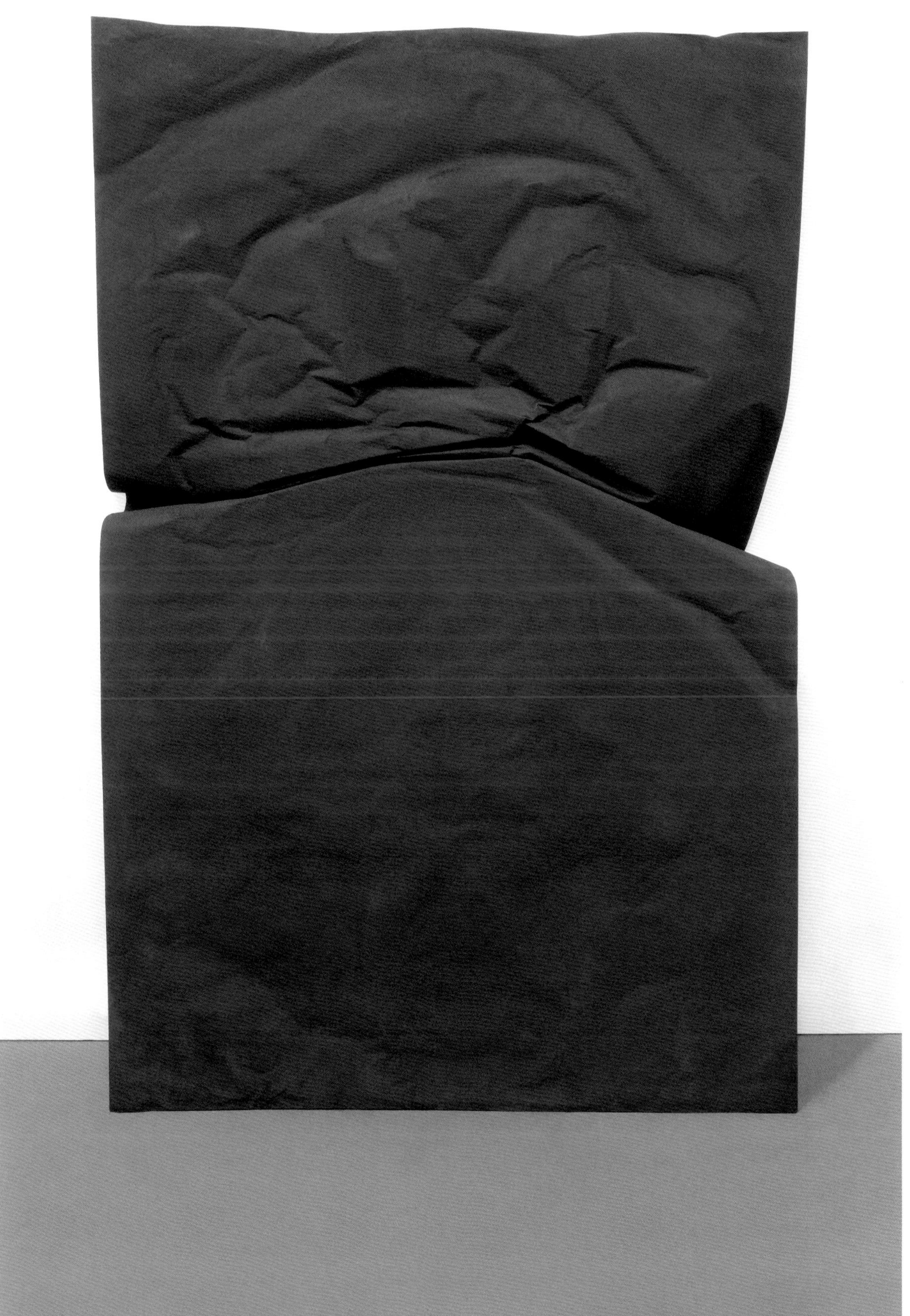

Charcoal Sheet 1 (Position 1), 2012
Charcoal and aqua-resin
73 × 48 × 7½ inches (185.4 × 121.9 × 19.1 cm)

DANH VO

b. 1975, Bà Rja, Vietnam

Pantoffel II, 2014
Gold, cardboard, and ink
Weight: 132 oz. (3742.1 g)

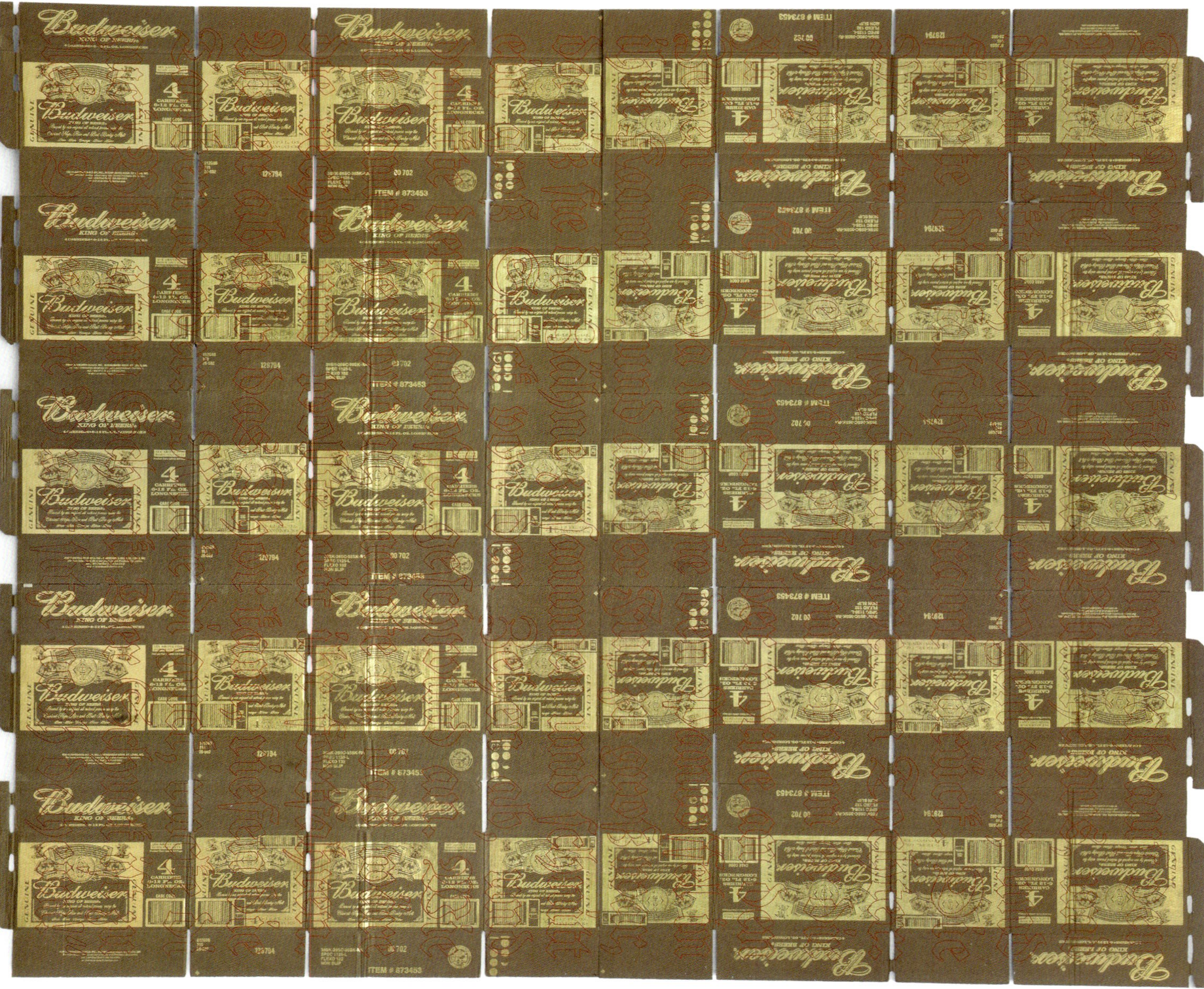

When Danh Vo was four years old his family fled Vietnam in a homemade boat. A few days later they were rescued, floating in the middle of the Gulf of Thailand, by a Danish cargo ship. The family then settled in Denmark, and Vo grew up in—though perhaps not a part of—European society.

His art, in turn, is a direct extension of this exodus, otherness, and alienation, and Vo probes notions of statehood, self-identity, sexuality, language, and symbolism using a variety of mediums.

Vo, who was born in 1975, attended the Royal Academy of Fine Arts in Copenhagen; after dropping out, he attended the Städelschule in Frankfurt and dtraction over the following decade, and today Vo, who now lives and works in Mexico City, has had dozens of major solo exhibitions, including shows at the Solomon R. Guggenheim Museum in New York, the Art Institute of Chicago, and the Kunsthaus Baselland.

All of Vo's work can be considered conceptual and much of it can be considered, in one way or another, performance. His ongoing, *Marriage Project*, for instance, entails marrying and then immediately divorcing close friends, after which Vo retains the paperwork of the brief unions and, more importantly, legally changes his name to include the surname of his one-time spouse. In doing so, Vo plays with the idea of marriage as a highly regulated institution of cultural and bourgeois hegemony, simultaneously subjugating participants while also elevating their privilege through tax breaks and other state-sponsored perks. In marrying European citizens, Vo is also playing on his own immigrant identity—each union is, in a sense, one step closer to assimilation.

Other projects, like *We The People* (2011–13) are manifested in material forms. After discovering that the copper cladding on the Statue of Liberty was just a few centimeters thick—that such a potent symbol of strength and freedom was in fact remarkably fragile—Vo commissioned a factory in China to reproduce an exact, thirty-ton copper copy of the Ellis Island statue. He then distributed fragments of the statue around the world, including this fragment of part of Lady Liberty's hair. The work underscores Vo's complicated relationship with Western democracy, and the symbolic statue's dissemination, not to mention its fragility, serves as a timely reminder of the tenuous, illusory nature of freedom itself. J. T.

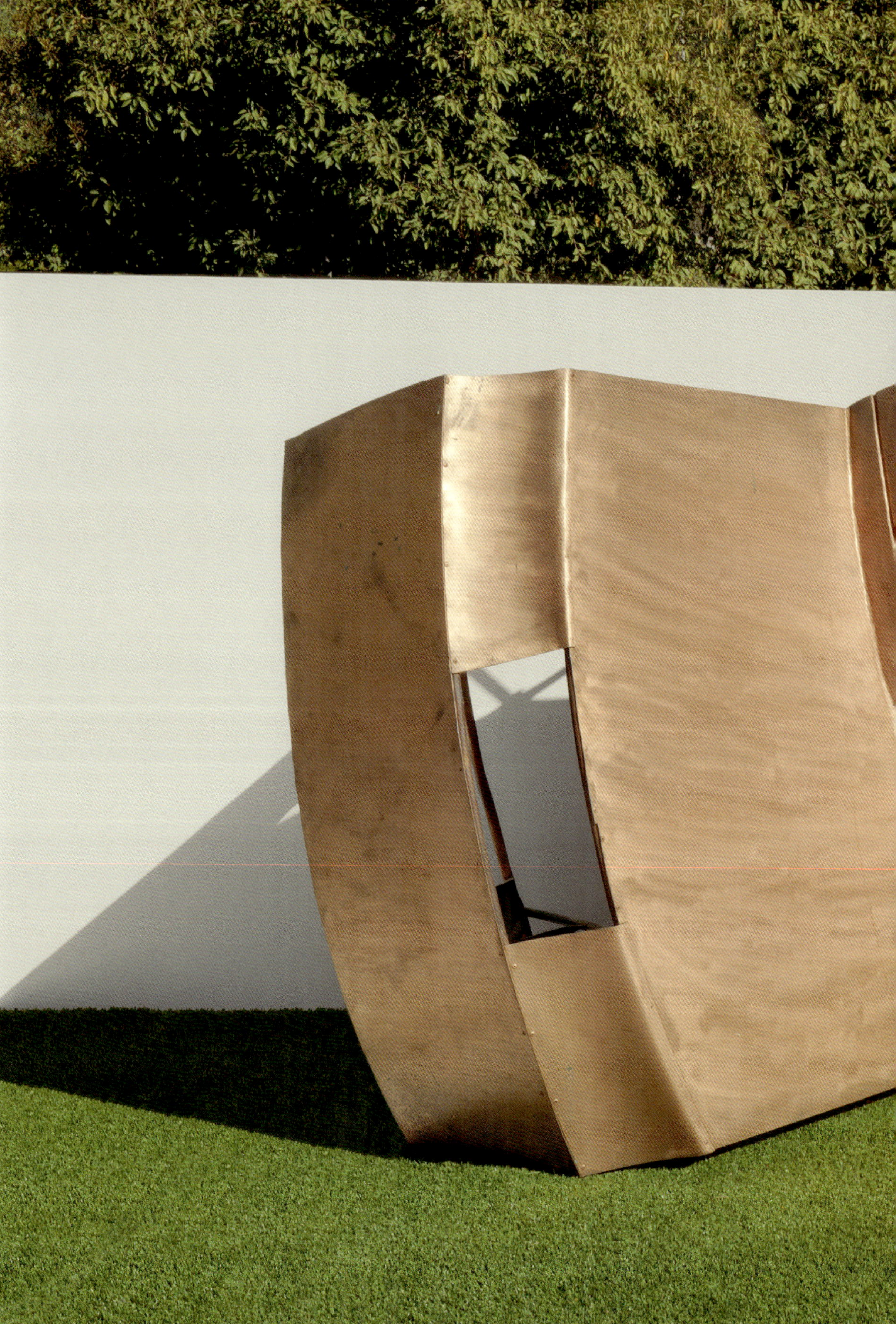

We The People (detail), 2011–13
Copper—8.4m2, 190kg

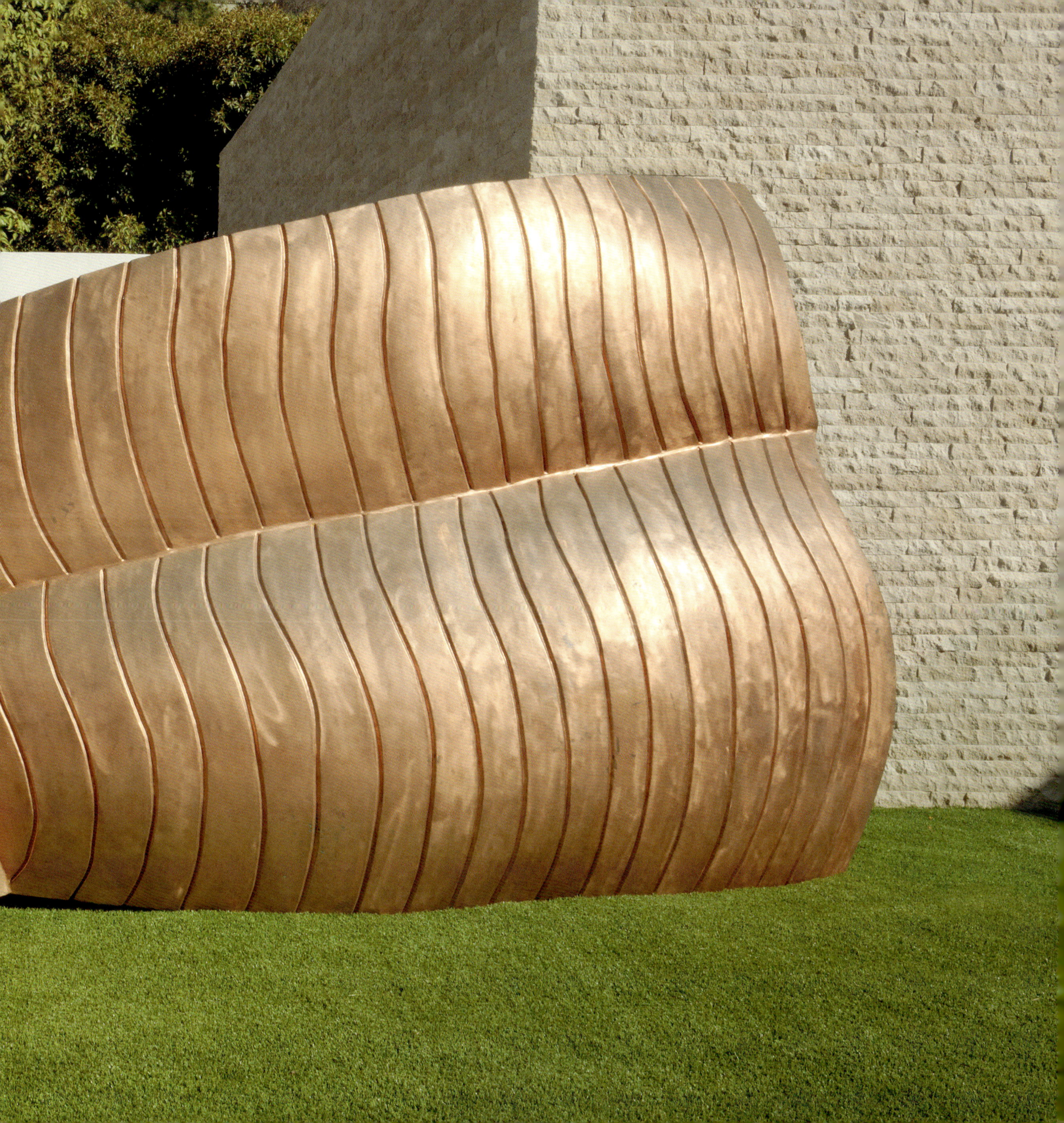

KELLEY WALKER

b. 1969, Columbus, GA

Kelley Walker's artistic output is varied enough that, inevitably, someone who likes one of his works will be turned off by another. Not content to stick to one motif, aesthetic, or theoretical concern, Walker—who could be classified as a post-Conceptual artist—dances between them all. There are recurring concepts, of course; Walker is preoccupied by medium specificity, creating layers between himself and his paintings by using laser printers, appropriating and transforming found imagery, using chocolate as paint and also a symbol.

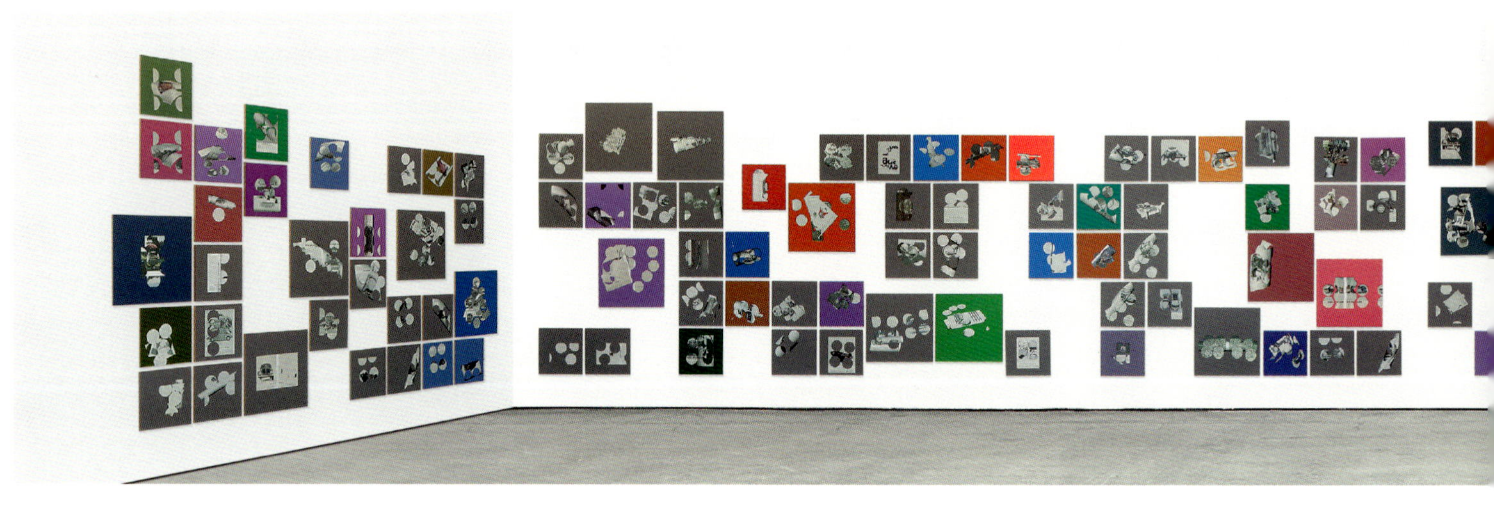

Untitled, 2013
196 panels of Pantone and four-color process silkscreen with acrylic ink on MDF
29 panels: 24 × 24 inches (61 × 61 cm) each
167 panels: 16 × 16 inches (40.6 × 40.6 cm) each

What distinguishes Walker from his peers is his willingness to experiment with new ideas, mediums, and ways of creating art.

Walker was born in 1969 in Columbus, Georgia, at the height of the Civil Rights movement. He graduated with a BFA from the University of Tennessee in Knoxville in 1995 and moved to New York soon after. His work first appeared in a gallery show in New York in 1999; in 2002, he was included in the influential *Painting as Paradox* show at Artists Space in New York. He's since been included in the 2006 Whitney Biennial and has had solo exhibitions at La Salle de Bains in Lyon, France, the Wiels–Centre d'art contemporain in Brussels, and the Manchester Art Gallery. His collaboration with Guyton, *Guyton/ Walker*, which both men consider to be a third, autonomous, art-making entity, has had solo shows at the Whitney Museum of American Art in New York, LA><ART in Los Angeles, and the Carpenter Center at Harvard University in Cambridge, Massachusetts.

Walker's *Black Star Press: Black Press, Black Star (rotated at 90 degrees clockwise)* (2006) nicely encapsulates his range. The work is a diptych of two digital prints depicting police brutality during race demonstrations, which Walker has splattered with chocolate. In creating these panels, Walker is perhaps underscoring the duality of the abstraction of history. The digital reconstruction of events is blurry (and, as Walker has appropriated the images, third-hand), the subjects and action are hard to see, and even their orientation is confusing. With the addition of chocolate—a concept that's trite, derogatory, and eminently straightforward—Walker nicely juxtaposes nuance with trope, modernity with ignorance, and perhaps most importantly, art with politics.

J. T.

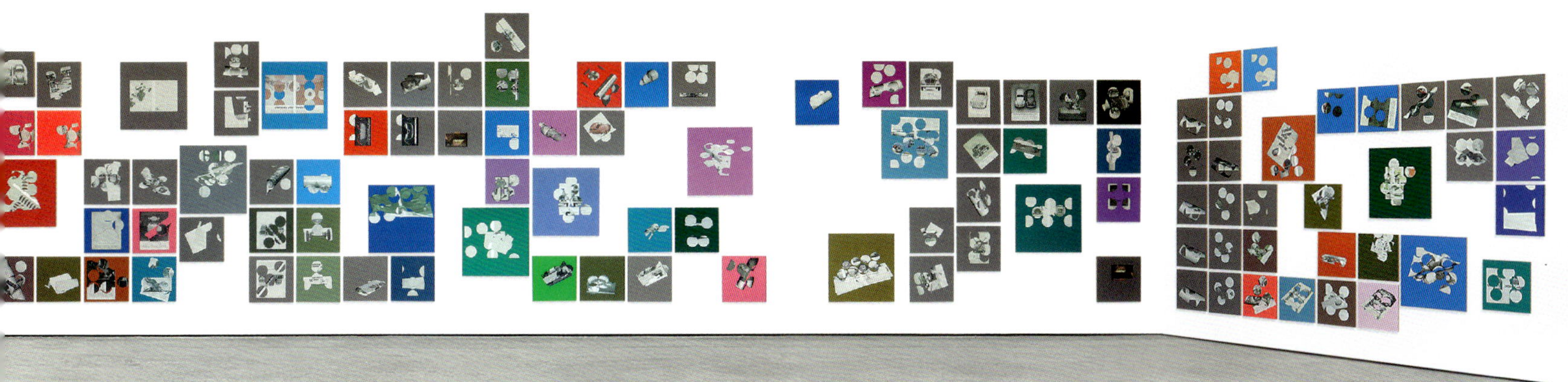

Untitled, 2007
Four-color process silkscreen on canvas with collage *VMan* (fall/winter 2007)
78 1/2 × 54 1/4 inches (199.4 × 137.8 cm)

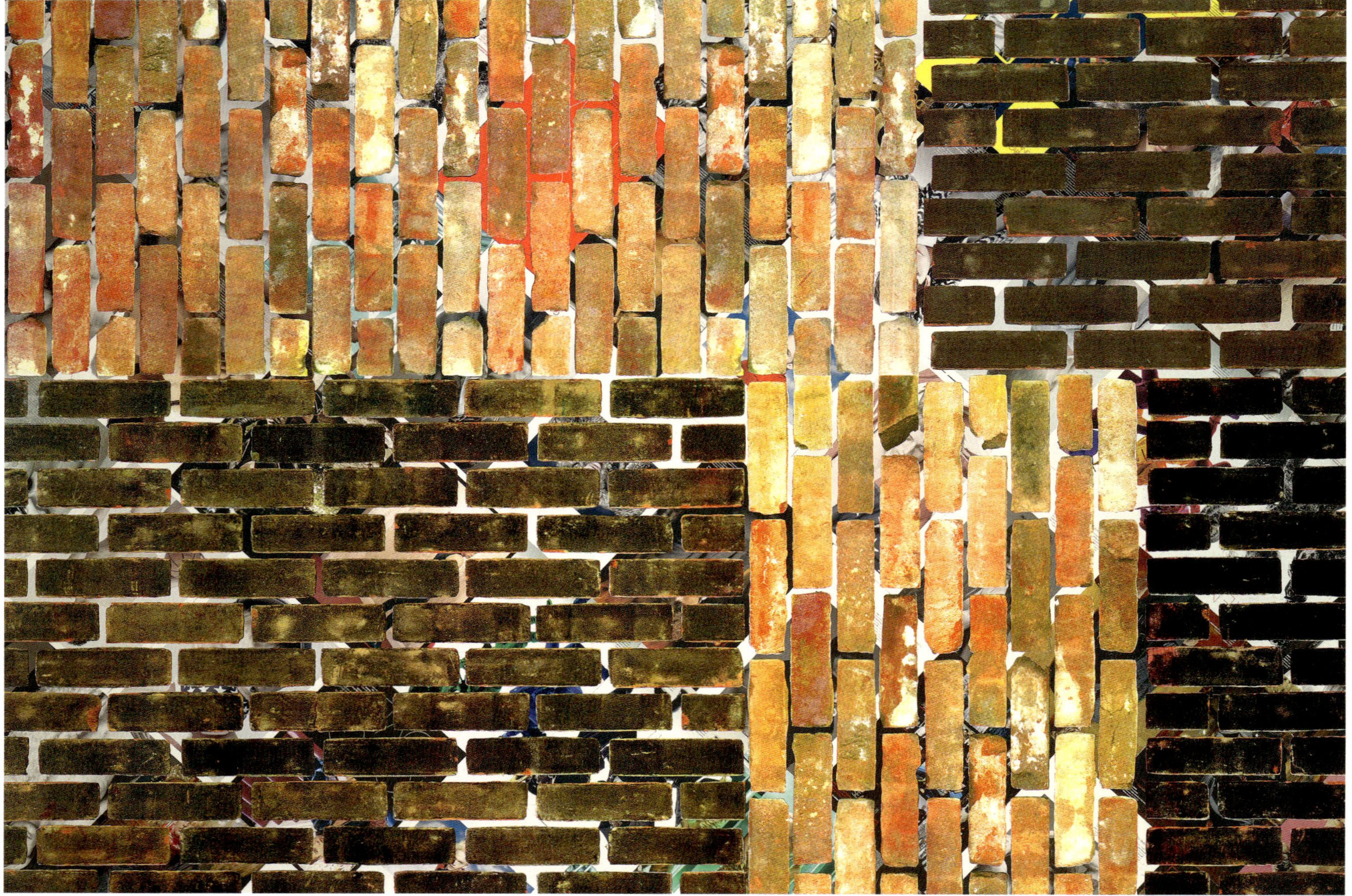

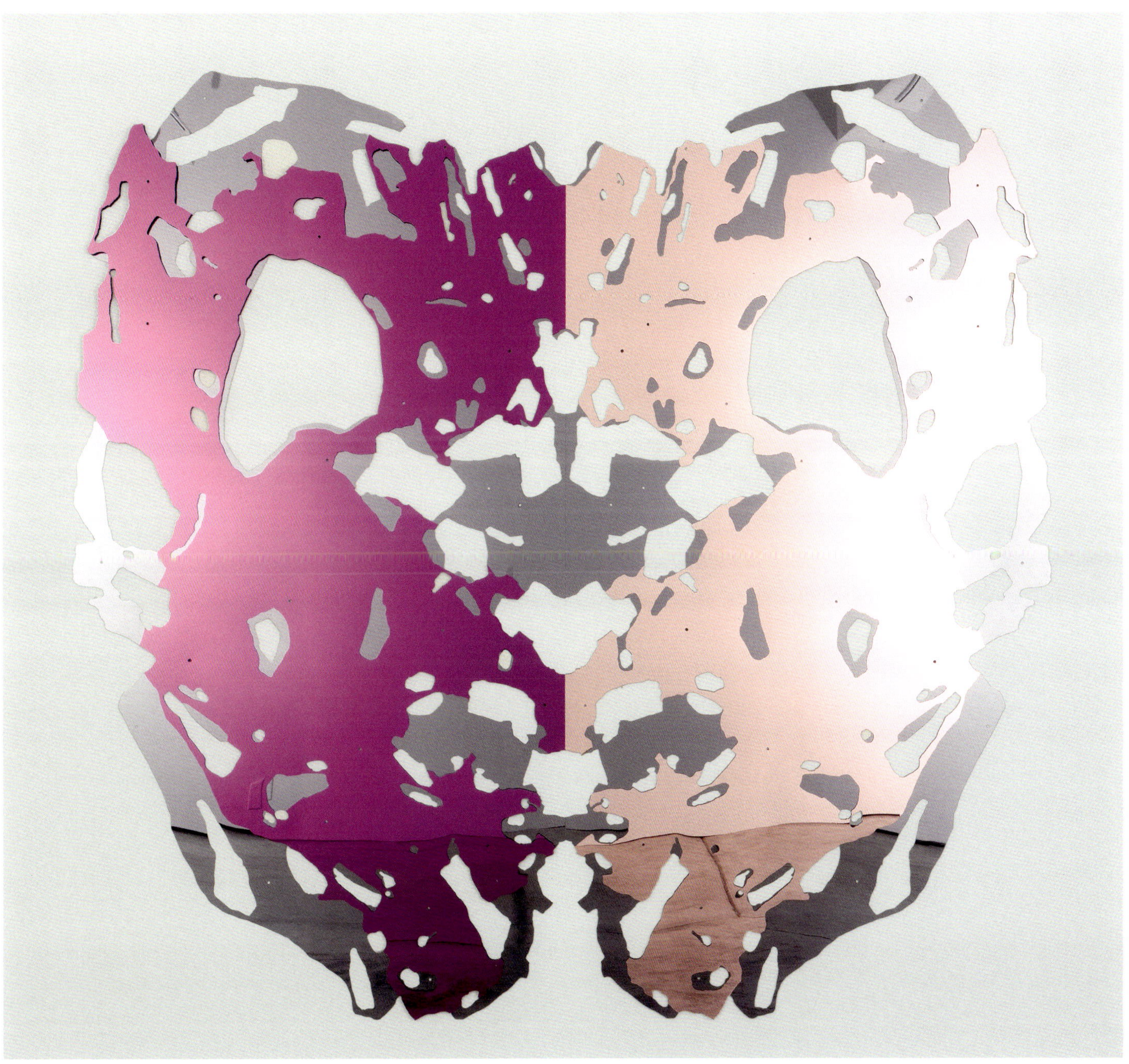

Untitled, c. 2002
4 panels of mirrored acrylic
92 × 48⅝ inches (233.7 × 123.5 cm) each
92 × 97⅜ inches (233.7 × 247.3 cm) overall

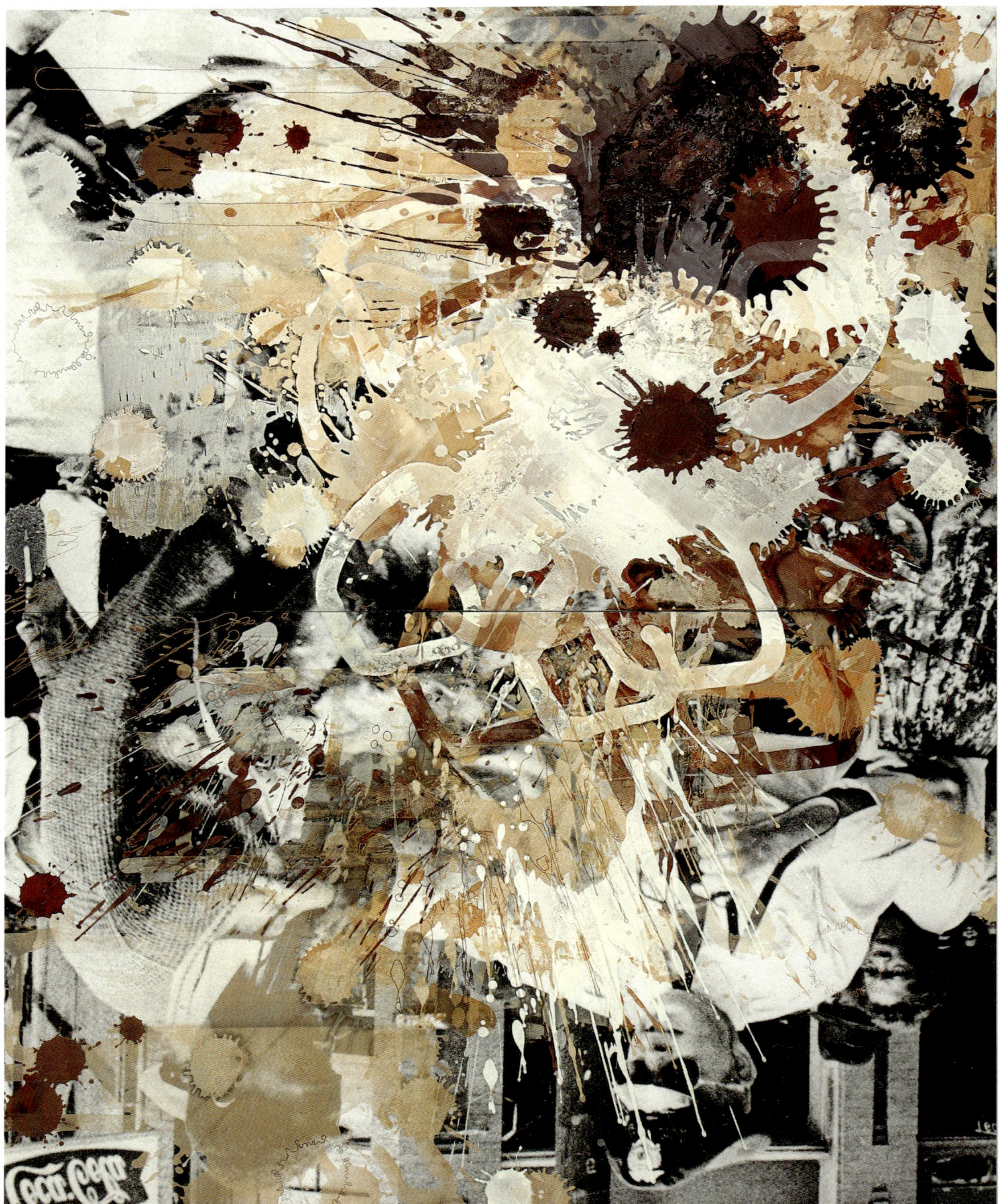

Black Star Press (rotated 180 degrees): Press Black, 2006
Digital print and chocolate on canvas
Two panels: 52½ × 82½ inches
(133.4 × 209.6 cm) each
105 × 82½ inches (266.7 × 209.5 cm) overall

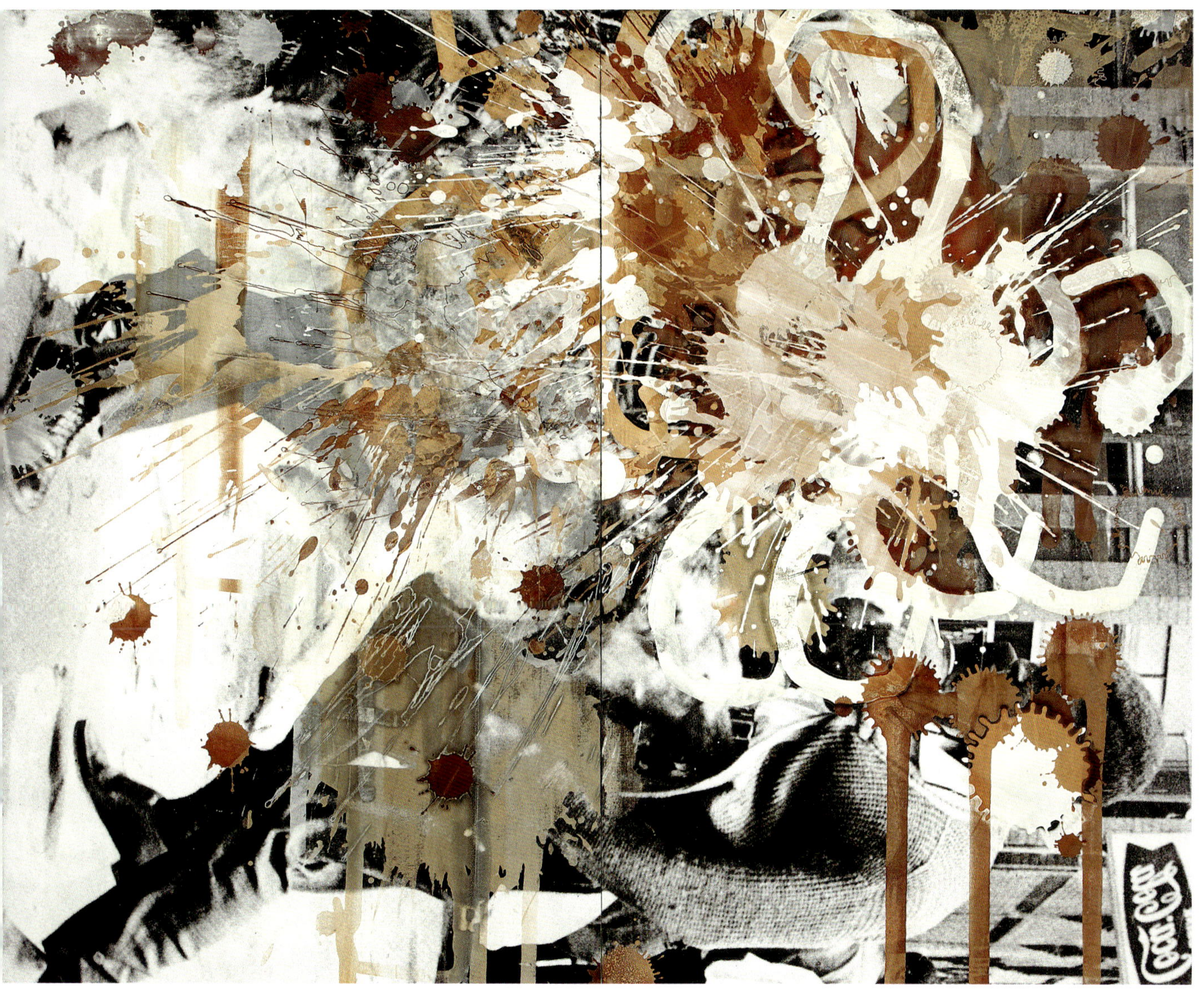
Coca-Cola

Some of the first artworks Franz West ever made were called "Adaptives" ("Passstücke"), a series he began in 1974. Rough, sculptural objects meant to be held (or worn), they occupied the liminal space between prosthetics, performance art, sculpture, and—crucially—humor. More importantly, they served as springboards for the rest of his career; many of the stylistic and theoretical threads from West's artistic output can be traced back to these raw early objects. It's not just that the Adaptives bear stylistic similarities to his later, more famous sculptures; it's that their ethos—an integration of art and life, no matter how nonsensical it seemed—stayed at the fore of his oeuvre.

West was born in 1947 in postwar Vienna and was exposed to the Viennese avant-garde during his adolescence. He studied at the Academy of Fine Arts in Vienna, graduating in 1982, at which point he embarked, casually at first, on a career as an artist. Success came initially in Europe, then the U.S. His first American museum show wasn't until 1989, when the exhibition *Possibilities* opened at MoMA PS1. The next year he represented Austria at the Venice Biennale, at which point his international reputation was permanently established. West's work is now in the collections of the most prominent major institutions with focuses on contemporary art, including the MAXXI in Rome, the Centre Georges Pompidou in Paris, and The Museum of Modern Art in New York. After a long illness, West died in Vienna in 2012.

West's art encompasses sculpture, painting, and installation, though the public is probably most familiar with his large-scale, painted aluminum works. Reacting in part to a tendency among contemporary artists to make public art that's monumental and slick, West set about creating objects of an altogether different sort.

Eidos (2009), for instance, while objectively quite large and intricate (it's over seventeen feet high), has the aesthetic quality of a DIY project—the soldering is visible between panels, a few sections appear to be dented, even the paint, a bubblegum pink, gives it a casual, playful air. *Eidos* succeeds not just by sending up corporate, generic art, but by embodying what makes West's art so special: it might have lofty theoretical underpinnings, but ultimately, it's something that anyone (and everyone) can look at and enjoy. J. T.

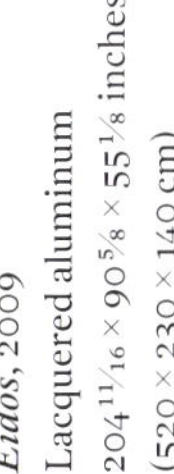

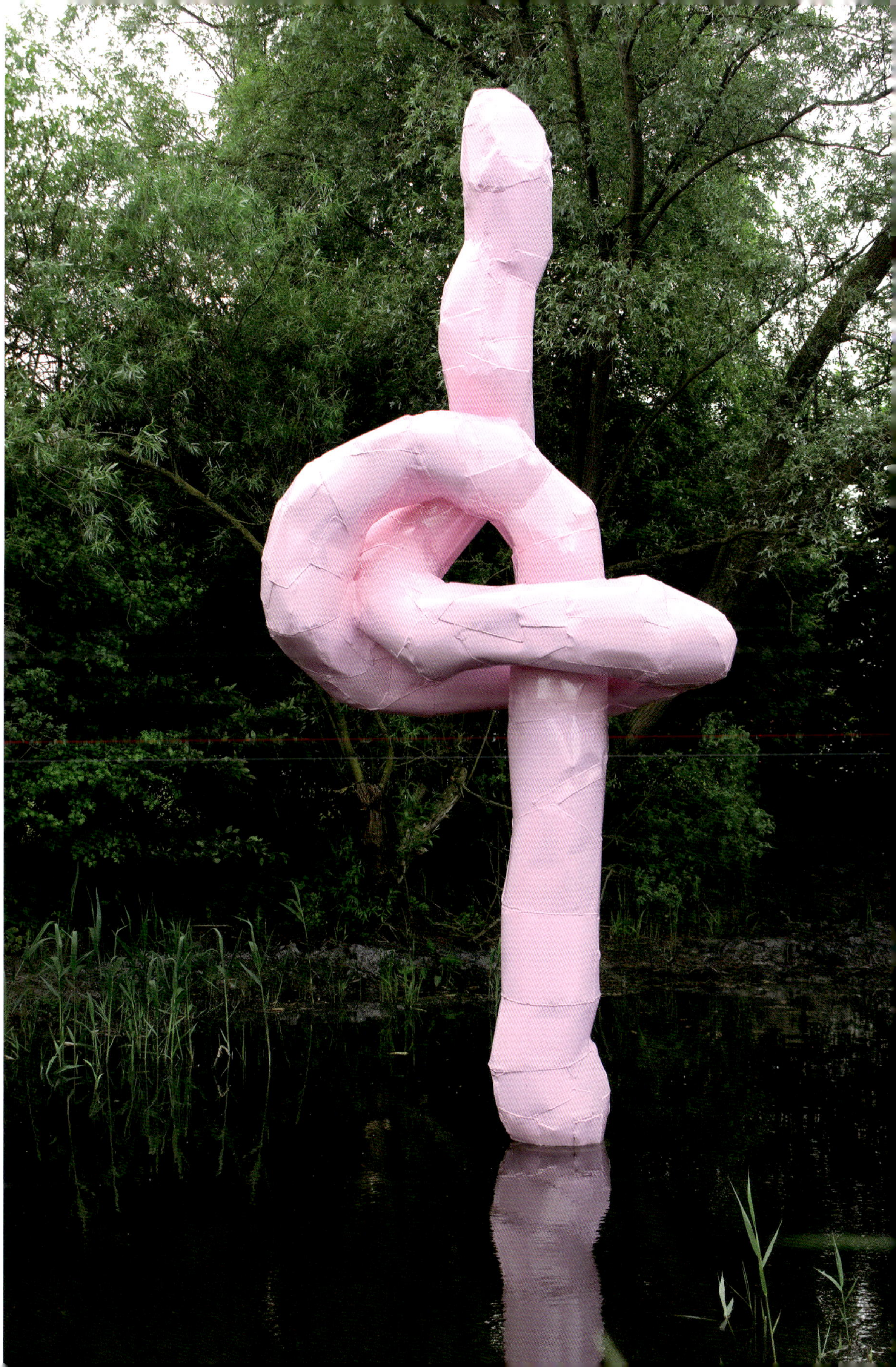

Eidos, 2009
Lacquered aluminum
204 11/16 × 90 5/8 × 55 1/8 inches
(520 × 230 × 140 cm)

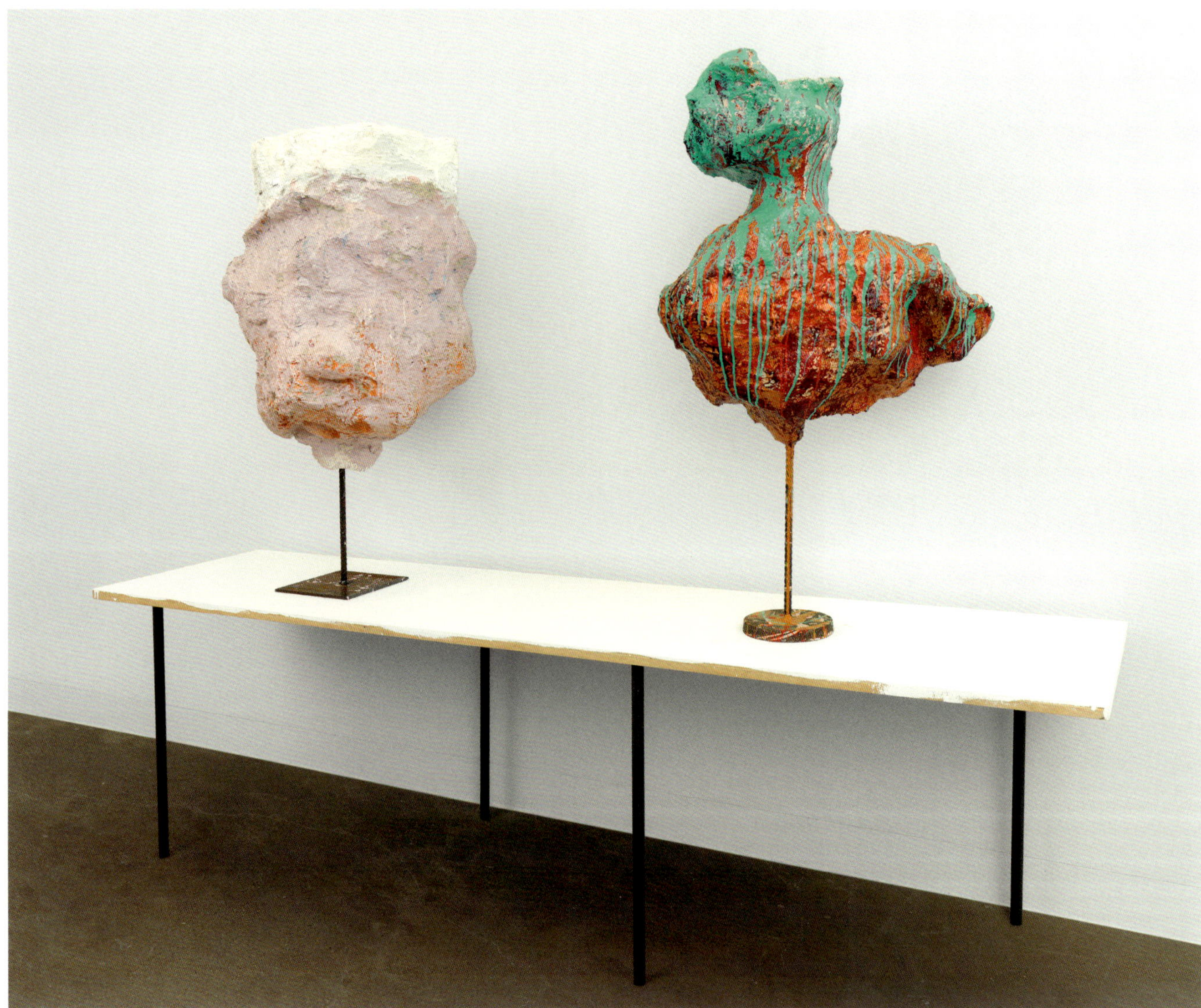

Table for 2 Sculptures, 2007
Acrylic paint, papier-mâché, steel, and wood
104 × 78 × 24 inches (264.2 × 198.1 × 61 cm)

Arbeitstisch in Aspik, 2009
Wood, acrylic lacquer, epoxy, and steel
29½ × 60 × 98⅜ inches
(74.9 × 152.4 × 249.9 cm)

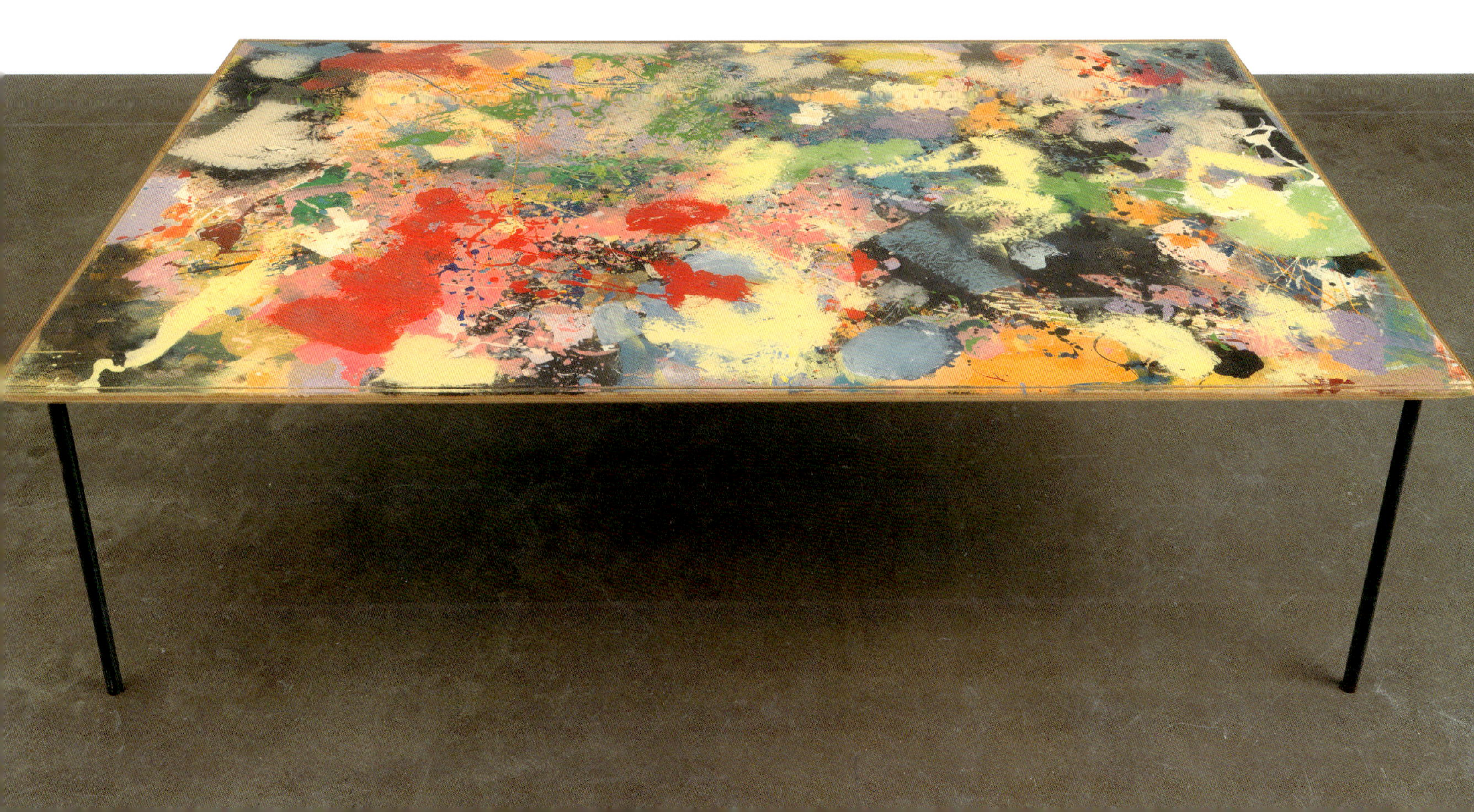

JONAS **WOOD**

b. 1977, Boston, MA

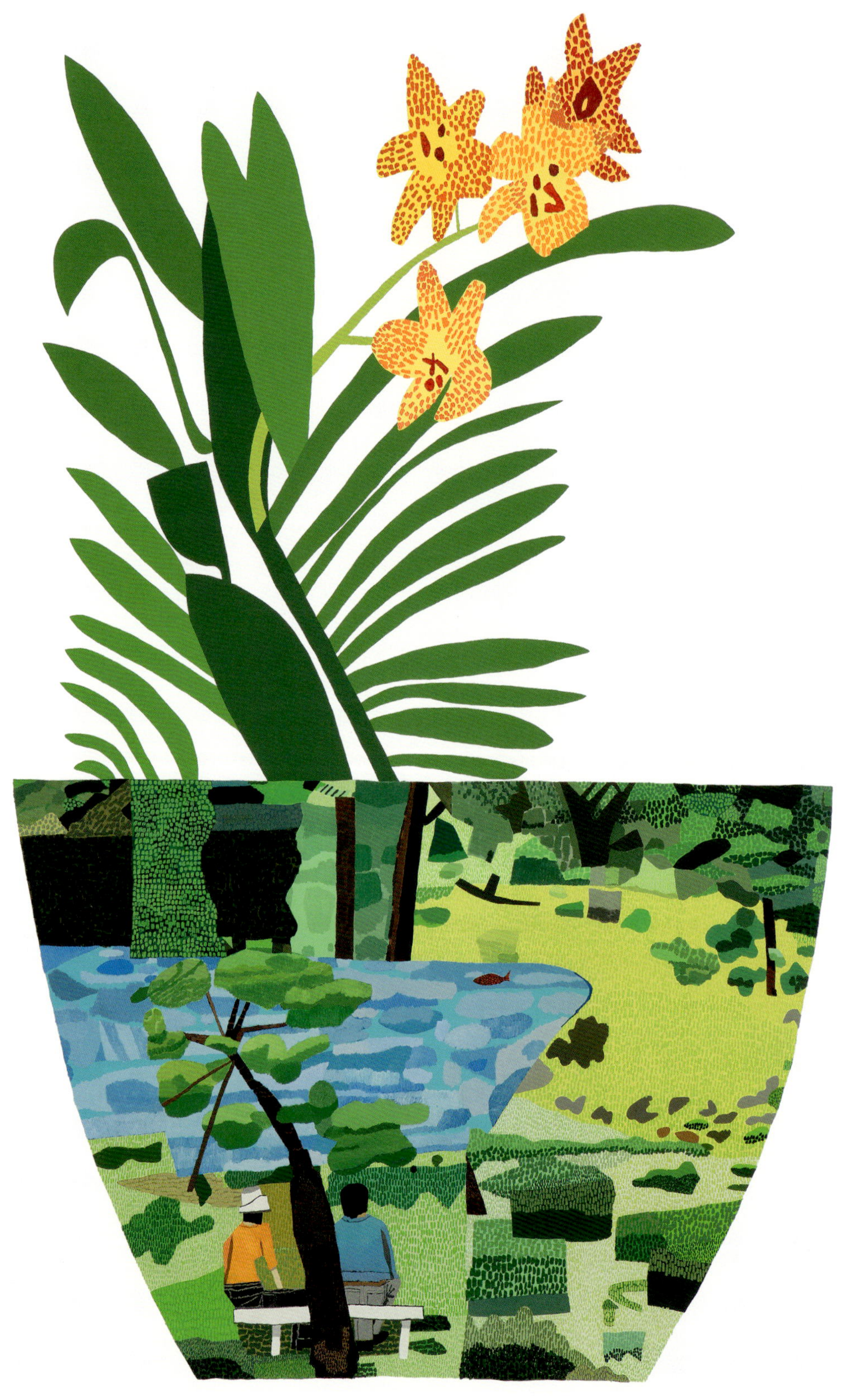

Landscape Pot with Yellow Orchid, 2014
Oil and acrylic on canvas
118 × 90 inches (299.7 × 228.6 cm)

Though Jonas Wood was born in Boston in 1977, it is the influence of Los Angeles, where he currently lives, which manifests in his work. Wood deftly and playfully toes the line between the aesthetics of modernist abstraction and sixties Pop. His canvases are densely populated with brightly coloured and crisply geometric plants, buildings, interiors, portraits, and athletic scenes, meticulously rendered and compressed through a distorted perspective. Reminiscent at times of Henri Matisse's cut-outs, Wood's abstract tendencies might also be likened to Alex Katz's portraits or David Hockney's simple depictions of modernist exteriors—also informed by the Californian landscape.

It comes as no surprise that Wood considers himself an inheritor of the modernist tradition, both in his rigorous preparation (which sees him enter the territory of photography, etching, and sketching), and in the joyful experience of viewing he strives to facilitate by animating scenes of and from everyday life. Wood plays in painting.

Wood earned a BA in psychology from Hobart and William Smith College in 1999 before changing gears and receiving an MFA in painting and drawing from the University of Washington in 2002. Since then, Wood's has had solo exhibitions at Anton Kern Gallery, the Hammer Museum, and the David Kordansky Gallery in Los Angeles.

Landscape Pot with Yellow Orchid (2014) gathers the defining characteristics of Wood's practice. Set against a white background, the canvas shows an abstracted orchid in a heavily decorated pot. The pot itself is the work's main focus, depicting two figures on a bench, who look out toward a vast and complex garden. The space wavers, and it becomes unclear whether the pot is painted as such or whether it opens onto the landscape in question. A lush palette of blues, greens, and yellows draw the eye through brushstrokes that vary from flat swathes of monochrome to a pointillist fusion of tones that creates depth and intrigue. Though Wood speaks to a great art historical lineage, his synthesising of these influences is wholly unique. J. H.

Hammer 8, 2010
Acrylic on canvas
90 × 108 1/8 inches (228.6 × 274.3 cm)

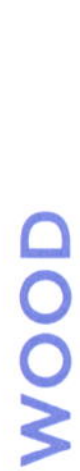

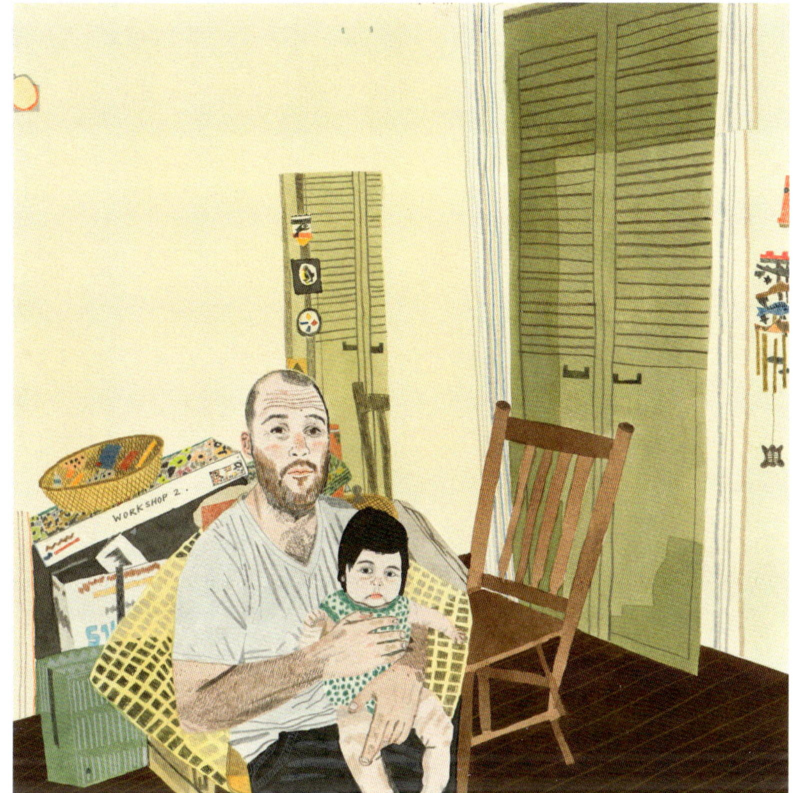

Self Portrait with Momo, 2014
Gouache and colored pencil on paper
20 1/4 × 20 inches (51.4 × 50.8 cm)

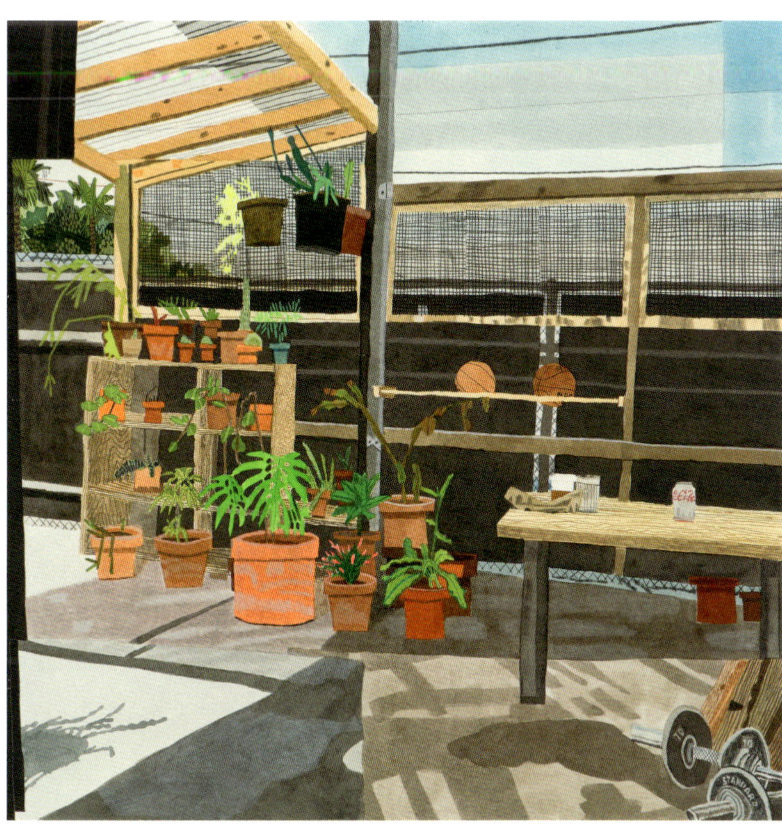

Blackwelder Studio Exterior, 2014
Ink, gouache, and colored pencil on paper
26 × 26 inches (66 × 66 cm)

CHRISTOPHER WOOL

b. 1955, Boston, MA

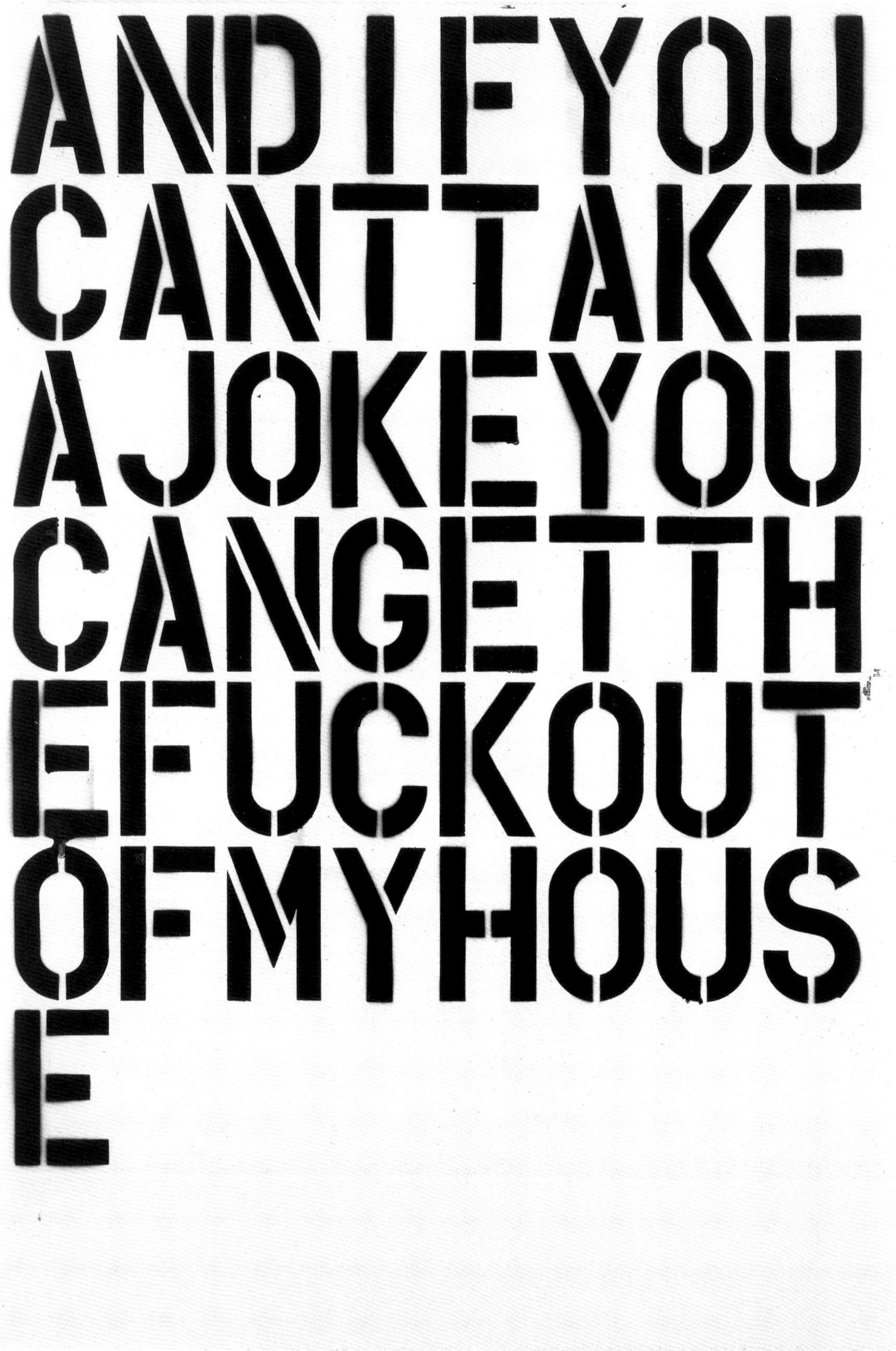

And if you, 1992
Enamel on aluminum
52 × 36 inches (132.1 × 91.4 cm)

Christopher Wool's paintings manage to combine the diverse and occasionally conflicting worlds of abstraction, Minimalism, and Conceptual art. Born in 1955, Wool grew up in Chicago, then moved east to get his BA from Sarah Lawrence College. After graduating in 1973, he settled in New York City at the precise moment that its art scene was undergoing an insurrection bordering on revolution. Punk was in its nascent stages, Conceptual art had nearly supplanted abstraction, and the city, which was teetering on the edge of bankruptcy, became the locus of a youthful, anti-establishment artistic community.

It was in this cultural ferment that Wool began to develop his artistic practice. Inspired by graffiti and popular signage—and reacting, at least in part, to the then-dominant perception that painting as a medium was outdated—Wool made paintings that brought the streets indoors.

In the mid 1980s, he used patterned paint rollers to create black-and-white panels whose lines were too smudged to be pretty and too chaotic to be decoration. A few years later, inspired by a white van spray-painted with graffiti that read "luv" and "sex," Wool began to make his iconic word paintings. Some of these paintings are single words—"Run," "Fool," "Riot"—others, like *And if you* (1992), are full phrases. These word paintings, all of which are black or blue enamel on white aluminum, bridge the divide between pure formalism—letters as shapes—and, perhaps more compellingly, literal messages from the artist to the viewer. Jokes, invective, philosophy—all are rendered by Wool as works of bold, uncompromised art.

Wool eventually returned to stenciled patterns. This time, however, his approach bordered on anarchic: Wool would take an image of an earlier patterned artwork, screen print that image onto another canvas, and then trace or erase the screen printed lines with a spray gun. This process is in evidence in *Untitled* from 1997. The flowers, ornament, and decoration of Wool's early art have collapsed in on themselves, the tensions and variances in his initial paintings brought to a logical if violent conclusion. J. T.

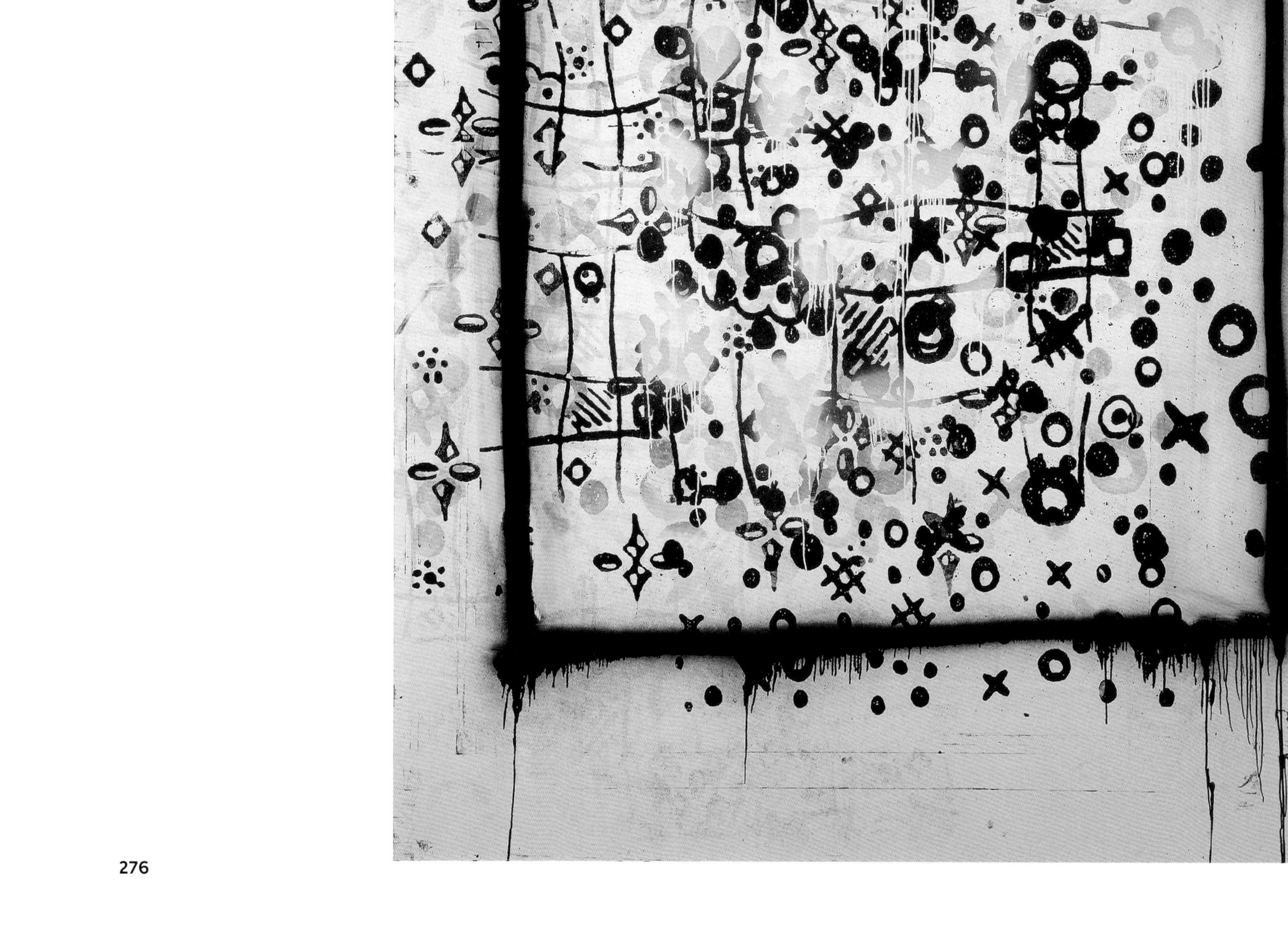

Untitled, 1997
Enamel on aluminum
108 × 72 inches (274.3 × 182.9 cm)

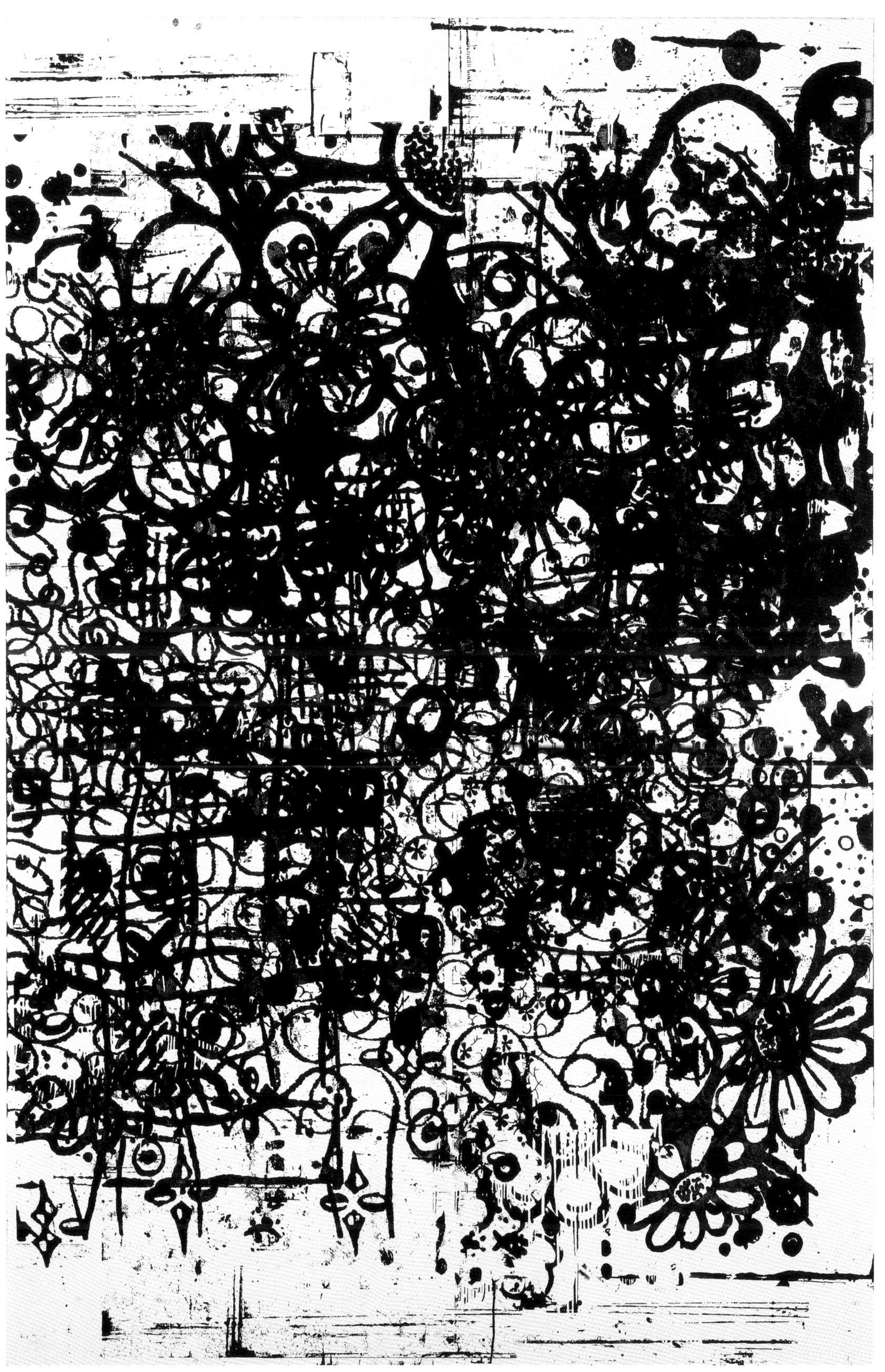

Mama Too Tight, 1999
Enamel on aluminum
108 × 72 inches (274.3 × 182.9 cm)

Untitled, 2012
Silkscreen ink on linen
120 × 96 inches (304.8 × 243.8 cm)

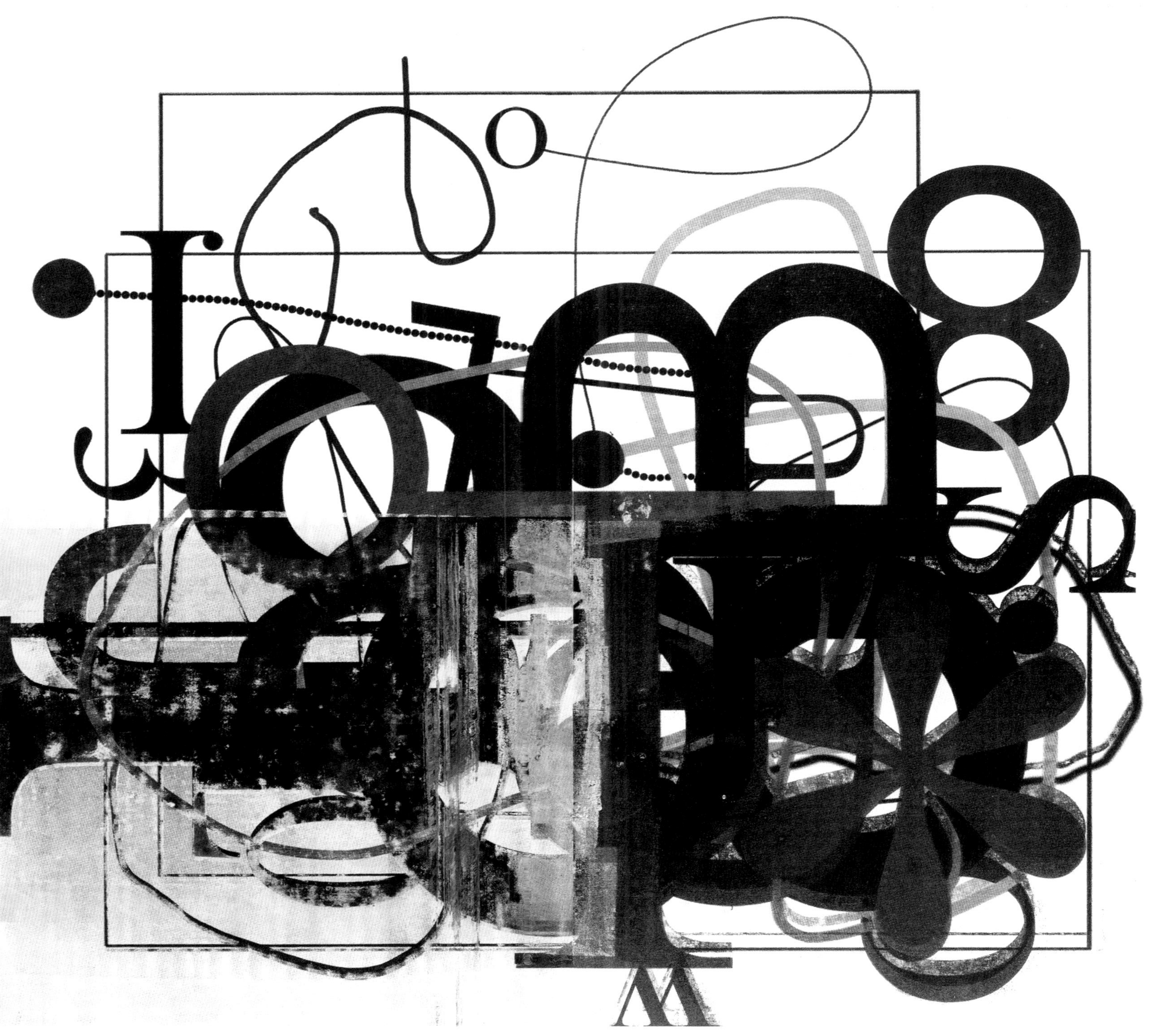

Untitled, 2014
Silkscreen ink and enamel on linen
106 × 96 inches (269.2 × 243.8 cm)

UNPACKING: THE MARCIANO COLLECTION

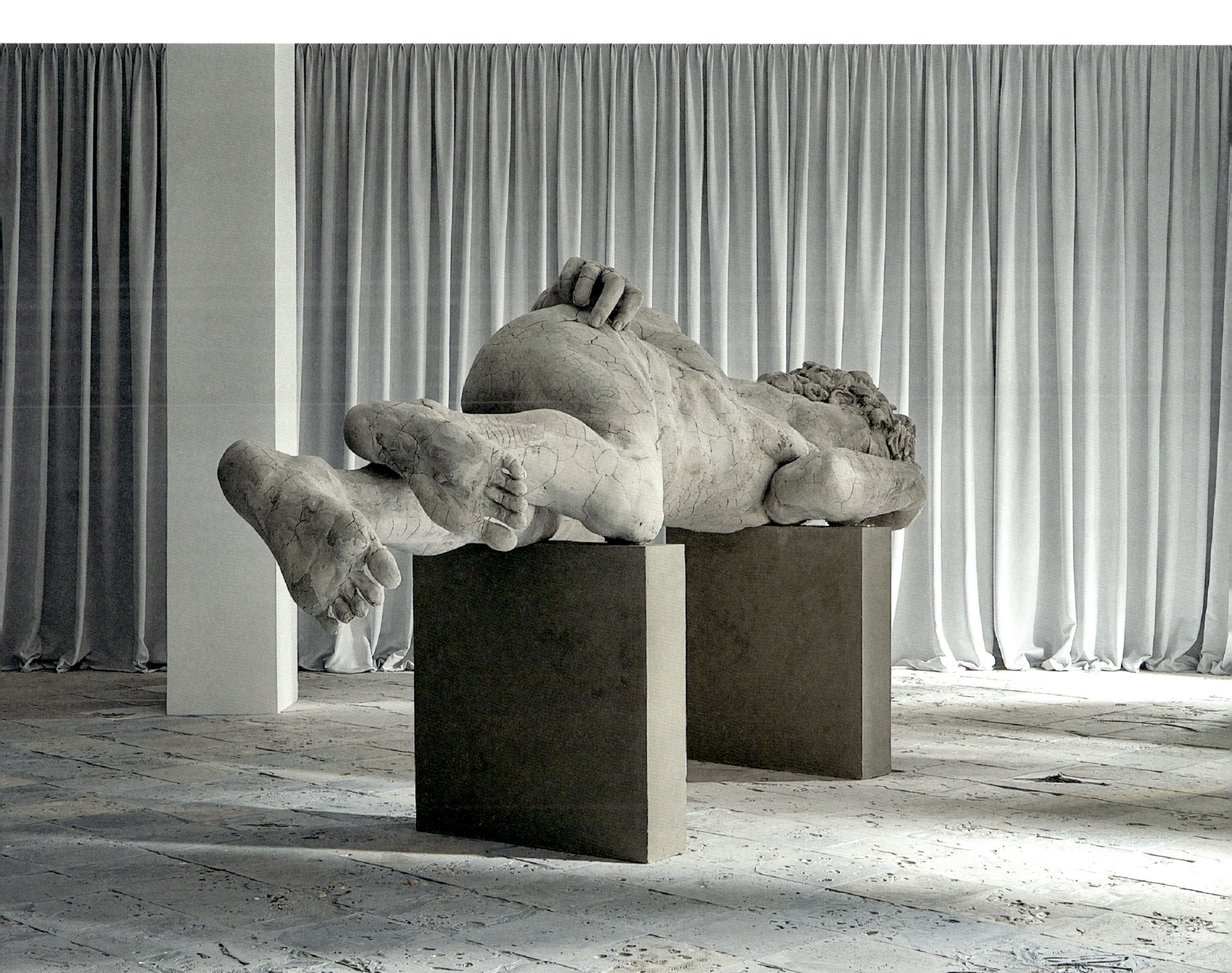

PHILIPP KAISER

Two years had passed since Walter Benjamin, the German philosopher and cultural critic, had divorced his wife, Dora, and moved out of his residence in the Grunewald district of Berlin into a furnished apartment with more than 2,000 of his books packed in crates. As he recounts in his 1931 essay, "Unpacking My Library," while emptying the boxes two years later, Benjamin finds himself reflecting on his relationship to property and collecting and invites the reader to join him "in the disorder of crates that have been wrenched open, the air saturated with the dust of wood, the floor covered with torn paper."[1] Euphoric, he forgets time and space and allows himself to be overwhelmed by the chaos, the "dam against the spring tide of memories which surges toward any collector as he contemplates his possessions."[2] The collector's relationship to objects, Benjamin concludes, is the most intimate one you could possibly have, because he is also the one who lives in them.

Entrusted with the wonderful task of organizing the first presentation of the Marciano Collection in the newly restored Scottish Rite Masonic Temple, my endeavor inevitably called to mind Benjamin. In this case, too, the "books" were not yet on the shelves of their new home—not yet touched by the mild boredom of order, as Benjamin wrote. Yet for all parallels, one cannot deny the differences—artworks freely defy categorizations and, as a result of their ambiguous nature, do indeed assert a discursive space, though they occupy it in a complex manner. Still, according to Benjamin, it is clear that any order is a balancing act of extreme precariousness.[3] And indeed this first presentation of only a small fraction of the Marciano Collection is poised between setting priorities while at the same time respecting the eclectic breadth. With this in mind, *UNPACKING: The Marciano Collection* must be read as an open arrangement that reflects its unusual context, a former Masonic lodge, as well as its first iteration, while not ignoring all the fraying that art has to offer.

1 Walter Benjamin, "Unpacking My Library: A Talk about Book Collecting," in Hannah Arendt, ed., *Illuminations: Essays and Reflections* (New York: Shocken Books, 1969), 59–67.

2 Ibid., 60.

3 Ibid., 59, 60.

ARCHAEOLOGICAL IMPULSE

In recent years, a striking number of artists have chosen to operate in the manner of amateur archaeologists, celebrating these performances—digging numerous holes and presenting and staging relics of allegedly lost cultures—in photographic, sculptural or installation works. Perhaps the most convincing work in this context is Adrian Villar Rojas's *Two Suns (II)* (2015) (fig. 1), a seventeen-foot replica of Michelangelo's David laid out on two supports, the remnant of a distant culture. Introverted, his eyes closed, it is unclear whether David has recovered from his battle with Goliath or whether he is dreaming, thinking he is elsewhere. The floor, which is covered with a minimalistic arrangement of cement tiles embedded with shells, butterfly wings, bicycle tires, and even an old iPod, along with the theatrical staging of the Renaissance sculpture both create an incomparable atmosphere that, in a way, transcends its own decay.

In Villar Rojas's surreal and post-human universe, the omnipresent and dominant culture of the West presents itself poetically in its stage of demise. Its monuments are, from the outset, ruins, and in this manner they remind us of Robert Smithson, a pioneer of Land Art. It is not just Smithson's specific

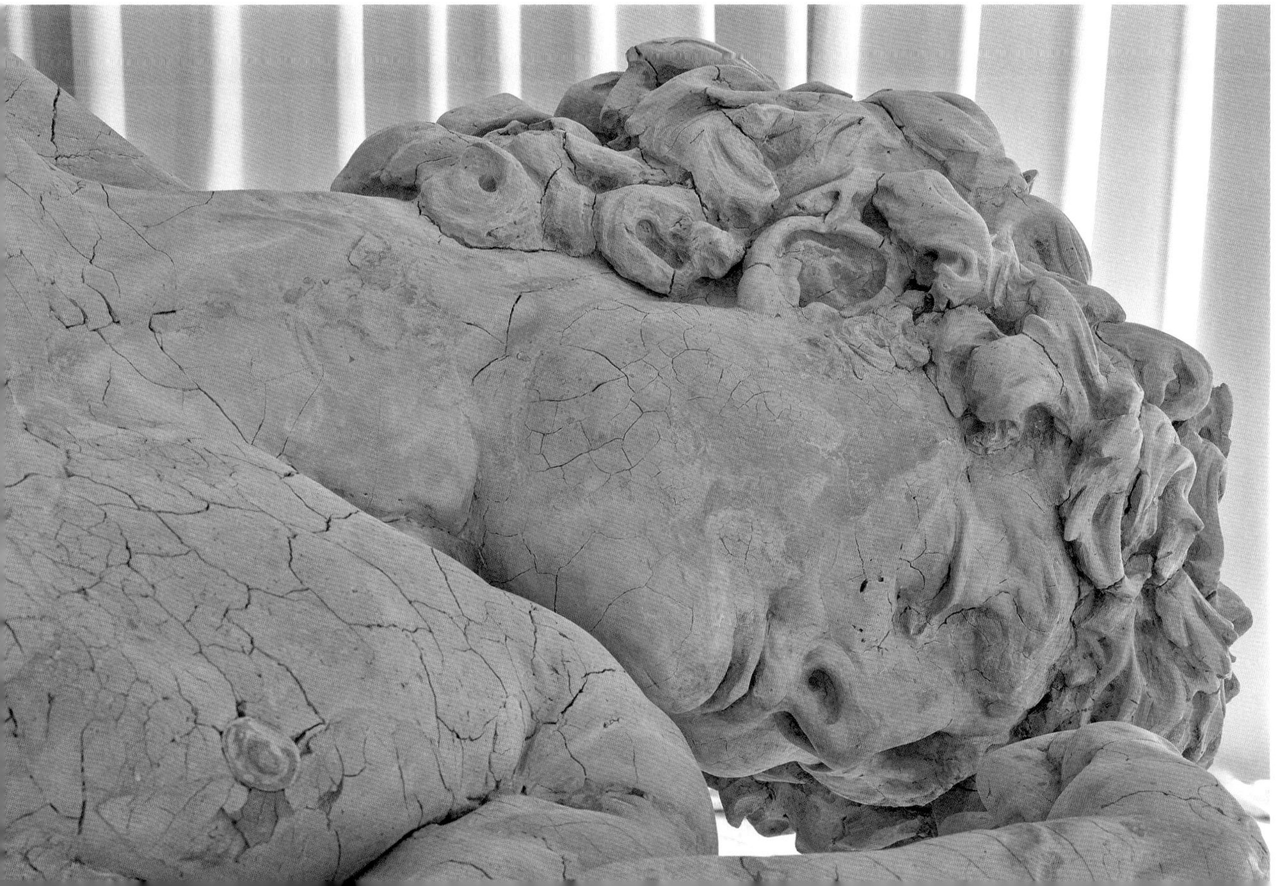

FIG. 1 Adrian Villar Rojas, ***Two Suns (II)*** (detail), 2015
Site-specific installation
Sculpture: 43 5/16 × 57 1/16 × 185 1/16 inches (110 × 145 × 470 cm)
Base: 40 3/16 × 9 13/16 × 41 5/16 inches (102 × 25 × 105 cm) (each)
Installation view, Marian Goodman Gallery, New York

interest in entropy—the irreversible process of decay of any formation as a result of the uncontrolled forces of nature—that fascinated entire generations of artists, but also the dystopian cosmos he traced in his visionary, sprawling writings, such as his 1966 essay, “The Crystal Land,” in which he recounts the first of his legendary excursions into the hinterland of New Jersey together with Donald Judd, describing the view of Manhattan as mineral and crystalline, brilliantly blending glacial and early history with science-fiction culture.

References to Smithson are ubiquitous in the collection, be it in Allora and Calzadilla’s *Petrified Pump Station No. 2* (2010), a post-apocalyptic ruin of the future that evokes fossil fuels and their obsolescence, or in Cyprien Gaillard’s sculptures, pictures, and rubbings (fig. 2). Gaillard’s work even engages in an explicit dialogue with Smithson’s notion of entropy: as part of a 2009 exhibition in The Hague, Gaillard excavated a German concrete bunker from World War II, which had been hidden in the sand near the beach, then, in a performative action, briefly displayed it as a kind of an anti-monument. His fascination with decay, ruins, destruction, and natural disasters as well as his iconographic vocabulary and his sculptural ready-mades—rusty excavator teeth and earthmover claws (see pages 64–65)—inevitably call to mind the legendary brute actions and works of historical, late 1960s Land Art, which accompanied the expansive wave of urbanization as reflective moments and temporary monuments.

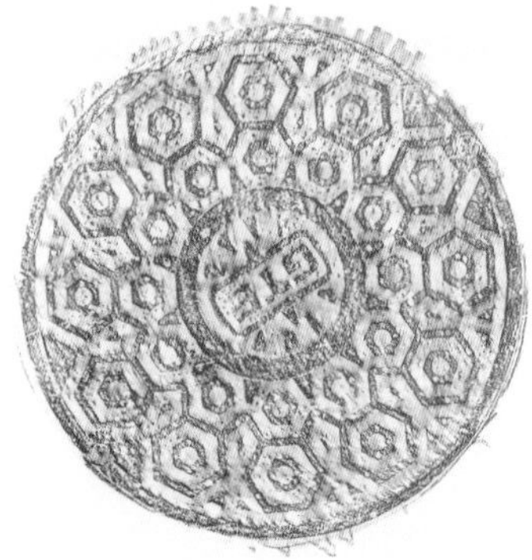

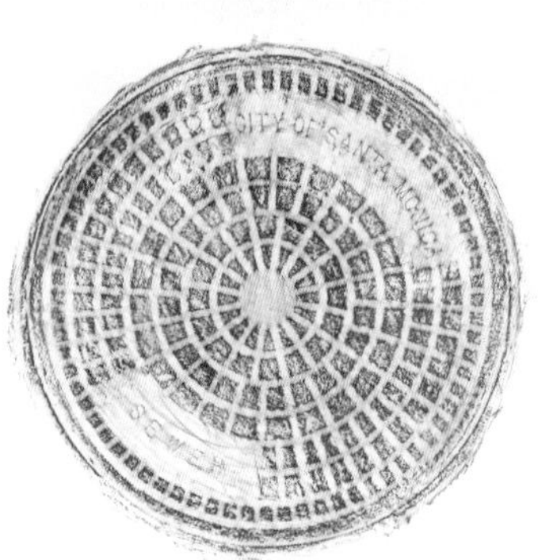

FIG. 2 Cyprien Gaillard, ***Gates GTE/CITY OF SANTA MONICA SEWER***, 2013
Frottage
112 1/4 × 54 inches (285.1 × 137.2 cm)

This archaeological and historiographical impulse was encapsulated a few years ago in the exhibition *The Way of the Shovel*; curator Dieter Roelstraete attributed the expanded historical awareness, on the one hand, to the increasing academization of art training and, on the other, to an epistemological reorientation in our society.[4] What is clear is that the historiographic turn in contemporary art has produced new narrative works, with artists turning to history because it is in crisis, both as an intellectual discipline and in our culture. The interest in dystopian contexts may, to some extent, appear transhistorical in this connection, for it is not microhistory, but rather the history of the glacial, great movements of the history of the earth and civilization that are important here.

Nonetheless the archaeological paradigm merits attention because the works essentially render something visible that was previously hidden, and, in doing so, locate themselves. In this sense, the archaeological impulse must be read as a metaphor for site-responsiveness. Though not site-specific—that is, conceived for a single, unique place—in the narrow sense of the term, the works mentioned do raise relevant issues of place and context. A prime example of this is Yael Bartana's cinematic epic *Inferno* (2013) (fig. 3). The twenty-two-minute film depicts the building of the Temple of Solomon in São Paolo by a Brazilian neo-Pentecostal church called the Universal Church of the Kingdom of God. At the beginning, the film shows followers of the cult adorned with baskets of fruit and flowers admiring and celebrating the temple as helicopters fly in sacred items of the Jewish faith, only to end with the imaginary, spectacular destruction of the temple and the subsequent church service. Bartana blends facts and

4 Dieter Roelstraete, "Field Notes," in *The Way of the Shovel* (Chicago: University of Chicago Press and Museum of Contemporary Art, Chicago, 2013), 21.

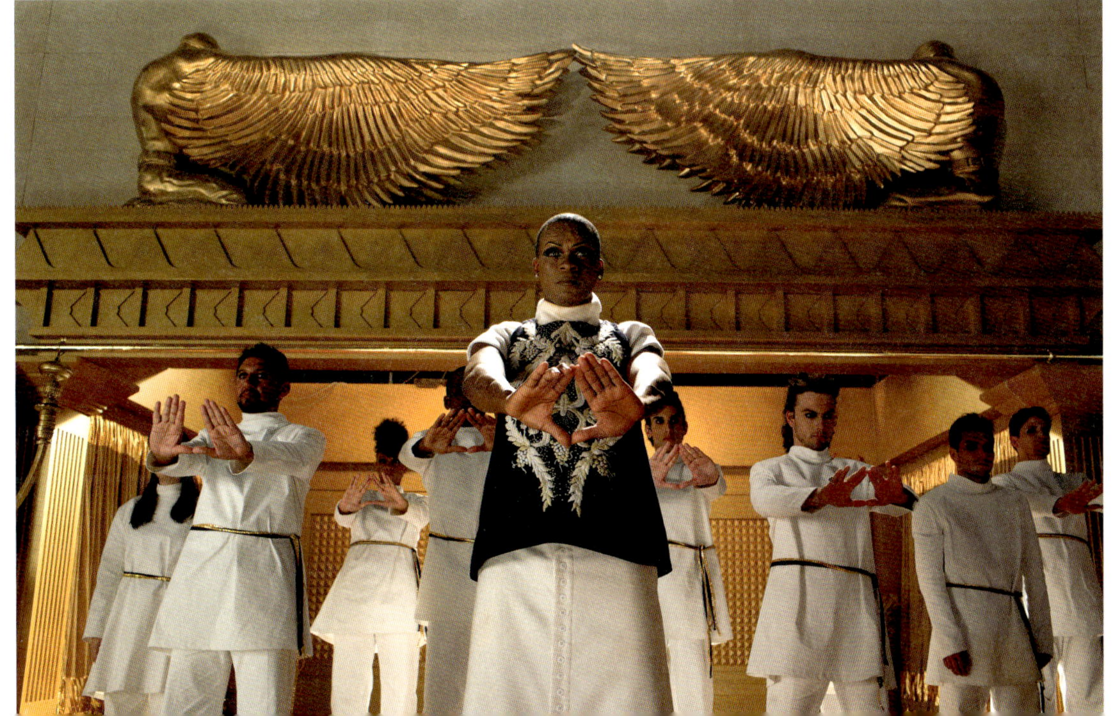

FIG. 3 Yael Bartana, *Inferno* (detail), 2013
Alexa camera transferred onto HD
22 min.
Edition 6 of 8, 3 AP

fiction, prophecy and history, referring to a "historical pre-enactment." The third Temple of Solomon erected by the evangelical Universal Church is a replica of the Temple of Solomon in Jerusalem, of which only the foundation, the Wailing Wall, remains. Led by Nebuchadnezzar II in the ninth century BC, the Babylonians famously destroyed this most sacred structure of Israel, which orthodox circles would like to have resurrected. Bartana's complex confrontation of the relatively young Brazilian church with the Jewish primal scene, which among other things resulted in the diaspora of the sixth century BC, becomes even more complex given the fact that *Inferno* is presented in a former Masonic temple. For the Freemasons, the spiritual rebuilding of the Temple of Solomon is essential because it is the model of the symbolic and spiritual temple of mankind. The contextual bonus of Bartana's film makes it clear that site-responsive works are anything but autonomous and contain a fundamental openness and readiness for semantic shifts.

Another example for a site-responsive work is Cindy Sherman's larger-than-life mural (fig. 4), which features a male protagonist who wears a large embroidered cape from the fraternal British order, Oddfellows. Like the Masons, the Oddfellows embraced mystical costuming. Sherman emphasizes the

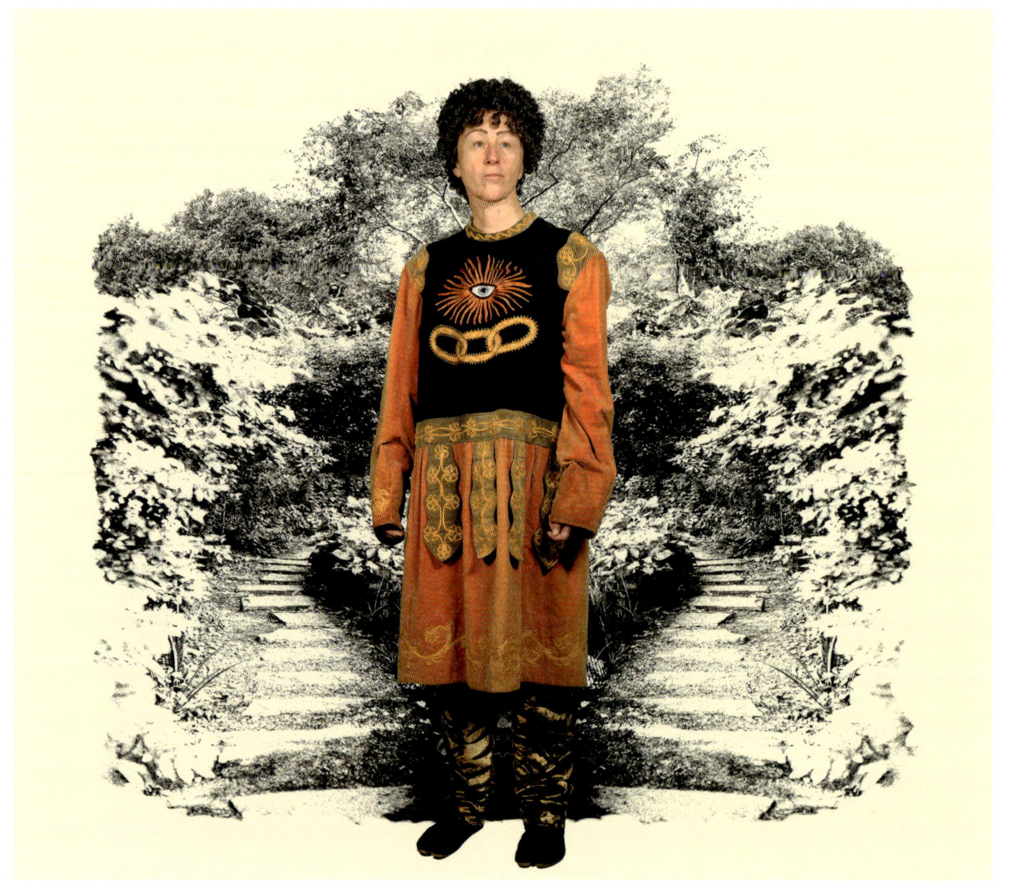

FIG. 4 Cindy Sherman, ***Untitled #549-E***, 2010
Pigment print on PhotoTex adhesive fabric
Dimensions variable

dialectics of placement while turning the character into an emblem positioned in the center on strictly symmetrical black and white ornamentation.

Ryan Trecartin and Lizzie Fitch's theatrical film environment *Ledge* (2014) (see page 247) responds in an even more specific way to its surroundings. It was shot and produced at the Marciano Art Foundation's Masonic temple before the renovations began. The work, comprised of five screens and a monitor inside a hybrid Cinerama Dome (which is also reminiscent of a stage, a camping tent, or a platform), presents indeterminable rambling without noticeable dramaturgy. Dressed in gaming outfits with targets on the backs, the film's figures explore the aged temple, in a way virtualizing and eliminating its reality and history from within.

PROCESSES AND UTOPIAN PROMISES

As previously mentioned, the inaugural exhibition of the Marciano Foundation addresses not just the unique context, but all the fraying that art has to offer as well. This implies that many works will be involved in intimate dialogues and monologues even without a contextual superstructure, and thus the first presentation of the collection includes an excellent group of post-Pop works by, among others, Christopher Wool, Paul McCarthy, Mike Kelley, Louise Lawler (fig. 5), Sterling Ruby, and Alex Israel, as well as a coherent group of post-Conceptual painting by artists ranging from Wade Guyton to Paul Sietsema to Laura Owens and Analia Saban. But because *UNPACKING: The Marciano Collection* is the

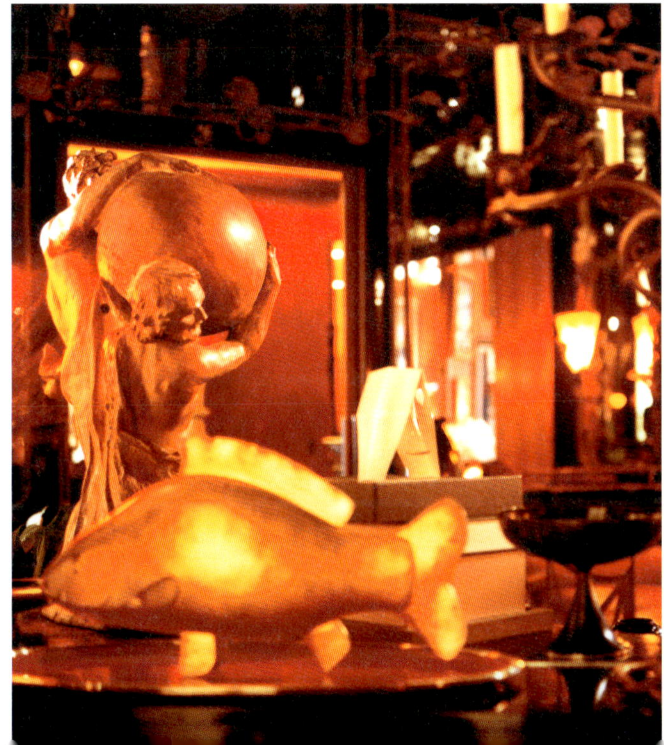

FIG. 5 Louise Lawler, ***Carpe d'or***, 2008/2010
Cibachrome face-mounted to plexi on museum box
$55\frac{1}{4} \times 47\frac{5}{8}$ inches (140.3 × 121 cm)

first iteration of the Marciano Collection in Los Angeles, it is of particular importance: the collection has never been shown, nor has there ever before been a presentation in the former Masonic temple. In this sense there is no memory, no past that could serve as a corrective of the present, and it may be a happy coincidence that a great many works in the collection implicitly and explicitly deal with processual constellations that, in the broadest sense, promise a "bright" future.

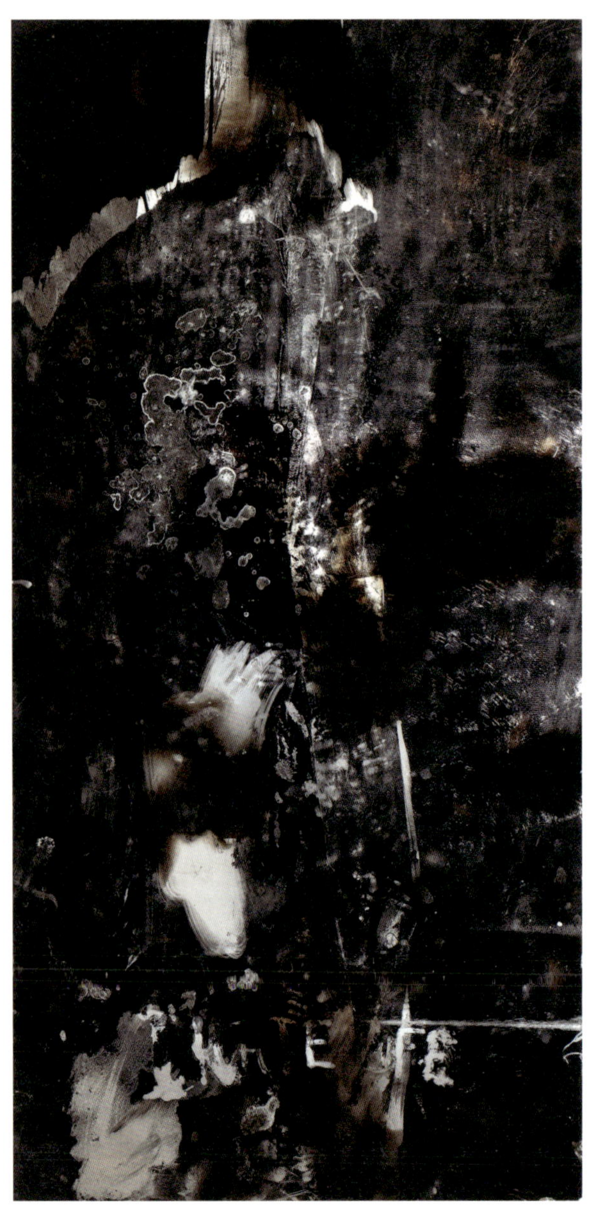

Process art emerged on the heels of Minimalism in the late 1960s. Its most noted manifestation was arguably the legendary 1969 exhibition at the Kunsthalle Bern, *When Attitudes Become Form*. From that point on, not just attitudes toward art, but sculpture as well, were reformed in such a way that the process of making, rather than the finished, perfect form, was now foregrounded. Works were declared artworks halfway through and, as a result, undoubtedly had a sketchy quality, while the boundaries of sculpture, object and painting were utterly eroded. Many years have since past, yet a look at the contemporary artistic production of recent years shows to what extent a young generation of artists has again reflected on the premises of the processual. Not so much with the aim to once again overcome the rigid boundaries that used to exist between art forms, since today those boundaries can hardly have claim to validity anymore, but rather to empirically explore the boundaries of mediality and materiality and to give prominent visibility to the unpredictable.

Processes usually end in the future, although, as we have seen based on Smithson's theory of entropy, they can also end in decay and ruin. A good example of this is Kaari Upson's long-term and recently completed Larry Project, which deals with a fictional character of the same name living in the Inland Empire of California (fig. 6). Larry's house, which was tragically destroyed by a fire, as well as his journals, his life, and his dreams all become starting points of a disastrously complex multimedia work that explores the dark and unfathomable aspects of the (fictional) life. Upson's charred relics evoke a better past but at the same time reflect remnants of a lived-in home and a promising life.

FIG. 6 Kaari Upson, ***Untitled***, 2011
Smoke on aluminum panel
96 × 48 inches (243.8 × 121.9 cm)

Unlike Upson, who uses architecture in the broadest sense as a resonant space of the psychological, Oscar Tuazon aims to establish a sculptural practice that positions itself between house and sculpture, wall and picture (fig. 7). His crude plaster pictures, which not only reveal the production process but also the rust marks of the embedded reinforcing bars, are allusions to architecture and metaphors of the permanent and the stable, presented as autonomous abstract painting not unlike the elegance of a Robert Ryman. In a way, the works double the wall on which they are mounted and create an implicit relation to its proportions and borders, though they, too, ultimately point to their own fading.

The dialectic nature of becoming and decaying, appearing and disappearing, seems to be intrinsic to any processual logic. Even when processes appear as visual, painterly constellations—as in the work of, say, Latifah Echakhch, Jacqueline Humphries, and Sergej Jensen (all of whom are represented in the Marciano Collection)—they always point in two directions: the future and the past. One reason for this is that many artists also attempt to articulate a new sensitivity to time and duration, with a certain ambiguity being happily accepted or, indeed, being stylized into a precondition. In this sense, the Process works and the entire first exhibition resemble one another: both are open arrangements that contain experimental yet imminent promise. It is the promise of an auspicious future.

FIG. 7 Oscar Tuazon, ***Bleach***, 2013
Plaster, blue paint, and steel
65 × 65¼ × 2 inches (165 × 165.5 × 5 cm)

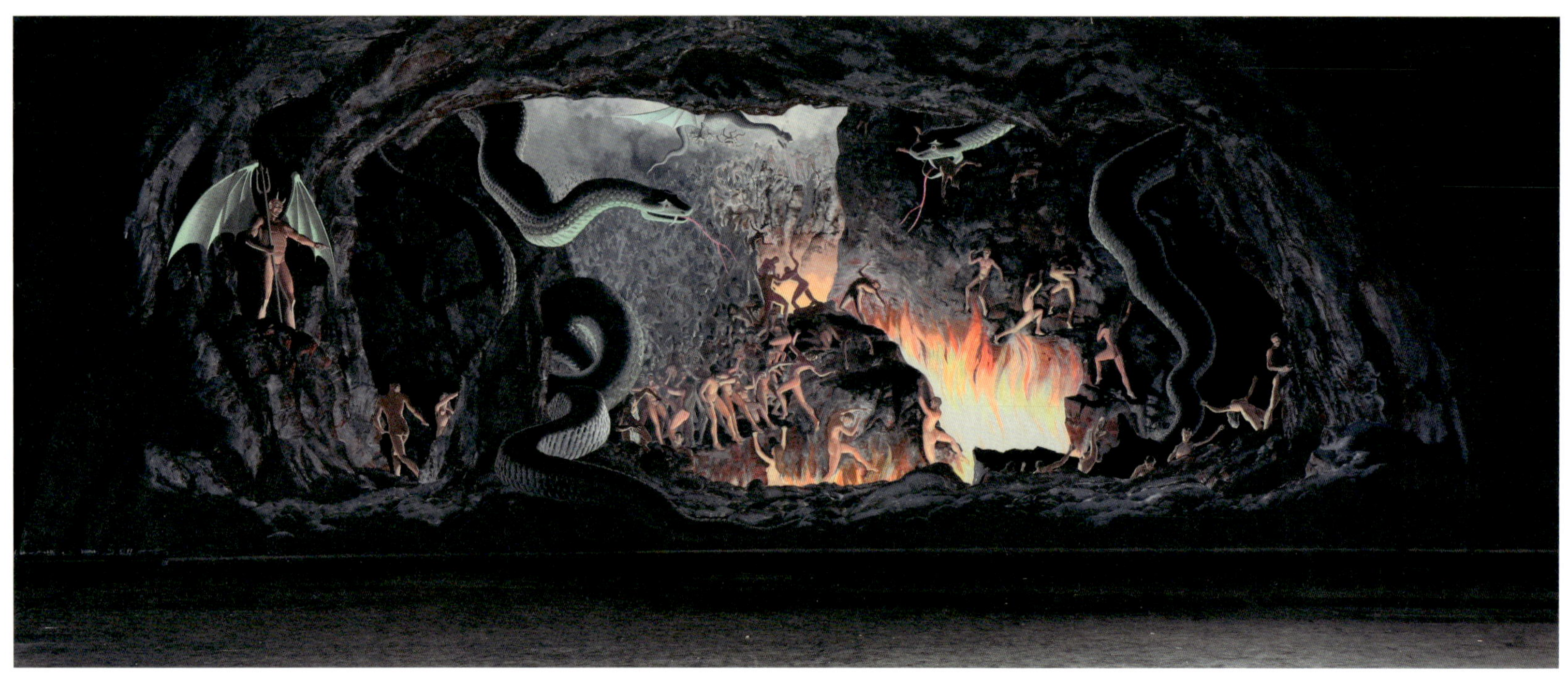

Theatrical backdrop, Scottish Rite Masonic Temple

THE WIG MUSEUM: JIM SHAW IN CONVERSATION WITH PHILIPP KAISER

SEPTEMBER 2016

PHILIPP KAISER Your show for the Marciano Art Foundation is called *The Wig Museum*. Wigs have appeared in your work before. What do they stand for and how would you describe your specific interest?

JIM SHAW Well, it varies from time to time. It began when I was just simply looking for wigs as an element of this mural I was doing, four pieces of which were in the style of 1970s prog rock album cover art, and one of them was going to have beehive hairdos standing in the air. I began to really get into the aesthetics of the hairdo artists because they do amazing stuff with these hairdos, and I began to make drawings. It seemed at that point the hairdos were standing for a force of nature as they did in the old forties and fifties comic books that I'd made delineating some of the Oist history, which also ties into the rock opera I'm planning for the exhibition, and I was kind of making them into these chaotic realms. But if you look at them as sculptures, they're shockingly amazing, that you can make hair do all this stuff. And there's this whole genre of black hairdressers who do crazy wig stuff and crazy hairdos; there's a book called *Hair Wars* about it. I'm kind of fascinated with the making of Rose Parade floats for the same reason because there's such a peculiar aesthetic and a lot of it's about, "Look what I did to defy gravity." Another thing is high-end dessert competitions. I have a friend who's a chocolatier, and he's the coach for the Olympic pastry chef competition team. They're all about defying gravity, so that weighs on their aesthetics. That's sort of the beginning of my interest in wigs.

But then after seeing that Masonic backdrop [in the Scottish Rite Temple] of the peculiarly shaped cloud inside the cathedral, I had this idea for a painting of a British jurist wig that was just kind of floating [René] Magritte-like in a jungle background. And that's sort of where I took off with this particular version of wigs as a symbol of authority. Certainly back then—you know Louis XIVth, George Washington, etc.—the wig was an important part of their authority, and if you were one of the lower classes, you probably didn't have a white wig.

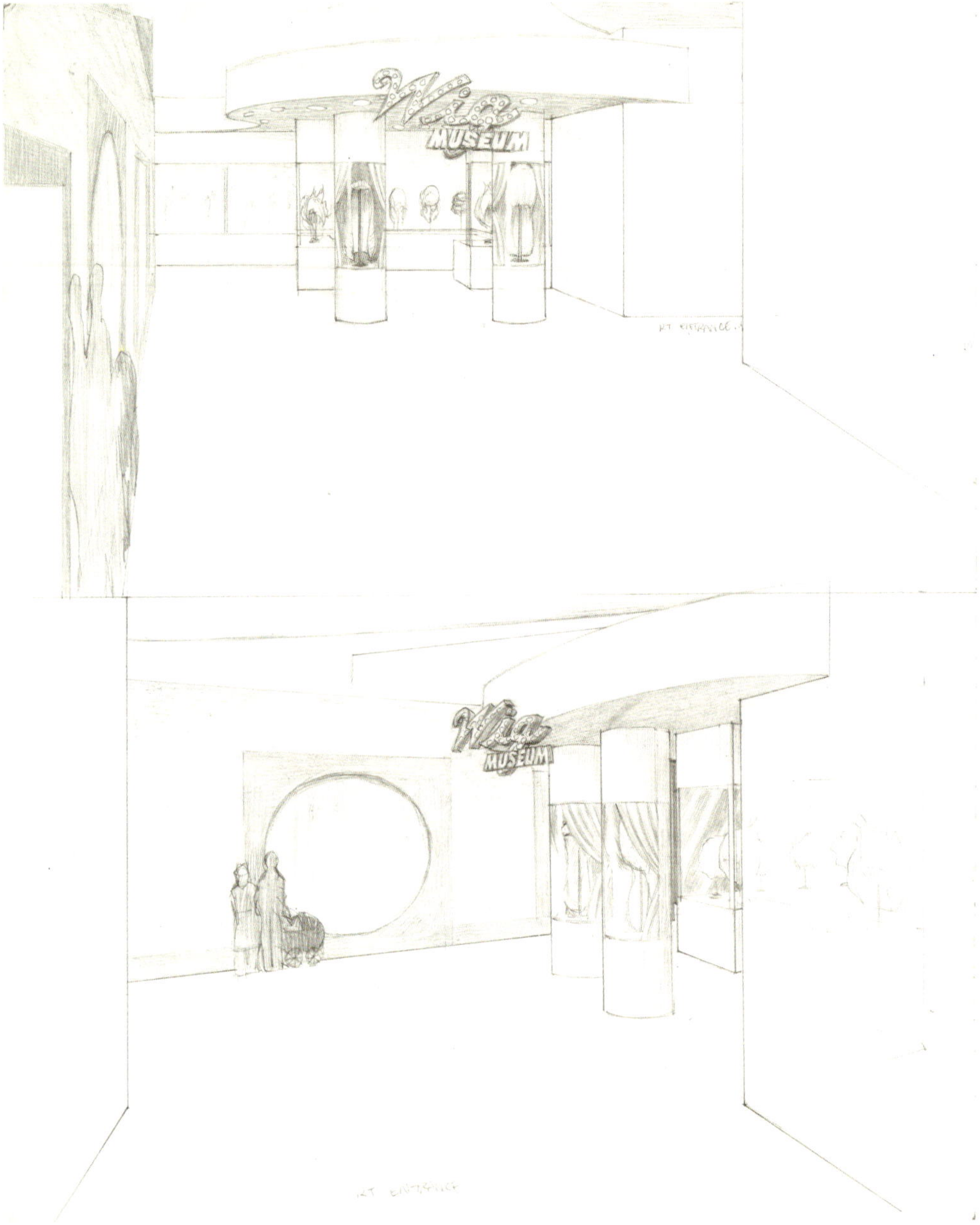

PK Are you saying they represent Anglo-Saxon power and control?

JS Yes. It represents something that I feel is coming to an end, for better or for worse. And so that's sort of the sub-theme of the whole thing. It is the end of control… as it's occurring now.

PK And that's also why you're turning it into a museum and historicizing the wigs?

JS Well, that's another form of control—the museum. I have to cast someone as the old curator.

PK [Laughter] Who's going to be the director of the wig museum?

JS I will have to find an older actor. I know a middle-aged actor who could do the voice.

PK How would you describe the museum? What is it going to look like in the exhibition?

JS It is kind of small because it'll be like a museum you'd find on Hollywood Boulevard. It's shown within this shopping district, which is represented by an unaltered backdrop of an actual shopping street, and because it's sort of the high-end shopping street, it represents the pinnacle of that civilization, the Anglo-American civilization. I hear that the queen actually owns most of the high street shopping in London around Piccadilly Circus, that's literally her real estate.

Jim Shaw, Study 1 for *The Wig Museum*, 2016
Pencil on paper
17 × 14 inches (43.2 × 35.6 cm)

PK Your exhibition takes place in the former auditorium where more than 2000 Freemasons celebrated their rituals in the past. Have you been to the temple before the remodel started? Did you find any wigs there?

JS Yes, I have, and it was very interesting. I had only been inside a Masonic temple on one or two occasions, but I'd never been able to go into the undersides of them, of course. A lot of stuff was gone by the time I got to the Scottish Rite Temple, but finding the wig and facial hair section was amazing. That's where all those ethnic heads come from that were in my *Hidden World* show. I don't know if there was an Anglo-Saxon head there, since it was mostly what would've been considered the sub-races or the…Racism was just enshrined in all levels. I mean even Rudolf Steiner believed in some of that stuff, because everybody did; it certainly made slavery convenient, it made colonialism convenient for everybody except the enslaved and the peons who were shunted to that low level.

In the sub-basement of this building, the Masons had a clinic for children with aphasia, and it included two-way mirrors so that they could observe the children. I have my doubts that anything so horrible happened there as would happen, as say in British hospitals involved in their pedophile scandals. It's like a perfect set up for that, but it doesn't mean it happened at this place. But it is another symbol of the authority that the wig carries with it, that you've got control over these kids in charity hospitals and reform schools, etc., and they may get abused and it can just turn them into hopeless, mental cases, and there is no justice for them.

PK Are you going to re-purpose some of the wigs you found there?

JS I'm hoping to. I also want to make some puppet wigs, which will become part of the stage show for the opera when it gets off the ground. I still need to write the texts that they will be speaking before they go into the museum.

PK You have presented your vast archive on several occasions. Did the Freemasons ever make it in your archive?

JS Oh, absolutely. I have bits and pieces, here and there. I've been to the Freemason neighborhood in London, where they have a Freemason's bar…

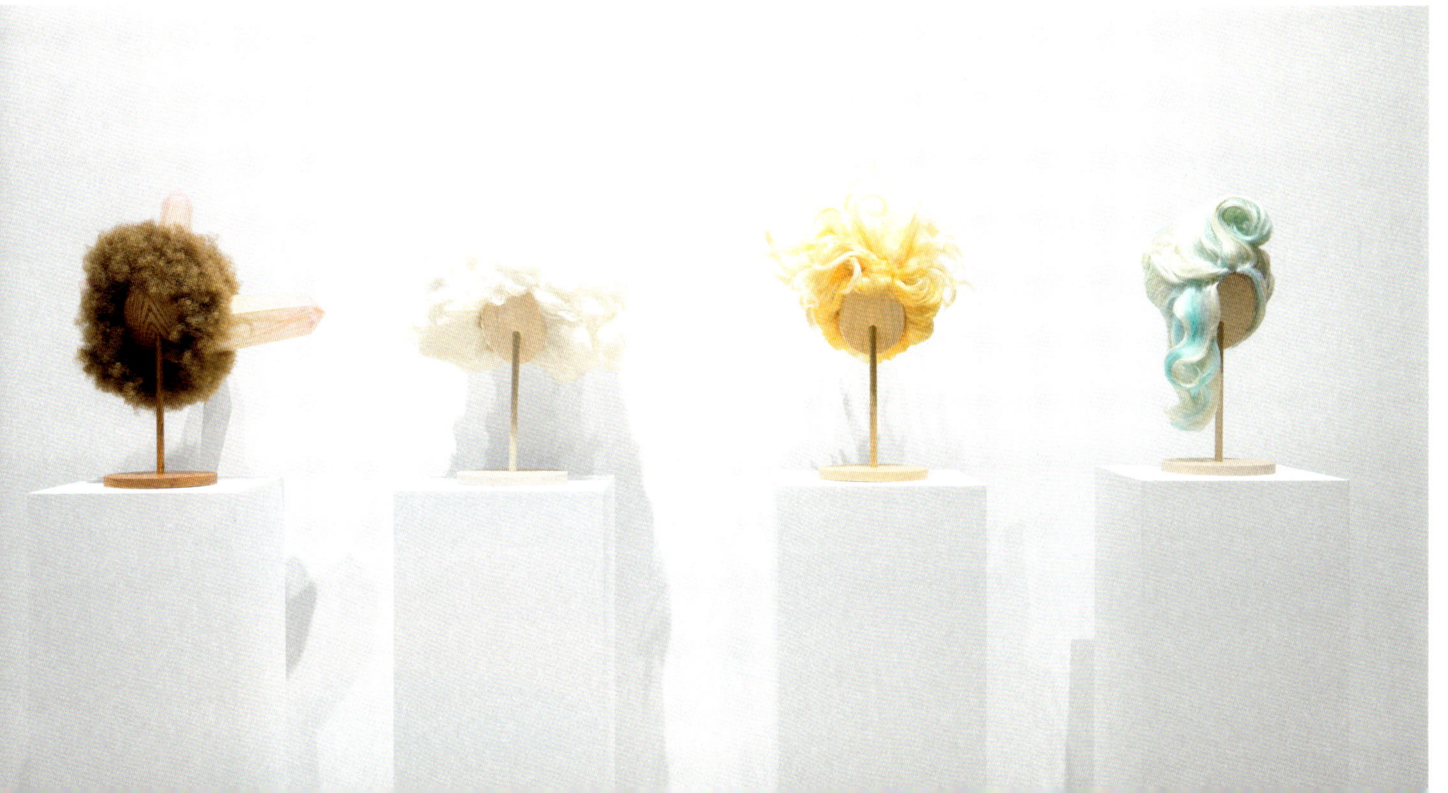

Jim Shaw, ***4 Element Wigs*** (female set), 2012
Four synthetic hair wigs with airbrush (Earth with fiberglass and Paverpol)
Dimensions variable
Installation view, *Jim Shaw: Entertaining Doubts*, MASS MoCA, March 28, 2015–February 7, 2016

PK Didn't it start there in 1717?

JS Unless it goes way back to ancient Egypt as claims are made…which you know, maybe it does? No one knows, really.

PK And what's in the archive exactly?

JS All kinds of archives. I was interested in the way that propaganda affects aesthetics, similar to the aesthetics of wigs. A lot of it is religious but there's also scientific material, crackpot science, and there's also Masonic stuff. The Masons were like the first Surrealists when it came to having floating eyeballs and shit like that. The way Americans re-purposed Surrealism, there were often columns involved, which is also a major symbol in the Masonic world. There are two or three columns, one has a sun, one has a moon. Since it's all secret stuff, I can only imagine or prefer to believe in this or that thing that's said about the Masons. I was never invited to become a Mason, but I found out my father was a Mason when he was in his late eighties. He never had any evidence of it around, unlike the other fraternal groups he joined, but I do have some of his Masonic medallions over there in velvet boxes. And my grandfather, I knew was a Shriner, since he did artwork for their Shriner events. He did cartoons of happy Shriners…

PK Let's talk about the show. You're turning the huge auditorium space into an encompassing environment. Your presentation includes some original backdrops that you found at the temple. When did you start using backdrops?

JS I started around 2004. My wife, Marnie, was looking for backdrops for one of her videos, and we looked at the "For Sale" section on this website where they had cracked, old and smelly, out of-date backdrops. I went, "Oh shit. I gotta do something about that." It was during the Iraq War buildup and the Iraq War, which in a lot of people's opinions including mine was just a cover for getting [George W.] Bush re-elected and making sure he maintained a parliamentary majority, and 9/11 handed him all this wonderful power to be abused. And, so I was doing stuff about the right-wing use of the Christian community basically manipulating voters into maintaining power

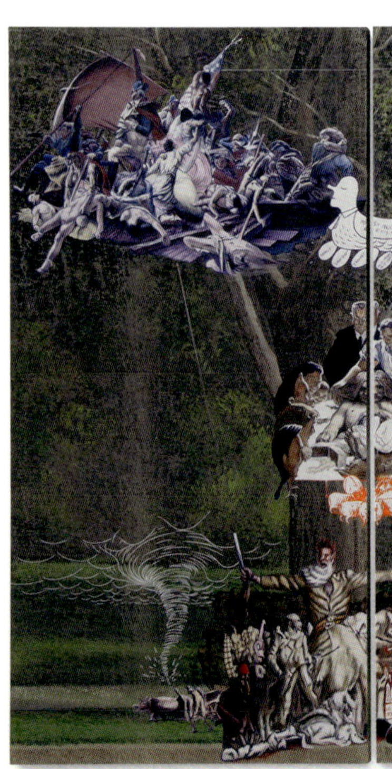
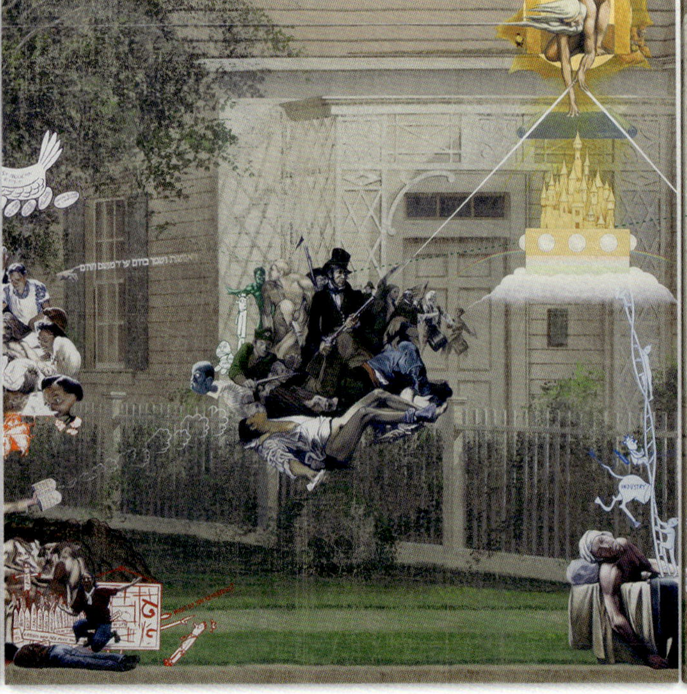
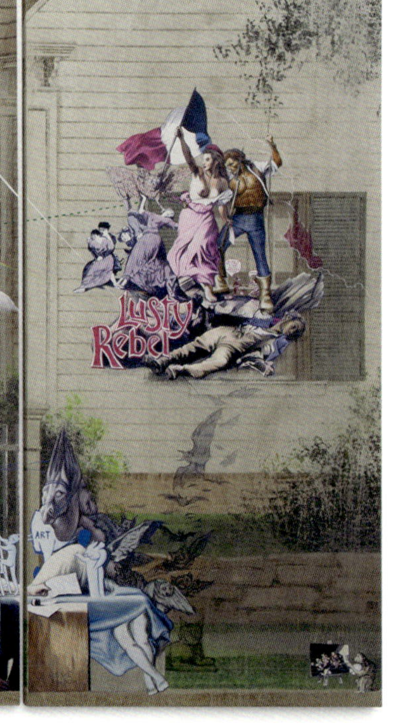

Jim Shaw, *Seven Deadly Sins*, 2013
Acrylic on muslin
96 × 194 (243.8 × 492.8 cm) overall
Marciano Collection

while selling away all of their jobs overseas. I was taking the sort of [Ronald] Reagan-esque, false ideas about the past and utilizing the actual backdrop as the metaphor for that false notion of the past. It's like a Magritte or a [James] Rosenquist except that there's a contrast between the original thing, which is full of cracks, and the thing that I paint on top, which hopefully isn't full of cracks. But I finally said, "I can't do anymore gigantic paintings." I don't have a gigantic studio. They don't fit in anybody's house, they barely fit in a museum. They're just too big. So I've been painting on smaller pieces of them.

At the temple there were many backdrops, some of them with two or three layers for foreground and background effects. They're very impressive, but they're not cracked and faded so I didn't want to paint on them.

PK Why not?

JS They were in perfect condition so there was never that distance. They [the Marcianos] also had a historian of Masonic stuff who said, "Oh you shouldn't let anybody paint on these." I was originally going to say, "I want to paint on them just because I didn't want to be the artist who didn't get to paint on them." But since nobody's going to paint on them, it's okay with me. I've painted on enough giant backdrops, and I don't need to paint on anymore. But I'm gonna stick some things in front of these and interact with them. So I'm creating sort of a [Hieronymus] Bosch-like hell within the world we live in—the shopping mall hell that is our contemporary life.

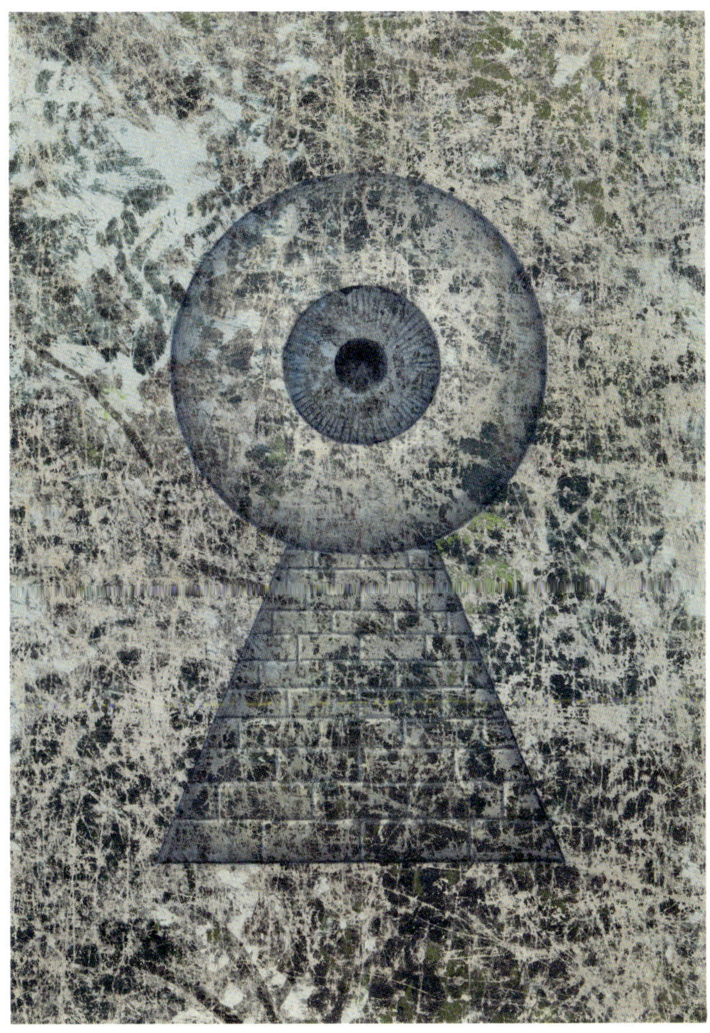

Jim Shaw, ***All-seeing Keyhole Eye***, 2013
Acrylic on muslin
32 × 22 inches (81.3 × 55.9 cm)
Marciano Collection

PK Your installation seems representative for your entire artistic cosmos and can be seen as a kind of mini retrospective. With its multilayered narratives and conspiracy theories, the installation feels like a three-dimensional collage. What is it about?

JS Well, the Freemasons are just a window onto the whole Northern European-centric world that we've been inhabiting, and which is now falling apart. I mean, it's not that I really believe that the Freemasons are an evil cabal of fat white men out to control us all. I think that the Northern European and American post-colonial world was already pretty good at controlling us all. And the control is disappearing on one end (i.e., the West) because of people deciding for libertarian reasons that they don't believe in authority or nation states anymore. Then on the other end, it's like… unless you're a well-heeled tyrant, you can't control what the people believe or you have failed states, real anarchy, and it's easier now for people who have extreme beliefs to take extreme actions.

PK Is the show an elegiac swan song?

JS I don't know if it's an elegy, but it's looking at that in some way or another. It's a metaphor, I guess. Also there's another Masonic related thing, which is an idea I read in a book called *The Secret History of the World*. It's a fairly straightforward thing, but it said that secret societies believe that the anti-Christ is currently among us and that the anti-Christ would be a figure that would have as much impact on the next two thousand year cycle, i.e. the Age of Aquarius, as Jesus had on the Age of Pisces. Of course, if you lived in China, I don't know how much effect Jesus had historically. But that's again Euro-centrically the thinking. And, I was compositing that with the whole idea of this as a cycle and thinking about who, or what, might possibly do that. I just decided that the iPhone is a symbol of the increasingly mechanical or cyber aspects of human life; that we have already, just through a few apps and the iPhone, altered our behavior to write in so many words on Twitter or make seven-

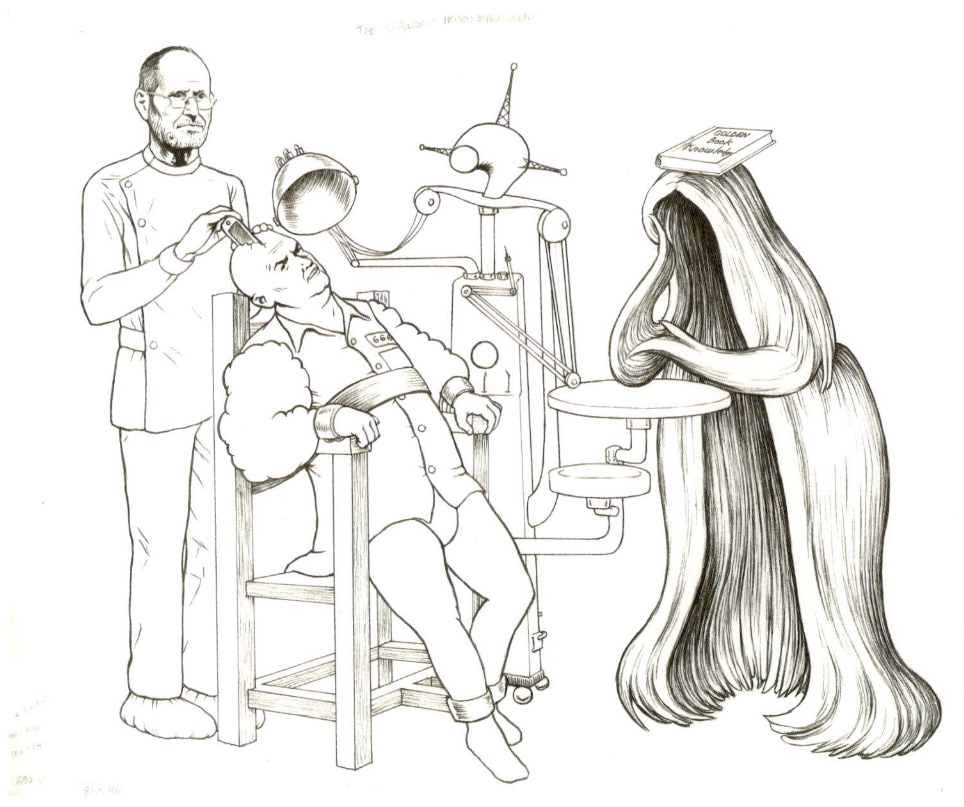

Jim Shaw, Study for *The Stanford Prison Experiment*, 2016
Ink on paper
14 × 17 inches (35.6 × 43.2 cm)

second videos on Vine. It's like, once that computer appendage exists it alters what we do and the way we write and think. If you get arrested nobody knows any phone numbers to call because they're all in their phone, so they haven't memorized them.

PK So how, in terms of conspiracy theories, does Steve Jobs come in to play?

JS Well, the other half is that supposedly in Islam, there's a character referred to by some as the anti-Christ. Maybe Jobs is not the anti-Christ literally, but within Islam there is, I forget his name, but he's the bad guy, and he will have one eye, and he will have been born between Iraq and Syria. And, I thought, "Oh, Steve Jobs. He's half Syrian, he invented the iPhone, which is sort of the one eye of the Cyclops." The weird thing is, it's the Cyclops of the thousand eyes, or a million eyes because it's also the end of authority. You can videotape the cops killing the unarmed person with it and show it on the news. So it works in different ways. And that's literally what ISIS supposedly believes, and plans on fighting the final battle of Armageddon in one of their more obscure enclaves, which they believe is where the final battle between the forces of good and evil will take. We, of course, are the forces of evil in their eyes, and we're playing into their hands by fighting them literally on the ground.

PK So, you're combining all these convoluted narratives to a bigger entity. It kind of reminds me of the very associative logic that you have in dreams.

JS Well, it's manic thinking. Magic thinking, manic thinking, to me they are the same. Just replace the g with an n. Maybe I learned it from Mike Kelley, but maybe I always did it. I mean, it's the way that I think the subconscious works, in puns, and maybe I'm getting old and I'm referencing art history more than I did in my youth.

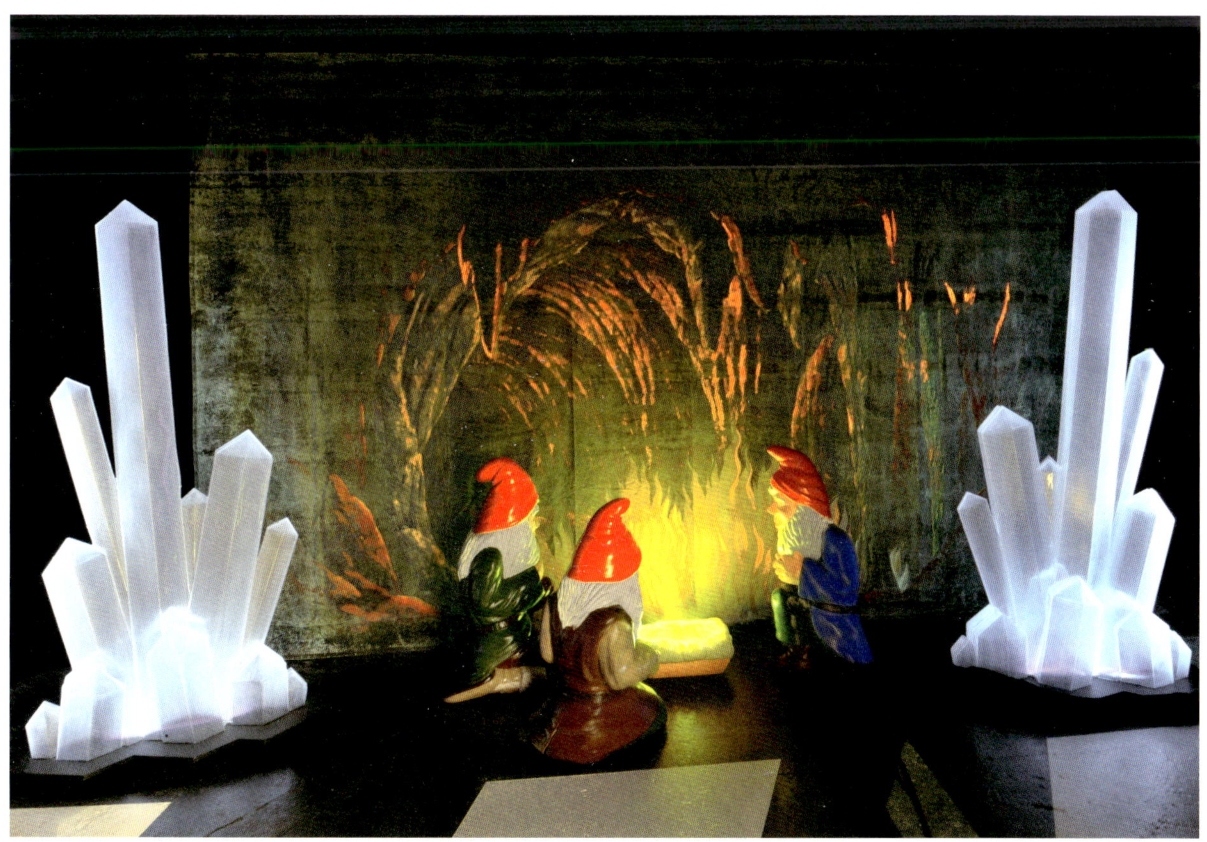

Jim Shaw, ***The Miracle of Compound Interest***, 2006
Mixed media installation
Dimensions variable
Installation view, *Jim Shaw: Left Behind*, CAPC musée d'art contemporain de Bordeaux, May 9–September 19, 2010

PK Magic and manic thinking seem to have a lot to do with Surrealism.

JS Yeah. But it also has to do with the stock market and how things aren't really worth what they're worth in the moment. You know, Enron stock wasn't worth what it was purported to be. Not only was it not worth it, the reason why it was so high was because they knew it wasn't worth it, and they had to lie to maintain their business model. It's like [Donald] Trump. Trump cannot release his tax returns because people would find out he's not as rich and successful as he says he is. And that's, you know, magical thinking; if he can convince people he's successful, they may vote for him.

PK Have you ever had a dream about Freemasons?

JS I've had dreams about secret societies and priests ritually killing children and things like that, but I don't know about Freemasons...

PK How do you usually capture the imagery of your dreams?

JS I just tape record it when I wake up. If you wait, you'll forget details. And if you write it down in the middle of the night you won't be able to read it unless you turn the light on, and then you can't get back to sleep. It takes less conscious effort to speak it than to write it. And the conscious effort can erase some of the interesting elements.

PK The conscious effort of writing, you mean?

JS Yes, translating images into words.

PK I assume that you have established a higher awareness of dreaming. Does that lead to better dreams or to more hysterical ones?

JS What leads to better dreams is something I haven't had much of since my daughter started regular school, which is sleeping in. During the summer times I get to sleep in, and in a year and three-quarters she'll be in college and I can sleep in again. It really deprives you of that luxury of extra dreaming. I mean, a lot of those dreams that you have under those circumstances are just kind of fluff compared to gnarly dreams that are, when you awaken, you go, "Oh that meant something, I've gotta deal with what they're dealing with there." Also, drawing them allows me to see some of the visual puns beyond the verbal puns. And the wig museum originated in a dream.

PK It did?

JS Yes, in my dream I was in Tijuana, and there were giant puppets, like shadow puppets out on the street and a hot dog place, and there was this wig museum there.

PK What else happened in the dream?

JS That was pretty much it. I think I may have gone into the wig museum.

PK Is the way it's built in the exhibition the way you saw it in your dream?

JS More or less...with the columns and the wigs. Yeah, I may not have the cut outs of the prostitute and John from the 1890s that were part of the dream or the hot dog stand, but it'll be part of the environment as you walk in. I like the theatrical entrance aspect, but it's kind of like a funhouse, too, a lot of weird angles and...it's kind of a dark ride, hopefully.

Jim Shaw, ***Not Since Superman Died***, 2014
Acrylic on muslin in eight pieces
270 × 600 inches (685.8 × 1524 cm) overall
Installation view, *Jim Shaw: Entertaining Doubts*, MASS MoCA, March 28, 2015–February 7, 2016

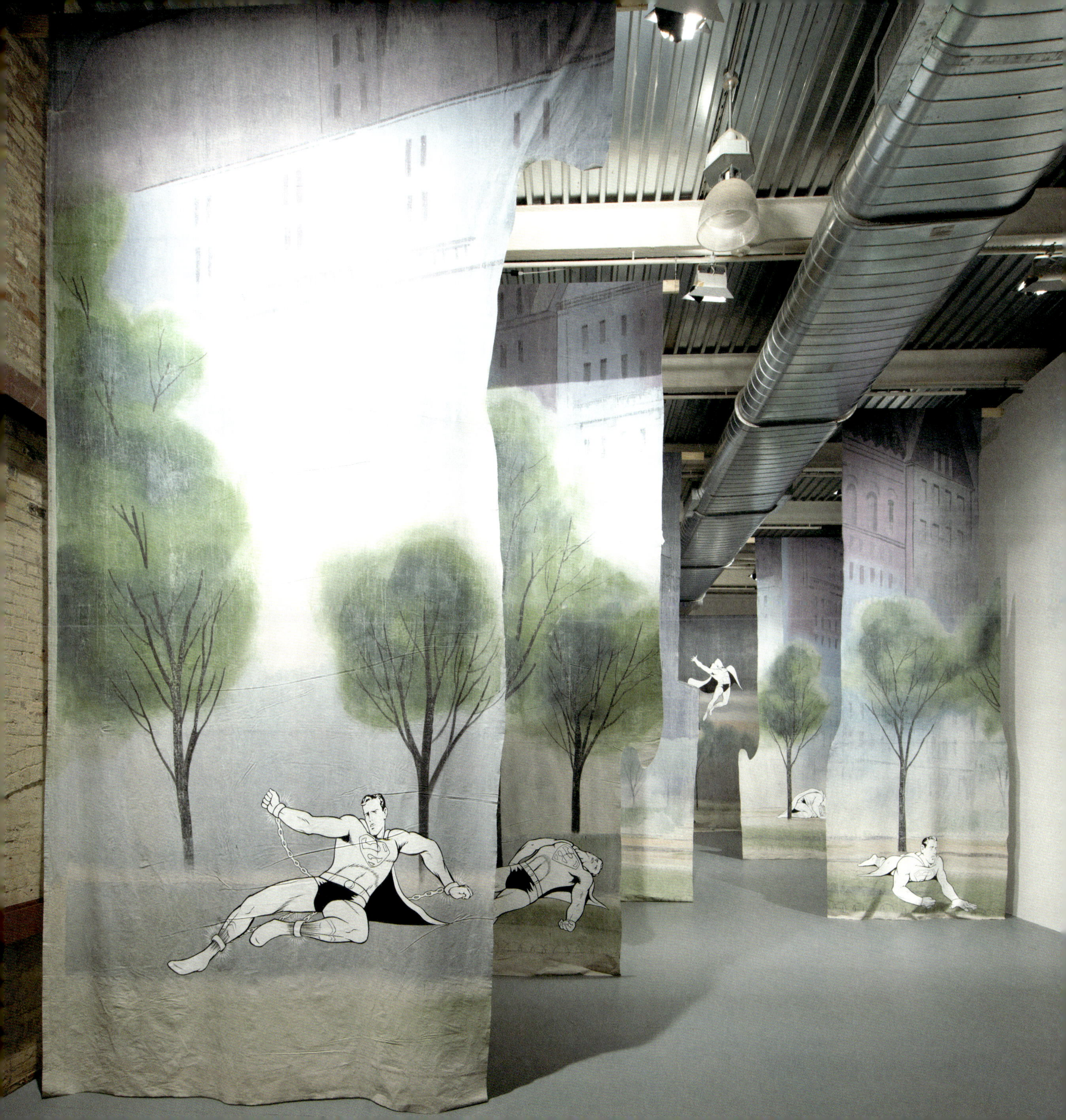

CHECKLIST OF THE EXHIBITION

(Checklist as of February 20, 2017)

JENNIFER ALLORA & GUILLERMO CALZADILLA
Petrified Petrol Pump No. 2, 2010
Limestone
Dimensions variable;
approx. 99½ × 54 × 26 inches
(252.7 × 137.2 × 66 cm)

EL ANATSUI
They Finally Broke the Pot of Wisdom, 2011
Found aluminum and copper wire
186 × 276 inches (472.4 × 701 cm) flat
Approx. 136 × 270 inches (345.4 × 685.8 cm) installed

YAEL BARTANA
Inferno, 2013
Alexa camera transferred onto HD
22 min.
Edition 6 of 8, 3 AP

WALEAD BESHTY
24-inch Copper (FedEx® Large Kraft Box ©2005 FEDEX 330510) First Overnight, Los Angeles–Miami trk#798173003782, November 27–28, 2009, Standard Overnight, Miami–New York trk#798196377030, December 7–8, 2009, Standard Overnight, New York–Beverly Hills trk#793169811939, January 11–12, 2010, Standard Overnight, Beverly Hills–St. Helena trk#793430416294, April 9–10, 2010, Priority Overnight, St. Helena–Beverly Hills trk#798559570416, April 14–15, 2010, 2009–
Polished copper, accrued FedEx shipping and tracking labels
24 × 24 × 24 inches (61 × 61 × 61 cm)

HUMA BHABHA
Lifetime, 2013
Cork, blue styrofoam, acrylic paint, oil stick, and wood
76 × 24 × 24 inches (193 × 61 × 61 cm)

CAROL BOVE
Untitled, 2012
Peacock feathers on linen, Plexiglas vitrine
96 × 48 × 5 inches (243.8 × 121.9 × 12.7 cm)

Peel's foe, not a set animal, laminates a tone of sleep, 2013
Brass and concrete
84 × 24 × 24 inches (213.4 × 61 × 61 cm)

Sixth Light Blue Sweater Painting, 2016
Acrylic on canvas
48 × 60 × 1¾ inches (121.9 × 152.4 × 4.4 cm)

TRISHA DONNELLY
Untitled, 2013
Granite azul Bahia
12 × 62¼ × 17⅜ inches
(30.5 × 158.1 × 44.1 cm)

LATIFA ECHAKHCH
Tannhäuser, 2013
Installation: backdrop of opera decors including wooden floor, 6 MDF modules, 6 spotlights, and 3 harps
158⅛ × 662⅝ × 313 inches
(401.5 × 1683 × 797 cm) overall

Branches became black, sky turn to a deep orange. Original shapes disappear in a blurred disorder., 2014
Ink on canvas
78¾ × 59 × 1 inches (200 × 150 × 2.5 cm)

All Over (80.06), 2016
Wool, cotton, aluminum, and wooden frame
79½ × 60⅝ × 2 inches (202 × 154 × 5 cm)

MATIAS FALDBAKKEN
SEE YOU ON THE FRONT PAGE OF THE LAST NEWSPAPER THOSE MOTHERFUCKERS EVER PRINT #6 (panel 2), 2014
Newsprint, India ink, tape, and wooden frame
62 × 43½ inches (157.5 × 110.5 cm)

SEE YOU ON THE FRONT PAGE OF THE LAST NEWSPAPER THOSE MOTHERFUCKERS EVER PRINT #6 (panel 7), 2014
Newsprint, India ink, tape, and wooden frame
62 × 43⅝ inches (157.5 × 110.5 cm)

CYPRIEN GAILLARD
Untitled, 2012
Screen print on oil on canvas
51⅛ × 59 inches (130 × 150 cm)

Gates GTE/CITY OF SANTA MONICA SEWER, 2013
Frottage
112¼ × 54 inches (285.1 × 137.2 cm)

MARK GROTJAHN
Untitled (Black and Grey Lined Face 810), 2009
Oil on cardboard mounted on linen
74½ × 56¼ inches (189.2 × 142.9 cm)

Untitled (Hidden Tea, Face 41.30), 2010
Oil on cardboard mounted on linen
101¼ × 72½ inches (257.2 × 184.2 cm)

Untitled (Non-Indian #1 Face 45.56), 2015
Oil on cardboard mounted on linen
50½ × 40½ inches (128.3 × 102.9 cm)

Untitled (Creamsicle Drawing in Two Parts: L: 85 10/16 × 47⅝ R 85½ × 47½ DO NOT SEPARATE 41.12), 2010
Color pencil on paper
Left: 85 10/16 × 47⅝ inches (217.5 × 121 cm)
Right: 85½ × 47½ inches (217.2 × 120.7 cm)

WADE GUYTON
Untitled, 2007
Epson UltraChrome inkjet on linen
84¼ × 69 inches (213.4 × 175.3 cm)

Untitled, 2008
Epson UltraChrome inkjet on linen
93 × 55 inches (236.2 × 139.7 cm)

Untitled, 2009
Epson UltraChrome inkjet on linen
84¼ × 69 inches (214 × 175.3 cm)

Untitled, 2012
Epson UltraChrome inkjet on linen
108¼ × 600 inches (275 × 1524 cm)

Untitled, 2012
Epson UltraChrome inkjet on linen
108¼ × 600 inches (275 × 1524 cm)

Untitled, 2015
Epson UltraChrome HDR on linen
84 × 69 inches (213.4 × 175.3 cm)

WADE GUYTON/KELLEY WALKER

Canstripe_ Crancherry_ Mattress, 2013
Mattress
80 × 60 × 8 inches (203.2 × 152.4 × 20.3 cm)

DAVID HAMMONS

Untitled, 2007
Fox fur coat with acrylic and spray paint
72 × 26 × 14 inches (182.9 × 66 × 35.6 cm)

Untitled, 2010
Acrylic on canvas and tarp
103 × 80 inches (261.6 × 203.2 cm)

Untitled, 2012
Acrylic on canvas and tarp
130 × 93 inches (330.2 × 236.2 cm)

RACHEL HARRISON

HOJOTOHO, 2012
Wood, polystyrene, cement, acrylic, and auger
95 × 23 × 25 inches (241.3 × 58.4 × 63.5 cm)

THOMAS HOUSEAGO

Striding Figure (Rome I), 2013
Bronze
155 × 67 × 94 inches (393.7 × 170.2 × 238.8 cm)
Edition 1 of 3, 2 AP

ALEX ISRAEL

Valet Parking, 2013
Oil painting on wall
Dimensions variable

Lens (Purple), 2015
UV protective plastic lens
84 × 96 × 14⅛ inches (213.4 × 243.8 × 35.9 cm)
Edition 1 of 4, 1 AP

RASHID JOHNSON

Untitled Anxious Men, 2015
White ceramic tile, black soap, and wax
73 × 94½ × 3 in. (185.4 × 240 × 7.6 cm)

MIKE KELLEY

Reconstructed History, 1989
17 gelatin silver prints
10 × 8 inches (25.4 × 20.3 cm) each

City 20, 2010
Tinted Urethane resin on illuminated base
12 × 31 × 31 inches (30.5 × 78.7 × 78.7 cm) overall

Kandor 18B, 2010
Foam coated with Elastomer, blown glass with water-based resin coating, tinted Urethane resin, wood, found objects, and lighting fixture
87 × 36 × 48 inches (221 × 91.4 × 121.9 cm)

Memory Ware #60, 2010
Foam, tinted resin, found jewelry, coffee pot, and plastic toys
47 × 81 × 12½ inches (119.4 × 205.7 × 31.8 cm)

LOUISE LAWLER

A.C.A.D.E.M.Y., 1987
Cibachrome mounted to Plexiglas on museum box
29 × 39½ inches (73.7 × 100.3 cm)
Edition 4 of 5

Pollyanna (adjusted to fit), 2007/2008/2012
Adhesive wall material
Variable dimensions constrained to match aspect ratio of wall

Carpe d'or, 2008/2010
Cibachrome face mounted to plexi on museum box
55¼ × 47⅝ inches (140.3 × 121 cm)

SHERRIE LEVINE

African Masks After Walker Evans: 1–24, 2014
24 Giclée inkjet prints
19⅛ × 13 inches (48.6 × 33 cm) each

GOSHKA MACUGA

Of what is, that it is; of what is not, that it is not 2, 2012
Wool tapestry
129⅞ × 435⅝ inches (330 × 1106 cm)
Edition 2 of 3, 1 AP

International Institute of Intellectual Co-operation, Configuration 15, End of Men: Madame Blavatsky, Mary Shelley, Guerilla Girls, Ada Lovelace, Donna Haraway, Olympe de Gouges, 2016
Bronze
150 × 125 × 125 inches (381 × 317.5 × 317.5 cm)

PAUL MCCARTHY

Chocolate Silicone Block Head, 1999–2000
Silicone
35⅞ × 43¼ × 27⅛ in. (91 × 110 × 69 cm)

Rebel Dabble Babble, Hollywood Sign, Inverted (large), 2011–12
Electrical light boxes and LED
62 × 328½ × 15⅜ inches (157.5 × 834.4 × 39.1 cm)

White Snow Head, 2012–13
Silicone (red), fiberglass, and steel
57 × 65 × 58 inches (144.8 × 165.1 × 147.3 cm)

White Snow, Balloon Dog, 2013
Sealed PVC polyvinyl chloride plastic, fan (cerulean blue)
62 × 33 × 82 inches (157.5 × 83.8 × 208.3 cm)

TAKASHI MURAKAMI

And then, and then and then and then and then, 1996
Acrylic on canvas mounted on board, in two parts
39⅜ × 39⅜ inches (100 × 100 cm) each

Oval Buddha Silver, 2008
Sterling silver and steel, marble base
Sculpture: 53⅝ × 31⅝ × 30⅝ inches (136.4 × 80.5 × 78 cm)
Base: 9¾ × 31¾ × 33 inches (24.8 × 80.6 × 83.8 cm)
Edition of 10

SUPERFLAT, 2009
Acrylic on canvas mounted on board
82⅓ × 63 × 2 inches (209 × 160 × 5.1 cm)

3m Girl (original rendering by Seiji Matsuyama, modeling by BOME and Genpachi Toaimura, full scale sculpture by Lucky-Wide Co., Ltd.), 2011–13
Fiberglass, reinforced plastic, and steel
106 5/16 × 38 3/16 × 47 3/16 inches
(270 × 97 × 120 cm)

Shangri-La Blue/Shangri-La Pink, 2012
Acrylic on canvas on aluminum frame
Two parts: 78 ¾ × 78 ¾ (200 × 200 cm) each

Double Helix Within Dark Matter, 2014
Acrylic on canvas
118 ⅛ × 157 ½ inches (300 × 400 cm)

ALBERT OEHLEN

Untitled, 1991
Oil and lacquer on canvas
93 ½ × 78 inches (237.5 × 198.1 cm)

Untitled, c. 1993–94
Oil on canvas
78 ¾ × 78 ¾ inches (200 × 200 cm)

Schnee, 1996
Oil on canvas
85 ⅞ × 114 ½ inches (218 × 291 cm)

Haken, 2003
Oil on canvas
86 ⅝ × 106 ¼ inches (220 × 270 cm)

Angela Molina, 2008
Oil and paper on canvas
67 × 110 inches (170 × 280 cm)

Untitled, 2009
Oil and paper on canvas
78 ¾ × 90 ½ inches (200 × 230 cm)

Untitled (Baum 3), 2014
Oil on Dibond
147 ⅝ × 98 7/16 inches (375 × 250 cm)

DAMIÁN ORTEGA

Building #4, 2009
Unique structure, eroded bricks, and metallic internal support
84 11/16 × 63 × 51 3/16 inches
(215 × 160 × 130 cm)

LAURA OWENS

Untitled, 2015
Acrylic, oil, Flashe, charcoal, screenprinting ink, pastel, clock motor, mechanical parts, pumice, aquarium rocks, buttons, cardboard, wallpaper, yarn, and collage on linen and hand-dyed linen
20 panels: 26 × 26 inches (66 × 66 cm) each

PHILIPPE PARRENO

Marquee (guirlande), 2014
Opaque Plexiglas, steel, incandescent lights and neon lights
64 ⅛ × 121 ⅞ × 67 ⅛ inches
(162.9 × 309.6 × 170.5 cm)

CHARLES RAY

Girl on Pony, 2015
Aluminum
84 × 60 × 3 ½ inches (213 × 152 × 9 cm)

STERLING RUBY

SP 93, 2010
Spray paint on canvas
125 × 185 inches (317.5 × 469.9 cm)

BC (3442), 2011
Collage, paint, bleach, and fabric on stretcher
90 × 56 × 2 inches (228.6 × 142.2 × 5.1 cm)

Modern Brass/Ketamine User, 2012
Ceramic
15 × 24 ½ × 15 inches (38.1 × 62.2 × 38.1 cm)

Stove 1, 2013
Stainless steel
54 × 12 × 33 inches (137.5 × 30.5 × 83.8 cm)

VAMPIRE 145 (Guess by Marciano 1), 2014
Fabric and fiberfill
85 × 39 ½ × 7 inches (215.9 × 100.3 × 17.8 cm)

ACTS/SURVIVAL HORROR, 2015
Clear urethane block, dye, wood, and formica
66 ¼ × 174 ½ × 35 inches
(168.3 × 445.8 × 88.9 cm)

SP308, 2015
Spray paint on synthetic canvas
Diptych: 100 × 144 × 2 inches
(254 × 365.8 × 5.1 cm) each

ANALIA SABAN

Erosion (Changing Room #2), 2012
Laser sculpted acrylic paint on canvas
38 × 58 × 2 inches (96.5 × 147.3 × 5.1 cm)

Bathroom Sink Template (Jade Marble), 2014
Marble
74 ⅝ × 44 inches (189.5 × 111.8 cm)

Cane Back Chair (with Back Weaving Rubbing), 2014
Linen and oil stick on chair
38 ½ × 18 ½ × 18 inches (97.8 × 47 × 45.7 cm)

JIM SHAW

All-seeing Keyhole Eye, 2013
Acrylic on muslin
32 × 22 inches (81.3 × 55.9 cm)

Seven Deadly Sins, 2013
Acrylic on muslin
96 × 194 (243.8 × 492.8 cm) overall

CINDY SHERMAN

Untitled #549-E, 2010
Pigment print on PhotoTex adhesive fabric
Dimensions variable

PAUL SIETSEMA

Painter's Mussel 4, 2011
Ink on paper in artist's frame
72 ¼ × 71 ½ inches (183.5 × 181.6 cm)

Painted coins, 2014
Ink and enamel on paper in artist's frame
32 × 34 ½ inches (81 × 88 cm)

Green painting, 2016
Enamel on linen
51 ½ × 47 ⅞ inches (131 × 122 cm)

RIRKRIT TIRAVANIJA

Untitled (Menos petróleo más valor / 14 de junio 2011), 2011
Acrylic and newspaper on linen
75 ⅓ × 68 inches (191.3 × 172.8 cm)

RYAN TRECARTIN/LIZZIE FITCH

Companion Quarry, 2013
Acrylic paint, cardboard, castors, cement, chain, contact cement, bricks, epoxy, epoxy putty, fake rock, foam, gel medium, hardware, hitch, metal pole, MDF, metal rods, paper, plaster, pigment, oars, rope, sand, screws, washers
62 × 53 × 84 inches (157.5 × 134.6 × 213.4 cm)

Drop Cause, 2013
Acrylic paint, aluminum, baby carrier, baseball cap, blue Solo cups, bolts, Bronco scaffold, carabineers, cardboard, epoxy, fiberglass, foam, gel medium, jeans, metal rod, paper, pigment, plastic, screws, silicone, socks, staples, stuffing, Vibram shoes, washers, zip ties
92 × 60 × 46 inches (233.7 × 152.4 × 116.8 cm)

Ledge, 2014
Unique sculptural theater with 6-channel HD Video and 5.1 soundtrack, 3D animations with Rhett LaRue
49:24 min.
Aluminum, ambient audiofiles, amps, anodizing pigment, cuben fiber, ethernet switches, foam, glue, grommets, mac mini, media players, no-see-um mesh fabric, paint, plastic, powdercoat, projectors, snaps, spacer mesh, speakers, staples, steel, rear projection fabric, reflective tape, rip-stop nylon fabric, rope, rubber, tape, thread, tubular webbing, various hardware, webbing, wireless programmable lights, wireless router, wood, and zippers
Dimensions variable

OSCAR TUAZON

People, 2012
Sugar maple tree, metal basketball backboard and hoop, and concrete wall
Dimensions variable

Playboy Papercrate, 2012/2013
Concrete
65 × 65 × 4¾ inches (165 × 165 × 12 cm)

Another False Wall, 2013
Plaster, cement, clay, and steel
65 × 65¼ × 2 inches (165 × 165.5 × 5.5 cm)

KAARI UPSON

Untitled, 2011
Smoke on aluminum panel
96 × 48 inches (243.8 × 121.9 cm)

Charcoal Sheet 1 (Position 1), 2012
Charcoal and aqua-resin
73 × 48 × 7½ inches (185.4 × 121.9 × 19.1 cm)

ADRIAN VILLAR ROJAS

Two Suns (II), 2015
Site-specific installation
Sculpture: 43⁵⁄₁₆ × 57¹⁄₁₆ × 185¹⁄₁₆ inches (110 × 145 × 470 cm)
Base: 40³⁄₁₆ × 9¹³⁄₁₆ × 41⁵⁄₁₆ inches (102 × 25 × 105 cm) each

DANH VO

We The People, 2011–13
Copper—8.4m2 - 190kg

Pantoffel II, 2014
Gold, cardboard, and ink
Weight: 132 oz. (3742.1 g)

KELLEY WALKER

Untitled, c. 2002
4 panels of mirrored acrylic
92 × 48⅝ inches (233.7 × 123.5 cm) each
92 × 97⅜ inches (233.7 × 247.3 cm) overall

Untitled, 2007
Laser-cut steel with gold leaf
58 × ⅛ inches (147.3 × .3 cm)

Untitled, 2007
Four-color process silkscreen on canvas with collage *VMan* (fall/winter 2007)
78½ × 54¼ inches (199.4 × 137.8 cm)

Untitled, 2009
Four-color process silkscreen with ink on canvas
60 × 12 inches (152.4 × 30.5 cm)

Untitled, 2013
196 panels of Pantone and four-color process silkscreen with acrylic ink on MDF
29 panels: 24 × 24 inches (61 × 61 cm) each
167 panels: 16 × 16 inches (40.6 × 40.6 cm) each

Untitled, 2014
Four-color process silkscreen with acrylic ink and collage *Domus* (December 2012) on canvas
100 × 58 inches (254 × 147.3 cm)

MARY WEATHERFORD

out by Coney, 2015
Flashe and neon on linen
117 × 104 inches (297.2 × 264.2 cm)

JONAS WOOD

Grid Pot with Pink Plant, 2016
Oil and acrylic on canvas
77¹⁵⁄₁₆ × 57⅞ inches (198 × 147 cm)

CHRISTOPHER WOOL

Untitled, 1997
Enamel on aluminum
108 × 72 inches (274.3 × 182.9 cm)

Mama Too Tight, 1999
Enamel on aluminum
108 × 72 inches (274.3 × 182.9 cm)

Untitled, 2012
Silkscreen ink on linen
120 × 96 inches (304.8 × 243.8 cm)

Untitled, 2014
Silkscreen ink and enamel on linen
106 × 96 inches (269.2 × 243.8 cm)

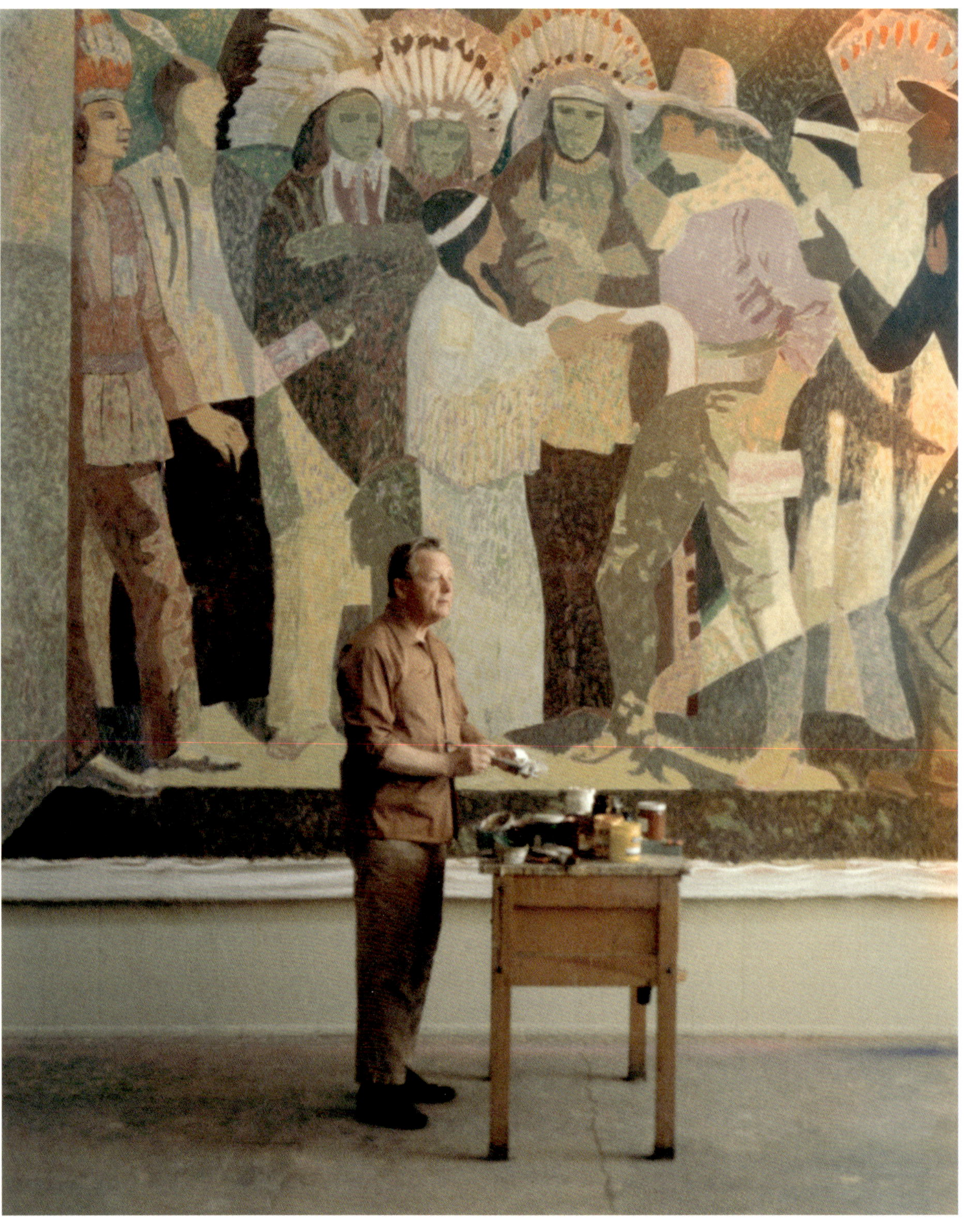

Millard Sheets painting mural for the Hollywood branch of a Home Savings and Loan, 1968

MILLARD SHEETS: ARTIST, EDUCATOR, ARCHITECTURAL DESIGNER

TONY SHEETS

The multifaceted Millard Sheets was one of the first of a group known as the California Scene Painters, part of a larger Regionalist movement from the 1930s to the 1960s that describes a representational style capturing scenes from everyday life. During the 1930s and 1940s, he and a small group of California artists developed a new style of watercolor painting and became known as the California Regionalist School. Throughout his life, Sheets would play a major role in bringing the art of California to the national arena.

Millard Sheets was born in Pomona, California, on June 24, 1907. After his mother's death from complications of childbirth, his grief-stricken father, John Sheets, sent Millard away to be raised by his maternal grandparents, Lewis and Emma Owen, on their horse ranch in Pomona. Interested in art at an early age, Sheets submitted a painting to the Los Angeles County Fair fine arts competition at age fourteen, winning first prize. His prowess prompted Polish artist Theodore B. Modra, who had retired in the area, to offer ongoing art lessons to the young Sheets.

After graduating from the Chouinard Art Institute (now the California Institute of the Arts) in 1929, Sheets immediately garnered the attention of Dalzell and Ruth Hatfield of the Dalzell Hatfield Galleries in Los Angeles. Among the most influential art dealers on the West Coast, the Hatfield's sponsored Sheets's first one-man exhibition that same year and helped launch the artist's painting career.

In 1929, Sheets also learned that he had won second place in the annual Edgar B. Davis art competition in San Antonio, Texas, which came with a cash prize of $1,750. He promptly made plans to travel to Europe for six months to study and paint. However, shortly before his graduation Sheets had met a young woman named Mary Baskerville and begun a whirlwind romance. With Mary's enthusiastic support for his European plans, and a promise that she would wait for him, Sheets departed for New York and then Europe, where he studied under master print maker Gaston Dorfinant in Paris.

Five months after Sheets returned to California in 1930, he and Mary Baskerville were married. Together they raised their four children in Claremont, California. Inveterate travelers, the pair visited fifty-six countries

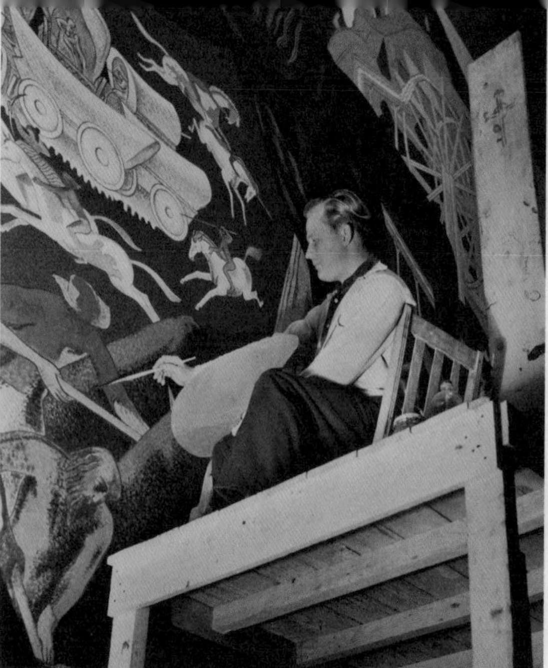

Millard Sheets painting a mural, c. 1939

throughout their lifetime, collecting art and subject matter along the way for his paintings and murals, as well as concepts for the many buildings he designed.

In 1931, Sheets became director for the annual Fine Arts Exhibition of the Los Angeles County Fair, a position he held until 1956. The following year, in 1932, he was invited to teach at Scripps College in Claremont, and by 1936 Scripps had made him the head of the art department. By 1939, however, the United States began to prepare for the inevitability of involvement in the Second World War, and Sheets put his skills as an architectural designer to use designing seventeen air cadet training schools for the United States Army Air Corps between 1939 and 1941.

During World War II, Sheets left Scripps to serve as a wartime artist and journalist for *Life* magazine. From 1943–44 he was stationed on the China-Burma-India front, an experience that affected him deeply. In contrast to his earlier works with neutral tones and brilliant shades that highlighted and punctuated the compositions, his wartime paintings featured somber tones. Sheets remarked of this time:

During the fighting and the time I spent in the C-B-1 Theater, I was too shaken and intellectually stunned to do any complete paintings. I made many, many sketches, though, as well as a real effort to remember each scene that particularly affected me. Then, once I returned to America, I painted frantically, for months, exorcising those demons.

Sheets returned from the war in 1944 and resumed his position at Scripps College until 1955, when the Los Angeles County Board of Supervisors approached him to become the director of the new Los Angeles County Art Institute. He accepted the position and spent the next five years reshaping the mission and format of the school, renaming it the Otis Art Institute (later renamed the Otis College of Art and Design). The school also later became part of New York's Parson's School of Design.

In 1953, he founded Millard Sheets Designs, which employed a working staff of licensed architects and engineers, draftsmen, and artists. With former student Susan Hertel serving as his assistant, the studio completed over one hundred murals and mosaics throughout the United States, in and on the buildings he designed such as

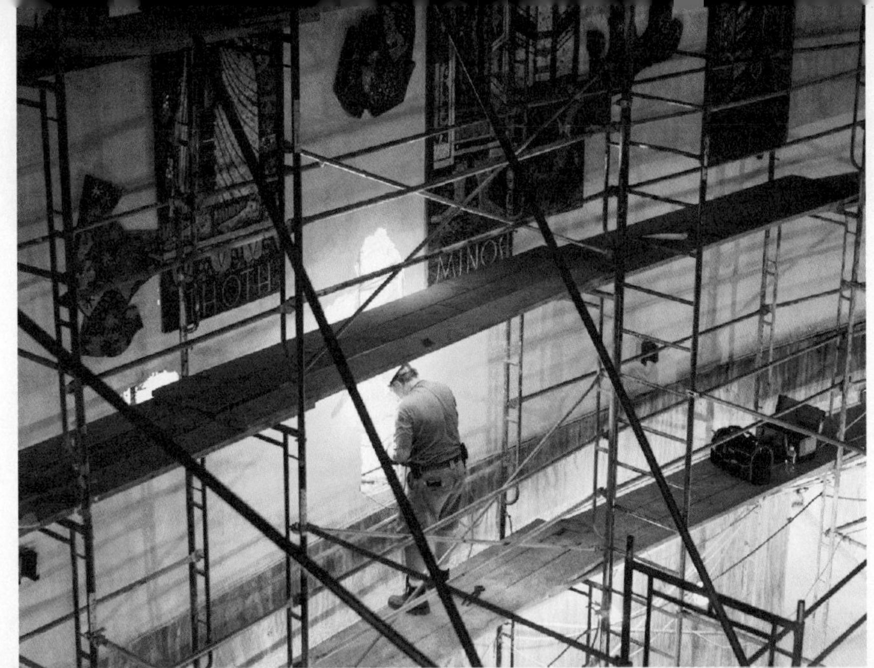

Tony Sheets removing mosaic from the north wall of the Scottish Rite Masonic Temple theater, 2014

the national American Insurance Company offices for the California financier, Howard Ahmanson, Ahmanson Bank and Trust Company in Beverly Hills, forty-two Home Savings and Loan Association Buildings, private residences, and the Scottish Rite Masonic Temples in Los Angeles and San Francisco, among many others.

In 1968, Sheets proposed a design for murals intended for the Los Angeles City Hall. Approved in 1972, his tile murals, "The Family of Man," now rest over the building's two main entrances. He also designed mosaics and murals for the Mayo Clinic in Minnesota, the granite "Word of Life" mural on the Hesburgh Library at the University of Notre Dame, the Detroit Public Library, and the Dome of the National Shrine of the Immaculate Conception in Washington, D.C., and the tile murals on the Rainbow Hilton in Honolulu, Hawaii.

During the early 1960s, Sheets participated as an American Art Specialist for the U.S. Department of State. His first assignment was to Turkey in 1960, where he served as a visiting artist, and the following year he went to the Soviet Union in the same capacity.

Throughout his life Sheets was a member of the National Watercolor Society, the American Watercolor Society, the National Academy of Design, the Society of Motion Picture Art Directors, and the Century Association of Art and Literature in New York, sharing his knowledge and love of art with others. Millard Sheets died on March 31, 1989, in Gualala, California.

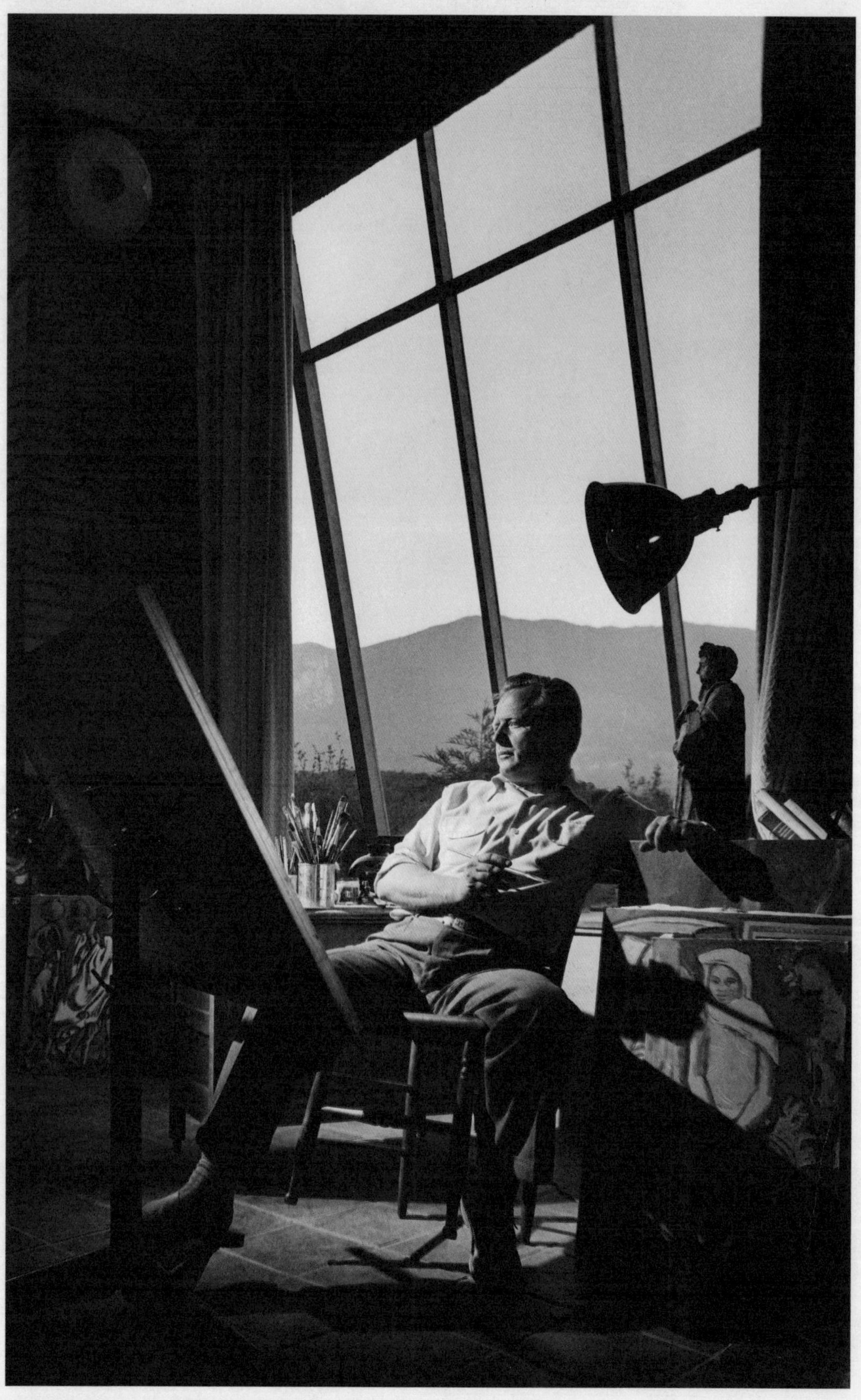

Millard Sheets in his Padua Hills home studio, for *LIFE Magazine*, 1948

AN INTERVIEW WITH MILLARD SHEETS

In this excerpt from a 1977 interview, Millard Sheets outlines the conversations that led to his commission to design the Scottish Rite Masonic Temple building on Wilshire Boulevard and details the complexity of the final architectural and artwork designs he used to represent Freemasonry.

Millard Sheets interviewed by George M. Goodwin, January 13 and 16, 1977 (Center for Oral History Research, University of California, Los Angeles, http://oralhistory.library.ucla.edu/viewItem.do?ark=21198/zz0008z9tz&title=Sheets,%20Millard)

The Scottish Rite cathedral was one of the most exciting projects I ever had anything to do with. It came to me in a strange way. The head of the Scottish Rite cathedral here in Los Angeles at the time, Judge Ellsworth Meyer, called me to ask me if I could go to dinner with a small group of people to discuss an interesting subject." I said, "Well, are you sure I could enter into the discussion?" He said, "Yes, we think you can." I said, "Do you wish to discuss the subject matter?" He said, "No, not until dinnertime." Well, I went to dinner at the [Los Angeles] Athletic Club with him. They said, "We are going to build a new temple." They called it a "cathedral." I said, "Well, what kind of a cathedral?" They said, "Scottish Rite." I was a little dopey. I thought it might be Masonic, but I wasn't sure. I said, "Well, where is your old one?" I thought that might give me a clue, and they told me where it was, down on Flower Street, something like that. Then I knew that they were talking about a Masonic temple.

They said, "We are trying to be very thorough before we go ahead with this job. We have met nine firms of architects, of which at least the principal men are members of our particular Masonry degree and also our particular temple. We've discussed the matter at length with each of them, and we've asked them for their idea of how they would approach this problem. You're the only one outside of the group that belong to the temple that we've interviewed. But we would like to discuss it with you." So they told me quite a bit about what has to be in a temple of this kind. I didn't dream that there was a huge auditorium and a huge dining room. The auditorium seats 3,000, and the dining room seats 1,500, and they have many lodge rooms and recreation rooms. It's a city, a tremendous thing. I said, "I'd have to know a lot more about you. As a matter of fact, the first question I would put at the top of my list is, 'Why do you think you need to build a big temple? What's wrong with the one you've got?' I don't know anything about the one you've got, except that I've seen the outside and it looks horrible. "But," I said, "that isn't the important thing. The important thing is why do you think you need a temple? Maybe the idea of Masonry isn't even practical today." They really looked so shocked at that! I said, "I have no idea, not being a Mason, but I certainly believe that you should really answer a lot of questions. I don't think it would make a damned bit of difference what I think you should do at this point, because I don't know, and I don't think any other designer or architect could tell you any better, unless of course they're active members and have a lot of strong feelings, which I don't have."

As a matter of fact, I was very busy, and I suddenly realized that about four months had gone by. I thought perhaps I had frightened them away completely by asking them the twenty-five or more questions of why they thought they ought to build a temple. Then the phone rang

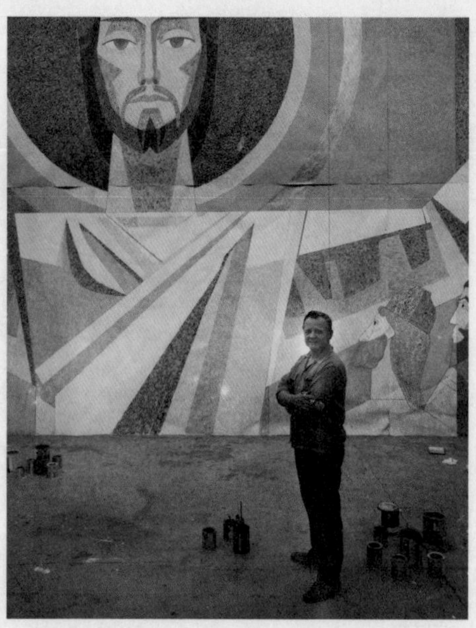

Millard Sheets in front of sketch for the "Word of Life" mural for the University of Notre Dame, c. 1964

and it was Judge Meyer, the head of the Scottish Rite. He said, "Well, we're ready to answer your questions." So we set up another dinner party, and it was an exciting evening. It was one of the really most exciting ones because they had done their homework. They had worked terribly hard on all of the questions and had, I thought, some imaginative answers. They were not in any way tying me or any other designer down, but they had some very good thoughts about the new relationship of Masonry to society and why they felt this was an important time to build the temple and why they wanted to truly represent the spirit of Masonry. So without further ado, I made many sketches, I think three different concepts, which I presented to a smaller committee that they had decided would be easier to operate with. I made the presentation of these three different concepts, from which they selected one. It was the one that we finally followed, but it grew considerably in the development, as most of these kinds of things do, both in character and in detail.

Well, I think I suggested to you that I was surprised by the tremendous number of things that had to be incorporated in this temple. First of all, the upper degrees of Masonry are given in an auditorium, and they are given in the form of plays. They have incredible costumes and magnificent productions of the basic concepts that are ethical and have at heart a religious depth, and they draw from many religions, as far as I understand. I'm not a Mason, but I do feel that it's a tremendous attempt toward the freedom of man as an individual, and the rights of man as an individual, and respect for various races and creeds. I won't say this is always obtained, but certainly that's been the spirit. They felt that they wanted to depict this in every form. That's the reason there's so much decoration involved in the temple. The huge mosaic on the exterior east end of the temple at that time was the largest mosaic I'd ever made. It starts out with the builders of the temple from the days of Jerusalem, and King Solomon, who built the temple, and Babylon. Then it jumps up to the Persian emperor, Zerubbabel. It showed the importance of [Giuseppe] Garibaldi, the Mason who broke away from the Roman Catholic Church because of what he felt was its limitations and dogmatism? Then there is King Edward VII in his Masonic regalia as one of the great grand masters. We had the changing of the guard at Buckingham Palace, which is part of the King Edward section. I think the final part of that mosaic shows the first grand master of California in his full regalia being invested in Sacramento. It's a kind of historical thing going way back to the ancient temple builders and coming right up through to actual California history, which the California sun at the top symbolizes.

The concept of the sculpture along the south facade, which I worked in collaboration with Albert Stewart to

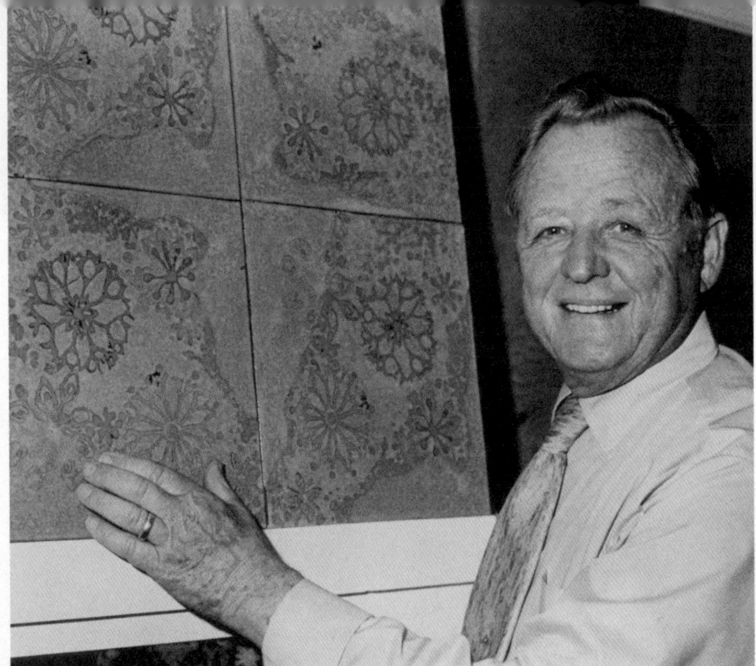

Millard Sheets showing off ceramic tile design, c. 1963–67

design, and then he made all of the models—it seems to me there were eight scale models, which I took to Rome and had carved by a very fine sculptor in solid travertine. These were, of course, eventually sent back and placed on the facade. And here again are all of the temple builders, each one representing a special builder going back to ancient Egypt and coming on through the time of King Solomon and the Persian emperor, up to and including George Washington. There are also Albert Pike, who was one of the very great men in the early part of the twentieth century or latter part of the nineteenth century, and Christopher Wren, who built the great cathedrals in England. The two St. Johns were interesting, because they were said to be patron saints, and they depicted two different meanings entirely. Then there's the Gothic builder, so it symbolizes the whole meaning of the building of the temple.

The double-headed eagle, which was the symbol for the Scottish Rite, which Albert Stewart designed, and I think it makes a stunning logo. We used it in four spots on the temple. Then all of the inscriptions that we did were carved in travertine, and the different insignias of the degrees are all parts of the actual rites themselves. On the inside, there are several sculptured and mosaic decorations on the interior of the auditorium. There's a large mural depicting the history of Masonry in California, starting with the first houses that were erected by Masons. It's all involved, and I can't remember all the details. There's also a large mural in the main reading room off the main library, which was not symbolic. It was the kind of thing I liked to do, a very interesting mood of some ancient trees, and it's a totally different type of mural. Then I did murals in the dining room. The temple is like a city. It has a huge auditorium where they hold performances for the degree. Then there are four lodge rooms upstairs, where the various blue lodges meet to give the lower degrees. There is a recreational floor that has nothing but library facilities and pool tables and a combination of reading room and card room. There is a very fine library, which we had a lot of fun designing. There are, of course, the locker rooms and all of the other things that make it a tremendous, big building. It is made up of four stories above ground and one below. There is a huge dining room on the top floor that seats 1,500 people, where you get an excellent view of the city. It's all under the overhang of that big roof that extends over the balcony areas. It's a stunning design, formed around its purpose.

FIG. 1 East wall mosaic, Scottish Rite Masonic Temple exterior, 2013

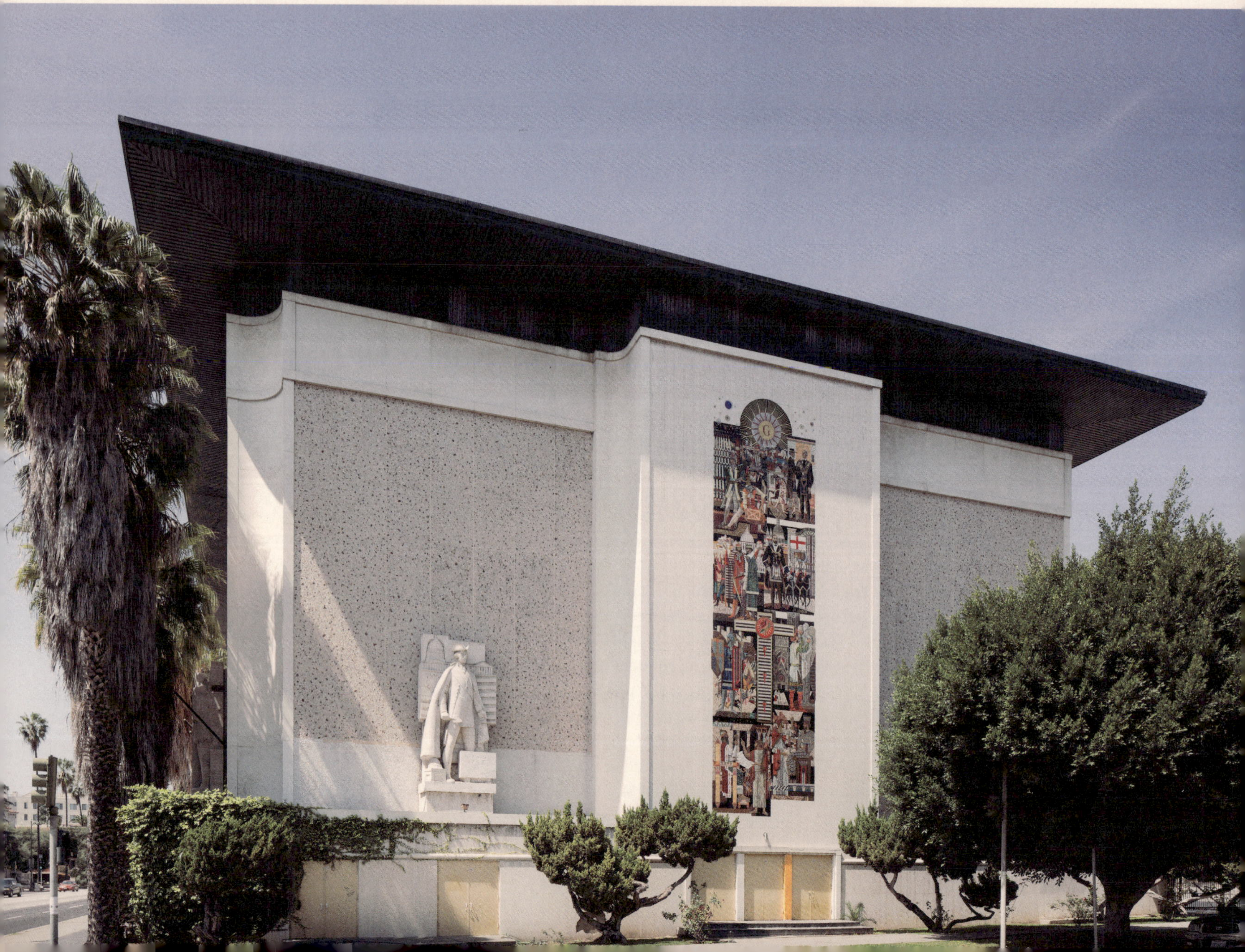

ART, FRATERNITY, AND LOS ANGELES

SUSAN L. ABERTH

The city of Los Angeles evokes many romantic and apocalyptic images to the popular imagination, but the visual culture of Freemasonry is likely not among them. Yet this fraternal organization, although supposedly shrouded in secrecy, has its symbols boldly emblazoned on Masonic lodges across this sprawling cityscape from Santa Monica to Glendale to Burbank. Often incorporating fanciful historic appropriations (such as the Mayan Revival style of the North Hollywood Lodge), these buildings rival the showy movie palaces that are their architectural neighbors. This is no accident, for long before Hollywood existed Masons were staging elaborate costumed rituals in front of fantastical painted backdrops. Indeed, many of the film industry's early pioneers, including Cecil B. DeMille, Louis B. Mayer, Darryl F. Zanuck, and Walt Disney, were Masons.

Built in 1961, Millard Sheets's Scottish Rite Masonic Temple at 4357 Wilshire Boulevard is one of the last of these theaters of ritual built in Los Angeles, its epic scale reflecting in part the final stages of the postwar economic prosperity enjoyed in the United States. At the time of its construction, membership in the Los Angeles Scottish Rite enjoyed healthy numbers, and the ambitious scale and luxurious fittings of the Wilshire Boulevard lodge reflected this. Though not a Mason himself, Sheets, a Southern California artist and architect, was impressed by the size of the commissioned project and noted, "the temple is like a city" unwittingly making biblical and architectural references in accordance with Masonic thought. The Wilshire building contained classrooms, meeting rooms, an impressive library, a 3,000-seat auditorium, and a dining hall that could serve up to 1,500 members. Sheathed inside and out in marble and travertine, the temple was modern in its sleek lines yet archaic in its monumentality—a perfect metaphor for an organization that valued the ancient, yet wanted to remain relevant to contemporary society.

As Stacy C. Hollander reflected in her essay for the American Folk Art Museum's recent groundbreaking exhibition on the subject, "The art of fraternity is at once universal and inscrutable. Mystical, evocative, and sometimes simply strange, it displays an amalgam of time-honored hieroglyphs that are familiar to all yet utterly at odds with the commonplace."[1] This is certainly true of the many sculpture groupings dispersed along the exterior wall of 4357 Wilshire Boulevard by Albert Stewart,

1 Stacy C. Hollander, "Signs and Wonders: The Art of Fraternity," in *Mystery and Benevolence: Masonic and Odd Fellows Folk Art from the Kendra and Allan Daniel Collection* (New York: American Folk Art Museum, 2016), 11.

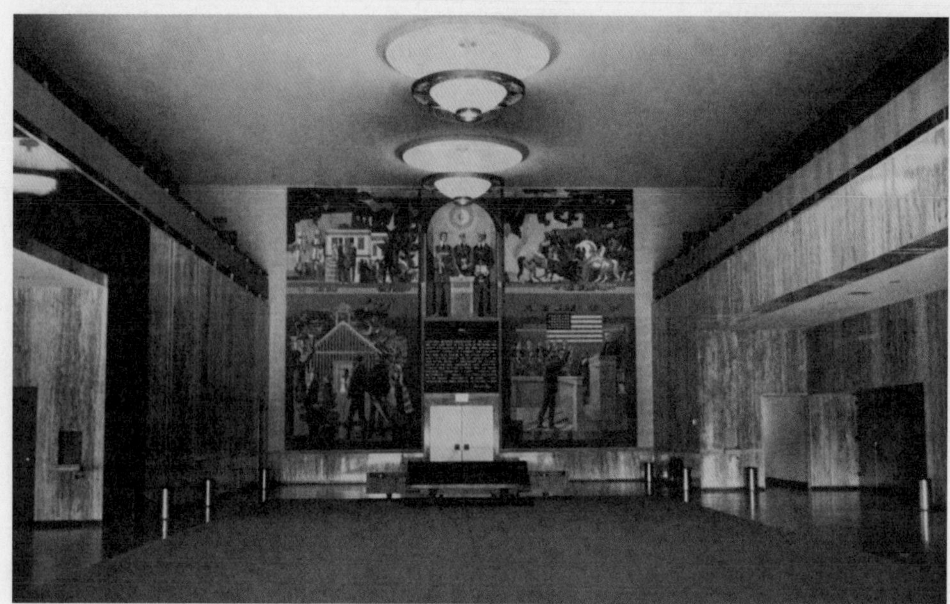

FIG. 2 View of Millard Sheet's *Freemasonry in California* mural, Scottish Rite Masonic Temple lobby, 1961

a friend and colleague of Sheets and head of the sculpture program at Scripps College in Claremont. These works depict individuals important to Freemasonry such as Albert Pike, a nineteenth-century Mason who in 1871 wrote a key text, *Morals and Dogma of the Ancient and Accepted Scottish Rite of Freemasonry*; George Washington who served simultaneously as the first president of the United States and the first Worshipful Master of Alexandria Lodge No. 22; and Christopher Wren, the great British Mason and architect. In addition there are figures from the ancient world that the Masons identified with such as Imhotep, the Egyptian considered to be the first architect; King Hiram of Tyre who sent Solomon materials and labor to help build the First Temple; and Zerubbabel King of Persia who laid the foundation of the Second Temple in Jerusalem. The theme of great builders and the history of the Masonic Scottish Rite are echoed in the nearly four-story mosaic on the east side of the temple (fig. 1).

The interior lobby of the building is similarly covered in elegant marble and travertine slabs and displays another large mural by Sheets (fig. 2), this time celebrating Masons in California. In fact, Freemasonry did play a role in the foundation of California. The many Masons among the state's Gold Rush settlers established lodges, and in 1850, built the Grand Lodge of California in Sacramento, the same year that California became a state.

When the Masons were forced to vacate the Wilshire Boulevard temple in 1994 (due to zoning issues) they left behind a small treasure trove of fraternal objects including books, photographs of past lodge members, and other paraphernalia, including several silk and satin banners created to identify specific lodges (figs. 3 and 4). Reminiscent of those used in medieval pageants and a source of fraternal pride, the banners were used both inside the lodge and, on occasion, during public spectacles. Embroidered with Masonic emblems in gold and silver braid and fringed at the bottom, they lent a festive air to ritual occasions. By far the most exciting things left behind pertained to the Masons secret theatrical performances, or rather the staging of the rituals of the Scottish Rite. The rituals of Masonry were a form of ethical instruction aimed at spiritual and moral self-improvement as one advanced through the degrees.

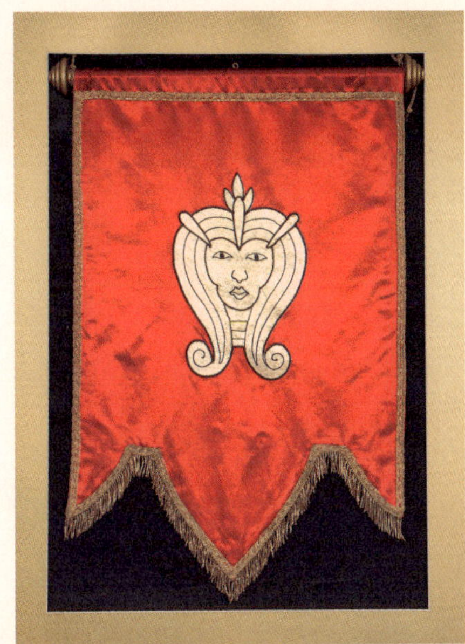

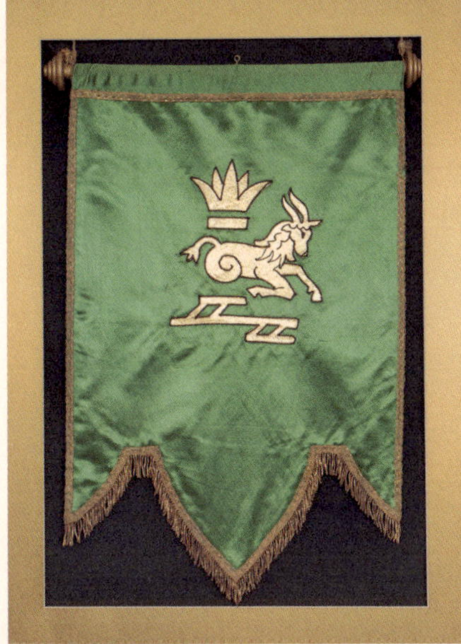

FIG. 3 Masonic banner with emblem
FIG. 4 Masonic banner with emblem

Appearing twice on the Wilshire building's exterior is the double-headed eagle, the symbol for the Scottish Rite, which differs from the regular three-degree lodges. Established in 1801, the Scottish Rite provided an additional twenty-nine esoteric degrees that led the candidate through intricate, dramatized historical and religious ritual journeys requiring full costumes and numerous scene changes. Men from all classes and professions could escape their stressful and regimented lives and, for a time, visit exotic locales, garner pompous and often outlandish titles, and engage in heroic deeds full of valor and mystery. The Scottish Rite Cathedral constructed in downtown Los Angeles between 1905 and 1906 (now gone) was, in its day, on the cutting edge of Masonic theater technology. Its enormous auditorium boasted eighty-four scenic drops. A number of these backdrops were relocated to the Wilshire lodge and are now in the custody of the Marciano Art Foundation. It is very rare for non-Masons to be able to see and study such backdrops, and these examples are particularly stunning.

The theater of fraternity conveyed ideas about masculinity in a number of ways. Besides women being physically absent, the degree narratives were devoid of not only female characters, but also any hint of feminized domestic spaces. Man's capacity to reason was emphasized along with his ability to control his world, attributes communicated most often through geometry, mathematics, and architecture. Each degree had specific buildings and historic time periods attached to it, ranging from Babylonian gardens, Persian palaces, Egyptian temples, ruined Gothic abbeys, and even Piranesi-like underground prisons. Symmetry, strict horizontal and vertical lines, and sharp geometric shapes underscored uncompromising masculinity, intellectual thought, and moral rectitude.

One of the most important degrees was the eighteenth where the initiate progressed from a Chamber of Reflection (as gloomy as it sounds with a skull and Bible) to the hill of Calvary, ending up in hell with snakes and demons. Masonic stage backdrops, often several for each degree, served to emphasize the theatrical thrill of moral progression. The Marciano Art Foundation's collection of Masonic backdrops is of particular importance when one considers the pivotal role Los Angeles played in the entertainment industry. For example, one

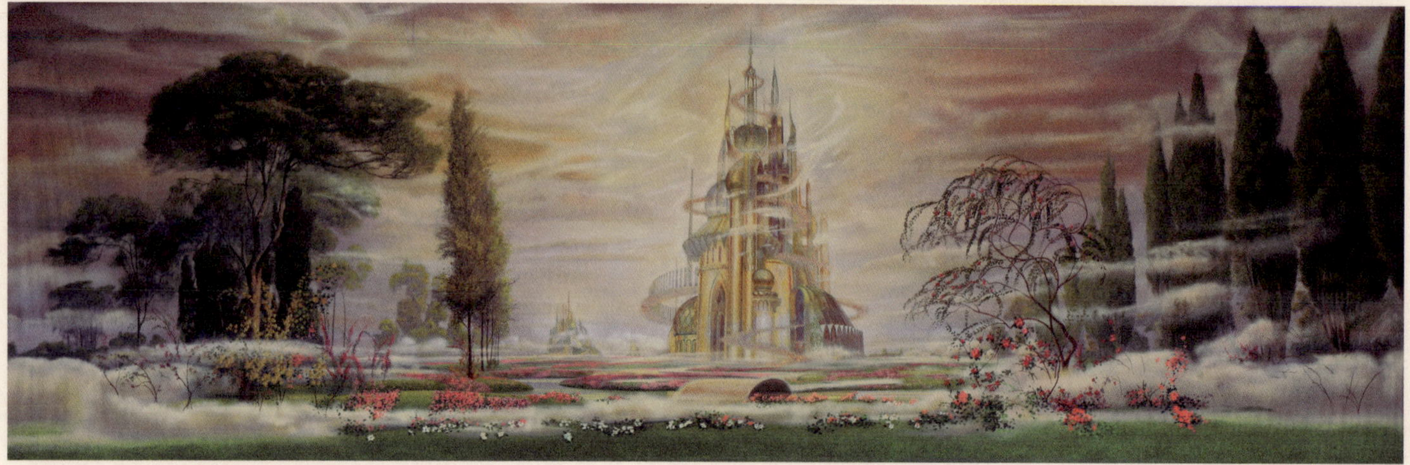

FIG. 5 Theatrical backdrop for Scottish Rite degree initiation, Scottish Rite Masonic Temple

particularly visionary backdrop displays what appears to be a magical city made up of glimmering golden towers and domes set within a field of blooming pink flowers. The likeness of this backdrop (fig. 5) to the one used in the scene from the *Wizard of Oz* film where Dorothy wakes up from her poppy-induced sleep and first sees the Emerald City is so close one wonders if the same theater company, if not the same people, painted them.

Further dramatizing these backdrops were the lavish costumes worn along with wigs, fake bushy eyebrows and mustaches all meant to transform a traveling salesman into a patriarch of old—one cannot help but think of the joy the men must have felt shedding their conventional business attire to done themselves in velvet robes festooned with jewels and other adornments (fig. 6). The great appeal of the Scottish Rite might have been the freedom men felt—among their "brothers" and within the "safe spaces" of the lodge where all were sworn to secrecy—to rid themselves of the restrictive one-dimensionality of conventional public demonstrations of masculinity.

The construction of the Temple of Solomon is the core metaphor of Freemasonry, and in looking at some of the smaller lodges associated with the Scottish Rite Temple, such as the Menorah Lodge (fig. 7), one can see that the membership contained a strong Jewish component. For this post-World War II construction, it is important to remember that many of its members fought in the war or were in some profound way touched by the Holocaust. How did the many Jewish members feel ritually reconstructing the Temple in Jerusalem, especially in light of the formation of the state of Israel? A good number of these men worked in the film business at all levels, and one wonders what the intersections were between Masonic stage drops, film, and dreams of a new nation? Much research remains to be done on these and other aspects of Freemasonry that might shed light on the political outreach via theatrical productions in Los Angeles.

It is a great irony that American youth, so adept at reading the logos of leading brands, appear to be blind to the semiotics of Freemasonry that frequently surround them. According to the *Los Angeles Times*, however,

below
FIG. 6 Scottish Rite costume, possibly for twenty-first degree initiation

right
FIG. 7 Photographic chart of Class and Officers of the Menorah Lodge No. 623, Free and Accepted Masons, Los Angeles, 1960

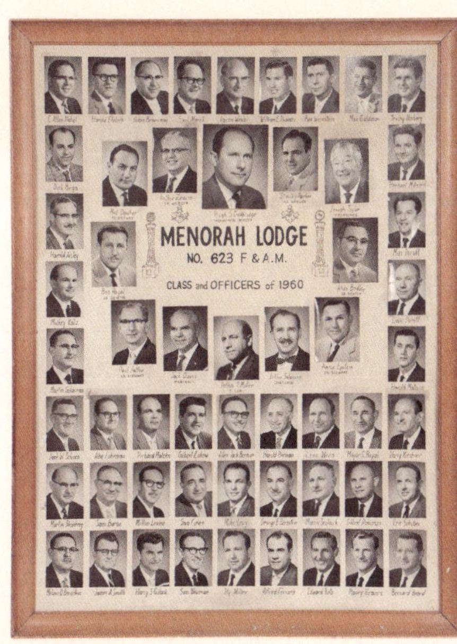

Freemasonry is making a steady comeback in the Los Angeles area among men of all ages and classes, including artists and hipsters. Intrigued by the artistic legacy of Freemasonry's outstanding architecture, creative types are also attracted to participating in a community based on ethics and public service as opposed to economic gain. These new members will not only keep this august organization alive, but also change it in ways that make it more relevant to the challenges of contemporary society. The arts have always been an important means of communication within Scottish Rite Masonry, and now the Maurice and Paul Marciano Art Foundation can continue this tradition in their own fashion, housed in their beautiful temple.

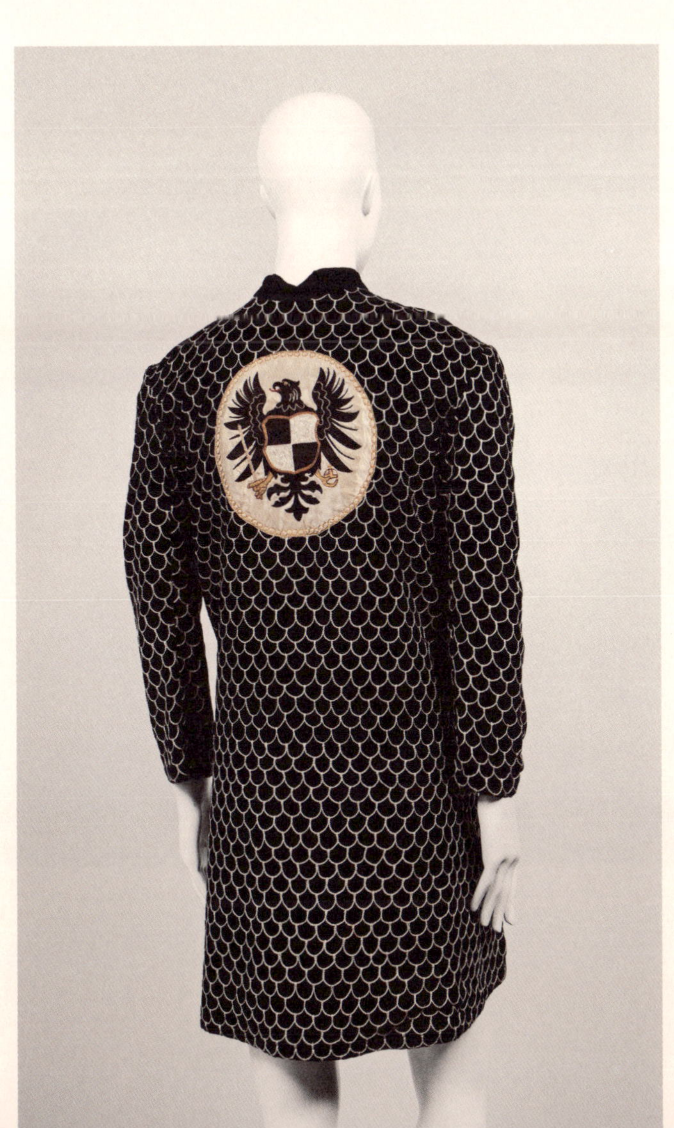

FIG. 1 Southeast corner, Scottish Rite Masonic Temple, 1961

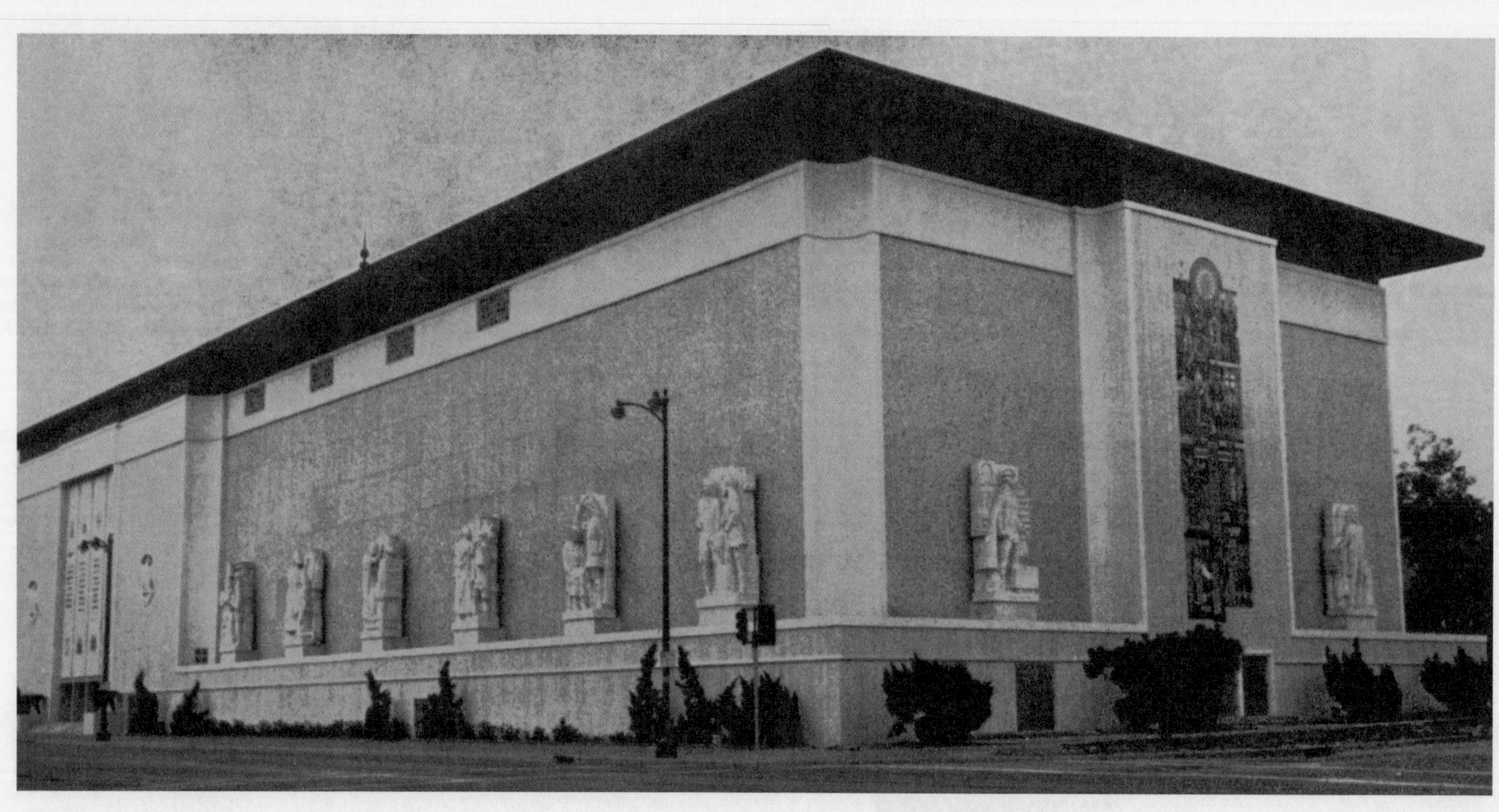

AN INVOLUNTARY COLLABORATION ACROSS TASKS AND TIME

KULAPAT YANTRASAST

They said Scottish Rite. I was a little dopey,
I thought it might be Masonic, but I wasn't sure.[1]

—Millard Sheets

COULD CONTEMPORARY ART LOVE HISTORY?

As I sat down to write this I had just returned from an international competition for a contemporary art museum where I engaged in a heated argument with a passionate juror who was upset by our proposal to symbolically wrap the museum with salvaged and referentially fabricated materials from building's historical locale. The juror argued that engaging historical fabric rendered the design not truly modern. I answered that I didn't feel the need to cut ties with history to be contemporary and added that many artists I admire seem keen to refer, appropriate, collaborate, and connect with history and with contexts.

The Marciano Art Foundation, I hope, is the prospect of that thought. The design takes on the memories, symbolism, and eccentricities of a building, of a city, and brings them together with a more contemporary spirit. Millard Sheets, the celebrated Southern Californian academic-artist-architect, designed the grand building as the Scottish Rite Masonic Temple in 1961 (fig. 1), with likely no awareness that one day the auditorium, the lodges, and the banquet dining room with an expansive view of the city would become perfect sites for art installation and spur another round of imaginative questioning and artistic exploration.

1 Millard Sheets interviewed by George M. Goodwin, January 13 and 16, 1977 (Center for Oral History Research, University of California, Los Angeles, *http://oralhistory.library.ucla.edu/viewItem.do?ark=21198/zz0008z9tz&title=Sheets,%20Millard*). All subsequent quotes from Millard Sheets are from this interview. See excerpt on pages 309–11.

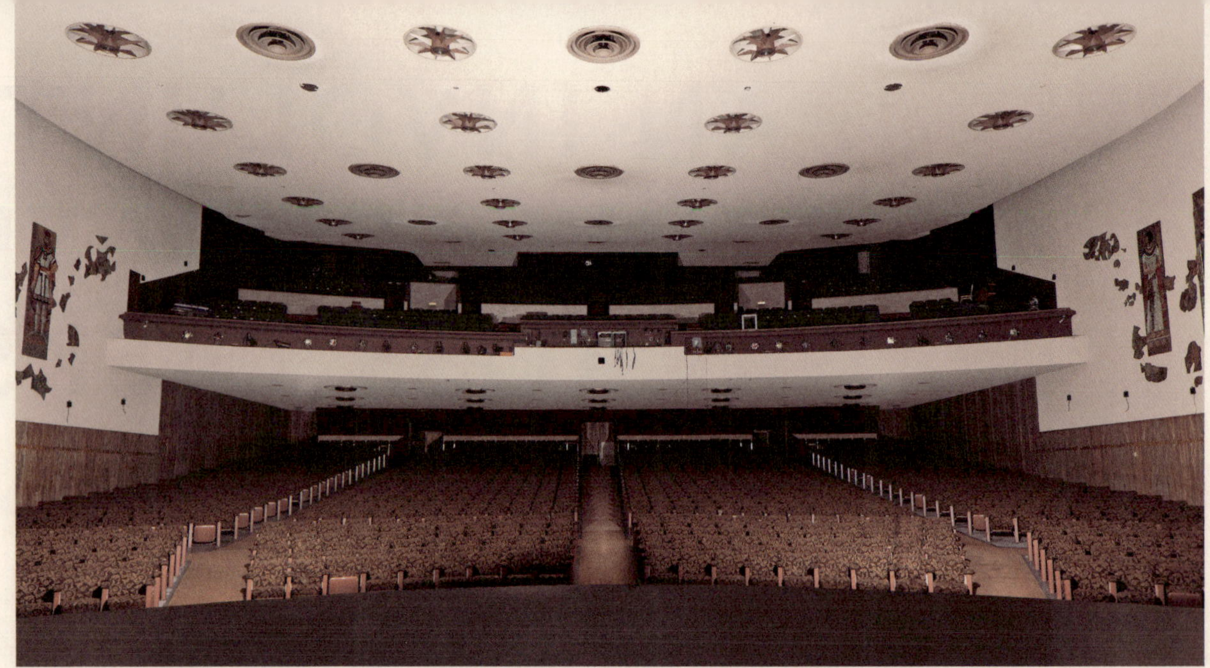

FIG. 2 Theater, Scottish Rite Masonic Temple, 2013

Why do you think you need to build a big temple?
What's wrong with the one you've got?
I don't know anything about the one you've got, except that
I've seen the outside and it looks horrible.

—Millard Sheets to Judge Ellsworth Meyer,
head of the Scottish Rite Cathedral Los Angeles, 1958[2]

2 Ibid.

In pursuing the project, Millard Sheets, a non-Mason cultural enthusiast, questioned why the Masons required such a big temple or "cathedral." The artist, avid watercolorist, educator, and successful designer, was tackling the design strategies as communications and symbols meant to connect the increasingly obsolete Masonry with the changing world. Referring to the temple many times as a city, Sheets, like any successful architect, listened and inquired before envisaging any building form, yet even he was surprised by the tremendous number of things and functions that the Masons required for this space.

The building was obviously well built, and the integral pride and spirit of Masonry symbolized and celebrated. One could not imagine a better building type to convert into an art space—all the high-ceiling rooms, wide-span structures, and extensive wall spaces with few windows—but the sense of closed exclusivity and esoteric social identity could potentially send it towards yet another isolated art bunker. We wanted to combat this perception, and, despite the building's solid presence, embrace Los Angeles in its own way. For Angelenos and beyond, I think, this history is fascinating—the juxtaposition and conjunction between the bones, body, and the DNA of the historic Masonic temple together with the strategic interventions and contemporary acupuncture throughout the building could present a new life of dynamic and mystifying presence.

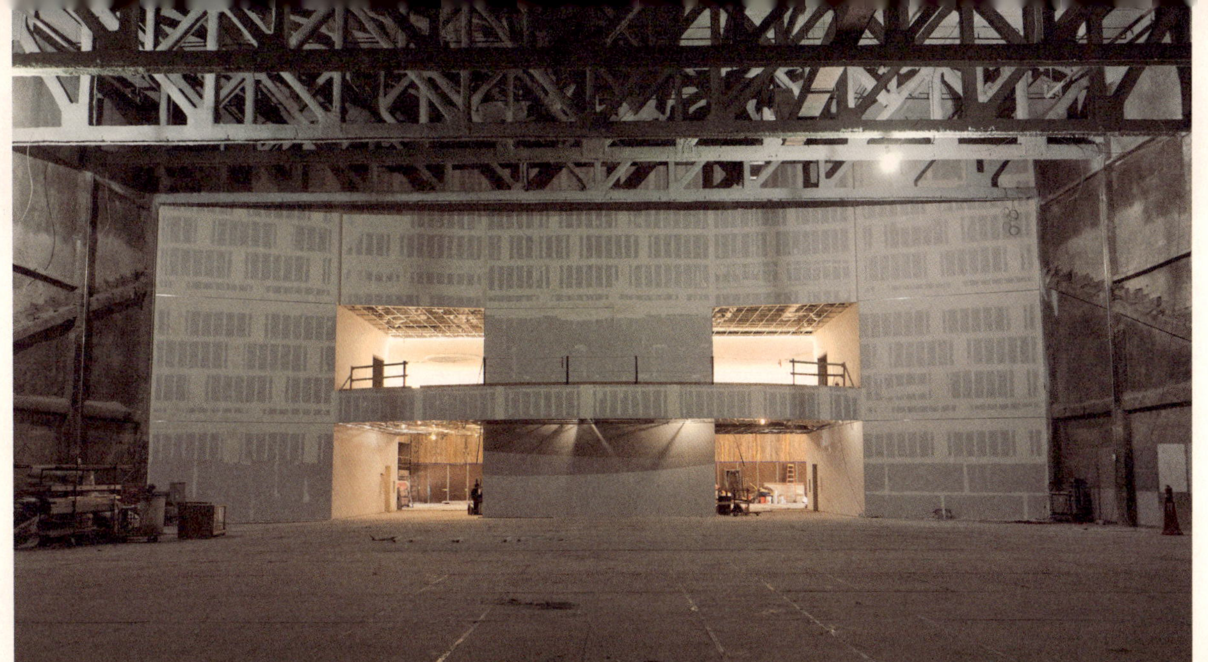

FIG. 3 Theater Gallery under construction, Marciano Art Foundation, 2016

FROM FRATERNAL TEMPLE TO ART PLAYGROUND

From the get-go the Foundation and wHY planned to keep the exterior integrity of the building as much as we could, restoring the grand mosaic on the east wall, which depicts the builders of the temple from the days of Jerusalem to Babylon to London and finally here in California, and assuring that all eight of the vandalized larger-than-life travertine sculptures of key Masonic figures from King Solomon to George Washington will still greet visitors along Wilshire Boulevard. Yet we also believe that for this building to truly serve contemporary art and its communities, the overall spaces required dynamic and dramatic transformation. Instantly my inspiration for the transition was an art playground—a place to experience and to explore, an innovative project space where collecting meets experimenting, and thus flexibility.

HACKABILITY IN THE THEATER OF RE-ENACTMENT

Flexibility has widely become the keyword for twenty-first-century museums as boundaries surrounding exhibition, art, and institution are constantly being pushed and even erased. I like to take a position on flexibility with an attitude—open, confident spaces with qualities and characters need to exist before any flex happens in them. The renovated building provides enough distinction for the experiences to be diverse and fun, while leaving the individual spaces open to be freely used by artists, curators, or the public.

One of the most impressive spaces in the Masonic temple is the theater (fig. 2), where for many years Masons re-enacted rituals and high-level ceremonies; the Masons believed in connecting themselves back to the origins, to the founders and forefathers. The theater was designed for more than 3,000 spectators with a huge back-of-house volume where tapestries of iconic scenes hung waiting to be lowered. Dramatic plays were rehearsed and presented with elaborate stage, sceneries, music, and lighting—a real immersive constructed experience.

Our conversion of the main gallery of roughly 15,000 square feet does a bit of that, but now, the flat-floor, exposed ceiling space is open for all (fig. 3). Designed to become one of the most impressive one-room art spaces in the city, its vast size and location, like the Tate Modern's Turbine Hall, provide an open and flexible

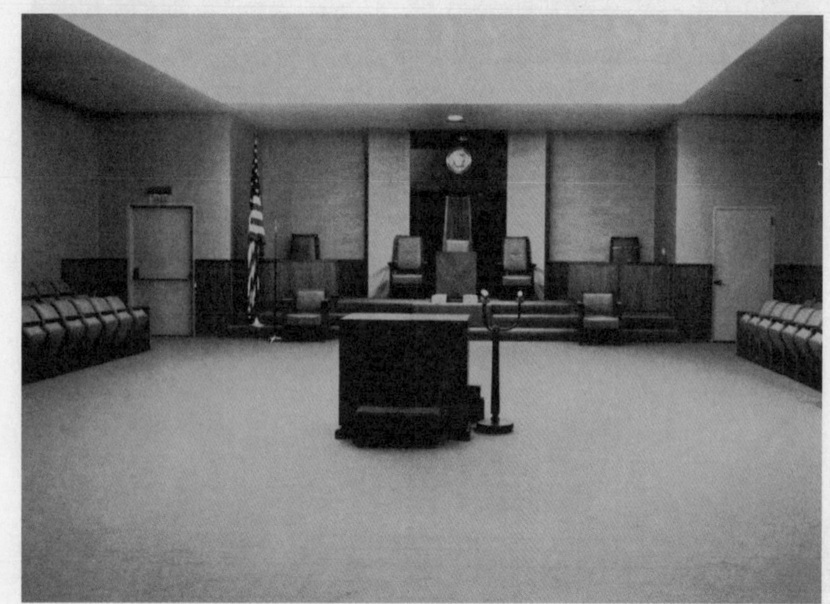

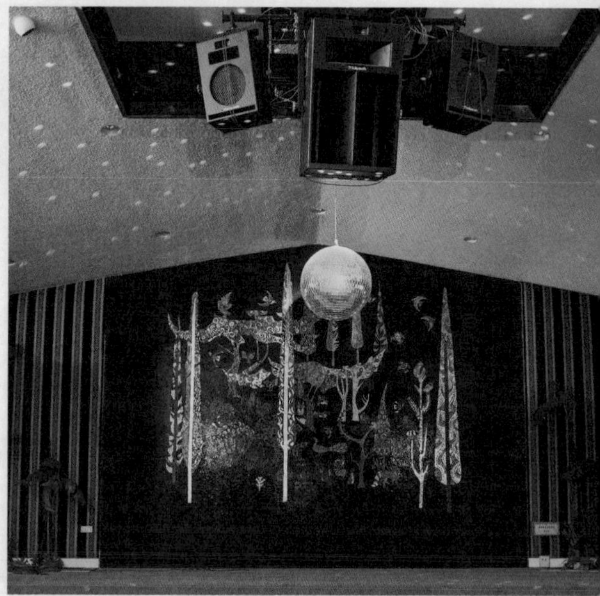

FIG. 4 Lodge, Scottish Rite Masonic Temple, 1961
FIG. 5 Banquet Hall mosaic, Scottish Rite Masonic Temple, 2013

space that simultaneously evokes its glorious past life. The rawness of the exposed structure is intentional, and the roughness of the space, deferential reminding us clearly of the Masons' spiritual anchor in construction as well as their love of origins and symbolic expressions.

ROUGHING IT IN, LODGING IN WITH THE ARTS

The Masons love their dramas—the stage and the narratives, the procession of arriving, socializing, and commanding focus. Handsome sets of documents, photographs, and Masonic paraphernalia left at the Temple are now preserved and presented in a simple and authentic manner in the renovated Masonic library. In the new transformation, the grand entry hall, restored yet nearly unchanged, will be accessed through the new west courtyard, making the entire ground floor fully accessible.

Originally, the west side of the temple's third floor contained three lodges where ceremonies and more intimate meetings were held (fig. 4). These rooms are now converted into adjoining individual galleries, with an exposed roof structure and simple finishes. In addition, a museum-size freight elevator is surgically inserted behind the existing elevators without altering any exterior view or interior integrity.

Adjacent to the three new galleries sits the former banquet dining room (figs. 5 and 6) that for decades hosted important dinners and ceremonies for as many as 1,500 guests. The space—almost an exact footprint of the auditorium beneath, but with a lower, gabled ceiling and expansive views of Los Angeles—has been converted into a large gallery filled with natural light from the wall of windows on either side that grant access on its north and south sides to outdoor terraces where the Hollywood sign peers through the trees. Memories of Masons in formal attire and festive costumes will now be replaced with the ever-growing collection of the Marciano Art Foundation I am a keen believer in making an art experience that is unique to a place, that art should not be isolated from its physical context. One could imagine seeing paintings from Ed Ruscha, Mark Grotjahn, or Jonas Wood in this light-fill Masonic-decorated gallery while looking out to the north with palm trees and the

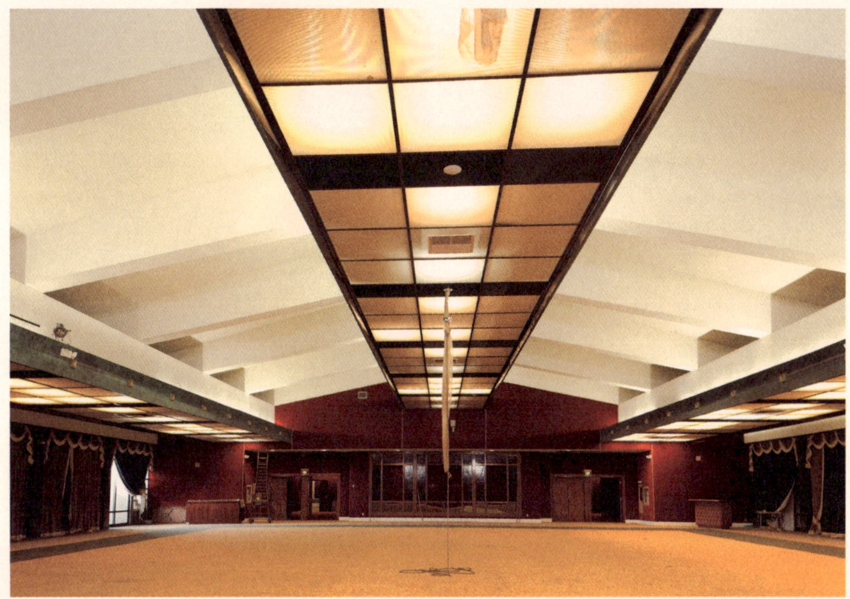

FIG. 6 Banquet Hall, Scottish Rite Masonic Temple, 2013

contour of Hollywood Hills in the afternoon light. And perhaps it's time for a substantial gallery where one can see artworks in a historic building in the full context of Los Angeles, where art and city are seen with the same eye, in the same moment.

LOS ANGELES DIDN'T HAVE ANYTHING LIKE THIS...

Today we have more and more art, but fewer unique places to see it or and make it. Now, the often-cited accusation that Los Angeles is ambivalent about embracing its history has found the best site to link the past and present. History will live in a different way, with the raw spirit of experimentation left to the artists. Somehow, it seems this kind of place should already have existed. Well, Sheets might have turned out to be right, Los Angeles didn't have anything like this—until now.

> *I felt that Los Angeles didn't have anything like this and there should be something that people would look at with a little different view…*
> *I felt if we could get some sense of bigness of spirit, it would be exciting.*[3]
>
> —Millard Sheets

3 Ibid.

Construction of Scottish Rite Masonic Temple, 1960

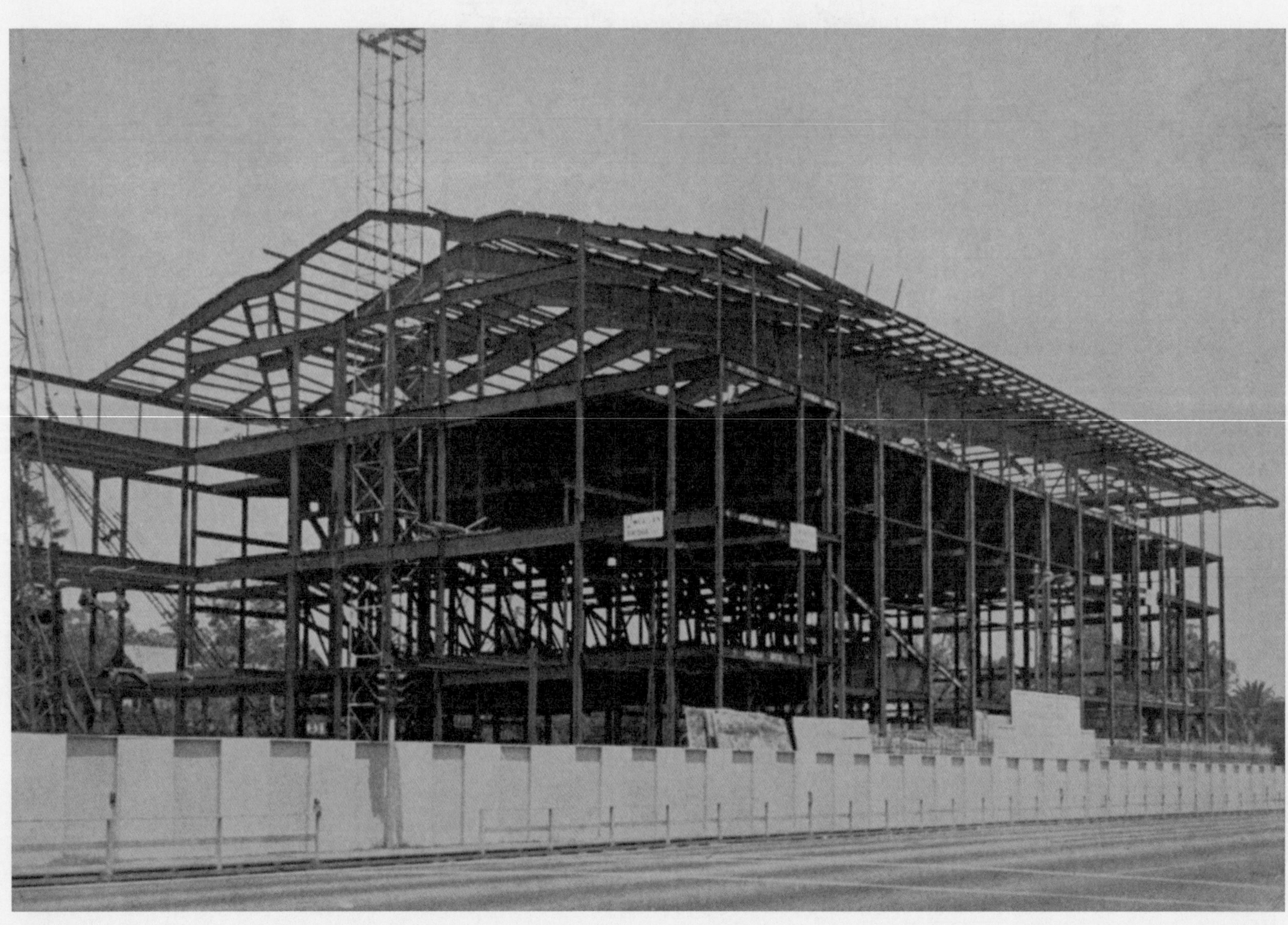

Construction of Scottish Rite Masonic Temple, 1960

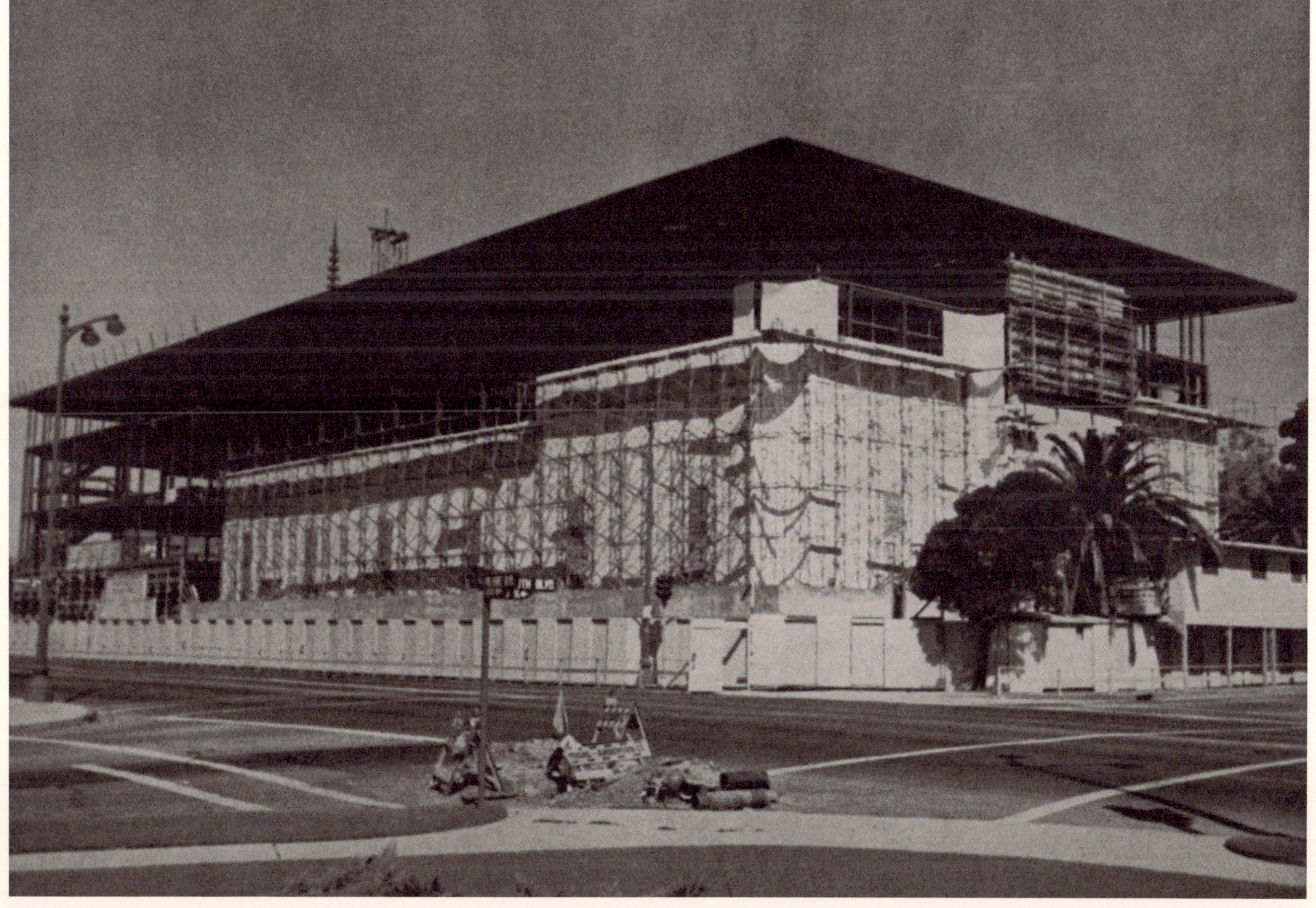

Northwest theater view, Scottish Rite Masonic Temple, 1961

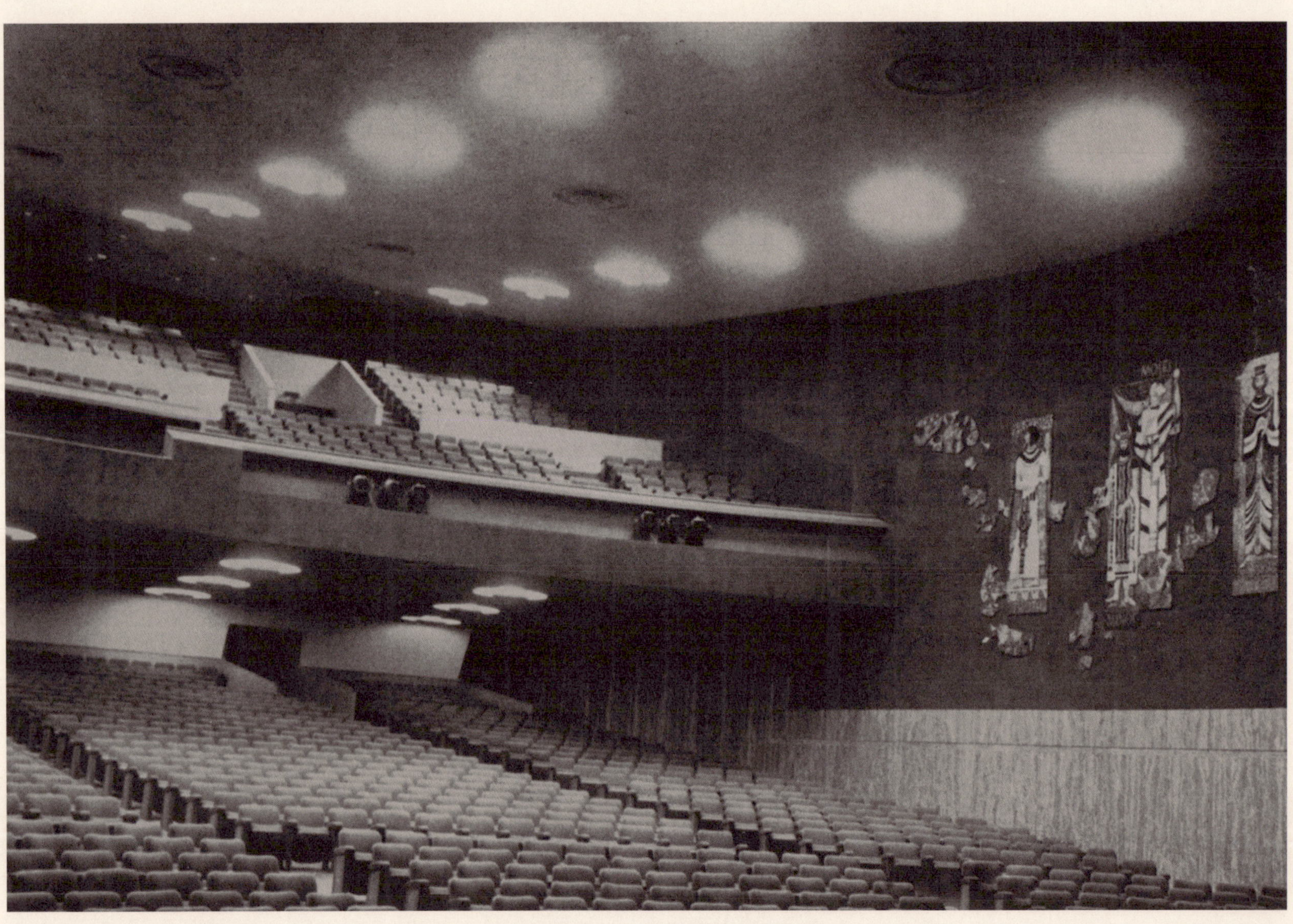

Banquet Hall, Scottish Rite Masonic Temple, 1961

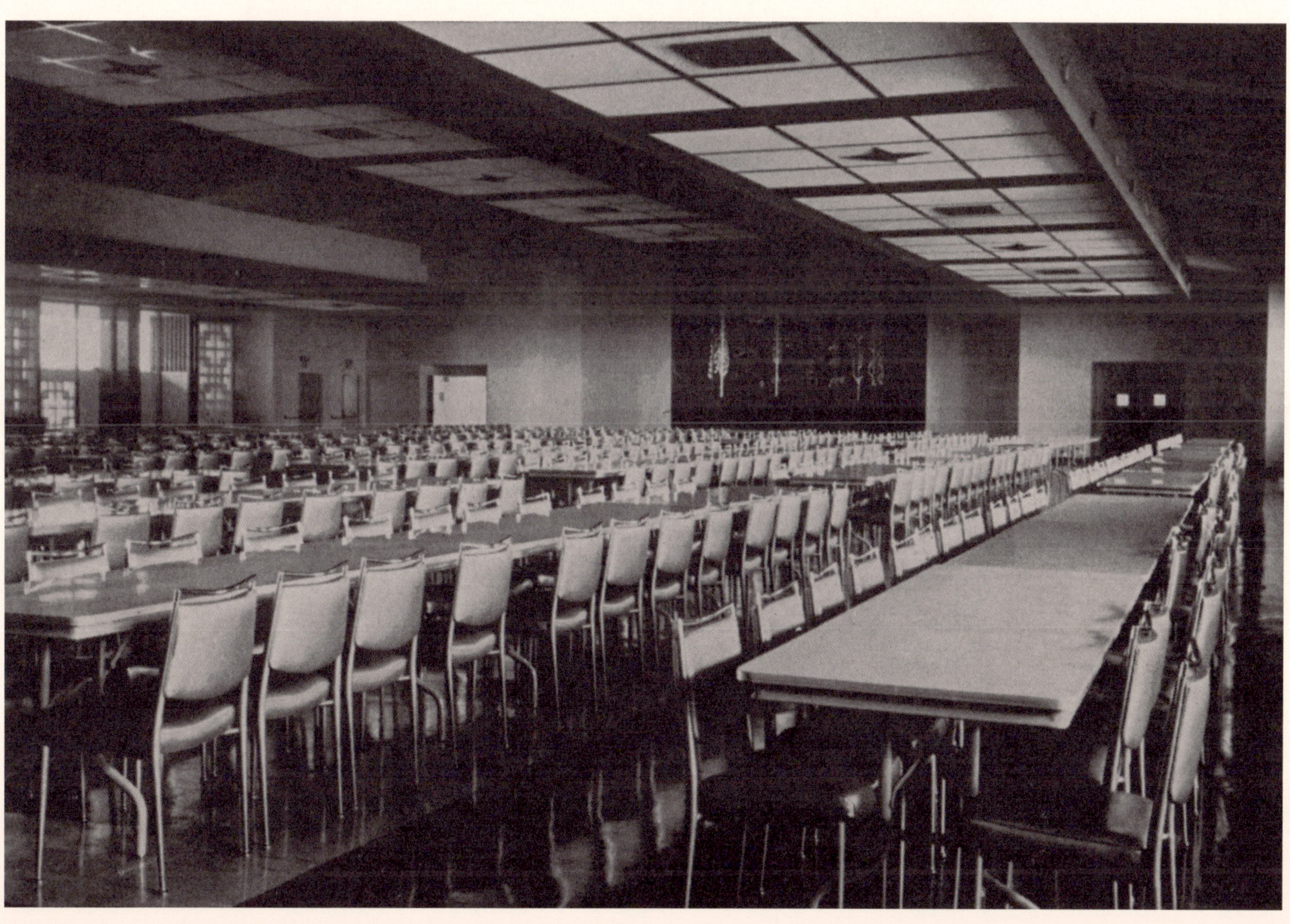

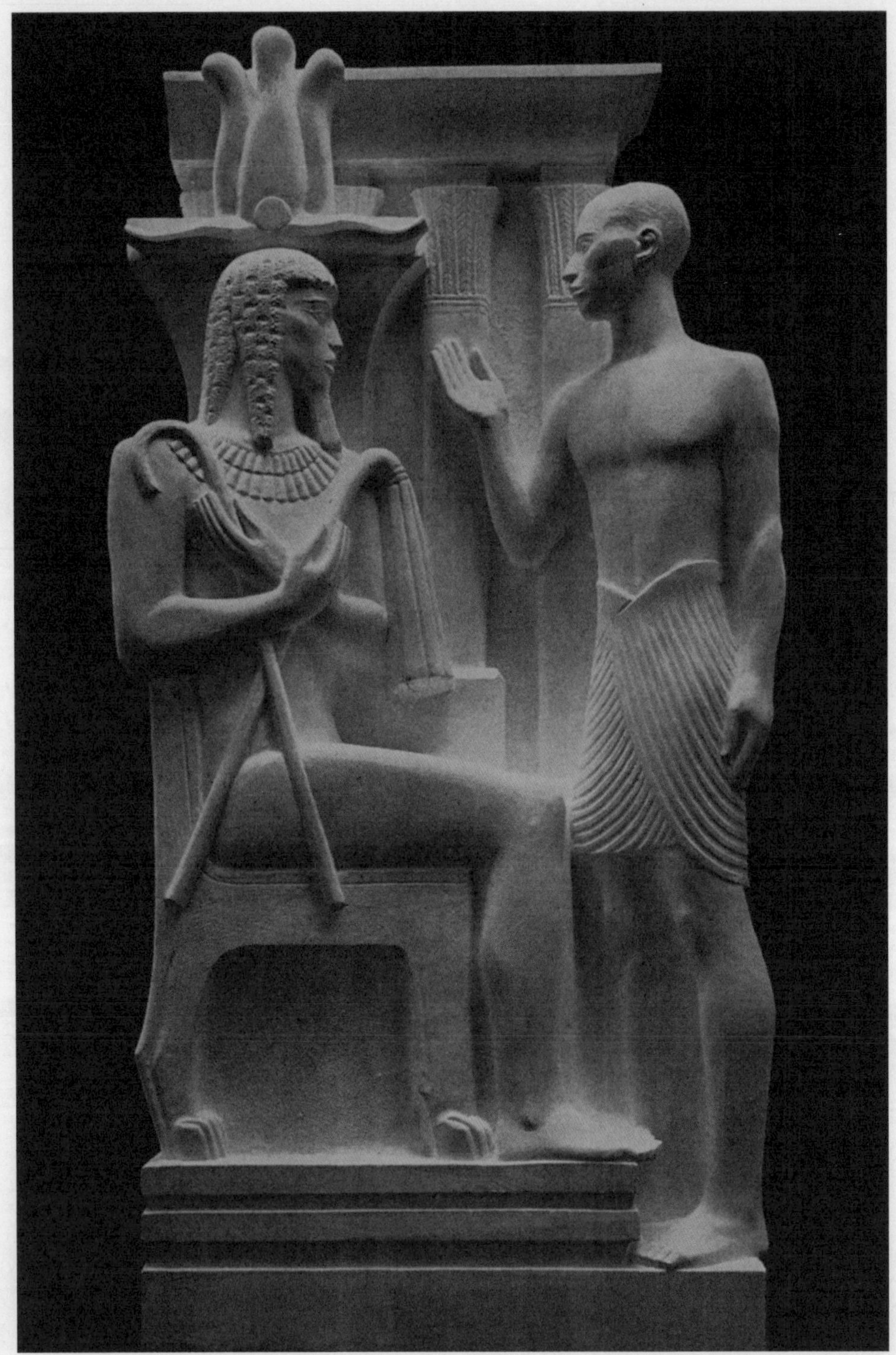

Scottish Rite Masonic stone figure, 1961

ACKNOWLEDGMENTS

This book would not have been possible without the help and expertise of colleagues and friends who were kind enough to dedicate their passion, expertise, energy, and time to this endeavor.

A huge amount of gratitude goes to Lorraine Wild, Xiaoqing Wang, and Green Dragon Office for the Foundation's beautifully designed logo and overall design of the Foundation's inaugural publication. Many thanks to our editor Stephanie Emerson for her remarkable organization, tireless fact-checking, comprehensive editing of text, and for keeping the project on schedule at all times.

We are extremely grateful to Philipp Kaiser for curating the Foundation's inaugural exhibition, *UNPACKING: The Marciano Collection,* and for contributing an essay to this catalogue. His consummate insight and vast curatorial experience were true gifts, and we are forever thankful for his guidance and support.

We would also like to thank our talented collaborators who contributed to this publication and to the formation of The Maurice and Paul Marciano Art Foundation: Kulapat Yantrasast for his thoughtfully prepared essay outlining the journey of redesigning the existing Scottish Rite Masonic Temple for reuse as a contemporary art exhibition space; Tony Sheets for his expertise and guidance regarding the work of his father, architect and artist Millard Sheets, for assisting with the conservation of numerous painted and mosaic murals found within the building, and for providing a comprehensive essay on Millard Sheets's life and work; and Susan L. Aberth for sharing her vast knowledge of Masonic history and practices, providing an essay to the publication, and curating the "Masonic Relic Room" at the Foundation, which features a curated selection of ritualistic and historical items left behind by the Freemasons.

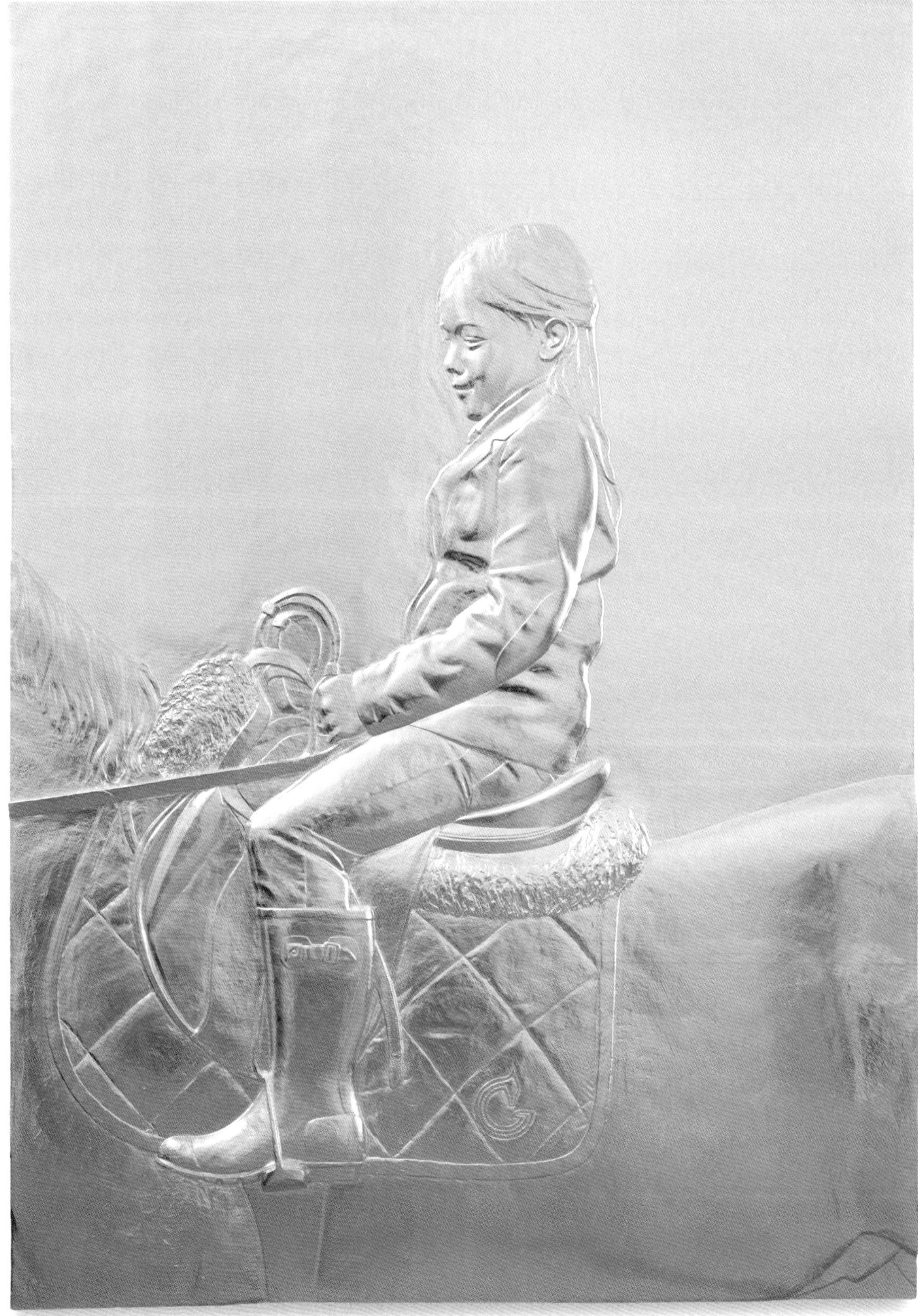

Charles Ray
Girl on Pony, 2015
Aluminum
84 × 60 × 3½ inches (213 × 152 × 9 cm)

We are grateful to the following writers for their contributions to the *Selected from the Collection* section of this publication: Jamin An, Lilly Casillas, Joseph Henry, Christine Robinson, and James Tarmy. Thank you also to Aardvark Press for providing the Foundation with high-quality prints of the Masonic copper archival image blocks found in the Scottish Rite Masonic Temple, and to DelMonico Books • Prestel for their distribution of the book as well as their reliable assistance navigating the marketing process.

We would also like to thank everyone who contributed to the transformation of the Scottish Rite Masonic Temple into the Marciano Art Foundation, specifically: Kulapat Yantrasast and Simone Lapenta of wHY Architecture & Design; The City of Los Angeles; Ian and Francine Jack; The Los Angeles Scottish Rite; Tony Sheets; Tanya Thompson; Turner Construction; John Welborne; and Brian Worley.

Bringing this publication to life would not have been possible without all of the hard work put forth by the Marciano Art Foundation staff. We would specifically like to thank Jamie G. Manné, the Foundation's Deputy Director, for her tireless efforts, insight, and vision in editing this volume; and Lauren Jack, the Foundation's Image Archivist, for expertly photographing the space throughout the construction process, managing all photography and securing all image rights and reproduction permissions required for this publication. We also would like to thank Olivia Marciano for her invaluable design input and editing.

Marciano Art Foundation thanks the following organizations for providing assistance and imagery for the publication: 303 Gallery; 365 Mission Road; Almine Rech Gallery; Andrea Rosen Gallery; Andrew Kreps Gallery; Anthony Meier Fine Art; Anton Kern Gallery; Archive Franz West; Blum & Poe; Galerie Chantal Crousel; Christie's; David Kordansky Gallery; David Zwirner; Foundation "De 11 Lijnen"; Gagosian Gallery; Galerie Max Hetzler; Galerie Neu; Galerie Gisela Capitain; Gavin Brown's enterprise; Gladstone Gallery;

Greene Naftali Gallery; Hauser & Wirth; Hauser Wirth & Schimmel; Jablonka Galerie; Jack Shainman Gallery; Kaikai Kiki Co., Ltd.; KUSAMA Enterprise; Kurimanzutto; Luhring Augustine; Luxembourg & Dayan; Maccarone; Marian Goodman Gallery; Matthew Marks Gallery; Metro Pictures; Mike Kelley Foundation for the Arts; Ota Fine Arts; Pace Gallery; Paula Cooper Gallery; Petzel Gallery; Phillips; Praz-Delavallade; Galerie Eva Presenhuber; Regen Projects; Sadie Coles; Salon 94; Shane Campbell Gallery; Simon Lee Gallery; Skarstedt Gallery; Sotheby's; Sprüth Magers; Tanya Bonakdar Gallery; Thomas Dane Gallery; Victoria Miro; White Cube; and Xavier Hufkens.

Lastly, the Marciano Art Foundation offers profound thanks to all the participating artists for graciously allowing the use of their works in this publication.

Maurice Marciano and Paul Marciano

CONTRIBUTORS

SUSAN L. ABERTH is an Associate Professor of Latin American Art at Bard College in New York. She is the author of *Leonora Carrington: Surrealism, Alchemy and Art* (London: Lund Humphries, 2005), as well as numerous essays for books, articles, and exhibition catalogues. Her specialties include Surrealism, occultism, and outsider art.

JAMIN AN is a Ph.D. candidate in art history at the University of California, Los Angeles. He specializes in contemporary art with additional interests in medieval and Byzantine art history.

LILLY CASILLAS holds a MA in curatorial practice from Central Saint Martins and a BA in art history from University of California, Berkeley. She specializes in modern and contemporary art with a special focus on Latin America.

JOSEPH HENRY is a Ph.D. candidate in the art history program at the Graduate Center of the City University of New York, where he specializes in modern and contemporary art. In particular, his research centers on performance and the arts of Germany and the United States.

PHILIPP KAISER is the former director of the Ludwig Museum in Cologne and former senior curator at Los Angeles's Museum of Contemporary Art. Kaiser is currently curator of the Swiss Pavilion for the 2017 Venice Biennale. He is the co-author of *Ends of the Earth: Land Art to 1974* (Munich: Prestel Publishing, 2012) and *Jack Goldstein x 10,000* (Munich: Prestel Publishing, 2012), among other publications.

JAMIE G. MANNÉ was born and raised in Los Angeles. With over ten years of experience working in the professional art world, she has managed the Marciano Art Collection since 2010 and now serves as the Marciano Art Foundation's Deputy Director. She lives in Los Angeles with her husband and three rescue dogs.

CHRISTINE ROBINSON is a Ph.D. candidate in art history at the University of California, Los Angeles, specializing in modern and contemporary art and the history of photography. She has held curatorial positions at The Museum of Contemporary Art, Los Angeles, and the Los Angeles County Museum of Art.

JIM SHAW is a Los Angeles–based artist and musician. He has had solo exhibitions at the New Museum in New York, MASS MoCA, and the Los Angeles County Museum of Art, among others. His work has also been included in numerous national and international group exhibitions, including both the Venice and Whitney Biennials.

TONY SHEETS is a sculpture and director of the Millard Sheets Center for the Arts at Fariplex at the Los Angeles County Fair. He is the son of the late Millard Sheets.

JAMES TARMY is the arts columnist for Bloomberg News in New York and has written about art, culture, and the art market for a variety of publications. He lives in Brooklyn.

KULAPAT YANTRASAST is founding partner and creative director of wHY, an interdisciplinary design studio with offices in Los Angeles, New York, and Louisville.

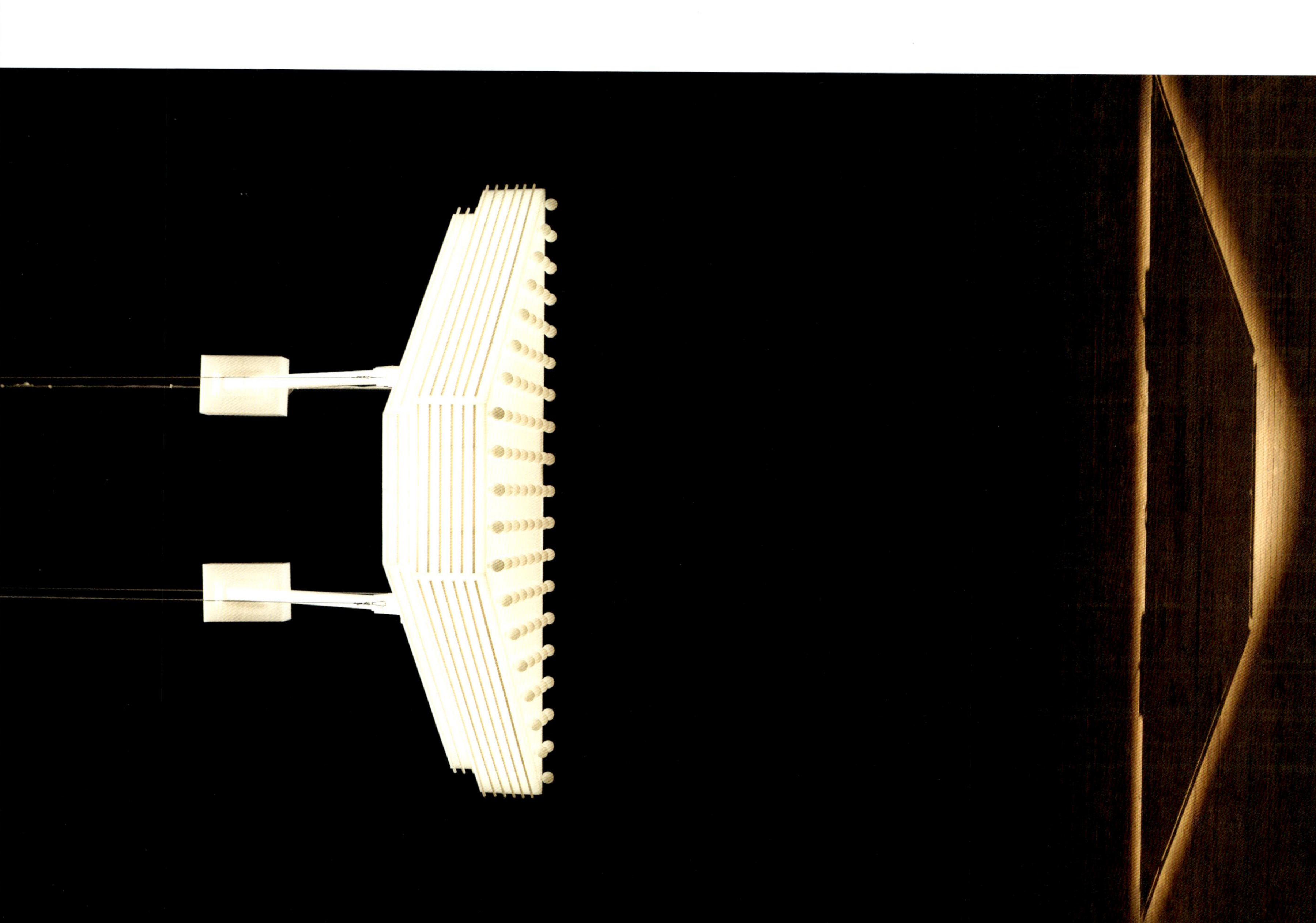

Philippe Parreno
Marquee (guirlande), 2014
Opaque Plexiglas, steel, incandescent lights, and neon lights
64 1/8 × 121 7/8 × 67 1/8 inches
(162.9 × 309.6 × 170.5 cm)
Installation view, *Philippe Parreno, H(N)Y PN(Y)OSIS*, Park Avenue Armory, New York

ILLUSTRATION CREDITS

Every effort has been made to obtain the permission of and to acknowledge the current owners of illustrated art. Errors or omissions in credit citations or failure to obtain permission if required by copyright law have been either unavoidable or unintentional. The publishers welcome any information that would allow them to correct future reprints.

All images © the artist in addition to the credits listed below.

Cover, pp. 36–39, 103, 153–57, back endsheet: Courtesy the artist and Hauser & Wirth; cover, p. 156: Photo Genevieve Hanson; front endsheet, pp. 92, 94–95: Courtesy of the artist and Almine Rech Gallery; front endsheet, p. 95: Photo Zarko Vijatovic; pp. 2, 312, 336 © James Ewing/OTTO; pp. 4, 24, 84, 85, 153, 200–1: Photo Fredrik Nilsen; pp. 4, 47, 191–94, 270–73: Courtesy of David Kordansky Gallery, Los Angeles, CA; p. 6: © Spencer Lowell; pp. 11–13: Courtesy 303 Gallery, New York, Victoria Miro Gallery, London, Galerie Eva Presenhuber, Zurich, and Regen Projects, Los Angeles; pp. 11, 27, 137, 138–39, 154, 191, 194, 196–97, 242, 270, 273, 288: Photo Brian Forrest; p. 13: Photo Charlie Coleman, Infinite 3D Ltd.; pp. 14–17: Courtesy of Allora & Calzadilla and kurimanzutto, Mexico City; pp. 14, 26, 56, 79, 258, 307, 315, 317, 320, 321, 322 (right), 323: Photo Lauren Jack; p. 19: Courtesy of the artist and Jack Shainman Gallery, New York; pp. 21–23, 59, 129, 133, 149, 238–41, 260–63: Courtesy Paula Cooper Gallery, New York; pp. 21, 23, 59, 149, 240–41, 260–61, 263: Photo Steven Probert; pp. 24–27, 29, 136–39, 175–77, 194–97, 200–1, 242: Courtesy Regen Projects, Los Angeles; p. 28: Image courtesy of Sotheby's. SOTHEBY'S, INC. LICENSE NO. 1216058. ©SOTHEBY'S, INC. 2016; pp. 31–33, 34–35: Courtesy of Carol Bove and Maccarone; p. 33 (right): Courtesy the Carol Bove, Maccarone New York/Los Angeles, and David Zwirner New York/London; pp. 41–43: Courtesy Gagosian Gallery; pp. 41–43, 160–61: Photo by Christopher Burke Studio; p. 45: © Artists Rights Society (ARS), NY, 2016. Courtesy Sprüth Magers; pp. 45, 164–65, 247, 294, 295: Photo by Joshua White/JWPictures.com; pp. 47, 82, 215, 220: Photo by Kristine Eudey; pp. 49–51: Courtesy Galerie Eva Presenhuber, Zurich. Photo by Stefan Altenburger Photography, Zurich; pp. 52–55: Image courtesy of Roe Ethridge and Andrew Kreps Gallery, New York; p. 56: Image courtesy Matias Faldbakken and Simon Lee Gallery; p. 58: Courtesy of Matias Faldbakken and Galerie Neu; p. 61: Image courtesy Urs Fischer and Gavin Brown's enterprise, New York/Rome; p. 63: Courtesy the artist and Sprüth Magers; pp. 64–65, 284: Courtesy Gladstone Gallery, New York and Brussels. Photo David Regen; pp. 66, 69–79: Courtesy of the artist and Blum & Poe, Los Angeles/New York/Tokyo. Photo by Douglas M. Parker Studio; pp. 68: Courtesy of Phillips; pp. 73–74; Photo Larry Lamay; pp. 74, 76–77: Courtesy Wade Guyton and Petzel, New York; pp. 75, 136: Photo Ron Amstutz; pp. 79–81: Courtesy of the artist and Salon 94, New York; pp. 82, 85, 168–69, 207–9: Courtesy of the artist and Gagosian Gallery; p. 84: Courtesy of Thomas Houseago and Xavier Hufkens, Brussels; pp. 87–89: Courtesy Pace Gallery; p. 91: Courtesy of Jaqueline Humpries and Greene Naftali, New York; pp. 97–98, 150–51, 184: © the artist and White Cube; p. 99: Courtesy of Sergej Jensen and Galerie Neu; pp. 101–2: Courtesy of David Kordansky Gallery, Los Angeles, CA. Photo by Martin Parsekian; pp. 107–11: Art © Mike Kelley Foundation for the Arts. All Rights Reserved/Licensed by VAGA, New York, NY; pp. 113–15: Courtesy of the artist and Blum & Poe, Los Angeles/New York/Tokyo; pp. 116–21: Courtesy KUSAMA Enterprise, Ota Fine Arts, Tokyo/Singapore and Anthony Meier Gallery; pp. 123–25, 287: Courtesy of Louise Lawler and Metro Pictures, New York; p. 127: All images courtesy Mark Leckey and Gavin Brown's enterprise, New York/Rome; pp. 130–31: Courtesy of Sherrie Levine and Simon Lee Gallery. Photo Todd White Art Photography, London; p. 132: Courtesy David Zwirner, New York, Simon Lee Gallery, London, Jablonka Galerie, Cologne; p. 134: Courtesy of the artist, Luhring Augustine, New York, Regen Projects, Los Angeles, and Thomas Dane Gallery, London; pp. 141–43: Courtesy of Nate Lowman and Maccarone; pp. 145–47: Image courtesy of Goshka Macuga and Andrew Kreps Gallery, New York; p. 155: Photo Antonio Cozza; pp. 158–65: © 2016 Takashi Murakami/Kaikai Kiki Co., Ltd. All Rights Reserved. Courtesy of the artist and Blum & Poe, Los Angeles/New York/Tokyo; pp. 167, 170–73: Galerie Max Hetzler archive; p. 171: Photo def-image.com; p. 168: Photo Stefan Rohner; p. 178: © Gabriel Orozco / kurimanzutto, Mexico City. Image courtesy of Sotheby's. SOTHEBY'S, INC. LICENSE NO. 1216058. © SOTHEBY'S, INC. 2016; pp. 180–81: kurimanzutto, Mexico City; p. 181: Photo Estudio Michel Zabé; 183–85, 199, 213–15: Courtesy Gladstone Gallery, New York and Brussels; pp. 187–89: Courtesy Laura Ownes/Gavin Brown's enterprise, New York/Rome/Sadie Coles HQ, London/Galerie Gisela Capitain, Cologne; p. 192: Photo Kevin Todora; p. 203: Courtesy of Seth Price, Petzel, New York, and 356 S. Mission Rd., Los Angeles. Photo Brica Wilcox; pp. 204–5: Courtesy of Seth Price and Petzel, New York; p. 211(left): Courtesy MDC Milano/London/Hong Kong. Photo EPW Studio; p. 211(left): Courtesy Gavin Brown's enterprise, New York/Rome; p. 216: Courtesy of the artist and Almine Rech Gallery; p. 217: Courtesy Galerie Eva Presenhuber, Zurich; pp. 218, 222–25: Courtesy Sterling Ruby Studio; pp. 218, 221–25: Photo Robert Wedemeyer; pp. 220–21: Courtesy the artist and Xavier Hufkens, Brussels; pp. 226, 230–31: Photo courtesy of the artist and Tanya Bonakdar Gallery, New York; pp. 228–29: Courtesy Analia Saban and Praz-Delavallade, Paris. Photo Rebecca Fanuele); pp. 233–35: Courtesy Matthew Marks Gallery; p. 237: Courtesy Gagosian Gallery. Photo Rob McKeever; pp. 239, 262: Photo Christie's Images/Images; pp. 244–45: Courtesy of Rirkrit Tiravanija and kurimanzutto, Mexico City; pp. 247–49: Courtesy Regen Projects, Los Angeles, and Andrea Rosen Gallery, New York; pp. 251–52: Courtesy of Oscar Tuazon and Maccarone; pp. 253, 289: Courtesy Galerie Eva Presenhuber, Zurich; pp. 255, 288: Courtesy Kaari Upson Studio; p. 256: Courtesy of Danh Vo and Marian Goodman Gallery; p. 258: Courtesy of Danh Vo and Galerie Chantal Crousel, Paris; pp. 264–65: Courtesy Thomas Dane Gallery, London; pp. 267–69: Archive Franz West N° DN 5407 © Archive Franz West; p. 267: Photo Hugo Maertens-Bruges; p. 268: Photo Adam Reich; p. 272: Courtesy of the artist, Anton Kern Gallery, New York, David Kordansky Gallery, Los Angeles, Shane Campbell Gallery, Chicago, and Gagosian Gallery; pp. 274–79, back cover: Courtesy of the artist and Luhring Augustine, New York; pp. 281, 283: Courtesy Adrián Villar Rojas, Marian Goodman Gallery. Photo Jörg Baumann; p. 285: Courtesy of Yael Bartana and Petzel, New York; p. 286: © Metro Pictures; pp. 290, 316: Photo Kevin Aguilar: pp. 292, 296: Courtesy of Jim Shaw; p. 293: Courtesy of Jim Shaw and Simon Lee Gallery, London/Hong Kong; pp. 293, 298: Photo Gregory Cherin; pp. 294–95, 297–98: Courtesy of Jim Shaw and Blum & Poe, Los Angeles/New York/Tokyo; p. 297: Photo Fredric Deval-mairie de Bordeaux; pp. 304–6, 308–11: Courtesy of Millard Sheets Family Archive; p. 308: ©LIFE Magazine; pp. 314, 318, 322, 324–28: Print courtesy of Aardvark Letterpress; p. 330: Courtesy Matthew Marks Gallery; p. 334: Courtesy Gladstone Gallery, New York and Brussels. Photo Andrea Rossetti.

UNPACKING THE MARCIANO COLLECTION

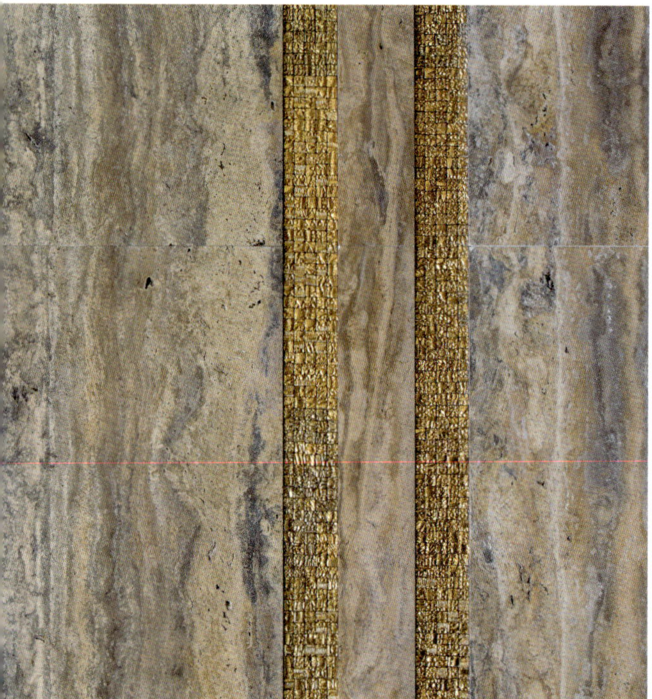

Front Cover: Paul McCarthy, ***White Snow Head*** (detail), 2012–13 (page 153)

Back Cover: Christopher Wool, ***Untitled*** (detail), 2014 (page 279)

Front Endsheet: Alex Israel, ***Valet Parking***, 2013. Oil painting on wall; dimensions variable

Back Endsheet: Mark Bradford, ***Dragon*** (detail), 2012 (page 39)

Frontispiece: South wall of Scottish Rite Masonic Temple, 2013

Page 4: Mary Weatherford, ***la niña***, 2014. Flashe and neon on linen; 117 3/8 × 103 5/8 × 3 3/4 inches (298.1 × 263.2 × 9.5 cm)

Above: Lobby wall of Scottish Rite Masonic Temple (detail), 2013

This edition copyright
© 2017 The Maurice and Paul Marciano Art Foundation

First published in 2017 by The Maurice and Paul Marciano Art Foundation and DelMonico Books • Prestel

The Maurice and Paul Marciano Art Foundation
4357 Wilshire Boulevard
Los Angeles, CA 90010
www.marcianoartfoundation.org

Co-founders
Maurice Marciano
Paul Marciano

Deputy Director
Jamie G. Manné

Associate Director
Olivia Marciano

Exhibitions Manager and Archivist
Lauren Jack

Project Manager and Editor
Stephanie Emerson

Designers
Lorraine Wild and Xiaoqing Wang, Green Dragon Office, Los Angeles

Color Separations
Echelon Color, Santa Monica, CA

Printed and bound by
Dr. Cantz'sche Druckerei Medien GmbH, Ostfildern, Germany

Typefaces
Caslon Egyptian
by John Morgan studio, London
Antwerp
by A2-Type, London

DelMonico Books, an imprint of Prestel Publishing, a member of Verlagsgruppe Random House GmbH

Prestel Verlag
Neumarkter Strasse 28
81673 Munich

Prestel Publishing Ltd.
14-17 Wells Street
London W1T 3PD

Prestel Publishing
900 Broadway, Suite 603
New York, NY 10003

www.prestel.com

ISBN: 978-3-7913-5620-4

Library of Congress Control Number: 2016961621

A CIP catalogue record for this book is available from the British Library.

All rights reserved. No part of this book may be reproduced, stored in a retrieval system or transmitted in any form or by any means electronic, mechanical, photocopying, recording or otherwise, without the written permission of the Marciano Art Foundation.

Every effort has been made to acknowledge correct copyright of images where applicable. Any errors or omissions are unintentional and should be notified to the Publisher, who will arrange for corrections to appear in any reprints.

10 9 8 7 6 5 4 3 2 1

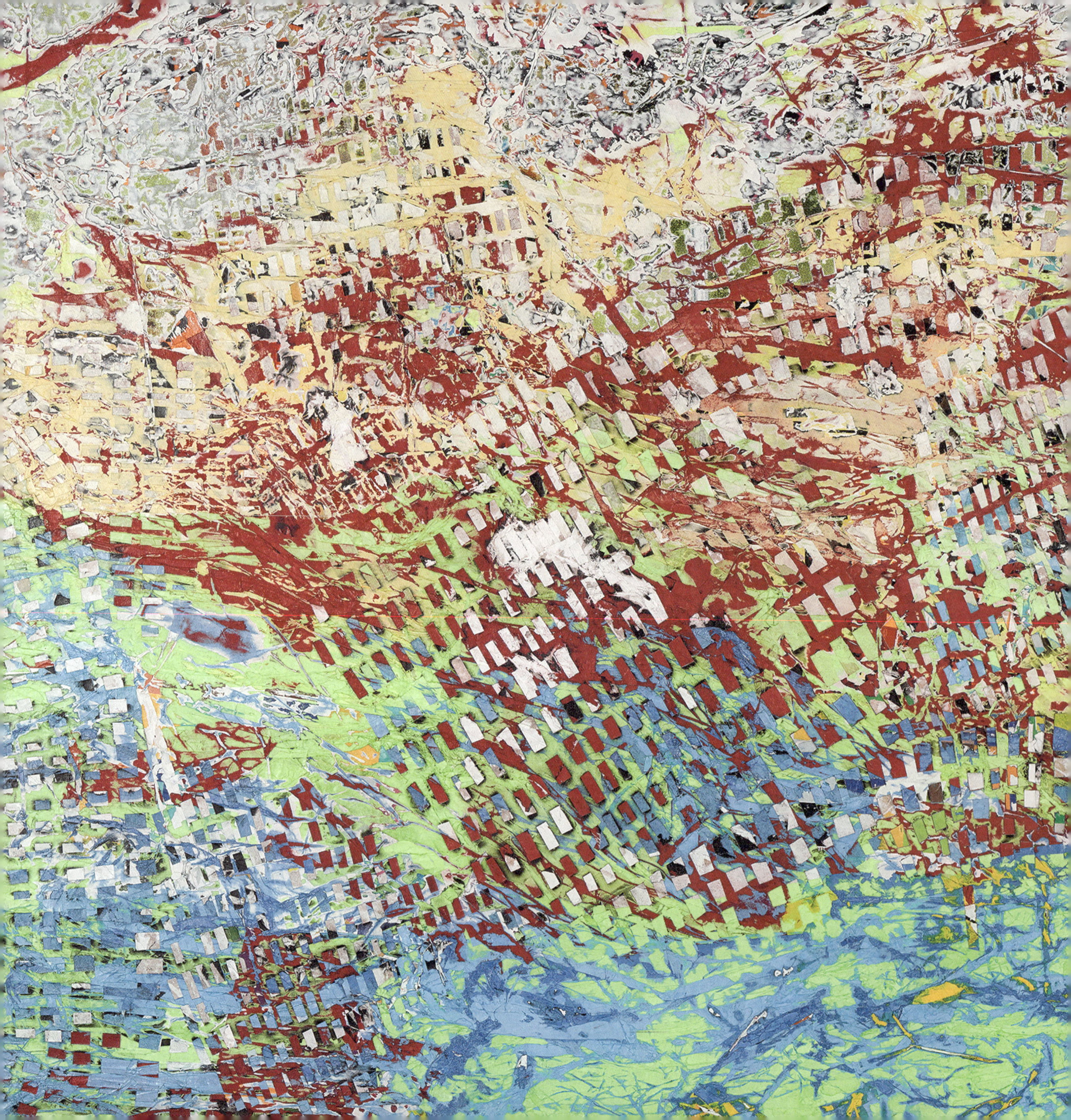